EXPOSITION and the
ENGLISH LANGUAGE

edited by
James L. Sanderson
Walter K. Gordon
Rutgers—The State University,
College of South Jersey

second edition

EXPOSITION and the
ENGLISH LANGUAGE
Introductory Studies

Prentice-Hall, Inc., Englewood Cliffs, New Jersey

ISBN: 0-13-298026-6

Library of Congress Catalog Card Number: 69-19993

10 9 8 7 6 5 4 3 2 1

PRENTICE-HALL INTERNATIONAL, INC., *London*
PRENTICE-HALL OF AUSTRALIA, PTY. LTD., *Sydney*
PRENTICE-HALL OF CANADA, LTD., *Toronto*
PRENTICE-HALL OF INDIA PRIVATE LIMITED, *New Delhi*
PRENTICE-HALL OF JAPAN, INC., *Tokyo*

Preface

This volume is an anthology of essays concerned with important aspects of the English language and arranged as examples of the major types of exposition. It is designed for use in courses whose purposes are the development of writing skills and the expansion of intellectual horizons. We believe the book contributes to the realization of these purposes both by the form and the content of the essays. The essays well exemplify the expository patterns that the student will most frequently use in his own writing. And in making him conscious of language as a subject of study in its own right, and of language's relationship to the history, indeed to the very possibility, of civilization, and of the importance of the responsible and effective use of language, the essays promote the kinds of intellectual awareness and discovery which have always been among the benefits and pleasures of liberal education.

We have selected the essays on the bases of their exemplification of good expository writing, their classroom utility, their interest for freshman students, and their intelligibility to students with little or no formal background in the study of English.

The book is divided into three major parts. Part One, INTRODUCTION TO EXPOSITION, presents the writing of expository prose as a process with discernible steps which the student can profitably follow. Part Two, EXPOSITORY TYPES, is divided into seven sections, each of which includes a discussion of a particular expository type, exercises, several essays exemplifying that type, and writing suggestions—essay subjects which are general and linguistic. Exercises as well as questions on expository technique, content, and vocabulary test the student's comprehension of individual essays and offer him opportunities to apply what he has learned. The essays in Part Two cover such major areas of linguistic concern as the historical development of

English, usage, phonology, current approaches to the study of English grammar, dialects, cultural influences on English, and semantics. Part Three, SPECIAL PROBLEMS IN LANGUAGE STUDY, studies language as it relates to propaganda and advertising, censorship, literature, and logic.

Our own experience with the book in its first edition, as well as that of our colleagues, convinces us that language study is not only a viable but also a highly successful core for a freshman course in writing. In this revision we have attempted to make the changes which our own experience and the comments of our students have suggested; in addition, we are indebted to a number of fellow teachers who have been generous enough to give us their reactions to the first edition and their recommendations for the second. We have profited by these responses and incorporated many of the recommendations in the present volume. We wish to thank the authors and publishers who gave us permission to reprint material from their publications, Misses Melanie Lusk and Dorothy Ward for their able secretarial services, and our wives, Ronny and Lydia, for their assistance in preparing exercises and in proofreading.

J. L. S.
W. K. G.

A Note to the Student

We wish it were otherwise, but it is best to concede at the very outset that developing one's skill as a writer is often a wearisome, discouraging, frustrating, and, sometimes, humbling undertaking. Strategists of positive thinking would no doubt counsel us to begin by extolling the thrill of the correctly placed comma and the self-approving joy in producing an ablative absolute; to conjure visions of the social adulation and financial emoluments awaiting each and every reader of Sanderson and Gordon, whether his or her destiny be successful engineer, forceful executive, subtle diplomat, or sophisticated wife, household executrix, and bluestocking of the cocktail table. Just ten minutes a day with *Exposition and the English Language* to a brilliant style—and, consequently, a larger share of your really deserved success! Alas, as members of a generation rumored to distrust anyone over thirty, you would immediately be suspicious of our blandishments—and having a few of your writing efforts appraised and returned by your instructor with margins awash with his red-inked disapproval would surely reveal the vapidity of such a sell.

This is not to say that writing is without its pleasures and rewards. Far from it. Some write because they must. They find a relief in satisfying a need that urges them to articulate their feelings and experiences, to share their visions with their fellows. In addition, many find a peculiarly rewarding aesthetic pleasure in imposing order on the clutter of their thoughts and communicating their ideas with precision and grace.

To such private satisfactions can be added the realization of some public goals that require clear and effective writing. Your work toward a college degree, for example, will demand verbal skills of a high order. You will be expected to listen attentively and to read critically, and you will also have to demonstrate through written examinations the range of your knowledge and your ability to explore a subject on your own, to organize the results, and to translate them into essays and reports, both long and short, which others can read with easy intelligibility. And in many of your future careers, occasions will often arise which demand a facility in written communication.

Writing, therefore, can be intrinsically pleasurable and extrinsically useful. But it remains a *skill,* a capability that must be developed and exercised, and one in which improvement must be measured in modest advances.

Many students are puzzled because effective writing is not an immediately easy accomplishment. After all, they have been speaking English for at least eighteen years. Why is it, when a student attempts to carry out a writing assignment that his hours of pencil sharpening and chewing, pacing about the room, opening and shutting the window, flicking on the television for a break from his arduous work, pausing for a quick snack, and then reluctantly returning to the mystical contemplation of the opposing wall frequently produce little more than the name of the would-be author in the upper righthand corner, followed by the course title, section number, and date—all, of course, elaborately embellished and underlined several times?

Part of the explanation of the difficulty experienced by many beginning writers—and a sizable number of experienced ones as well—is their comparative lack of practice with a special form of English. For every word we write we speak thousands upon thousands, and we forget that our easy facility with spoken English is the result of years of experimentation and practice. Furthermore, the writer must do without the very rich and meaningful context usually given the spoken word through the eloquence of hand gestures, the subtle language of facial expressions, and the delicate distinctions of intonation, those hundreds of spontaneous and largely unpremeditated nonverbal assets that insure our audience's understanding of our words and, indeed, convey meaning in their own right. Consequently, as writers we sometimes feel like singers attempting to perform without benefit of chorus or orchestra an opera with which we are not very familiar.

What we say in conversations is largely automatic and depends little on self-conscious thought. Any failure to communicate is usually quickly apparent to us from the baffled expression of our audience or a direct question, and we can try other forms of statement until we find one that works. As writers, however, we become self-conscious about communication. We begin to understand that we must anticipate the possible difficulties our readers may have in understanding us and that we must exercise a conscious choice in vocabulary, grammar, and sentence structure to insure that our statements will convey our intended meaning.

And the freshman writer faces added difficulty. He is usually in an unfamiliar situation, one that can almost paralyze his efforts, unless he adjusts properly and constructively to it. We all know that we can, and do, talk for hours without saying anything very substantive—and without suffering any particular embarrassment. But a composition for an English class is another matter. The student is expected to say something significant, to *perform,* to be interesting and articulate about a subject of mature importance. More forbidding yet, he must perform before an almost certainly critical audience, perhaps some ominous Thurberesque woman or grim Gradgrind poised to pounce upon his slightest stylistic infelicity and to decorate his essay with criticisms ranging from sacred to profane admonitions.

Despite such difficulties thousands of college students each year improve their written English, and there is no reason for you not being one of them— if you will accept criticism as a means to improvement rather than as a smart to be nursed in sullen silence, be patiently content with gradual improvement, and understand that writing one essay as well as you possibly can is the best preparation for writing the next.

J. L. S.
W. K. G.

Contents

Preface   v

A Note to the Student   vii

part one: INTRODUCTION
TO EXPOSITION   3

The Analytical Reading of Exposition   27

Politics and the English Language   George Orwell   28

part two: EXPOSITORY TYPES   49

ENUMERATION   53

Writing Suggestions: Enumeration   56

The Theory and Study of Language

1. *What Do Linguists Do?*   Neil Postman and Charles Weingartner   59
2. *Language and the Study of Language*   W. Nelson Francis   68
3. *Perspectives on Language*   Joshua Whatmough   75
4. *Theories Concerning the Origin of Language*   Stuart Robertson
    and Frederick G. Cassidy   85

Writing Suggestions: Enumeration   90

DEFINITION   95

Writing Suggestions: Definition   101

Problems in Definition and Usage

5. *Language Defined*   Edward Sapir   103
6. *The Definition and Determination of "Correct" English*
      Robert C. Pooley   117
7. *Right* vs. *Wrong*   Robert A. Hall, Jr.   128
8. *Don't Leave Your Language Alone*   Ernst Pulgram   140
9. *The Nature of Slang*   Stuart Berg Flexner   152
10. *Lingua California Spoken Here*   William Fadiman   169
11. *Gobbledygook*   Stuart Chase   174

The Dictionary

12. *What is a Dictonary?*   Jacques Barzun   188
13. *About the Dictionary*   Philip B. Gove   196

Writing Suggestions: Definition   203

        PROCESS   207

Writing Suggestions: Process   211

The Process of Verbal Communication

14. *Encoding and Decoding Linguistic Messages*   William G. Moulton   213

The Development of English

15. *The English Language in Process*   Margaret Schlauch   223
16. *Word-Making in Present-Day English*   R. C. Simonini, Jr.   254
17. *Etymology and Meaning*   Simeon Potter   264
18. *The Development of the English Dictionary*   Harold Whitehall   274

Writing Suggestions: Process   282

        ANALYSIS: DIVISION AND CLASSIFICATION   287

Writing Suggestions: Analysis   292

The Sounds of English

19. *The Classification of Speech Sounds*   Charlton Laird   293
20. *The Problem of Spelling Reform*   Mario Pei   306
21. *Sound Changes*   Arthur Bronstein   316

The Structure of English

22. *Revolution in Grammar*   W. Nelson Francis   331
23. *Intonation*   Paul Roberts   351
24. *Generative Grammar: Toward Unification and Simplification*
      Owen Thomas   359

25. *Meaning—Structural and Otherwise* Donald J. Lloyd
    and Harry R. Warfel   371

The Classification of Languages and Dialects

26. *The Classification of Languages* George Philip Krapp   382
27. *The Main Dialects of the U.S.A.* Jean Malmstrom
    and Annabel Ashley   394

Writing Suggestions: Analysis   405

    CAUSE AND EFFECT   409

Writing Suggestions: Cause and Effect   415

Influences on the American Language

28. *How We Got Our Dialects* Falk Johnson   417
29. *Noah Webster and the American Language* Albert C. Baugh   423
30. *The Influence of the Frontier on American English* Thomas Pyles   432
31. *The Genteel Tradition and the Glorification of the Commonplace*
    Albert H. Marckwardt   437
32. *Some Cultural Influences on Modern English* Albert C. Baugh 454

Writing Suggestions: Cause and Effect   462

    COMPARISON AND CONTRAST   465

Writing Suggestions: Comparison and Contrast   469

British and American Usage

33. *The Unity of English* Margaret Nicholson   471
34. *American and British Differences in Pronunciation* Thomas Pyles   477

Semantics

35. *The Useful Use of Words* Irving J. Lee   483
36. *Extensional and Intensional Meaning* S. I. Hayakawa   491

Writing Suggestions: Comparison and Contrast   497

    ILLUSTRATION   499

Writing Suggestions: Illustration   505

Language and Bias

37. *A Semantic Parable* S. I. Hayakawa   507
38. *Bias Words* F. A. Philbrick   513
39. *Linguistic Factors in Prejudice* Gordon Allport   521

Writing Suggestions: Illustration   533

part three: SPECIAL PROBLEMS
IN LANGUAGE STUDY   537

Language and Persuasion

40. *Propaganda Devices*   W. H. Werkmeister   539
41. *The Semantic Environment in the Age of Advertising*
    Henryk Skolimowski   555

Language and Morality

42. *Censorship*   Henry J. Abraham   565

Language and Literature

43. *Figurative Language*   Clement Wood   577

    Selected Poems and Short Story
        On First Looking into Chapman's Homer   John Keats   591
        Sonnet 73   William Shakespeare   591
        Lord Randall   Anonymous   592
        Since There's No Help   Michael Drayton   592
        Death, Be Not Proud   John Donne   593
        A Dirge   James Shirley   593
        I Wandered Lonely as a Cloud   William Wordsworth   594
        The Latest Decalogue   Arthur Hugh Clough   595
        To Autumn   John Keats   595
        Ozymandias   Percy Bysshe Shelley   596
        Cargoes   John Masefield   596
        The Sun Rising   John Donne   597
        The Canonization   John Donne   598
        The Collar   George Herbert   599
        On the Late Massacre in Piemont   John Milton   600
        To His Coy Mistress   Andrew Marvell   600
        Dover Beach   Matthew Arnold   601
        The Major-General's Song   W. S. Gilbert and Arthur Sullivan   602
        The Snake   Emily Dickinson   603
        Young Goodman Brown   Nathaniel Hawthorne   604

44. *Interpreting the Symbol*   Charles Child Walcutt   613

    Selected Poems and Short Story
        To the Virgins, To Make Much of Time   Robert Herrick   623
        The Eagle   Alfred, Lord Tennyson   624
        The Lamb   William Blake   624
        The Tyger   William Blake   624
        To Daffodils   Robert Herrick   625
        Because I Could Not Stop for Death   Emily Dickinson   626
        Stopping by Woods on a Snowy Evening   Robert Frost   626
        Araby   James Joyce   627

Language and Logic

45. *Deductive Reasoning*   Richard D. Altick   632
46. *The Process of Induction*   Max Black   642
47. *Pitfalls in Analogy*   Robert H. Thouless   647
48. *Linguistic Fallacies*   Daniel J. Sullivan   656

part one

INTRODUCTION TO EXPOSITION

O N the basis of the writer's intention, discourse may be classified into four broad categories: narration, description, exposition, and argumentation.

Narration recounts the movement of a sequence of events from one point in time to another. The writer's intention is basically to tell the reader *what* occurred and *how* it occurred. Although we usually think first of the novel, short story, or epic poem as examples of narration, the intention to recount some action or development is also realized in diverse works of non-fiction, such as Marchette Chute's biography *Shakespeare of London,* John Stuart Mill's *Autobiography,* and Thor Heyerdahl's account in *Kon-tiki* of his voyage across the Pacific on a raft.

Description attempts to give the reader a sense impression of an object, person, or place, and thus informs the reader of the appearance, taste, feel, sound, or smell of some object.

On the basis of its effect upon the reader, description may be classified as either subjective or objective. In the first type, the writer attempts to describe an object in order to arouse a response in his reader like that the reader might experience in the presence of the object. To accomplish his purpose, the writer of subjective description uses language that is vivid and rich in suggestive power. Frequently, in addition to enumerating the concrete details of the object, the writer employs simile, metaphor, and other figures of speech which appeal to the senses and emotions of the reader. The

3

following passage from "The Fall of the House of Usher," by Edgar Allan Poe, is a good example of subjective description.

> The room in which I found myself was very large and lofty. The windows were long, narrow, and pointed, and at so vast a distance from the black, oaken floor as to be altogether inaccessible from within. Feeble gleams of encrimsoned light made their way through the trellised panes, and served to render sufficiently distinct the more prominent objects around; the eye, however, struggled in vain to reach the remoter angles of the chamber, or the recesses of the vaulted and fretted ceiling. Dark draperies hung upon the walls. The general furniture was profuse, comfortless, antique, and tattered. Many books and musical instruments lay scattered about, but failed to give any vitality to the scene. I felt that I breathed an atmosphere of sorrow. An air of stern, deep, and irredeemable gloom hung over and pervaded all.

In objective description, however, the writer does not attempt to arouse an emotional response in his reader. He appeals to the reader's intellect and is primarily interested in giving him a factual account of the appearance of the subject. The following "wanted" notice is an example of objective description.

> WANTED FOR ARSON. GEORGE SMITH, alias James Barnes, alias Philip Jones. Male Caucasian. Ht. 5'10"; wt. 165. Thinning brown hair, brown eyes; dark, pock-marked complexion. Usually wears small mustache. 2" scar over left eyebrow; index finger missing from right hand. Has small anchor tattoo on left forearm. Considered dangerous.

Exposition attempts to explain a subject. Through such methods as analysis, definition, comparison and contrast, and illustration, it seeks to inform the reader about such subjects as the meaning of some term, the operation of some mental or physical process, or the similarities and differences between two objects, persons, or institutions.

Argumentation, the fourth form of discourse, seeks to convince the reader of the truth or falsity of some view or of the desirability or undesirability of some action. The writer of argumentation usually envisions a further result of his effort—the persuasion of his reader to assent to or to adopt, to dissent from or to renounce, some particular course of action. Although in many instances argumentation employs the techniques of the other three forms of discourse, it is distinguished from them chiefly by the response it seeks in its reader. Whereas narration, description, and exposition consider entertainment or enlightenment as ends, argumentation seeks to involve the will of its reader, to win his agreement or commitment. The brief that a lawyer prepares in behalf of his client, many of the speeches delivered in Congress, and the televised debates between political opponents are examples of this form of discourse.

THE FORMS OF DISCOURSE
IN COMBINATION

Although each form of discourse has its own purpose and special techniques, in practice the four forms are seldom mutually exclusive. Generally, two or more forms are represented in a piece of writing. In *Great Expectations,* for example, Dickens often interrupts his narrative in order to describe one of his characters, as in the following passage:

> Casting my eyes on Mr. Wemmick as we went along, to see what he was like in the light of day, I found him to be a dry man, rather short in stature, with a square wooden face, whose expression seemed to have been imperfectly chipped out with a dull-edged chisel. There were some marks in it that might have been dimples, if the material had been softer and the instrument finer, but which, as it was, were only dints. The chisel had made three or four of these attempts at embellishment over his nose, but had given them up without an effort to smooth them off. I judged him to be a bachelor from the frayed condition of his linen, and he appeared to have sustained a good many bereavements; for he wore at least four mourning rings, besides a brooch representing a lady and a weeping willow at a tomb with an urn on it. I noticed, too, that several rings and seals hung at his watch-chain, as if he were quite laden with remembrances of departed friends. He had glittering eyes— small, keen, and black—and thin wide mottled lips. He had had them, to the best of my belief, from forty to fifty years.

And in the same novel Dickens incorporates exposition in order to identify characters for the reader, explain their background, or account for their presence in a particular situation. In the second paragraph of the novel, Pip, the central character, informs us about his family, as follows:

> I give Pirrip as my father's family name, on the authority of his tombstone and my sister—Mrs. Joe Gargery, who married the blacksmith. As I never saw my father or my mother, and never saw any likeness of either of them (for their days were long before the days of photographs), my first fancies regarding what they were like, were unreasonably derived from their tombstones. The shape of the letters on my father's gave me an odd idea that he was a square, stout, dark man, with curly black hair. From the character and turn of the inscription, "Also Georgiana Wife of the Above," I drew a childish conclusion that my mother was freckled and sickly. To five little stone lozenges, each about a foot and a half long, which were arranged in a neat row beside their grave, and were sacred to the memory of five little brothers of mine—who gave up trying to get a living exceedingly early in that universal struggle—I am indebted for a belief I religiously entertained that they had all been born on their backs with their hands in their trousers-pockets, and had never taken them out in this state of existence.

Similarly, the writer of exposition sometimes uses narrative, perhaps in the form of a parable or an illustrative anecdote, and describes the persons, places, or objects about which he wishes to inform his reader.

EXPOSITION

Although the forms of discourse usually appear in combination, the student can benefit by studying each separately. Skill in all four forms is useful to a writer, in the way that the ability to execute all the strokes is essential to a good tennis player. But just as the tennis player must practice his serve or backhand individually in order to improve his game, so the writer needs to gain experience and to master each individual part of the total writing process. The form of discourse with which this book is concerned is exposition. Some further discussion of the special features of exposition is appropriate before we proceed to the examples of expository writing in the essays that follow.

As was indicated above, exposition seeks to explain a subject, to inform the reader about that subject. Exposition attempts to answer the kinds of questions which the inquiring mind is always posing: What is it? What caused it? Who is responsible for it? How does it happen? What is its purpose? What is its meaning? What is its value? Of what is it composed? How does it work? What is it like? How does it differ from. . . ?

Exposition has many uses. Most of the writing college students do is expository. For example, examinations, book reviews, critical essays, and term papers are all forms of exposition. In many of the careers college graduates pursue—in medicine, law, government, and industry—the writing of exposition is often required.

THE PROCESS OF COMPOSITION

The writing of an expository composition may be divided into four principal steps: (1) finding and developing a subject; (2) organizing the subject material; (3) writing a first draft; (4) revising and writing a final draft.

Many fledgling writers find the first step the most difficult. Finding a lively and appropriate subject seems to them as desperately hopeless an undertaking as finding their way through a complex labyrinth. Sometimes the instructor will provide a suitable topic and even give in detail the approach he wishes you to take in a given assignment. Obviously, it is important to follow such leads and to respond to them in your writing. But in many of the writing situations you will encounter in college you will have to supply your own subject. The following suggestions may help you past what may at first seem a formidable barrier.

SOURCES OF SUBJECTS

Where can you find subjects for essays? However commonplace and unpromising it may seem at first, the best immediate source of subjects for freshman exposition assignments is your own personal experience. Subjects chosen from your own experience are advantageous because they usually require a minimum of research, eliminate worries over plagiarism (since the experiences and ideas are yours), and permit you to concentrate on the art of writing. In considering your *personal experience,* think not merely of the raw data of the external events of your life or of your inner impressions and reactions, but of the experiences in which you have found some meaning, or about which you have made some judgment or evaluation, or on the basis of which you have come to some conclusion. These are experiences with potential interest and meaning for your reader as well as yourself.

Although you may not be aware of it, you have a bank of rich experience that you can draw on for writing subjects. Your mind is like a large computer in which you have unconsciously stored a vast number of memories, impressions, and attitudes, which a little stimulation will retrieve for your conscious consideration. Even a casual inventory of your past will call to mind some of the hundreds of people you have known—teachers, ministers, school chums, relatives, neighbors, dates; or moments luminous with memorable significance for you—moments, for example, of success and achievement, of intellectual or emotional discovery, of embarrassment, disillusionment, and disappointment, of sadness and tragedy, of joy and exhilaration.

Turning from an inward to an outward contemplation of yourself and your environment of home and family and of the larger worlds of society and nation, you will discover a host of additional subjects which can be vividly and interestingly treated. Think, for example, of the latest battle at home over your sister's wearing a micro-miniskirt to a formal wedding, of the parental ultimatums on the length of your hair and the infrequency of your haircuts, or of any of the instances that reveal glaringly the "generation gap." Take a look at the front page of any comprehensive newspaper and you will find a varied catalogue of ills and misadventures, of street violence, casual and organized; of accidental and deliberate cruelty; of flirtations with and addiction to drugs; of racial strife, oppression, and misunderstanding; of political campaigns; of religious debates over dogma, ecclesiastical discipline, and the social role of organized religion; of threats of global and reports of localized war; of nuclear, social, racial, and population explosions; of attacks by young people on social mores and institutions; and of old men making martyrs of themselves or others.

Your interests and involvement in contemporary American culture will provide additional sources of subject material. Consider your enthusiasms or antipathies for current clothing, hair, and cosmetic styles, rock-music groups and folk singers, standup comics and improvisational comic groups, motion pictures, television shows, entertainment celebrities and "personalities," records, books, magazines, pop art, op art, psychedelic art, and so on.

If you will open your eyes and ears and summon up any kind of sensitive remembrance of things past in your life, you will be overwhelmed by interesting subjects. With such an abundance the lament that you can't think of anything to write about will change to one that you have too many good possibilities.

Let us, then, assume that somewhere in the welter of possible subjects you find a particularly promising one. How do you develop it into an essay discussion? Development is a process, too, with certain discernible steps. Although the order in which they occur sometimes differs with individuals, we shall treat the steps as distinct and give them in the most usual order. When you have a subject, you should (1) consider the possibilities of narrowing and limiting it; (2) formulate a controlling idea for your essay; and (3) amplify that idea.

NARROWING AND LIMITING

Adequate development of a subject requires a reasonably thorough discussion of its important aspects. One expects a treatment with density of detail and inclusiveness. If your subject is too broad for the limits of a writing assignment, you will find that you cannot adequately discuss it. If you attempt, for example, to discuss "Modern Literature" in a 500–600 word essay, the result will inevitably be superficial and incomplete. The subject is simply too large. Within this word limit, however, you might succeed in defining and discussing the theme of Ernest Hemingway's "The Killers," in analyzing the character of Phineas or of Eugene in John Knowles's *A Separate Peace,* or the symbolic meaning of the conch shell in William Golding's *Lord of the Flies*. Narrowing the subject to fit the limits of a writing assignment is an essential first step in writing a good essay.

Narrowing a topic is sometimes aided by a deliberate pencil-and-paper analysis, in which the writer takes the subject apart and notes as many of its components and implications as he can. As an example, suppose you wish to write an essay of 500–600 words on "Highway Traffic Safety." Such a subject might seem promising. But even the brief analysis which follows reveals that the topic is too general and broad and includes many smaller subjects.

GENERAL SUBJECT: Highway Traffic Safety

Restricted: The Problem
Causes of Accidents
Prevention of Accidents

Further restricted:

I. The Problem of Motor Vehicle Accidents
   A. Accident totals for 1966, 13,600,000
      1. 44,200 fatal accidents
      2. 1,200,000 nonfatal injury accidents
      3. 12,400,000 property damage
   B. Accident deaths
      1. All U.S. wars 1900–1966, approximately 1,107,000; motor vehicle accidents 1900–1966, 1,600,000
      2. Fatalities in 1967, 53,000—one every 10 minutes
      3. Increase from 1957 to 1967 of 37 percent
   C. Accident injuries
      1. Disabling injuries in 1966, 1,900,000—one every 17 seconds
      2. Disabling injuries in 1967, 1,900,000—one every 17 seconds
   D. Costs (medical, insurance, property, loss of wages) in 1967, $11,000,000,000

II. Causes of Highway Accidents
   A. Poor highway design
   B. Overcrowded highways
   C. Unsafe automobiles
   D. Poorly trained drivers
   E. Reckless driving
      1. Excessive speed
      2. Inattention
      3. Drunken driving

III. Prevention of Accidents
   A. Rigid law enforcement
      1. Suspension of driving licences
      2. Compulsory automobile inspection
      3. Effective highway patrol
         a. Radio patrol cars
         b. Helicopters
         c. Radar
   B. Improved highway design
      1. Parkway design
      2. Medial barriers
      3. Elimination of blind entrances
      4. Separation of truck and passenger routes
   C. Improved automobile design
      1. Safety devices
         a. Shoulder belts
         b. Lap belts
         c. Special locks on doors
         d. Collapsible steering wheels
      2. Safety design
         a. Wider, unobstructed windshields
         b. Better brakes

    D. Agencies active in accident prevention
        1. Agencies of Federal, state, and municipal governments
        2. Private agencies
           a. National Safety Council
           b. Automobile clubs
           c. Insurance companies
           d. Automobile manufacturers
    E. Driver education
        1. Professional driving instruction courses
        2. High school driver-training programs
        3. Examination of drivers
           a. Physical examination
           b. Performance examination
           c. Theoretical examination
           d. Reexaminations

In attempting to treat the broad topic "Highway Traffic Safety," you may reasonably be expected to discuss several or all of the points noted above. Thus, by omitting "Causes of Highway Accidents" or "Prevention," you will open yourself to criticism because in choosing your topic you have promised more than you can perform. But, if you comment on all the points, your essay will be hopelessly superficial. Within a 500–600 word limit you simply cannot discuss each point in sufficient detail. Rather than attempting to write on the broad subject "Highway Traffic Safety," then, you will fare much better by developing a more *limited* aspect of this subject—the use of radar in detecting speeding violations, for example, or the effectiveness of the driver-training program in your high school.

Some students resist narrowing a topic because they feel they cannot possibly write five or six hundred words on a restricted subject. This inability, or presumed inability, to amplify is a fairly common difficulty for beginning writers, and instructors sometimes find touching evidence of this problem in such marginal notations in their students' essays as *175, 283, 392,* marking the breathless and exhausted march toward the goal of 500 words. We shall say something about amplification later, but it is important first that you appreciate the necessity of fitting the dimensions of your subject to your writing assignment, of narrowing your obligations to those that you can fulfill within the limits of your essay.

A CONTROLLING IDEA

The second step in development is the formulation of a *controlling idea.* Such a concept may be of two main types: a thesis or a purpose statement. By *thesis* we mean an assertion, judgment, or evaluation that the writer proposes concerning his subject and then supports, defends, or proves in his essay. Suppose, for example, that you wish to develop the subject of gun-control legislation for an essay. You might formulate any number of theses like the following:

> By making it difficult for known criminals, dope addicts, and alcoholics to obtain firearms, gun-control legislation can reduce the incidence of violent crimes in the United States.

> Gun-control legislation is undesirable because it unnecessarily penalizes the law-abiding citizen and does not effectively restrain the criminally inclined.

> The possession of firearms should not be denied to Americans because such an action would infringe upon their basic constitutional rights and unnecessarily curtail their personal freedom.

Each of these makes an assertion and indicates the basis for that assertion. The main body of an essay developing a thesis would support the assertion and, very much like argumentation, attempt to win the reader's agreement by the cogency of discussion.

A thesis is dynamic in that it implies an *anti*thesis, which suggests the stance of a debater arguing for a resolution and against an opposing view. But there are many writing situations in which such an attitude is not necessarily appropriate. One thinks, for example, of essay answers to examination questions: "Discuss the influence of Melville's experiences at sea on his fiction," or "Explain the meaning of *laissez faire* and 'supply and demand.'" Other writing assignments may call for a report of findings or recommendations. In such situations the controlling idea takes the form of a statement of purpose, either explicitly formulated or clearly implied: "The purpose of this essay is to discuss the function of water imagery in 'Lycidas,'" or "The purpose of this essay is to make recommendations for the improvement of the health services of the college." In achieving such a purpose, you might regard your essay as a reply to a specific request. Someone has asked you to do something; and your essay is your attempt to comply with the request.

Determining a controlling idea is a vital step. It is a wise practice actually to write the idea and to include it in the introduction to your essay, although as you gain experience in writing you may wish to imply the controlling idea rather than to state it explicitly in your composition. This idea directs your thought and that of your reader; it serves as a guide in insuring the relevance of the items in the main body of your essay, and it gives unity and stability to the whole composition.

The value of a controlling idea is illustrated in the following essays.

LAERTES

As everyone knows, *Hamlet* has always been one of Shakespeare's most popular plays. It was first performed around 1600 in England on one of the open-air stages in London. Shakespeare was born in 1564 in Stratford-on-Avon, and although not much is known about his early life, he definitely had had a lot of experience in the theatre by the time *Hamlet* was written.

In the play *Hamlet* Laertes is the son of Polonius and the brother of Ophelia. Shortly after the play opens Laertes asks Claudius, the King of Denmark, who has succeeded to the throne on the death of his brother, for permission to return to Paris to continue his studies. The play is set in medieval Denmark. At this time it was customary for a subject to ask his king's permission to be absent from the court. After a brief consultation with Polonius, Claudius grants Laertes permission to go to Paris.

One of the most delightful scenes in all of Shakespeare occurs in Act II, Scene 1, of *Hamlet,* where Laertes tells his sister and father good-bye. Hamlet has been paying attention to Ophelia and Laertes advises her to be on her guard against Hamlet. He is afraid Hamlet is simply toying with Ophelia's affections.

Ophelia is one of the most truly pathetic characters in all of Shakespeare. She is a young and attractive girl who is destroyed by forces she never really understands.

Her father forces her to break off with Hamlet. After Polonius' death she becomes very neurotic and eventually drowns.

The successful portrayal of such a heroine shows Shakespeare's great mastery of human characterization. It also tells us about the great skill of the Elizabethan actors. The part of Ophelia was played in Shakespeare's day by a male actor, probably a young boy, for no women were permitted on the English stage until the Restoration period when the court of the "merry monarch," Charles II, who had returned from exile in France, changed the Puritan attitudes in London life.

In this amusing scene Polonius gives Laertes his famous speech of advice, which includes the famous business about "This above all," etc., etc., etc. After Polonius' long speech Laertes says good-bye and leaves.

Later in the play Polonius, not trusting the ways of young people on their own, sends a spy to Paris to find out what Laertes' activities are and who his friends are. He is a forgetful old man, and his scene with Reynaldo is quite amusing and funny although it is sometimes left out in modern productions.

Following his father's death, Laertes returns to Denmark and, urged on by Claudius, kills Hamlet in a treacherous manner, and loses his own life at the same time.

In the very last scene of the play, another young man, who in some ways reminds one of Laertes and of Hamlet, Fortinbras, enters to become the King of Denmark and to restore order, and to have the dead bodies carried off the stage (which had no curtain).

Laertes was an important figure in two of the most exciting scenes of the entire play. The first was the fight with Hamlet in the graveyard. The second was in the duel scene in Act V.

This admittedly exaggerated attack on intelligibility shows, among other things, how the absence of a controlling idea can impair an essay. Although this example is extreme, your instructor probably has a few samples like it in his file of compositional horrors, and its weaknesses are similar to those found in any composition without the undergirding of a controlling idea. This essay seems to be about Laertes, but it constantly drifts off into matters irrelevant to Laertes, and its author never develops any idea with enough detail.

Consider the second essay.

LAERTES AS FOIL

Shakespeare's characterization of Laertes adds vitality to *Hamlet*. Laertes is an attractive, energetic young courtier, respectful of his father and, if a bit stuffy in his readiness to give Ophelia advice, genuinely concerned about his sister's welfare. In addition, Laertes plays an important part in the action, for it is Laertes who provokes Hamlet into fighting in the graveyard scene, plots Hamlet's death with Claudius, and actually kills Hamlet in the climactic duel scene. But Laertes' most interesting function is that of foil to Hamlet.

Just as a jeweler will display a string of pearls or a diamond broach against a black background, causing the brilliance of the gems to be more striking, so Shakespeare makes the qualities of certain of his characters more pronounced by setting them next to other characters with whom they markedly differ. Laertes offers such a study of contrasts with Hamlet. We have a keener awareness of Hamlet because of his differences with Laertes.

Laertes and Hamlet share enough similarities to make comparing them meaningful. Early in the play they are brought together before our eyes when in Act I, Scene ii, Claudius considers Laertes' request to return to Paris to continue his studies and Hamlet's to return to the university in Wittenberg. They are both youthful courtiers. They both show an interest in Ophelia and a concern for her. And they are also respectful and dutiful sons. Toward the end of the play, Claudius speaks of the interest Hamlet has developed in fencing because he has learned of Laertes' skill and accomplishment as a fencer. Shakespeare deliberately keeps us aware of these two young men as figures worthy of comparison.

But such similarities as these only make more real the significant differences between Laertes and Hamlet, accentuating certain important qualities in the Prince who is the central figure in the play. While Laertes goes on his way to Paris with the blessing of the King and of his father, Hamlet is strongly urged to remain in Denmark against his wishes. Where we see the happy and affectionate farewell between Polonius and his son, we remember Hamlet bereft of a father and bidding farewell to his father's ghost, who urges his son not to a prudent conduct, but to revenge.

Differences of outlook and temperament are made even more apparent when Laertes returns to Denmark on the death of Polonius, breathing fire, stirring up the people, and clamoring for revenge for the death of his father. While we have heard Hamlet *talk* of sweeping to his revenge and *thinking* about punishing Claudius for the murder of his father, we see Laertes barely restrained by Claudius in taking his revenge immediately on returning to Denmark, and then restrained only because his satisfaction is near at hand. When the two young men meet in the graveyard scene, both are emotionally overwrought, but in the struggle which ensues, it is Laertes who goes for Hamlet's throat. Finally, Laertes eagerly embraces Claudius' plot of the rigged dueling match with Hamlet, and no passive tool of Claudius, he makes the outcome certain by poisoning the tip of his unbated rapier.

This rashness, impetuosity, and forceful commitment to action are important components deepening the earlier impressions of Laertes in the play, and they are qualities which make Laertes' actions credible, but more important, and more subtly, these qualities set off the character of Hamlet as a pensive, reflective man, whose subtle mind and delicate distinctions mark him as a creature superior to Laertes and his kind, but also—and perhaps here is Hamlet's "tragedy"—make him at the same time all the more vulnerable to the menace which they mindlessly pose.

The second essay may not be a perfect piece of writing, and you may find much with which to disagree, details that you would have added or interpreted differently, but you will probably agree that, in contrast to the first essay, you have a fairly clear understanding of the writer's position and how the various parts of the essay support his position. Your understanding is largely the result of a central controlling idea—Laertes as foil—to which the subordinate ideas in the essay relate.

AMPLIFICATION

We come now to the third step in developing your subject. Having narrowed the subject and formulated a controlling idea, you must now amplify that idea.

It is important not to confuse "amplification," or development, with padding. Repetitious writing or puffed-up discourse, whose main features are the wordiest way of saying something, is not interesting to anyone. Amplification should be thought of as a public justification for private views, a making concrete and convincing assertions that might otherwise lack clarity and conviction. Some lazy and unimaginative writers feel they have fulfilled their obligation by tossing off a string of general statements and assertions. Let the reader supply his own particulars! Such a writer might be content, for example, to pass on to another aspect of his essay after no more than the following statement:

> The driver-training program at Central High School included some interesting classroom presentations.

"What kind of presentations?" the reader (or certainly the instructor) will demand. Did the teacher show films of poor driving techniques? Did he use scale-model automobiles to illustrate the proper way of passing another car? Did a representative of the National Safety Council visit the class and startle the students with statistics about highway deaths or show pictures of the gruesome results of accidents? In short, the easy but uninteresting and really uninformative generality "some interesting classroom presentations" makes the essay superficial—and dull.

With a written statement of your controlling idea before you, let your mind play with its implications. Permit your free association to work on it, remembering to jot down as many of the ideas that come to you as possible. Don't worry about their order or their spelling or their neatness. The important thing is to get something down on paper, with which you can then work.

After making an unstructured collection of ideas and experiences, attempt a more logical analysis, and again note the results on your scrap paper. Examine the important terms of your controlling idea, and write definitions for each term, setting forth its special properties, its formal meaning, its function, and its appearance. Does the controlling idea have divisions? Does it have subdivisions? If so, what are they? Is the controlling idea the effect or result of something else? What effects or consequences may it have? What specific, concrete examples can you think of to support or illustrate your concept? How is it similar to or different from other concepts? Posing and answering such questions will provide more items than you may wish to retain in your essay, but among them will be the constituent elements for the main body of your composition. You will then be ready for the second principal stage of composition—organizing your material.

Before discussing this step, however, let's try this kind of amplification for a specific controlling idea. Let's assume that you have been asked to write an essay of 500–600 words for which you must supply both subject and approach. Following the counsel offered earlier, you have interviewed yourself and find recurring in your thoughts certain recollections of the first weeks of your freshman year, particularly an insistent dislike of the whole freshman orientation program in which you were a reluctant participant. Deciding to focus on the orientation program and to use as your controlling idea your dislike of it, you might devise the following working idea: "The freshman orientation program at Ringo College was a waste of time."

Your problem now is to amplify, or to find the implications of the controlling idea and the means of supporting it. By letting your free associations collect on the page before you, you might produce a list like this:

> exhausting walks from bldg. to bldg.
> rain one day (smelly clothes in the lecture hall)
> blood sample taken by nurse (five jabs at vein)
> lasted three days
> aptitude tests
> learned school songs and where to buy used books

A more deliberate analysis might produce the following items:

DEFINITION:
> freshman orientation a process of familiarizing the student with necessary information about his college

ANALYSIS:
consisted of lectures by administrative people, teachers, and upperclassmen
health exam
testing
socializing

ENUMERATION OF DETAILS:
speeches by President Smythers, Dean Wilson, Prof. Jackson (Psych. Dept.),
president of student council
health exam—X-ray, blood test, complete health record
tours of library, of campus, of new science bldg.
talk by dean of students
reviews of freshman handbook
three dances and two receptions

EFFECTS:
boredom
information about eligibility for sports interesting
met other freshmen and some upperclassmen
learned what teachers to avoid
exhausted, depressed

CAUSES:
games at dances forced you to meet new people
talks and lectures too long, too repetitious
foolish having to walk from place to place to hear lectures
student guides met us late, took us to wrong places
program spread out over too much time
most information would have been picked up anyway when school began

COMPARISON AND CONTRAST:
at Sewickey College, high school friend liked orientation
lasted one day and night
social night with a name band and a popular comedian
good banquet
discussion of a book everyone had read

ILLUSTRATION:
poor planning
went to lecture hall to hear president
loudspeaker didn't work
could hardly hear anything he said
talk lasted one hour and fifteen minutes
not enough seats for everyone
heat terrible
president was late in arriving
talk more like a sermon

The results of this procedure do not, of course, constitute a composition, but they provide you with the basic elements for one, probably more than you will actually need or want to use.

ORGANIZATION

The second major step in writing a composition is organizing the components of the essay.

A composition must have a distinct integrity of its own; that is, it must have outer limits and inner structure. This is another way of stating the ancient requisite that effective discourse must have a beginning, a middle, and an end. The following diagram shows a basic and common pattern for a composition.

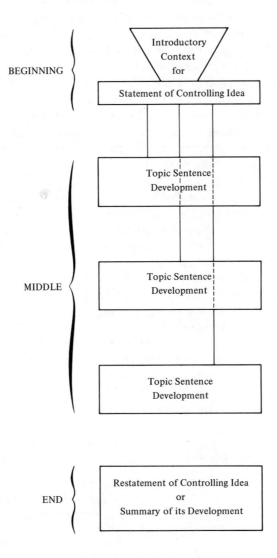

Such a pattern may strike you as too rigid and formal, and you will certainly find experienced writers departing from it. But it is well in the early stages of developing your writing to master a conventional and workable pattern before taking liberties with it.

The "beginning" in most freshman essays consists of one paragraph. Its principal function is to arrest the attention of the reader and to give him a context that will make the controlling idea intelligible. The beginning is a rhetorical strategy to arouse the reader's interest and to guide his understanding. You must be careful that your introduction really introduces, that it is not filled with irrelevant, vapid, mere space-filling padding. But an effective introduction will keep the statement of your thesis or purpose from appearing too baldly functional and ungracefully abrupt.

Many students find writing the introductory paragraph difficult. If you have unusual trouble, postpone writing the introduction until you revise your first draft. By that time an effective opening will probably have occurred to you. But a number of standard openers may serve you. You might begin with a classical or a contemporary quotation which is pertinent to your subject, a question or a series of questions which your controlling idea answers, a statement about a situation which you will refute or confirm, an account of a shocking or typical incident, a series of statistics which your idea will explain or interpret, an explanation of your interest or ability to discuss your subject, or an explanation of the background of your concept.

The "end" is frequently a brief concluding paragraph which restates your controlling idea in somewhat different form, or, without being repetitious, briefly summarizes the significance of the main body. Again, a concluding paragraph is a rhetorical strategy which gives emphasis and a sense of completeness and utilizes an ancient pedagogical technique: having told the audience what you are going to tell them and having told them, you tell them what they have heard. But a concluding paragraph may often be unnecessary, particularly in very brief essays. Then the last paragraph of the main body may conclude the essay, signaling the end by transitional markers like *finally* and *in conclusion*.

Your major organizational problem will be in ordering the parts of the main body of your essay. The amplification of your controlling idea will provide a number of items which you will have to arrange in some meaningful way. You will have to look for related ideas, group them in coordinate and subordinate categories, and exclude the extraneous or trivial items which may have slipped in.

Consider the following list of unorganized ideas relating to the controlling idea, "Summer jobs are a valuable experience for students":

busboys	employment agencies
camp counselors	high school counselors'
learn responsibility	recommendations
unpleasant working conditions	road work

gardening   earn spending money
risks of accidents   swimming instructors
want ads   clerical work
lack of summer rest   typists
lack of summer recreation   file clerks
meet new friends   department store sales clerks
learn to adjust to new situations door-to-door salesmen
lose contacts with friends   milk routes
learn to take orders   earn good work recommendations
earn money for college tuition   construction work

Were you to try to write a composition on the basis of these unorganized items the problems would be head-splitting and the results chaotic. Consider now the same material analyzed into groups and subgroups of related ideas:

I. Kinds of Summer Employment for Students
    A. Food service
        1. Busboys
        2. Waiters
        3. Cooks
        4. Dishwashers
    B. Camp work
        1. Swimming instructor
        2. Boating instructor
        3. Counselors
    C. Clerical work
        1. Typists
        2. File clerks
    D. Sales jobs
        1. Department stores
        2. Door-to-door
        3. Milk routes
    E. Manual work
        1. Road work
        2. Gardening
        3. Construction
II. Leads for Summer Jobs
    A. Want ads
    B. High school counselors
    C. Employment agencies
III. Advantages of Summer Jobs
    A. Learn responsibility
    B. Learn to take orders
    C. Meet new friends
    D. Build up a work record
    E. Earn good recommendations
    F. Earn money for tuition
    G. Earn money for personal expenses
    H. Learn to adjust to new situations

IV. Disadvantages
    A. Lose contact with friends
    B. Lack of rest and relaxation before school
    C. Possibly unpleasant working conditions
    D. Risks of accidents

Such an analysis may help you narrow your topic further and modify your controlling idea. It will greatly facilitate your writing your first draft.

The way in which a writer organizes his essay is influenced by his purpose in writing, the nature of his subject, and what he judges the most effective means of communicating his thoughts. As each composition poses unique organizational problems, it is pointless to generalize about the *best* kind of organization. But it is useful to mention some of the options at your disposal. You may wish to follow a chronological pattern and consider each aspect of a subject in a time sequence. Or, if your subject involves the description of some object or scene, you may follow a spatial pattern: proceed from top to bottom, left to right, inside to outside, and so on. You may, on the other hand, have a series of items to enumerate in a sequential fashion, in which case you can proceed from the least to the most important, the earliest to the most recent, the farthest to the nearest, or the least vivid to the most startling. Again, you may wish to use one of the logical patterns. For example, you can treat your subject inductively by first discussing details and then drawing conclusions from them; or you can proceed deductively, beginning with a general statement and then applying it to specific instances. Other kinds of logical patterns are cause to effect, effect to cause, comparison and contrast, and definition and differentiation.

There are, then, a number of patterns which you may utilize. What is of chief importance is that you organize your material in *some* way and that you make the divisions apparent to the reader. Just as punctuation aids him in grasping the units of thought within sentences and paragraphs, clear demarcations of the elements of your discussion assist him in following, understanding, and assimilating the presentation of your ideas.

An outline, such as the one above, is indispensable for the orderly development of your subject. Some students resist using outlines and prepare them *after* they have written their compositions, merely to satisfy the letter of a particular compositional assignment. But an outline is only useful as a tool, as an efficient means to a desirable end. The student who writes first and outlines afterwards is improperly using a valuable aid.

An outline is valuable in several ways. First, as in the example above, an outline reduces a number of related items to understandable groupings; it establishes classes of data and subordinates members within those classes. Second, it gives you an overall view of the basic elements of your material and a chance to try alternative patterns of arrangement, which are impossible when the basic elements are scattered over several pages. Third, the outline is an important aid in preserving unity in your composition and insuring that the components are clearly pertinent to the controlling idea. It is in the outline that you can most easily detect an item which, upon closer examination, proves to be irrelevant. In the outline duplication or the need for further amplification can be easily seen.

WRITING THE FIRST DRAFT

The first draft translates your outline into coherent discourse. If you have outlined with care, you will find that the Roman numerals of your outline will usually furnish the substance of the topic sentences of your paragraphs and that the various subdivisions of the principal headings will constitute the bodies of the paragraphs. The greater the detail with which you have worked out your outline the greater the ease with which you will turn it into prose discourse.

But the major business at hand is to write. Let your pen or pencil go as rapidly as possible or your fingers fly on the typewriter keys. Do not pause to think about conventions of punctuation and spelling, usage, grammar, or other inspiration-killing considerations. The important thing is to write, to turn your ideas into a visible form that you can later revise and correct. No one else will see this rough draft, so it can be as messy as your visions and revisions require. It is your working material, something that you will tinker with, cross out, add to, alter, and elaborate.

Writers differ in their ways of writing first drafts. Some sit, some stand, some pace up and down and write in transit. Some favor hard pencils, some soft; some goosequill pens, some typewriters. Some must have music, others absolute silence. Some favor yellow paper, some white; some magenta ink, some black. No single recommendation can be made about this part of the process, and you should find your own most satisfying way of doing it. Prudence suggests, however, that you leave ample margins and plenty of space between lines for corrections, that you write on only one side of each page, and that you number the pages.

Having written your first draft, read through it and make whatever corrections seem called for—and stop. Put it aside for a time. Always try to budget your time so that you may relax your attention between the various stages of composition. Your mind unconsciously continues to work on your writing assignment and, when you return to your work after a rest, you will suddenly see new and better possibilities for effective paragraph arrangement and sentence construction, or summon up the right illustration or the word for which you had been groping. You will find that what at first seemed an acceptable sentence is awkward, that an eloquent patch of writing inspired in the early hours of the morning is, in the soberer light of the following afternoon, chiefly remarkable for its irrelevance or unintelligibility.

REVISION AND THE FINAL DRAFT

Return to the first draft and read through it; decipher whatever notes you have left for yourself in the margins and incorporate whatever changes seem desirable. Most writers then write a second and, sometimes, a third rough draft. This may strike you as unnecessarily laborious procedure, but good writing is almost always the product of much rewriting and revision. It is interesting to note, in this regard, that Ernest Hemingway rewrote the closing paragraph of *A Farewell to Arms* nearly forty times before he was satisfied with it, and James Joyce is reported to have been satisfied with a day of writing if he produced *one* sentence of which he completely approved.

With the neater and more legible second draft before you, look for further possibilities of meaningful revision. Among them will be revision of grammar, syntax, and diction, the deletion or addition of material, and the improvement of coherence.

By grammar we mean here both a kind of "linguistic etiquette," as W. Nelson Francis puts it, and the means by which relationships between words are indicated and by which meaningful statements are constructed in English. Revision of grammar in the first sense corrects departures from standard idiomatic expressions and conventional English usage in such matters as plural forms, subject-verb agreement, pronoun and reference and case, and verb forms. In the second sense revision seeks to arrange sentences, or *grammatical structures,* in the most appropriate and effective way.

English is a very flexible language, which frequently offers alternative verbal structures which can convey essentially the same information. Active constructions, for example, can be transformed into passive: "The bullet hit the man," "The man was hit by the bullet." And an infinitive phrase can be replaced with a gerund: "John likes to swim," "John likes swimming." By attaching affixes to certain words and by changing their position and function, we can generate different structures:

He put a bandage on the wound that was serious.
He bandaged the serious wound.

He was not experienced in the use of guns.
He was inexperienced in using guns.

The cover of the book is decorated with geometrical figures.
The decoration of the book's cover is geometrical figures.
Geometrical figures decorate the book cover.

I divided the pie into fair shares.
I divided the pie fairly.

I saw a man out for a walk in the park in the afternoon.
I saw a man who was walking in the park in the afternoon.

I saw a man walking in the park in the afternoon.
I saw a man taking an afternoon walk in the park.

In revising syntax, you should look for the most effective position of words, phrases, and clauses, so that modifiers modify the appropriate word or phrase, elements give the desired emphasis, punctuation accurately signals syntactical divisions, and dull, monotonous sentence structures are avoided. Consider, for example, the following possible syntactical variants:

Only the young fireman offered to save the old man.
The young fireman only offered to save the old man.
The young fireman offered only to save the old man.
The young fireman offered to save only the old man.
The only young fireman offered to save the old man.

The tall swaying trees were gracefully serene.
The swaying tall trees were serenely graceful.

Walking in the street, the automobile hit the man.
The automobile hit the man walking in the street.

The man with the lady who had a black coat departed quickly.
The man who had a black coat departed quickly with the lady.
The man departed quickly with the lady who had a black coat.
The man with the lady, who had a black coat, departed quickly.

In revising diction, replace colorless, omnibus words with more specific, vivid expressions:

The man left the building.
The drunk crashed through the screen door.

The nice man gave the nice boy a nice present.
The friendly minister handed a shiny hunting knife to the courteous student.

Good diction further calls for the elimination of clichés and the unmixing of mixed metaphors that otherwise produce a ludicrous effect, such as Mrs. Richard Nixon's statement concerning her husband's gubernatorial campaign in California, "Dick is going to take off the gloves and nail down these vicious smears."

Elimination and addition are other matters to consider in revision. As painful as it sometimes is to discard a pleasing passage from your essay, try to be as objective as possible—and as ruthless as necessary—in order to keep your writing relevant to your purpose. Irrelevant material not only weakens the effect of your writing but also confuses and misleads your reader. Look, too, for redundancies, for patches of wordiness where a precise word may replace a phrase or clause, and for unnecessary repetition in idea and word. Search for areas that require additional development, statements that need clarification and assertions that demand further support.

Revision for coherence attempts to make clear the relationship of the components of an essay to each other. Good organization, of course, contributes to coherent writing, but transitional words and phrases show most easily how the elements in a composition relate to each other and to the whole essay. Some of the principal relationships and the expressions that signal them follow:

ENUMERATIVE: in addition to, and, also, second, moreover, furthermore, next, in summary, besides

TEMPORAL: first, next, then, later, before, after, when, soon, thereafter, immediately preceding, subsequently

SPATIAL: in front of, behind, before, near to, on the right, to the left, over, above, beneath, behind

CONSEQUENTIAL: as a result, thus, therefore, consequently, then, hence

COMPARATIVE: similarly, like, in like manner, just as, in the same way

ILLUSTRATIVE: for example, for instance, such as

Such expressions give writing a continuity and smooth flow. They are to the elements of a paragraph or a composition what mortar is to the bricks in a wall.

After revising the second draft, you are ready to write the final copy. Make this version as neat and as legible as possible; such qualities indicate your respect for your audience and suggest the care you have expended on your work. If at all possible, type the final copy—and reread it carefully before submitting it. You will frequently find small, but potentially embarrassing typing errors (for example, a school bulletin declared that the tuition for summer session was $225.00, including bed and broad," and an inattentive proofreader did not correct the following: " 'On Moscow streets . . . there are few young men around. As soon as the young men are of age they are whiskyed away into the service.").

The procedures we have presented here will enable you to communicate your insights and experiences in an efficient manner. With practice you will develop facility in writing and proceed from self-conscious application of directions to smooth, continuous writing, an act that can become increasingly spontaneous, painless, and pleasurable.

Exercises

1. Divide each of the following topics into as many subtopics as you can: communism, adolescence, government, careers.

2. By using the following pattern, frame five theses, each on a different subject:

The constitution of the Student Council should be revised because it fails to specify the duties and powers of its officers and the Council's relationship to faculty and administrative bodies in the college.

3. By using the following pattern, frame five theses, each on a different subject:

Although student protests have sometimes been very disruptive and costly, they have been valuable in forcing administrations to provide more imaginative and relevant studies for their students.

4. Frame a thesis concerning your high school Senior Class Trip and amplify the thesis in as much detail as you can. (If convenient, this undertaking might be a cooperative effort by the class in which each person contributes ideas in developing the thesis.)

5. From the series of items produced in 4. above, select the most promising and arrange them in an outline.

6. The sequence of "athletic organization," "baseball team," and "St. Louis Cardinals" proceeds from general to more and more specific. Complete the blanks below with increasingly specific words or phrases.

GENERAL			SPECIFIC
book	___	___	___
dwelling	___	___	___
transportation	___	___	___
disease	___	___	___
medical personnel	___	___	___

7. Indicate several more vivid and concrete substitutes for each of the italicized words or phrases in the sentences below.

a. *The animal consumed* the *food.*

b. The *creatures noted* the *natural phenomena.*

c. *The household article* was *removed* from the *enclosure.*

8. Make the corrections or revisions you think are needed in the following sentences.

a. George told his father that he had received no mail.

b. My friend John Smith a person I had known in college joined me on March 13 1967 for lunch in Burton a small quaint town in England.

c. All those who had accompanied us and traveled with us to New York objected to stopping on the return trip back to Pittsburgh to eat their evening meal because of the fact that they wanted to catch the 9:10 P.M. evening train.

d. Striking workers can be dangerous.

e. Children who are disrespectful sometimes require compassion.

f. When I was in college as a student I had to compile and bring together a list of titles of books and of magazine articles published in journals and periodicals which pertained to the general subject of the effects and consequences of smoking.

g. I stared at the man while he spoke intently.

h. We talked for a long time he told me he was having a good time however he seemed subdued unhappy and depressed.

i. My father liked to quote Dr Johnson's comment concerning Rousseau A man who talks nonsense so well, must know that he is talking nonsense.

j. Stand back shouted the policeman do you want to smother him

k. Students who are homesick frequently do poor work.

l. I was introduced to an actor with a beard that completely captivated me.

m. The two prisoners who were awaiting trial asked a man who seemed frightened of them for cigarettes.

n. The natives we talked to often became very friendly to us.

o. The teacher looked at the boy with a pained expression.

p. Walking around the corner, the speeding car struck the child.

q. His two ambitions are to graduate from college and finding a good-paying job.

r. When only eight years old, his mother died.

s. He asked that his petition be acted upon immediately and the restoring of his name to the class roll.

t. He was encouraged by the good grade on his last examination, I think he will begin to do much better work now.

The Analytic
Reading of Exposition

Writing is a skill that may be cultivated and improved by deliberate practice. But for centuries, careful, attentive reading has also been regarded as a complementary and highly useful aid in improving one's writing. English schoolboys during the Renaissance laboriously sought (or were driven to pursue) a good Latin style by close reading and imitation of famous Latin authors. To this end they sometimes made "double translations," whereby they first translated the Latin into English and then, without consulting the original, translated the English back into Latin, measuring their success by the closeness of their Latin to that of the original. In his *Autobiography* the enterprising Benjamin Franklin reports a similar effort by which he perfected his style through imitating that of the *Spectator* essays. After a close reading of one of the essays, during which he attempted to absorb its structure, diction, sentence patterns, and content, he would attempt to rewrite the essay from his recollection. Through these exercises he sought to make something of Addison's grace and clarity a part of his own style.

Whatever one may think of such deliberate exercises in imitative writing, reading is an important adjunct to fluency and facility in writing. Just as in learning to speak we repeat what we have heard, so in writing, if somewhat less spontaneously, we write what we have read. Individuals differ in their capacity to relate their reading experience to their writing. Some easily absorb the conventions of punctuation and spelling, appropriate their author's vocabulary for their own purposes, and become increasingly aware of the rich subtleties of syntax and the potential for grammatical structures, all of which they turn to good account when they write. Others find the transfer less facile and the need for a guide to mediate between them and the printed page more pressing. But careful and extensive reading is an important aid for all writers.

This book encourages an approach to writing development through practice and careful reading. But before turning to the materials in the remainder of the book, we shall say something briefly about the careful, analytic reading we here recommend and suggest through a series of questions how it might be applied to a substantial piece of writing.

Responsible reading has three qualities: it is analytic, interpretive, and critical. Analytic reading seeks to understand the underlying structure of a work, that is, its basic elements and their relationship to each other. Interpretive reading attempts to comprehend the author's meaning, to understand his ideas and the vocabulary in which he expresses them. Critical reading tests the author's views by the reader's own sense of logic and consistency, his experience, and his judgment.

The following essay, a minor classic of exposition, will give you an opportunity to read an essay in these three ways. Its author was George Orwell (1903–1950) who, besides living a strenuously interesting life in Burma and the bohemian quarters of London and Paris, and fighting in the Spanish Civil War, distinguished himself as a novelist, satirist, essayist, and literary critic. He is most frequently remembered today as the author of *Animal Farm* (1945) and *1984* (1949), disturbing satires of twentieth-century totalitarianism.

GEORGE ORWELL

Politics and the English Language

Most people who bother with the matter at all would admit that the English language is in a bad way, but it is generally assumed that we cannot by conscious action do anything about it. Our civilization is decadent and our language—so the argument runs—must inevitably share in the general collapse. It follows that any struggle against the abuse of language is a sentimental archaism, like preferring candles to electric light or hansom cabs to aeroplanes. Underneath this lies the half-conscious belief that language is a natural growth and not an instrument which we shape for our own purposes.

Now, it is clear that the decline of a language must ultimately have political and economic causes: it is not due simply to the bad influence of this or that individual writer. But an effect can become a cause, reinforcing the original cause and producing the same effect in an intensified form, and so on indefinitely. A man may take to drink because he feels himself to be a failure, and then fail all the more completely because he drinks. It is rather the same thing that is happening to the English language. It becomes ugly and inaccurate because our thoughts are foolish, but the slovenliness of our language makes it easier for us to have foolish thoughts. The point is that the process is reversible. Modern English, especially written English, is full of bad habits which spread by imitation and which can be avoided if one is willing to take the necessary trouble. If one gets rid of these habits one can think more clearly, and to think clearly is a necessary first step towards political regeneration: so that the fight against bad English is not frivolous and is not the exclusive concern of professional writers. I will come back to this presently, and I hope that by that time the meaning of what I have said here will have become clearer. Meanwhile, here are five specimens of the English language as it is now habitually written.

These five passages have not been picked out because they are especially bad—I could have quoted far worse if I had chosen—but because they illustrate various of the mental vices from which we now suffer. They are a little below the average, but are fairly representative samples. I number them so that I can refer back to them when necessary:

(1) I am not, indeed, sure whether it is not true to say that the Milton who once seemed not unlike a seventeenth-century Shelley had not become, out of an experience ever more bitter in each year, more alien [*sic*] to the founder of that Jesuit sect which nothing could induce him to tolerate.
          Professor Harold Laski (Essay in *Freedom of Expression*)

(2) Above all, we cannot play ducks and drakes with a native battery of idioms which prescribes such egregious collocations of vocables as the Basic *put up with* for *tolerate* or *put at a loss* for *bewilder*.
          Professor Lancelot Hogben (*Interglossa*)

(3) On the one side we have the free personality: by definition it is not neurotic, for it has neither conflict nor dream. Its desires, such as they are, are transparent, for they are just what institutional approval keeps in the forefront of consciousness; another institutional pattern would alter their number and intensity; there is little in them that is natural, irreducible, or culturally dangerous. But *on the other side,* the social bond itself is nothing but the mutual reflection of these self-secure integrities. Recall the definition of love. Is not this the very picture of a small academic? Where is there a place in this hall of mirrors for either personality or fraternity?
          Essay on psychology in *Politics* (New York)

(4) All the "best people" from the gentlemen's clubs, and all the frantic fascist captains, united in common hatred of Socialism and bestial horror of the rising tide of the mass revolutionary movement, have turned to acts of provocation, to foul incendiarism, to medieval legends of poisoned wells, to legalize their own destruction of proletarian organizations, and rouse the agitated petty-

bourgeoisie to chauvinistic fervor on behalf of the fight against the revolutionary way out of the crisis.

Communist pamphlet

(5) If a new spirit *is* to be infused into this old country, there is one thorny and contentious reform which must be tackled, and that is the humanization and galvanization of the B.B.C. Timidity here will bespeak canker and atrophy of the soul. The heart of Britain may be sound and of strong beat, for instance, but the British lion's roar at present is like that of Bottom in Shakespeare's *Midsummer Night's Dream*—as gentle as any sucking dove. A virile new Britain cannot continue indefinitely to be traduced in the eyes or rather ears, of the world by the effete languors of Langham Place, brazenly masquerading as "standard English." When the Voice of Britain is heard at nine o'clock, better far and infinitely less ludicrous to hear aitches honestly dropped than the present priggish, inflated, inhibited, school-ma'amish arch braying of blameless bashful mewing maidens!

Letter in *Tribune*

Each of these passages has faults of its own, but, quite apart from avoidable ugliness, two qualities are common to all of them. The first is staleness of imagery; the other is lack of precision. The writer either has a meaning and cannot express it, or he inadvertently says something else, or he is almost indifferent as to whether his words mean anything or not. This mixture of vagueness and sheer incompetence is the most marked characteristic of modern English prose, and especially of any kind of political writing. As soon as certain topics are raised, the concrete melts into the abstract, and no one seems able to think of turns of speech that are not hackneyed: prose consists less and less of *words* chosen for the sake of their meaning, and more and more of *phrases* tacked together like the sections of a prefabricated hen-house. I list below, with notes and examples, various of the tricks by means of which the work of prose-construction is habitually dodged:

DYING METAPHORS

A newly invented metaphor assists thought by evoking a visual image, while on the other hand a metaphor which is technically "dead" (e.g., *iron resolution*) has in effect reverted to being an ordinary word and can generally be used without loss of vividness. But in between these two classes there is a huge dump of worn-out metaphors which have lost all evocative power and are merely used because they save people the trouble of inventing phrases for themselves. Examples are: *Ring the changes on, take up the cudgels for, toe the line, ride roughshod over, stand shoulder to shoulder with, play into the hands of, no axe to grind, grist to the mill, fishing in troubled waters, on the order of the day, Achilles' heel, swan song, hotbed.*

Many of these are used without knowledge of their meaning (what is a "rift," for instance?), and incompatible metaphors are frequently mixed, a sure sign that the writer is not interested in what he is saying. Some metaphors now current have been twisted out of their original meaning without those who use them even being aware of the fact. For example, *toe the line* is sometimes written *tow the line.* Another example is *the hammer and the anvil,* now always used with the implication that the anvil gets the worst of it. In real life it is always the anvil that breaks the hammer, never the other way about: a writer who stopped to think what he was saying would be aware of this, and would avoid perverting the original phrase.

OPERATORS OR VERBAL FALSE LIMBS

These save the trouble of picking out appropriate verbs and nouns, and at the same time pad each sentence with extra syllables which give it an appearance of symmetry. Characteristic phrases are *render inoperative, militate against, make contact with, be subjected to, give rise to, give grounds for, have the effect of, play a leading part (role) in, make itself felt, take effect, exhibit a tendency to, serve the purpose of, etc., etc.* The keynote is the elimination of simple verbs. Instead of being a single word, such as *break, stop, spoil, mend, kill,* a verb becomes a *phrase,* made up of a noun or adjective tacked on to some general-purposes verb such as *prove, serve, form, play, render.* In addition, the passive voice is wherever possible used in preference to the active, and noun constructions are used instead of gerunds (*by examination of* instead of *by examining*). The range of verbs is further cut down by means of the *-ize* and *de-* formations, and the banal statements are given an appearance of profundity by means of the *not un-* formation. Simple conjunctions and prepositions are replaced by such phrases as *with respect to, having regard to, the fact that, by dint of, in view of, in the interests of, on the hypothesis that;* and the ends of sentences are saved from anticlimax by such resounding commonplaces as *greatly to be desired, cannot be left out of account, a development to be expected in the near future, deserving of serious consideration, brought to a satisfactory conclusion,* and so on and so forth.

PRETENTIOUS DICTION

Words like *phenomenon, element, individual* (as noun), *objective, categorical, effective, virtual, basis, primary, promote, constitute, exhibit, exploit, utilize, eliminate, liquidate,* are used to dress up simple statements and give an air of scientific impartiality to biased judgments. Adjectives like *epoch-*

making, epic, historic, unforgettable, triumphant, age-old, inevitable, inexorable, veritable, are used to dignify the sordid processes of international politics, while writing that aims at glorifying war usually takes on an archaic color, its characteristic words being: *realm, throne, chariot, mailed fist, trident, sword, shield, buckler, banner, jackboot, clarion.* Foreign words and expressions such as *cul de sac, ancien régime, deus ex machina, mutatis mutandis, status quo, gleichschaltung, weltanschauung,* are used to give an air of culture and elegance. Except for the useful abbreviations *i.e., e.g.,* and *etc.,* there is no real need for any of the hundreds of foreign phrases now current in English. Bad writers, and especially scientific, political and sociological writers, are nearly always haunted by the notion that Latin or Greek words are grander than Saxon ones, and unnecessary words like *expedite, ameliorate, predict, extraneous, deracinated, clandestine, subaqueous* and hundreds of others constantly gain ground from their Anglo-Saxon opposite numbers.[1] The jargon peculiar to Marxist writing (*hyena, hangman, cannibal, petty bourgeois, these gentry, lacquey, flunkey, mad dog, White Guard,* etc.) consists largely of words and phrases translated from Russian, German or French; but the normal way of coining a new word is to use a Latin or Greek root with the appropriate affix and, where necessary, the *-ize* formation. It is often easier to make up words of this kind (*deregionalize, impermissible, extramarital, non-fragmentary* and so forth) than to think up the English words that will cover one's meaning. The result, in general, is an increase in slovenliness and vagueness.

MEANINGLESS WORDS

In certain kinds of writing, particularly in art criticism and literary criticism, it is normal to come across long passages which are almost completely lacking in meaning.[2] Words like *romantic, plastic, values, human, dead, sentimental, natural, vitality,* as used in art criticism, are strictly meaningless, in the sense that they not only do not point to any discoverable

---

[1] An interesting illustration of this is the way in which the English flower names which were in use till very recently are being ousted by Greek ones, *snapdragon* becoming *antirrhinum, forget-me-not* becoming *myosotis,* etc. It is hard to see any practical reason for this change of fashion: it is probably due to an instinctive turning-away from the more homely word and a vague feeling that the Greek word is scientific.

[2] Example: "Comfort's catholicity of perception and image, strangely Whitmanesque in range, almost the exact opposite in aesthetic compulsion, continues to evoke that trembling atmospheric accumulative hinting at a cruel, and inexorably serene timelessness. . . . Wrey Gardiner scores by aiming at simple bull's-eyes with precision. Only they are not so simple, and through this contented sadness runs more than the surface bitter-sweet of resignation." (*Poetry Quarterly.*)

object, but are hardly ever expected to do so by the reader. When one critic writes, "The outstanding feature of Mr. X's work is its living quality," while another writes, "The immediately striking thing about Mr. X's work is its peculiar deadness," the reader accepts this as a simple difference of opinion. If words like *black* and *white* were involved, instead of the jargon words *dead* and *living,* he would see at once that language was being used in an improper way. Many political words are similarly abused. The word *Fascism* has now no meaning except in so far as it signifies "something not desirable." The words *democracy, socialism, freedom, patriotic, realistic, justice,* have each of them several different meanings which cannot be reconciled with one another. In the case of a word like *democracy,* not only is there no agreed definition, but the attempt to make one is resisted from all sides. It is almost universally felt that when we call a country democratic we are praising it: consequently the defenders of every kind of régime claim that it is a democracy, and fear that they might have to stop using the word if it were tied down to any one meaning. Words of this kind are often used in a consciously dishonest way. That is, the person who uses them has his own private definition, but allows his hearer to think he means something quite different. Statements like *Marshal Pétain was a true ·patriot, The Soviet Press is the freest in the world, The Catholic Church is opposed to persecution,* are almost always made with intent to deceive. Other words used in variable meanings, in most cases more or less dishonestly, are: *class, totalitarian, science, progressive, reactionary, bourgeois, equality.*

Now that I have made this catalogue of swindles and perversions, let me give another example of the kind of writing that they lead to. This time it must of its nature be an imaginary one. I am going to translate a passage of good English into modern English of the worst sort. Here is a well-known verse from *Ecclesiastes:*

> I returned and saw under the sun, that the race is not to the swift, nor the battle to the strong, neither yet bread to the wise, nor yet riches to men of understanding, nor yet favour to men of skill; but time and chance happeneth to them all.

Here it is in modern English:

> Objective consideration of contemporary phenomena compels the conclusion that success or failure in competitive activities exhibits no tendency to be commensurate with innate capacity, but that a considerable element of the unpredictable must invariably be taken into account.

This is a parody, but not a very gross one. Exhibit (3), above, for instance, contains several patches of the same kind of English. It will be seen that I have not made a full translation. The beginning and ending of the sentence follow the original meaning fairly closely, but in the middle the concrete illustrations—race, battle, bread—dissolve into the vague phrase "success or failure in competitive activities." This had to be so, because no modern writer of the kind I am discussing—no one capable of using phrases like "objective consideration of contemporary phenomena"—would ever tabulate his thoughts in that precise and detailed way. The whole tendency of modern prose is away from concreteness. Now analyze these two sentences a little more closely. The first contains forty-nine words but only sixty syllables, and all its words are those of everyday life. The second contains thirty-eight words of ninety syllables: eighteen of its words are from Latin roots, and one from Greek. The first sentence contains six vivid images, and only one phrase ("time and chance") that could be called vague. The second contains not a single fresh, arresting phrase, and in spite of its ninety syllables it gives only a shortened version of the meaning contained in the first. Yet without a doubt it is the second kind of sentence that is gaining ground in modern English. I do not want to exaggerate. This kind of writing is not yet universal, and outcrops of simplicity will occur here and there in the worst-written page. Still, if you or I were told to write a few lines on the uncertainty of human fortunes, we should probably come much nearer to my imaginary sentence than to the one from *Ecclesiastes*.

As I have tried to show, modern writing at its worst does not consist in picking out words for the sake of their meaning and inventing images in order to make the meaning clearer. It consists in gumming together long strips of words which have already been set in order by someone else, and making the results presentable by sheer humbug. The attraction of this way of writing is that it is easy. It is easier—even quicker, once you have the habit—to say *In my opinion it is not an unjustifiable assumption that* than to say *I think*. If you use ready-made phrases, you not only don't have to hunt about for words; you also don't have to bother with the rhythms of your sentences, since these phrases are generally so arranged as to be more or less euphonious. When you are composing in a hurry—when you are dictating to a stenographer, for instance, or making a public speech—it is natural to fall into a pretentious, Latinized style. Tags like *a consideration which we should do well to bear in mind* or *a conclusion to which all of us would readily assent* will save many a sentence from coming down with a bump. By using stale metaphors, similes and idioms, you save much mental effort, at the cost of leaving your meaning vague, not only for your reader but for yourself. This is the significance of mixed metaphors. The sole aim of a metaphor is to call up a visual image. When these images clash—as in *The Fascist octopus has sung its swan song, the jackboot is thrown into the melting pot*—it can be taken as certain that the writer is not seeing a mental image of the objects he is naming; in other words he is not really thinking. Look again at the examples I gave at the beginning of this essay. Professor Laski (1) uses five negatives in fifty-three words.

One of these is superfluous, making nonsense of the whole passage, and in addition there is the slip *alien* for akin, making further nonsense, and several avoidable pieces of clumsiness which increase the general vagueness. Professor Hogben (2) plays ducks and drakes with a battery which is able to write prescriptions, and, while disapproving of the everyday phrase *put up with,* is unwilling to look *egregious* up in the dictionary and see what it means; (3), if one takes an uncharitable attitude towards it, is simply meaningless: probably one could work out its intended meaning by reading the whole of the article in which it occurs. In (4), the writer knows more or less what he wants to say, but an accumulation of stale phrases chokes him like tea leaves blocking a sink. In (5), words and meaning have almost parted company. People who write in this manner usually have a general emotional meaning—they dislike one thing and want to express solidarity with another—but they are not interested in the detail of what they are saying. A scrupulous writer, in every sentence that he writes, will ask himself at least four questions, thus: What am I trying to say? What words will express it? What image or idiom will make it clearer? Is this image fresh enough to have an effect? And he will probably ask himself two more: Could I put it more shortly? Have I said anything that is avoidably ugly? But you are not obliged to go to all this trouble. You can shirk it by simply throwing your mind open and letting the ready-made phrases come crowding in. They will construct your sentences for you—even think your thoughts for you, to a certain extent—and at need they will perform the important service of partially concealing your meaning even from yourself. It is at this point that the special connection between politics and the debasement of language becomes clear.

In our time it is broadly true that political writing is bad writing. Where it is not true, it will generally be found that the writer is some kind of rebel, expressing his private opinions and not a "party line." Orthodoxy, of whatever color, seems to demand a lifeless, imitative style. The political dialects to be found in pamphlets, leading articles, manifestos, White Papers and the speeches of under-secretaries do, of course, vary from party to party, but they are all alike in that one almost never finds in them a fresh, vivid, home-made turn of speech. When one watches some tired hack on the platform mechanically repeating the familiar phrases—*bestial atrocities, iron heel, bloodstained tyranny, free peoples of the world, stand shoulder to shoulder*—one often has a curious feeling that one is not watching a live human being but some kind of dummy: a feeling which suddenly becomes stronger at moments when the light catches the speaker's spectacles and turns them into blank discs which seem to have no eyes behind them. And this is not altogether fanciful. A speaker who uses that kind of phraseology has gone some distance towards turning himself into a machine. The appropriate noises are coming out of his larynx, but his brain is not involved as it would be if he were choosing his words for himself. If the speech he is making is one that he is accustomed to make over and over again, he may be almost unconscious of what he is saying, as one is when one utters the responses in church. And this reduced state of consciousness, if not indispensable, is at any rate favorable to political conformity.

In our time, political speech and writing are largely the defense of the indefensible. Things like the continuance of British rule in India, the Russian purges and deportations, the dropping of the atom bombs on Japan, can indeed be defended, but only by arguments which are too brutal for most people to face, and which do not square with the professed aims of political parties. Thus political language has to consist largely of euphemism, question-begging and sheer cloudy vagueness. Defenseless villagers are bombarded from the air, the inhabitants driven out into the countryside, the cattle machine-gunned, the huts set on fire with incendiary bullets: this is called *pacification*. Millions of peasants are robbed of their farms and sent trudging along the roads with no more than they can carry: this is called *transfer of population* or *rectification of frontiers*. People are imprisoned for years without trial, or shot in the back of the neck or sent to die of scurvy in Arctic lumber camps: this is called *elimination of unreliable elements*. Such phraseology is needed if one wants to name things without calling up mental pictures of them. Consider for instance some comfortable English professor defending Russian totalitarianism. He cannot say outright, "I believe in killing off your opponents when you can get good results by doing so." Probably, therefore, he will say something like this:

While freely conceding that the Soviet régime exhibits certain features which the humanitarian may be inclined to deplore, we must, I think, agree that a certain curtailment of the right to political opposition is an unavoidable concomitant of transitional periods, and that the rigors which the Russian people have been called upon to undergo have been amply justified in the sphere of concrete achievement.

The inflated style is itself a kind of euphemism. A mass of Latin words falls upon the facts like soft snow, blurring the outlines and covering up all the details. The great enemy of clear language is insincerity. When there is a gap between one's real and one's declared aims, one turns as it were instinctively to long words and exhausted idioms, like a cuttlefish squirting out ink. In our age there is no such thing as "keeping out of politics." All issues are political issues, and politics itself is a mass of lies, evasions, folly, hatred and schizophrenia. When the general atmosphere is bad, language must suffer. I should expect to find—this is a guess which I have not sufficient knowledge to verify—that the German, Russian and Italian languages have all deteriorated in the last ten or fifteen years, as a result of dictatorship.

But if thought corrupts language, language can also corrupt thought. A bad usage can spread by tradition and imitation, even among people who should and do know better. The debased language that I have been discussing is in some ways very convenient. Phrases like *a not unjustifiable assumption, leaves much to be desired, would serve no good purpose, a consideration which we should do well to bear in mind,* are a continuous temptation, a packet of aspirins always at one's elbows. Look back through this essay, and for certain you will find that I have again and again committed the very faults I am protesting against. By this morning's post I have received a pamphlet dealing with conditions in Germany. The author tells me that he "felt impelled" to write it. I open it at random, and here is almost the first sentence that I see: "[The Allies] have an opportunity not only of achieving a radical transformation of Germany's social and political structure in such a way as to avoid a nationalistic reaction in Germany itself, but at the same time of laying the foundations of a co-operative and unified Europe." You see, he "feels impelled" to write—feels, presumably, that he has something new to say—and yet his words, like cavalry horses answering the bugle, group themselves automatically into the familiar dreary pattern. This invasion of one's mind by ready-made phrases (*lay the foundations, achieve a radical transformation*) can only be prevented if one is constantly on guard against them, and every such phrase anaesthetizes a portion of one's brain.

I said earlier that the decadence of our language is probably curable. Those who deny this would argue, if they produced an argument at all, that language merely reflects existing social conditions, and that we cannot influence its development by any direct tinkering with words and constructions. So far as the general tone or spirit of a language goes, this may be true, but it is not true in detail. Silly words and expressions have often disappeared, not through any evolutionary process but owing to the conscious action of a minority. Two recent examples were *explore every avenue* and *leave no stone unturned,* which were killed by the jeers of a few journalists. There is a long list of flyblown metaphors which could similarly be got rid of if enough people would interest themselves in the job; and it should also be possible to laugh the *not un-*formation out of existence,[3] to reduce the amount of Latin and Greek in the average sentence, to drive out foreign phrases and strayed scientific words, and, in general, to make pretentiousness unfashionable. But all these are minor points. The defense of the English language implies more than this, and perhaps it is best to start by saying what it does *not* imply.

To begin with it has nothing to do with archaism, with the salvaging of obsolete words and turns of speech, or with the setting up of a "standard English" which must never be departed from. On the contrary, it is especially

---

[3] One can cure oneself of the *not un-* formation by memorizing this sentence: *A not unblack dog was chasing a not unsmall rabbit across a not ungreen field.*

concerned with the scrapping of every word or idiom which has outworn its usefulness. It has nothing to do with correct grammar and syntax, which are of no importance so long as one makes one's meaning clear, or with the avoidance of Americanisms, or with having what is called a "good prose style." On the other hand it is not concerned with fake simplicity and the attempt to make written English colloquial. Nor does it even imply in every case preferring the Saxon word to the Latin one, though it does imply using the fewest and shortest words that will cover one's meaning. What is above all needed is to let the meaning choose the word, and not the other way about. In prose, the worst thing one can do with words is to surrender to them. When you think of a concrete object, you think wordlessly, and then, if you want to describe the thing you have been visualizing you probably hunt about till you find the exact words that seem to fit it. When you think of something abstract you are more inclined to use words from the start, and unless you make a conscious effort to prevent it, the existing dialect will come rushing in and do the job for you, at the expense of blurring or even changing your meaning. Probably it is better to put off using words as long as possible and get one's meaning as clear as one can through pictures or sensations. Afterwards one can choose—not simply *accept*—the phrases that will best cover the meaning, and then switch round and decide what impression one's words are likely to make on another person. This last effort of the mind cuts out all stale or mixed images, all prefabricated phrases, needless repetitions, and humbug and vagueness generally. But one can often be in doubt about the effect of a word or a phrase, and one needs rules that one can rely on when instinct fails. I think the following rules will cover most cases:

(*i*)   Never use a metaphor, simile, or other figure of speech which you are used to seeing in print.
(*ii*) Never use a long word where a short one will do.
(*iii*) If it is possible to cut a word out, always cut it out.
(*iv*) Never use the passive where you can use the active.
(*v*)   Never use a foreign phrase, a scientific word or a jargon word if you can think of an everyday English equivalent.
(*vi*) Break any of these rules sooner than say anything outright barbarous.

These rules sound elementary, and so they are, but they demand a deep change of attitude in anyone who has grown used to writing in the style now fashionable. One could keep all of them and still write bad English, but one could not write the kind of stuff that I quoted in those five specimens at the beginning of this article.

I have not here been considering the literary use of language, but merely language as an instrument for expressing and not for concealing or preventing thought. Stuart Chase and others have used this as a pretext for advocating a kind of political quietism. Since you don't know what Fascism is, how can you struggle against Fascism? One need not swallow such absurdities as this, but one ought to recognize that the present political chaos is connected with the decay of language, and that one can probably bring about some improvement by starting at the verbal end. If you simplify your English, you are freed from the worst follies of orthodoxy. You cannot speak any of the necessary dialects, and when you make a stupid remark its stupidity will be obvious, even to yourself. Political language—and with variations this is true of all political parties, from Conservatives to Anarchists— is designed to make lies sound truthful and murder respectable, and to give an appearance of solidity to pure wind. One cannot change this all in a moment, but one can at least change one's own habits, and from time to time one can even, if one jeers loudly enough, send some worn-out and useless phrase—some *jackboot, Achilles' heel, hotbed, melting pot, acid test, veritable inferno* or other lump of verbal refuse—into the dustbin where it belongs.

After carefully reading and rereading Orwell's essay, consider the following questions, which you may profitably ponder in studying any piece of exposition.

Structure

1. What are the major structural components of the essay?

2. Does the essay have a major controlling idea? If so, state the idea in one sentence and show how each of the components relates to it.

3. Which components contain subordinate parts? What are they? Prepare a topic outline of the major component and supporting ideas of the essay.

Interpretation

4. Be prepared to define or explain the meaning of the following in Orwell's context: decadent, canker, atrophy, traduced, effete, brazenly, inadvertently, hackneyed, reverted, evocative, euphonious, quietism.

5. What does Orwell mean by "bad English"?

6. Orwell lists such things as "Pretentious Diction" and "Meaningless Words" as "tricks" by which "the work of prose-construction is habitually dodged." Explain and illustrate each of these "tricks."

7. Examine the following statements and explain why Orwell would object to them.

a. One of the teacher's functions is to water the flames of genius which he discovers in his students.

b. When the plan has jelled, it will be geared to the needs of the community.

c. He had hoped to jump on board Smith's political bandwagon, but, unfortunately, it never got off the ground.

d. Unemployment compensation is the golden egg the lazy want to milk.

8. What four questions does "a scrupulous writer" ask himself about his writing?

9. "In our time, political speech and writing are largely the defense of the indefensible." Explain.

Content

10. Do you agree that "the decline of a language must ultimately have political and economic causes"?

11. Do you concede the *fact* of language decay? Do you find instances of fuzzy, unclear, meaningless statements in political debates and statements or in art and music criticism?

12. Is language "a natural growth and not an instrument which we shape for our own purposes" or is it, as Orwell contends, something which we can consciously change in any significant degree?

13. Is Orwell's dislike of Latinate expressions intelligible? What difference does the national origin of a term make?

14. Do you think it likely any significant change in man's behavior will come from a more precise and sincere use of language?

15. If the abuse of language is as profound and widespread as Orwell suggests, is there any reason to be optimistic that it can be remedied?

16. Do you think Orwell's contention that language can corrupt thought has any validity?

Expository Technique

1. Comment on the unity of this essay, indicating how, if you think it does, the controlling idea unifies the work.

2. Are there "introductory" and "concluding" sections? If so, how do they relate to each other?

3. In developing his essay, Orwell utilizes many of the traditional devices of expository writing. What examples of definition, explanation of cause and effect, illustration, comparison and contrast, enumeration, and analysis can you find?

4. Discuss the coherence of this essay and the means by which it is achieved.

5. Discuss Orwell's success in clarifying his views through specific details and examples.

6. Comment on any examples of vivid diction, images, metaphors, and analogies in the essay.

7. Find what you consider to be one of the best paragraphs in the essay and comment on its unity, organization, method of development, and coherence.

8. Orwell suggests that he probably inadvertently violates in this essay some of his own recommendations for clear writing. Do you find any such instances?

Exercises

Read each of the following student compositions and be prepared to appraise their effectiveness as expository writing.

FRIENDSHIP

Every individual has their own personal meaning for friendship, in general, it means having a companion, someone to be with and confide in, and in whom you have confidence.

Until my senior year in high school I was in a "crowd", of all friends—or what at the time I believed to be friends. I confided with, studied with, went out socially with, and was in extra-curricular activities with them. However in my senior year I became extremely interested and active in the student government and was elected to the Student Senate. My new job brought with it not only prestige but added duties in which I was unable to include my friends. I never intentionally excluded them, but because they were not in the Senate it was impossible for them to be on the committees of which I was in charge.

I found that I had to work exceptionally hard scholastically because I was not only working for myself but I was more or less a symbol in front of 3500 other students and was compared not only by them but by the members of the faculty.

I was never over jealous of my friends' accomplishments and I never felt they had any reason to be jealous of mine for I believe every individual has something he alone must excel in. As a friend I stuck behind the members of the crowd when they set out to do something because I always felt that they would do the same for me. But when the time came for election of a new president I found that friendship could be a very disillusioning condition. I found that I knew very little about the character of these people I called my friends, and thought I knew so well. Instead of backing me up they fought against me—not because they felt I wasn't qualified, but because they were unable to attain a position of this level they did not want me to have this honor. For the first time I realized that the dissension between my friends in childhood and adolescence was caused primarily by personal jealousies which could not be hidden and that people won't necessarily be fighting for something but will fight against something even though they know they are wrong.

Looking back on this period of time I feel that although the entire circumstance may have been ridiculous it was also one of the most significant things which had happened. It made me open my eyes—to understand people a little better, although not completely, for I feel that in a lifetime I could never understand them completely, and most important it made me realize that a true friend is the most precious thing in life and that they are very hard to find. I feel now, that the "crowd" was part of a stage in growing up, it was a status symbol to say you were in a "crowd." As for friendship, I was their friend and they were mine to the extent that we were companions for each other. At present, I wouldn't give all the gold and silver in the world to have that crowd back, for they are now, as they actually were then, nothing more than mere acquaintances just like nine out of ten people I'm friendly with are acquaintances—people with whom I have friendly discussions.

The literal definition of friendship will never change, however, to every individual the importance, the significance and the emotional feeling behind choosing a friend, I believe, will continually change until the individual has acquired a stable set of ideals.

THE EFFECT OF 16TH CENTURY RELIGION ON SCIENCE

At the beginning of the sixteenth century, Protestantism was still in its infancy and the Roman Church was still all powerful.

The ancient Greek science had almost completely confined itself to reasoning out the answers to problems, many times purely on religious grounds. Although there were men who used observation to determine the truth or fallacy of their hypotheses, such as Hipparchus, they were a minority and usually were only tolerated as long as their views coincided with the generally accepted views.

Late in the fifteenth century, a man was born who was destined to help overthrow the power of the church and to lay the foundation for the establishment of the experimental method as an integral part of science. This man was Nicolas Copernicus.

The sixteenth century church still advocated the view that man was the most important of God's creations, therefore, the earth must be the center of the universe. And also that, since everything God created must be perfect, the stars and planets must move around the earth in circles, which were thought to be the most perfect figure.

Copernicus, with a stroke of genius, realized that the observed motions of the stars and planets could be explained much more simply by assuming that the earth and planets moved around a stationary sun. But even in Copernicus, the religious prejudices of the age were too strong to permit him to assume anything but circular orbits for the planets. The resulting error in his theory would have made him abandon it except for the intervention of some protestant clergy. And even this great genius apparently had no intentions of justifying theory merely on the grounds that it worked. In the *De Revolutionibus* he argues that the sun, and not the earth, really deserves the place of honor at the center of universe because it is the sustainer of all life.

Although it took until Johann Kepler to get the experimental method firmly entrenched, this was the beginning of a revolution in science and of the overthrow of the absolute power of the church.

The publicity given to this revolution in scientific thinking by the church's condemnation, undoubtedly helped to hasten what was inevitable in any event.

THE VERNACULAR OF THE CLIP AUCTIONEER

For the past two years I have been using a language at my place of employment which is most unusual for its great versatility. The cant of the clip auctioneer, consisting of no more than fifty words, can convey hundreds of messages and instructions to a worker without anyone else in hearing distance knowing what is going on. Being an auction clerk for a local clip auctioneer, I have become fairly well acquainted with the peculiarities of this particular jargon.

First it would be well to differentiate the clip auctioneer from a regular auctioneer, although I am confident you would be able to do this yourself if you have ever availed yourself of the former's services. The regular auctioneer actually has his merchandise up for bid, while the clip auctioneer "sells" his wares under the guise of an auction. To the customer one is ethical while the other is unethical. Now that the distinction between the two is clear, let us consider the clip auctioneer's occupation.

The first task a "C-man" (clip auctioneer) faces is that of "gathering an audience" (obtaining some customers). This is accomplished by "distributing" (throwing out randomly) "plush" (cheap factory seconds such as razor blades, toothbrushes, combs, and sewing needles). As soon as enough "moochers" (customers) are seated, their trust and confidence in the C-man must be gained. This is usually accomplished by the distribution of "higher line" (more expensive) merchandise at no cost. For example, a $3.00 lighter in the house goes up at such a good bargain, and the clip man, to show his appreciation, gives both the lighter and the money to the lucky customer. The important point in this process is that money is *always* collected. It is the C-man's prerogative to refund the money along with the merchandise.

This technique continues with higher line merchandise being given away each time. An ashtray, an alarm clock, a dinner set, all find their way into the hands of a few fortunate customers at no cost in the manner described in the preceding paragraph. Hence, the audience believes fate has smiled upon them and they will get the whole store for nothing at the C-man's wonderful "advertising campaign" (the entire scheme). But their enthusiasm is short-lived when they discover that they have been "nailed" (sold merchandise) by each paying five dollars for a cheap billfold, twenty for a seven-dollar wristwatch, and occasionally fifty for a set of silver and a hundred for a Japanese sewing machine. The catch is that this time they don't get both the merchandise and their money. They get only what they bargained for, the merchandise, all the time thinking they were getting something for nothing. Finally, the clip man makes a hasty retreat with his scads of money, the auction clerks settle any beefs, and the advertising campaign for that hour is over.

The preceding description is what occurs during an ideal spiel, but since the majority of the advertising campaigns are not ideal, the clip man must give instructions to his clerks over the microphone so that everything runs smoothly. His vocabulary consists mainly of the following words:

beef—a complaint

B.O.—a person that wants to back out of the deal he has made; one who wants his money back.

C-man—a clip auctioneer

dig out—give back

dipstick—a customer in the audience with money. (The auction clerk usually can estimate how much cash a person has in his billfold as he stands by the seated customer waiting to be paid for some item. Knowing this, a C-man can concentrate or "work" on certain individuals.)

fuzz—a policeman

heavyweight—a troublemaker

high line—expensive merchandise

hustle—collect

larry—broken merchandise, such as a clock or radio; anything no good

line—money; half-dollar; half of anything ("Ten line" would be five dollars, "twenty line" would be ten dollars.)

low line—cheap, not expensive

moocher—a customer, usually one who expects everything for nothing

nailers—merchandise which is actually sold

plush—worthless merchandise

R.G.—a regular moocher, one that comes back frequently just for the free merchandise

R.B.—also stands for a regular moocher. This term is used when a moocher comes back so often he knows the meaning of R.G.

rucket—a commotion

sherry—get rid of

spiel—the talk

story—the spiel or talk

yoyo—bounce out; throw out

These constitute the bulk of the C-man's vocabulary. However, with these few terms the auctioneer can express a multitude of ideas to his clerks during the sale. It has been my observation that people tend to disregard words they hear and do not understand much in the manner as they skip over words they read and do not recognize. It is apparently for this reason that a C-man can say the following without the customers even batting an eyelash.

"Sherry the B.O. in ten line row."
   Trans. Get rid of the backout in the fifth row.
"Low line merchandise for eight line."
   Trans. Cheap merchandise selling for four dollars.
"Yoyo the R.G. in 2 line row."
   Trans. Throw out the regular in the first row.
"Dig out six line to the heavyweight in six line row."
   Trans. Give back three dollars to the troublemaker in the third row.

These are but a few of the many things a C-man can say to his clerks without being detected by the general public. The unusual words, however, can always be heard. So if you hear terms like "line," "plush," and "hustle," chances are you are in a C-joint. If you don't want to leave penniless, my advice to you would be: "Sherry in a hurry, I mean, leave as soon as possible!"

part two

EXPOSITORY
TYPES

IN ORDER to fulfill the purpose of exposition, that is, to explain a subject, a writer may employ several basic methods. Sometimes known as expository types or expository patterns, these methods include enumeration, definition, description of process, analysis by·division and classification, cause and effect, comparison and contrast, and illustration. In the following pages each of these methods will be defined and discussed and then illustrated in essays by experienced writers.

In the preliminary stages of the study of writing techniques, it is useful to regard essays as "pure" examples of expository types. You should remember, however, that most writers use the seven types in various combinations, utilizing first one and then another to achieve their purposes. Essays are usually expository composites, since almost any subject can be effectively developed by any or all of the techniques discussed in the seven sections which comprise Part Two of this book. An essay on Nazism, for example, might *enumerate* the philosophical and political antecedents to Nazism, describe the *process* by which it evolved, *define* its nature as it appeared in Hitler's Germany, *classify* the social groups who most earnestly espoused it, trace the *causes* for its initial success and the *effects* of its ultimate failure, *compare* its downfall with that of other totalitarian ideologies, or *illustrate* its tyranny by referring to the maltreatment of the Jews. In order to write effectively, then, the writer must be ready to use whatever tools he feels will best accomplish his ends.

The seven expository types are illustrated in essays concerned with important aspects of the English language: its essential nature, historical development, grammatical structure, kinship with other languages, dialectical subdivisions, and problems of usage, as well as the forces affecting English, and the kinds of meaning communicated by its words.

Enumeration

ENUMERATION is the presentation of a series of related items. It is a familiar pattern in daily communication. When we make an invitation list or place a grocery order, we are enumerating. Similarly, we enumerate when we specify the attractive qualities of a friend or the talents of a performer whom we admire. Enumeration is also a common and fairly simple way to explain a subject in expository writing.

Although capable of myriad variation in practice, enumeration most commonly appears in expository writing in three principal situations, which may be *enumerated* as follows: (1) the citation of particular instances or specific details which support the validity of or clarify a general statement or assertion; (2) the multiple exemplification or illustration of a central idea; and (3) the listing of concrete details that describe a subject.

In using enumeration as an expository device it is important to remember that the items must have a significant relationship to each other or to the statement that they support or clarify. Enumeration should not produce a disparate collection of discrete, unrelated items. Whether the relationship of the items is explicit or implicit, the unity and coherence of the paragraph or essay must be preserved through careful, purposive selection.

ORGANIZATION

The elements in an essay or paragraph of enumeration may be arranged in several ways. The order may be either deductive or inductive; that is, the items may lead *from* or *to* a general statement. In addition, the items may be placed in chronological or in some spatial order, or arranged in order of ascending importance or vividness. The reader's sense of order and coherence will be aided by transitional words (*first, second, next,* and so on) which clearly indicate the various items in the series.

EXAMPLES OF ENUMERATION

The following paragraphs illustrate the three types of enumeration. In the first, Professor Albert C. Baugh cites a number of words added to the English language during the twentieth century, all of which support the assertion in the first sentence of the paragraph.

The twentieth century permits us to see the process of vocabulary growth going on under our eyes, sometimes, it would seem, at an accelerated rate. At the turn of the century we get the word *questionnaire* and in 1904 the first hint of *television*. In 1906 the British launched a particular battleship named the *Dreadnaught*, and the word *dreadnaught* passed into popular use for any warship of the same class. A year later we got the word *raincoat* and about the same time *Thermos bottle*. This is the period when many of the terms of aviation that have since become so familiar first came in—*airplane, aircraft, airman, monoplane, biplane, hydroplane, dirigible,* and even *autogiro. Nose-dive* belongs to the period of the war. About 1910 we began talking about the *futurist* and the *postimpressionist* in art. *Intelligentsia* as a designation for the class to which superior culture is attributed, and *bolshevik* for a holder of revolutionary political views were originally applied at the time of the First World War to groups in Russia. At this time *profiteer* and in America *prohibition* arose with specialized meanings. Meanwhile *foot-fault, fairway, plus fours, fox trot, auction bridge,* and *contract* were indicative of popular interest in certain games and pastimes. The 1933 supplement to the *Oxford Dictionary* records *Cellophane* (1921), *Celanese* (1923), and *rayon* (1924), but it does not yet know the *Mazda lamp. Mazda* is a trade-mark which few people probably realize is derived from the name of the Zoroastrian god of the light-giving firmament. Only yesterday witnessed the birth of *crooner, nudist, air-conditioned, plastic* (the noun), *nylon* (originally a trade name), *transistor, Deepfreeze, record changer, tape recorder, automation, prefabricated,* and such popular American expressions as *coffee break* and *baby sitter*. To-morrow will witness others as the exigencies of the hour call them into being.*

A good example of multiple exemplification occurs in the following paragraph from Emerson's essay "Self-Reliance." The paragraph enumerates variations on the idea of "civilized" man's impoverishment.

The civilized man has built a coach, but has lost the use of his feet. He is supported on crutches, but lacks so much support of muscle. He has a fine

* From A HISTORY OF THE ENGLISH LANGUAGE, Second Edition, by Albert C. Baugh. Copyright © 1957 by Appleton-Century-Crofts, Inc. Reprinted by permission of the publishers.

Geneva watch, but he fails of the skill to tell the hour by the sun. A Greenwich nautical almanac he has, and so being sure of the information when he wants it, the man in the street does not know a star in the sky. The solstice he does not observe; the equinox he knows as little; and the whole bright calendar of the year is without a dial in his mind. His note-books impair his memory; his libraries overload his wit; the insurance-office increases the number of accidents; and it may be a question whether machinery does not encumber; whether we have not lost by refinement some energy, by a Christianity, entrenched in establishments and forms, some vigor of wild virtue. For every Stoic was a Stoic; but in Christendom where is the Christian?

The marshalling of descriptive details is shown to skillful effect in Mark Twain's vivid description of a Mississippi riverboat.

Assembled there, the people fasten their eyes upon the coming boat as upon a wonder they are seeing for the first time. And the boat *is* rather a handsome sight, too. She is long and sharp and trim and pretty; she has two tall, fancy-topped chimneys, and a gilded device of some kind swung between them; a fanciful pilothouse, all glass and gingerbread, perched on top of the texas deck behind them; the paddle boxes are gorgeous with a picture or with gilded rays above the boat's name; the boiler deck, the hurricane deck, and the texas deck are fenced and ornamented with clean white railings; there is a flag gallantly flying from the jack staff; the furnace doors are open and the fires glaring bravely; the upper decks are black with passengers; the captain stands by the big bell, calm, imposing, the envy of all; great volumes of the blackest smoke are rolling and tumbling out of the chimneys—a husbanded grandeur created with a bit of pitch pine just before arriving at a town; the crew are grouped on the forecastle; the broad stage is run far out over the port bow, and an envied deck hand stands picturesquely on the end of it with a coil of rope in his hand; the pent steam is screaming through the gauge cocks; the captain lifts his hand, a bell rings, the wheels stop; then they turn back, churning the water to foam, and the steamer is at rest.

Exercises on Enumeration

1. Dr. Eliot Shapiro, principal of P.S. 92 in New York (formerly P.S. 119), is quoted in a recent book as saying of his underprivileged students,

They look lively, don't they? And they're very charming . . . The way they look conceals the fact they're dying. It's not like being killed by a car. There's no blood on them, and because there is no visible injury, nobody in the middle classes is aghast at the sight. Nobody gets really involved.

Write a theme in which you list the actions you believe Dr. Shapiro might suggest the middle class take to reclaim his "dying" students.

2. Using *one* of the sentences below as a thesis, indicate in outline form how you would support it.

a. Despite their widespread adoption in American secondary schools today, the

College Boards have many limitations which make their use unfair to the students required to take them.

b. For several reasons students are in general agreement on the essential fairness, impartiality, and necessity of the College Board Examinations.

3. Make a list of five ways in which your generation differs from that of your father. Organize the five items into a clear and logical pattern. Indicate how you would develop each item into a paragraph of an essay.

4. Show how the device of expository enumeration can be used in treating some aspect of your major field of interest.

5. Examine some object carefully (e.g., a face on the cover of a magazine, a record album cover, a costume, a blossom) and enumerate its physical qualities in detail. Scrutinize its shape, color, width, size, texture, etc. and organize the characteristics into a list which is accurate, clear, and complete.

6. Arrange the following statistical information, reported in *Time* (July 12, 1968), into an outline which enumerates the arguments for (or against) government-sponsored, noncommercial television.

In 1968, 2000 advertisers will spend 3.1 billion dollars in television advertising which will reach 95% of the U.S. homes. On a typical weekday each of the three major networks will telecast 600 commercial messages, and the total time taken up by commercials will be approximately as follows:

	Between 7 A.M.–4 P.M.	(maximum of 16 commercials per hour allowed)
NBC	2 hrs., 4 mins.	
CBS	2 hrs., 7 mins.	
ABC	1 hr., 56 mins.	

	Between 4 P.M.–1 A.M.	(maximum of 10 commercials per hour allowed during "prime time," 7:30–11:00 P.M.)
NBC	3 hrs., 48 mins.	
CBS	3 hrs., 41 mins.	
ABC	3 hrs., 46 mins.	

Writing Suggestions: Enumeration

1. _____(Radical Student Organizations, Black Power Leaders, Civil Rights Organizations, Peace Corps Programs, UNESCO Activities, Reforms in the Roman Catholic Church, Activities of the Minute Men Organizations, Minor Political Parties)

2. Consequences of_____(Inflation, Obesity, Failure, Infidelity, Divorce, Student Unrest, Poverty, Slum Life)

3. Undesirable Features of_____(Parents, a Large Family, Sexual Revolution, Freedom, Responsibility, a Democratic Society, Lobbies, Political Campaigns, Police Brutality, Mob Rule, Violating the Law, Segregation, Integration)

4. Examples of_____(the Button Vogue, Witty Graffiti, Daring Styles of Dress, the Defeminization of Women, the Feminization of Men, Loss of Values, Tensions of Twentieth Century Life, the Hypocrisy of Diplomacy, Contribution to World Peace by the United Nations, Crucial Decision in the Arab-Israeli War, Violent Comic Books, Indecent Best Sellers, the New Frankness of Expression in the Movies [or on Television or the State], Professional Athletes Who Are Businessmen)

5. The Responsibilities of_____(Steadies, Teachers, Parents, Churchmen, Police, Politicians, the Press, Union Leaders, Columnists, Entertainers)

6. The Aims of_____(SDS, CORE, SCLC, SNCC, Urban League, Socialist Labor Party, American Independent Party, Birch Society)

7. The Qualities of_____(an Educated Person, a Good College Department, a Good Administrator, a Friend, a Successful Date, Leadership, Maturity)

(Additional writing suggestions on linguistic subjects are on pages 90–91.)

The Theory
and Study of Language

1.

NEIL POSTMAN
CHARLES WEINGARTNER

What Do Linguists Do?

Linguistics . . . is conducting yourself in a particular manner—a scientific manner—when you study language. But what exactly are linguists interested in studying? What are the aspects of language and language behavior which have come under investigation by men who are called linguists? After all, most disciplines are concerned in some way with language problems. Are anthropologists linguists? Are psychologists linguists? Are philosophers? Literary critics? Engineers? Physicists? Our answer is, They are *when they are using scientific procedures to inquire into the role of language in human affairs*. In fact, some of the great contributors to the linguistic enterprise have conducted their inquiries from a background of other disciplines. For example: Sapir and Whorf from anthropology, I. A. Richards from literary criticism, Korzybski from engineering, Bridgman from physics, Piaget from psychology, Russell and Wittgenstein from philosophy. This roster of important linguists may come as a surprise to those who tend to view linguistics as (almost solely) an activity of grammarians. But linguistics is far too important a process to be left entirely or even principally in the hands of grammarians, as we shall have occasion to discuss in a moment.

By considering some of the definitions of linguistics offered by important language-inquirers, we can achieve some understanding of the variety of studies made by men who form part of the community of linguistic scholars.

One ought to begin with Leonard Bloomfield, generally regarded as the most important figure in linguistics in this century. In his book *Language* (first published in 1914), Bloomfield defines linguistics as the study of language in a scientific way. By defining linguistics as a process of inquiry (as we have), Bloomfield meant to allow (as we would) a broad scope to investigators, and his book reveals the wide range of subjects he felt to be legitimate areas of investigation. He includes discussions of phonology (sound systems), grammatical forms, syntax, dialect geography, language history, and language change.

One of Bloomfield's great colleagues in the development of linguistics was Edward Sapir, whose background was largely in anthropology. In a speech delivered in 1928 at a joint meeting of the Linguistic Society of America, the American Anthropological Association, and the American Association for the Advancement of Science, Sapir urged linguists to become aware of what their science may mean for the interpretation of human conduct in general. "It is difficult for a modern linguist to confine himself to his traditional subject matter," Sapir said, meaning by traditional subject matter comparative and historical studies. "Unless he is somewhat unimaginative," Sapir continued, "he cannot but share in some or all of the mutual interests which tie up linguistics with anthropology and culture history, with sociology, with psychology, with philosophy, and, more remotely, with physics and physiology." Sapir thus staked out an even wider field for linguists than perhaps Bloomfield was willing to do. (Bloomfield, for example, strongly cautioned against linguists associating themselves with certain "schools of psychology.")

Sapir's most distinguished student, Benjamin Lee Whorf, took his teacher's remarks to heart, and redefined linguistics in a way that would permit the exploration of untouched areas of language. In an article written in 1936, titled "A Linguistic Consideration of Thinking in Primitive Communities," Whorf wrote:

> The ethnologist engaged in studying a living primitive culture must often have wondered: What do these people think? How do they think? Are their intellectual and rational processes akin to ours or radically different? But thereupon he has probably dismissed the idea as a psychological enigma and has sharply turned his attention back to more readily observable matters. And yet the problem of thought and thinking in the native community is not purely and simply a psychological problem. It is quite largely cultural. It is moreover largely a matter of . . . language. It is approachable through linguistics, and, as I hope to show, the approach requires a rather new type of emphasis in linguistics, now beginning to emerge through the work of Sapir, Leonard Bloomfield, and others . . . What needs to be clearly seen by anthropologists, who to a large extent may have gotten the idea that linguistics is merely a highly specialized and tediously technical pigeonhole in a far

corner of the anthropological workshop, is that linguistics is essentially the quest of meaning. It may seem to the outsider to be inordinately absorbed in recording hair-splitting distinctions of sound, performing phonetic gymnastics, and writing complex grammars which only grammarians read. But the simple fact is that its real concern is to light up the thick darkness of the language, and thereby of much of the thought, the culture, and the outlook upon life of a given community.

Whorf's studies of exotic languages, notably the language of the Hopi Indians of Arizona, eventually led to the formulation of what is still the most provocative hypothesis in the linguistic enterprise: the idea that the structure of the language one habitually uses influences the manner in which one perceives and understands his environment.

To Whorf, linguistics is essentially "the quest of meaning." To I. A. Richards, "General Linguistic," as he calls it, is a similar quest, although his particular search took him to different materials and challenged him to look for different things. In *Practical Criticism,* published in 1929, Richards wrote:

It is the oddest thing about language, whose history is full of odd things (and one of the oddest facts about human development) that so few people ever sat down to reflect systematically about meaning. For no daring or original steps are needed to carry our acquaintance with these matters at least one step further than the stage at which it usually remains. A little pertinacity and a certain habit of examining our intellectual and emotional instruments as we use them, is all that is required. From the point of view thus attained one would expect that our libraries would be full of works on the theory of interpretation, the diagnosis of linguistic situations, systematic ambiguity and the function of complex symbols; and that there would be Chairs of Significs or of General Linguistic at all our Universities. Yet, in point of fact, there is no respectable treatise on the theory of linguistic interpretation in existence, and no person whose professional occupation it is to inquire into these questions and direct study in the matter. For grammatical studies do not trespass upon this topic. Surely systematic investigation of the uses of language may be expected to improve our actual daily use of it, at least in the same measure that the study of plant-physiology may improve agriculture or human physiology assist medicine or hygiene.

By quoting Sapir, Whorf, and Richards at some length, we have run the risk of losing your interest. But not without good reason. It is extremely important that the concerns of linguists be seen as covering a very wide field. Whorf's and Richard's remarks about the limitations of grammar are germane. In our view, it would be a disaster if linguistics became identified solely with inquiries into grammatical problems, a disaster not only for the vitality of the discipline, but particularly for the teaching of English. And yet, if our communications with teachers of English are an indication, linguistics has already become for many simply a synonym for "new grammars" or "new theories of grammar." Such a state of affairs parallels the belief held by some that psychiatry is synonymous with psychoanalysis. The identification of linguistics with grammar has probably occurred because so many linguists of more recent vintage than Bloomfield, Sapir, Whorf, and Richards have confined their inquiries to grammar. Their definitions of linguistics therefore reflect their limited perspective. "Linguistics is the study of the internal structure of language," goes one. "Linguistics is the scientific study of the structure of sentences," goes another. "The task of linguistics is to produce adequate grammatical theories" is still another.

We must emphasize that insofar as such definitions help linguists to focus their attention on special aspects of language, there can be no objection to them. Definitions such as these have produced a wealth of reliable data, provocative questions, and imaginative theories about grammar. In some ways, grammar is the most active (even if not the most interesting) field in the linguist's terrain. But the equation of linguistics and grammar not only excludes the work of major language scholars; it also sharply diminishes the relevance of linguistics to the study and teaching of English. We wish to stress a conception of linguistics that (1) has a high status among linguists themselves, and (2) provides the greatest possible utility for the work of the schools.

What, then, are the subject matters of linguistics? How, in fact, have linguists of varying interests and backgrounds collectively defined the "role of language in human affairs"?

Without claiming to be exhaustive, we list below, along with brief explanations, aspects of language and language behavior that have attracted the attention of linguists.

As Bloomfield indicated, the *phonology* (sounds), *morphology* (word forms), and *syntax* (phrases and sentences) of languages are legitimate areas of investigation for linguists. The inquiries made are of two kinds, descriptive and historical. For example, there is the question, "What were (or are) the significant sounds of a language at a specific time (including now)? There is also the question, "What are the patterns or dynamics of change in the sound system of a language over a period of time?" The second type of question—the historical—was asked frequently by linguists in the nineteenth century, when they called themselves comparative philologists. The first type of question has been more frequently asked in this century by men calling themselves descriptive linguists. Inquiries by both kinds of linguists have produced studies in *language history*, in which questions about the origins of words and the relationships among languages have been studied.

As Bloomfield also indicated, *dialect geography* is another area of investigation. The data sought here concern the variations of pronunciation, syntax, and vocabulary among the regional dialects of a language. Such inquiries may also focus on the language variations among different economic and social classes and vocational groups, although the term *linguistic sociology* would perhaps be more appropriate for these studies.

Usage denotes inquiries into the attitudes of speakers of a language toward certain words and structures. In other words, the linguist tries to find out what kind of social status certain pronunciations, grammatical forms, and expressions have among different groups.

Lexicography refers generally to the process of compiling dictionaries. Lexicographers are mainly concerned with inquiring into the meanings as well as the pronunciations, grammatical functions, history, and spellings of words. Of course they rely heavily on studies in *usage, dialect geography,* and *language history* for their work. At the same time, they have developed techniques of their own for obtaining data about the meanings that have been given to words by the speakers of a language.

Semantics is related to lexicography, but usually implies broader inquiries into the uses of language and the meanings of words. Whereas lexicographers tend to ask, "What does a word mean?" semanticists ask, "What do we mean by 'mean'?" For example, inquiries have been made into such questions as, What are the functions and varieties of statements? When can a statement be called "meaningful"?

Some linguists have tried to push themselves beyond such questions to even more difficult ones (and, some say, with predictably precarious results). For example, In what ways does language—its grammatical structure and lexicon—influence our nervous system? or, to put it another way, To what extent is our nervous system a product of language habits? Alfred Korzybski preferred to place these questions under the heading *neurolinguistics*. Later, he used the term *general semantics*.

As we have already indicated, similar questions were asked by Whorf. By common but not unanimous consent, the terms *metalinguistics* and *psycholinguistics* have been used to designate inquiries of this type.

The work of I. A. Richards practically defies labeling. Although he was an early contributor to questions of semantics, probably his most important inquiries are those he made into the behavior of readers. For Richards, the question "What does a literary work mean?" tends to be misleading and unproductive. He substituted for it the question "How do readers make meanings when confronted by literary works?" From our point of view, there are no more exciting or relevant inquiries into language behavior than those conducted by Richards.

There remains for us to mention those studies conducted into the development of language in children, to which the chief contributor has probably been Jean Piaget. The *psychology of language* or *language development* is an appropriate designation for such inquiries.

The chart you will find on the next two pages will provide a visual overview of the subject matters that have been studied by linguists. A few additional remarks need to be made now about the areas we have listed.

	DIALECT STUDY	GRAMMAR	DESCRIPTIVE LINGUISTICS	LANGUAGE HISTORY
1900				
1910				George Krapp
1920				Otto Jespersen
1930		Henry Sweet H. Poutsma	Edward Sapir	Henry Wyld

1940	H. L.
	Mencken
		George Curme
		Otto Jespersen
		Charles C. Fries
			Leonard
			  Bloomfield
			Kenneth Pike
				Leonard
				  Bloomfield

1950	Hans
	Kurath
		Zellig Harris	Martin Joos
			Bernard Bloch
			George Trager
			Edgar Sturtevant
			George Trager &
			  Henry Lee
			Smith Jr.
				Albert
				  Marckwardt

1960	G. Brooks
	Raven
	McDavid
		George Trager &
		  Henry Lee
		Smith Jr.
		Harold Whitehall
		Paul Roberts
		Noam Chomsky
		W. Nelson Francis
		Archibald A. Hill
		James Sledd
		Eugene A. Nida
		Robert B. Lees
			Zellig Harris
			Henry A. Gleason
			Roman Jakobson
			Morris Halle
			Charles Hockett
				Samuel Moore
				Albert Baugh
				John Firth
				Henry
				  Hoenigswald

	Angus Macintosh Harold Orton	Emmon W. Bach J. Katz & Paul Postal Norman Stageberg	Andre Martinet	Winfred Lehmann Thomas Pyles

64

USAGE	LEXICOGRAPHY	SEMANTICS	PSYCHOLINGUISTICS
		Charles Peirce	
		Michel Breal Bertrand Russell	
		V. Welby Ludwig Wittgenstein	
		C. K. Ogden I. A. Richards Alfred N. Whitehead	Edward Sapir Jean Piaget H. Head
H. W. Fowler Sterling Leonard	William Craigie		
Herbert Horwill Arthur Kennedy Albert Marckwardt & Fred Walcott Charles C. Fries	William Neilson Allen W. Read Mitford Mathews C. Barnhart Harold Wentworth	Alfred Korzybski Rudolph Carnap A. J. Ayer Stuart Chase Hugh Walpole	L. S. Vygotsky

Robert Pooley
Ernest Gowers
		S. I. Hayakawa
		Irving Lee
		Charles Morris
		Wendell Johnson
		Susanne Langer
		Anatol Rapaport
			Benjamin Lee
			  Whorf
			Ernst Cassirer
			O. Hobart
			  Mowrer
			George Miller

Bergen Evans &
  Cornelia Evans
Robert Hall Jr.
		Dorothy Lee
		S. Ullmann
		Benjamin Lee
		  Whorf
			L. A. Jeffress
			Charles Osgood
			Thomas Sebeok
			Eric Lennenberg
			J. M. Roberts
			Harry Hoijer
			Bronislaw
			  Malinowski
			B. F. Skinner
			Roger Brown
			Joseph Church

Margaret Bryant	Philip Gove James Sledd		Sol Saporta John R. Carroll Edward Hall

65

First, the subject matters of linguistics appear to be growing in quantity and complexity, as Sapir hoped they would. Ten years from now the areas under investigation by linguists may be twice as large as the number we have identified. Theoretically, there is no limit to the varieties of inquiries that can be made into the role of language in human affairs. As I. A. Richards observed, our libraries should be filled with works on the subject. And it is likely that they will be, although many kinds of inquiries must be postponed until there are adequate instruments with which to conduct them. There is nothing unusual in science about the proliferation of subject matters. Below, for example, is a passage from an article by Marjorie Grene which explains what modern biologists are like:

> The difference between [the two fronts of biology] is illustrated by their different research procedures. In the laboratories of molecular geologists one can find blackboards full of calculations, expensive electronic equipment, carefully isolated preparations of various tissues of micro-organisms or metabolic substances; but anything that looks like a plant or an animal is conspicuously absent. True, molecular geneticists still perform breeding experiments, but for this purpose they usually use bacteria phage or other borderline organisms invisible to the naked eye. Even in electron microscopy, where techniques of looking, of "pure observation," are undoubtedly crucial, the structures "seen" are far removed from ordinary vision.
>
> Ethnologists, on the contrary, must spend hour after hour and week after week devotedly *watching* animals—living animals—in laboratory conditions, in zoos, or best of all, in the wild, managing or submitting to environments which differ greatly from species to species. They do, of course, perform experiments of great ingenuity and sophistication, interfering with the environment of their subjects in such a way as to infer from altered or constant behavior the fundamental patterns of action which certain situations call forth. For example, they spend much time trying to discover whether a given pattern of action is "innate" or "learned." In every case, however, their concern is not with tissue cultures, proteins, or genes, but rather with the actions of whole, individual animals or groups of animals. However abstract and elaborate their theoretical explanations of such behavior may be, they always talk about *what animals do,* and this is a very different subject matter from that of their molecule-oriented colleagues. Indeed, the ethologist more nearly resembles his more old-fashioned colleague, the morphologist; both are engaged in the study of perceptible patterns in things that are visible and audible on the surface of our world.

In linguistics, the situation is somewhat similar. Just as there are biologists who appear to be physicists, or chemists, or mathematicians, or good old-fashioned zoologists, there are linguists who appear to be physicists, or mathematicians, or psychologists, or just good old-fashioned comparative philologists. All of which leads us to a second point about the areas of inquiry we have identified: If you feel that the fields we have marked off are not sufficiently exclusive or precise, bear in mind that the categories of research in science are often quite arbitrary and do not in practice lend themselves to precise demarcation. To refer again to the passage about biologists: The ethologist is hard to distinguish from the morphologist. The molecular biologist is hard to distinguish from the molecular geneticist. Similarly, in linguistics, the lexicographer may be hard to distinguish from the semanticist, the semanticist from the psycholinguist, the dialect geographer from the usage scholar, and so on.

Third, linguists in each of the fields we mentioned have tended to emphasize different activities of the scientific process. For example, those concerned with phonology have been particularly effective in developing their techniques of observation and a taxonomy for classifying data. Those working in the field of grammar, especially in recent years, have been most active in developing what they call a theory of grammar, and have paid less attention than their predecessors to description. Some linguists, like Korzybski and Whorf, and to some extent I. A. Richards, have contributed to the linguistic enterprise mainly by formulating suggestive hypotheses and lines of inquiry. Thus, in a certain sense, not all of these fields of inquiry are equally "scientific." Some areas are further along in the refinement of procedures than are other areas. Linguists working in phonology have developed their describing procedures to a far more precise and systematic degree, than, say, those working on problems of meaning. But having said this, we must hastily add that all linguistic inquirers assume that one of their important objectives is to improve their methods of investigation, and they all accept the general ground rules of science.

Vocabulary

hypothesis, pertinacity, ambiguity, germane, demarcation, ethnologist, morphologist, taxonomy

Review Questions

1. What definitions of linguistics are given by Bloomfield, Sapir, Whorf, and Richards?
2. Name six areas of language and language behavior which have attracted the attention of linguists. Cite specific examples of some of the problems you think the investigator might encounter in each of these areas.
3. What difficulty is there in categorizing the various fields of linguistic study?
4. To what extent is linguistics a science? To what extent is it not?

Expository Technique

1. Comment on the effectiveness of the question-and-answer technique used in the first paragraph.

2. Note that the second paragraph is very brief. Why did the authors not expand it?

3. In the paragraphs which define *usage, lexicography,* and *semantics,* the authors use no transitional devices. Why?

4. Is the lengthy analogy between linguistics and biology a good one? Why?

(Exercises relating to Essays 1, 2, and 3 are on pages 84–85.)

2.

W. NELSON FRANCIS

Language and the Study of Language

I. THE NATURE OF LANGUAGE

This book is about the English language—its nature, its history, its vocabulary, its writing system, and to some degree its use. It differs from most books used in the broad and vaguely defined school and college subject called "English" in that its purpose is to supply information, discuss ideas, and stimulate curiosity about our language rather than give directions and advice about how to use it. It is true that people who know something about language are likely to be more thoughtful and skillful about how they use it. But it is also true that language is interesting in itself. After all, it is a universal form of human behavior, and all of us are interested in what people, including ourselves, do.

English is, of course, only one of the many languages, perhaps as many as three thousand, which are spoken today. These languages are very differ-

Reprinted from *THE ENGLISH LANGUAGE: An Introduction* by W. Nelson Francis. By permission of W. W. Norton & Company, Inc. Copyright © 1963, 1965 by W. W. Norton & Company, Inc.

ent one from another. Indeed, it is primarily the fact that they are so different as to be mutually unintelligible that allows us to call them separate languages. A speaker of one of them, no matter how skillful and fluent, cannot communicate with a speaker of another unless one of them, as we say, "learns the other's language." Yet these differences, great as they are, are differences of detail—of the kinds of sounds used and the ways of putting them together. In their broad outlines, in their basic principles, and even in the way they approach certain specific problems of communication, languages have a great deal in common. It is thus possible to make some observations about languages in general before we come to the specific qualities of English in particular.

In the first place, any language is *arbitrary*. This means that there is nothing—or at most very little—in the nature of the things we talk about that dictates or controls the language we use to talk about them. When we are children we do not know this. We believe that the connection between an act or an object and the word which refers to it is somehow a natural and inevitable one. If you ask a child why he calls a certain object a *clock*, he will probably answer, "Because it *is* a clock." We can see the error of this belief in this childlike form. But it is likely to persist in a somewhat more sophisticated form in the minds of those who have not thought or studied about language. All of us have heard people make statements like "The real name for these things is *crullers*, but I call them *doughnuts* because everybody else around here does." Note the assumption that there is a *real*—natural or inevitable—name for something, even though nobody uses it. Only when we learn a foreign language do we become completely disabused of this notion. When we discover that *horloge* and *Uhr* seem to other people just as natural names for a timepiece as *clock*, we come to realize that none of them is really natural, but all are arbitrary.

Primitive peoples often build much of their religious and cultural behavior on this belief in the natural relationship of word and thing. For example, they believe that to know the name of an object, person, or deity is to gain a certain control over it: in "Ali Baba and the Forty Thieves," the words "Open Sesame!" cause the stone doors of the cave to move aside. Conversely, certain powers in the universe are thought to dislike the use of their names by mortals. Words are therefore tabooed, or euphemisms and descriptive phrases are invented such as *the little people* instead of *fairies*. The Greeks came to call those vengeful mythological creatures whose "real name" was *Erinyes* (or Furies) the *Eumenides* (or "good-tempered ones").

Although we consider ourselves too civilized for such superstitious behavior, vestiges of it remain in our conduct still. Many people will not speak of "death" or "dying" but use expressions like "passing away," "going to rest." A group of words that virtually everybody knows, most of them referring to universal bodily functions, are taboo in polite society, though polysyllabic synonyms for them are quite all right. Many of us knock on wood or cross our fingers when we say certain things, pretending—usually humorously—that this conduct will counteract the risk incurred by using powerful or dangerous words. But on our rational side we know that the only real connection between the word and the thing is in the minds of the people who speak our language.

There is, of course, a small area of language which is less arbitrary than the rest because it makes use of imitation. A child may call a clock a *tick-tock* or a train a *choo-choo*. Even here, however, there is a considerable degree of arbitrariness. The pendulum clock in the room where I am writing is making a rhythmic sound, but it certainly would not be described as "tick-tock" by an impartial—Chinese or Martian—observer. And the disappearance of the steam locomotive has removed from the scene anything making a sound even remotely resembling "choo-choo." Even supposedly imitative words of this sort are usually learned from others rather than made up in spontaneous imitation of other sounds.

Secondly, language is *conventional*. Its effectiveness rests upon a kind of unspoken public agreement that certain things will be done in certain definite ways. This is one consequence of its arbitrariness. Speakers of English are agreed upon calling a certain animal a *horse*. This is an arbitrary agreement. The principal function of language, communication, would break down if everybody insisted on using his own private arbitrary names for things. It is true that the agreement is often not complete. People may argue over whether or not whales are fish or spiders are insects. Such arguments, however, are wholly within the conventional field of language. They are concerned not with the basic agreements about words but with how much of the world of things a given word can be agreed upon to cover, which, in turn, may vary with the circumstances. It suits biologists to limit the class of things which they agree to call insects to those which have six legs, but most of us in our daily lives are agreed on including the eight-legged spiders as well. It is sometimes necessary, therefore, to specify what convention we are operating under at any given time. That is, when we are using language carefully, we must define our terms.

A third important quality of language is that it is *culturally transmitted*: it is passed on from generation to generation as a form of learned, rather than physically inherited, behavior. Nobody inherits the ability to use a particular language; everybody must learn it from other people who have themselves learned it at an earlier time. This learning begins in infancy and continues in varying intensity throughout life. The biggest part of the job is done between the ages of one and six, but it is not necessary to remind students that a good part of both their formal and their informal education consists of extending and sharpening their use of language.

An important consequence of this quality of language is that since individual people differ greatly in their capacity to learn, they also differ greatly in their command of language. This is true of all culturally transmitted activities—dancing, for example, or drawing. Some people simply have more aptitude for them, or have received more training, or both. At one end of the scale are those whose use of language and interest in it are the minimum needed to get them through routine work and simple play. At the other are writers (especially poets), actors, and others for whom the elaborate and subtle use of language is the central activity of life. Most of us fall somewhere between, depending on the nature of our work and play.

A second consequence is that like other aspects of human culture, language is subject to change. Our clothes, our food, our tools, and our speech vary from generation to generation just as they do from age to age. This change is sometimes fast and sometimes slow, sometimes radical and sometimes superficial, but it goes on all the time. Its causes are many and varied, and some of them are not fully understood. There may be a kind of slow, imperceptible, glacierlike drift, such as that which has brought about the differences in pronunciation between the English of America and the English of England. Or there may be striking innovation, taken up and circulated by fashion, like that which has added such new expressions as *hipster, blast off,* and *cosmonaut* to our vocabulary. The cumulation of such changes, going on in different ways in different places, may eventually cause what were once local versions of the same language to become distinct, mutually unintelligible languages like French and Spanish, or English and German. We don't know in how many different places language began—perhaps several, perhaps only one—but we do know that the great diversity of tongues among the peoples of the world today is almost wholly due to this process of divergent change.

The fourth and last general quality of language that will be mentioned here is that it has a very complicated *multiple structure.* This is necessary if language is to discharge the most important function that is asked of it: the communication of an infinite number of different messages, made up from a small number of vocal signals which can be learned by any human of normal intelligence. Language, in other words, is open-ended; there is no limit to the number of things that can be said. This is made possible by the mathematical possibilities of combination. Out of a relatively small group of sounds—fewer than a hundred—that any normal person can learn to produce can be made hundreds of thousands of words, which in turn can be combined according to the rules of grammar into a virutally endless number of different sentences. All languages have this complex, many-layered structure. That is what makes them adequate to the needs of their users. Contrary to some popular impressions, the word and sentence structure of the language of the most primitive peoples is highly complex. Anyone who undertakes to study an American Indian language, with its long, intricately complicated word structure and its delicate nuances of grammar, many of them very different from those we are used to in English, discovers immediately how preposterous is the widespread notion that the first Americans communicated largely by grunts, by sign-language, and by smoke signals. No matter where language is used—in the jungles of Africa or South America, the mountains of Tibet, or the islands of the Pacific—it has a complex, versatile, and adaptable structure.

II. THE ENGLISH LANGUAGE TODAY

The three thousand or so languages of the world differ greatly in practical importance, as measured by the number of people who speak them and the part they play in world affairs. Some are spoken by only a few hundred people, others by hundreds of millions. Some are dying out, either because the groups who speak them are dwindling or, more commonly, because the speakers have adopted another, more useful language, and the new generation does not bother to learn the old one. This last situation is what is bringing about the rapid disappearance of many American Indian languages in our time. On the other hand, some languages are growing in importance as the people who speak them increase in number and influence in the world. English is now one of these great and growing world languages.

We whose native speech is English seldom think how fortunate we are. The speech community of English, comprising all those who use it as their regular means of communication, numbers over three hundred million persons, any one of whom can converse (admittedly sometimes with difficulty) with any other. In addition, large numbers of people whose native speech is not English go to the trouble of learning it in order to be able to communicate with the native English speakers—or in some cases, with each other. More people learn English in India than in England, though for all of them it is a second language, learned laboriously at school. There are something like seventy thousand teachers of English in Japan alone. The result of widespread use of English is that even in the mid-twentieth-century world of international trade, cheap and quick travel, and vast military movement, the average American almost never finds himself in a position where he is forced to make himself understood in another language beside English. The American tourist in France expects to get by on English, while the American shopkeeper or hotel clerk at home likewise expects to use English with the French tourist. The American child goes to school with his working language well under control, and usually gives no school time to the learning of another language until eighth or ninth grade. Compare his position with that of the Ilocano child from northern Luzon. When he first goes to school, he starts at once to learn Tagalog, the national language of the Philippines; in the second grade, he begins to learn English as well; from the fourth grade on, all his instruction is conducted in English. At an age when most American children have seldom if ever heard a foreign language spoken, the Indian, Swiss, or Filipino child is a proficient speaker of one or more languages beside his own.

It is inevitable that a language like English, spoken by so many people scattered from one end of the world to the other, should have many varieties, differing rather widely from one another. The most obvious varieties are regional dialects, some of which go far back in history. When the various Germanic tribes, commonly lumped together as Anglo-Saxons, migrated from the continent of Europe to the island of Britain in the fifth and sixth centuries, they already spoke somewhat different varieties of their common tongue. Since they tended to settle in tribal groups, these differing dialects became associated with various regions of the new homeland. Differences between them increased during the Middle Ages and have survived into our own time. As a result, the native speech of the plain folk, especially in the country, shows great diversity within the relatively small area of the British Isles. We can all tell a Scot from an Irishman and both of them from a Cockney, and as Americans we may have trouble understanding any of them. Other varieties of English are spoken in various parts of America, and in other parts of the world where English has been carried. All of these regional dialects have in common most of their grammar and vocabulary and the main features of their pronunciation; otherwise we would have to call them separate languages rather than varieties of a single language, English. But each has its own peculiarities, which sound unfamiliar, odd, and sometimes comical to speakers of other varieties.

Another form of diversity which English shows is based on the social class and amount of education of its speakers. Even in a single area, such as New York City or coastal New England, there is a wide and obvious difference between the speech of the educated professional and business people and that of factory workers, farm laborers, fishermen, and the like. This kind of difference is commonly spoken of as the difference between "good English" and "bad English." Insofar as educated English has a larger vocabulary and permits the expression of more subtle and complex ideas, this value judgment is a sound one. But it should be emphasized that uncultivated English serves quite adequately to meet the more limited demands put upon it, and hence among those who use it, it is not "bad" at all.

Our language shows variety in a third way, somewhat less obvious than the first two. If we stop to think about it, we are aware that not every word, expression, or sentence pattern is appropriate to every occasion. "Dinner is served, madam," "Dinner's ready," and "Come and get it!" are all equally communicative, but each one evokes a different mental picture of the environment where it might appropriately be heard. These divergent modes of speech, ranging from the artificial "frozen" forms of prayer and legal documents, through formal, informal, and colloquial to slang, have been called *functional varieties* or *styles* of language. Each is appropriate to the relationship existing between the speaker, the subject, and the person spoken to. The formal notice in Pullman cars reads "Quiet is requested for the benefit of those who have already retired"; a mother says to the noisy child, "Shh! Daddy's asleep"; a student admonishes his dormitory neighbor, "Shut up, my room-mate's sacked out." Each of these, quite proper in its own situation, would seem comic or rude in another. We all have to learn, as part of our social training, which functional variety or style of language to use in any social situation. When in doubt we usually use a somewhat formalized variety of the informal style characteristic of conversation among acquaintances who are not intimate enough for easy colloquial or slang.

By now it should be apparent that what we refer to in the easy and common phrase "the English language" is a complicated thing indeed. Our attitude toward it will be most realistic and practical if we think of it as the sum total of three hundred million ways of speaking, on the one hand very different, on the other sharing enough features in common so that any one of the three hundred million can communicate, albeit often with some difficulty and misunderstanding, with any other. The English language is not to be found in dictionaries and grammar books: it is to be found built into the brains of three hundred million native speakers. If they and the countless millions who have learned English as a second language were all to be wiped out, the English language would be as extinct as the dinosaur. Books would provide valuable fossil-like clues, permitting scholars to reconstruct many things about it. But the language itself is alive only so long as there are people who naturally and easily speak it when they need to communicate. Dictionaries and grammar books are nothing more than records of certain aspects of the language at given points in its ever-changing history.

Vocabulary

arbitrary, disabused, tabooed, vestiges, cumulation, nuances, albeit

Review Questions

1. What does Francis mean when he calls all language "arbitrary"? Cite examples from English and at least one foreign language of this aspect of language.

2. How are language habits similar to other social conventions, such as those relating to dance and dress?

3. Is there a relationship between the worldly sophistication of a people and the complexity of their language structure?

4. Enumerate three forms of diversity within the English language.

5. Comment on the sentence, "The English language is not to be found in dictionaries and grammar books: it is to be found built into the brains of three hundred million native speakers."

Expository Technique

1. What transitional devices signal the introduction of each of the four characteristics of language discussed in Part I of this essay?

2. How is Part II of this essay related to Part I?

3.

JOSHUA WHATMOUGH

Perspectives on Language

What is language? It is customary to begin with definitions. But philosophically a definition comes at the end of an investigation. If we begin by defining language, that is because language has been investigated from more than one point of view already. We might indeed be clear first about the nature of a definition. To define is to set forth the proper or peculiar qualities of an object, the features that give it its character and quality. But to define is also to differentiate an object, to set forth the features that distinguish it from other objects with which it might be confused. Again a definition is not bound to be permanent, but may be changed. The ancients regarded vinegar as typical of acid substances, but vinegar is impure acetic acid; acetic acid (the acid of vinegar) in modern chemistry is $HC_2H_3O_2$, of which only one of the hydrogen (H) atoms has acid properties—an acid being a salt of hydrogen, in the language of chemistry a substance which gives a hydrogen ion in solution, or which neutralizes bases yielding water. In general, an acid

From *LANGUAGE: A Modern Synthesis*, by Joshua Whatmough. Originally published in the United States by St. Martin's Press, Inc. and The New American Library of World Literature, Inc. Copyright 1956 by Joshua Whatmough. Reprinted by permission of Verona Taylor Whatmough.

is "a molecule with a positive field which is capable of neutralizing a basic molecule having a 'free' electron pair." In ordinary conversation, of course, the term 'acid' is not restricted by the scientific definition.

Now, to define language with precision is far less easy than to define acid or other chemical terms. This is because many scientific inquirers are interested in language, philosophers, psychologists, physicists, logicians, literary critics, neurologists, sociologists, as well as linguists, to name no others. There is also, just now, widespread interest in language and in meaning on the part of many intelligent men and women, no matter whether they regard an understanding of the nature and function of language as directly important for their daily work or not. No wonder, then, if many different definitions are made by different thinkers. But there need not be one, and only one, definition of language; and the different definitions advanced are not exclusive. They bring out different aspects of language, and supplement one another instead of excluding one another. Everything depends on the investigator's point of view and interest at the time he makes his definition.

To many, language is the most important form of human communication, and this is the broadest way of regarding it. Certainly language is human, and human only. Insects, birds, and some mammals as well as man do communicate; but they do not talk. And language is normally, though not invariably, a form and a means of communication. Humans also use other means of communication, such as a red light, or a flag; but these are interpreted in language. 'Communication' means that an organism is affected by an external event and makes a reply to it. Clearly both the reply and the original event, in many cases itself also an utterance, are quite commonly what we understand by language: 'Is it raining?' (utterance) 'Not much' (response).

To others, language is first and foremost a form of symbolism. Here again we must stop to ask a question. What is a symbol? A symbol is a surrogate. We speak of mathematical symbols, for example x for any number, x^y for any number multiplied by itself any other number of times, i.e. x^y is the continued product of y x's, or x multiplied by itself $(y-1)$ times; Σ for any sum, and so on; or logical symbols, as a or b as variables in a statement or proposition, and then $\bar{a}$ to mean 'not a,' $a \vee b$ for 'a or b,' $\supset$ for implication as $a \supset b$ to mean 'a implies b,' and so forth. But all these surrogates have one feature in common. There is nothing in the nature of things that gives them the meanings stated; that is something *we* have given them, by agreement or convention, so that the symbol acquires a certain arbitrary character. This is something quite different from a *sign*. A sign has a direct relation to its object, like water dripping from the trees as a sign of rain; but the *word* rain (which obviously is not rain, or a sign of rain, for I can say it indoors, or for that matter I can say it repeatedly, even outdoors, without getting wet) is a symbol of 'rain' or 'raining,' as in our question *Is it raining? Not much!* or (to vary the event and therefore the response) *Not at all!*

Moreover, any consistent or coherent group of symbols, as in a language or dialect, is *systematic*. Like a family or society, it is not a merely accidental collection of stray individuals. The nature of symbols is such that to speak of an unsystematic symbolism is to fall into a contradiction in terms. Certainly linguistic symbols which are combined in such a way that the ties between them are unsystematic or are even bizarre—that is linguistic symbols unrelated to one another but merely juxtaposed—make nonsense; they cease to function as symbols. A haphazard jumble of symbols, say a pied text, is a mathematician's, or musician's, or a mere writer's or talker's, nightmare —but still a nightmare. An isolated symbol, on the other hand, remains just that to all eternity. The symbol for implication implies nothing by itself but implication in the abstract, and there it must rest; probability is probability in relation to something. All higher order abstractions are symbolic—'justice,' 'freedom,' 'goodness,' 'truth' and the like. Neither their content nor their form is directly or independently experienced, but only in relation to that which they symbolize; which is the reason why they are so much either distrusted or blindly worshipped, like the ideal of autonomy which destroyed the ancient Greek city-states.

But there remains one other factor even in this definition of language. Language is not only a systematic symbolism. Music is that, and also like language uses sound, and at times, as in singing, combines its own rhythm and melody with language. Language is a *verbal* systematic symbolism. That is to say, it makes use of verbal elements and structures, in brief, of what we commonly call words and of their arrangements. It will be better to postpone for a while any definition of words, or of what, in some languages such as Eskimo, behave pretty much as words do in others such as English. For the present it will be enough to take an example, say 'table.' There we have a symbol of a certain object; the symbol is also a word; that is, it is a verbal symbol. So, in like manner, *and* or *beer* or *have* or *embryo* or *drunk* or *man*. Now when we have occasion to use such a verbal symbol, we do so in a systematic way. Thus the verbal symbols 'table and embryo have drunk beer,' placed in that sequence are so unsystematic in arrangement as to symbolize nothing, unless possibly dementia on the speaker's part; but 'the man has drunk beer,' by adhering to the system, retains the symbolic integrity of each symbol, and the arrangement enhances their symbolic values.

The same is true at each step; *table* is a symbol, *letab* is not. It is not even necessary to add that *elbat* or *letab* is not a symbol in English, implying that it is, or may be, in some other language. What we have said so far is true of languages, or of a language, as well as of language at large; for every case is a given case when you come to it, and this is true of languages as of everything else, from cabbages to kings. To raise the question of system or no-system of a symbol outside its own systematic symbolism is idle. How deep-seated this principle is may be seen by taking the following groups of Latin words:

saxum 'stone' but *sexum* (acc. sing.) 'sex,' and *sex* 'six'
lacus 'lake' but *locus* 'place'
līquens 'clear' but *lĭquens* 'fluid,' *lŏquens* 'speaking,' and *līquans* 'liquefying.'

Lucretius, like all the ancient atomists, was aware of all this, and fond of it as an illustration of his theories: *ignis* is 'fire,' which may be had from *lignum* 'firewood' by disturbing or subtracting from or adding to the constituent particles of the words as well as of the substances! The principle may be illustrated from the system of any language whatever. It is astonishing how few of the primary units, that is the speech-sounds, will serve, and how little strain is put upon them, or upon the user, by quite severe demands for efficiency in their use. Even a child, or even a very dull adult, can easily make this powerful instrument serve all his needs.

But there are other ways of looking at language. One other way of putting what has just been said about the systematic character of linguistic symbolism is to say that language is a form of order, a pattern, a code. That is to say, at any given status of its history, a language is found to show a statistical regularity which may be put in terms of formulae that are concerned with classical probability of frequency of occurrence of the constituent elements, and of permitted combinations of them within the pattern of a particular language. Objectively, therefore, a language may be described as a body of physically discrete events in which relations of similarity occur in a statistically definable pattern. The sequence of events is governed by probabilities of occurrence; i.e. proceeds by probability, ranging from 0 to 1, in a series of mass phenomena showing repetitive events. The successive steps in the process are dependent also upon preceding steps. Finally, a sufficiently large sample of the sequence is representative of the whole, precisely because the events are repetitive. For example, in modern written English the occurrence of the symbol *q* guarantees that the symbol which follows it will be *u*; the symbol *th* in English may be followed by *a, e, i, o, u, r, w, y* but not by *l* (unless in borrowed words) or *x* or any of the other English alphabetic symbols. *Thx* would be a zero probability in genuinely English words; *tha* and the rest will always be less than 1. Even *th-* (as in *then*) is not followed by *r*, but only *th-* (as in *thin*); likewise English *shr-* occurs, but not *shl-*, or *pw-*: if you hear *pwivate* 'private' from a few speakers [w] is a variant, phonematically speaking, of [r]. The probability that *th* will be followed by *e* is considerably higher than that it will be followed by *u*. This is a very simple illustrative example.

In modern English, if a permissible sequence of symbols that makes a word, for example the series *f u r i o u s ,* is followed by anything at all, then those following symbols are already prescribed and limited; in this case they must be *l y* or *n e s s* (not normally *e r* or *e s t*) and nothing else, for example not *t h* (like *w i d e : w i d t h*). In other words, the symbols *l y* or *n e s s,* in this particular sequence, are determined by what went before.

But in all this, there is one feature of language that must never be lost sight of. *Language is first and foremost a means of transmitting information,* and its study a branch of the study of symbols and of the signs and objects that they symbolize. Language is made up of messages purposively produced in such a way as to be decoded word-by-word in the easiest, i.e. most economical, possible fashion. The length and arrangement of linguistic structures such as words, the nature and relation of speech-sounds (phonemes) one to another, the length and relation of constituent clauses in a sentence or period, all these have evolved in such a way as to promote an economical, but powerful, means of communication.

Language is also a form of social behavior. If all normal humans talk, and only humans, they also talk to one another. At the moment I am talking to my reader, as much as if I were 'on the air'; there is a greater time-lag in a printed book, as in a recording, than there is in face-to-face talk, the telephone, or direct, unrehearsed radio. A letter is written not to its writer, but to his family or friends or business acquaintances, to his tailor or grocer, to the tax-collector, and so forth. If I make notes for my own subsequent use, then I am practically two different persons, in different places or at different times, one here and now, the other somewhere else in the future. Some forms of language, shall we say those partially tabooed (but often infuriating or laughable) varieties of language, profanity and obscenity, have been made the objects of psychological study. Perhaps it is a mistake to treat them solely as matters of individual psychology. When language, or verbal behavior, is taken up by the psychologist, it is or should be as a matter of social as well as of individual conduct. Linguistic phenomena are conditioned by the social group, by circumstances which are socially determined—both the linguistic patterns of the community, and extralinguistic group habits, e.g. customs such as taboo or courtesy or the like.

To say that language may be studied as a form of behavior by no means admits that the school of psychology known as behaviorist is unreservedly supported by linguistics or by all linguists, or that a behaviorist interpretation of linguistic phenomena is the correct and only one. The serious objection to behaviorism is that it fails to take adequate account of intelligence. Intelligence consists in the power to make a new departure instead of repeating the old habit, to take a new step. A high degree of intelligence is always abnormal, and it occurs in the individual. How can behaviorists explain any initial success which they may themselves experience by their own professed theory that initial success is to be explained only in terms of chance and habit? A behaviorist who sets himself the purpose of proving that purpose does not exist is in the impossible position of starting himself into flight by tugging on his own bootstraps; he seems not to have noticed that the more frequently something has been tried, the less likely it is to recur if it has been unsuccessful, so that an intelligent result calls for deviation from normal habit. This is true also of language. Even on the mathematical view, a striking utterance is found, on inspection, to disturb commonplace encoding and decoding processes, as in T. S. Eliot's 'The yellow fog' (not 'dog') 'that rubs its back upon the window-panes.'

A notion of language that was common, at least by implication, in the nineteenth century, is held by nobody today, though many of the old ways of expression are constantly met with. We speak of mother languages, sister languages, dead and living languages. These expressions clearly suggest the view of language as an organism. But a moment's reflection must always have shown that the expressions are figurative only. Languages do not intermarry and produce offspring; to talk of a 'family' of languages means that a number of mutually unintelligible languages all represent divergent forms that can be shown historically to go back to a common original, that they possess a common stock of words, forms, sentence-structure, and speech-sounds, all greatly modified in the course of time, the relationships of which one to another can be accounted for only on the assumption that they represent a previous single, more-or-less homogeneous, speech. Provided that this fact is clearly understood, there is little harm in talking about this or that 'family' of languages.

But the whole matter was often put in the terms of a family-tree relationship. This idea was fostered in part by the evolutionary theories associated with the name of Darwin which were very much in the air in the middle of the nineteenth century. It was also encouraged by the work of a prominent philologist of the time, August Schleicher, who happened also to be a botanist, and was tempted to apply not only his scientific attitude of mind to his theorizing about language, which was all to the good, but also the current ideas of genetic relationships among plants or animals, which was misleading. Yet language certainly is an activity of living organisms, and through them shows remarkable power of adaptation to a changing environment.

But if language is not itself an organism, neither is it a mechanism. Many modern linguists are confirmed believers in a mechanist theory of language which shuns all mental interpretations and all mentalist terms. The theory of course claims to be objective. But it is difficult to admit the validity of the claim. For then we are asked to accept language about language about language about language . . . (and so on to infinity), and all of it starting from the hypothesis that language is nothing more than a matter of mechanical stimulus and response. If the theory were correct it would refute itself; for it would, on its own showing, be reduced to being a response or series of responses made by a certain linguist or linguists to certain stimuli, chiefly verbal. Such responses might tell us something about the linguist or linguists concerned and even about his or their use of language, but hardly anything about language as such. It is impossible to explain x by x; an unknown cannot be interpreted by itself. The mechanist theory aims at strictly scientific method, and therefore pretends to use only direct observation of communicating individuals; but in practice it leans heavily on indirect observation through records of all kinds. It tends also to restrict itself to observing and discussing the effects of language on the behavior of the individual, notwithstanding the fact that verbal behavior is essentially social. It is difficult to see how a mechanical theory of communication can ever escape the charge of solipsism: the mechanist always overlooks the fact that he himself, an organism like any other, is doing the observation, so that his much-vaunted objectivity is false.

As for the quaint notion that language arose from primitive facial gestures, and therefore does not differ fundamentally from other muscular behavior, not only does the idea rest on nothing stronger than conjecture; it naively assumes the validity of an absurdly simple solution to an extremely complicated problem. A truly philosophical account of language must comprehend, for example, poetic as well as scientific discourse, the power of human intellect as well as the chit-chat of everyday conversation.

But it will not do to fly to the opposite extreme and regard language as pure intellection. In scientific discourse, in logic, a large part of the total utterance serves intellectual operations, in mathematics close to 100 per cent (a definite article, demonstrative pronoun, the substantive verb, short phrases or sentences, and the like here and there in a page of mathematics perhaps are supererogatory); in poetry and creative writing generally, in aesthetic discourse too, a high percentage may still be said to be concerned with intellect. But in ordinary conversation as much as 90 to 95 per cent of what we say is neutral, and the meaning is carried largely by the overtones of the remainder—say such words as 'friend,' or 'enemy,' that arouse the emotions. Even here there is still a crude correspondence between the structure of the utterance and the structure of experience. But in some commercial and political propaganda any such correspondence may be not seriously attempted at all. There is often a pretense at making the statements informative, but it is a pretense unworthy of human intellect. It is, however, precisely the intervention of the individual cerebral (or mental) event between stimulus and response that effectively rescues language from being an automatic mechanist affair, even when it proceeds from the mouth of a dictator.

Finally, it has been suggested that language is a relation, or (better) a means of establishing and sustaining relations between members of a community, large or small—a village or hamlet, or on a world-wide scale. This is another, and in a way a more concrete, statement of what is meant by saying that language is a form of social behavior. Think of a human being as a point on a plane; and of what he says as projected like a double cone with the point on the plane, the cones produced above and below the plane and the axes variable; suppose also a number of such points, each corresponding to a human being, close together or more widely separated, as the case may be, on the plane. The cones will intersect. And the farther each cone is projected into space, the greater the volume of intersection. Even cones widely separated, people who are, if you like, 'poles apart,' may be brought into contact by the spreading influence of what they say, especially if they use modern techniques of communication, including the light-swift radio. The members of a family, however, clan, village, city, or nation—the latter usually, if not always, having a single language—are bound together not less by language than by law and government; and, under modern conditions, more than by religion and some other institutions such as education or 'amusement.'

But no matter in which of these different ways we look at language, we shall always find that all languages have certain characteristics which make language what it is. For example, there is the high degree of convention that characterizes linguistic symbolism—its features are conventional rather than arbitrary, for they are evolutionary. Then again, every language has its pattern, to which it adheres consistently. Diverse as are the aspects of language, and even more varied as are actual language-patterns, and the national languages that are utterly incomprehensible, without learning, to their several groups of speakers, still there are universals, fundamental and intrinsic to language, that appear in every particular language that has been examined.

Very early in life each normal human being becomes aware of his own existence, conscious of self and environment, and may continue so as long as he lives. Language is indeed part of this environment, and though we believe it to be a derivation from the background of human nature and experience, it has become relatively independent of the immediate environment. We may conveniently separate, therefore, from all other events (and their relations) those events which constitute that which is said about them.

The domain of this second kind of events, namely linguistic, is limitless; for clearly not only does it run the gamut from everyday conversational discourse to philosophy and mathematics, but there may be constructed a hierarchy of language in which we have language about language about language and so on—like a set of Chinese boxes. We distinguish, therefore, between (a) language at large and (b) language that is concerned with the interpretation of language and with logic; further we distinguish (c) language that is concerned with the description, history, and comparison of languages (linguistics); and (d) language which reports on sciences preliminary or auxiliary to the study of language (e.g. acoustics or phonetics) in the sense of linguistics proper (description, history, and comparison).

Any field of knowledge which is being actively cultivated may be expected to produce new crops, and in the field of linguistics spectacular results have been won in recent decades. In the eighties of the last century leading linguists insisted on strict historical method in tracing the relationship between, for example, Hindi *punch* 'five' (hence applied to a drink compounded of five ingredients) and English *five* and French *cinq,* all of which are the modern representatives of one and the same original word, which can be shown (by the same methods) to be connected with the English *fist* and *finger,* so that *five* has to do with counting on your fingers (and thumbs) or toes, five to each hand or foot. The theory which embodied the method was that historical changes or substitutions of sounds are absolutely regular and must be stated in terms which adhere strictly to this principle. This was definitely a new departure, and the leading spirits behind it were called 'new grammarians.' At that time there were hardly any other concepts behind the study of general linguistics.

Now we have new methods again, logical, psychological, physical, structural, statistical and mathematical, which are giving a tremendous impulse to the study and understanding of language.

Vocabulary

surrogate, bizarre, juxtaposed, pied, dementia, solipsism, gamut, hierarchy

Review Questions

1. Comment on the symbolic nature of language.
2. Why is it more difficult to define *language* with precision than most terms from the chemical and physical sciences?
3. Discuss the idea that language is a form of social behavior.
4. Enumerate the characteristics of language cited by Whatmough.
5. What does the author mean when he says that language is neither an organism nor a mechanism?

Expository Technique

1. This essay begins by defining "definition" as a setting forth of the "proper or peculiar qualities of an object." Show how the remainder of the essay rhetorically develops this idea by enumerating the features of language that give it its particular character and quality.
2. How does Whatmough insure that his enumeration is not merely a *random* list of characteristics?
3. What is the conclusion of this essay? How is it prepared for?

Exercises

1. Which of the following words would be most relevant to the linguistic concerns of a lexicographer, semanticist, dialect geographer, grammarian, and language historian:

psychedelic	calf	O.K.	cocktail
manufacture	oxen	bazooka	bitch
nigger	creek	xerography	ain't
realtor	filibuster	pancake	greasy
pajamas	khaki	woman	blitzkreig

2. W. Nelson Francis observes that language is arbitrary, conventional, culturally transmitted, and structurally complex. Compile a list of words, phrases, and sentences heard during a forty-eight hour period which exhibit these aspects of English. Be prepared to comment on each item in your enumeration.

3. Dictionaries "are nothing more than records of certain aspects of the language at given points in its ever-changing history." Go to your college library, find dictionaries from the eighteenth, nineteenth, and twentieth centuries, and cite the qualities that mark each dictionary as a record of its period.

4. What is the difference between a sign and a symbol? Which are the following?

the cross	the flag
the written word *cross*	the hammer and sickle
the spoken word *cross*	parched land
the letter *X*	beauty
black as an indication of mourning	S.O.S.

5. Make a list of as many nonverbal signs of danger, such as a flashing red light and a bell buoy, as you can.

6. Try to communicate the following ideas *without* the use of spoken language:

a. The teacher's chair is brown.

b. I am usually here during the summer, but I go south for the winter.

c. Have twentieth-century morals and ethics deteriorated to the point where a change in orthodox religion is warranted?

Which of these ideas is the most difficult to communicate by nonverbal means? Why? Which is the least difficult? Why? What does this reveal about the nature of language?

7. Consult one of the following works dealing with gestures and prepare an oral class report:

R. L. Birdwhistell, *Introduction to Kinesics* (Washington, 1952).

E. T. Hall, *The Silent Language* (New York, 1959).

"The High Price of Silent Insults," *Time* (April 9, 1965), 67–68.

Weston La Barre, "Paralinguistics, Kinesics, and Cultural Anthropology," in *Approaches to Semiotics,* ed. T. A. Sebeok (London, 1964), pp. 191–220.

R. L. Rosekrans, "Do Gestures Speak Louder than Words?" *Colliers* (March 4, 1955), 56–57.

Jurgen Ruesch and Weldon Kees, *Non-Verbal Communication* (Berkeley, 1956).

8. Kinesics is the study of nonlinguistic bodily movements or actions which convey meaning, such as handshaking, backslapping, winks, whistles, grimaces, and applause. Make a list of kinesic gestures you have observed in your parents, teachers, and friends.

4.

STUART ROBERTSON
FREDERICK G. CASSIDY

Theories Concerning the Origin of Language

When we talk at length to animals—as Alice in Wonderland does to her cat Dinah, which is not even present—we do not expect to be understood; like a baby babbling, or like Wordsworth's solitary reaper singing to herself, we often make sounds merely for the enjoyment of utterance. In short, language has an important expressive function, as well as the communicative one. Much of what we say in social intercourse, while ostensibly communicative, is no more than vaguely so and is quite as much expressive. The words we use in greeting or in being pleasant to people are not to be taken literally; they, and the tone in which they are said, are mostly a means of establishing a friendly atmosphere.

It is probably safe to conjecture that expressive sounds preceded communicative language, since they require a single speaker only, and the noises made are not necessarily conventionalized. As a speaker repeatedly made sounds, however, he might well find them falling into habitual patterns— like the songs of some birds—and another creature, hearing them in connection with particular situations, might interpret them accordingly. Thus the person expressing himself would quite incidentally be communicating.

From Stuart Robertson & Frederick G. Cassidy, THE DEVELOPMENT OF MODERN ENGLISH, SECOND EDITION © 1954. Reprinted by permission of Prentice-Hall, Inc., Englewood Cliffs, New Jersey.

When, for example, he howled with hunger, smaller creatures would keep out of his way. So expression would pass insensibly into communication as the expression became more willful or as one creature's expression brought a reply from another. Cries evoked by pain, fear, anger, love-longing, and such elemental sensations were surely as much the property of primitive man as of modern man and the lower animals. Out of some such crude beginnings must have come the highly developed structure of language—a primarily social thing as we know it, and primarily communicative rather than expressive.

This leads us to ask what theories have been offered of the origin of language, and to glance at some of the better-known ones. The first, now completely discredited, is that which finds the origin of language in a divine fiat. Thus, Plato, in what is perhaps the earliest extant explanation of the beginnings of speech, insists that "names belong to things by nature," and hence "the artisan of words" must be "only he who keeps in view the name which belongs by nature to each particular thing."[1] The implication is that the original perfect language, which humans must rediscover or re-create, is the work of the ruler of the universe, the great "law-giver." Imperfections in human language are thus explained as failures to discover the original "natural" or divine words. Curiously parallel to this is the view of the origin of language that was long the orthodox Hebrew (and Christian) theory, likewise maintaining that language originated in a divine act. It was supposed that God gave to Adam a language fully developed—this was, of course, believed to be Hebrew—and that the confusion of tongues at the building of the Tower of Babel accounted for the variations in human speech. This explanation, it is surely unnecessary to add, has long since been given up, by theologians as by linguists. Language is looked upon today as one of the things achieved by the human creature in the course of his long development—but one so fundamentally human, as we have said, that it is a distinguishing characteristic setting him apart from the lower animals.

Of the more recent theories based on this assumption one encounters two types, resulting from two approaches. The earlier approach sought, by examining the vocabulary of languages as we know them, to isolate the most primitive (least conventionalized) types of words, and to build a theory of origins on these. The more recent approach has been through speculative reconstruction of the broader situation which might have led to the discovery or application of vocal communication. As an example of the first we may look at the echoic (or as it is nicknamed, the "bow-wow") theory. This maintained that primitive language was exclusively onomatopoetic; that is, that its words were directly imitative of the sounds of nature or of animals, all the word-stock being thought to have originated in a way

---

[1] *Cratylus,* Loeb ed. (New York), p. 31.

parallel to the child's calling a dog "bow-wow" or a duck "quack-quack." There is undoubtedly some truth in this; but it should be noticed that sheer echoisms are not words; they become words when they are conventionalized in terms of the sound-patterns of the imitator's language. Thus to a German the cock crows "Kikeriki"; to a Frenchman "Cocorico"; to an Englishman "Cock-a-doodle-doo"—not because cocks crow differently in Germany, France, and England, but because these forms are the imitations conventional to each language. Furthermore, once an echoism, duly conventionalized, has entered a language, it is subject to the same kinds of language-change as any other word, and may thus be altered in the course of time until its echoic origin is no longer perceived. The word *cow* is not obviously echoic, because its vowel sounds have changed (with all similar sounds) within the past six hundred years. In Old English, however, its ancester was *cū,* which more clearly suggests its probable echoic origin.

The obvious objection to the "bow-wow" theory is that it does not explain more than a part, and not the largest part, of language. Not even early or "primitive" languages have been shown to be composed chiefly or altogether of onomatopoetic words. The languages of primitive or savage peoples, indeed, turn out upon examination to be quite as conventional as those of civilized peoples. Thus the "bow-wow" theory, though it contains some truth, claims too much.

Similarly, other discarded theories may contain an element of truth. The principal ones are the so-called "pooh-pooh" (or interjectional) theory, which derives language from instinctive ejaculatory responses to such emotions as pain or joy; and the "ding-dong" theory, which holds that language began with a mystically harmonious response, on the part of man's hitherto silent vocal organs, to a natural stimulus which was fated thus to call forth its perfect expression—"everything that is struck, rings." The obvious criticism of the interjectional theory is the difficulty of bridging the gap between interjections (which on the whole are relatively isolated phenomena in speech) and the main body of language. Indeed, it has been held that this is precisely the chasm that separates animal speech, "exclusively exclamatory," from that of men.[2] It is difficult to see how the theory of interjections accounts for much more than the interjections themselves. The other theory is reminiscent of the ancient Greek belief that words exist by nature, rather than by convention, and that there is a necessary and inherent connection between words and the ideas for which they stand. In its eighteenth- and nineteenth-century phases, this theory (once maintained but later rejected by Max Müller) seems no more acceptable as a complete explanation of the origin of language than it does in its Platonic form.

[2] Cf. C. H. Grandgent, "The Why and How of Speech," *Getting a Laugh* (Cambridge, Mass., 1924), p. 78.

To this account of past theories may be added, in brief summary, the speculations of two twentieth-century students of language. Otto Jespersen's hypothesis[3] based in part on the study of the language of children and of primitive races but chiefly on the history of language, is that emotional songs were the germs of speech. In particular he felt that the emotion of love[4] called forth the earliest songs, that these songs—and others evoked by different emotions (a chant of victory, for example, or a lament for the dead)—were inevitably accompanied by what were at first meaningless syllables, and that the circumstance that the same sounds were used on similar occasions brought about the first association of sound and meaning.

Sir Richard Paget, assenting to the general belief that the earliest form of human communication is gesture, has proposed the *oral gesture* theory. This holds that

> . . . human speech arose out of a generalized unconscious pantomimic gesture language—made by the limbs and features as a whole (including the tongue and lips)—which became specialized in gestures of the organs of articulation, owing to the human hands (and eyes) becoming continuously occupied with the use of tools. The gestures of the organs of articulation were recognized by the hearer because the hearer unconsciously reproduced in his mind the actual gesture which had produced the sound.[5]

This theory differs from others in considering gesture not as a concomitant of speech, but as the source or at least the articulating factor of speech; it proposes a causal relationship where none had been seen before. There is, of course, no way of either proving or disproving this. Even if we agree that gesture preceded speech as a means of communication, the one need not be accepted as the cause of the other.

The conclusion of the whole matter is that the origin of language is an unsolved and doubtless insoluble enigma.[6] Whatever the origin may have been, it is too remote to admit of more than conjectures about it, of differing degrees of plausibility. Yet the fact that he may never arrive at the truth

---

[3] *Language* (New York, 1924), pp. 412–442.

[4] Professor Arthur E. Hutson reports that his students have dubbed this, by analogy, the "woo-woo" theory.

[5] *Human Speech* (New York, 1930), p. 174. By an interesting coincidence, the same theory was arrived at independently and almost simultaneously in Iceland, by Alexander Jóhanneson; see his *Origin of Language*.

[6] There are, of course, a great many more theories than have been mentioned here. Sturtevant, for example, argues that "voluntary communication can scarcely have been called upon except to deceive; language must have been invented for the purpose of lying." *An Introduction to Linguistic Science* (New Haven, 1947), p. 48. For a brief summary of theories, see Gray, *Foundations of Language,* p. 40. . . .

should not prevent the scientist from making and testing hypotheses. If he gains nothing absolute, at least he dismisses untenable theories and keeps the question alive. As Jespersen has pointed out,[7] "questions which . . . *can* be treated in a scientific spirit, should not be left to the dilettanti." Thus while it is right to reject premature solutions, it is "decidedly wrong to put the question out of court altogether"—as some recent linguists have tended to do.

There is no historical reason or logical necessity, then, to find a single explanation for all types of words. Some were no doubt exclamatory, others imitative; most have changed so entirely from their early form that it cannot be recovered. All we can feel fairly safe about is that at some point the human creature discovered something that the lower animals had not discovered: the symbolic process. His noises could be made to stand for things not present to his senses. Gradually he elaborated this into a system, conventionalizing more and more and combining the symbolic sounds in new ways.

But if the *how* of language can never be known, there can be little doubt as to the *why*. Language must have arisen out of a social necessity— the need for communication between man and man. As soon as human creatures began to live in interdependent groups this need must have been a very powerful stimulus. Perhaps, for a time, communication was achieved by gesture alone. But this would have had serious limitations, through darkness, any obstruction that kept one person from seeing another, or the occupation of the limbs that did not leave them free for gestures. Sound, on the other hand, was subject to none of these difficulties, and vocal sound was accessible to almost everybody. And once meaningful speech had been discovered it must have proved its worth as a unifying possession of the whole community. Everyone who could use these symbols would be a member of the group; those who could not, or whose speech-symbols were different, were outsiders. Thus language in the abstract becomes concrete, and we can speak of *a* language, or *the* English language, as the possession of a certain "speech-community." Many of the deepest things in our natures become attached to the particular language which, by accident of birth, happens to be our own. And contrariwise, a difference in language prevents us too often from realizing that other men are, in most ways, very much like ourselves.

Vocabulary

ostensibly, insensibly, artisan, orthodox, linguist, onomatopoetic, ejaculatory, enigma, untenable, dilettanti, symbolic

[7] *Language,* pp. 96–99.

Review Questions

1. Identify the following: Plato, Max Müller, Otto Jespersen, Sir Richard Paget.

2. What is the difference between "expressive" and "communicative" language?

3. How are the theories of Plato and of the Hebrew scriptures concerning the origin of language parallel?

4. How do the echoic and the interjectional theories account for the origin of language? Why is each regarded as inadequate?

5. To what extent do Robertson and Cassidy believe the evolution of language exemplifies the old adage "Necessity is the mother of invention"?

Expository Technique

1. In the sections in which Robertson and Cassidy discuss theories of the origin of language, what principle(s) of organization or arrangement do they employ?

2. Is there a contradiction between the first and last paragraphs of this essay? Why? Why not?

Exercises

1. Reread the discussion of the echoic and interjectional theories on the origin of language, making whatever brief notes you deem useful. Then, without consulting the essay by Robertson and Cassidy, write a paragraph that begins with and develops the following topic sentence:

Though not regarded by most students of language as completely adequate, two theories, the echoic and the interjectional, have been proposed to explain the origin of language.

2. An entertaining essay which develops further the ways in which echoisms become conventionalized in sound patterns in various European languages is by Noel Perrin and appeared in *The New Yorker* (January 27, 1962), 28–29. Read the essay and prepare a brief summary to be presented as an oral class report.

3. If there is a small child (one to three years old) in your family or among your acquaintances, observe the development of his language. Is his language mostly expressive or communicative? What examples of echoic and interjectional expressions do you note?

Writing Suggestions: Enumeration

1. How ——————— (Beers, Perfumes, Soft Drinks, Bourbons, Dog Foods, Soaps, Cars) Are Named

2. Animal Communication Systems (Investigate current thought on the kinds of communication used by bees, bats, birds, porpoises, or ants.)

3. The Gestural Language of _____ (Baseball, Football, Basketball, Hockey, Tennis)

4. Nonverbal Communication Systems (Drums, Whistles, Smoke, Bells)

5. Proposals for a World Language

6. The Advantages of English as a World Language

7. Out-of-Date Assumptions about Language

8. Varieties of English

9. Approaches to the Study of Language

10. Speculations about the Origin of Language

11. Misconceptions about Language

12. Alphabets

Definition

DEFINITION is frequently the best way to explain a word or concept because to define is to set limits, to clarify the unknown in terms of the known, to answer the question, What is it? Since we must know the meanings of words and ideas before we can hope to use and understand them in any kind of written expression, definition is the most basic of the expository types. Writers, therefore, often begin their essays with precise definitions, for they are aware that only confusion and misunderstanding can result if a reader misinterprets their use of important terms. Definition, then, may be essential to the effective communication of ideas.

The commonest method of giving the meaning of a word is by giving its *synonym,* and we employ this procedure when we define *temerity* as *boldness* or *empty* as *unoccupied.* It is true that no two words are exactly synonymous (someone, for example, might be called "empty-headed" but never "unoccupied-headed"), but *unoccupied* is close enough in denotation to *empty* to be helpful in establishing its meaning.

A more explicit method of definition is *classification.* Here the term to be defined is placed in a class and then distinguished from other members of that class, much as in biology a species is placed within a genus and then differentiated from other species within that genus. Note how this procedure is followed in these examples:

WORD	CLASS (GENUS)	HOW WORD DIFFERS FROM OTHER MEMBERS OF THE SAME CLASS (SPECIES)
canoe	a small boat	which is long, narrow, and pointed at both ends, without rudder or sails, and propelled by paddles.

95

WORD	CLASS (GENUS)	HOW WORD DIFFERS FROM OTHER MEMBERS OF THE SAME CLASS (SPECIES)
democracy	a system of government	in which the supreme power is retained by the people either directly (absolute democracy) or indirectly (representative democracy).

A third method of definition is by *example*. A person may not know the meaning of *crustacean,* but if he is told that shrimps, lobsters, and crabs are crustaceans, he will probably understand the term. In a similar manner one might define *philanthropist* by citing such examples as Ford, Guggenheim, and Carnegie. In order for this method to be effective, the reader, although unaware of the meaning of the general class term, must be familiar with some specific members of that class. The major disadvantage of definition by example is that the examples cited may have several characteristics in common, and the reader may be uncertain of which is the essential one. As a consequence, this method of defining is most effectively used in conjunction with one of the other two rather than by itself.

Both the dictionary and the essay of definition employ the three types of definition, but the lexicographer and the essayist differ in purpose and technique. It will be helpful to note these differences in order to understand definition as a means of exposition. First, the editor of a dictionary is concerned with the meanings of *words;* the essayist is concerned not only with the meanings of words but also with the *ideas* which they represent. The dictionary, for instance, defines the word *meaning* very briefly as *what is indicated or signified,* but C. K. Ogden and I. A. Richards have written an entire book entitled *The Meaning of Meaning,* which investigates the complex concept of meaning and its implications, and which involves the semantic problem of the threefold relationship of thoughts, words, and things.

A second difference between lexicographers and essayists in their use of definition is the degree of objectivity attained by each. Modern dictionaries are products of a composite mind and have been compiled by men who have examined hundreds of contexts in which words have appeared. Only after extensive analysis and comparison is meaning rendered, and then as concisely as possible. The essayist who employs definition as a means of exposition, however, is usually not as scientific in his approach as the lexicographer, and his essay is more subjective and discursive than dictionary entries. That definitions vary comparatively little between one dictionary and another is evidence of the lexicographer's objectivity, whereas different essays of definition on the same subject vary widely, even contradicting each other in many cases. In brief, the dictionary-maker reports; the essayist editorializes.

SPECIAL PROBLEMS IN DEFINITION

There are several kinds of pitfalls in definition which the writer of exposition should avoid. The first is *circularity,* the use of the term being defined or some form of it in the definition. In both of the following sentences note that the definitions add nothing to our understanding of the term being defined:

> Justice is the principle by which men deal justly with each other.
> A definition is that which defines.

A second error to be avoided is that of *nonparallel grammatical form.* Both the term to be defined and the definition must be expressed in terms of identical grammatical structure. Thus, nouns should always be defined by nouns, adjectives by adjectives, etc.

> *Incorrect:* Voting is when you try to elect a civil official.
> (Gerund is defined by an adverbial clause.)
> *Correct:* To vote is to express formally a choice for a candidate, proposal, or bill.
> (Infinitive is defined by an infinitive.)

Two other errors, which can be considered together because of their close relationship, are *overrestriction* and *overinclusion.* A definition is said to be overrestricted when the meaning given is too narrow to cover everything that might be denoted by the term to be defined. Consider, for example, this definition of *citizen*:

> A citizen is an individual who gains his political rights by birth.

Although this definition may be true and can describe one kind of citizen, it is overrestrictive because it does not include citizens who gain their political rights through means other than birth, such as naturalization. An overinclusive definition operates in exactly the opposite manner and gives a meaning which is too broad, for it includes possibilities which are not denoted by the term to be defined. Consider this example:

> A citizen is an individual who resides in a country.

Again, although this definition may be true under certain circumstances, it is faulty, this time because it includes too many people not denoted by the term *citizen*. Under this definition all aliens living in the United States would be regarded as American citizens. The deficiencies in these examples can be corrected by framing a definition which is broad enough to encompass means of gaining citizenship in addition to birth and yet narrow enough to restrict citizenship to a smaller group than all those who reside in a country. Such a definition is the following:

> A citizen is an individual who owes allegiance to a state or nation and who is entitled to full political rights therein.

Finally, definitions should always clarify the term to be defined, never obscure it. To define *network,* as Samuel Johnson does, as "anything reticulated and decussated at equal intervals with interstices between the intersections" is to befuddle the reader with ponderous Latinate diction. In summation, definitions should be neither circular, grammatically nonparallel, overrestrictive, overinclusive, nor needlessly complicated. If definitions are clear and precise, they will serve their functions as aids to clear thinking and effective communicators of ideas.

ORGANIZATION

Definitions as in essays may vary greatly in length—from only a sentence or two to many paragraphs or even the entire essay; but whether definition is used only briefly or as the body of the whole essay, it will usually be developed by means of one or more of the other expository types. Thus, in an essay entitled "What Is a Criminal?" the writer might develop his definition by citing examples of criminals, like Capone and Dillinger; or by describing the process by which a youth in the slums becomes a thief; or by comparing criminals with so-called law-abiding citizens; or by analyzing prison statistics to produce a composite of the criminal type; or by discussing the causes of anti-social behavior—all of these could be means of defining his subject. In short, the organization of the essay of definition is integrally connected with the other five types of exposition, and the writer's final choice of organizational pattern will depend upon his specific subject and his approach to it.

AN EXAMPLE OF DEFINITION

In the following excerpt Bergen and Cornelia Evans define a common aspect of language usage: the cliché.

THE MEANING OF CLICHÉ*

Cliché is a French word meaning a stereotype block and is used in English to describe those phrases (there are thousands of them), originally idioms, metaphors, proverbs, or brief quotations, which overuse and, sometimes, changing circumstances have rendered meaningless. Many of them just fill out the vacancies of thought and speech. A man goes to say *far* and he says *far and wide.* Speech is a difficult thing. We spend more time learning to talk than anything else we do. It is an effort, an unceasing effort. There is strong resis-

---

tance in us to it and the inertia which this resistance sets up is probably the chief cause of our use of clichés.

Many clichés are alliterative, that is, their words begin with the same sound. We do not say we are *cool*, but *cool as a cucumber*. Unless one is *slow but sure*, things go to *rack and ruin* and he may be thrown out *bag and baggage*.

Historical changes have made many clichés utterly meaningless. What does *fell* mean in *one fell swoop?* Or *halcyon* in *halcyon days?* Or *moot* in *moot point?* Yet these and hundreds of other phrases, totally devoid of meaning to those who speak them, are heard every day.

Many clichés were once original and clever, but repetition by millions, possibly billions, of people for hundreds and even thousands of years in some instances has worn all originality and cleverness away. They were fresh-minted once, but are now battered beyond acceptability. And their use is doubly bad because it characterizes the user as one who thinks he is witty, or would like to be thought witty, and yet is a mere parroter of musty echoes of long-dead wit. His very attempt to sound clever shows him to be dull.

Our speech is probably more crammed with clichés today than ever before. The torrent of printed and recorded matter that is dumped on us every day in newspapers and from radio and television is bound to be repetitious and stereotyped. The brightest day in the world's history never produced one-millionth, in fresh, original, and honest expression, of the bulk of what cascades over us every day. All this stuff is prepared in furious haste. There is neither time nor energy for care or thought and the inevitable result is a fabric woven of stereotyped phrases. Ninety per cent of what the public reads and hears is expressed in fossilized fragments and, naturally, ninety per cent of its own expression, apart from the necessities of life, is also expressed in them.

This makes the task of the man who wants to speak and write clearly and honestly a difficult one. He must be on his guard all the time, especially against anything that seems particularly apt. That doesn't mean that he is never to use a current phrase or even a hackneyed one. It may be, for example, that after consideration he really does want to say that the pen is mightier than the sword. And if he does, he'd better say it in the cliché form than in some labored circumlocution. But he mustn't expect to be thought clever for saying it. And, of course, he may deliberately choose to speak in clichés in order that his speech may be common and familiar.

Wits often use clichés as the basis of their wit, relying on the seeming familiarity of the phrase and the expectation of its inevitable conclusion to set the trap for the innocent reader—such as Oscar Wilde's "Punctuality is the thief of time" or Samuel Butler's "It's better to have loved and lost than never to have lost at all"—but that is a wholly different thing.

Exercises on Definition

1. Comment upon the degree of objectivity of each of the following definitions of *home:*

a. Home is where the heart is. (Proverb)

b. It takes a heap of living to make a house a home. (Edgar A. Guest)

c. Home is a place where when you have to go there they have to take you in.
(Robert Frost)

d. Home is a family's place of residence.
(*Webster's Seventh New Collegiate Dictionary*)

e. Home is the girl's prison and the woman's workhouse. (Bernard Shaw)

2. In a far-reaching decision the United States Supreme Court ordered that integration of America's public school system be carried out with "deliberate speed." Does *deliberate* mean *slow, unhurried, reflective, cautious, prudent?* All of these? Are the ideas contained in the words *slow speed* mutually contradictory?

3. Define the following terms and distinguish each from the terms indicated in parentheses:

a. freedom (*license, right*)

b. justice (*law*)

c. imitate (*reproduce, copy*)

d. radicalism (*extremism*)

4. Differentiate between the words in each of the following classes:

a. Boats: punt, canoe, skiff, rowboat, kayak

b. Governments: monarchy, theocracy, oligarchy, anarchy

c. Doctors: gynecologist, psychiatrist, pathologist, roentgenologist, otolaryngolist

d. Dogs: cur, whelp, mongrel, puppy

5. Compare the definitions in each of the following paragraphs. What techniques does each definition represent? Which is the more effective? Why?

a. If I were asked to describe as briefly and popularly as I could, what a University was, I should draw my answer from its ancient designation of a *Studium Generale,* or "School of University Learning." This description implies the assemblage of strangers from all parts in one spot;—*from all parts;* else, how will you find professors and students for every department of knowledge? and *in one spot;* else how can there be any school at all? Accordingly, in its simple and rudimental form, it is a school of knowledge of every kind, consisting of teachers and learners from every quarter. Many things are requisite to complete and satisfy the idea embodied in this description; but such as this a University seems to be in its essence, a place for the communication of thought, by means of personal intercourse, through a wide extent of country.
(John Henry Newman, *The Idea of a University*)

b. Democracy is the line that forms on the right. It is the don't in Don't Shove. It is the hole in the stuffed shirt through which the sawdust slowly trickles; it is the dent in the high hat. Democracy is the recurrent suspicion that more than half of the people are right more than half of the time. It is the feeling of privacy in the voting booths, the feeling of communion in the libraries, the feeling of vitality everywhere. Democracy is the score at the beginning of the ninth. It is an idea which hasn't been disproved yet, a song the words of which have not gone bad. It's the mustard on the hot dog and the cream in the rationed coffee.
(E. B. White, *The Wild Flag*)

Writing Suggestions: Definition

1. What is a _____ (College, Community, Fraternity, Sorority, Pressure Group, Constituency, Home)?

2. My Concept of a Good _____ (Examination, Advisor, Teacher, College, Draft Board, Police Department)

3. The Meaning of _____ (*Camp, Soul, Soul Food, Trip, Underground, Mod*)

4. A Definition of _____ (Courage, Poverty, Democracy, Comedy, Tragedy, Farce, Race)

(Additional writing suggestions on linguistic subjects are on page 203.)

Problems in Definition and Usage

5.

EDWARD SAPIR

Language Defined

Speech is so familiar a feature of daily life that we rarely pause to define it. It seems as natural to man as walking, and only less so than breathing. Yet it needs but a moment's reflection to convince us that this naturalness of speech is but an illusory feeling. The process of acquiring speech is, in sober fact, an utterly different sort of thing from the process of learning to walk. In the case of the latter function, culture, in other words, the traditional body of social usage, is not seriously brought into play. The child is individually equipped, by the complex set of factors that we term biological heredity, to make all the needed muscular and nervous adjustments that result in walking. Indeed, the very conformation of these muscles and of the appropriate parts of the nervous system may be said to be primarily adapted to the movements made in walking and in similar activities. In a very real sense the normal human being is predestined to walk, not because his elders will assist him to learn the art, but because his organism is prepared from birth, or even from the moment of conception, to take on all those expenditures of nervous energy and all those muscular adaptations that result in walking. To put it concisely, walking is an inherent, biological function of man.

Not so language. It is of course true that in a certain sense the individual is predestined to talk, but that is due entirely to the circumstance that he is born not merely in nature, but in the lap of a society that is certain, reasonably certain, to lead him to its traditions. Eliminate society and there is every reason to believe that he will learn to walk, if, indeed, he survives at all. But it is just as certain that he will never learn to talk, that is, to communicate ideas according to the traditional system of a particular society. Or, again, remove the new-born individual from the social environment into which he has come and transplant him to an utterly alien one. He will develop the art of walking in his new environment very much as he would have developed it in the old. But his speech will be completely at variance with the speech of his native environment. Walking, then, is a general human activity that varies only within circumscribed limits as we pass from individual to individual. Its variability is involuntary and purposeless. Speech is a human activity that varies without assignable limit as we pass from social group to social group, because it is a purely historical heritage of the group, the product of long-continued social usage. It varies as all creative effort varies—not as consciously, perhaps, but none the less as truly as do the religions, the beliefs, the customs, and the arts of different peoples. Walking is an organic, an instinctive, function (not, of course, itself an instinct); speech is a non-instinctive, acquired, "cultural" function.

There is one fact that has frequently tended to prevent the recognition of language as a merely conventional system of sound symbols, that has seduced the popular mind into attributing to it an instinctive basis that it does not really possess. This is the well-known observation that under the stress of emotion, say of a sudden twinge of pain or of unbridled joy, we do involuntarily give utterance to sounds that the hearer interprets as indicative of the emotion itself. But there is all the difference in the world between such involuntary expression of feeling and the normal type of communication of ideas that is speech. The former kind of utterance is indeed instinctive, but it is nonsymbolic; in other words, the sound of pain or the sound of joy does not, as such, indicate the emotion, it does not stand aloof, as it were, and announce that such and such an emotion is being felt. What it does is to serve as a more or less automatic overflow of the emotional energy; in a sense, it is part and parcel of the emotion itself. Moreover, such instinctive cries hardly constitute communication in any strict sense. They are not addressed to any one, they are merely overheard, if heard at all, as the bark of a dog, the sound of approaching footsteps, or the rustling of the wind is heard. If they convey certain ideas to the hearer, it is only in the very general sense in which any and every sound or even any phenomenon in our environment may be said to convey an idea to the perceiving mind. If the involuntary cry of pain which is conventionally represented by "Oh!" be looked upon as a true speech symbol equivalent to some such idea as "I am in great pain," it is just as allowable to interpret the appearance of clouds as an equivalent symbol that carries the definite message "It is likely to rain." A definition of language, however, that is so extended as to cover every type of inference becomes utterly meaningless.

The mistake must not be made of identifying our conventional interjections (our oh! and ah! and sh!) with the instinctive cries themselves. These interjections are merely conventional fixations of the natural sounds. They therefore differ widely in various languages in accordance with the specific phonetic genius of each of these. As such they may be considered an integral portion of speech, in the properly cultural sense of the term, being no more identical with the instinctive cries themselves than such words as "cuckoo" and "killdeer" are identical with the cries of the birds they denote or than Rossini's treatment of a storm in the overture to "William Tell" is in fact a storm. In other words, the interjections and sound-imitative words of normal speech are related to their natural prototypes as is art, a purely social or cultural thing, to nature. It may be objected that, though the interjections differ somewhat as we pass from language to language, they do nevertheless offer striking family resemblances and may therefore be looked upon as having grown up out of a common instinctive base. But their case is nowise different from that, say, of the varying national modes of pictorial representation. A Japanese picture of a hill both differs from and resembles a typical modern European painting of the same kind of hill. Both are suggested by and both "imitate" the same natural feature. Neither the one nor the other is the same thing as, or, in any intelligible sense, a direct outgrowth of, this natural feature. The two modes of representation are not identical because they proceed from differing historical traditions, are executed with differing pictorial techniques. The interjections of Japanese and English are, just so, suggested by a common natural prototype, the instinctive cries, and are thus unavoidably suggestive of each other. They differ, now greatly, now but little, because they are builded out of historically diverse traditions, phonetic systems, speech habits of the two peoples. Yet the instinctive cries as such are practically identical for all humanity, just as the human skeleton or nervous system is to all intents and purposes a "fixed," that is, an only slightly and "accidentally" variable, feature of man's organism.

Interjections are among the least important of speech elements. Their discussion is valuable mainly because it can be shown that even they, avowedly the nearest of all language sounds to instinctive utterance, are only superficially of an instinctive nature. Were it therefore possible to demonstrate that the whole of language is traceable, in its ultimate historical and psychological foundations, to the interjections, it would still not follow that language is an instinctive activity. But, as a matter of fact, all attempts so to explain the origin of speech have been fruitless. There is no tangible evidence, historical or otherwise, tending to show that the mass of speech elements and speech processes has evolved out of the interjections. These are a very small and functionally insignificant proportion of the vocabulary of language; at no time and in no linguistic province that we have record of do we see a noticeable tendency towards their elaboration into the primary warp and woof of language. They are never more, at best, than a decorative edging to the ample, complex fabric.

What applies to the interjections applies with even greater force to the sound-imitative words. Such words as "whippoorwill," "to mew," "to caw," are in no sense natural sounds that man has instinctively or automatically reproduced. They are just as truly creations of the human mind, flights of the human fancy, as anything else in language. They do not directly grow out of nature, they are suggested by it and play with it. Hence the onomatopoetic theory of the origin of speech, the theory that would explain all speech as a gradual evolution from sounds of an imitative character, really brings us no nearer to the instinctive level than is language as we know it to-day. As to the theory itself, it is scarcely more credible than its interjectional counterpart. It is true that a number of words which we do not now feel to have a sound-imitative value can be shown to have once had a phonetic form that strongly suggests their origin as imitations of natural sounds. Such is the English word "to laugh." For all that, it is quite impossible to show, nor does it seem intrinsically reasonable to suppose, that more than a negligible proportion of the elements of speech or anything at all of its formal apparatus is derivable from an onomatopoetic source. However much we may be disposed on general principles to assign a fundamental importance in the languages of primitive peoples to the imitation of natural sounds, the actual fact of the matter is that these languages show no particular preference for imitative words. Among the most primitive peoples of aboriginal America, the Athabaskan tribes of the Mackenzie River speak languages in which such words seem to be nearly or entirely absent, while they are used freely enough in languages as sophisticated as English and German. Such an instance shows how little the essential nature of speech is concerned with the mere imitation of things.

The way is now cleared for a serviceable definition of language. Language is a purely human and non-instinctive method of communicating ideas, emotions, and desires by means of a system of voluntarily produced symbols. These symbols are, in the first instance, auditory and they are produced by the so-called "organs of speech." There is no discernible instinctive basis in human speech as such, however much instinctive expressions and the natural environment may serve as a stimulus for the development of certain elements of speech, however much instinctive tendencies, motor and other, may give a predetermined range or mold to linguistic expression. Such human or animal communication, if "communication" it may be called, as is brought about by involuntary, instinctive cries is not, in our sense, language at all.

I have just referred to the "organs of speech," and it would seem at first blush that this is tantamount to an admission that speech itself is an instinctive, biologically predetermined activity. We must not be misled by the mere term. There are, properly speaking, no organs of speech; there are only organs that are incidentally useful in the production of speech sounds. The lungs, the larynx, the palate, the nose, the tongue, the teeth, and the lips, are all so utilized, but they are no more to be thought of as primary organs of speech than are the fingers to be considered as essentially organs of piano-playing or the knees as organs of prayer. Speech is not a simple activity that is carried on by one or more organs biologically adapted to the purpose. It is an extremely complex and ever-shifting network of adjustments—in the brain, in the nervous system, and in the articulating and auditory organs —tending towards the desired end of communication. The lungs developed, roughly speaking, in connection with the necessary biological function known as breathing; the nose, as an organ of smell; the teeth, as organs useful in breaking up food before it was ready for digestion. If, then, these and other organs are being constantly utilized in speech, it is only because any organ, once existent and in so far as it is subject to voluntary control, can be utilized by man for secondary purposes. Physiologically, speech is an overlaid function, or, to be more precise, a group of overlaid functions. It gets what service it can out of organs and functions, nervous and muscular, that have come into being and are maintained for very different ends than its own.

It is true that physiological psychologists speak of the localization of speech in the brain. This can only mean that the sounds of speech are localized in the auditory tract of the brain, or in some circumscribed portion of it, precisely as other classes of sounds are localized; and that the motor processes involved in speech (such as the movements of the glottal cords in the larynx, the movements of the tongue required to pronounce the vowels, lip movements required to articulate certain consonants, and numerous others) are localized in the motor tract precisely as are all other impulses to special motor activities. In the same way control is lodged in the visual tract of the brain over all those processes of visual recognition involved in reading. Naturally the particular points or clusters of points of localization in the several tracts that refer to any element of language are connected in the brain by paths of association, so that the outward, or psychophysical, aspect of language is of a vast network of associated localizations in the brain and lower nervous tracts, the auditory localizations being without doubt the most fundamental of all for speech. However, a speech-sound localized in the brain, even when associated with the particular movements of the "speech organs" that are required to produce it, is very far from being an element of language. It must be further associated with some element or group of elements of experience, say a visual image or a class of visual images or a feeling of relation, before it has even rudimentary linguistic significance. This "element" of experience is the content or "meaning" of the linguistic unit; the associated auditory, motor, and other cerebral processes that lie immediately back of the act of speaking and the act of hearing speech are merely a complicated symbol of or signal for these "meanings," of which more anon. We see therefore at once that language as such is not and cannot be definitely localized, for it consists of a peculiar symbolic relation— physiologically an arbitrary one—between all possible elements of consciousness on the one hand and certain selected elements localized in the auditory, motor, and other cerebral and nervous tracts on the other. If language can be said to be definitely "localized" in the brain, it is only in that general and rather useless sense in which all aspects of consciousness, all human interest and activity, may be said to be "in the brain." Hence, we have no recourse but to accept language as a fully formed functional system within man's psychic or "spiritual" constitution. We cannot define it as an entity in psycho-physical terms alone, however much the psycho-physical basis is essential to its functioning in the individual.

From the physiologist's point of view we may seem to be making an unwarrantable abstraction in desiring to handle the subject of speech without constant and explicit reference to that basis. However, such an abstraction is justifiable. We can profitably discuss the intention, the form, and the history of speech, precisely as we discuss the nature of any other phase of human culture—say art or religion—as an institutional or cultural entity, leaving the organic and psychological mechanisms back of it as something to be taken for granted. Accordingly, it must be clearly understood that this introduction to the study of speech is not concerned with those aspects of physiology and of physiological psychology that underlie speech. Our study of language is not to be one of the genesis and operation of a concrete mechanism; it is, rather, to be an inquiry into the function and form of the arbitrary systems of symbolism that we term languages.

I have already pointed out that the essence of language consists in the assigning of conventional, voluntarily articulated, sounds, or of their equivalents, to the diverse elements of experience. The word "house" is not a linguistic fact if by it is meant merely the acoustic effect produced on the ear by its constituent consonants and vowels, pronounced in a certain order; nor the motor processes and tactile feelings which make up the articulation of the word; nor the visual perception on the part of the hearer of this articulation; nor the visual perception of the word "house" on the written or printed page; nor the motor processes and tactile feelings which enter into the writing of the word; nor the memory of any or all of these experiences. It is only when these, and possibly still other, associated experiences are automatically associated with the image of a house that they begin to take on the nature of a symbol, a word, an element of language. But the mere fact of such an association is not enough. One might have heard a particular word spoken in an individual house under such impressive circumstances that neither the word nor the image of the house ever recur in consciousness without the other becoming present at the same time. This type of association does not constitute speech. The association must be a purely symbolic one; in other words, the word must denote, tag off, the image, must have no other significance than to serve as a counter to refer to it whenever it is necessary or convenient to do so. Such an association, voluntary and, in a sense, arbitrary as it is, demands a considerable exercise of self-conscious attention. At least to begin with, for habit soon makes the association nearly as automatic as any and more rapid than most.

But we have traveled a little too fast. Were the symbol "house"— whether an auditory, motor, or visual experience or image—attached but to the single image of a particular house once seen, it might perhaps, by an indulgent criticism, be termed an element of speech, yet it is obvious at the outset that speech so constituted would have little or no value for purposes of communication. The world of our experiences must be enormously simplified and generalized before it is possible to make a symbolic inventory of all our experiences of things and relations and this inventory is imperative before we can convey ideas. The elements of language, the symbols that ticket off experience, must therefore be associated with whole groups, delimited classes, of experience rather than with the single experiences themselves. Only so is communication possible, for the single experience lodges in an individual consciousness and is, strictly speaking, incommunicable. To be communicated it needs to be referred to a class which is tacitly accepted by the community as an identity. Thus, the single impression which I have had of a particular house must be identified with all my other impressions of it. Further, my generalized memory or my "notion" of this house must be merged with the notions that all other individuals who have seen the house have formed of it. The particular experience that we started with has now been widened so as to embrace all possible impressions or images that sentient beings have formed or may form of the house in question. This first simplification of experience is at the bottom of a large number of elements of speech, the so-called proper nouns, or names of single individuals or objects. It is, essentially, the type of simplification which underlies, or forms the crude subject of, history and art. But we cannot be content with this measure of reduction of the infinity of experience. We must cut to the bone of things, we must more or less arbitrarily throw whole masses of experience together as similar enough to warrant their being looked upon —mistakenly, but conveniently—as identical. This house and that house and thousands of other phenomena of like character are thought of as having enough in common, in spite of great and obvious differences of detail, to be classed under the same heading. In other words, the speech element "house" is the symbol, first and foremost, not of a single perception, nor even of the notion of a particular object, but of a "concept," in other words, of a convenient capsule of thought that embraces thousands of distinct experiences and that is ready to take in thousands more. If the single significant elements of speech are the symbols of concepts, the actual flow of speech may be interpreted as a record of the setting of these concepts into mutual relations.

The question has often been raised whether thought is possible without speech; further, if speech and thought be not but two facets of the same psychic process. The question is all the more difficult because it has been hedged about by misunderstandings. In the first place, it is well to observe that whether or not thought necessitates symbolism, that is speech, the flow of language itself is not always indicative of thought. We have seen that the typical linguistic element labels a concept. It does not follow from this that the use to which language is put is always or even mainly conceptual. We are not in ordinary life so much concerned with concepts as such as with concrete particularities and specific relations. When I say, for instance, "I had a good breakfast this morning," it is clear that I am not in the throes of laborious thought, that what I have to transmit is hardly more than a pleasurable memory symbolically rendered in the grooves of habitual expression. Each element in the sentence defines a separate concept or conceptual relation or both combined, but the sentence as a whole has no conceptual significance whatever. It is somewhat as though a dynamo capable of generating enough power to run an elevator were operated almost exclusively to feed an electric doorbell. The parallel is more suggestive than at first sight appears. Language may be looked upon as an instrument capable of running a gamut of psychic uses. Its flow not only parallels that of the inner content of consciousness, but parallels it on different levels, ranging from the state of mind that is dominated by particular images to that in which abstract concepts and their relations are alone at the focus of attention and which is ordinarily termed reasoning. Thus the outward form only of language is constant; its inner meaning, its psychic value or intensity, varies freely with attention or the selective interest of the mind, also, needless to say, with the mind's general development. From the point of view of language, thought may be defined as the highest latent or potential content of speech, the content that is obtained by interpreting each of the elements in the flow of language as possessed of its very fullest conceptual value. From this it follows at once that language and thought are not strictly coterminous. At best language can but be the outward facet of thought on the highest, most generalized, level of symbolic expression. To put our viewpoint somewhat differently, language is primarily a pre-rational function. It humbly works up to the thought that is latent in, that may eventually be read into, its classifications and its forms; it is not, as is generally but naïvely assumed, the final label put upon the finished thought.

Most people, asked if they can think without speech, would probably answer, "Yes, but it is not easy for me to do so. Still I know it can be done." Language is but a garment! But what if language is not so much a garment as a prepared road or groove? It is, indeed, in the highest degree likely that language is an instrument originally put to uses lower than the conceptual plane and that thought arises as a refined interpretation of its content. The product grows, in other words, with the instrument, and thought may be no more conceivable, in its genesis and daily practice, without speech than is mathematical reasoning practicable without the lever of an appropriate mathematical symbolism. No one believes that even the most difficult mathematical proposition is inherently dependent on an arbitrary set of symbols, but it is impossible to suppose that the human mind is capable of arriving at or holding such a proposition without the symbolism. The writer, for one, is strongly of the opinion that the feeling entertained by so many that they can think, or even reason, without language is an illusion. The illusion seems to be due to a number of factors. The simplest of these is the failure to distinguish between imagery and thought. As a matter of fact, no sooner do we try to put an image into conscious relation with another than we find ourselves slipping into a silent flow of words. Thought may be a natural domain apart from the artificial one of speech, but speech would seem to be the only road we know of that leads to it. A still more fruitful source of the illusive feeling that language may be dispensed with in thought is the common failure to realize that language is not identical with its auditory symbolism. The auditory symbolism may be replaced, point for point, by a motor or by a visual symbolism (many people can read, for instance, in a purely visual sense, that is, without the intermediating link of an inner flow of the auditory images that correspond to the printed or written words) or by still other, more subtle and elusive, types of transfer that are not so easy to define. Hence the contention that one thinks without language merely because he is not aware of a coexisting auditory imagery is very far indeed from being a valid one. One may go so far as to suspect that the symbolic expression of thought may in some cases run along outside the fringe of the conscious mind, so that the feeling of a free, non-linguistic stream of thought is for minds of a certain type a relatively, but only a relatively, justified one. Psycho-physically, this would mean that the auditory or equivalent visual or motor centers in the brain, together with the appropriate paths of association, that are the cerebral equivalent of speech, are touched off so lightly during the process of thought as not to rise into consciousness at all. This would be a limiting case—thought riding lightly on the submerged crests of speech, instead of jogging along with it, hand in hand.

The modern psychology has shown us how powerfully symbolism is at work in the unconscious mind. It is therefore easier to understand at the present time than it would have been twenty years ago that the most rarefied thought may be but the conscious counterpart of an unconscious linguistic symbolism.

One word more as to the relation between language and thought. The point of view that we have developed does not by any means preclude the possibility of the growth of speech being in a high degree dependent on the development of thought. We may assume that language arose pre-rationally —just how and on what precise level of mental activity we do not know— but we must not imagine that a highly developed system of speech symbols worked itself out before the genesis of distinct concepts and of thinking, the handling of concepts. We must rather imagine that thought processes set in, as a kind of psychic overflow, almost at the beginning of linguistic expression; further, that the concept, once defined, necessarily reacted on the life of its linguistic symbol, encouraging further linguistic growth. We see this complex process of the interaction of language and thought actually taking place under our eyes. The instrument makes possible the product, the product refines the instrument. The birth of a new concept is invariably foreshadowed by a more or less strained or extended use of old linguistic material; the concept does not attain to individual and independent life until it has found a distinctive linguistic embodiment. In most cases the new symbol is but a thing wrought from linguistic material already in existence in ways mapped out by crushingly despotic precedents. As soon as the word is at hand, we instinctively feel, with something of a sigh of relief, that the concept is ours for the handling. Not until we own the symbol do we feel that we hold a key to the immediate knowledge or understanding of the concept. Would we be so ready to die for "liberty," to struggle for "ideals," if the words themselves were not ringing within us? And the word, as we know, is not only a key; it may also be a fetter.

Language is primarily an auditory system of symbols. In so far as it is articulated it is also a motor system, but the motor aspect of speech is clearly secondary to the auditory. In normal individuals the impulse to speech first takes effect in the sphere of auditory imagery and is then transmitted to the motor nerves that control the organs of speech. The motor processes and the accompanying motor feelings are not, however, the end, the final resting point. They are merely a means and a control leading to auditory perception in both speaker and hearer. Communication, which is the very object of speech, is successfully effected only when the hearer's auditory perceptions are translated into the appropriate and intended flow of imagery or thought or both combined. Hence the cycle of speech, in so far as we may look upon it as a purely external instrument, begins and ends in the realm of sounds. The concordance between the initial auditory imagery and the final auditory perceptions is the social seal or warrant of the successful issue of the process. As we have already seen, the typical course of this process may undergo endless modifications or transfers into equivalent systems without thereby losing its essential formal characteristics.

The most important of these modifications is the abbreviation of the speech process involved in thinking. This has doubtless many forms, according to the structural or functional peculiarities of the individual mind. The least modified form is that known as "talking to one's self" or "thinking aloud." Here the speaker and the hearer are identified in a single person, who may be said to communicate with himself. More significant is the still further abbreviated form in which the sounds of speech are not articulated at all. To this belong all the varieties of silent speech and of normal thinking. The auditory centers alone may be excited; or the impulse to linguistic expression may be communicated as well to the motor nerves that communicate with the organs of speech but be inhibited either in the muscles of these organs or at some point in the motor nerves themselves; or, possibly, the auditory centers may be only slightly, if at all, affected, the speech process manifesting itself directly in the motor sphere. There must be still other types of abbreviation. How common is the excitation of the motor nerves in silent speech, in which no audible or visible articulations result, is shown by the frequent experience of fatigue in the speech organs, particularly in the larynx, after unusually stimulating reading or intensive thinking.

All the modifications so far considered are directly patterned on the typical process of normal speech. Of very great interest and importance is the possibility of transferring the whole system of speech symbolism into other terms than those that are involved in the typical process. This process, as we have seen, is a matter of sounds and of movements intended to produce these sounds. The sense of vision is not brought into play. But let us suppose that one not only hears the articulated sounds but sees the articulations themselves as they are being executed by the speaker. Clearly, if one can only gain a sufficiently high degree of adroitness in perceiving these movements of the speech organs, the way is opened for a new type of speech symbolism—that in which the sound is replaced by the visual image of the articulations that correspond to the sound. This sort of system has no great value for most of us because we are already possessed of the auditory-motor system of which it is at best but an imperfect translation, not all the articulations being visible to the eye. However, it is well known what excellent use deaf-mutes can make of "reading from the lips" as a subsidiary method of apprehending speech. The most important of all visual speech symbolisms is, of course, that of the written or printed word, to which, on the other side, corresponds the system of delicately adjusted movements which result in the writing or typewriting or other graphic method of recording speech. The significant feature for our recognition in these new types of symbolism, apart from the fact that they are no longer a by-product of normal speech itself, is that each element (letter or written word) in the system corresponds to a specific element (sound or sound-group or spoken word) in the primary system. Written language is thus a point-to-point equivalence, to borrow a mathematical phrase, to its spoken counterpart. The written forms are secondary symbols of the spoken ones—symbols of symbols—yet so close is the correspondence that they may, not only in theory but in the actual practice of certain eye-readers and, possibly, in certain types of thinking, be entirely substituted for the spoken ones. Yet the auditory-motor associations are probably always latent at the least, that is, they are unconsciously brought into play. Even those who read and think without the slightest use of sound imagery are, at last analysis, dependent on it. They are merely handling the circulating medium, the money, of visual symbols as a convenient substitute for the economic goods and services of the fundamental auditory symbols.

The possibilities of linguistic transfer are practically unlimited. A familiar example is the Morse telegraph code, in which the letters of written speech are represented by a conventionally fixed sequence of longer or shorter ticks. Here the transfer takes place from the written word rather than directly from the sounds of spoken speech. The letter of the telegraph code is thus a symbol of a symbol. It does not, of course, in the least follow that the skilled operator, in order to arrive at an understanding of a telegraphic message, needs to transpose the individual sequence of ticks into a visual image of the word before he experiences its normal auditory image. The precise method of reading off speech from the telegraphic communication undoubtedly varies widely with the individual. It is even conceivable, if not exactly likely, that certain operators may have learned to think directly, so far as the purely conscious part of the process of thought is concerned, in terms of the tick-auditory symbolism or, if they happen to have a strong natural bent toward motor symbolism, in terms of the correlated tactile-motor symbolism developed in the sending of telegraphic messages.

Still another interesting group of transfers are the different gesture languages, developed for the use of deaf-mutes, of Trappist monks vowed to perpetual silence, or of communicating parties that are within seeing distance of each other but are out of earshot. Some of these systems are one-to-one equivalences of the normal system of speech; others, like military gesture-symbolism or the gesture language of the Plains Indians of North America (understood by tribes of mutually unintelligible forms of speech) are imperfect transfers, limiting themselves to the rendering of such grosser speech elements as are an imperative minimum under difficult circumstances. In these latter systems, as in such still more imperfect symbolisms as those used at sea or in the woods, it may be contended that language no longer properly plays a part but that the ideas are directly conveyed by an utterly unrelated symbolic process or by a quasi-instinctive imitativeness. Such an interpretation would be erroneous. The intelligibility of these vaguer symbolisms can hardly be due to anything but their automatic and silent translation into the terms of a fuller flow of speech.

We shall no doubt conclude that all voluntary communication of ideas, aside from normal speech, is either a transfer, direct or indirect, from the typical symbolism of language as spoken and heard or, at the least, involves the intermediary of truly linguistic symbolism. This is a fact of the highest importance. Auditory imagery and the correlated motor imagery leading to articulation are, by whatever devious ways we follow the process, the historic fountain-head of all speech and of all thinking. One other point is of still greater importance. The ease with which speech symbolism can be transferred from one sense to another, from technique to technique, itself indicates that the mere sounds of speech are not the essential fact of language, which lies rather in the classification, in the formal patterning, and in the relating of concepts. Once more, language, as a structure, is on its inner face the mold of thought. It is this abstracted language, rather more than the physical facts of speech, that is to concern us in our inquiry.

There is no more striking general fact about language than its universality. One may argue as to whether a particular tribe engages in activities that are worthy of the name of religion or of art, but we know of no people that is not possessed of a fully developed language. The lowliest South African Bushman speaks in the forms of a rich symbolic system that is in essence perfectly comparable to the speech of the cultivated Frenchman. It goes without saying that the more abstract concepts are not nearly so plentifully represented in the language of the savage, nor is there the rich terminology and the finer definition of nuances that reflect the higher culture. Yet the sort of linguistic development that parallels the historic growth of culture and which, in its later stages, we associate with literature is, at best, but a superficial thing. The fundamental groundwork of language—the development of a clear-cut phonetic system, the specific association of speech elements with concepts, and the delicate provision for the formal expression of all manner of relations—all this meets us rigidly perfected and systematized in every language known to us. Many primitive languages have a formal richness, a latent luxuriance of expression, that eclipses anything known to the languages of modern civilization. Even in the mere matter of the inventory of speech the layman must be prepared for strange surprises. Popular statements as to the extreme poverty of expression to which primitive languages are doomed are simply myths. Scarcely less impressive than the universality of speech is its almost incredible diversity. Those of us that have studied French or German, or better yet, Latin or Greek, know in what varied forms a thought may run. The formal divergences between the English plan and the Latin plan, however, are comparatively slight in the perspective of what we know of more exotic linguistic patterns. The universality and the diversity of speech lead to a significant inference. We are forced to believe that language is an immensely ancient heritage of the human race, whether or not all forms of speech are the historical outgrowth of a single pristine form. It is doubtful if any other cultural asset of man, be it the art of drilling for fire or of chipping stone, may lay claim to a greater age. I am inclined to believe that it antedated even the lowliest developments of material culture, that these developments, in fact, were not strictly possible until language, the tool of significant expression, had itself taken shape.

Vocabulary

illusory, circumscribed, prototype, warp, woof, tantamount, glottal, rudimentary, genesis, acoustic, sentient, throes, gamut, coterminous, facet, preclude, despotic, fetter, adroitness, latent, pristine

Review Questions

1. In what ways is language a biological function similar to walking? In what ways is it not?

2. Why does Sapir believe a cry of pain is not "speech"?

3. Can it be said language is a localized biological activity? Why?

4. What problems of communication are inherent in the fact that in the word-symbol *house* lie "thousands of distinct experiences . . . ready to take in thousands more"?

5. What is the relationship of a written language to its spoken counterpart?

6. Describe some of the linguistic transfers to nonverbal means of communication.

Expository Technique

1. This essay uses several different methods of defining *language*. Cite the author's use of three different techniques and show how he develops his definition in each case.

2. Why is it necessary that so much time be spent on a discussion of interjections and sound-imitative words before presenting a "serviceable definition of language"?

3. "Language as a structure is on its inner face, the mold of thought" is a controlling idea for the latter part of the essay. Specifically, how does Sapir relate this idea to his discussion of Morse code and gesture languages?

Exercises

1. Sapir believes that interjections are "a very small and functionally insignificant proportion of the vocabulary of language." Consider the following interjections. What sort of attitude do they most frequently convey? Could other parts of speech be easily substituted for them?

ah	alas, bah	bravo	encore	fie	gosh
hurrah	indeed	lo, oh	ouch	ugh	whoopee

2. Engage in a ten-minute debate with a classmate on the subject "Is Thought Possible Without Language?"

3. . . . ____ ____ ____ . . . is the Morse equivalent for S.O.S. Explain how this is a "symbol of a symbol of a symbol."

4. Read one of the following books and report on a code or cipher system described therein:

William F. Friedman, *Military Cryptanalysis* (New York, 1942).
Helen F. Gaines, *Cryptanalysis* (New York, 1956).
David Kahn, *The Code Breakers* (New York, 1967).

6.

ROBERT C. POOLEY

The Definition and Determination of "Correct" English

In the year 1712 Dean Swift wrote a letter to the Earl of Oxford outlining a plan for the foundation of an English academy similar to the French Academy for the purpose of regularizing and establishing correct English. Although his plan was received with interest, it was never acted upon, and many later attempts to found an academy have failed. The purists of the later eighteenth century did much of what Swift desired, but fortunately for the life and vigor of our tongue it has never been submitted to the restraint

From *Teaching English Usage* (New York, 1946), by Robert C. Pooley. Reprinted with the permission of the National Council of Teachers of English and Robert C. Pooley.

of a board of authorities. Several theories of "correctness" in English have therefore been formulated and have influenced writers and teachers of the past and present. One of the most important of these theories was that enunciated by George Campbell in 1776, that "correctness" rests in good custom, defined as "national," "reputable" and "present." This definition was accepted by practically all the nineteenth-century grammarians (although they frequently did it violence in specific instances), and may be found in a number of the high-school composition books of the present day. Another theory, really a modification of Campbell's, proposed by Fitzedward Hall and other nineteenth-century students of language, is that "good usage is the usage of the best writers and speakers." This definition is also very widely used in the textbooks of today, and is probably the expressed or implied standard of good English in almost every American schoolroom. Both of these definitions, useful as they have been and are, present many difficulties in application to the teaching of current usage.

The chief difficulty lies in the interpretation of the terms "reputable" and "the best writers and speakers." For example, nearly all grammar books list as undesirable English the use of the split infinitive, the dangling participle or gerund, the possessive case of the noun with inanimate objects, the objective case of the noun with the gerund, the use of *whose* as a neuter relative pronoun, and many others; yet all of these uses may be found in the authors who form the very backbone of English literature and who are "reputable" and the "best writers" in every sense of the words. If the standard-makers defy the standards, to whom shall we turn for authority? Moreover, the use of literary models tends to ignore the canon of *present* usage, for by the time an author has come to be generally recognized as *standard* his usage is no longer *present*. And among present speakers, who are best? The writer has heard a large number of the most prominent platform speakers of the day, yet he has still to hear one who did not in some manner violate the rules of the books. Are all great writers and speakers at fault, or is it possible that the rules are inaccurate?

The way out of this perplexity is to shift the search for standards away from "authorities" and traditional rules to the language itself as it is spoken and written today. Just as the chemist draws his deductions from the results of laboratory experiments, the biologist from his observation of forms of life, and the astronomer from his telescope, so must students of language draw their deductions from an observation of the facts of language. In establishing the laws of language, our personal desires, preferences, and prejudices must give way to the scientific determination and interpretation of the facts of language. What language we use ourselves may take any form we desire, but the making of rules and the teaching of rules must rest upon objective facts. We must take the attitude of a distinguished scholar who said recently of *due to,* "I don't like it, but there is no doubt about its establishment in English."

If we discard the authority of rules and of "reputable" writers, to what can we turn for a definition of "correct" English? At the outset it must be acknowledged that there can be no absolute, positive definition. "Correct English" is an approximate term used to describe a series of evaluations of usage dependent upon appropriateness, locality, social level, purpose, and other variables. It is a relative term, in decided contrast with the positive nature of (1) *reputability,* the determination of good usage by reference to standard authors; (2) *preservation,* the obligation to defend and maintain language uses because they are traditional, or are felt to be more elegant; (3) *literary,* the identification of good usage with formal literary usage. By discarding these traditional conceptions, and turning to the language itself as its own standard of good usage, we may find the following definition adequate for our present needs. *Good English is that form of speech which is appropriate to the purpose of the speaker, true to the language as it is, and comfortable to speaker and listener. It is the product of custom, neither cramped by rule nor freed from all restraint; it is never fixed, but changes with the organic life of the language.*

Such a definition is linguistically sound because it recognizes the living, organic nature of language; it is historically sound, for the language of the present is seen to be the product of established custom; it is socially sound in recognizing the purpose of language and its social acceptability in *comfort* to speaker and writer.

Teachers of English will recognize that the acceptance of this or a similar definition of good English necessitates great changes in the presentation of usage in textbooks and in the classroom. Those who are accustomed to rule and authority, to an absolute right and wrong in language, will find great difficulty in making the mental readjustment imperative for a relative rather than an absolute standard of usage. Much of the conventional teaching of grammar and correctness will have to be vastly modified or discarded. There will be much confusion and some distress. But eventually there will grow up in the schools a new theory of good English so closely knit with the language itself that the perplexity now arising from the discrepancies between rule and usage will no longer have cause for existence. But in discarding an absolute right and wrong for a relative standard of appropriateness and social acceptability, we shall have to determine the areas or levels of language usage, to define and illustrate them, and to apply them as standards for the written and spoken English in the schools. . . .

It is obvious that when such terms as *appropriate, customary, comfortable,* or *socially desirable* are used in defining the nature of good English usage, the conception of a single standard or level of correctness can no longer prevail. Speech is a form of human behavior, and like all forms of human behavior, is subject to almost infinite variety. But in even the most primitive societies human behavior is made subject to certain restraints, determined and maintained by the social group. Some of these are fundamental, essential to the life of the group, like the prohibition of murder; others are ceremonial in character, applying to all members of the group at certain times, or to some members of the group at all times. In somewhat similar fashion language usages are subjected to the restraints of society. At all times those who speak a language are required to keep within the limits of intelligibility in order to be understood; language which departs from custom so far as to be incomprehensible defeats its own purpose. But in addition to fundamental understanding there are ceremonial distinctions in language to be found in the most primitive societies; the language of the council fire or religious observance differs in vocabulary and tone from that of the hunt or the harvest. In civilized societies the same principle prevails, except that greater complexity of life calls forth a wider range of differentiations in usage. It will cause no surprise upon reflection to realize that we all more or less unconsciously distinguish three or more gradations or levels in our language usage; there is the informal intimate speech of the home and of our hours of recreation; the slightly restrained speech of semi-public occasions, like conversation with strangers; and the carefully chosen, deliberate language of public address on formal occasions. Each of these has its analogue in writing. Moreover, business and professional people are very apt to employ a technical vocabulary among their colleagues, sometimes almost incomprehensible to the uninitiated. It seems beyond doubt reasonable, therefore, that this differentiation of language usage, a fundamental law of language, should be our first consideration in the study of "correct" English and in the presentation of English usage in the classroom. The purpose of this chapter is to define and illustrate the levels of English usage and to point out their relative values in the social group.

THE ILLITERATE LEVEL

The words and phrases typical of this level of English usage mark the user as belonging definitely outside the pale of cultivated, educated society. They have no standing whatever in literature, except in the dialect conversation of characters deliberately portrayed as illiterate or uncultivated. Although comparatively few in number, they are widespread and extremely common in the speech of the uneducated. They cannot be tolerated in the classroom except in deliberate attempts to reproduce the conversation of illiterate characters.

EXAMPLES

If I had *of* come, he wouldn't *of* done it.
I got the measles *off* Jimmie.
He *give* me the book. (past tense)
They *was*, we *was*, you *was*
I *is*, you *is*, they *is*, them *is*
He *come, done, seen, run*, etc.
Have went, have came, have did, have saw, have ran, have drank, etc.
The double negative, as in: *didn't have no, won't never, can't never, couldn't
  get no*, etc.
Them books
Youse
I *ain't*, you *ain't*, etc.
Growed, knowed, blowed, seed, etc.
That there, this here
He looked at me and *says*
Leave me do it.
He did *noble, good, swell*, etc.

THE HOMELY LEVEL

The words and phrases typical of this level are outside the limits of standard, cultivated usage, yet are not completely illiterate. They characterize the speech of many worthy men and women with some claim to literacy, who by the accident of birth, occupation, or geographical location are denied the society of more cultivated persons. The children in many of our rural schools come from homes in which the parents speak the English of this level. It behooves the teacher, therefore, to have an understanding sympathy for this type of speech, and while zealously seeking to build up in the children a dialect more closely approaching standard English, to refrain from ridiculing the speech of the home or from characterizing it unreservedly as "bad English." Tactful understanding will do far more than rigid purism in creating among these children a respect for the more standard forms of speech and a desire to attain a higher standard of usage.

EXAMPLES

He *don't* come here any more.
I *expect* you're hungry.
Stop the bus; I *want out*.
Mary's mother, *she* isn't very smart.
I *got* an apple right here in my hand.
I *haven't hardly* time.
We *can't scarcely* do it.

Just where are we *at?*
He *begun, sung, drunk, eat,* etc.
The various forms of confusion in *lie* and *lay, sit* and *set, rise* and *raise*
I *want for* you to do it.
The dessert was made with *whip cream.*
He comes *of a Sunday.*
John *was raised* in Kentucky.
This is *all the farther* we can go.
Calculate (or cal'late, reckon) for *guess, suppose*
A light-*complected* girl
Hadn't he ought to do it?

To this homely level of English speech belong also the local dialect uses not generally recognized over the United States, like the *to home* for *at home,* of New England; the *admire* for *like* of the South; the *loco* for *crazy* of the West; and the characteristic idioms of the mountaineers in the Blue Ridge and Ozark ranges.

STANDARD ENGLISH, INFORMAL LEVEL

The range of standard English is necessarily very wide. It must include all the words, phrases, forms, and idioms employed by the great mass of English-speaking people in the United States whose dialect lies between the homely level and the decidedly literary level. It must be wide enough to include the variations of language usage common among people of education; the speech of the home, of the hours of business and recreation, as well as that of the party and formal reception. In written form it must include the most informal of personal correspondence to the formal phrasing of the business and social note. Standard English is, in fact, *the language;* it is present, ordinary, comfortable usage, with sufficient breadth in limits to permit of the shades of difference appropriate to specific occasions.

The informal level of standard English includes words and phrases commonly used by people of culture and education in their more informal moments, but which are generally excluded from formal public address, social conversation with strangers, and formal social correspondence. Informal standard English should be the normal usage of the teacher in the classroom and the goal which is set for the pupils to attain. A large part of the confusion arising from the teaching of usage in schools has been the result of trying to maintain the formal standard dialect, appropriate to careful writing, for the conversational needs of the schoolroom. There is no more need for children to be bookish in their schoolroom speech than for the teacher herself to be bookish in her intimate conversation.

The examples listed here for the informal standard level include only those items which may be employed informally but which are generally excluded from formal standard English.

EXAMPLES

He *blamed* the accident *on* me.
The *picnic* was a failure, *due to* a heavy shower.
No one knows what *transpires* in Washington.
Does anyone know *if* he *was* there?
I have never seen anyone act *like* he does.
His attack on my paper was most *aggravating*.
Most everyone is familiar with this picture.
Where can you get *these kind* of gloves?
We had just two dollars *between* the four of us.
I *can't help but* go to the store.
Who did you send for?
John is the *quickest* of the two.
They were *very pleased* with the new house.
It was *good and cold* (*nice and warm*) in the room.
I *will try and do* it.
They invited John and *myself*.
Did you *get through with* your work?
As *long as you have come*, we can start.

STANDARD ENGLISH, FORMAL LEVEL

It is quite in accord with the customs of language usage that "correct" English have considerable variety in range of appropriateness, two levels of which are distinguished in this study by the terms *informal* and *formal* standard English. In general the leading characteristics of the more formal level of standard English are (1) greater restraint in vocabulary, with the avoidance of words distinctly informal in tone; (2) greater attention to formal agreement in number, both in subject-verb and pronoun-antecedent relationships, in tense sequence, and in case-agreement of pronouns; (3) greater attention to word order, particularly with respect to the position of modifying words, phrases, and clauses, and the use of a more complex sentence structure.

In the schoolroom this formal level of standard English should be the goal set for careful theme-writing, especially in what is commonly called the "thought theme," whether expository or argumentative. Narration and the various kinds of informal essays, as well as friendly letters, need not be held to the more exacting requirements of the formal standard level. It is, however, of great importance that children recognize the characteristics of both levels, and are able to use either appropriately.

To this level of English usage belong not only the public speech and formal writing of educated people, but also much of the printed material generally classed as "literature." Writing designed primarily for communication, as for example new articles, editorials, textbooks, and other expository compositions, unless distinctly technical or artistic in aim, employ the usages of the formal standard level.

It is rather difficult to offer many distinctive examples of formal standard usage, inasmuch as it is characterized by a general tone of restraint and care more than by the use of certain expressions. A few examples, however, may be found which are quite typical of the formal standard level.

EXAMPLES
I *shall* be glad to help you.
Neither of the party *was* injured.
Here are three *whom* we have omitted from the list.
I *had rather* stay at home.
We *had* better complete this investigation.
Under the circumstances, he did as well as might be expected.
The use of connectives like *furthermore, notwithstanding, despite, inasmuch as, on the contrary*

THE LITERARY LEVEL

It must be granted at the outset that the definition of the literary level of English usage employed in this study is somewhat arbitrary, and is more narrow in scope than the definitions of many textbooks. But since much of the difficulty in the teaching of English usage centers about the confusion of the terms *literary, standard,* and *correct* English, a most earnest attempt has been made in this book to differentiate the terms and to clarify their meanings and applications. It is therefore assumed that what is commonly called "correct" English includes the usages of at least three levels: the informal standard, the formal standard, and the literary levels, the correctness of any specific item in any given instance being dependent upon its appropriateness. The first two levels have been defined; it remains to describe the third.

Literary English is taken to mean that form of speech or writing which in aim goes beyond mere utility to achieve beauty. It differs from formal standard English not so much in kind as in purpose and effect. In diction it seeks not only accuracy in meaning but also a subjective quality of suggestion aroused by the sound of the word or the associated ideas and feelings. In form it goes beyond mere orderliness to achieve rhythm, symmetry, and balance. In every respect it surpasses the ordinary prose of communication in the attainment of aesthetic values transcending the needs of everyday expression.

An illustration of the difference between standard formal English and literary English may be seen in the opening sentence of Lincoln's "Gettysburg Address." Had Lincoln said, "Eighty-seven years ago our ancestors established on this continent a new nation, inspired by the spirit of liberty, and actuated by the theory that all men are created equal," he would have met adequately the demands of clear, formal communication. But in his phrasing, "Four score and seven years ago, our fathers brought forth on this continent a new nation, conceived in liberty, and dedicated to the proposition that all men are created equal," there are to be found those characteristics of the literary style which transcend communication. The literary tone of *fourscore and seven, fathers, dedicated to the proposition* is at once apparent; the associations awakened by the words *brought forth, conceived,* and *dedicated* give them emotional depths unsounded by *established, inspired,* or *actuated;* moreover, the sentence as a whole moves with an effect of solemnity achieved only by the happy arrangement of accents and the sonorous quality of the vowels employed. These qualities combine to make this sentence artistic, literary prose of the highest order.

It is obvious that the literary level cannot be made a requirement for all students in schoolroom composition. It is too much the product of mental maturity and highly developed skill to be attainable by the average student, or indeed, by the average teacher. Therefore, while examples of beautiful prose should be given to pupils to study, and the few who are gifted should be encouraged to strive toward the development of a literary tone and style, the great body of school children should be expected to do no more than to cultivate the clear, direct English of communication, together with a feeling for the appropriateness of word and idiom to the purpose intended. Students in whom these perceptions have been engendered will always use "correct," adequate English.

Vocabulary

perplexity, purist, canon, analogue, behoove, arbitrary, aesthetic, sonorous

Review Questions

1. Why is it fortunate that English "has never been submitted to the restraint of a board of authorities"?

2. Pooley remarks that the two theories of "correctness" in English enunciated by George Campbell and Fitzedward Hall "present many difficulties in application to the teaching of current usage." What are some of these difficulties?

3. What is a *split infinitive*? A *dangling participle*?

4. Is the author opposed to the idea of standards of correct English?

5. Pooley maintains that "Good English is that form of speech which is appropriate to the purpose of the speaker, true to the language as it is, and comfortable to speaker and listener." What is meant by each of these characteristics?

6. What are the principal levels of English usage?

7. What are the leading characteristics of the more formal level of standard English?

8. How does *literary* English differ from *formal standard* English?

Expository Technique

1. Cite as many different uses of definition in this essay as you can.

2. Pooley generally develops his paragraphs by citing particulars in support of a general idea. Find three examples. What other techniques does he use?

3. What use does Pooley make of enumeration?

4. Make an outline of this well-unified essay showing how each level of usage is an integral organizational part of the whole.

Exercises

1. Read Jonathan Swift's *A Proposal for Correcting, Improving, and Ascertaining the English Tongue* (1712) and prepare a summary to be presented as an oral class report.

2. For each of the expressions Pooley cites as examples of usages typical of the *illiterate level* (page 121) give the corresponding expression appropriate to the *formal level of standard English*.

3. For each of the expressions Pooley cites as examples of usages typical of the *informal level* (page 123) give the corresponding expression appropriate to the *formal level*.

4. Read John H. Kenyon, "Cultural Levels and Functional Varieties of English," *College English*, X (1948), 31–36. Prepare a summary of Kenyon's remarks to be presented as an oral class report.

5. Read the following passages and determine which level, according to Pooley's classification, each represents. Indicate in each instance the basis upon which your designation is made.

a. Eccentricity has always abounded when and where strength of character has abounded; and the amount of eccentricity in a society has generally been proportional to the amount of genius, mental vigor, and moral courage which it contained. That so few now dare to be eccentric, marks the chief danger of the time.

b. If the day and the night are such that you greet them with joy, and life emits a fragrance like flowers and sweet-scented herbs, is more elastic, more starry, more immortal,—that is your success.

c. You don't know about me without you have read a book by the name of *The Adventures of Tom Sawyer;* but that ain't no matter. That book was made by Mr. Mark Twain, and he told the truth, mainly. There was things which he stretched, but mainly he told the truth. That is nothing. I never seen anybody but lied one time or another, without it was Aunt Polly, or the widow, or maybe Mary. Aunt Polly—Tom's Aunt Polly, she is—and Mary, and the Widow Douglas is all told about in that book, which is mostly a true book, with some stretches, as I said before.

d. Whenever a word comes to have a disagreeable sense, some synonym begins to take its place in the ordinary language. The synonym may be a new word borrowed for the express purpose, but it is more commonly a word already established, which may suffer a slight change of meaning, perhaps by being more generalized. Thus, when *knave* began to acquire a disagreeable signification, *servant,* from the French, took its place. *Servant* was already in the language, but was a somewhat more dignified and special word than *knave.* In modern usage, with the spread of democratic feeling, there has been, particularly in America, a tendency to abandon this word *servant* in favor of *help,* or *domestic,* or some other less plain-spoken term.

e. I cannot praise a fugitive and cloistered virtue, unexercised and unbreathed, that never sallies out and seeks her adversary, but slinks out of the race, where that immortal garland is to be run for, not without dust and heat.

f. Dear Bill,

Many thanks for letting George and I borrow your car last Saturday for the trip to the shore. We had a swell time, though we couldn't help but wish you were along, too. We ran into some friends on the beach who invited George and myself to dinner. Great fun. I will write you more next week.

g. [Death] comes equally to us all and makes us all equal when it comes. The ashes of an oak in the chimney are no epitaph of that oak to tell me how high or how large it was; it tells me not what flocks it sheltered while it stood, nor what men it hurt when it fell. The dust of great persons' graves is speechless too, it says nothing, it distinguishes nothing; as soon the dust of a wretch whom thou wouldst not as of a prince whom thou couldst not look upon will trouble thine eyes if the wind blow it thither; and when a whirlwind hath blown the dust of the churchyard into the church, and the man sweeps out the dust of the church into the churchyard, who will undertake to sift those dusts again and to pronounce, this is the patrician, this is the noble flour, and this the yeomanly, this the plebeian bran.

6. Many writers of fiction have utilized levels of usage in their writing in order to accomplish various effects. Read one of the following and define the level or levels which are employed and for what, if any, special purpose.

Sherwood Anderson, "I'm a Fool," from *Horses and Men* (New York, 1923).
Ring Lardner, "Haircut" and "Alibi Ike," in *The Collected Short Stories of Ring Lardner,* Modern Library edition (New York, 1941).
George Milburn, "The Apostate," from *No More Trumpets* (New York, 1933).
Damon Runyon, "My Father," from *Runyon First and Last* (New York, 1949).

J. D. Salinger, *The Catcher in the Rye* (New York, 1951).

Mark Twain, "Scotty Briggs and the Parson," from *Roughing It* (New York, 1875).

7. Write a letter of application to a prospective employer in which you state your qualifications to fill a particular position. Then, write a second letter to a close friend in which you tell him what job you have applied for and why you think you could fill its requirements. Designate the level of each of the letters and indicate how each level is achieved.

8. "Translate" the opening line of Hamlet's meditation upon suicide, "To be, or not to be: that is the question," into expressions appropriate to the various levels of usage designated by Pooley.

7.

ROBERT A. HALL, JR.

Right vs. *Wrong*

"How many of these frequent errors in English do YOU make?"

"Do YOU say KEW-pon for KOO-pon, ad-ver-TISE-ment for ad-VER-tise-ment, or AD-ult for ad-ULT?"

"Almost everybody makes these blunders in English: *between you and I, it's me, those kind of books.*"

"Even the greatest writers sin against the laws of grammar."

We have all seen advertisements in newspapers or magazines, with messages like those just quoted, implying to the reader "Shame on you if you are one of those who sin!"—and, of course, offering to teach him better. It is easy, on the one hand, to see that those who talk or advertise in this way and offer to cure our errors in pronunciation or grammar are simply appealing to our sense of insecurity with regard to our own speech. On the other hand, we must also admit that this sense of insecurity does exist, in almost all except those who are hardened against criticism and disapproval, and renders us easily susceptible to appeals of this kind. Our problem now is, to look at some of the ways in which we are supposed to be speaking wrongly, and to

From *Leave Your Language Alone* (Ithaca, N. Y., 1950). Copyright, 1950, by Robert A. Hall, Jr. Reprinted by permission of the author.

see whether there really exists a choice between "right" and "wrong," and, if so, what "right" and "wrong" consist of.

Our first approach may be made through very ordinary, everyday instances of "mistakes" like *I ain't, he don't, we seen him, you done it* or *hisn.* Most of us know that these are pretty widely condemned as "errors," when used instead of the corresponding *I am not* or *I'm not, he doesn't, we saw him, you did it, his.* But what is it that makes them "mistakes" or "errors"? If we drive through a traffic light, steal somebody's property, or kill someone, we know exactly what provides sanctions against these actions: the law of the land; and we know what will punish us if we disobey the law: the government. Is there any law of the land to set up rules about our speech, or any branch of the government that will enforce them? Obviously not. There are books that contain rules for speaking and writing, and there are people who will raise objections and criticise us if we fail to follow these rules; but those books and those people have no legal authority over us (outside of the rather special and limited situation in the schoolroom, where of course the teacher can give us a bad mark for not obeying the rules). Not only have they no legal authority, they have no authority whatsoever conferred on them by any power. Some countries, it is true, have had regulators of language with a kind of authority, such as the national Academies of France and Spain, which were set up by the king with the specific duty of "regulating and preserving the purity of the language." Even in those countries, very few people ever took the Academies' authority over language too seriously; but, technically speaking, their authority did exist in a way. But no such authority has ever existed in any English-speaking country, nor does it seem likely that speakers of English would ever be willing to accept the decrees of an Academy or similar institution or of a Ministry of Education.

And yet, if we say *I ain't, you done it,* or *hisn,* we *are* likely to run into trouble. Trouble with whom?—with everybody? No. A foreigner using some completely abnormal turn of phrase, such as *this must we first do,* will confuse the ordinary speaker of English considerably, and will run no chance of finding anybody who would accept that as normal English. He would have trouble with everybody. But with *I ain't* and the like, some people would not be in the slightest upset; in fact, more than a few would find those "incorrect" forms more normal than the supposedly "correct" usage that they "ought" to be following themselves and insisting on in others. With some other people, however, our use of *he don't* and similar expressions may get us into more or less serious trouble. Our hearers may correct us on the spot, and tell us "Don't say *I ain't,* say *I'm not;* not *hisn,* but *his";* or, even though they may not correct our usage then and there, they are nevertheless likely to hold it against us, and to allow it to determine their attitude toward us in one way or another. They may, perhaps, not consider us their social equals; they may not invite us to their home again; they may object to our marrying into their family; they may pick someone else, who says *I'm not* and *his,* to give a job or a promotion to; or some other form of unfavorable reaction may result from our using a form or word which is the wrong one for the given situation.

Usually, we are told and we believe that "correctness" is a characteristic of educated, intelligent people, whereas "incorrectness" is the special quality of uneducated, ignorant, or stupid people. But notice that exactly the type of situation we described above, where someone arouses an unfavorable reaction because of his language, can arise from the use of "correct" speech where the hearer does not use that kind of speech, or has a prejudice or other objection against it. It can be just as much of a *faux pas* to say *I saw him,* where your hearer expects and wants *I seen him,* as the other way around. One friend of mine found that, when he went to work in a Houston ship-yard during the second World War, he was regarded as a snob for saying *those things* instead of *them things,* and he did not get full cooperation from his fellow-workers until he started to say *them things.* There are even some ways of speaking, some turns of expression, such as *am I not?,* which, no matter how "correct" they may be in theory, are just too artificial for almost any situation.

Notice also that the forms themselves are of equal worth as expressions of the ideas you are are trying to communicate. *You done it* is just as good an expression of "doing" something, in past time, as *you did it,* and no present-day speaker of English will ever be confused as to what you mean. The same is true for *he don't* instead of *he doesn't;* for *we seen him* instead of *we saw him;* and for a host of others. In some cases, one might even argue that the "incorrect" form is actually somewhat preferable from the point of view of clarity or simplicity. The form *his,* in "correct" speech, is both an adjective (*his book*) and a pronoun (*that's his*); whereas the "incorrect" form *hisn* and the others parallel to it ending in *-n* (*hern, ourn, yourn, theirn*) are clearly marked, by their ending, as being possessive pro-nouns and nothing else. The argument runs similarly for *ain't.* To make the present-tense forms of the verb *be* negative, we must use, in "correct" speech, three different forms: *I'm not, he isn't, we* (*you, they*) *aren't;* whereas the "incorrect" *ain't* offers us one single form, exactly parallel to *can't, won't* or *don't* and equally convenient. *He doesn't* instead of *he don't* is also an extra complication, seen to be needless when compared with *can't* or *won't.* We might make similar arguments in favor of other "incorrect" forms as well.

What is it, then, that makes some forms "incorrect" and others not? This is not a matter of legal or quasi-legal authority, as we have seen. It is not a matter of universal condemnation, nor yet of incomprehensibility; in fact, some "incorrect" forms, as we have just pointed out, would be clearer or simpler than the corresponding "correct" forms. It all boils down, really, to a question of acceptability in certain classes of our society, in those classes which are socially dominant and which set the tone for others. Whether a form is accepted or rejected does not depend on its inherent merit nor yet on any official approval given it, but purely on whether its hearers like it or not—on whether they will react favorably or unfavorably towards a person they hear using it. "Correct" can only mean "socially acceptable," and apart from this has no meaning as applied to language.

The social acceptability, and hence "correctness," of any form or word is determined, not by reason or logic or merit, but solely by the hearer's emotional attitude towards it—and emotional attitudes naturally differ from person to person, from group to group, from social class to social class. Forms and words also change in social acceptability in the course of time: in the early seventeenth century, conservative speakers and purists objected violently to *ye* and *you*, used in speaking to one person, instead of the earlier *thou* and *thee;* and there must have been a time when *cows*, instead of the older plural *kine*, seemed an objectionable innovation.

Nevertheless, the difference in social acceptability between *I ain't* and *I am not*, between *hern* and *hers*, and so forth, is a real fact. If my child is likely to run into trouble later on for saying *I done it* or *hisn*, I will try to keep him from getting into the habit of using those forms which are actually not acceptable socially and which may cause others to react unfavorably towards him. But, if I am sensible about it, I will realize that the reason I want him to avoid these "incorrect" forms is not any inherent badness or evil character that they may have, but a purely practical consideration, that of their social acceptability. His choice of language will be used by others as a purely arbitrary means of classifying him socially among the sheep or the goats. All we need to do in the case of *I ain't*, etc., is to re-word the traditional instructions, and say that we avoid using such turns of speech, not because they are "bad" or "wrong" or "ungrammatical," but because they are socially unacceptable. Of course, as soon as people in any given group stop treating, say, *he don't* as socially unacceptable, it automatically becomes "correct."

There is a close parallel between acceptable usage in language and "correct" behavior in other social customs, such as personal garb or table manners. What is it that makes it perfectly good manners to eat some things, such as bread-and-jam, with the fingers, and not others, like meat or vegetables? Certainly not the decree of any official or self-appointed authority; and certainly not any inherent feature or characteristic of what we eat or do not eat with the fingers. Some things that we eat with our fingers are much more messy than others that we would always take up with knife and fork. Here again, it is social acceptability that determines whether we may or may not eat a given item of food with our fingers, or wear a four-in-hand tie with a tuxedo. This acceptability varies from place to place, and from one period of time to another. Thus, in England it is perfectly good manners to pile your peas up on the back of your fork, using your knife as a pusher, and to eat the peas from the back of the fork; but it is very much frowned upon to keep changing the fork from the left hand to the right and back again, as Americans normally do. And the permissibility of, say, table behavior is constantly changing; for instance, I was brought up always to eat bacon with knife and fork or in a sandwich, whereas by now it has become much more widely "correct" to eat it with the fingers.

For cases like those we have been discussing up to now, the situation is clear: we will avoid forms like *I seen him, he don't* because they are used as shibboleths, disregard of which may lead to unfortunate results for us in our living and relations with others. There are many instances, however, where reality and what we are taught do not correspond as to the actual "correctness," the actual acceptability, of what we are told to avoid. Take the case of *it's me.* Grammarians tell us that a rule exists that "the verb *to be* never takes a direct object," and that hence we must always say *it is I* and never *it's me.* The rule itself is found in plenty of grammar books, but that is no guarantee of its accuracy or relevance; in reality, this rule is meaningless as a statement of the facts of English usage. It was taken over by English grammarians from Latin grammar, where it is an accurate statement of the facts of Latin usage: in Latin, you said *sum egō* "[it] am I," never *sum mē* "[it] am me." The facts of actual acceptable usage in English are quite different: we normally say, and have said for hundreds of years, *it's me, it's us,* and so forth.

This is not merely an unsupported assertion on my part; statistical studies have been made which show *it's me* to be by far the most frequent and normal usage in current English, as compared with *it is I.* Professor Charles C. Fries made a detailed study of many such points as are often the objects of dispute and condemnation, in his *American English Grammar,* by analyzing thousands of letters which had been written to the War Department by people of all levels of education and social standing. He found very clear documentary proof that many forms and many constructions that are often condemned are actually in perfectly good standing in the usage of educated persons, and hence by definition acceptable or "correct." He found, for instance, that it is normal to say *it's me, these kind of things, none of the children are here, everybody should take off their hat,* in standard English, and that there is no real difference in such respects between standard and vulgar speech. The story is told of a certain very puristic lady—let's call her Miss Fidditch—who was teaching her class very strictly to avoid *it's me:*

MISS FIDDITCH. You must always say *it is I.* The inflexible rule of grammar is that the verb *to be* never takes a direct object.

(*A few minutes later.*)
PRINCIPAL (*outside the door, knocking*). Who's there?
MISS FIDDITCH. It's me—Miss Fidditch.

Miss Fidditch was right when she said *it's me,* naturally and normally, in
a give-and-take conversational situation and without reflecting; she was
wrong when she tried to force on her class an artificial, unrealistic rule that
applied to no one's, not even her own, usage in actual fact. And we all know
the old story about the grammarian who said "Never use a preposition to
end a sentence with."

We are often told that such-and-such a form or combination of forms
is "in accordance with the rules of logic," which make other competing
forms or combinations "illogical" and hence inadmissible. Such a rule as
"*everyone* or *everybody* is singular and hence a word referring to it must
be in the singular" is an instance of this, or the rule that "a double negative
makes a positive" and that hence we mustn't say *I didn't see nobody* except
when we really did see somebody. It is perfectly true that, in strictly ordered
systems like mathematics or symbolic logic, a violation of the rules of discourse will introduce confusion and make a statement into its opposite or
into something else from what was intended. The purists' error here lies in
identifying language and logic, and expecting normal linguistic usage to
be strictly logical. As a matter of fact, no language ever was strictly logical,
nor can we make it so by preaching at its speakers. To begin with, we
should have to define what "logical" meant—and we would find that each
different language would, from the outset, give its speakers different ideas
as to what "logic" is. To us, for instance, it seems logical, and, in fact, in-
escapable to say *one book,* but *two books, three books, five books,* using the
form *books* when we refer to more than one of them, and thus distinguishing between "one" and "more than one" or (to use the traditional grammatical terms) singular and plural. To someone brought up speaking Hungarian, that difference seems useful in general—a Hungarian will say *könyv*
for "book" and *könyvek* for "books," with *-ek* indicating the plural for him
just as *-s* does for us—but when he has a numeral to tell him how many
books there are, he uses, not the plural, but the singular form of the word
for "book." The Hungarian says *egy könyv* "one book," *két könyv* "two
book," and likewise *három könyv* "three book," *öt könyv* "five book" and
so forth. To him it seems silly, needless and illogical to say "five books"
where the indication of plurality is already given by the number, so that
"five book" will do just as well. Which is more logical, English or Hungarian, in this respect? One could argue both ways, and perhaps the Hungarian way of saying "two book, three book" might prove to be more strictly
logical. It all depends on what you are brought up to say.

The same thing holds for such points as the "double negative," which
many persons condemn violently—*I didn't see nobody* instead of *I didn't*

see anybody. They tell us that "logically" a double negative makes a positive, and that therefore *I didn't see nobody* "really" means *I did see somebody*. Here again, our traditional grammar rule is based on Latin, as it is in so many other instances—as if the rules of Latin could be applied to English. In Latin, those who spoke it about the time of Caesar, Cicero and Augustus normally took a double negative to mean a positive. So for them, *nōn nihil* "not nothing" meant "something," and *nōn vīdī nēminem* "I didn't see nobody" could only have meant "I saw somebody." That was right, logical and natural *for them,* because that was the way they used Latin. But later, in the course of the centuries, those who spoke Latin and the Romance languages which developed out of Latin, got in the habit of using a double negative with *negative* meaning. In Spanish, for instance, it is downright incorrect (because nobody will accept it) to say such a thing as *vi a nadie* in the meaning of "I saw nobody." You *must* say *no vi a nadie,* literally "I didn't see nobody," with the two negatives *no* "not" and *nadie* "nobody," whenever *nadie* "nobody" follows the verb; otherwise what you say is meaningless. It may be "illogical," and it may be "incorrect" from the point of view of Latin grammar; but in Spanish, French and Italian, for instance, the requirement of a double negative is so absolute that no one would be able to get away with condemning it on the grounds of logic. The reason that the point can be raised at all in modern English is that we have a divided usage: in actual current speech, when there is no emphasis, a double negative and a single negative both have a negative meaning, and everybody will understand what we mean whether we say *I didn't see nobody* or *I saw nobody* or *I didn't see anybody*. But when we are putting emphasis on the verb or the pronoun, then *I DIDN'T see NObody* does have positive meaning, and would be normal as an answer, say, in contradiction to *You saw nobody*. The drift of our language is inevitably toward the use of the double negative; this is as normal and natural as anything else in English, and as logical in English as it is in Spanish and French.

Now with regard to this second group of "wrong" usages, the situation is essentially different from that of *ain't* and *hisn*. Such forms as *ain't* are both socially unacceptable and condemned by purists; whereas *it's me* and *those kind of things,* although grammarians may condemn them, are nevertheless in normal, everyday use by socially accepted people and hence are socially acceptable and by definition "correct." And when it comes to such pronunciations as KEW-pon, ad-ver-TISE-ment, AD-ult, the purists' condemnations are absolutely fanciful, without any rhyme or reason whatsoever. Both KEW-pon and KOO-pon, both ad-ver-TISE-ment and ad-VER-tise-ment, both AD-ult and ad-ULT are normal, regular, and acceptable variants; to call either member of these pairs "correct" and the other "incorrect" is quite arbitrary. Language is not an either-or proposition, in which no variation, no deviation from a strictly maintained party line, is permissible;

in many instances, such as those of *coupon* and *advertisement,* more than one alternative exists and both are equally acceptable or "correct." . . .

Another objection that we often hear made against such a usage as *it's me* (instead of *it is I*) or *none of the boys are here* (instead of *none of the boys is here*) is that it is "ungrammatical" or that it does not "conform to the rules of grammar." The assumption involved here, whether we state it openly or not, is that there is such a thing as a body of rules, which are as fixed and unchangeable as the laws of the Medes and the Persians, which are called "grammar" and to which all language must conform or else be condemned as "ungrammatical." As a matter of fact, no such body of rules exists, or ever could exist. What passes for "grammar" in the usual textbook is really a conglomeration of rules, most of them taken from Latin grammars, some of them not, but often misstating the facts about English. We have already seen that the rule "the verb *to be* never takes a direct object" is a very good statement of the actual facts of Latin, but has no relation to the actual facts of English; and likewise for the double negative. Nor is there any reason why Latin should be taken as a model for all other languages, whether related or not. People used to think, and some still do, that Latin should be a universal model for language; the reason for this is that all during the Middle Ages in Western Europe, the language of learning and religion happened, through a historical accident, to be Latin. Educated people, just because they happened to get their education through Latin rather than through their native language, came to the conclusion that high intellectual activity and use or imitation of Latin were inseparable. We can easily see that such an idea was rather naive, and based on a false identification of two unrelated factors in the situation. Actually, Latin is just a language like any other, with its faults and shortcomings as well as its virtues, and its rules are far from being universally applicable. How would a speaker of Hungarian react to being told that he must say *három könyvek* "Three books" just because that is the way they say it in Latin or English or some other language?

Many other "grammar rules," although not derived from Latin grammar, are still quite inaccurate and unfounded: the best example of this is the "shall" and "will" rules that we are taught with regard to the future of English verbs. Most of us can never remember those rules, and are always uneasy about whether we are or are not making a mistake in their application: is it *I shall go* or *I will go, he should go* or *he would go?* We have been told that there is some difference in the meaning of each member of these pairs, that one of them indicates "determination" and the other "simple futurity"—but which? As a matter of fact, there is no wonder that we can't remember—because such a distinction does not really exist: in normal speech we would usually say *I'll go, he'd go, we'll go.* Even with the full forms, there is no distinction in meaning, except the artificial distinction that we may have been taught to make. Where did the grammar books get this rule? A seventeenth-century English grammarian, one John Wallis, sitting in his study, dreamed the rule up, manufactured it out of whole cloth, and put it in his book; and later grammarians have copied and re-copied it, each from his predecessor. Its relation to the facts of the English language is completely null, and its origin classifies it among works of fiction rather than of science.

And even with rules that do state normal, current usage accurately— have they any authority beyond that of simple statements of fact? We have already seen that there is no legal sanction, not even any semi-legal academic backing, for any claim to "authority" in language and its use. Suppose that usage should change, and that what we now say universally (such as *he goes, she sings*) should go out of fashion and be replaced by some other usage which we now wouldn't accept (like *he go, she sing*). Would the old be "right" and the new be "wrong"? By no means; if people's habits and usage change, then there is no "authority," no law that can keep them from doing so, and the new is just as good as the old. Not necessarily better, of course: neither better nor worse, but just different. Some of us are inclined to think that because a habit, a custom, or a thing is old, it must necessarily be better than something new. This was the prevailing attitude all through ancient times and the Middle Ages, and has lasted even up to now in some matters like those of language; it is the only reason some grammarians have for preferring one usage to another.

Another norm that is often set up for deciding disputed points is the usage of great writers: do we find *it ain't, he don't* or split infinitives in great writers, men who must have had great knowledge of their own language in order to write their great books? First of all, though, we must ask *which* great writers—those of the present, or those of the past? Our choice is difficult here; if we go too far back, the literary language is obviously archaic, and nobody nowadays, not even the most conservative grammarian, would recommend every feature of Milton's or Dr. Johnson's prose for our modern usage. If we come too close to the present, it is hard to tell just who is a really great writer and who is not; and, even if we have our great writers picked out, we find that very often they use freely the very forms we want to condemn, especially the more "realistic" writers like Steinbeck and Farrell. Then let's restrict our choice of great writers to, say, the late nineteenth and early twentieth century, so that they will fit what we want to prescribe. Even so, we find that their actual usage was considerably freer than we want to think. Hence the defensive accusations we often hear dogmatic purists make, that "even the greatest writers" make this, that or the other "mistake."

Furthermore, just how much bearing does great literature and its language have on normal everyday usage? That great literature gives us examples of the *artistic* use of language, we can easily grant; and that studying the way a Thomas Hardy or a Henry James has manipulated his language will be of use to us if we want to write literature—likewise granted. But such men as Hardy or James (to say nothing of authors like Carlyle or Meredith) are not typical, they are exceptional, in their language as in their content; and the very fact that they are exceptional disqualifies them as examples for everyday, normal, non-literary usage. Wouldn't it be nice if we all tried to talk like great literature in our daily contacts? It would be almost like trying to handle everyday affairs in the style of grand opera.

The entire attempt to set up absolute standards, rigid norms, for regulating people's language is destined to failure from the outset, because, as we have seen in this essay, (1) there is no authority that has either the right or the ability to govern people's usage; and (2) such an authority, even when it has been set officially (as were the French and Spanish academies), can never find valid standards by which to govern usage. Logic, Latin grammar, the usage of literature, appeals to authority as such—none have any applicability. In our country, especially, attempts to prescribe rules, to set up a normative grammar, have been very widespread, and have battened on our insecurities, on our fears for our social standing in the face of linguistic shibboleths. But all such attempts have been, and will continue to be, failures.

Is there any definition at all that we can give for "good" language? Only, I think, something like this: "good" language is language which gets the desired effect with the least friction and difficulty for its user. That means, of course, that "good" language is going to vary with the situation it is used in. In elegant or puristically inclined society, "good" usage will include *it isn't he, he doesn't,* and also *this kind of people, it is I,* since those forms will get the best results in favor and compliance with what we desire. In normal everyday situations with normal everyday people, *it isn't him, he don't, these kind of people, it's me* will be good usage, since ordinary people speak that way normally; and we won't be too worried about saying *damn!* unless our hearers have specific objections. With people who customarily say *it ain't him, he don't, we seen them, hisn,* those forms will be good usage, provided they serve to get results most effectively.

One type of confusion which often crops up at this point, and which we should be on our guard against, is that between language and style. We are often inclined to think that "correctness" is the same thing as good style, particularly in writing. Actually, the two are not the same, though the situation is parallel for both. "Good" style is simply that style of speaking or writing which is most effective under any given set of circumstances. When we speak of "good style," what we usually mean is clarity, absence of ambiguity, orderly structure, and the like—and these are, indeed, important in most situations. But they are not the same thing as type of language, and "good style" is possible in any dialect. Aesthetic considerations—whether a given way of expressing ourselves is pleasing or not to our listeners or readers—of course enter into the picture, too, with regard to "good" style. But all matters of aesthetics depend so much on individual preference, and differ so much not only from one language to another but from one speaker to another, that no one can presume to set up objective standards for them, nor legislate or make authoritative pronouncements on what is or is not pleasing to the ear or to the eye.

"Right" and "wrong," then, have no meaning, as applied to language, apart from the situations in which language is used. That is, by definition, we can never be wrong in our own language, when we use it as we have grown up speaking it, among our own family and friends. The ditch-digger who says *him and me ain't got none* and who uses swear-words and "four-letter" words freely is absolutely right—in his own language. His type of speech is not necessarily right for the language of other groups, just through the very fact that they speak differently. But when we condemn the ditch-digger's speech, we do so, not because of any inherent demerit of the way he talks, but because we take his speech as being characteristic of his social class. This factor in our speech attitudes is a relic from earlier antidemocratic times, which accords very poorly with other aspects of our modern aspirations to true democracy.

When a person who has grown up using *him and me ain't got none* speaks in his normal, natural way and is told he is "wrong," therefore, all that this really means is that he is using these forms in a situation where his usage would make things harder rather than easier for him. But most often—in fact, we can say usually—neither the person making the "error" nor the one criticizing him understands this. As a result, speakers who have not been brought up speaking "correctly" are made to feel inferior, and either have to make a strong (and often poorly guided) effort to change their habits of speech, or else take shelter behind defensive feelings of hostility, mockery, etc., towards the approved type of speech. Current prescriptions of "right" and "wrong" thus serve only to divide our society, and to increase further the split between upper and lower, favored and unfavored classes—just at the time when greater unity, not greater division, is our crying need.

In short: the entire structure of our notions about "correctness" and "right" *vs.* "wrong" in language is not only inaccurate, erroneous and useless; it is definitely harmful, and we would do well to outgrow it. When purists tell us that we are using "bad" or "incorrect" or "ungrammatical" language, they are simply telling us that what we say would not be acceptable in the upper social levels; sometimes they are right as to the facts of the case, and sometimes they are just talking through their hats. What our purists give us in the way of rules and laws to observe has no authority, no validity aside from their own preference, and is often based on specious pseudo-logic or on the structure of a distantly related language, Latin, which has no relevance to English. If an "error" or "mistake" is frequent, if almost everybody makes it, if it is found in even the greatest writers, then it is no error: as the great Byzantine emperor and law-codifier Justinian put it, *commūnis error facit iūs*—a mistake that everybody makes is no longer a mistake. We need to look at our language realistically, not feeling "inferior" about it and taking nobody's word as to its being "right" or "wrong." Often enough, we may find we need to change our usage, simply because social and financial success depends on some norm, and our speech is one of the things that will be used as a norm. In a situation like this, it is advisable to make the adjustment; but let's do so on the basis of the actual social acceptability of our speech, not because of the fanciful prescriptions of some normative grammarian or other pseudo-authority.

Vocabulary

sanction, *faux pas,* quasi-, innovation, arbitrary, shibboleth, naive, prescribe, batten, pseudo-

Review Questions

1. Which do you feel is the "correct" method of indicating plurality—the Hungarian or the English?

2. What are some of the norms which have been established to decide disputed points of usage?

3. Why does Hall think that all attempts to set up rigid standards in order to regulate usage are "destined to failure from the outset"?

4. Do you think Hall's judgment that such an expression as *am I not* is "too artificial for almost any situation" is inconsistent with the point of view toward correctness which he advocates in his essay?

5. How does Hall answer his question, "What is it, then, that makes some forms 'incorrect' and others not?"

6. What is your reaction to the following statement by Hall: *"You done it* is just as good an expression of 'doing' something, in past time, as *you did it"*?

7. What differentiation, according to Hall, should be made between "correctness" and "good style"?

8. When linguistic adjustments are desirable, what criterion for the changes would Hall apply?

9. Why does Hall's essay *not* give students the right to assume that anything goes in the writing of their essays?

Expository Technique

1. With what sort of concrete details are the first six paragraphs developed?

2. Consider the definition of good language as language which achieves the desired effect with the least friction and difficulty for the user. How does Hall prepare the reader for this view?

3. Is this essay organized inductively or deductively? Explain.

4. In his final paragraph Hall states that the entire structure of our thoughts about correctness in language is inaccurate and harmful. What does *structure* mean here?

(Exercises relating to Essays 7 and 8 are on pages 151–152.)

8.

ERNST PULGRAM

Don't Leave
Your Language Alone

We must make up our minds what we mean by linguistic usage. If it be defined merely as the practice of the majority, we shall have a very dangerous rule, affecting not merely style but life as well, a far more serious matter. For where is so much good to be found that what is right should please the majority? The practice of depilation, of dressing the hair in tiers, or of drinking to excess at the baths, although they may have thrust their way into society, cannot claim the support of usage, since there is something to blame in all of them. . . . So too in speech we must not accept as a rule of language words and phrases that have become a vicious habit with a number of persons. . . . I will therefore define usage in speech as the agreed practice of educated men, just as where our way of life is concerned I should define it as the agreed practice of all good men.[1]

> (A Latin grammarian of the 1st century of our era)

The lack of aesthetic sense produced by an excessive preoccupation with utility

From *Quarterly Journal of Speech*, XXXVIII (December 1952), 423–430. Reprinted by permission of the Speech Association of America and the author.
[1] Quintilianus, *De Institutione Oratoria* 1.6. 44–45.

shows also in the matter of speech. Educated people throughout Europe, and peasants on the Continent and in Scotland and Ireland, have a certain beauty of diction: language is not merely a means of communication, but a vehicle for expressing the emotions of joy or sorrow, love or hate, that are the material of poetry. Words, many of them, have beauty; they have a history, and we are, each in our own day, responsible for handing on an unimpaired tradition in diction and enunciation. It is rare to find this feeling among Americans. If you make your meaning clear, what more can be desired? Accordingly their vocabulary is small, and sounds which should be distinguished are blurred. The only good thing about the American language is the slang. Fortunately it is just this that the English are most disposed to copy.[2]

(A contemporary English philosopher)

In all our activities we are guided, or at least strongly influenced, by the practices which are considered right, or correct, or polite by the society into which we happen to be born. . . . The conventions of language are simply part of this whole body of convention which is woven into our lives. . . . Ordinarily, the failure to observe the conventions of language does not interfere seriously with the *plain sense* part of meaning. The person who talks with his mouth full of food usually can be understood; but his listeners are unlikely to be favorably impressed by what he is saying or to hope that he will continue his communication. In much the same way, though a reader may be temporarily confused by a lack of punctuation, by misplaced modifiers, or by faulty parallelism, he can usually grasp the *plain sense* of the passage in spite of these obstacles. He will, however, feel an irritated disrespect for the writer who makes his communication needlessly difficult, and will be offended by the writer's apparent *attitude* of discourtesy and disregard for his reader. Under these circumstances, the writer's *intention* will almost certainly be defeated: a reader is not easily persuaded or convinced by one with whom he is irritated, nor is he likely to trust the information of a writer who seems imprecise or incompetent.[3]

(Authors of a recent Freshmen English text)

"The merit of what a person says . . . is not affected in any way by the way in which they say it." "A dictionary or grammar is not as good an authority for your speech as the way you yourself speak." "There is nothing wrong with your language." "Leave your language alone."[4]

(A modern American linguist)

Most opinions on linguistic usage can be fitted into one of the four attitudes represented by these quotations. Quintilian's is the grammarian's and moral-

---

[2] Bertrand Russell, "The Political and Cultural Influence," in a volume of essays: *The Impact of America on European Culture* (Boston, 1951), pp. 13–14. Reprinted by permission of Beacon Press.

[3] Newman B. Birk and Genevieve B. Birk, *Understanding and Using English,* 2nd ed. (New York, 1951), pp. 56–58. Reprinted by permission of The Odyssey Press, Inc.

[4] Robert A. Hall, Jr., *Leave Your Language Alone* (Ithaca, N.Y., 1950), pp. 236, 6, title of chapter 14, title of book, respectively.

izer's approach. Whether we like it or not, a great deal of teaching is still done in his spirit; and, whether we like it or not, the method has not been as utter a failure as many latter-day linguists will have us believe. The fact is that writing and speaking according to a conventional adherence to rules which in popular usage have long since been altered or abandoned, lends in the opinion of all hearers and readers, regardless of their own speech standards, an air of literacy and elegance to the linguistic utterance. There is no doubt, however, that at any given date many grammatical rules are antiquated and superfluous, and no longer serve the purpose of even elevated and learned style. Let us say, then, that Quintilian's precepts have become inoperative in their stringency and rigid absoluteness, and, above all, distasteful to linguists and many teachers of language because of the implications of terms like *good, bad, vicious, dangerous, right.*

Bertrand Russell's opinion is that generally held by the layman; it consists in part—to avail myself of Russell's indulgence and guarded approval of American slang—of hogwash. With all due and profound respect for Bertrand Russell, I must say that when he wrote that paragraph he did not know whereof he spoke. It would be easy, though it would lead too far afield, to demolish much of his argument: the beauty of diction of the peasants of the Continent and Scotland and Ireland (not England?) is romantic, but (even aesthetically) intangible; to say that language with some is only a means of communication and not a vehicle for expressing emotions of joy or sorrow, love or hate, is tantamount to saying that such persons do not know these emotions; that words have a beauty and history is true enough, but that we should endeavor to pass on to posterity an unimpaired tradition in diction and pronunciation (and meaning too, I suppose), is not only impossible since language changes apart from and in spite of all human efforts, but also no more useful an enterprise than trying to impose on our children and children's children our current fashions of clothing; that such feeling among Americans (as a nation) is rare, is as untrue as it is irrelevant; and that the Americans' (collectively) vocabulary is small is so unsubstantiated a statement as to be meaningless, and if it were not meaningless it would be false.

This brings us to a book written by two teachers of English, whose aim is to transmit to their students a feeling for the appropriateness of linguistic usage. I refrain from calling it correctness for fear of having it misunderstood in Quintilian's absolute and moral sense. What the Birks mean, I daresay, is the kind of elastic correctness which is variably appropriate to different occasions. Since they assume that a student comes to school in order to be guided rather than left alone ("Mother, do I *have* to do all day just what I *want* to do?" said the little boy on his way to Progressive School), and to learn, in various fields of endeavor, that kind of proficiency which later will benefit him and the society in which he lives, the Birks, as teachers of English, also wish to impart to him a knowledge of his native language which will be appropriate under various professional and social exigencies. Basically, philosophically, and morally speaking, how properly to accept or decline a formal invitation is a bit of quite useless *linguistic* information, and I am sure that the Birks will agree with me. Yet they do offer to teach their students this too: not because they think it an essential and fundamental element of human linguistic behavior, but because in our society it is a piece of equipment, a formula, a tool which, though not indispensable, is most convenient. In the same sense the Birks teach "correct" grammar. It is something our society demands of what it calls educated persons. Rebellion, isolationism, separatism in language, while ethically and morally defensible and often understandable, vitiate the fundamental purpose for which an utterance has been made, that is, broadly speaking, to *influence* the hearer or reader.

It is often said (to Bertrand Russell's just displeasure, though not only Americans harbor such barbarous views) that as long as one gets the meaning across, all is well. This is, of course, untrue: communication is only the minimum function of language. If someone says or writes a sentence like "Somebody opens their mouth,"[5] leaving it to the context to inform me whether he means "Somebody opens his mouth" or "Somebody opens their mouths" or "Some persons open their mouths," I shall, under certain conditions, and no matter how obvious the meaning and no matter whether another language can or cannot make such grammatical distinctions, be irritated, hence not as openly receptive to the writer's or speaker's argument as I could have been. True enough, a great many persons will not be vexed by this manner of talking or writing; perhaps the majority will not. If I am, do I occupy Quintilian's aristocratic position, *viz.* the majority, *qua* majority, is not necessarily the arbiter of what is "good" and "bad"? In matters of, say, television programs, comic books, popular music, slick magazines, I gladly admit to being what the majority would call highbrow, or even snobbish—but I am sure that I find myself in excellent company, that of my readers, for instance.

In fact, the author of the fourth introductory quotation would join me, I am confident. However, when it comes to language, he thinks that the majority, *qua* majority, should rule or at least not be interfered with, because that would be undemocratic. I do of course not believe as Quintilian perhaps did, that linguistic usage can be intrinsically, *per se,* good or bad; the true source of my highbrow irritation on reading such sentences as those I quoted from Mr. Hall is my opinion that this way of putting words together is not appropriate to the occasion. If Mr. Hall in his own book writes in this manner, he consciously deviates from an aesthetic, not merely

[5] Hall, *op. cit.,* p. 235.

a grammatical, norm which he knows as well as anyone. In other words, in a book whose style is generally formal, even though not solemnly academic, the author feels compelled, in deference to his title "Leave your language alone," to go slumming every now and then, as if to prove to his readers that he is a regular guy: "He had already learned them . . . by the time he comes to school," "Nobody will understand each other,"[6] etc. Such excursions into poor linguistic neighborhoods fit the book no more than ski shoes and woolen socks fit a strapless evening gown. It can be done; it is neither reprehensible, nor stupid, nor amoral—but what is the good of it?

Someone might object here that, by introducing aesthetics, I am speaking of literary style which is extraneous to a discussion of "correct" usage. I do not think it is at all. I believe that it is as unsatisfactory to divorce style and taste from linguistic arguments which profess to deal with something more than the mere physical material of human speech, as it is to restrict oneself to describing the chemical composition of the colors used by Michelangelo without reference to their effect. The peculiar mixture of paints, while indeed chemically analyzable beyond and outside of "good" and "bad," derives its sense only from the purpose and the composition of the whole work; precisely so our putting together of sounds and words, while indeed phonetically and syntactically analyzable beyond and outside of "good" and "bad," becomes appropriate, pleasing, disgusting, "wrong," only with reference to the aim and intent of the whole utterance.

The position and purpose of Hall are quite different from those of the Birks. Hall approaches the problem of grammatical correctness in terms of descriptive linguistics, and comes therefore to the valid conclusion that, since there is no linguistic sense, nor ethical value in what the grammarians prescribe, we could make a case for paying no attention to these "authorities." However, he makes his mistake by converting the findings of the analysis of the material into prescriptions on the use of the material. This is like telling Michelangelo that, since colors and paints are neither good nor bad *per se,* he should not worry himself sick and waste his time over how to use them to make a painting. The Birks on the other hand, while knowing as well as does Hall that grammatical rules are neither "good" nor "bad," neither irrefrangible nor eternal, and while pointing this out to their students, feel that as teachers of English rather than descriptive linguistics they must compromise a rigidly scientific, analytical stand and equip the student with such tools and skills that he can behave, as speaker and writer, intelligently and appropriately, though not in blind obedience to so-called authorities, and so that he can compose a pleasing and effective work which transcends the sum of its composing parts.

[6] *Ibid.,* pp. 187–188, 6.

Mr. Hall's book is a well written (in terms of grammar, apart from studied lapses, as well as content) popular introduction to linguistics, except where it becomes propagandistic and prescriptive. The author did himself an injustice by entitling it *Leave Your Language Alone,* firstly, because the volume contains a lot more than the chatty title promises, and secondly, because he does not really mean what the title says. And whenever he does very self-consciously and sporadically use what most would normally call bad English (as Hall himself would call it if it were submitted in a doctoral thesis by one of his students), he has in mind, he says, inflicting upon the reader the beneficial effects of a shock treatment, which he prescribes for users of English who hold the absurd notion that grammar is a necessary item in one's linguistic equipment. One would say, then, that the radical Mr. Hall leads his readers straightway and uncompromisingly into linguistic anarchy, expounding his electrifying theses in a revolutionary manifesto which, though utopian both in its biblical righteousness and in its regrettable impracticality, can be defended on linguistic and philosophical grounds. Unfortunately, we are disappointed, for somehow Hall cannot bring himself to shock his reader, or himself, very often or very consistently. So that, if he advises you to leave your language alone, he neither lets himself go enough to set an example of anti-grammarian debauchery, nor does he really want to incite you to linguistic revolution because, he says, you might get hurt. Now the title is clear and sweeping enough, and so are the quotations at the beginning of this article. Why then does Mr. Hall's angry fist—"Tear off the rusty shackles of linguistic authoritarianism!"—change into a wagging finger— "—but don't get your hands dirty. . . ."? Because Hall admits, for example, that the punishment for the use of "bad grammar" is social stigma which may get you into all sorts of real difficulties;[7] because he allows that there is such a thing as *sub*-standard usage,[8] which one can only interpret as meaning that at least *some* people's language is at least *sometimes* so nasty that *they* had better not leave *their* language alone; and because, while he is ready to concede that the "ditch-digger who says *him and me ain't got none* and who uses swear words and 'four-letter' words is absolutely right—in his own language,"[9] Hall does not wish his son to leave his language alone to the same extent, for ". . . if my child is likely to run into trouble later on for saying *I done it* or *hisn* I will try to keep him from getting into the habit of using these forms which are actually not acceptable socially and which may cause others to react unfavorably towards him."[10] Mr. Hall has a real theoretical aversion, as one can plainly see, toward so-called authorities and such institutions as the French or Spanish Academy which meddle with language; indeed he is glad to note that ". . . no such authority has ever existed in any English-speaking country, nor does it seem

---

[7] *Ibid.,* pp. 13–14.   [8] *Ibid.,* pp. 60 *et passim.*   [9] *Ibid.,* p. 27.   [10] *Ibid.,* p. 13.

likely that speakers of English would ever be willing to accept the decrees of an Academy or similar institution or of a Ministry of Education."[11] (A fascinating bit of theory on the eternity of the sentiments of incorruptibility and tyrannophobia among speakers of English. Too bad Mr. Hall did not state his point with as much proof as conviction, especially as to whence speakers of English derive virtues of that sort: from their Anglo-Saxon racial superiority, or from their language? Anthropologists and linguists should not be left in suspense.) Yet with all his disdain of rules and authorities, in reviewing a bibliography the same Hall writes this:

> . . . the compilers [of this bibliography] consistently misplace the *Jr.* which many persons in the English-speaking world (including your reviewer) regard as an essential part of their names. The syntactic formula for the use of this element is: full name (i.e. given name[s] or initial[s] $+$ surname, whether in this order or inverted) $+$ *Jr.* If the surname only is listed, *Jr.* is not included. Thus *J(osephus) Nettlepink Jr.* or *Nettlepink, Josephus, Jr.,* but simply *Nettlepink*—not *Nettlepink Jr.,* as found passim in the CIPL bibliographies. Use of this last construction produces, at least in some readers, the same kind of irritation that comes from being addressed as *Mr. Prof. Dr. Nettlepink.*[12]

Is this the same Hall who tells us to leave our language alone, that there is nothing wrong with out language, that we should throw away grammars and dictionaries, that we are the only and best authorities on what is right or wrong? Is he worried about the misplacing of *Jr.,* does he offer a "syntactic formula" on how to write (of all things) a name, does he let himself be irritated if certain rules (made by whom?) are overlooked? How very disappointing in an iconoclast. Which Hall (not Hall *Jr.*) shall we believe? Well, anyhow, that's the end of the revolution.

But now that we have Hall's own word for it that there are various degrees of correctness (his distinction between "standard" and "vulgar"[13] is an oversimplification—there are numerous levels in each), let us ask a vital question: Who is to tell the ditch-digger's son just what degree of deviation from what rules may "cause others to react unfavorably towards him"? His father cannot do it. Hence we send him to school. If the Birks teach him he will learn the difference in language between the bare physical necessities of communication on one hand, and on the other hand the added niceties of convention and artistry and aesthetic predilections of his society; if true linguistic anarchists teach him, he will come out of

---

[11] *Ibid.,* p. 10.

[12] Robert A. Hall, Jr., review of *Bibliographie linguistique des années 1939–1947,* vol. 2, and *Bibliographie linguistique de l'année 1948 et complément des années 1939–1947, Language,* XXVII (1951), 611, n. 2.

[13] Hall, *Leave Your Language Alone,* p. 15.

school still talking like his old man and the hell with grammar; but if he studies Hall, he will turn schizophrenic—unless he takes the road to the caustic and disillusioning conclusion that Hall believes that what is good enough for the ditch-digger's boy is not good enough for the professor's son: this, I daresay, Mr. Hall does not seriously contemplate.

Indeed, Mr. Hall wishes to be very democratic. Unfortunately, his democratic crusade flies the flag of Education (with capital E). Says he:

> If we condemn the ditch-digger's speech, we do so, not because of any inherent demerit of the way he talks, but because we take his speech as being characteristic of his social class. This factor in our speech attitude is a relic from earlier, antidemocratic times, which accords very poorly with other aspects of our modern aspirations to democracy.[14]

If that is so, then Hall should not perpetuate in practice, albeit condemn in theory, such antidemocratic attitudes by teaching his son how *not* to talk like a ditch-digger. Moreover, though democracy obviously must decline to promote hatred of the common man, it can hardly disapprove of our hating his commonness—such as, for example, when he belches at the table. True, in some societies this may express enjoyment of the meal and be accepted as a compliment by the smiling hostess; in our civilization, like it or not, this is not the case. Surely the spirit of conciliatory relativity that permeates anthropology and sociology, as well as other sciences, does scarcely in all earnestness advocate the necessity of promiscuous adoption, in addition to indulgent comprehension, of all possible phenomena of social life.[15]

No doubt we shall be told that ignorance of the niceties of grammar is not the same thing at all as lack of taste or lack of manners, that language is a tool and that, to repeat Hall's dictum, "the merit of what a person says . . . is not affected in any way by the way in which they say it."[16] Hall knows this is not true—but perhaps he likes the folksy appeal of the phrase—for he says elsewhere: "If little Johnny uses a form that is

---

[14] *Ibid.*, p. 27.

[15] Cf. Margaret Mead, "Human Differences and World Order," *World Order: Its Intellectual and Cultural Foundations,* ed. F. Ernest Johnson (New York, 1945), p. 44. "One of the principal differences between anthropology and religion, and it is true of any religion, including in some cases ordinary, garden-variety ethical philosophers who have none, is the belief that has grown up in the past twenty-five years that anthropologists are ethical relativists, that say to their students, 'You see over there they eat their grandmother and over here they do not. So obviously it doesn't make much difference whether you eat your grandmother or not.' Anthropologists do not do this." This is comforting though difficult reading: Miss Mead should not have "left alone" that first sentence of hers.

[16] Hall, *op. cit.,* p. 236.

really not standard, we can point it out to him and get him to change, not on an authoritarian basis, but on the basis of actual usage among people whose speech is acceptable."[17] But who is to decide what is "really" not standard? Is it a matter of majority usage and approval? The majority says *ain't,* but we are told that Mr. Hall's son must not. *Who* is to say *what* people's speech is "acceptable" and acceptable to *whom?* Apparently somebody will have to act as an authority after all, sometimes even in defiance of the majority's usage.

Since as human beings we are born only with the faculty of speech, not with a language nor with any notion of style, both language and style must be acquired through learning, not through leaving anything alone. If left alone, the ditch-digger will always remain a ditch-digger, and that is all his son is ever going to be. The first condition for being anything else is, next to mental fitness, acquiring a fitting language, with the necessary vocabulary and an appropriate grammar and style.

Apart from Mr. Hall's failure to be consistent in his preaching, to say nothing of practicing what he preaches, it might be worthwhile to examine whether a good case could not actually be made, at least theoretically, for the desirability of relinquishing class standards, as it were, of linguistic usage. However since, as we have seen, and as Mr. Hall himself shows very well in several places in his book, the linguistic utterance *per se* cannot be evaluated apart from non-linguistic criteria, such as current grammatical rules, prevailing stylistic and aesthetic preferences, purpose of the communication, we must needs conclude that the best we can hope for from a purely linguistic reform is that it might alter our *attitude* toward language, but not that it will improve *language.* And in fact it is Mr. Hall's professed intention, as it is that of other reformers like him, to remedy social rather than linguistic inequities: the latter cannot exist. I quite agree that "we condemn the ditch-digger's speech not because of any inherent demerit of the way he talks, but because we take his speech as being characteristic of his social class"[18]—or rather, I should say (and this is essential!) of his (presumed) coarseness, lack of education, ignorance, even illiteracy. In other words, our prejudice, though provoked by linguistic idiosyncrasies of the speaker, will be of a social and/or intellectual nature. Should we, or indeed could we at all, change our attitude toward the linguistic behavior of our fellow men to such an extent and in such a manner as not to pre-judge them by the way they talk? I believe this is even less feasible than our refraining from judging, sometimes indeed misjudging, a person by his clothes, his features, his manners, his movements. In fact, when all other criteria deceive us, a man's speech and writing—unless he dissimulates his natural language ways (and it is easier to wear the King's clothes than to

[17] *Ibid.,* p. 190.   [18] *Ibid.,* p. 27.

talk the King's English)—are the safest indications of what manner of man he may be. Ask any actor, especially a radio actor, who must rely on voice characterization exclusively. And if we all walked away naked, anyone should be able to distinguish by the manner and content of their speech, the intelligent from the stupid, the educated from the unlettered.

But let us go even one step further. Let us assume the nearly miraculous, namely that it has actually become impossible, through the efforts of some social reformers and through linguistic equalization, to judge a man by his linguistic habits, because we either actually all talk alike (either like professors, or like ditch-diggers), or because one can through some miracle no longer be sure whether what contemporary society calls "correct" usage is any more typical of professors than of ditch-diggers (and this would require more than occasional linguistic slumming on the part of the professors). Would this state of affairs in any manner whatever necessarily imply any sort of social equalization, or at least freedom from social prejudices? Of course it would not, for we have at best removed merely the symptoms of a disease, but not its causes. Language and man's attitude toward language are only symptomatic of the state of a society, but not actively responsible for it.

All linguistic reforms and practical applications of the linguist's knowledge, regardless of whether they aim at retarding or dispatching the natural rate of linguistic change (and some have said lately that this rate is constant; in any event, there *is* change), will therefore produce only linguistic but not social effects. Moreover, it is highly doubtful whether such reforms can be successful at all, until and unless they have acquired enough social prestige. And to acquire such prestige does not mean acceptance by a majority, but rather approval by those persons, generally the minority of the intellectual and alas! social élite, who are worth emulating. And there we have come back again to the concepts of an élite, of emulation, of good and bad, of correctness and "bad" English. It seems indicated, therefore, that we should concentrate on social rather than on linguistic reforms, if our purpose is to improve the state of humanity, the state of language being beyond, and impervious to, improvement. Language will adjust itself to social conditions, not *vice versa*.

But if the Birks, and I with them, say that we might as well teach today's children today's best standard of English, as approved by society, some might accuse us all of being reactionaries, conservatives, people who don't like to see things change, whereas they, the reformers, are progressives. I for one should resent being called a reactionary or even a conservative on the evidence of my wanting to teach students appropriate grammar rather than encourage them to leave their language alone (though I doubt that even I should worry them too much with the analytic formula for the use of *Jr.*). My only answer is that I am indeed in favor of all changes which have any chance of promoting human welfare and wisdom: adequate wages, sufficient medical care for all, abolition of Jim Crow, education for the ditch-diggers' sons if they are smart enough though poor, and many considerably less innocuous ones. But I do not particularly care to waste my efforts on championing causes that promise what they cannot attain: like social justice and democracy through language reform, peace on earth through an international language,[19] and similar bargain-basement panaceas and short-cuts to salvation. Consequently, I should rather dedicate my linguistic efforts to the learning of how to use a language, native or foreign, well, that is, efficiently, effectively, and pleasingly. This is a skill, indeed an art, which must be learned like any other skill and art, and it includes a knowledge of how best to manipulate the basic tools and techniques. Those are admirably explained by the Birks, whereas Hall denies their necessity, at least in his title, and sporadically throughout his book. For the time being, therefore, I shall advise students to study English with the Birks and not with Hall.

Vocabulary

antiquated, stringency, tantamount, exigency, vitiate, *viz.,* arbiter, *per se,* amoral, extraneous, irrefrangible, manifesto, utopian, debauchery, authoritarianism, stigma, tyrannophobia, iconoclast, predilection, schizophrenic, caustic, conciliatory, promiscuous, indulgent, relinquishing, idiosyncrasy, feasible, dissimulate, emulation, innocuous, panacea

Review Questions

1. Which of the levels of usage as defined by Pooley (pages 117–125) does Pulgram's essay best represent? In what ways is the essay characteristic of this level?

2. List in columnar form the major linguistic ideas, attitudes, and assumptions contained in Hall's "Right *vs.* Wrong" and Pulgram's attempted refutation of each. Which of the writers is the more convincing?

3. In one sentence summarize each of the four attitudes toward usage expressed in the quotations at the beginning of Pulgram's essay.

4. Do you think that Pulgram's comparison between a speaker's use of words and Michaelangelo's use of paints is a good one? Why?

5. Why does Pulgram disagree with Hall's contention that "correct" usage and style be regarded as entirely separate matters?

6. Why does Pulgram describe such expressions in Hall's writing as "He had

[19] Cf. Ernst Pulgram, "An International Language—When?" *Modern Language Journal,* XXXII (January 1948), 50–68.

already learned them . . . by the time he comes to school" and "Nobody will understand each other" as "excursions into poor linguistic neighborhoods"?

7. In discussing *Leave Your Language Alone,* Pulgram asserts that Hall's book becomes prescriptive in places. What does he mean? To what extent does *prescriptive* apply to Pulgram's own attitude toward good usage?

8. Comment on the validity of Pulgram's charge that, if followed, Hall's suggestions would lead us into "linguistic anarchy."

9. Pulgram asks a "vital question": "Who is to tell the ditch-digger's son just what degree of deviation from what rules may 'cause others to react unfavorably towards him'?" Do you think Pulgram adequately answers the question?

10. Toward the end of his essay, Pulgram makes the following statement:

If left alone, the ditch-digger will always remain a ditch-digger, and that is all his son is ever going to be. The first condition for being anything else is, next to mental fitness, acquiring a fitting language, with the necessary vocabulary and an appropriate grammar and style.

What terms in this passage might Hall rightly request that Pulgram be more specific about?

11. Comment on Pulgram's views concerning the relationship between language and society.

Expository Technique

1. How would you define the tone of Pulgram's essay? Does it ever become sarcastic?

2. This essay begins with four quotations, each expressing a different attitude toward correct usage. Is this an effective means to begin such an essay? How does Pulgram integrate these quotations into the body of his text?

3. Throughout this essay Pulgram employs parentheses to enclose personal observations and attitudes. Is this device overused? Why?

4. Carefully analyze the final paragraph. Is it a good conclusion? Why? Why does Pulgram qualify his final sentence with "For the time being"?

Exercises

1. If you were Robert Hall, Jr., how would you write a rejoinder to Ernst Pulgram's "Don't Leave Your Language Alone"? Prepare a five-minute presentation to the class on what you think Hall might say. *After* preparing the report, consult the *Quarterly Journal of Speech,* XXXIX (February 1953), 42–44, for the answer he actually wrote, summarize his brief essay, and be prepared to comment on its effectiveness.

2. Controversy similar to the Hall-Pulgram debate has raged for over a decade. Report to the class on your findings concerning similar exchanges between Donald J. Lloyd and Jacques Barzun, *American Scholar,* XX (Summer 1951),

279–288, 289–293, and also between Wilson Follett, *Atlantic Monthly,* CCV (February 1960), 73–76, and Bergen Evans, *Atlantic Monthly,* CCV (March 1960), 79–82.

3. Many critics feel that much of the validity of Hall's argument is dependent upon determining what the usage pattern of a given social segment is. Consider how you would do this for college professors and ditch-diggers and make a list of the difficulties you might incur in trying to establish what "good English" is in each of these groups. Or, do you believe that Hall's criterion of linguistic relativity makes it impossible to generalize?

4. Read one of the following essays dealing with specific usage disputes and comment on its major points.

Robert J. Geist, " 'There is' Again," *College English,* XIV (December 1954), 188f.

John S. Kenyon, "One of Those Who Is . . . ," *American Speech,* XXVI (October 1951), 161–165.

——, "On Who and Whom," *American Speech,* V (February 1930), 253–255.

Ann E. Nichols, "The Past Participle of *Overflow: Overflowed* or *Overflown?*" *American Speech,* XLI (October 1966), 52–55.

N. E. Osselton, "Introductory 'This,' " *English Studies,* XLVIII (1967), 231–234.

Russell Thomas, "*Showed* as Past Participle," *College English,* XI (December 1949), 157f.

9.

STUART BERG FLEXNER

The Nature of Slang

American slang, as used in the title of this dictionary, is the body of words and expressions frequently used by or intelligible to a rather large portion of the general American public, but not accepted as good, formal usage by the majority. No word can be called slang simply because of its etymological history; its source, its spelling, and its meaning in a larger sense do *not* make it slang. Slang is best defined by a dictionary that points out who uses slang and what "flavor" it conveys.

I have called all slang used in the United States "American," regardless of its country of origin or use in other countries.

In this preface I shall discuss the human element in the formation of slang (what American slang is, and how and why slang is created and used). . . .

The English language has several levels of vocabulary:

Standard usage comprises those words and expressions used, understood, and accepted by a majority of our citizens under any circumstances or degree of formality. Such words are well defined and their most accepted spellings and pronunciations are given in our standard dictionaries. In standard speech one might say: *Sir, you speak English well.*

Colloquialisms are familiar words and idioms used in informal speech and writing, but not considered explicit or formal enough for polite conversation or business correspondence. Unlike slang, however, colloquialisms are used and understood by nearly everyone in the United States. The use of slang conveys the suggestion that the speaker and the listener enjoy a special "fraternity," but the use of colloquialisms emphasizes only the informality and familiarity of a general social situation. Almost all idiomatic expressions, for example, could be labeled colloquial. Colloquially, one might say: *Friend, you talk plain and hit the nail right on the head.*

Dialects are the words, idioms, pronunciations, and speech habits peculiar to specific geographical locations. A dialecticism is a regionalism or localism. In popular use "dialect" has come to mean the words, foreign accents, or speech patterns associated with any ethnic group. In Southern dialect one might say: *Cousin, y'all talk mighty fine.* In ethnic-immigrant "dialects" one might say: *Paisano, you speak good the English,* or *Landsman, your English is plenty all right already.*

Cant, jargon, and *argot* are the words and expressions peculiar to special segments of the population. *Cant* is the conversational, familiar idiom used and generally understood only by members of a specific occupation, trade, profession, sect, class, age group, interest group, or other sub-group of our culture. *Jargon* is the technical or even secret vocabulary of such a sub-group; jargon is "shop talk." *Argot* is both the cant and the jargon of any professional criminal group. In such usages one might say, respectively: *CQ-CQ-CQ . . . the tone of your transmission is good; You are free of anxieties related to interpersonal communication;* or *Duchess, let's have a bowl of chalk.*

Slang[1] is generally defined above. In slang one might say: *Buster, your line is the cat's pajamas,* or *Doll, you come on with the straight jazz, real cool like.*

Each of these levels of language, save standard usage, is more common in speech than in writing, and slang as a whole is no exception. Thus, very few slang words and expressions (hence very few of the entries in this dictionary) appear in standard dictionaries.

American slang tries for a quick, easy, personal mode of speech. It

---

[1] For the evolution of the word "slang," see F. Klaeber, "Concerning the Etymology of Slang," *American Speech*, April, 1926.

comes mostly from cant, jargon, and argot words and expressions whose popularity has increased until a large number of the general public uses or understands them. Much of this slang retains a basic characteristic of its origin: it is *fully* intelligible only to initiates.

Slang may be represented pictorially as the more popular portion of the cant, jargon, and argot from many sub-groups (only a few of the sub-groups are shown below). The shaded areas represent only general overlapping between groups.

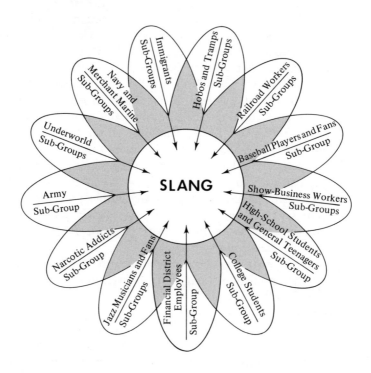

Eventually, some slang passes into standard speech; other slang flourishes for a time with varying popularity and then is forgotten; finally, some slang is never fully accepted nor completely forgotten. *O.K., jazz* (music), and *A-bomb* were recently considered slang, but they are now standard usages. *Bluebelly, Lucifer,* and *the bee's knees* have faded from popular use. *Bones* (dice) and *beat it* seem destined to remain slang forever: Chaucer used the first and Shakespeare used the second.

It is impossible for any living vocabulary to be static. Most new slang words and usages evolve quite naturally: they result from specific situations. New objects, ideas, or happenings, for example, require new words to describe them. Each generation also seems to need some new words to describe the same old things.

Railroaders (who were probably the first American sub-group to have a nationwide cant and jargon) thought *jerk water town* was ideally descriptive of a community that others called a *one-horse town*. The changes from *one-horse town* and *don't spare the horses* to a *wide place in the road* and *step on it* were natural and necessary when the automobile replaced the horse. The automobile also produced such new words and new meanings (some of them highly specialized) as *gas buggy, jalopy, bent eight, Chevvie, convertible,* and *lube*. Like most major innovations, the automobile affected our social history and introduced or encouraged *dusters, hitch hikers, road hogs, joint hopping, necking, chicken* (the game), *car coats,* and *suburbia*.

The automobile is only one obvious example. Language always responds to new concepts and developments with new words.

Consider the following:

wars: *redcoats, minutemen, bluebelly, over there, doughboy, gold brick, jeep.*
mass immigrations: *Bohunk, greenhorn, shillalagh, voodoo, pizzeria.*
science and technology: *'gin, side-wheeler, wash-and-wear, fringe area, fallout.*
turbulent eras: *Redskin, maverick, speak, Chicago pineapple, free love, fink, breadline.*
evolution in the styles of eating: *applesauce, clambake, luncheonette,   hot dog....*
dress: *Mother Hubbard, bustle, shimmy, sailor, Long Johns, zoot suit, Ivy League.*
housing: *lean-to, bundling board, chuckhouse, W.C., railroad flat, split-level, sectional.*
music: *cakewalk, bandwagon, fish music, long hair, rock.*
personality: *Yankee, alligator, flapper, sheik, hepcat, B.M.O.C., beetle, beat.*
new modes of transportation: *stage, pinto, jitney, kayducer, hot shot, jet jockey.*
new modes of entertainment: *barnstormer, two-a-day, clown alley, talkies, d.j., Spectacular.*
changing attitudes toward sex: *painted woman, fast, broad, wolf, jailbait, sixty-nine.*
human motivations: *boy crazy, gold-digger, money-mad, Momism, Oedipus complex, do-gooder, sick.*
personal relationships: *bunky, kids, old lady, steady, ex, gruesome twosome, John.*
work and workers: *clod buster, scab, pencil pusher, white collar, graveyard shift, company man.*
politics: *Tory, do-nothing, mug-wump, third party, brain trust, fellow traveler, Veep.*
and even hair styles: *bun, rat, peroxide blonde, Italian cut, pony tail, D.A.*

Those social groups that first confront a new object, cope with a new situation, or work with a new concept devise and use new words long before the population at large does. The larger, more imaginative, and useful a group's vocabulary, the more likely it is to contribute slang. To generate slang, a group must either be very large and in constant contact with the dominant culture or be small, closely knit, and removed enough from the dominant culture to evolve an extensive, highly personal, and vivid vocabulary. Teen-agers are an example of a large sub-group contributing many words. Criminals, carnival workers, and hoboes are examples of the smaller groups. The smaller groups, because their vocabulary is personal and vivid, contribute to our general slang out of proportion to their size.

Whether the United States has more slang words than any other country (in proportion to number of people, area, or the number of words in the standard vocabulary) I do not know.[2] Certainly the French and the Spanish enjoy extremely large slang vocabularies. Americans, however, do use their general slang more than any other people.

American slang reflects the kind of people who create and use it. Its diversity and popularity are in part due to the imagination, self-confidence, and optimism of our people. Its vitality is in further part due to our guarantee of free speech and to our lack of a national academy of language or of any "official" attempt to purify our speech. Americans are restless and frequently move from region to region and from job to job. This hopeful wanderlust, from the time of the pioneers through our westward expansion to modern mobility, has helped spread regional and group terms until they have become general slang. Such restlessness has created constantly new situations which provoke new words. Except for a few Eastern industrial areas and some rural regions in the South and West, America just doesn't look or sound "lived in." We often act and speak as if we were simply visiting and observing. What should be an ordinary experience seems new, unique, or colorful to us, worthy of words and forceful speech. People do not "settle down" in their jobs, towns, or vocabularies.

[2] The vocabulary of the average American, most of which he knows but never uses, is usually estimated at 10,000–20,000 words. Of this quantity I estimate conservatively that 2,000 words are slang. Slang, which thus forms about 10 per cent of the words known by the average American, belongs to the part of his vocabulary most frequently *used*.

The English language is now estimated to have at least 600,000 words; this is over four times the 140,000 recorded words of the Elizabethan period. Thus over 450,000 *new words or meanings* have been added since Shakespeare's day, without counting the replacement words or those that have been forgotten between then and now. There are now approximately 10,000 slang words in American English, and about 35,000 cant, jargon, and argot words.

Despite this quantity, 25 per cent of all communication is composed of just nine words. According to McKnight's study, another 25 per cent of all speech is composed of an additional 34 words (or: 43 words comprise 50 per cent of all speech). Scholars do differ, however, on just which nine words are the most popular. Three major studies are: G. H. McKnight, *English Words and Their Background*, Appleton-Century-Crofts, Inc., 1923 (for spoken words only); Godfrey Dewey, "Relative Frequency of English Speech Sounds," *Harvard Studies in Education*, vol. IV, 1923 (for written words only); and Norman R. French, Charles W. Carter, and Walter Koenig, Jr., "Words and

Nor do we "settle down" intellectually, spiritually, or emotionally. We have few religious, regional, family, class, psychological, or philosophical roots. We don't believe in roots, we believe in teamwork. Our strong loyalties, then, are directed to those social groups—or sub-groups as they are often called—with which we are momentarily identified. This ever-changing "membership" helps to promote and spread slang.

But even within each sub-group only a few new words are generally accepted. Most cant and jargon are local and temporary. What persists are the exceptionally apt and useful cant and jargon terms. These become part of the permanent, personal vocabulary of the group members, giving prestige to the users by proving their acceptance and status in the group. Group members then spread some of this more honored cant and jargon in the dominant culture. If the word is also useful to non-group members, it is on its way to becoming slang. Once new words are introduced into the dominant culture, via television, radio, movies, or newspapers, the rapid movement of individuals and groups spread the new word very quickly.

For example, consider the son of an Italian immigrant living in New York City. He speaks Italian at home. Among neighborhood youths of similar background he uses many Italian expressions because he finds them always on the tip of his tongue and because they give him a sense of solidarity with his group. He may join a street gang, and after school and during vacations work in a factory. After leaving high school, he joins the navy; then he works for a year seeing the country as a carnival worker. He returns to New York, becomes a longshoreman, marries a girl with a German background, and becomes a boxing fan. He uses Italian and German borrowings, some teen-age street-gang terms, a few factory terms, slang with

Sounds of Telephone Conversations," *Bell System Technical Journal,* April, 1930 (telephone speech only). Their lists of the most common nine words are:

MC KNIGHT'S SPEECH	DEWEY'S WRITTEN	BELL TELEPHONE CONVERSATIONS
	a	a
and	and	
be		
have		
	in	
		I
	is	is
it	it	it
		on
of	of	
	that	that
the	the	the
to	to	to
will		
you		you

a navy origin, and carnival, dockworker's, and boxing words. He spreads words from each group to all other groups he belongs to. His Italian parents will learn and use a few street-gang, factory, navy, carnival, dockworker's, and boxing terms; his German in-laws will learn some Italian words from his parents; his navy friends will begin to use some of his Italian expressions; his carnival friends a few navy words; his co-workers on the docks some carnival terms, in addition to all the rest; and his social friends, with whom he may usually talk boxing and dock work, will be interested in and learn some of his Italian and carnival terms. His speech may be considered very "slangy" and picturesque because he has belonged to unusual, colorful sub-groups.

On the other hand, a man born into a Midwestern, middle-class, Protestant family whose ancestors came to the United States in the eighteenth century might carry with him popular high-school terms. At high school he had an interest in hot rods and rock-and-roll. He may have served two years in the army, then gone to an Ivy League college where he became an adept bridge player and an enthusiast of cool music. He may then have become a sales executive and developed a liking for golf. This second man, no more usual or unusual than the first, will know cant and jargon terms of teen-age high-school use, hot-rods, rock-and-roll, Ivy League schools, cool jazz, army life, and some golf player's and bridge player's terms. He knows further a few slang expressions from his parents (members of the Jazz Age of the 1920's), from listening to television programs, seeing both American and British movies, reading popular literature, and from frequent meetings with people having completely different backgrounds. When he uses cool terms on the golf course, college expressions at home, business words at the bridge table, when he refers to whiskey or drunkenness by a few words he learned from his parents, curses his next-door neighbor in a few choice army terms —then, he too is popularizing slang.

It is, then, clear that three cultural conditions especially contribute to the creation of a large slang vocabulary: (1) hospitality to or acceptance of new objects, situations, and concepts; (2) existence of a large number of diversified sub-groups; (3) democratic mingling between these sub-groups and the dominant culture. Primitive peoples have little if any slang because their life is restricted by ritual; they develop few new concepts; and there are no sub-groups that mingle with the dominant culture. (Primitive sub-groups, such as medicine men or magic men, have their own vocabularies; but such groups do not mix with the dominant culture and their jargon can never become slang because it is secret or sacred.)

But what, after all, are the advantages that slang possesses which make it useful? Though our choice of any specific word may usually be made from habit, we sometimes consciously select a slang word because we believe that it communicates more quickly and easily, and more personally, than does a standard word. Sometimes we resort to slang because there is no one standard word to use. In the 1940's, *WAC, cold war,* and *cool,* (music), could not be expressed quickly by any standard synonyms. Such words often become standard quickly, as have the first two. We also use slang because it often is more forceful, vivid, and expressive than are standard usages. Slang usually avoids the sentimentality and formality that older words often asume. Taking a girl to a *dance* may seem sentimental, may convey a degree of formal, emotional interest in the girl, and has overtones of fancy balls, fox trots, best suits, and corsages. At times it is more fun to go to a *hop.* To be *busted* or without a *hog* in one's *jeans* is not only more vivid and forceful than being penniless or without funds, it is also a more optimistic state. A *mouthpiece* (or *legal beagle*), *pencil pusher, sawbones, boneyard, bottle washer* or a course in *biochem* is more vivid and forceful than a lawyer, clerk, doctor, cemetery, laboratory assistant, or a course in biochemistry—and is much more real and less formidable than a legal counsel, junior executive, surgeon, necropolis (or memorial park), laboratory technician, or a course in biological chemistry.

Although standard English is exceedingly hospitable to polysyllabicity and even sesquipedalianism, slang is not. Slang is sometimes used not only because it is concise but just because its brevity makes it forceful. As this dictionary demonstrates, slang seems to prefer short words, especially monosyllables, and, best of all, words beginning with an explosive or an aspirate.[3]

We often use slang *fad* words as a bad habit because they are close to the tip of our tongue. Most of us apply several favorite but vague words to any of several somewhat similar situations; this saves us the time and effort of thinking and speaking precisely. At other times we purposely choose a word because it is vague, because it does not commit us too strongly to what we are saying. For example, if a friend has been praising a woman, we can reply "she's *the bee's knees*" or "she's a real *chick*," which can mean that we consider her very modern, intelligent, pert, and understanding—or can mean that we think she is one of many nondescript, somewhat confused, followers

[3] Many such formations are among our most frequently used slang words. As listed in this dictionary, *bug* has 30 noun meanings, *shot* 14 noun and 4 adjective meanings, *can* 11 noun and 6 verb, *bust* 9 verb and 6 noun, *hook* 8 noun and 5 verb, *fish* 14 noun, and *sack* 8 noun, 1 adjective, and 1 verb meaning. Monosyllabic words also had by far the most citations found in our source reading of popular literature. Of the 40 words for which we found the most quotations, 29 were monosyllabic. Before condensing, *fink* had citations from 70 different sources, *hot* 67, *bug* 62, *blow* and *dog* 60 each, *joint* 59, *stiff* 56, *punk* 53, *bum* and *egg* 50 each, *guy* 43, *make* 41, *bull* and *mug* 37 each, *bird* 34, *fish* and *hit* 30 each, *ham* 25, *yak* 23, *sharp* 14, and *cinch* 10. (Many of these words, of course, have several slang meanings; many of the words also appeared scores of times in the same book or article.)

of popular fads. We can also tell our friend that a book we both have recently read is *the cat's pajamas* or *the greatest*. These expressions imply that we liked the book for exactly the same reasons that our friend did, without having to state what these reasons were and thus taking the chance of ruining our rapport.

In our language we are constantly recreating our image in our own minds and in the minds of others. Part of this image, as mentioned above, is created by using sub-group cant and jargon in the dominant society; part of it is created by our choice of both standard and slang words. A sub-group vocabulary shows that we have a group to which we "belong" and in which we are "somebody"—outsiders had better respect us. Slang is used to show others (and to remind ourselves of) our biographical, mental, and psychological background; to show our social, economic, geographical, national, racial, religious, educational, occupational, and group interests, memberships, and patriotisms. One of the easiest and quickest ways to do this is by using counter-words. These are automatic, often one-word responses of like or dislike, of acceptance or rejection. They are used to counter the remarks, or even the presence, of others. Many of our fad words and many student and quasi-intellectual slang words are counter-words. For liking: *beat, the cat's pajamas, drooly, gas, George, the greatest, keen, nice, reet, smooth, super, way out,* etc. For rejection of an outsider (implying incompetence to belong to our group): *boob, creep, dope, drip, droop, goof, jerk, kookie, sap, simp, square, weird,* etc. Such automatic counters are overused, almost meaningless, and are a substitute for thought. But they achieve one of the main purposes of speech: quickly and automatically they express our own sub-group and personal criteria. Counter-words are often fad words creating a common bond of self-defense. All the rejecting counters listed above could refer to a moron, an extreme introvert, a bird-watcher, or a genius. The counters merely say that the person is rejected—he does not belong to the group. In uttering the counter we don't care what the person is; we are pledging our own group loyalty, affirming our identity, and expressing our satisfaction at being accepted.

In like manner, at various periods in history, our slang has abounded in words reflecting the fear, distrust, and dislike of people unlike ourselves. This intolerance is shown by the many derogatory slang words for different immigrant, religious, and racial groups: *Chink, greaser, Heinie, hunkie, mick, mockie, nigger, spik.* Many counters and derogatory words try to identify our own group status, to dare others to question our group's, and therefore our own, superiority.

Sometimes slang is used to escape the dull familiarity of standard words, to suggest an escape from the established routine of everyday life. When slang is used, our life seems a little fresher and a little more personal.

Also, as at all levels of speech, slang is sometimes used for the pure joy of making sounds, or even for a need to attract attention by making noise. The sheer newness and informality of certain slang words produces a pleasure.

But more important than this expression of a more or less hidden esthetic motive on the part of the speaker is slang's reflection of the personality, the outward, clearly visible characteristics of the speaker. By and large, the man who uses slang is a forceful, pleasing, acceptable personality. Morality and intellect (too frequently not considered virtues in the modern American man) are overlooked in slang, and this has led to a type of reverse morality: many words, once standing for morally good things, are now critical. No one, for example, though these words were once considered complimentary, wants to be called a *prude* or *Puritan*. Even in standard usage they are mildly derisive.

Moreover, few of the many slang synonyms for drunk are derogatory or critical. To call a person a standard drunk may imply a superior but unsophisticated attitude toward drinking. Thus we use slang and say someone is *boozed up, gassed, high, potted, stinking, has a glow on,* etc., in a verbal attempt to convey our understanding and awareness. These slang words show that we too are human and know the effects of excessive drinking.

In the same spirit we refer to people sexually as *big ass man, fast, John, sex pot, shack job, wolf,* etc., all of which accept unsanctioned sexual intercourse as a matter of fact. These words are often used in a complimentary way and in admiration or envy. They always show acceptance of the person as a "regular guy." They are never used to express a moral judgment. Slang has few complimentary or even purely descriptive words for "virgin," "good girl," or "gentleman." Slang has *bag, bat, ex, gold digger, jerk, money mad, n.g., old lady, square,* etc.; but how many words are there for a good wife and mother, an attractive and chaste woman, an honest, hard-working man who is kind to his family, or even a respected elderly person? Slang—and it is frequently true for all language levels—always tends toward degradation rather than elevation. As slang shows, we would rather share or accept vices than be excluded from a social group. For this reason, for self-defense, and to create an aura (but not the fact) of modernity and individuality, much of our slang purposely expresses amorality, cynicism, and "toughness."

Reverse morality also affects slang in other ways. Many use slang just because it is not standard or polite. Many use slang to show their rebellion against *boobs, fuddy-duddies, marks,* and *squares.* Intellectuals and politicians often use slang to create the "common touch" and others use slang to express either their anti-intellectualism or avant-garde leanings. Thus, for teen-agers, entertainers, college students, beatniks, jazz fans, intellectuals, and other large groups, slang is often used in preference to standard words and expressions. Slang is the "official" modern language of certain vociferous groups in our population.

In my work on this dictionary, I was constantly aware that most American slang is created and used by males. Many types of slang words—including the taboo and strongly derogatory ones, those referring to sex, women, work, money, whiskey,[4] politics, transportation, sports, and the like—refer primarily to male endeavor and interest. The majority of entries in this dictionary could be labeled "primarily masculine use." Men belong to more sub-groups than do women; men create and use occupational cant and jargon; in business, men have acquaintances who belong to many different sub-groups. Women, on the other hand, still tend to be restricted to family and neighborhood friends. Women have very little of their own slang.[5] The new words applied to women's clothing, hair styles, homes, kitchen utensils and gadgets are usually created by men. Except when she accompanies her boy friend or husband to *his* recreation (baseball, hunting, etc.) a woman seldom mingles with other groups. When women do mingle outside of their own neighborhood and family circles, they do not often talk of the outside world of business, politics, or other fields of general interest where new feminine names for objects, concepts, and viewpoints could evolve.

Men also tend to avoid words that sound feminine or weak. Thus there are sexual differences in even the standard vocabularies of men and women. A woman may ask her husband to put out the *silver, crystal,* and *china*—while the man will set the table with *knives, forks, spoons, glasses,* and *dishes.* His wife might think the *table linen* attractive, the husband might think the *tablecloth* and *napkins* pretty. A man will buy a *pocketbook* as a gift for his wife, who will receive a *bag.* The couple will live under the same roof, the wife in her *home,* the man in his *house.* Once outside of their domesticity the man will begin to use slang quicker than the woman. She'll get into the *car* while he'll get into the *jalopy* or *Chevvie.* And so they go: she will learn much of her general slang from him; for any word she associates with the home, her personal belongings, or any female concept, he will continue to use a less descriptive, less personal one.

Males also use slang to shock. The rapid tempo of life, combined with the sometimes low boiling point of males, can evoke emotions—admiration, joy, contempt, anger—stronger than our old standard vocabulary can convey. In the stress of the moment a man is not just in a standard "untenable

---

[4] It would appear that the word having the most slang synonyms is *drunk.*

[5] Women who do work usually replace men at men's jobs, are less involved in business life than men, and have a shorter business career (often but an interim between school and marriage). The major female subgroups contributing to American slang are: airline stewardesses, beauty-parlor operators, chorus girls, nurses, prostitutes, and waitresses.

position," he is *up the creek*. Under strong anger a man does not feel that another is a mere "incompetent"—he is a *jerk*.

Men also seem to relish hyperbole in slang. Under many situations, men do not see or care to express fine shades of meaning: a girl is either a *knock-out* or a *dog*, liquor either *good stuff* or *panther piss*, a person either has *guts* or is *chicken*, a book is either *great* or nothing but *crap*. Men also like slang and colloquial wording because they express action or even violence: we *draw pay, pull a boner, make a score, grab some sleep, feed our face, kill time*—in every instance we tend to use the transitive verb, making ourselves the active doer.

The relation between a sub-group's psychology and its cant and jargon is interesting, and the relation between an individual's vocabulary and psychological personality is even more so. Slang can be one of the most revealing things about a person, because our own personal slang vocabulary contains many words used by choice, words which we use to create our own image, words which we find personally appealing and evocative—as opposed to our frequent use of standard words merely from early teaching and habit. Whether a man calls his wife *baby, doll, honey, the little woman, the Mrs.,* or *my old lady* certainly reveals much about him. What words one uses to refer to a mother (*Mom, old lady*), friend (*buddy, bunkie, old man*), the bathroom (*can, John, little boy's room*), parts of the body and sex acts (*boobies, gigi, hard, laid, score*), being tired (*all in, beat*), being drunk (*clobbered, high, lit up like a Christmas tree, paralyzed*), and the like, reveal much about a person and his motivations.[6]

The basic metaphors, at any rate, for all levels of language depend on the five senses. Thus *rough, smooth, touch; prune, sour puss, sweet; fishy, p.u., rotten egg; blow loud; blue, red, square*. In slang, many metaphors refer to touch (including the sense of heat and cold) and to taste.

Food is probably our most popular slang image. Food from the farm, kitchen, or table, and its shape, color, and taste suggest many slang metaphors. This is because food can appeal to taste, smell, sight, and touch, four of our five senses; because food is a major, universal image to all people, all sub-groups; because men work to provide it and women devote much time to buying and preparing it; because food is before our eyes three times every day.

Many standard food words mean money in nonstandard use: *cabbage, kale, lettuce*. Many apply to parts of the body: *cabbage head, cauliflower ear, meat hooks, nuts, plates of meat*. Many food words refer to people: *apple, cold fish, Frog, fruitcake, honey, sweetie pie*. Others refer to general situa-

---

[6] For just the last example, *clobbered* may indicate that a drinker is punishing himself, *high* that he is escaping, *lit up like a Christmas tree* that he is seeking attention and a more dominant personality, and *paralyzed* that he seeks punishment, escape or death.

tions and attitudes: to *brew* a plot, to receive a *chewing out,* to find oneself *in a pickle* or something not *kosher,* to be unable to *swallow* another's story, to ask *what's cooking?* Many drunk words also have food images: *boiled, fried, pickled;* and so do many words for nonsense: *applesauce, banana oil, spinach.* Many standard food words also have sexual meaning in slang. The many food words for money, parts of the body, people, and sex reveal that food means much more to us than mere nourishment. When a *good egg brings home the bacon* to his *honey,* or when a *string bean* of a *sugar daddy* takes his *piece of barbecue* out to get *fried* with his hard-earned *kale,* food images have gone a long way from the farm, kitchen, and table.

Sex has contributed comparatively few words to modern slang,[7] but these are among our most frequently used. The use of sex words to refer to sex in polite society and as metaphors in other fields is increasing. Sex metaphors are common for the same conscious reasons that food metaphors are. Sex appeals to, and can be used to apply to, most of the five senses. It is common to all persons in all sub-groups, and so we are aware of it continually.

Slang words for sexual attraction and for a variety of sexual acts, positions, and relationships are more common than standard words. Standard non-taboo words referring to sex are so scarce or remote and scientific that slang is often used in referring to the most romantic, the most obscene, and the most humorous sexual situations. Slang is so universally used in sexual communication that when "a man meets a maid" it is best for all concerned that they know slang.[8] Slang words for sex carry little emotional connotation; they express naked desire or mechanical acts, devices, and positions. They are often blunt, cynical and "tough."

The subconscious relating of sex and food is also apparent from reading this dictionary. Many words with primary standard meanings of food have sexual slang meanings. The body, parts of the body, and descriptions of each, often call food terms into use: *banana, bread, cheese cake, cherry, jelly roll, meat,* etc. Beloved, or simply sexually attractive, people are also often called by food names: *cookie, cup of tea, honey, peach, quail, tomato,* etc. This primary relation between sex and food depends on the fact that they are man's two major sensuous experiences. They are shared by all personalities and all sub-groups and they appeal to the same senses—thus there is bound to be some overlapping in words and imagery. However, there are too many

[7] Many so-called bedroom words are not technically slang at all, but are sometimes associated with slang only because standard speech has rejected them as taboo. However, many of these taboo words do have further metaphorical meanings in slang: *jerk, screw you,* etc.

[8] On the other hand, Madame de Stael is reported to have complimented one of her favorite lovers with "speech is not his language."

standard food words having sexual meanings in slang for these conscious reasons to suffice. Sex and food seem to be related in our subconscious.

Also of special interest is the number of slang expressions relating sex and cheating. Used metaphorically, many sex words have secondary meanings of being cheated, deceived, swindled, or taken advantage of, and several words whose primary meaning is cheating or deceiving have further specific sexual meanings: *cheating, make, royal screwing, score, turn a trick,* etc. As expressed in slang, sex is a trick somehow, a deception, a way to cheat and deceive us. To curse someone we can say *screw you,* which expresses a wish to deprive him of his good luck, his success, perhaps even his potency as a man.[9] Sex is also associated with confusion, exhausting tasks, and disaster: *ball buster, screwed up, snafu,* etc. It seems clear, therefore, that, in slang, success and sexual energy are related or, to put it more accurately, that thwarted sexual energy will somehow result in personal disaster.

Language is a social symbol. The rise of the middle class coincided with the period of great dictionary makers, theoretical grammarians, and the "correct usage" dogma. The new middle class gave authority to the dictionaries and grammarians in return for "correct usage" rules that helped solidify their social position. Today, newspaper ads still implore us to take mail-order courses in order to "learn to speak like a college graduate," and some misguided English instructors still give a good speaking ability as the primary reason for higher education.

The gap between "correct usage" and modern practice widens each day. Are there valid theoretical rules for speaking good English, or should "observed usage" be the main consideration? Standard words do not necessarily make for precise, forceful, or useful speech. On the other hand, "observed usage" can never promise logic and clarity. Today, we have come to depend on "observed usage," just as eighteenth- and nineteenth-century social climbers depended on "correct usage," for social acceptance.

Because it is not standard, formal, or acceptable under all conditions, slang is usually considered vulgar, impolite, or boorish. As this dictionary

---

[9] See F. P. Wood, "The Vocabulary of Failure," *Better English,* Nov., 1938, p. 34. Failure in one's personality, school, job, business, or an attempted love affair are all expressed by the same vocabulary. One gets the *brush off,* the *gate,* a *kiss off,* or *walking papers* in both business and personal relationships. As the previous discussion of counter-words demonstrates, slang allows no distinction or degree among individual failures. Incompetence does not apply to just one job or facet of life—either one belongs or is considered unworthy. This unworthiness applies to the entire personality, there are no alternative avenues for success or happiness. One is not merely of limited intelligence, not merely an introvert, not merely ugly, unknowing, or lacking in aggression—but one is a failure in all these things, a complete *drip, jerk,* or *square.* The basic failure is that of personality, the person is not a mere failure—he is an outcast, an untouchable; he is taboo.

shows, however, the vast majority of slang words and expressions are neither taboo, vulgar, derogatory, nor offensive in meaning, sound, or image. There is no reason to avoid any useful, explicit word merely because it is labeled "slang." Our present language has not decayed from some past and perfect "King's English," Latin, Greek, or pre-Tower of Babel tongue. All languages and all words have been, are, and can only be but conventions mutually agreed upon for the sake of communicating. Slang came to America on the Mayflower. In general, it is not vulgar, new, or even peculiarly American: an obvious illustration of this is the polite, old French word *tête,* which was originally slang from a Latin word *testa*—cooking pot.

Cant and jargon in no way refer only to the peculiar words of undesirable or underworld groups. Slang does not necessarily come from the underworld, dope addicts, degenerates, hoboes, and the like. Any cultural subgroup develops its own personal cant and jargon which can later become general slang. All of us belong to several of these specific sub-groups using our own cant and jargon. Teen-agers, steel workers, soldiers, Southerners, narcotic addicts, church-goers, truck drivers, advertising men, jazz musicians, pickpockets, retail salesmen in every field, golf players, immigrants from every country, college professors, baseball fans—all belong to typical sub-groups from which slang originates. Some of these sub-groups are colorful; most are composed of prosaic, average people.

Many people erroneously believe that a fundamental of slang is that it is intentionally picturesque, strained in metaphor, or jocular. Picturesque metaphor (and metonymy, hyperbole, and irony) does or should occur frequently in all levels of speech. Picturesque metaphor is a frequent characteristic of slang, but it does not define slang or exist as an inherent part of it. The picturesque or metaphorical aspect of slang is often due to its direct honesty or to its newness. Many standard usages are just as picturesque, but we have forgotten their original metaphor through habitual use. Thus slang's *jerk* and *windbag* are no more picturesque than the standard *incompetent* and *fool. Incompetent* is from the Latin *competens* plus the negating prefix *in-* and = "unable or unwilling to compete"; *fool* is Old French, from the Latin *follis* which actually = "bellows or wind bag"; slang's *windbag* and the standard *fool* actually have the same metaphor.

As for picturesque sounds, I find very few in slang. Onomatopoeia, reduplications, harsh sounds and pleasing sounds, even rhyming terms, exist on all levels of speech. Readers of this dictionary will find no more picturesque or unusual sounds here than in a similar length dictionary of standard words. Many slang words are homonyms for standard words.

As has been frequently pointed out, many slang words have the same meaning. There seems to be an unnecessary abundance of counter-words, synonyms for "drunk," hundreds of fad words with almost the same meaning, etc. This is because slang introduces word after word year after year from many, many sub-groups. But slang is a scatter-gun process; many new words come at the general public; most are ignored; a few stick in the popular mind.

Remember that "slang" actually does not exist as an entity except in the minds of those of us who study the language. People express themselves and are seldom aware that they are using the artificial divisions of "slang" or "standard." First and forever, language is language, an attempt at communication and self-expression. The fact that some words or expressions are labeled "slang" while others are labeled "jargon" or said to be "from the Anglo-Saxon" is of little value except to scholars. Thus this dictionary is a legitimate addition to standard dictionaries, defining many words just as meaningful as and often more succinct, useful, and popular than many words in standard dictionaries.

Vocabulary

etymological, ethnic, innovations, wanderlust, solidarity, adept, sesquipedalianism, aspirate, rapport, introvert, esthetic, aura, vociferous, untenable, hyperbole, prosaic, jocular, metonymy, homonymns

Review Questions

1. Why does the author believe slang can best be defined in terms of who uses it and the flavor it conveys rather than by its derivation, spelling, or meaning?

2. Differentiate between standard usage, colloquialisms, dialects, cant, jargon, and argot.

3. Comment on the three cultural conditions that contribute to the creation of a large slang vocabulary.

4. What are the most common sources of slang expressions?

5. How is slang similar to standard usage? How is it different?

6. Discuss the statement "Slang . . . always tends toward degradation rather than elevation." Cite examples.

7. The London *Times* has stated that the object of slang "is really always to provide a new and different way of saying what can be perfectly well said without it." How valid is this observation?

Exercises

1. H. L. Mencken has observed that part of the vocabulary of slang is composed of "old words, whether used singly or in combination, that have been put to new uses, usually metaphorical."

a. List ten words which have new meanings accepted in Standard English usage and which also have slang meanings (e.g., *dope, crazy*). Indicate in each case the meaning of the slang term.

b. List ten examples of slang phrases which are composed of words accepted in Standard English usage (e.g., *snap course, out of it*). Indicate the meaning of each.

2. Some slang terms are produced by abbreviating terms found in Standard English usage (e.g., *beaut* for *beauty*). Cite five examples of such slang formations.

3. In an article on slang at the University of Kansas (*American Speech*, XXXVIII [October 1963], 163–177), Alan Dundes and Manuel R. Schonhorn found that most collegiate slang can be divided into two areas: social and academic. What slang words or phrases are current on your campus for the following:

SOCIAL	ACADEMIC
one who puts a damper on a party	studying diligently for an examination
a rough and noisy party	an easy course
an effeminate young man	cheating on an examination
a very pretty female date	failing an examination
an unattractive female date	a studious classmate
describing something in superlative terms	wasting time

4. Read the above article and bring a report of it to class. See also Henry Kratz, "What Is College Slang?" *American Speech*, XXXIX (October 1964), 188–195; and Lawrence Poston, "Some Problems in the Study of Campus Slang," XXXIX (May 1964), 114–123.

5. In an article describing slang in Harlem ("Last Word from Soul City," *New York Times Magazine*, [August 23, 1964], p. 62), Junius Griffin lists fourteen different terms for *white man* (*Whitey, ofay, wheat, paleface, anemic, strawman, mop, peckerwood, hunky, Mister Charley, Charley Square, patty, patty boy,* and *them*). Are there as many terms for *Negro* in the white man's vocabulary? Cite some. Before consulting the article, try to give the meaning of the following words:

Soul Brother	charge account	hit
Uncle Tom	kill a brick	out of sight
CORE Cat	bust	snow
Mau Man	fox	pluck
soul food	bombed	

6. Consult the *Dictionary of American Slang*, compiled by Harold Wentworth and Stuart Berg Flexner (New York, 1967), and report to the class the definition(s) and background information given for *brace, brag-rags, calaboose, egghead, freebie, Homberg Heaven, ivory-hunter, rug-cut, stew.*

7. There are more entries in the *Dictionary of American Slang* for *drunken-*

ness than for any other word. How many can you cite? Do any of them indicate *degrees* of intoxication?

8. What examples of "rhyming slang" expressions, like *trig the wig, flash the hash, boo hoo, footsie-wootsie,* and *eager-beaver,* can you cite?

9. Consult *A Dictionary of Slang and Unconventional English,* preferably the 5th edition (London, 1961), compiled by Eric Partridge, and report to the class the definition(s) given for *foal and filly dance, geluk, gentleman, commoner, pegger, smole, swiz.*

10. Examine the *Dictionary of American Underworld Slang,* compiled by Hyman E. Golding and others (New York, 1950). Make notes of ten expressions and their meanings and report them to your class.

10.

WILLIAM FADIMAN

Lingua California Spoken Here

It has been well established that the technical jargon of an industry or profession frequently attains sufficient currency and respectability to be integrated into our everyday language. Lexicographers accept the inevitable, and the lingo and cant of some enterprises are ultimately, if sometimes reluctantly, admitted to the formal haven of the dictionary. But on occasion an individual business vocabulary forms a pattern that never becomes a part of this language accretion process. It remains essentially isolated and aloof, an outlander's speech. Thus an entire system of communication may come into being which only makes sense to its practitioners, the members of the ingroup. It is this private, highly personalized mode of verbal and written intercourse that characterizes the innovative idiom of Hollywood.

The entertainment industry is exceptionally prolific and imaginative in its invention of new words and the transformation of old ones, yet its coinages have never entered fully into contemporary speech. Its flourishing collection of odd phrases, strange condensations, curious abbreviations, and esoteric verbal symbols is relatively unknown to the public. For an uninitiated citizen to try to fathom Hollywood argot or the language of the film trade paper *Variety* is to come unexpectedly upon the Tower of Babel.

The exuberance, buoyancy, and sheer playfulness of show business talk would seem to make it simple to comprehend, but it continues to defy understanding even by the most sophisticated outsiders. Indeed, Hollywood as a whole has hardly been honored for its mastery of language, either oral or written. It is more celebrated for its Mrs. Malaprops (male and female) than for any stray Demosthenes or Cicero it may have in its midst. But, not withstanding this alleged cultural inadequacy, it has given birth to more colorful phrases and neologisms than any other segment of our population unless it be the underworld.

The examples applicable to a particular craft within the film industry itself are diverting and uncommon, but their use is strictly limited to technicians. The domain of the electrician, or "juicer," has its own peculiar vocabulary in which lighting experts are called "gaffers" and installations are made by "riggers" with the aid of assistants dubbed "carbon monkeys." These, however, do not infiltrate normal conversation. This is equally true of their glittering world of lights, in which the largest and the smallest lamps are known respectively as "ash cans" and "inky dinks," a miniature spotlight is a "baby," a diffusion light is a "goon," and still other specific light sources are referred to as "crackerboxes," "friers," and "dishpans." The sound specialists have still another vernacular containing a series of onomatopoetic words identifying imperfections in a sound recording as "bloops," "gargles," and "wow-wows." Unexpected sound defects are styled "gremlins" or "termites," and an uninvited echo is hailed as a "polly."

I pass hurriedly and almost disdainfully over the array of contractions and compressions employed in Hollywood, for these reveal nothing of the dynamism or the pyrotechnics of which show people are capable. Such truncated trivia as "sked" for schedule," "subsid" for subsidiary, "admish" for admission, "spec" for spectacle, "niterie" for night club, "celeb" for celebrity, or "sesh" for session denote nothing but lip laziness. They exist solely by omission of syllables or letters, instances of what grammarians call syllabic syncope. They have neither vitality nor novelty. Nor are they invariably indigenous to Hollywood; they demonstrate little but the same slovenliness of speech found with alarming frequency throughout America.

It is the more generic words of show business parlance, those that reflect ingenuity rather than sloth, that are more revelatory of the bizarre, creative diction of film workers. It is in this realm of colloquialisms, nomenclature, epithets, nicknames, and idioms that Hollywood demonstrates its striking penchant for authentic style and eloquence.

No Hollywood film that has achieved a wide audience is greeted with the drab encomium of being called a hit or a success. It is either a "wow" or a "wham" or a "sock" or a "boff" or a "blitz" or a "sizzler" or a "whammo." It may also be deemed "snappy" or "torrid" or "blooming" or "hotsy" or "tall" or "brisk" or "whopping" or "lusty" or "fancy" or "red hot" or "happy" or "rosy" or "lush," surely a series of sounds that sing their song of triumph more effectively than the lusterless locutions of ordinary acclaim. Should you find this gleaming cavalcade of words inadequate or limiting in any way, a picture that thrives at the box office may also be pronounced "sturdy" or "hefty" or "lively" or "trim" or "stout" or "frisky" or "hardy" or "handsome" or "happy" or "zingy." It may likewise be regarded as "mighty" or "busy" or "sweet" or "lofty" or "slick" or "potent" or "bustling" or "loud" or "soaring" or "crisp" or "bountiful."

Nor is Hollywood any less fecund in describing those films that attain only a modicum of public approval. These are reported as being "modest" or "sad" or "slim" or "tame" or "pale" or "NSG." If they are out-and-out failures it is obvious that they are "nixed" and will have to "exit" or be "bumped" or "folded" or "shuttered" or "pulled" or "shrouded" or "yanked" or do an "el foldo."

It is in the literary sphere of its activities that Hollywood manifests—as indeed it should—an even greater verve and flair. A scenarist does not write a screenplay; he "pens" it. But the composition of a story outline does not bear this distinction, it is invariably "knocked out." Any screenplay that lacks the sheen provided by brilliant dialogue is patently in need of a "dull polish." If, on the other hand, its sophistication and subtlety give rise to a fear that it may not appeal to a mass audience, it is advisable to "dumb it up a little." The inevitable resolution of a carefully posited series of events is succinctly termed the "pay-off." The hero and heroine who quarrel constantly during a film, only to embrace each other lovingly at the finale, are indulging in a fighting romance. No Hollywood writer would consider his screenplay complete unless he included a dramatic device to lend it novelty, a device known as a "gimmick." And this gimmick is especially valuable to strengthen, or "hypo," the central dramatic element, or the "weenie." Should a story seem overcrowded with characters, the process of depopulation is referred to as the "write-out." A narrative concept is not considered or reflected upon or thought about; it is "attacked." Certainly it is never discussed; it is "kicked around."

In areas distinct from writing there are also ingenious and fascinating expressions. A publicity representative carries on his duties as a "flack" or a "tub thumper." Nor, in pursuit of his profession, does he praise a picture; he either "trouts" it or he "puffs" it or he "plugs" it or he gives it "the pitch." The story analysts who read advance proofs of books for film purposes are "galley slaves." Specialists in a field of knowledge do not advise or counsel; they "expert." A deal is "firmed," not closed, and the subsequent contract is a "pact" which is "inked" rather than signed. An option is not exercised; it is "hoisted." A film does not open in a theatre; it either "bows" or "preems," depending upon its commercial importance. Nor does it play for a week; instead it holds for a "stanza" or a "frame." The director does not direct nor the producer produce; they both "helm" or "rein." An assistant director in charge of extras is a "sheepherder" and no performer ever acts; he "thesps" or "emotes." A pretty girl with an abundance of sex appeal is either a "tidy unit" or a "cobra."

This largesse in language reaches new heights when a singer emerges as a "chirper" or "thrush" who "pipes" or "bleats" and "shellacs" or "waxes" a platter when she makes a recording. Much more than incidentally, if the record is a success she enjoys a "disclick." A drive-in theatre is transformed into an "ozoner" by Hollywood's word magic. A conference is a "huddle," and when you participate in it you "make the scene." Any idea is necessarily a "wrinkle." Anything gratuitous is automatically "cutto." A performer is not hired but "lassoed." A dance is a "strut," and every laugh is a "yock." Here is a land where an actor who works simultaneously in two pictures is a "bicycler." Hollywood does not start or begin or commence a picture but "buds" it; it does not disagree with a captious critic but "blasts" him; it eschews flying in favor of "winging" or "avioning" or "skying"; it would rather "lens" a picture than photograph it; and it "Tommys the tanks" instead of having its films exhibited in small towns. (This latter expression has historical basis stemming from the 1880's when more than 150 theatrical companies playing "Uncle Tom's Cabin" were operating throughout the country.)

Perhaps George Bernard Shaw's bequest to create a new alphabet to simplify the English language might better have been granted to Hollywood, for no community displays greater zeal in rendering our tongue more efficiently, effecting economy of expression, and endowing it with color, power, and flexibility.

Cinemese or Hollywoodese may well be a semanticist's horror, a pedagogue's nightmare, and a philologist's despair; but it remains a delight to those thousands who consider it as peculiarly their own. Here is a language to relish and savor and enjoy accessible to everyone but "civilians" or those who are not show folk. To Hollywood, these civilians remain tragic, pathetic, bereft, unenlightened members of the human race doomed to speak only the King's English. Never will they experience the freewheeling glory of the LINGUA CALIFORNIA. Never will these Philistines know the wonder of a tongue that is at one and the same time a wow and a wham and a sock and a boff and a blitz and a sizzler and a whammo!

Vocabulary

accretion, innovative, prolific, coinages, esoteric, dynamism, syncope, indigenous, penchant, encomium, locutions, fecund, gratuitous, captious, bereft

Review Questions

1. Identify Mrs. Malaprop, Demosthenes, Cicero.
2. Name two forces which have exerted an influence on "Lingua California."
3. Cite two characteristics which differentiate show-business vernacular from other types of slang.

Expository Technique

1. In this essay slang is defined mainly by classification and example. Which is the more effective? Why?
2. What techniques does Fadiman use to insure that his definition by illustration does not become tedious?
3. Make an outline of this essay showing its various subdivisions. What transitional devices does the author use to move from one part of his discussion to the next?

Exercises

1. Consult one of the following articles and prepare a summary to present as an oral class report:

Louise Ackerman, "Truckers' Lingo Again," *American Speech*, XXXI (October 1956), 236.

R. W. Apple, Jr., "G.I.'s Vocabulary in Vietnam is Beaucoup Exotic," *New York Times* (November 3, 1965), p. 2.

Al Berkman, *Singer's Glossary of Show Business Jargon* (Hollywood, 1961).

Howard B. Bonham, Jr., *Football Lingo: The Dictionary of Football* (Memphis, 1963).

Maurice A. Crane, "Vox Bop," *American Speech*, XXXIII (October 1958), 223–226.

Marshall W. Frazier, "Truck Drivers' Language," *American Speech*, XXX (May 1955), 91–94.

Robert S. Gold, *A Jazz Lexicon* (New York, 1964).

Roberta Hanley, "Truck Drivers' Language in the Northwest," *American Speech*, XXXVI (December 1961), 271–274.

Zander Hollander, *Baseball Lingo* (New York, 1959).

Peter B. Hukill, "The Spoken Language of Medicine," *American Speech*, XXXVI (May 1961), 145–148.

Bruce Jackson, "Prison Folklore," *Journal of American Folklore*, LXXVIII (October-December 1965), 317–319.

James L. Jackson, "Amelioration of Some Slang Terms: Have Present Teen-agers Gone 'Ape' or 'Chicken'?" *American Speech*, XXXVI (May 1961), 149–151.

Horst Jarka, "The Language of Skiers," *American Speech*, XXXVIII (October 1963), 202–208.

George Monteiro, "Truckers' Language in Rhode Island," *American Speech*, XXXVIII (February 1963), 42–46.

William E. Schultz, "Football Verbiage," *American Speech*, XXVI, (October 1951), 229–231.

David Shulman, "Baseball's Bright Lexicon," *American Speech*, XXVI (February 1951), 29–34.

"Surf's Up!" *Time*, LXXXII (August 9, 1963), 49.

11.

STUART CHASE

Gobbledygook

Said Franklin Roosevelt, in one of his early presidential speeches: "I see one-third of a nation ill-housed, ill-clad, ill-nourished." Translated into standard bureaucratic prose his statement would read:

> It is evident that a substantial number of persons within the Continental boundaries of the United States have inadequate financial resources with which to purchase the products of agricultural communities and industrial establishments. It would appear that for a considerable segment of the population, possibly as much as 33.3333* of the total, there are inadequate housing facilities, and an equally significant proportion is deprived of the proper types of clothing and nutriment.

This rousing satire on gobbledygook—or talk among the bureaucrats— is adapted from a report[1] prepared by the Federal Security Agency in an attempt to break out of the verbal squirrel cage. "Gobbledygook" was coined by an exasperated Congressman, Maury Maverick of Texas, and means using two, or three, or ten words in the place of one, or using a five-syllable word where a single syllable would suffice. Maverick was censuring the forbidding

From *Power of Words*. Copyright, 1953, 1954, by Stuart Chase. Reprinted by permission of Harcourt, Brace & World, Inc.

* Not carried beyond four places.

[1] This and succeeding quotations from F.S.A. report by special permission of the author, Milton Hall.

prose of executive departments in Washington, but the term has now spread to windy and pretentious language in general.

"Gobbledygook" itself is a good example of the way a language grows. There was no word for the event before Maverick's invention; one had to say: "You know, that terrible, involved, polysyllabic language those government people use down in Washington." Now one word takes the place of a dozen.

A British member of Parliament, A. P. Herbert, also exasperated with bureaucratic jargon, translated Nelson's immortal phrase, "England expects every man to do his duty":

England anticipates that, as regards the current emergency, personnel will face up to the issues, and exercise appropriately the functions allocated to their respective occupational groups.

A New Zealand official made the following report after surveying a plot of ground for an athletic field:[2]

It is obvious from the difference in elevation with relation to the short depth of the property that the contour is such as to preclude any reasonable developmental potential for active recreation.

Seems the plot was too steep.

An office manager sent this memo to his chief:

Verbal contact with Mr. Blank regarding the attached notification of promotion has elicited the attached representation intimating that he prefers to decline the assignment.

Seems Mr. Blank didn't want the job.

A doctor testified at an English trial that one of the parties was suffering from "circumorbital haematoma."

Seems the party had a black eye.

In August 1952 the U.S. Department of Agriculture put out a pamphlet entitled: "Cultural and Pathogenic Variability in Single-Condial and Hyphaltip Isolates of Hemlin-Thosporium Turcicum Pass."

Seems it was about corn leaf disease.

On reaching the top of the Finsteraarhorn in 1845, M. Dollfus-Ausset, when he got his breath, exclaimed:

---

[2] This item and the next two are from the piece on gobbledygook by W. E. Farbstein, *New York Times*, March 29, 1953.

The soul communes in the infinite with those icy peaks which seem to have their roots in the bowels of eternity.

Seems he enjoyed the view.

A government department announced:

Voucherable expenditures necessary to provide adequate dental treatment required as adjunct to medical treatment being rendered a pay patient in in-patient status may be incurred as required at the expense of the Public Health Service.

Seems you can charge your dentist bill to the Public Health Service. Or can you?

LEGAL TALK

Gobbledygook not only flourishes in government bureaus but grows wild and lush in the law, the universities, and sometimes among the literati. Mr. Micawber was a master of gobbledygook, which he hoped would improve his fortunes. It is almost always found in offices too big for face-to-face talk. Gobbledygook can be defined as squandering words, packing a message with excess baggage and so introducing semantic "noise." Or it can be scrambling words in a message so that meaning does not come through. The directions on cans, bottles, and packages for putting the contents to use are often a good illustration. Gobbledygook must not be confused with double talk, however, for the intentions of the sender are usually honest.

I offer you a round fruit and say, "Have an orange." Not so an expert in legal phraseology, as parodied by editors of *Labor*:

I hereby give and convey to you, all and singular, my estate and interests, right, title, claim and advantages of and in said orange, together with all rind, juice, pulp, and pits, and all rights and advantages therein . . . anything hereinbefore or hereinafter or in any other deed or deeds, instrument or instruments of whatever nature or kind whatsoever, to the contrary, in any wise, notwithstanding.

The state of Ohio, after five years of work, has redrafted its legal code in modern English, eliminating 4,500 sections and doubtless a blizzard of "whereases" and "hereinafters." Legal terms of necessity must be closely tied to their referents, but the early solons tried to do this the hard way, by adding synonyms. They hoped to trap the physical event in a net of words, but instead they created a mumbo-jumbo beyond the power of the layman, and even many a lawyer, to translate. Legal talk is studded with tautologies, such as "cease and desist," "give and convey," "irrelevant, incompetent, and immaterial." Furthermore, legal jargon is a dead language; it is not spoken and it is not growing. An official of one of the big insurance companies calls their branch of it "bafflegab." Here is a sample from his collection:[3]

> One-half to his mother, if living, if not to his father, and one-half to his mother-in-law, if living, if not to his mother, if living, if not to his father. Thereafter payment is to be made in a single sum to his brothers. On the one-half payable to his mother, if living, if not to his father, he does not bring in his mother-in-law as the next payee to receive, although on the one-half to his mother-in-law, he does bring in the mother or father.

You apply for an insurance policy, pass the tests, and instead of a straightforward "here is your policy," you receive something like this:

> This policy is issued in consideration of the application therefor, copy of which application is attached hereto and made part hereof, and of the payment for said insurance on the life of the above-named insured.

ACADEMIC TALK

The pedagogues may be less repetitious than the lawyers, but many use even longer words. It is a symbol of their calling to prefer Greek and Latin derivatives to Anglo-Saxon. Thus instead of saying: "I like short clear words," many a professor would think it more seemly to say: "I prefer an abbreviated phraseology, distinguished for its lucidity." Your professor is sometimes right, the longer word may carry the meaning better—but not because it is long. Allen Upward in his book *The New Word* warmly advocates Anglo-Saxon English as against what he calls "Mediterranean" English, with its polysyllables built up like a skyscraper.

Professional pedagogy, still alternating between the Middle Ages and modern science, can produce what Henshaw Ward once called the most repellent prose known to man. It takes an iron will to read as much as a page of it. Here is a sample of what is known in some quarters as "pedageese":

> Realization has grown that the curriculum or the experiences of learners change and improve only as those who are most directly involved examine their goals, improve their understandings and increase their skill in performing the tasks necessary to reach newly defined goals. This places the focus upon teacher,

---

[3] Interview with Clifford B. Reeves by Sylvia F. Porter, *New York Evening Post,* March 14, 1952.

lay citizen and learner as partners in curricular improvement and as the individuals who must change, if there is to be curriculum change.

I think there is an idea concealed here somewhere. I think it means: "If we are going to change the curriculum, teacher, parent, and student must all help." The reader is invited to get out his semantic decoder and check on my translation. Observe there is no technical language in this gem of pedageese, beyond possibly the word "curriculum." It is just a simple idea heavily ototverbalized.

In another kind of academic talk the author may display his learning to conceal a lack of ideas. A bright instructor, for instance, in need of prestige may select a common sense proposition for the subject of a learned monograph—say, "Modern cities are hard to live in" and adorn it with imposing polysyllables: "Urban existence in the perpendicular declivities of megalopolis . . ." et cetera. He coins some new terms to transfix the reader— "mega-decibel" or "strato-cosmopolis"—and works them vigorously. He is careful to add a page or two of differential equations to show the "scatter." And then he publishes, with 147 footnotes and a bibliography to knock your eye out. If the authorities are dozing, it can be worth an associate professorship.

While we are on the campus, however, we must not forget that the technical language of the natural sciences and some terms in the social sciences, forbidding as they may sound to the layman, are quite necessary. Without them, specialists could not communicate what they find. Trouble arises when experts expect the uninitiated to understand the words; when they tell the jury, for instance, that the defendant is suffering from "circumorbital haematoma."

Here are two authentic quotations. Which was written by a distinguished modern author, and which by a patient in a mental hospital? You will find the answer at the end of this essay.

1. Have just been to supper. Did not knowing what the woodchuck sent me here. How when the blue blue blue on the said anyone can do it that tries. Such is the presidential candidate.
2. No history of a family to close with those and close. Never shall he be alone to be alone to be alone to be alone to be alone to lend a hand and leave it left and wasted.

REDUCING THE GOBBLE

As government and business offices grow larger, the need for doing something about gobbledygook increases. Fortunately the biggest office in the world is working hard to reduce it. The Federal Security Agency in

Washington,[4] with nearly 100 million clients on its books, began analyzing its communication lines some years ago, with gratifying results. Surveys find trouble in three main areas: correspondence with clients about their social security problems, office memos, official reports.

Clarity and brevity, as well as common humanity, are urgently needed in this vast establishment which deals with disability, old age, and unemployment. The surveys found instead many cases of long-windedness, foggy meanings, clichés, and singsong phrases, and gross neglect of the reader's point of view. Rather than talking to a real person, the writer was talking to himself. "We often write like a man walking on stilts."

Here is a typical case of long-windedness:

Gobbledygook as found: "We are wondering if sufficient time has passed so that you are in a position to indicate whether favorable action may now be taken on our recommendation for the reclassification of Mrs. Blank, junior clerk-stenographer, CAF 2, to assistant clerk-stenographer, CAF 3?"
Suggested improvement: "Have you yet been able to act on our recommendation to reclassify Mrs. Blank?"

Another case:

Although the Central Efficiency Rating Committee recognizes that there are many desirable changes that could be made in the present efficiency rating system in order to make it more realistic and more workable than it now is, this committee is of the opinion that no further change should be made in the present system during the current year. Because of conditions prevailing throughout the country and the resultant turnover in personnel, and difficulty in administering the Federal programs, further mechanical improvement in the present rating system would require staff retraining and other administrative expense which would seem best withheld until the official termination of hostilities, and until restoration of regular operations.

The F.S.A. invites us to squeeze the gobbledygook out of this statement. Here is my attempt:

The Central Efficiency Rating Committee recognizes that desirable changes could be made in the present system. We believe, however, that no change should be attempted until the war is over.

This cuts the statement from 111 to 30 words, about one-quarter of the original, but perhaps the reader can do still better. What of importance have I left out?

Sometimes in a book which I am reading for information—not for

---

[4] Now the Department of Health, Education, and Welfare.

literary pleasure—I run a pencil through the surplus words. Often I can cut a section to half its length with an improvement in clarity. Magazines like *The Reader's Digest* have reduced this process to an art. Are long-windedness and obscurity a cultural lag from the days when writing was reserved for priests and cloistered scholars? The more words and the deeper the mystery, the greater their prestige and the firmer the hold on their jobs. And the better the candidate's chance today to have his doctoral thesis accepted.

The F.S.A. surveys found that a great deal of writing was obscure although not necessarily prolix. Here is a letter sent to more than 100,000 inquirers, a classic example of murky prose. To clarify it, one needs to *add* words, not cut them:

> In order to be fully insured, an individual must have earned $50 or more in covered employment for as many quarters of coverage as half the calendar quarters elapsing between 1936 and the quarter in which he reaches age 65 or dies, whichever first occurs.

Probably no one without the technical jargon of the office could translate this: nevertheless, it was sent out to drive clients mad for seven years. One poor fellow wrote back: "I am no longer in covered employment. I have an outside job now."

Many words and phrases in officialese seem to come out automatically, as if from lower centers of the brain. In this standardized prose people never *get jobs,* they "secure employment"; *before* and *after* become "prior to" and "subsequent to"; one does not *do,* one "performs"; nobody *knows* a thing, he is "fully cognizant"; one never *says,* he "indicates." A great favorite at present is "implement."

Some charming boners occur in this talking-in-one's-sleep. For instance:

> The problem of extending coverage to all employees, regardless of size, is not as simple as surface appearances indicate.
> Though the proportions of all males and females in ages 16–45 are essentially the same . . .
> Dairy cattle, usually and commonly embraced in dairying . . .

In its manual to employees, the F.S.A. suggests the following:

INSTEAD OF	USE
give consideration to	consider
make inquiry regarding	inquire
is of the opinion	believes
comes into conflict with	conflicts
information which is	confidential
of a confidential nature	information

Professional or office gobbledygook often arises from using the passive rather than the active voice. Instead of looking you in the eye, as it were, and writing "This act requires . . ." the office worker looks out of the window and writes: "It is required by this statute that . . ." When the bureau chief says, "We expect Congress to cut your budget," the message is only too clear; but usually he says, "It is expected that the departmental budget estimates will be reduced by Congress."

> *Gobbled:* "All letters prepared for the signature of the Administrator will be single spaced."
> *Ungobbled:* "Single space all letters for the Administrator." (Thus cutting 13 words to 7.)

ONLY PEOPLE CAN READ

The F.S.A. surveys pick up the point that human communication involves a listener as well as a speaker. Only people can read, though a lot of writing seems to be addressed to beings in outer space. To whom are you talking? The sender of the officialese message often forgets the chap on the other end of the line.

A woman with two small children wrote the F.S.A. asking what she should do about payments, as her husband had lost his memory. "If he never gets able to work," she said, "and stays in an institution would I be able to draw any benefits? . . . I don't know how I am going to live and raise my children since he is disable to work. Please give me some information. . . ."

To this human appeal, she received a shattering blast of gobbledygook, beginning, "State unemployment compensation laws do not provide any benefits for sick or disabled individuals . . . in order to qualify an individual must have a certain number of quarters of coverage . . ." et cetera, et cetera. Certainly if the writer had been thinking about the poor woman he would not have dragged in unessential material about old-age insurance. If he had pictured a mother without means to care for her children, he would have told her where she might get help—from the local office which handles aid to dependent children, for instance.

Gobbledygook of this kind would largely evaporate if we thought of our messages as two way—in the above case, if we pictured ourselves talking on the doorstep of a shabby house to a woman with two children tugging at her skirts, who in her distress does not know which way to turn.

RESULTS OF THE SURVEY

The F.S.A. survey showed that office documents could be cut 20 to 50 per cent, with an improvement in clarity and a great saving to taxpayers in paper and payrolls.

A handbook was prepared and distributed to key officials.[5] They read it, thought about it, and presently began calling section meetings to discuss gobbledygook. More booklets were ordered, and the local output of documents began to improve. A Correspondence Review Section was established as a kind of laboratory to test murky messages. A supervisor could send up samples for analysis and suggestions. The handbook is now used for training new members; and many employees keep it on their desks along with the dictionary. Outside the Bureau some 25,000 copies have been sold (at 20 cents each) to individuals, governments, business firms, all over the world. It is now used officially in the Veterans Administration and in the Department of Agriculture.

The handbook makes clear the enormous amount of gobbledygook which automatically spreads in any large office, together with ways and means to keep it under control. I would guess that at least half of all the words circulating around the bureaus of the world are "irrelevant, incompetent, and immaterial"—to use a favorite legalism; or are just plain "unnecessary"—to ungobble it.

My favorite story of removing the gobble from gobbledygook concerns the Bureau of Standards at Washington. I have told it before but perhaps the reader will forgive the repetition. A New York plumber wrote the Bureau that he had found hydrochloric acid fine for cleaning drains, and was it harmless? Washington replied: "The efficacy of hydrochloric acid is indisputable, but the chlorine residue is incompatible with metallic permanence."

The plumber wrote back that he was mighty glad the Bureau agreed with him. The Bureau replied with a note of alarm: "We cannot assume responsibility for the production of toxic and noxious residues with hydrochloric acid, and suggest that you use an alternate procedure." The plumber was happy to learn that the Bureau still agreed with him.

Whereupon Washington exploded: "Don't use hydrochloric acid; it eats hell out of the pipes!"

Note: The second quotation on page 178 comes from Gertrude Stein's *Lucy Church Amiably.*

[5] By Milton Hall.

Vocabulary

adjunct, literati, solons, tautologies, pedagogues, lucidity, declivities, megalopolis, prolix, efficacy, toxic, noxious

Review Questions

1. Find examples of the use of definition, illustration, and classification in Chase's essay.
2. Who was Mr. Micawber?
3. How does Chase differentiate between gobbledygook and double talk?
4. Make a list of three ways in which Chase believes we can avoid gobbledygook in writing.

Exercises

1. Translate each of the following passages into its original form. Note in each case that the selections lose effectiveness in the gobbledygook version.
   a. Vermilion-hued cumulus formations observed during matinal hours cause considerable agitation to mariners, while the appearance of a visible garnet mass of vapor during nocturnal periods produces euphoria among those who traverse aqueous bodies.
   b. All substances which exhibit a reflection of light particles emanating in dazzling profusion are not necessarily composed of a dense, metallic, chemical element which possesses a high degree of ductility and malleability.
   c. A pair offers possibility of companionship, while triple identities considered as an aggregate assume the overpowering characteristics of a multitude.
   d. Lavation is in proximity to a state of piety.
   e. A warm-blooded, plumed vertebrate which activates its energies quickly from a state of nocturnal hibernation is able to seize by force or stratagem the slender, soft-bodied, segmented animal which lives by burrowing underground.
   f. An overabundance of culinary experts often vitiates the bouillon.
   g. The art of combining vocal or instrumental sounds or tones in varying melody, harmony, rhythm, and timbre in order to form structurally complete expressive compositions mollifies the uncultivated primitive.
   h. Individuals who inhabit domiciles composed of frangible substances containing silicon compounds should be wary of casting hard nonmetallic mineral matter.
   i. Undue velocity produces lavish prodigality.
   j. It is not considered prudent to enumerate an individual's stock of domestic fowl in advance of the termination of the period of gestation.

k. It is not judicious for an individual to engage in lachrymation concerning an unintentional overflow of lacteous substances.

l. A nonmetallic mineral substance of definite density which is in the process of periodical revolution in orbit does not assemble quantities of lichenous material.

m. A group of three *mus musculi,* afflicted with the distressing malady of being unable to perceive with their ocular organs, has been observed to demonstrate unusual powers of locomotion and extreme agility. This triumvirate pursued the spouse of an agrarian developer, who severed the animals' caudal appendages with a sharp utensil used in the slaughter or dressing of animals; and it has been observed by onlookers that a spectacle of this particular rarity exceeded any experience they had ever encountered by its sheer singularity.

2. Try to find examples of gobbledygook in one of the following fields: art, education, law, medicine, politics. In each example be prepared to show how the passage could have been better expressed in fewer words and/or less pompous diction.

3. The cliché is a different kind of stylistic shortcoming (see George Orwell's essay in Part One and Bergen and Cornelia Evans's definition on pages 98–99). Its trite and stale qualities are amusingly revealed in a concentrated way in the following dialogue, "The Cliché Expert Testifies on Politics,"* by Frank Sullivan. Do the examples Sullivan uses fit the Evans's definition of the cliché? Would you disagree with Sullivan about the cliché-status of any of these expressions?

Q. MR. ARBUTHNOT, I hear you've become a campaign orator.

A. Fellow American, you have heard correctly. I've been on the stump all fall.

Q. In that case you ought to be up on your campaign-oratory clichés.

A. Well, sir, it is not my wont to brag, but I believe I may say with all due modesty that I can point with pride and view with alarm as sententiously and bombastically as any senator who ever thrust one arm in his frock coat and with the other called upon high heaven to witness the perfidy of the Other Party.

Q. Describe your candidate, Mr. Arbuthnot.

A. My candidate is a man four-square, a true representative of the people, a leader worthy of the trust which has been placed in him, and a standard-bearer who will carry the banner of our ga-reat and ga-lorious party to victory.

Q. Is he a man of prophetic vision?

A. He is indeed. He is also a man of sterling character and a champion of the rights of the people.

Q. What kind of champion?

A. A stalwart champion.

Q. What is he close to?

---

* From *A Rock in Every Snowball* by Frank Sullivan, by permission of Little, Brown and Co. Copyright 1945 by Frank Sullivan.

A. The soil.

Q. Is his name Jones?

A. It is not. I have nothing against Mr. Jones personally, but I can't see where he's fitted to be President.

Q. Why not?

A. He may be a first-rate businessman, but what does he know about government?

Q. Then your candidate's name is Brown.

A. Not at all. I'm a lifelong Democrat and I've always voted the straight Democratic ticket, but this year I'm taking a walk.

Q. Why?

A. Because old party lines are disappearing. What this country needs is a *businessman* in the White House.

Q. Then your man is Jones, after all.

A. Jones is all right personally, but I don't like the crowd he's tied up with.

Q. What crowd?

A. Oh, the public utilities, the Old Guard, and so on. Besides, what does he know about foreign affairs?

Q. Mr. Arbuthnot, I can't figure out *where* you stand. Let's get back to your campaign-oratory clichés. What kind of questions have you been discussing?

A. Burning questions. Great, underlying problems.

Q. What have you arrayed yourself against?

A. The forces of reaction. There must be no compromise with the forces of reaction.

Q. And now, Mr. Arbuthnot, may I ask you to characterize these times?

A. These are troubled times, sir. We are met here today in an hour of grave national crisis.

Q. What do you, as a campaign orator, propose to do in this grave hour?

A. I shall demand, and denounce, and dedicate. I shall take stock. I shall challenge, pledge, stress, fulfill, indict, exercise, accuse, call upon, affirm, and reaffirm.

Q. Reaffirm what?

A. My undying faith in the principles laid down by the Founding Fathers. And I shall exercise eternal vigilance that our priceless heritage may be safeguarded.

Q. Admirable, Mr. Arbuthnot. And that reminds me: What is it you campaign orators rise above?

A. Narrow partisanship. We must place the welfare of our country above all other considerations, including our desire to win.

Q. Mr. Arbuthnot, how do you campaign orators dedicate yourselves?

A. We dedicate ourselves anew to the task that lies before us.

Q. How does your party approach this task?

A. With a solemn realization of the awful responsibility that rests upon us in this hour of unprecedented national stress.

Q. When our country is—

A. Sore beset by economic ills.

Q. How else do you approach the task?

A. With supreme confidence that our ga-reat party will prove worthy of its ga-lorious tradition.

Q. And if your party failed to approach the task in that spirit, Mr. Arbuthnot, would you say that—

A. It would indeed be recreant to its sacred trust.

Q. Ah. But you feel that it won't be recreant?

A. No, my fellow American, a tha-a-o-u-sand times no! The ga-reat party of Washington, and Jefferson, and Lincoln, and Wilson, and Roosevelt, and Cleveland, and Grant, Garfield, Hayes, and Arthur will not fail our country in this, her hour of need.

Q. Hurrah for Jones!

A. The candidate of Big Business?

Q. Then hurray for Brown!

A. He wants to be a dictator.

Q. Then three rousing cheers for Green!

A. If elected, he couldn't even control his own party.

Q. Then hurray for Smith!

A. Elect him and you'll *never* get rid of him.

Q. I'm afraid there's no pleasing you today, Mr. Arbuthnot. Would you mind telling me who's to blame for our country's hour of need?

A. The Other Party.

Q. What has the Other Party proved?

A. Its utter incapacity to govern. Its record is an unbroken record of failure, of forgotten campaign pledges, of callous disregard for the welfare of the country.

Q. What is the Other Party undermining?

A. The American way of life. It is spending vast sums of the taxpayers' money.

Q. For what?

A. To build up a huge political machine. It has aroused class hatred. Fellow American, in this solemn hour, when the sacred institutions of democracy are challenged on every side and the world is rent by strife, I charge the Other Party with having betrayed the pee-pul of these Yew-nited States.

Q. What must the pee-pul do?

A. They must rise in their wrath and elect my candidate.

Q. Mr. Arbuthnot, perhaps you'll tell us just what kind of leader the hour calls for?

A. A leader who will lead this country out of the wilderness, eliminate waste and extravagance in government, do away with red tape and bureaucratic inefficiency, solve the problem of unemployment, improve living conditions, develop purchasing power, raise the standard of living, provide better housing, and insure national defense by building a navy and air force second to none.

Q. What about the farmer?

A. The farmer must have relief.

Q. What kind of relief?

A. Farm relief. Labor must have the right to organize. Economy must be the watchword. Mounting deficits must cease; so must these raids on the public treasury. I view with alarm the huge and unwarranted increase in our national debt. Generations yet unborn! Those who would undermine our sacred institutions! Bore from within! Freedom of speech! Monroe doctrine! I call upon every patriotic American—

Q. Regardless of race or creed?

A. Be quiet! . . . regardless of race or creed, from the snow-capped peaks of the Rockies—

Q. To the pine-clad shores of Maine?

A. Shut *up!* . . . to the pine-clad shores of Maine to have faith in the American way of life. Subversive doctrines! Undesirable aliens! Lincoln!

Q. What kind of Lincoln?

A. The Immortal Lincoln! The Immortal Washington! The Immortal Jefferson! The time for evasions has passed. We must face the facts, put our shoulders to the wheel, put our house in order, meet the challenge of the dictators, carry aloft the torch of liberty, fulfill our high destiny, face the future with confidence, and march forward to victory at the polls in November.

a. This essay defines *cliché* by illustrating it. Is the meaning of the term clear by the end of the dialogue?

b. It is generally agreed that clichés weaken writing and should be avoided. But whether a particular phrase is to be regarded as a cliché or as an acceptable idiomatic expression is sometimes disputed. In this connection, read Bergan Evans, "Fell Swoop on a Fine Cliché Kettle," *New York Times Magazine* (July 27, 1958), pp. 13 ff., and the reply to Evans in the same publication by Joseph Wood Krutch (August 31, 1958), pp. 13 ff. Summarize each article for an oral class report, noting especially Krutch's disagreement with Evans.

c. Frank Sullivan has written a number of other amusing articles for the *New Yorker* Magazine illustrating the clichés used in writing about various subjects. Read one of the articles listed below and, using it as a model, prepare a similar one of your own for some interest or activity with which you are familiar.

"The Cliché Expert Testifies on the Atom" (November 17, 1945), pp. 27–29.
"The Cliché Expert Testifies on Campaign Oratory" (September 4, 1948), pp. 20–22.
"The Cliché Expert Testifies on the Tabloids" (October 2, 1948), pp. 26–28.
"The Cliché Expert Testifies on the Drama" (October 6, 1951), pp. 32–34.

d. Read one of the following short stories and prepare a brief oral class report on the use and the effect of clichés in the story.

O. Henry, "Calloway's Code," *The Complete Works of O. Henry* (Garden City, 1937).
Ring Lardner, "Some Like Them Cold," *Round Up: The Stories of Ring Lardner* (New York, 1933).
George Milburn, "The Apostate," *No More Trumpets* (New York, 1953).

The Dictionary

12.

JACQUES BARZUN

What is a Dictionary?

Webster's Third New International Dictionary (which I refuse to call W3 as if life were too short for words) has been in circulation more than a year and has received from the start the kind of critical attention that a work of that size and importance deserves. There have been reviews, descriptive, admiring and hostile; there have been newspaper editorials, including one in the *New York Times* which exemplified by parody the doctrine of the new edition; and there have been articles in literary and general magazines, which pointed a moral while treating the fundamental question: What is a dictionary? Mr. Dwight MacDonald in the *New Yorker* and Mr. Wilson Follett in the *Atlantic* delivered, with abundant examples, the most philosophic of the attacks on the new work, and Mr. Bergen Evans, among others, offered rebuttal and counterattack. Both sides have written with heat —the heat of indignation—except when they meant to be freezingly cold with the cold of contempt.

All this is gratifying. For it shows that despite the many signs of linguistic indifference in daily life, some people at least still feel strongly about language and can be roused to battle about it. The debate has not been confined to print, and it is not over; it is very much alive in living rooms, students' rooms, editorial rooms. When it came up as a subject of interest at a meeting of the board of *The American Scholar,* everyone present felt that its importance warranted notice from one of us, and I was delegated to express the board's "position." This was extraordinary, for more than one reason. Never in my experience has the Editorial Board desired to reach a

Reprinted from THE AMERICAN SCHOLAR, XXXII, No. 2 (Spring 1963). Copyright © 1962 by the United Chapters of Phi Beta Kappa. By permission of the publishers.

position; it respects without effort the individuality of each member and contributor, and it expects and relishes diversity. What is even more remarkable, none of those present had given the new dictionary more than a casual glance, yet each one felt that he knew how he stood on the issue that the work presented to the public.

That astonishing and possibly premature concurrence within a group of writers whose work almost invariably exhibits judicial tolerance and the scholarly temper defines the nature and character of the new Webster: it is undoubtedly the longest political pamphlet ever put together by a party. Its 2662 large pages embody—and often preach by suggestion—a dogma that far transcends the limits of lexicography. I have called it a political dogma because it makes assumptions about the people and because it implies a particular view of social intercourse. This is indeed why any page of the work provokes immediate resistance or assent. No one who thinks at all can keep from being a partisan. And the explosive charge contained in the definitions and examples (let alone the prefatory matter) is reinforced by the intellectual theory that underlies the political and social views. That theory is the scientism of the linguists, which is bound to divide thinking people still more sharply into adherents and enemies. The issue comes down to this: Are the products of the human mind (in this instance language) to be treated like natural objects? The answer Yes means that whatever "the people" utter is a "linguistic fact" to be recorded, cherished, preferred to any reason or tradition. The new dictionary might thus be called avant-garde, not to say surrealist. To which its detractors say: "It is voluminous, but gives no light."

No doubt this explanation of the passions aroused by the new Webster will seem to some far-fetched and abstract. How can the definition of a simple word such as "of" betray the political and moral biases I have inferred? Quite simply: the populism and scientism of the new lexicon appear together, for example, in the twenty-first use of "of," as an alteration of "have"—"I should of come." This is given as representing, "especially in written dialogue, a supposed dialectal or substandard speech." The word "supposed" is laden with prejudice, and one is amazed at the suggestion that this "of" occurs in writing only. Since this usage occurs frequently in speech, as everybody knows, one is bound to wonder whether its inclusion in a famous dictionary does not confer upon it the lexicographer's blessing. Certainly there is an implied defense of these "of's," who are also the have nots.

So much for democratic feeling. Now to its concomitant. The previous illustrations of "of" are each introduced by the designation: "used as a function word to indicate . . . ." The phrase is therefore repeated twenty times, although the word being defined—"of"—is never repeated but is represented by the sign ~. This is science. In the same way proper names and adjectives are never capitalized but carry the indication "usu. cap." This is system. Science and system play throughout the work a strongly rhetorical part. They do not save space; much less do they serve the reader's convenience. The use of a sign for the word we are interested in is a subtle attack on The Word, just as it is a blow struck against the sentence. The dictionary ceases to be a book for readers interested in words and sentences; it becomes an imitation ～ the technical handbooks ～ physics and chemistry. By this means words are stripped of a quality they have had since the dawn of civilization and are reduced to algebraic signs. I am not using a figure of speech: it is a mathematical yearning that induces the linguist to invent the term "function word" for preposition, conjunction, auxiliary verb and the like; just as it is algebraic and not verbal usage that leads the modern pedant to insist that we write: "In his *The Wasteland* . . . ," as if the joining of "his" and "the" were indispensable to an equation that would come out wrong by the omission of either.

These common examples bring us to the questions implied in What is a dictionary? namely: What is language? What are words? The so-called scientific doctrine which has killed grammar and rhetoric in the schools asserts a number of incompatible things about language: that it is a system of sounds used for communication and therefore changeable at will; that it is a natural entity which grows and evolves, and therefore follows natural, not arbitrary laws. Linguistics, it is clear, is playing at technology as well as science. It goes on to teach that the sounds of language can be given symbolic representation in written forms, thanks to which the evolution of both sounds and forms can be traced over millennia and across continents; yet the science also holds that language is speech and speech alone; hence the ways and opinions of writers have no more importance in linguistics than ideas have in Marxist materialism: both are the empty froth carried down the powerful stream of history. It follows that the English language comprises whatever is intelligible to any group that thinks it is speaking English—Puerto Rican children in New York, native bureaucrats in India or Nigeria, Ozark mountaineers, B.B.C. announcers, judges of the United States Supreme Court, and unfortunate idiots with cleft palates.

There is undeniable grandeur in this acceptance of Babel, which strives to emulate the scientist's acceptance of all phenomena. And it is indeed true that since the pioneer work of Henry Sweet, the prototype of Higgins in Shaw's *Pygmalion,* much has been learned as a result of applying the scientific hypothesis to speech. But there are difficulties in the attempt to equate physical events and language, and it is in trying to escape these difficulties that the linguists whose theology is embodied in the new Webster become arbitrary and absurd. Their scientific detachment deserts them; they begin to champion the underdog linguistic forms against the socially approved, and they show the precariousness of their position by growing abusive and baring fangs when it is challenged.

A science obviously cannot admit that from the outset language is something more than speech, and words something more than a device for communication. Words are nevertheless anything but neutral symbols like numbers. They breed fancies and sport individual features. Feelings attach to words, as may be tested by calling a stranger a harsh name. And the feeling is not in the word, since the same word in an identical tone may be applied to a friend with affectionate intent and be received by him with equanimity. Nor, despite all the new schoolbooks on Structural English, does clear communication suffice to establish a form of words as part of the language. The latest Webster can imply by its hospitableness to barbarism that there is no such thing as good English, no correctness in grammar, syntax or diction, yet it is not English to say: "What age have you?" "How much hour is it?" "It makes cold this night." The system of words and ideas that constitutes a language has quirks of its own and remains a mystery. It *looks* as if it could be changed at will; it *looks* as if it followed natural laws—vowel shifts, slurrings, inversion and substitution of consonants, et cetera; it *looks* as if logic had no hand in its alterations; it *looks* as if reasoning were at work making forms alike and introducing distinctions; it *looks* as if mere repetition in use warranted a word or a form; it *looks* as if convenience were an irresistible cause of change—all of these are true and all false. The merest glance at history proves and disproves each of these propositions. "Invite" as a noun has been in use for two hundred and fifty years without becoming good usage. Our Webster itself calls it "now chiefly dial," which is, I think, an error. In my experience the word is colloquial and faintly depreciatory; but why so, when it is formed from the verb as regularly as "request" or "demand," and when it is (or would be) equally convenient? No one can tell. Again, "them" as a demonstrative adjective ("Hand me them pliers") is certainly the people's choice. It was so as far back as Chaucer, yet the majority vote it has obtained in every generation still leaves it, in Webster's term, "substand."

Evidently caprice is at work, a whim of iron which no scientific observation or dogmatic authority can reduce to order. But what one concludes from this can take one in divergent ways: one can become a linguist or remain sensitive to the varieties of linguistic experience. The linguist blinds himself to the truth that language is a very mixed affair, like art, love, government, history; which is to say life at its most comprehensive. Language indeed comes closest to being the envelope of life; it is the web, certainly, of conscious life. As such it is not abstractly detachable, like the segments of physical experience conveniently cut off for study by science. This difference explains why it is that the linguist has no sooner affirmed the folly of a normative grammar and dictionary than he is forced to mutter "substandard" at every other word. In this, to be sure, the linguist is a child of the age: "incorrect" being a horrid, undemocratic term, he replaces it by "substandard," which is fraternal and scientific. This is the formula by which we have turned in the poor in exchange for the underprivileged and backward countries for undeveloped areas. But little is changed in fact. There is a norm, a standard, in the languages of civilized nations, for the same reason that there are manners and customs. The difficulty of ascertaining at any moment what is right in these modes of action does not abolish the idea of rightness, any more than the variability of manners abolishes manners themselves. Many people neglect to say "please" and "thank you," but their omission does not constitute a new absence of norm; it only defines their boorishness. And this perception is not limited to the last effete representatives of a dying civilization, or books of etiquette would not be the perennial best sellers that they are. One of the chief vices of the new Webster is that it flouts the strong impulse toward rightness that animates the very masses whom the lexicographer means to flatter by his laxity charged with condescension.

To be charitable as well as fair we must ask whether the new lexicography is not in fact responding to contemporary tendencies in ourselves, rather than imparting to us the results of objective research. Take the assumption that speech is primary. The proposition is obviously true historically, but is it true as a social fact after three thousand years of written literature? It was surely not self-evident at the beginnings of lexicography, which was undertaken by and for the literate. Anyone who uses words by profession knows how important it is to preserve language from confusion through misuse. A writer's or an orator's difficulties come from the inadequacies of the audience as much as from those of the tongue he uses. And when literature has slowly clarified his medium for him, the good writer feels that he has entered into a contract with all his predecessors *not* to debase the coinage they have bequeathed to him.

This view might still prevail if modern literature itself had not first become impatient, "realistic," and tried with ever greater fidelity to reproduce the vocables of the marketplace. The playwright has always done this by fits and starts, yet without influencing the learned's notion of language. It was Scott and the novel descended from him that introduced first "dial" and then "colloq" and finally "vulg," to a point where one must keep Partridge's *Dictionary of Slang* by one's side and learn thieves' cant to appreciate the highest forms of the new in prose or poetry. From the moment that reality is equated with the average, science and democracy and linguistic devaluation form a single cultural tendency.

For it is this translation of reality into realism that undermines both formality and form in the use of language. In the novels of Sinclair Lewis, whose ear for the demotic was remarkable, phonetic renderings often replace words and phrases; Babbitt is made to say: "Zizesaying." Similarly, when the new Webster seeks examples of adjectival "them" it quotes the novels of educated writers—Helen Eustis and Helen Glasgow. The whole nineteenth century, the whole Romantic revolution in poetry, lies behind the accelerated deformation of words which the new linguist thinks he discovered by scientific methods. At one end of the span, Wordsworth and Victor Hugo democratize literature by adapting the tone, diction and subjects of street ballads, and at the other end, Lewis Carroll, Mallarmé and Joyce put the quietus to syntax and usage by punning and distorting and confusing the words of the tribe.

In this task of demolition they were aided by the engineers and tradesmen who were forging new words out of half-understood Greek and Latin roots to denote processes and products. The litter of "telephone," "Kodak," and their kind continues to increase, adding acronyms and portmanteaus (for example, Unicef and Puritron) in shapes and in numbers that will soon require a separate glossary, a second volume of Webster.

Even before that point is reached, we grasp what the modern answer is to the question we started with: What is a dictionary? As *Webster's Third New International* shows, a dictionary is a heterogeneous list of vocables, abbreviations, acronyms, ready-made phrases, trade and proper names, which have been selected on current populist-scientific principles as constituting "the language." Such a dictionary is certainly not a list of the words generally spoken by speakers of English. DNOC is not a word, nor does it stand for a spoken portion of the language, since it represents "dinitro-ortho-cresol," which is unspeakable. The so-called dictionary is thus in part a manual of formulas; in part a handbook for editors, scientists and other professionals. For the under-read it is also a semi-encyclopedia which has an entry for "dialectical materialism," and one for "fermat's principle," in which it is careful to decapitalize Fermat at the head of the entry and recapitalize him within, adding the date of his death.

This new-style dictionary of the English language includes many foreign words other than those that have been naturalized into English—the unpronounceable *oeuvre,* for example. In such cases, which are relatively numerous, popular approval does not seem to function as the guardian at the gates. But then profession and performance are hard to match in a book so strangely conceived. I have shown that the criterion of spoken usage— "language is speech"—breaks down at the point where the thousands of many-syllabled scientific compounds irrupt and overrun the page. The same criterion is disregarded in the pronunciations offered after such words as are, in fact, spoken. For these pronunciations, given in a factitious phonetic alphabet, are widely deviated from by speakers of English. From Virginia to Texas, millions of people regularly produce in common words sounds that are unknown to this "international" dictionary of "the English language." The pronunciations that it does give are consequently an arbitrary norm for which observable reality gives dubious warrant.

On the plane of observation itself, this composite glossary is equally questionable in its reports. It grows garrulous about "ain't," saying: "though disapproved by many and more common in less educated speech, used orally in most parts of the U.S. by many cultivated speakers, esp. in the phrase *ain't I*." This statement goes counter not only to my experience but also to that of a dozen "more educated" people whom I have asked. Except in the jocular mode, "ain't" is never used by those Webster calls cultivated. And one is brought up short by the introduction of these categories. Do they not violate the scientific-populist scheme? More or less educated to do what?— cultivated in what respect? Could it be "educated to speak well and write correctly? cultivated in the use of English words and grammatical forms?" No linguist ever answers such impertinent questions. The structuralist keeps saying that whatever choice and arrangement of words is "effective" is or will be good speech. The lexicographer, who eagerly records as alternative meanings of a word the misconceptions of the illiterate, repeats that any meaning can be attached to any sound, so why fuss as long as we manage to "communicate." But effectiveness is never gauged or defined, and the loss of distinctions, of precision, of elegance is never brought within the scope of "communication." It is mere taste—aesthetics no less.

This willful neglect puts language in a unique position, alien to science, art and nature too. We shore up the hills and contain the flooding streams, but we let language rip, recognizing nothing as error. The lexicographer would not tolerate error in the *scientific* vocabulary: use "absorb" for "adsorb" and he will pounce on you; no use pleading that the two words are so much alike. But use "connive" for "contrive," and he will applaud— the language is growing! It's alive and evolving! Growth apparently means making two words do the work of one: "fortuitous" and "fortunate"; "precipitous" and "precipitate"; "disinterested" and "uninterested"; "infer" and "imply"; "companion" and "cohort"; "complete" and "fulsome"; "difference" and "differential"; "elementary" and "elemental"—in short, a later Webster could probably cut in half the abundance of the old English vocabulary and no one would feel the differential.

The social forces and private emotions that promote this general decay, misnamed growth or evolution, are not peculiar to the English language and were not invented by the science-proud partisans of linguistic anarchy. English has in fact resisted longer than other modern European languages, such as French, perhaps because English was more elastic and hybrid to begin with. I cannot hope to give here a full view of influences that have been undoing the work of the lettered generations. The triumph of the written word at the expense of oral traditions; the enlargement of the electorate; the establishment of public schools for all; the spread of specialism with its attendant jargons; the new pride of the common man, which makes him a pedant; the learned ignorance of technicians and tradesmen; the singular ideals and conventions developed by the press; the gigantic growth of advertising keeping pace with that of industry; the corresponding revolt against standardization, which incites everyone to be "himself" by defying good manners, to be "creative" by distorting language, and to flout the machine by revelling in symbol and metaphor—all these things and more that could be pointed to have played a part in the impoverishment that our language discloses about our life.

Webster's Third New International Dictionary of the English Language is thus the representation between covers of a cultural revolution. From its tendentious title—the work being neither Webster's nor international, and only now and then a dictionary—to its silly systems and petty pedantries, the book is a faithful record of our emotional weaknesses and intellectual disarray. It should contribute mightily to that healthful annihilation of a way of thought and feeling, to that *tabula rasa* from which new cultural movements spring. Meanwhile the book belongs in every "cultivated" reader's library of humor. I did not read every page, but at least once in every page that I read I laughed.

Vocabulary

lexicography, dogma, partisan, avant-garde, surrealist, detractors, laden, concomitant, millennia, depreciatory, caprice, effete, flouts, bequeathed, vocables, demotic, quietus, acronyms, portmanteaus, factitious, garrulous, jocular, tendentious, *tabula rasa*

Review Questions

1. What inconsistencies does Barzun find in *Webster's Third New International Dictionary?*
2. Compile a list of Barzun's objections to *Webster's Third.*
3. Do you agree that the compilers of *Webster's Third* are "science-proud partisans of linguistic anarchy"?
4. Near the end of the essay Barzun lists nine forces that have "been undoing the work of the lettered generations." Briefly show how each has operated in this regard. Is it possible to stop, retard, or alter these forces?
5. What is Barzun's definition of a dictionary?

Expository Technique

1. What is the tone of this essay? Find examples of sarcasm, humor, and irony.

2. What is the effect of lumping together as speakers of English Ozark mountaineers, BBC announcers, Supreme Court justices, and idiots with cleft palates?

3. Barzun claims that *caprice* is at work in the compilation of *Webster's Third*. Why do you think he selected this word rather than one of its synonyms *vagary, whim,* or *fancy?*

(Exercises relating to Essays 12 and 13 are on pages 199–203.)

13.

PHILIP B. GOVE

About the Dictionary

The function of a dictionary is to help the person who consults it. A thousand people who consult it could have a thousand different reasons. Predictably, some will be helped and some will not be. The consulter of a dictionary should not open it to find out who won the Ivy League football championship two years ago or how to make New England rum. He would not find out how many pheasants a licensed hunter can shoot in South Dakota in one season or what towns in Kansas have local option. He would not discover how many sonnets Wordsworth wrote or how many Terry clocks are still ticking. If he were to look expectantly for such information, he would at best merely be revealing his utter unfamiliarity with dictionaries; more seriously he could be disqualifying himself for a scholarship.

If, however, a consulter wants to know what use Eleazar Wheelock might have had for a *Gradus ad Parnassum,* he might find the answer in a dictionary. He might be able to find the population of South Dakota and the area of Kansas. Even these questions, however, lie in a special area not

Reprinted from *THE AMERICAN SCHOLAR,* XXXII, No. 4 (Autumn 1963). Copyright © 1962 by the United Chapters of Phi Beta Kappa. By permission of the publishers.

strictly lexical. If a dictionary expressly restricts itself to the generic vocabulary, a consulter who looks in it for nongeneric information is asking it to perform a service for which it was not built. I am restricting my statement about the function of a dictionary to our generic English vocabulary.

An ideal dictionary would seem to me to be one in which a genuine consulter can find right off a satisfactory answer to a proper question. The matter of a proper question should concern spelling, pronunciation, etymology, meaning, function, or status, for these are the six kinds of information generally given explicitly or implicitly for each word. By far the most important of these is meaning, which for most words is the chief concern of a lexicographer. Status is of three kinds: (1) temporal (if a word is obsolete or archaic, it is so labeled; otherwise it is current); (2) regional (if a word is found in only one region of the English-speaking world, it is so labeled; otherwise it is general); and (3) stylistic (if a word is in some degree clearly not standard, this may be indicated by a label or note).

A genuine consulter is one who needs to know something about a word he has heard or read or who wants to know how to use a word in speaking or writing. Since readers in our civilization outnumber writers several thousand to one, the most important function of a dictionary is to help a reader to find out what a word means so that a passage read can be understood, so that what its author intended can be figured out. A consulter of a dictionary who does not have a context into which to fit a word he looks up is not a genuine consulter. He may be motivated by a desire to criticize or to find out how a word is treated, or by several other secondary or tertiary interests. He is not looking in a dictionary for a key to open a door to understanding. His findings, although sometimes made articulate, if not vociferous, are relatively trivial.

If a consulter is a writer, his dictionary readers are likely to put on a particular word in a particular context. A dictionary does not undertake to tell him what someone thinks his readers ought to understand. There is no point in telling anybody that the word *arrival* ought to be reserved for a "coming to shore by water" if no one understands or uses it that way. A dictionary is not concerned with telling a writer how he should write. That is a writer's business, in which he serves as his own arbiter.

The difficulties of using a dictionary are often attributed to the dictionary maker, as if he were responsible for all the complications in the language. Our language is infinitely complex and difficult. No one person can ever master it. There is no formula for making it easy and simple and no panacea for those who stumble around in it in a daze. The reducing of this complexity to some kind of ordered presentation which can most of the time give a consulter the guidance he seeks is one of the lexicographer's chief accomplishments. When a dictionary fails a consulter, it is often either the consulter or the language which is responsible.

For whom is an unabridged dictionary made? Not for foreigners and not for children. The definitions in it are not written under an assumption that the consulter may be totally unacquainted with the company a word keeps. Outside of contests and quizzes (or bets) words do not exist by themselves; they are surrounded by other words and live in a context of associated and related ideas, from which a consulter takes to the dictionary some little bit of understanding. The definition he finds helps him to fit a word into a frame. If it fails to help him, because the subject is difficult or unfamiliar, he may give up, for lack of ability or background. Not all words are for everybody. Definitions in an unabridged dictionary are written for adults of all kinds and degrees of interest and intelligence. Yet every user of the language is continually getting into semantic problems over his depth.

For the majority of situations in which a dictionary is consulted for meaning, words may be roughly divided into three groups: (1) Hard words which circumstances make immediately important: "The doctor prescribed synthesized *cortisone.*" "*Recidivism* is a serious criminal problem in some urban communities." "*Existentialism* is a subjective philosophy." (2) Words frequently seen, usually understood loosely, but suddenly or recurrently unstable (for the individual): *synthesize, urban* and *subjective* in the preceding sentences. (3) Common familiar words which unexpectedly need to be differentiated (*break* vs. *tear, shrub* vs. *bush*) or specifically clarified, such as *fable, adventure, shake, door, remainder, evil.* Most people get by without having to clarify these common words in the third group until they become an issue. Without an issue definitions of these common words are frequently jumped on because the word looks easy to the uninitiated, although in practice they are usually more difficult than hard words to define.

A lexicographer understands that a dictionary can be misused and misinterpreted, but he keeps his mind on its proper use, on words rather than on people, and tries with all his diligence and percipience to tell the truth about their behavior. The only area in which the truth may be found is actual usage. In fine, the function of a dictionary is to reflect the facts of usage as they exist. A dictionary neither permits nor prevents. If a consulter goes to it to find out whether he can or cannot say or write anything different from what he finds there, his self-subjection is a preconceived notion and the consequences are his personal responsibility.

Vocabulary

generic, arbiter, panacea, uninitiated, percipience

Review Questions

1. To what extent does Gove believe that the dictionary should contain non-generic information?

2. Gove's definition of the ideal dictionary in the third paragraph of his essay raises the additional problems of identifying *genuine* consulters, describing the nature of *satisfactory* answers, and defining *proper* questions. Does the remainder of his essay make any attempt to clarify his definition? How?

3. What are the six kinds of information a dictionary should give for each word?

4. Comment on Gove's dictum that "the function of a dictionary is to reflect the facts of usage as they exist." What are the implications of this view?

Exercises

1. Read the prefatory material in your dictionary and answer the following questions:
   a. What is the date of publication of your dictionary? Why is the date important?
   b. How does your dictionary indicate the pronunciation of the words it defines?
   c. If two or more pronunciations are listed for a word, what, if any, significance should be attached to the order in which the pronunciations are given?
   d. If several meanings are recorded for a word, what, if any, significance should be attached to the order in which they appear?
   e. What do the following terms mean and how are they employed in your dictionary: *colloquial, slang, obsolete, archaic, dialectic?*
   f. How does your dictionary indicate whether words and phrases borrowed from foreign languages are regarded as foreign or naturalized English expressions? Which of the following expressions are considered by your dictionary as foreign and which naturalized: *faux pas, clique, bravado, ersatz, risqué, ex cathedra, Zeitgeist, naive, chic, dossier, enfant terrible, en masse, cliché, bolshevik, corpus delicti?*
   g. Does your dictionary provide etymological information? If so, copy the information given for *brawl* and *client*.

2. Consult the meanings given by your dictionary for the following: *bayonet, canter,* and *milliner*. What do the three terms have in common?

3. According to your dictionary, what is the derivation of the following terms: *bowdlerize, boycott, brougham, caesarean, chauvinism, pander, quisling, tantalize?*

4. What plural forms does your dictionary give for the following: *datum, phenomenon, campus, formula, gymnasium?*

5. Which of the following does your dictionary print as (*a*) hyphenated, (*b*) single words, (*c*) multiple words: *sister in law, pre medical, attorney at law, court martial, co operate, long suffering, in as much, long winded, high school, non support, post man?*

6. What kind of information in addition to the purely linguistic does your dictionary contain?

7. Examine the following entry for *slang* from *The Oxford English Dictionary.** Explain the significance of this work. Why would it be useful as an aid in

† **Slang,** *sb.*[1] Chiefly *Sc. Obs.* Also 6 **slaing.** [a. MDu. or MLG. *slange* (Du. *slang*, G. *schlange*) serpent, cannon, etc.] A species of cannon; a serpentine or culverin. (Cf. SLING *sb.*[2])
1521 LD. DACRE in *Archaeologia* XVII. 205 A Saker, two Faucons,..viij. small Serpentyns.., a grete Slaing of Irn. **1539** in *Archaeologia* XI. 439 Four score shotte of leade for a slang, 16 shotte of leade for a saker. **1549** *Compt. Scot.* vi. 41 Mak reddy 30ur .. slangis, & half slangis, quartar slangis. *c* **1600** R. BANNATYNE *Memor.* (1836) 133 Small brasen peices, slanges of irone, and vtheris mae peices that was tane fra the toun.

Slang (slæŋ), *sb.*[2] *dial.* [Of obscure origin. Some dialects have the form *sling*; further variations are *slanget* (*slanket*) and *slinget* (*slinket*).] A long narrow strip of land.
The precise sense varies a little in different localities.
1610 HOLLAND *Camden's Brit.* I. 715 There runneth forth into the sea a certaine shelfe or slang, like unto an out-thrust tongue. **1764** in *Rep. Comm. Inq. Charities* XXVIII. 145 Two slangs of ground. **1804** J. EVANS *Tour S. Wales* 300 Formerly the lands of this district [near Fishguard] were divided into very narrow slangs, which were unenclosed. **1839**- in dialect glossaries (Northampt., Shropsh., Heref.). **1885** *Field* 4 Apr. 426/2 He struggled across a couple of grass fields into the slang adjoining Brown's Wood.

Slang (slæŋ), *sb.*[3] [A word of cant origin, the ultimate source of which is not apparent. It is possible that some of the senses may represent independent words. In all senses except 1 only in slang or canting use.
The date and early associations of the word make it unlikely that there is any connexion with certain Norw. forms in *sleng-* which exhibit some approximation in sense.]

1. The special vocabulary used by any set of persons of a low or disreputable character; language of a low and vulgar type. (Now merged in c.)
In the first quot. the reference may be to customs or habits rather than language: cf. the use of SLANG *a.* 2 b.
1756 TOLDERVY *Hist. 2 Orphans* I. 68 Thomas Throw had been upon the town, knew the slang well. **1774** KELLY *School for Wives* III. ix, There is a language we [bailiffs] sometimes talk in, called slang. **1809** E. S. BARRETT *Setting Sun* I. 106 Such grossness of speech, and horrid oaths, as shewed them not to be unskilled in the slang or vulgar tongue of the lowest blackguards in the nation. **1824** SCOTT *Redgauntlet* ch. xiii, What did actually reach his ears was disguised..completely by the use of cant words, and the thieves-Latin called slang. *a* **1839** PRAED *Poems* (1864) II. 117 And broaches at his mother's table The slang of kennel and of stable.

b. The special vocabulary or phraseology of a particular calling or profession; the cant or jargon of a certain class or period.
1802-12 BENTHAM *Ration. Judic. Evid.* (1827) IV. 306 Giving, in return for those fees, scraps of written lawyer's slang. **1834** H. J. ROSE *Apol. Study of Divinity* (ed. 2) 15 However tempting the scientific *slang*, if I may so term it, of the day may be. **1857** KINGSLEY *Lett.* (1878) II. 43, I have drawn, modelled in clay and picture fancied, so much in past years, that I have got unconsciously into the slang. **1872** GEO. ELIOT *Middlem.* xi, Correct English is the slang of prigs who write history and essays. And the strongest slang of all is the slang of poets.

c. Language of a highly colloquial type, considered as below the level of standard educated

speech, and consisting either of new words or of current words employed in some special sense.
1818 KEBLE in Sir J. T. Coleridge *Mem.* (1869) 75 Two of the best [students] come to me as a peculiar grinder (I must have a little slang). **1848** THACKERAY *Van. Fair* xliii, I am too old to listen to the banter of the assistant-surgeon and the slang of the youngsters. **1868** DORAN *Saints & Sinners* I. 107 He [Latimer] occasionally employed some of the slang of the day to give force to his words. **1887** R. N. CAREY *Uncle Max* xv, If I had ever talked slang, I might have said that we chummed together famously.
attrib. and *Comb.* **1846** MRS. GORE *Engl. Char.* (1852) 139 Like a door from which some slang-loving roué has wrenched the knocker. **1850** *N. & Q.* Ser. 1. 369/2 That great slang-manufactory for the army, the Royal Military College, Sandhurst.

d. Abuse, impertinence. (Cf. SLANG *v.* 3, 4.)
1825 LOCKHART in *Scott's Fam. Lett.* (1894) II. 297 This Mr. H. gave grand slang to the Porters, etc., who crowded the vessel on our anchoring : 'Your fingers are all thumbs, I see', etc.

† **2.** Humbug, nonsense. *Obs.*—[1]
1762 FOOTE *Orator* I. Wks. 1799 I. 192 Have you seen the bills?..What, about the lectures? ay, but that's all slang, I suppose; no, no. No tricks upon travellers.

† **3.** A line of work; a 'lay'. *Obs.*—[1]
c **1789** G. PARKER *Life's Painter* 120 How do you work now?..O, upon the old slang, and sometimes a little lully-prigging.

4. A licence, *esp.* that of a hawker.
1812 J. H. VAUX *Flash Dict., Slang,*..a warrant, license to travel, or other official instrument. **1865** *Slang Dict.* 234 'Out on the slang,' i. e. to travel with a hawker's licence. **1896** *Westm. Gaz.* 9 Dec. 2/1 You don't want for much to start with;..½ sovereign..for a (slang) licence is plenty.

5. A travelling show.
1859 *Slang Dict.* 94 *Slang,* a travelling show. **1873** LELAND *Egypt. Sketch Bk.* 63 There is a great deal of the Rommany or Gipsy element .. wherever the 'slangs' or exhibition affairs show themselves.

b. A performance.
1861 MAYHEW *Lond. Lab.* III. 101, I am talking of a big pitch, when we go through all our 'slang', as we say.

c. *attrib.,* as slang cove, cull, a showman.
c **1789** G. PARKER *Life's Painter* 130 To exhibit any thing in a fair or market,..that's called slanging, and the exhibiter is called the slang cull. **1851** MAYHEW *Lond. Lab.* I. 353 We did intend petitioning.., but I don't suppose it would be any go, seeing as how the slang coves (the showmen) have done so, and been refused.

6. A short weight or measure. (Cf. SLANG *a.* 3.)
1851 MAYHEW *Lond. Lab.* I. 32/2 There's plenty of costers wouldn't use slangs at all, if people would give a fair price. *Ibid.* II. 90/1 Some of the street weights, a good many of them, are slangs.

Slang (slæŋ), *sb.*[4] *Cant.* [app. a. Du. *slang* snake, etc.: see SLANG *sb.*[1]]

1. A watch-chain; a chain of any kind.
G. *schlange* is similarly used in canting language.
1812 in J. H. VAUX *Flash Dict.* *c* **1866** VANCE *Chickaleary Cove* (Farmer), How to do a cross-fan for a super or slang. **1884** *Pall Mall G.* 29 Dec. 4/2 The slang (chain) should be taken with the watch, if possible, by snipping..the button-hole that it is fixed in.

2. *pl.* Fetters, leg-irons.
1812 J. H. VAUX *Flash Dict., Slangs,* fetters, or chains of any kind used about prisoners. **1823** 'J. BEE' *Dict.*

* From the entry for Slang in the *Oxford English Dictionary,* by permission of the Clarendon Press, Oxford.

Turf, **Slangs** are the greaves with which the legs of convicts are fettered. **1883** *York & York Castle* 276 Each set of these slangs or leg irons, weighing perhaps from twelve to fifty pounds.

So **Slanged** *ppl. a.*, fettered.
1812 in J. H. VAUX *Flash Dict.*

Slang (slæŋ), *a.* (and *adv.*). [Related to SLANG *sb.*3]

1. Of language, etc.: Having the character of, belonging to, expressed in, slang.

1758 *J. Wild's Adv. to Successor* (Hotten), The master who teaches them should be a man well versed in the cant language, commonly called the slang patter. **1798** *Anti-Jacobin* 5 Mar., The following stanzas..in the Slang or Brentford dialect. **1810** *Ann. Reg.* 296 The police-officers are of opinion that the robbery..is what is called, in slang language, *a put-up robbery*. **1817** *Edin. Rev.* XXVIII. 512 Now this style is the reverse of one made up of slang phrases. **1861** *Q. Rev.* No. 220. 468 The translation..is studded with the colloquialisms, and sometimes even slang expressions, of Charles II 's time. **1892** STEVENSON *Across the Plains* 24 Set phrases, each with a special and almost a slang signification.

2. Given to the use of slang; of a fast or rakish character; impertinent.

1818 MOORE *Diary* 1 Dec., The conversation to-day of rather a commoner turn than usual on account of these slang bucks. **1858** TROLLOPE *Dr. Thorne* xxiv, The set with whom he lived at Cambridge were the worst of the place. They were fast, slang men, who were fast and slang, and nothing else. **1862** WHYTE MELVILLE *Ins. Bar* xi, Forgetting in his indignation to be either slang or cool. **1864** *The Realm* 30 Mar. 7 Daring, saucy girls, slang and fast.

Comb. 1856 WHYTE MELVILLE *K. Coventry* xii, A slang-looking man with red whiskers.

b. Of dress: Loud, extravagant; more showy or obtrusive than accords with good taste. *?Obs.*

1828 *Sporting Mag.* XXII. 444 Without the slightest appearance of slang or flash toggery about him. **1849** ALB. SMITH *Pottleton Legacy* (1854) 11 A smart scarf, a very new hat, a slang coat, and a massive watch-chain. **1858** WHYTE MELVILLE *Interpreter* x, His dress was peculiarly neat and gentlemanlike, not the least what is now termed 'slang'.

c. Of tone, etc.: Slangy, rakish.

a **1834** COLERIDGE *Notes & Lect.* (1849) I. 47 Let some wit call out in a slang tone,—'the gallows!' and a peal of laughter would damn the play. **1840** HOOD *Up Rhine* 62 A slang air..and the use of certain significant phrases.. current in London. **1847** ALB. SMITH *Chr. Tadpole* xxix.

(1879) 263 The slang tone in which these words were uttered produced another burst of laughter.

3. *Costers' slang.* Of weights and measures: Short, defective.

1812 J. H. VAUX *Flash Dict.*, *Slang weights or measures*, unjust, or defective ones. **1851** MAYHEW *Lond. Lab.* I. 32/2 The slang quart is a pint and a half. *Ibid.*, The slang pint holds in some cases three-fourths of the just quantity.

b. *adv.* So as to give short measure.

1851 MAYHEW *Lond. Lab.* I. 32/2 He could always 'work slang' with a true measure.

Slang (slæŋ), *v. colloq.* or *slang.* [f. SLANG *sb.*3 or *a.*, in various senses.]

1. *?intr.* To exhibit at a fair or market.
c **1789** [see SLANG *sb.*3 5 c].

2. a. *trans.* To defraud, cheat. **b.** *intr.* (also with *it*). To employ cheating; to give short measure.

1812 J. H. VAUX *Flash Dict.*, *Slang*, to defraud a person of any part of his due, is called *slanging* him; also to cheat by false weights or measures, or other unfair means. **1812** *Sporting Mag.* XXXIX. 284 He *slanged* the *dragsman*,.. which means that he sneaked away from the coach. **1851** MAYHEW *Lond. Lab.* I. 32/2 So the men slangs it, and cries '2*d.* a pound', and gives half-pound. *Ibid.* 474/2 What he's made by slanging, and what he's been fined.

3. *intr.* To utter, make use of, slang; to rail in abusive or vulgar language.

1828 LYTTON *Pelham* xlviii, We rowed, swore, slanged with a Christian meekness and forbearance. **1842** LD. HOUGHTON in Wemyss Reid *Life* I. 285 Having so furiously slanged against the wickedness of war. **1868** W. R. GREG *Lit. & Soc. Judgm.* 141 Mr. Carlyle slangs like a blaspheming pagan; Mr. Kingsley like a denouncing prophet.

4. *trans.* To abuse or scold violently.

1844 ALB. SMITH *Adv. Mr. Ledbury* i, He could..slang coal-heavers..better than anybody else in London. **1853** R. S. SURTEES *Sponge's Sp. Tour* v, His off-hand way of blowing up and slanging people. **1888** BURGON *Lives 12 Good Men* II. xi. 314 He sent for the offender..and in the most slashing style 'slanged', even threatened him.

Hence **Sla·nging** *vbl. sb.*

1856 LEVER *Martins of Cro' M.* 250, I feel certain that I could stand any..quantity of what is genteelly called 'slanging'. **1864** MISS YONGE *Trial* xvii, I never had such a slanging in my life! **1895** *Athenæum* 7 Sept. 316/3 The slanging all round which they give one another.

Slang, obs. or Sc. pa. t. of SLING *v.*

---

reading the works of Chaucer, Shakespeare, and Milton? In what way might the legal profession use the *OED*?

8. Using the *OED*, determine the meaning of each of the italicized expressions in the following lines taken from Shakespeare's plays.

a. For who would bear the whips and scorns of time

. . . .

When he himself might his *quietus* make
With a bare *bodkin*?
(*Hamlet*, III, i)

b. What *hempen home-spuns* have we swagg'ring here?
(*A Midsummer Night's Dream*, III, i)

c. . . . for who shall go about
To *cozen* fortune and be honourable
Without the *stamp* of merit?
(*The Merchant of Venice*, II, ix)

d. 'Twas told me you were rough and *coy* and sullen.
And now I find report a very liar;
For thou are pleasant, *gamesome, passing* courteous. . . .
(*The Taming of the Shrew*, II, i)

e. [Nurse to Capulet] Go, you *cot-quean*, go,

> Get you to bed. Faith, you'll be sick to-morrow
> For this night's watching.
>
> (*Romeo and Juliet*, IV, iv)

9. What is the earliest meaning recorded in the *OED* for each of the following: *girl, fond, nice?*

10. What is the date of the earliest citation given in the *OED* for each of the following: *blackmail, mollycoddle* (verb), *trust* ("a business organized to reduce or defeat competition")?

11. Consult *A Dictionary of American English on Historical Principles* and *A Dictionary of Americanisms.* How is each similar to the *OED?* How is each different from the *OED?*

12. Consult the main card catalogue in your library and determine what specialized dictionaries are held by your library in the following fields: chemistry, education, fine arts, music, philosophy, physics, psychology, and religion. Compare the definition(s) of one word given in any of these specialized dictionaries with its treatment in the *OED* and *Webster's Third New International Dictionary.* How do the treatments differ? What justification for the existence of such specialized dictionaries can you offer?

13. Commenting on the basic concepts of modern linguistic science, Dr. Philip Gove has cited the following precepts as those which must be understood by all makers and users of dictionaries:

a. Language changes constantly.

b. Change is normal.

c. Spoken language is the language.

d. Correctness rests upon usage.

e. All usage is relative.

Which of these concepts might a "traditionalist" attack? Which might he ask be discussed further?

14. Copy the entries in *Webster's Third New International Dictionary,* for the words listed below, and be prepared to discuss them in class in the light of what you think the function of a dictionary to be:

ain't	gimmick	pad
dig	corny	irregardless
finalize	imply, infer	dollarwise
hipster	shall, will	boo-boo
goof	pneumonoultramicroscopicsilicovolcanoconiosis	zyzzogeton

15. The following paragraph appeared in an editorial in the *New York Times* (October 12, 1961) which somewhat facetiously claimed that it was "correct" English because, based on its criterion of usage, *Webster's Third New International Dictionary* had included this diction. Pretend you are the editor of *Webster's Third* and write a response to the *Times* defending yourself against the charges of permissiveness and lack of standards. For the letter Dr. Philip Gove actually wrote see *New York Times* (November 5, 1961).

A passel of double-domes at the G. & C. Merriam Company joint in Springfield, Mass., have been confabbing and yakking for twenty-seven years—which is not intended to infer that they have been doing plenty work—and now they have finalized *Webster's Third New International Dictionary, Unabridged,* a new edition of that swell and esteemed word book.

16. Report on the critical reception of *Webster's Third New International Dictionary.* Among the many reviews and discussions are those which follow; others may be found by consulting the *Readers' Guide to Periodical Literature.*

Bergen Evans, *Atlantic Monthly,* CCIX (May 1962), 57–62.
Wilson Follett, *Atlantic Monthly,* CCIX (January 1962), 73–77.
Dwight Macdonald, *New Yorker,* XXXVIII (March 10, 1962), 130–160.
Mario Pei, *Saturday Review,* XLV (July 21, 1962), 44f., 55f.

17. Be prepared to engage in a five-minute debate in class with a fellow student on the subject "Dictionaries—Reporters or Lawgivers?"

Writing Suggestions: Definition

LINGUISTIC SUBJECTS
1. What is _____ (Good English, Substandard English, Diction, Slang, Argot, Cant, Cliché, Gobbledygook, Style)?
2. The Vernacular of _____ (Hot Rods, the Race Track, Fraternities, Sororities, Poker Players, Hunting, Teenie-boppers, L.S.D., "Discotalk," Wall Street, Motorcycle Clubs, Surfing, Skiing, Sky Diving, the Ghetto, Fishing, the Space Age, Narcotics Addicts)
3. Read one of the following works and write an essay on the author's use of slang, showing how it is or is not particularly effective to his purpose:

Nelson Algren, *Man with the Golden Arm* (New York, 1950).
Allen Ginsberg, *Howl* (San Francisco, 1956).
Jack Kerouac, *On the Road* (New York, 1959).
J. D. Salinger, *The Catcher in the Rye* (New York, 1951).

Process

THE EXPOSITION of a process recounts the steps leading to the completion of some action. It deals with a dynamic subject, one involving change or development. A static subject like a watch may be described, defined, analyzed, or compared to or contrasted with another timepiece. But such subjects as *how* the watch works, *how* it is manufactured, or *how* it should be cleaned would be the concern of the writer of expository process.

Correctly understood, a process is more than a series of events related only by the fact that one event follows another. Like narrative, process has a beginning, a middle, and an end. Viewed either in prospect or in retrospect, the succession of steps leads to some conclusion. It is the writer's responsibility to show what each of the steps into which he has analyzed the process contributes to the conclusion.

On the basis of the writer's purpose, process may be divided into two kinds: informational and directional. The first is cast in the indicative mood: the writer seeks to *inform* his reader of the way some process is, or was, carried out. He discusses, for example, the major steps involved in publishing a newspaper, enacting a law, or producing a Broadway musical. The directional process is cast in the *imperative* mood: the writer gives the reader directions for the performance of some action. He is told how to place a long-distance telephone call, to execute the Australian crawl stroke, to maintain a piece of machinery, or to perform a surgical operation.

SPECIAL PROBLEMS IN EXPLAINING
A PROCESS

In order for his explanation of a process to be clear, the writer must carefully consider the knowledge which his reader may be presumed to have concerning the process. Especially if his explanation involves technical terminology, he must be sure that he clearly defines terms and describes equipment with which the reader may be unfamiliar.

The writer must also remember that the mind may easily be overwhelmed by a multiplicity of detail. We are better able to comprehend and to retain three or four major ideas with pertinent subordinate ideas grouped under each than to recall sixteen or more points of seemingly equal importance. In analyzing the process into its various steps, the writer should attempt to see larger relationships among the individual steps in the total process. That sometimes baffling process by which a freshman registers at a university, for example, might involve the following:

1. Meet with adviser
2. Obtain registration materials
3. Complete personal-data card for adviser
4. Select courses for semester
5. Fill out schedule card
6. Secure adviser's signature on schedule card
7. Report for medical examination
8. Complete medical-history card
9. Physical examination
10. Chest X-ray
11. Blood test
12. Complete registration at gymnasium
13. Have identification photograph made
14. Present schedule card to registrar
15. Present course card to representative of English department
16. Present course card to representative of French department
17. Present course card to representative of history department
18. Present course card to representative of biology department
19. Present course card to representative of physical education department
20. Pay tuition bill at treasurer's desk.

Given directions in the above form, the student might understandably find it difficult to keep them all in mind. But if they were grouped as indicated below, the steps would be easier to remember and the whole process simpler to complete:

I. Report to Adviser
   A. Obtain registration materials

      B. Complete personal-data card for adviser
      C. Select courses for semester
      D. Fill out schedule card for adviser's signature
  II. Report to Infirmary
      A. Complete medical history
      B. Complete physical examination
      C. Have chest X-ray taken
      D. Have blood test made
 III. Report to Gymnasium
      A. Have identification photograph made
      B. Present signed schedule card to registrar
      C. Present course cards to departmental representatives
      D. Pay tuition at treasurer's desk

ORGANIZATION

Dividing the process into its significant steps provides the major organizational framework for an essay which explains a process. The discussions of each of the steps constitute the major units of the essay. Because time is involved in a process, the arrangement of the units is chronological. Some variation within the past-to-present pattern, however, is possible and sometimes desirable. A writer may wish, for example, to organize his material in a present-to-past pattern: to begin with the end result of the process and to retrace the steps through which it developed. Then, too, it is sometimes necessary to interrupt the step-by-step account of the process. A writer explaining the manufacture of a pipe organ, for instance, might pause in his account in order to describe some implement used by the organ craftsmen or to comment on the superiority of one method of construction over another.

AN EXAMPLE OF PROCESS

In the following selection, the noted linguist S. I. Hayakawa discusses the process by which editorial staffs of modern dictionaries collect their data and derive definitions.

HOW DICTIONARIES ARE MADE*

It is an almost universal belief that every word has a correct meaning, that we learn these meanings principally from teachers and grammarians (except that most of the time we don't bother to, so that we ordinarily speak "sloppy English"), and that dictionaries and grammars are the supreme authority in matters of meaning and usage. Few people ask by what authority the writers of dictionaries and grammars say what they say. The docility with which most people bow down to the dictionary is amazing, and the person who says, "Well, the dictionary is wrong!" is looked upon as out of his mind.

Let us see how dictionaries are made and how the editors arrive at definitions. What follows applies, incidentally, only to those dictionary offices where first-hand, original research goes on—not those in which editors simply copy existing dictionaries. The task of writing a dictionary begins with the reading of vast amounts of the literature of the period or subject that it is intended to cover. As the editors read, they copy on cards every interesting or rare word, every unusual or peculiar occurrence of a common word, a large number of common words in their ordinary uses, and also the sentences in which each of these words appears, thus:

---

pail
The dairy *pails* bring home increase of milk
Keats, *Endymion*
I, 44–45

That is to say, the context of each word is collected, along with the word itself. For a really big job of dictionary writing, such as the *Oxford English Dictionary* (usually bound in about twenty-five volumes), millions of such cards are collected, and the task of editing occupies decades. As the cards are collected, they are alphabetized and sorted. When the sorting is completed, there will be for each word anywhere from two to three to several hundred illustrative quotations, each on its card.

To define a word, then, the dictionary editor places before him the stack of cards illustrating that word; each of the cards represents an actual use of the word by a writer of some literary or historical importance. He reads the cards carefully, discards some, rereads the rest, and divides up the stack according to what he thinks are the several senses of the word. Finally, he writes his definitions, following the hard-and-fast rule that each definition *must* be based on what the quotations in front of him reveal about the meaning of the word. The editor cannot be influenced by what *he* thinks a given word *ought* to mean. He must work according to the cards, or not at all.

The writing of a dictionary, therefore, is not a task of setting up authoritative statements about the "true meanings" of words, but a task of *recording,* to the best of one's ability, what various words *have meant* to authors in the distant or immediate past. *The writer of a dictionary is a historian, not a lawgiver.* If, for example, we had been writing a dictionary in 1890, or even as late as 1919, we could have said that the word "broadcast" means "to scatter" (seed and so on) but we could not have decreed that from 1921 on, the commonest meaning of the word should become "to disseminate audible messages, etc., by wireless telephony." To regard the dictionary as an "authority," therefore, is to credit the dictionary writer with gifts of prophecy which neither he nor anyone else possesses. In choosing our words when we speak or write, we can be *guided* by the historical record afforded us by the dictionary, but we cannot be *bound* by it, because new situations, new experiences, new inventions, new feelings, are always compelling us to give new uses to old words. Looking under a "hood," we should ordinarily have found, five hundred years ago, a monk; today, we find a motorcar engine.

Exercises on Process

1. List five "informational" and five "directional" processes with which you are familiar. Then analyze one of each kind into as many individual steps as you can, and, as was done in the example concerning college registration, reduce the numerous steps in each process to four or five with subdivisions.

2. Write a paragraph on one of the larger steps for each process.

3. As briefly and clearly as you can, write directions for someone unfamiliar with your campus to go from your classroom to the library and to find a book and to check it out.

4. From your own experience write directions for the placing of a pay telephone call, and for obtaining a cup of coffee, with extra cream and sugar, from a vending machine.

5. Direct another member of the class in lacing and tying his shoes or in putting on her lipstick.

6. Find examples of directions which you cannot understand or follow, or which are less clear than they might be, for example, directions for assembling children's toys.

Writing Suggestions: Process

1. The Process of _____ (Enacting Legislation, Judicial Appeal, Running a Mail-Order Business, Selecting a Faculty, Picking a Major, Electing a Candidate, Surveying Public Opinion, Measuring Advertising Effectiveness)

2. The Operations of _____ (the National Catholic Office for Motion Pictures, an Atomic Reactor, a Publishing House, a Police Review Board)

3. How to _____ (Learn a Foreign Language, Read a Book, Fail a Course, Prepare for Final Examinations, Finance a Literary Magazine, Find a Date, Lose Weight, Gain Weight, Organize a Student Protest, Destroy a University, Get Out of Vietnam, Reduce Crimes of Violence, Reduce Air Pollution, See Europe on $5 a Day, Enjoy a Foreign City, Prepare for a Job Interview)

4. How to Select a _____ (College, Career, Mate, Car, Wardrobe, Hair Style, Restaurant, Vacation Spot, Insurance Policy, Course)

5. How _____ (Records Become "Hits," Slums Develop, Books Be-

come Best-Sellers, News Media Influence Opinion, an Actor Gets a Part, Bias Develops, a Lobby Influences Congress, the Zip Code Works)

6. How the Decision was Made to _____ (Drop the First Atomic Bomb, Enter the Vietnam Conflict, Intervene in the Dominican Republic, Call for Police Intervention at Columbia University)

(Additional writing suggestions on linguistic subjects are on pages 282–284).

The Process of
Verbal Communication

14.
WILLIAM G. MOULTON

Encoding and
Decoding Linguistic Messages

How language changes through time, how it varies through space, how it differs from one social group to another, and most of all how it *works*—these things are studied in linguistics. Because modern linguistics has roots which go back to the early nineteenth century and beyond, many people are familiar with some of the things which interested linguists then and still interest them today.

They find it understandable that a linguist should try to find the line which separates those areas in New England where *barn* is *"barrn"* (with *r*) from those areas where it is *"bahn"* (without *r*); and they may even envy him a bit when he goes to an Indian reservation or South America or Africa to investigate some hitherto undescribed tongue and thus add his little bit to our meager knowledge of the world's 2,000 to 4,000 languages. (No one knows how many there are.)

But when a linguist says that he is doing some research which he hopes will help us understand a little better how it is that "two people are able to talk together," most people shake their heads in puzzlement.

Yet how two people are able to talk together is, of course, the central problem. During the 1930's and 1940's, most American linguists attacked it by trying to work out better techniques of discovering the structure of lan-

From *NEA Journal* (January 1965). Reprinted by permission of the National Educational Association and the author.

guage—any language—and of analyzing and classifying what they found. Then, in the late 1950's there came a rather dramatic swing in another direction: away from mere classification of data toward a search for universals and a broad, inclusive "theory of language."

In a sense this has been merely a return to some of the prime interests of our nineteenth century predecessors—Wilhelm von Humboldt, for example. It has also brought American linguistics out of the scholarly isolation from which it suffered for a time, and into closer contact with such related disciplines as psychology and philosophy. (The contact with anthropology has always been close.)

How *are* two people able to talk together? Since most of us never ask this question, but take the matter for granted, it is useful to consider just what goes on. Let us assume that we have a speaker A and a hearer B, that A says something to B, and that B understands him without difficulty. Here an act of communication via language has taken place. But *how* did it take place? What went on inside of A? How did the communication move from A to B? And what went on inside of B? The process seems to consist of at least eleven different steps. [See the diagram on page 217.]

1. Semantic Encoding.   We assume that A has some sort of "meaning" (or whatever we want to call it) which he wishes to convey to B. His first step is to get this meaning into proper shape for transmission in the language he is using (English, we shall say). Since this is like putting a message in shape to fit the code in which it is to be sent, we can call the process *semantic encoding.*

If A wants to talk to B about some sort of timepiece, his encoding will depend on whether he means the kind that hangs on the wall or stands on a table (a *clock*), or the kind that is carried in the pocket or worn on the wrist (a *watch*). In German the single semantic unit *Uhr* includes both types. If he wants to ask whether B "knows" something, he can use the single semantic unit *know*. Spanish would force him to choose between *conocer* (for a person, place, or thing) and *saber* (for a fact).

As these examples show, each language "slices the pie of reality" in its own capricious way. In English, we group a host of different objects, of many types, colors, sizes, and shapes, into the semantic unit *stool*. If to a stool we add a back, however, it suddenly becomes the semantic unit *chair*. If we widen it so that two or more people can sit on it, it is a *bench*. If to a chair we add upholstery, it is still a *chair*. But if to a bench we add upholstery, it suddenly becomes a *sofa*.

Using a bold and imprecise metaphor, we can think of every language as a vast sieve with thousands of semantic slots in it. Any idea which we want to express in that language first has to be put through this sieve. And every language has a special sieve of its own. The discipline which studies such metaphorical sieves is semantics. (A semanticist would describe his valuable and difficult work more elegantly, but this is a reasonable approximation to part of what he does.)

2. Grammatical Encoding. Once speaker A has found the proper semantic units for his message, he must next arrange them in the particular way the grammar of his language requires. If in English he wants to get across the idea of "dog," "man," and "bite"—with the dog and not the man doing the biting—he has to encode it in the order *dog bites man*; the order *man bites dog* gives quite a different message.

The grammatical code of Latin employs totally different devices. For the meaning "dog bites man" it marks the unit "dog" as nominative (*canis*), the unit "man" as accusative (*virum*), and it can then combine these words with *mordet* "bites" in any order whatever. For the opposite message it would mark "dog" as accusative (*canem*), "man" as nominative (*vir*), and it could then again combine these with *mordet* in any order at all.

English grammar signals the difference between subject and object by means of word order; Latin grammar signals it by means of inflectional endings; other languages use still other devices.

The basic units used in grammatical encoding are called morphemes (from Greek *morphē* "form"). Morphemes may be either words: *dog, bite, man,* or parts of words: the *-s* of *bites,* the *-ing* of *biting,* etc. Some clearly correspond to semantic units: *dog, bite, man;* with others, however, the semantic connection is less clear, e.g. *-s, -ing.* Still others seem to have no semantic connection at all, the *to* of *try to come,* for example, or the *-ly* of *quickly.*

Morphemes are then arranged grammatically into such higher level units as words: *bites, biting, quickly* (some morphemes are of course already words: *dog, bite, man, quick*); then phrases of various sorts, e.g. *the dog* (which can function, among other ways, as a "subject"); then clauses of various sorts (in English, such constructions contain a subject and predicate); and finally sentences, which are marked in some way as not being parts of still larger constructions.

Recent interest in grammar has focused on the following familiar and yet astonishing (and somehow disturbing) fact—any speaker can say, and any hearer can understand, an infinite number of sentences; and, indeed, many of the sentences we say and hear have never been said before.

How does our grammar provide for this enormous variety and flexibility? If we merely want to reach infinity quickly, we need only allow ourselves to use the word *and* over and over again. There are, however, two far more elegant devices. One is that of *embedding:* putting a construction inside a construction, etc., like a Chinese puzzle. A classic example is the old nursery tale: "This is the cat that killed the rat that ate the malt (and so on and on and on) . . . that lay in the house that Jack built."

Still more elegant is *transformation,* whereby a basic sentence type may be transformed into a large variety of derived constructions. Thus *the dog bites the man* can be transformed into: *the dog bit (has bitten, had bitten, is biting, was biting, has been biting, can bite,* etc.) *the man; the man is bitten (was bitten, has been bitten,* etc.) *by the dog; (the dog) that bites* (etc.) *the man; (the man) that the dog bites; (the man) that is bitten by the dog; (the dog) that the man is bitten by;* etc.

3. Phonological Encoding. When grammatical encoding has been completed, the message enters the phonological component of the code as a string of morphemes, and these must now be encoded for sound. This is accomplished by encoding each morpheme into one or more basic phonological units or phonemes (from Greek *phōnē̆* "sound"). The morpheme *-s* of *bites* is converted to the phoneme /s/, *check* to /ček/, *stone* to /stōn/, *thrift* to /θrift/, etc.

(Written symbols for phonemes are customarily placed between slant lines to distinguish them from the letters of regular spelling and from the symbols used in phonetic transcription. Just what symbols are used for phonemes is unimportant; one must merely have a different symbol for each phoneme in the language.)

This device of encoding morphemes into *one or more* phonemes each is an extraordinarily powerful one, and in terms of sheer economy it is hard to overestimate its importance. If a language used only one phoneme per morpheme, it could have only as many morphemes as it has phonemes. But if a language uses from one to five phonemes per morpheme (as in the above English examples), the number of possible morpheme shapes soon becomes astronomical.

For a stock of twenty phonemes the figure is 3,368,420; for thirty phonemes it is 25,137,930; and for forty phonemes (English has between thirty and forty, depending on just how you figure them) it reaches the fantastic total of 105,025,640 possible morpheme shapes.

We have given these figures to show what an enormous economy is achieved by having in human language this "duality principle," as it has been called: first an encoding into morphemes, and then a separate encoding of morphemes into *one or more* phonemes each.

There is, however, a very bad flaw in our figures: We have assumed that it is possible for phonemes to occur in any mathematically possible sequence, such as (for English) /ppppp/, /fstgk/, etc. But English of course does not do this; like every language, it places very strict limitations on possible sequences of phonemes. Nevertheless, even with the strictest sorts of limits, the duality principle permits every language to form far more morpheme shapes than it will ever use.

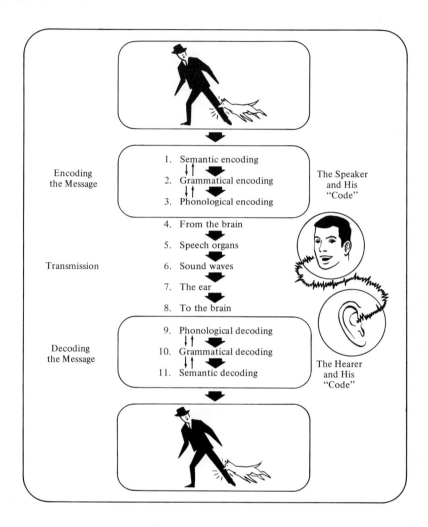

If we take English to be a thirty-phoneme language (it has more than thirty, no matter how you figure them), permit no morpheme shape of more than five phonemes (*glimpse*/glimps/ actually has six), and assume that only one out of every 1,000 possible sequences can be used, we still end up with a total of 25,137 possible morpheme shapes (the above 25,137,930 divided by 1,000)—enough to take care of any language.

If we remind ourselves that English words can easily consist of three or more morphemes (e.g. *un-friend-li-ness*), it is clear that we are also provided with an overabundance of possible word shapes—more than enough for Lewis Carroll to invent "slithy toves did gyre and gimble in the wabe," using a few of the thousands of available word shapes which had not previously been claimed.

In the preceding paragraphs we have assumed, for purposes of presentation, that a message is neatly encoded first semantically, then grammatically, and then phonologically. But since normal speech is full of false starts, hesitations, grammatical slips, and the like, it seems clear that we behave a good deal more like the young lady who, when told that she should "think before she spoke," replied with rare honesty: "But I can't do that! How do I know what I'm going to say until I start talking?"

If we do *not* normally plan out our entire message before we start sending it, then we must possess some sort of feedback device which permits us to "monitor" the message as it is sent and to make necessary adjustments as we proceed—adjusting a present tense verb to agree with its singular subject, for example.

4. From Brain to Speech Organs. When phonological encoding has been completed, the message has been changed from a string of morphemes to a string of phonemes. Speaker A must now somehow program and send on down to his speech organs a set of instructions telling them what movements to make so as to turn each phoneme into sound. We can compare this with the way paper tapes are punched to provide instructions to automatic typewriters, telegraph transmitters, computers, and the like. Programmed in this way, the message is sent sequentially from the brain to the speech organs.

5. Movements of the Speech Organs. Triggered by successive innervations, the speech organs (vocal cords, tongue, lips, etc.) now perform the proper series of movements. As they do so, an interesting and rather disturbing thing happens. We have assumed that, when the message is sent to the speech organs, it is transmitted in the form of a string of separate instructions, one for each phoneme.

If the message is the word *pin* /pin/, for example, there are first instructions for producing a /p/, then for producing an /i/, and then for producing an /n/. This seems, at least, to be the most reasonable assumption. If the speech organs responded ideally to these instructions, they would first assume the position for /p/, then move jerkily and instantaneously to the position for /i/, then jerkily and instantaneously to the position for /n/.

Common sense tells us that they cannot do this, and X-ray moving pictures of the speech organs in action prove it beyond a doubt. Instead of moving instantaneously from one position to the next, the speech organs bobble back and forth in a constant flow of motion which does not seem to consist of any specific number of segments at all.

A remarkable transformation has taken place. Where the message previously consisted of a string of discrete segments—three, we assume, in the case of /pin/—it has now been "smeared" into a continuum. As the speech organs move into position to produce the /p/, they already anticipate part of the position for the following /i/. (The reader can test this by whispering the *p*'s of *peer, par, poor*; the sound of each *p* shows clearly which vowel would follow if he went on with the rest of the word.)

As the speech organs then move into the /i/ they carry over part of the position of the /p/ and anticipate part of the position for the following /n/. (We normally "nasalize" such a vowel slightly.) And when the speech organs get to the /n/, they still have part of the position of the proceeding /i/. This drastic change in the shape of the message may seem quite harmless now, but it means that later on this "smeared continuum" of sound will have to be turned back into a string of discrete segments if the message is to be recovered. This is what must take place at stage 9, "phonological decoding."

When the speech organs interact so as to produce a speech sound, they are said to articulate the sound. The study of this aspect of the speech event, *articulatory phonetics,* has long been a highly developed research field.

6. Vibrations of the Air Molecules. As the speech organs articulate, they set the air molecules into vibration and produce audible sound. The study of this aspect of the speech event is *acoustic phonetics*. Here again a great deal of research has been done, and some remarkable advances have been achieved, especially since World War II.

7. Vibrations of the Ear. When the vibrations of the air molecules reach hearer B's eardrum, they produce corresponding vibrations which are then transmitted via the three bones of the middle ear to the cochlear fluid of the inner ear. The study of this aspect of the speech event is *auditory phonetics*. It is usually combined with study of the ear in general, and with the study of auditory perception (which of course involves also the activity of the brain farther up the line).

8. From Ear to Brain. Though this stage is in a sense the mirror image of stage 4, "From brain to speech organs," there are two important differences.

First, when the message went from A's brain to his speech organs, it was transmitted as a string of discrete segments; but since it was then turned into a "smeared continuum" by A's speech organs, this is the shape in which it now reaches B's brain.

Second, speaker A was able to send the message only because, somewhere inside his head, he possessed the proper code; hearer B, however, can receive all the energy in the message whether he knows the code or not—though of course he can do nothing further with it unless he *does* know the same code. We can "hear" all there is to hear in a foreign language message;

we can "understand" the message only if we also know the foreign language code.

9, 10, 11. *Phonological, Grammatical, and Semantic Decoding.* Though we surely use these three different types of decoding when we hear and understand a message, the evidence suggests that we do not use them in a step-by-step procedure but rather race back and forth from one to the other, picking up all the information we can get.

Suppose, for example, that we receive a message which we tentatively decode phonologically as, "I hope this'll suture plans." A quick check with the grammatical component of the code reveals that there is indeed a morpheme *suture* marked "transitive verb" (that is to say, we know that one can "suture something"), so all is well for the moment. But a check farther up the line in the semantic component tells us that one just does not "suture plans," so something must be wrong.

Back we race to the phonological component. Again the message (held in the meantime by some sort of storage device) is decoded as having the phonemic structure "I hope this'll suture plans." But a second check in the grammatical component now reveals that the phoneme sequence "suture plans" can be grammatically either one of two different things: *suture plans* or *suit your plans.* So we check this *second* possibility in the semantic component of the code. This now "makes sense"—and we accept it.

Our brain can function so swiftly that all of this happens in a flash. Only rarely does this "searching process" take so long that it interferes with our understanding of the speaker's next sentence.

In addition to the message itself, our decoding brings us information of three other types. First, there is information about the identity of the speaker (the quality of his voice tells us that it is Jones and not Smith who is speaking), his state of health (hoarse voice, stuffed up nose), and the like. Such things are presumably the same in all languages and hence not part of any code.

Second, there is the kind of information we often refer to as "it wasn't what he said but how he said it"—things indicating that the speaker is angry, excited, sarcastic, unctuous, etc. Since such matters are different in English from what they are in French or Vietnamese, they are clearly part of the English language in the wider sense of the term. (They also make a fascinating subject for linguistic study.)

Third, there is information as to where the speaker comes from and what social and educational class he belongs to. If he uses the phonological encoding "thoity-thoid," this will suggest that he comes from Brooklyn or thereabouts; if he says "thihty-thihd" we may suspect that he comes from the vicinity of Boston.

If he uses the grammatical encoding "I seen him when he done it," we will place him at a relatively low social and educational level—even though (and this is an interesting point) the message comes through just as clearly as if he had said "I saw him when he did it." Matters of this third sort are also part of the English language in the wider sense of the term.

In the above description of a speech event, the part which is of most fundamental interest to the linguist is of course the code itself: its phonological component (here great progress was made in the 1930's and 1940's), its grammatical component (again great progress at that time, and a whole new approach opening up since the late 1950's), and its semantic component (long neglected by American linguists, though there has been a recent revival of interest).

When one looks back upon it all, one is perhaps inclined to say: What is it good for? Is it just a game? To the linguist it is more than a game: It is a thing of beauty and wonder, and it needs no more justification than this. At the same time, with a bit of a sigh, he will say that (like such long "useless" fields as astronomy) it *can* be of practical value. It has obvious applications to foreign language teaching and—with great help from the teachers themselves—these applications are now being exploited.

If presented clearly and simply (and this has in general not been the case—nor is it easy) it seems likely that it could also be applied usefully to the teaching of reading and writing, and to the teaching of the English language at all levels. Tentative applications of this sort have already been made; with cooperation on all sides, perhaps they can lead to truly useful results.

Vocabulary

capricious, astronomical, monitor, programmed, continuum, innervation, discrete, transcription

Review Questions

1. Identify Wilhelm von Humboldt.
2. Moulton uses and explains a number of technical linguistic terms. Explain the following:

morpheme	transformation	phoneme	semantic
embedding	phonological	duality principle	smeared continuum

semantic, grammatical, and phonological encoding
articulatory, acoustic, and auditory phonetics

3. Into how many steps does Moulton analyze the process of verbal communication? What are they?

4. What justification does he offer for this kind of elaborate analysis and study of language?

Expository Technique

1. Comment on the introduction of this essay. Where does a clear statement of the controlling idea occur? How does what precedes it relate to that idea?

2. Part of Moulton's technique involves the use of examples, analogies, and metaphor. Find examples of each.

3. Would you say that there is a "tone" to this essay, that is, a manifestation of the author's attitude? If so, how would you describe it? What produces it?

4. What rhetorical questions can you find?

5. Comment on the basic expository type represented by this essay, on the central organizing device, and on any ways in which the organization might have been modified to advantage. (Would, for example, the steps have been better grasped and retained had Moulton presented them as three larger units, Encoding, Transmission, and Decoding, each followed by subdivisions?)

5. Study the paragraph on page 216 beginning "There is, however, a very bad flaw in our figures." Point out words and phrases which promote coherence within the paragraph.

6. Find examples of words and phrases which link paragraphs or larger units of the essay.

Exercises

1. Construct a model, similar to that on page 217, which will illustrate a process which you will explain in class. For suggested topics see pages 211 and 212.

2. Find out what you can about attempts to produce translation machines. What difficulties have the design engineers encountered; how have they tried to solve them. If sufficient information is available, construct a model which will illustrate the working principles of such a machine.

The Development of English

15.

MARGARET SCHLAUCH

The English Language in Process

IMPORTANCE OF STUDYING
ENGLISH HISTORICALLY

. . . Our English language is . . . such a curious mixture from many sources that a brief sketch of its biography is really essential to an understanding of its structure today. Moreover there is an interesting parallel to be drawn between the development of the language and the vicissitudes of the people speaking it. If we trace the history of English, we shall observe historical relationships which also obtain in the histories of other languages.

THE ROMAN PERIOD

Under the later Roman emperors, as everyone knows, Britain was a Roman province with a flourishing colonial culture. The population was predominantly Celtic, to be sure, and spoke a language akin to modern Welsh. The native dialect no doubt persisted in the countryside, but the cities grew up about former Roman camps and included many Roman families, patrician and plebeian, who used Latin habitually. They did so even when they intermarried with the British or employed them as workers and slaves. All the amenities of Latin culture were enjoyed in the cities of this distant province: baths, forums, or market places, comfortable villas with plumbing and tessellated floors, schools of rhetoric, theaters, and li-

From *THE GIFT OF TONGUES*, by Margaret Schlauch. Copyright 1942 by Margaret Schlauch. Reprinted by permission of The Viking Press, Inc.

223

braries. The Roman army was famous for making itself at home and mingling with native populations everywhere, with or without official formalities. It deserves indeed much of the credit for spreading Vulgar Latin as an international language among the common people of the ancient world. Cultured Britons were Roman citizens and used the recognized dominant language of the empire with slight modifications. In due time they were adopting the new religion, Christianity, which was rapidly becoming the chief Roman faith in the fourth century.

THE ANGLO-SAXONS

The ancestor of the English language appeared first in Albion when some tribes from Northern Germany, the Angles, Saxons, and Jutes, began to harry the shores and invade the island. This happened in the middle of the fifth century A.D. The raids were part of a larger diffuse movement known to historians as the *Völkerwanderung* or folk migrations. From the shores of the Black Sea to the coasts of Britain, the northern boundaries of the *Imperium Romanum* were harassed by restless Germanic peoples: Ostrogoths, Visigoths, Vandals, Franks, Langobards, Burgundians, and the so-called Anglo-Saxons, who sought foothold within the provinces. Roman resistance was weakened for many reasons, and the Germanic peoples were able to establish themselves in the heart of some of the most fertile sections. The struggle was at its height when the Angles and Saxons began the invasion of Britain. The mother cities, Rome and Constantinople, could give no help. More than that: Rome was obliged to call on the British provincial army to give aid on the continent. So Britain was doubly exposed. By the year 500 the Germanic invaders were established. There was an end of the sophisticated urban culture of the Romans, with their debates and theaters, their laws, government, army, and incipient Christian Church.

The newcomers were pagans, worshipers of Woden and other Teutonic gods. Their organization was tribal rather than urban. They were described by contemporaries as tall, blond, and blue-eyed. In the early days of the "Germanic peril" it had been the fashion for Roman matrons to dye their hair or wear wigs in imitation of barbaric blondness. By this time, however, the threat had become grim earnest; no mere subject for coiffeurs' modes.

The languages spoken by all the Germanic tribes about 450 A.D. were closely alike. They might more properly be called dialects of a General Germanic tongue shared by all, as English now is divided into dialects throughout the English-speaking world. The Germanic dialects had in turn . . . sprung from a fairly unified (lost) ancestor which we call Primitive Germanic.

EARLY OLD ENGLISH

We have no written documents in the Anglo-Saxon or Old English of the first few hundred years. Later, when Christianity was re-established in Britain in the early seventh century, schools, books, and the art of writing followed it. From two sources the newly converted Anglo-Saxons received instruction in these amenities. The missionaries from Rome acted as pedagogues chiefly in the south, in the kingdoms of Kent, Sussex, Wessex, and Mercia. In Northumbria some excellent work was done by Irish Christian missionaries, whose influence was felt in places like Lindisfarne, Yarrow, and Whitby. The alphabet taught here shows clearly its kinship with the Old Irish characters still used in Modern Gaelic. The first blooming of Old English literature occurred in this north country in the latter seventh and the eighth centuries. To the northern English schools of writing belonged Cynewulf, Caedmon, the Venerable Bede (who, like Alcuin, wrote in Latin), and the unknown author of *Beowulf*. Epic poems were written on the native heroic pagan traditions, and Christian themes were also treated in lyrical and heroic style—all in the Northern dialect. Unfortunately this glorious promise was cut short by the violence of the Danish invasions, beginning at the end of the eighth century. Monastic schools were reduced to smoking ruins, the learned writers scattered or killed, and precious manuscripts were destroyed.

WEST SAXON

A revival of letters occurred later, despite the persistent fierce onslaughts of the Danes, in the kingdom of Wessex under King Alfred. The king was acutely aware of the need for education among his followers. According to his own account, even the clergy had sunk into a distressing condition of illiteracy. It was his wish "that all the freeborn youth of England who have sufficient means to devote themselves thereto, be set to learning so long as they are not strong enough for any other occupation, until such time as they can well read English writing. Let those be taught Latin whom it is proposed to educate further, and promote to higher office."

The language spoken by Alfred and his court was the Wessex or West Saxon dialect of Old English. It may be compared to Modern German in many respects. It had similarly inflected nouns with four cases in the singular and plural. There were approximately half a dozen different schemes of declension. In Modern German it is necessary to know what declension a noun "belongs to" in order to give it the proper forms in a sentence (according to use or "construction"); this too was true of Old English. The similarity of pattern is clear if one compares the inflection of two cognate or related words meaning "stone," a masculine noun:

	SINGULAR		PLURAL	
	OLD ENG.	GERM.	OLD ENG.	GERM.
Nom.	*stān*	*Stein*	*stānas*	*Steine*
Gen.	*stānes*	*Steines*	*stāna*	*Steine*
Dat.	*stāne*	*Steine*	*stānum*	*Steinen*
Acc.	*stān*	*Stein*	*stānas*	*Steine*

There are reasons for the differences to be noted in the plurals. However, the kinship is clear enough. Modern German is a conservative first cousin of Old English.

A Roman missionary trying to learn Anglo-Saxon for purposes of persuasion had to remember which of about six patterns to follow with every new noun acquired. It would have been felt to be a bad blunder if, for instance, he had used the *"-e"* ending of the plural of a feminine noun to make a plural for *stān*. In precisely the same way Americans who learn German are constantly in danger of falling into barbarous error if they choose the wrong pattern in inflecting a newly acquired noun. Since articles and adjectives presented forms for every case, gender, and number, and each form had to be carefully chosen so as to agree with the coming noun, the difficulty was greatly increased.

A Latin-speaking missionary might find all this entirely natural and understandable, since his native speech was also highly inflected, but he would have been puzzled by the existence of two separate and distinct declensions for all adjectives, the "strong" and the "weak." The former was used when the adjective alone preceded a noun, as in "good man"; the latter when an article or demonstrative came before the adjective, as in "the good man." Latin had no such distinction, but German had and still has:

	STRONG SINGULAR DATIVE	WEAK SINGULAR DATIVE
O.E.	*gōdum menn* "[to] good man"	*pǣm gōdan menn* "[to] the good man"
Germ.	*gutem Manne*	*dem guten Manne*

OLD ENGLISH VERBS

In the system of verbs one can see many resemblances between Old English and German. Both languages show a large number of verbs, called "strong," which indicate changes in tense by internal vowel change. The pattern is a very ancient one based on the vowel gradations of the old parent language (Indo-European). Some words still show the basic similarity of pattern:

	INFINITIVE	PAST	PAST PARTICIPLE
O.E.	*rīdan*	*rād, ridon*	*riden*
Germ.	*reiten*	*ritt*	*geritten*
Eng.	ride	rode	ridden
O.E.	*bindan*	*band, bundon*	*bunden*
Germ.	*binden*	*band*	*gebunden*
Eng.	bind	bound	bound
O.E.	*etan*	*æt, ǣton*	*eten*
Germ.	*essen*	*ass*	*gegessen*
Eng.	eat	("et") ate	eaten

In both German and Old English too, there existed a second, larger group of verbs which used a different method for forming tenses. These "weak" verbs used a suffix instead: an added syllable containing a dental consonant. In modern German the suffix is always *-te,* but in Old English it varied. The possible forms were *-de, -ode, -te.* The past tense of Old English *dēman,* "to deem, to judge," was *dēmde,* "deemed"; of *lōcian,* "to look," it was *lōcode;* of *sēcan,* "to seek," it was *sōhte,* "sought."

OLD ENGLISH SOUNDS COMPARED TO MODERN GERMAN

The close relation between Old English and German is further indicated by constant relations in the sound pattern. When you encounter a strange word in the former you can often guess quite accurately what its cognate is in Modern German. Certain consonants have shifted away from the common Germanic position of an earlier day, but the kinship is still clear.*

O.E. *drincan* resembles German *trinken* (drink) d: t
   " *þencan* [θɛŋkʲan] resembles German *denken* (think) þ: d
   " *twelf* resembles German *zwölf* (twelve) t: z [ts]
   " *dēop* resembles German *tief* (deep) p: f

By applying a few simple correspondences like these you can use German to help you learn Old English, or Old English to help you learn German.

* Bracketed characters refer to sound symbols in the International Phonetic Alphabet. For a detailed description of the I. P. A. see the essay by J. S. Kenyon, pp. 166–175.

Moreover, even the vowels show fairly consistent parallelism. The Old English *ā* [ɑ:] parallels Modern German *ei*, pronounced [ai], in a multitude of words: *stān, Stein* (stone); *bān, Bein* (bone); *ān, ein* (one), etc. So with the Old English diphthong *ēa* [ɛ:a] and Modern German *au* [aʊ]: *hēap, Haufen* (heap); *lēapan, laufen* (run, leap); *ēac, auch* (also, eke). It is useful to compile your own list as you proceed.

To be sure, minor changes in both languages have by now obscured some of the neat correspondences. Old English was particularly prone to assimilations of various sorts: palatalizations which changed [k] into [tʃ]— as you will note in the pair of words "church," *Kirche*—and subtle changes in vowels, also of an assimilatory character. The causes of these changes become apparent, usually, when the Old English forms are compared with others in the related Germanic dialects. For practical purposes Modern Dutch is even more useful than Modern German in showing family similarities.

A few lines of Old English, from a Biblical translation, will illustrate some of the characteristics of the language:[1]

Ond Pharāōnes dohter cwæð tō hire: "Underfōh þis cild ond fēd hit mē, ond ic sylle þē pīne mēde." þæt wīf underfēng þone cnapan, ond hine fēdde ond sealde Pharāōnes dehter.	And Pharaoh's daughter quoth to her: "Receive this child and feed it (for) me, and I (shall) give thee thy meed." The woman took the boy and fed him and gave (him) to Pharaoh's daughter.
Ond hēo hine lufode ond hæfde for sunu hyre, ond nemde his naman Moises, ond cwæð: "Forþāmþe ic hine of wætere genam."	And she loved him and had (him) as her son, and named his name Moses, and quoth: "Because I took him (out) of water."
Exodus 2:9–10	(Literal translation)

CONNECTIONS WITH INDO-EUROPEAN

Even in this short passage there are a few words which show the more remote kinship of Old English with languages outside the closely knit Germanic family. No specialized knowledge is required in order to see these similarities:

O.E. *sunu* (son) corresponds to Russian *syn*, Sanskrit *sūnú*.
   "   *nama* (name) corresponds to Latin *nōmen*, Greek *onoma*.
   "   *dohtor* (daughter) corresponds to Greek *thugátēr*, Sanskrit *duhitá*.
   "   *mē* (me) corresponds to Latin *mē*, Russian *me'nʲa*.

[1] Note that þ, ð stand for [θ] and [ð] indiscriminately. The letter *h* stood for a rougher sound than ours today, something like [χ].

It is by resemblances such as these that the wider relationships are established among the various families called Indo-European.

INFLUENCE OF LATIN ON OLD ENGLISH

Once the language of the Anglo-Saxons began to be written and to be studied along with Latin, it was brought into contact with the wide currents of world culture still pulsing strongly from the great center of Rome. The influence was felt in several ways. First of all, the study of classical Roman writers, which was more enthusiastic and intense than many readers may suppose, made Old English authors conscious of style and sentence structure in their own language. They began to cultivate certain effects they had admired in writers like Virgil, Ovid, and the prose historians. That is why the great prose translations and even the original works fostered in Old English by King Alfred have the air of being done by cultured, sophisticated writers, who knew very well what effect they were striving for. At times their admiration of Roman prose style led to unfelicitous imitation. When the translator of *Apollonius of Tyre* writes "all these things thus being done" *đisum eallum đus gedōnum*) in the dative case, he is trying slavishly to follow a famous Latin construction in the ablative case: something like *hīs omnibus ita factīs*. It just doesn't fit. The effect remains foreign and awkward. But other writers combined planned intricacy and simplicity with more success. There are passages in the Alfredian translations of Bede, St. Gregory, Boethius, and Orosius which represent a happy marriage of Roman rhetoric with native English usage in sentence structure. In describing the death of Cædmon, the Old English version of Bede's history shifts from elaborate description to the direct recording of Cædmon's simple request: "*Beraþ mē hūsl tō*" (Bring me last sacrament). Nothing could be more English, including the ancient and entirely legitimate ending of a sentence with a preposition or adverb-particle. Thus while vigor of native idiom was retained, the very architecture of English was somewhat modified, at least among the cultured few at the courts and churches and schools, by association with the Roman literary heritage.

In the second place, the Old English vocabulary was enriched by a number of direct loans from Latin. The implanting of Christianity brought a number of direct transfers from one language to the other. Most have survived to this day. The list includes:

abbot	hymn	organ	shrive
altar	martyr	pope	synod
angel	mass	priest	relic
candle	noon	psalm	temple
deacon	nun	shrine	

Flourishing trade with Roman merchants continued the borrowings which had begun long ago on the continent when Germanic tribes first encountered salesmen from the Mediterranean. To the list above belong words like *cycene* (kitchen) from *coquīna; disc* (dish) from *discus; cīese* (cheese) from *cāseus; pund* (pound) from *pondus; mynet* ("mint" of money), from *moneta; copor* (copper) from *cuprum; tigele* (tile) from *tegula; strǣt* (street) from *strāta via;* and *ynce* (inch) from *unica.*

The debt to Roman word material was increased in another less obvious manner. For abstract learned concepts the Anglo-Saxon writers frequently coined words out of simple forms already existent in their own language. But they did this by translating literally the elements of the Latin words. . . . Thus the Old English vocabulary was increased under Roman inspiration without sacrifice of native ingredients. German has often followed the same method of constructing new learned words out of native elements, with an eye to the Latin model. The similar method of compounding appears in these typical examples:

O.E.	GERMAN	ENGLISH
efen-sārgian	*mit-leiden*	com-miserate
fore-sprǣc	*Vor-wort*	pre-face
mid-wyrhta	*Mit-arbeiter*	col-laborator
ofer-ferian	*über-führen*	trans-fer
wið-standan	*wider-stehen*	op-pose
ūt-drǣfan	*aus-treiben*	ex-pel

Old English writers were thus exploring the possibilities of elaborate compounding in order to express new ideas. They never went very far in this direction—not so far, say, as some modern German writers—but it is possible that the tendency might have led to unwieldy polysyllables if Old English had developed into Modern with no disturbances from without.

INFLUENCE OF DANISH

There was one other foreign language besides Latin which exercised a measurable influence on Old English. The long-continued attacks by Danes and other Scandinavians on the English coasts were attended by some measure of success. At one time a Danish king, Knut or Canute, actually ruled the country. Large settlements were established, especially in the northern districts. They eventually remained on a peaceful footing, and the settlers merged with the English population. Before losing their identity entirely, however, they contributed a list of loan words to the English vocabulary.

Most of them are so homely and practical that we may be sure that the immigrants rapidly attained neighborly status with the people they had but recently been harrying. Words borrowed at this period include "husband," "fellow," "law," "take," "store," "gate," "skill," "sky," "ransack," "call," "thrive," "skull." A personal pronoun was taken over bodily. We owe our plural forms, "they, their, them" to the Scandinavian *þeir, þeira, þeim* which gradually displaced Old English *hīe, hīera, hem* (confusingly like the singular masculine pronoun). The loans show the intimacy finally achieved by northern settlers who must have been at first bitterly resented.

LATE OLD ENGLISH

By the end of the Old English period, then, England had what might be called a recognized literary language, already used for several hundreds of years for important creative and translated writings. By the year 1000, however, certain changes were beginning to affect the literary language. The multiplicity of endings was gradually being reduced. Cases originally kept distinct were beginning to fall together with identical terminations. You could no longer be sure, without relying more and more on context, whether a given form meant a dative singular or a dative plural. If the confusion was appearing in formal documents written by men at least semi-learned, it was no doubt far more widespread among the unlearned. And very soon the process of confusion or leveling was speeded up by an important political event.

THE NORMAN CONQUEST

In 1066, as every school child knows, England was invaded and conquered by William, Duke of Normandy, commonly called "the Bastard." He used as pretext a doubtful claim to the English crown after the death of Edward the Confessor, "last of the Saxon Kings." The army attendant upon William was chiefly composed of Normans, men speaking a provincial dialect of French but related by blood to the Danes. Their forefathers, most of them, had migrated from Scandinavia and conquered the land of Normandy even as they themselves were now proposing to conquer England. Their success meant more than a mere change in dynastic rule for the inhabitants of Britain. The old local kingdoms and tribal organizations were swept away—such as had survived the period of unified Danish rule. In their stead the whole of England, excluding Scotland and Wales, was placed under a single complex feudal system of administration.

FEUDALISM IN ENGLAND

Feudalism of course was a highly stratified organization of society. In France there were already many ranks or orders of men, from the lowly unfree serf, up through free traders and workers, landless knights, land-owning knights, little barons, big barons, and recognized kings. Military service and other obligations were the basis of land ownership. Rights and prerogatives were at times vague or conflicting, and hence gave rise to fierce combats. Feudal France was divided into great duchies, each with a heredi-tary overlord at his head. Roughly speaking the dialects of medieval French corresponded to these feudal divisions. Within the confines of each duchy there was not a great deal of difference between the language of the lower and the higher orders, except insofar as differences of interest and preoccu-pation tended to mark off the stores of words used. The husbandman talked about agricultural matters, using more or less simple sentences studded with the technical terms of his job; the knight employed a more aristocratic vo-cabulary referring to tournaments, etiquette, literature, and art (within limits!), terms of inheritance, and the techniques of warfare; but in general they spoke the same dialect within the same region. The regional dialect divisions were probably much more noticeable than class divisions, apart from limited items of specialized vocabulary.

BILINGUAL ENGLAND

When William of Normandy transferred this feudal organization to England, the linguistic situation became more complex. At once the lowest orders were doubly marked, not only by inferior economic position but also by the use of a separate, despised tongue. Since the Church, which con-ducted most of the schooling of the time, was also taken over by Norman-French bishops, abbots, and other prelates, instruction in English practically ceased. Most of the native speakers became necessarily illiterate and re-mained so for several generations. The recording of English came to an abrupt stop almost everywhere. While English thus remained unrecorded in writing and uncorrected by formal teaching, it tended to change more rapidly than it had been doing before 1066. The leveling of forms, now ac-celerated, produced a greatly simplified grammar. Many of the distinctions of Old English were lost in the process. Earlier writers like Sir Walter Scott have probably exaggerated the cleavage between Norman French and English, and the length of time it endured. But it was sufficiently marked at least to intensify the drive towards simplicity, already noticeable in Old English.

EARLY MIDDLE ENGLISH

English re-emerged as a literary language in the hands of churchly writers in the latter twelfth century. These men, schooled primarily in Latin and Norman French, merely adapted the classroom spelling of these upper-class languages to the native idiom. Some few may have known a little about the Old English written before 1066, especially in places where efforts had been made to keep the old *Anglo-Saxon Chronicle* up to date under the Normans. In all cases they tried to write what they actually heard, phonetically. Where inconsistencies arose they were due to regional dialects in English itself, or to a conflict between French and traditional English orthography. In Old English, for instance, the word *hūs* for "house" was pronounced with a single long vowel [hu:s], and was so written. In the so-called Middle English period, from 1100 to 1400, it was still being pronounced as before, but under French influence the spelling became *hous* for [hu:s]. We can be fairly certain of the pronunciation because of the general consistency. Some writers, moreover, were interested enough in the problem to indicate the reasons for their spelling, and what it was supposed to represent.

CHANGES IN GRAMMAR

With the reduction of Old English declensions the English sentence fell increasingly into the word order habitual with us today: subject, predicate, complement. Otherwise it would have been impossible, eventually, to distinguish one part from the other. (Old English sentences had used the inverted order and delayed clausal verbs to be found in Modern German.) Almost all the nouns were attracted into the declension represented by *stān,* with a plural in *-as* later weakened into *-es.* Only a few survived in the other declensions. The vowels of unaccented endings were reduced to the obscure sound [ə], written *-e-.* The verbs retained endings not unlike those current in the time of King Alfred:

Ī singe	*we singen*[2]
þū singest	*yē singen*
hē singeth	*þei singen*

The adjectives retained vestiges of inflection, even slightly differentiating strong forms from weak; but the elaborate declensions of Old English

[2] This is the Midland form of the plural. In the South it was *singeth,* in the North *singes.* The distinction is typical of many others which demarked the dialects from one another.

adjectives were forgotten. The reduction of endings to short, unstressed syllables gave the language a trochaic and dactylic effect.

CHANGES IN SOUNDS

Although the consonants survived with little change, there was some shifting in the quality of the vowels. Old diphthongs were simplified and new ones arose. Old long vowels were shortened and short ones were lengthened under special conditions and for special reasons which need not be rehearsed here. In general the resulting new vowels were pronounced as in Modern Italian, Spanish, or German: in short, with the so-called "continental" values. Thus:

ā was [ɑ:] as in "father";
ē was [e:] or [ɛ:] as in "they" or "there," respectively;
ī was [i:] as in "machine";
ō was [o:] (not [oʊ]) as in "lone";
ū was [u:], sometimes written "ou," as in "rouge";
ȳ was identical with ī in pronunciation.

All vowels were intended to be spoken, except when two coming together in a sentence were elided (*thē intente* became *th' intente,* with three syllables to the second word). Diphthongs were pronounced by giving the above values to the separate parts: thus *"au"* represented [ɑ] plus [u] in one syllable. When you have grasped these few principles you can read Middle English aloud and enjoy the music of it along with the sense.

PERSISTENCE OF OLD ENGLISH WORDS

The earliest Middle English texts were still composed with an almost pure English vocabulary. The spelling, too, was conservative for a time, especially in the South, so that a casual glance at some of the early texts (ca. 1200) leaves the impression that Old English was still being written. A closer examination, however, shows that the simplification of forms was already far advanced at this time. Here is a short passage from a poem written in the South about 1170. It deals in a quaint medieval manner with the transitoriness of earthly happiness, yet there is a perennial appeal about its grave simplicity:

> Ich æm elder þen ich wes a wintre and a lore;
> Ic wælde more þanne ic dude; mi wit ah to ben more.
> Wel lange ic habbe child i-beon a weorde and ech a dede;

þeh ic beo a wintre eald, to ying I eom a rede. . . .
Ylde me is bestolen on ær ic hit awyste;
Ne mihte ic iseon before me for smeche ne for miste.

(I am older than I was in winters and in lore; I have more strength than I
did; my wit ought to be more. For a long time I have been a child in word
and eke in deed; though I be in winters old, too young I am in rede. Old age
has stolen on me before I ever wist it; I could not see before me for the smoke
and for the mist.)

Some of the lyrics retain pure English vocabulary at an even later date,
because they deal with warm intimate things which we still prefer to express
with the "Anglo-Saxon" part of our language.

Wynter wakeneth al my care,
Nou thise leves waxeth bare;
Oft I sike and mourne sore   [sigh and mourn sorely]
    When hit cometh in my thoht
    Of this worldes joie, hou hit geth al to noht.

Nou hit is, an nou hit nys,
Al so hit ner were, ywys;
That moni mon seith, soth hit ys:
    Al goth bote Godes wille:
    Alle we shule deye, thoh us like ylle.   [though it displeases us]

FRENCH LOAN WORDS

Meanwhile, however, French was still the language of court, school,
diplomacy, and Parliament. Even as late as the fourteenth century some
outstanding English men of letters wrote exclusively in French. The English
vocabulary could not long remain unaffected by this environment. What had
at first been a mere infiltration of French words into English increased until
by 1300 it was flood-tide. The new terms came from many occupations: from
law, philosophy, theology, and military science; cookery, weaving, architecture, book-making; and the trade in wool, wine, and other commodities.
Many of the more learned importations were long words which must have
seemed by their vagueness imposing and slightly awesome to English ears.
French words like *contritioún, transubstantioún, reverénce, penaúnce, obli-
gacioún, dominacioún* must have arrived with double impressiveness: first
because they referred to lofty matters of religion and government which the
common man uneasily shies away from; and second because they simply
sounded different from the native vocabulary. During the years when it was
chiefly the language of illiterates, English had naturally veered away from
the tendency to form lengthy compound abstractions out of native elements.

Only a few like *rihtwysnesse* ("righteousness") and *agenbit* ("remorse") had survived. On the whole the native vocabulary had conserved best the basic non-abstract terms and hence turned now to an alien treasury for the needed terminology of learning.

The loans were conspicuous for another reason besides their length. They still preserved the French accentuation on the last syllable, in direct opposition to the English tendency to throw accents forward. Even when this English tendency began to affect the French importations, a strong secondary stress was retained on the last syllable: *con-trí-ci-oùn, ré-ve-rèn-ce, dó-mi-ná-ci-oùn*. The struggle between French and English tendencies in accentuation produced a wave-like rise and fall of stress which added even more dignity, it may well be, to the physical impressiveness of the words. The alternation of strongly stressed root syllables in native English, followed by the shrinking unstressed endings, was already contributing to the same effect. Out of these divergent sources came the iambic-trochaic movements of English which Chaucer used so brilliantly in his narrative verse.

THE COMBINED VOCABULARY IN CHAUCER

And Chaucer illustrates, too, the aesthetic uses to be made of the new polyglot vocabulary. No one knew better than he how to juxtapose, contrast, or temporarily isolate the dual elements of fourteenth-century English. In this respect he may be compared to his own advantage with many modern poets. At one time Chaucer permits the full grandeur of the French poly-syllables to roll out:

> For of *fortúnes* sharpe *adversité*
> The worste kynde of *infortúne* is this:
> A man to han been in *prospérité*,
> And it remembren when it passed is.
> > (*Troilus and Cressida,* III, l. 1625 ff.)

This poignant comment on human felicity, paraphrased from Dante, gains in dignity from the use of the italicized Romance words. At the same time, the last line has a simplicity of everyday speech, the more effective by contrast; and the delayed verb in the archaic Old English style gives it a falling cadence which heightens the wistfulness. The same artful contrast of poly-syllabic dignity and native simplicity is found in many other Chaucerian passages. In the ballade called "Fortune" he begins:

> This wrecched worldes *trānsmutácioùn*
> As wele or wo, now povre and now *honoúr*

> Withouten ordre or wys *discrécioùn*
> *Govérned* is by Fórtunès *erroúr*.

He laments the passing of a happier day when people told the truth and their word was as good as their bond:

> Sometyme this world was so stedfast and stable
> That mannes word was *obligácioùn*. . . .
>
> ("Lak of Stedfastnesse")

You will notice that the melody of Chaucer's lines depends on a correct rendering of the unaccented syllables. Unless the vowels are pronounced in these, the verse is harsh and unmetrical. Give due value to the unstressed vowels (including final -*e's*), however, and retain strong secondary stress at the end of French loan words, and you will have verse as musical and diversified as any in English.

In less exalted moods Chaucer often undertook to describe the lives and persons and small adventures of common folk. Here his brilliant realism was re-enforced by an appropriate vocabulary and a sentence structure echoing the cadences of ordinary speech. In drawing the picture of an elderly carpenter's young wife, with her gay amorous ways, her "likerous eye" and her "middle gent and smal" as any weasel's, he concludes gustily:

> Hir mouth was sweete as bragot or the meeth, [ale or mead]
> Or hoord of apples leyd in hey or heeth.   [hay or heath]
> Wynsynge she was, as is a joly colt,
> Long as a mast, and upright as a bolt. . . .
> Hir shoes were laced on hir legges hye.
> She was a prymerole, a piggesnye   [primrose or "pig's-
> For any lord to leggen in his bedde,   eye" (a flower)]
> Or yet for any good yeman to wedde.

The homely details and comparisons expressed in everyday language— "sweet as apples laid in heath or hay"—are enough to make the reader's mouth water, as indeed they were intended to do. And the simple vocabulary of ordinary life is beautifully used when the same fair Alison rebuffs (but not permanently!) an amorous overture by her boarder, a handsome young student:

> [She] seyde, "I wol nat kisse thee, by my fey!
> Why, lat be," quod she, "lat be, Nicholas,
> Or I wol crie 'out, harrow' and 'allas'!
> *Do wey youre handes,* for youre curteisye!"
>
> ("Miller's Tale," *CT,* A3261 ff.)

With the English vernacular being handled in so masterful a manner, it had surely reached legal majority and could no longer be regarded as a subject dialect. Conversely, it was because English had already won recognition that Chaucer devoted his genius to it rather than French or Latin. Significantly enough, Parliament was first opened in English in 1362, and the chronicler Trevisa tells us the native language was used in the schools in 1385. Both events fell in Chaucer's lifetime.

THE FIFTEENTH CENTURY

Soon after Chaucer's death, in the fifteenth century, there was a renewed drift towards simplification in English. Final unaccented vowels, by 1400 already reduced to a very slight murmur, were entirely lost. Still more nouns were shifted to the majority declension (with plurals in -s) out of the small group left in the minority declensions. More and more verbs were shifted to the weak conjugation from those still retaining the internal vowel change. For a time, of course, there was a choice of forms: Malory could decide between either "he clave" or "he clefte" in telling how one knight smote another asunder, as they were so frequently engaged in doing in the *Morte d'Arthur*. Similar fluctuations arose between "he clomb" and "he climbed"; "he halp" and "he helped." Some of the quaint surviving constructions out of Old English, such as impersonal verbs with the dative, the inflected genitive case for nouns denoting things, and the double negative, began to fall into disuse. They persist in the fifteenth century, indeed even into the sixteenth, but they are felt increasingly to be archaic survivals.

Where Chaucer said:	Later English has:
He *nevere* yet *no* vileynye *ne* sayde In al his lif unto *no* manner wight. *Me* [to me] were levere a thousand fold to dye.	He never said *any*thing villainous about *any*body In all his life to *any* person. *I'd* liefer [rather] die a thousand times over.

Where Chaucer said:	Later English has:
Me thynketh *it* acordaunt to resoun. Our present *worldes lyves* space. . . . In hope to stonden in his *lady* [gen. sing. fem.] grace. . . .	*It* seems reasonable *to me*. The space *of* our present life *of* [in] this world. In hope to stand in his *lady's* grace.

Another important usage became increasingly prevalent in the fifteenth and early sixteenth century: the bolstering of verbs with a number of auxiliaries derived from "do" and "be." In Middle English a question was asked with the simple form of the verb in inverted position: "What say you? What think you?" For a couple of centuries after 1400 this was still done habitually, but more and more people fell into the habit of saying "What do you say? What do you think?" The "do" was colorless and merely brought about a deferment of the main verb. In effect it makes our English usage somewhat like Russian, which says "What you say? What you think?" without any inversion of the verb before the subject. In simple statements the "do" forms were used for situations where we no longer feel the need for them. An Elizabethan would say "I do greatly fear it" (an unrestricted statement). We should use the less emphatic "I fear it greatly." Compare Shakespeare's

> I *do prophesy* the election lights
> On Fortinbras; he has my dying voice—

and many other instances.

During the same period there began the gradual spread of the so-called progressive conjugation, with forms of "to be": "I *am coming; he is sitting* down." These two special forms of English conjugation have developed an intricate etiquette, with many modifications of usage, which cause great trouble to the foreign student. One of the last distinctions he masters is the one between "I eat breakfast every morning" and "I am eating breakfast now"; between "I believe that" and "I do indeed believe that."

One of the most fateful innovations in English culture, the use of the printing press, had its effects on the language in many ways. The dialect of London, which had for over a century been gaining in currency and prestige, took an enormous spurt when it was more or less codified as the language of the press. As Caxton and his successors normalized it, roughly speaking, it became the language of officialdom, of polite letters, of the spreading commerce centered at the capital. The local dialects competed with it even less successfully than formerly. The art of reading, though still a privilege of the favored few, was extended lower into the ranks of the middle classes. With the secularizing of education later on, the mastery of the printed page was extended to still humbler folk. Boys who, like William Shakespeare, were sons of small-town merchants and craftsmen, could learn to read their Virgil and Ovid and Holy Writ even if they had no intention of entering the Church. Times had distinctly changed since the thirteenth century. It may be added that changes in society—the gradual emergence of a mercantile civilization out of feudalism—gave scope to printing which it would never have had in the earlier Middle Ages. The invention was timely in more than one sense.

All this may have been anticipated by the early printers. Their technological innovations may have been expected to facilitate the spread of culture.

But they could not have foreseen that the spelling which they standardized, more or less, as the record of contemporary pronunciation, would have been perpetuated for centuries afterwards. Today, when our pronunciation has become quite different, we are still teaching our unhappy children to spell. as Caxton did. Respect for the printed page has become something like fetish-worship. A few idiosyncrasies have been carefully preserved although the reason for them is no longer understood. When Caxton first set up the new business in London he brought with him Flemish workers from the Low Countries, where he himself had learned it. Now the Flemish used the spelling "gh" to represent their own voiced gutteral continuant, a long-rolled-out sound [γ] unlike our English [g]. English had no such sound at the time, but the employees in Caxton's shop were accustomed to combining the two letters, and continued to do so in setting up certain English words. In words like "ghost" and "ghastly" it has persisted, one of the many mute witnesses to orthographical conservatism.

HUMANISM AND CLASSICAL INFLUENCES

English vocabulary continued to be diversified as printing and increased communication with the continent diversified its cultural needs and interests. The Renaissance (a term we shall not attempt to define here) brought with it widened interest in pagan classical learning. It was not so much an innovation as an extension of the already lively medieval interest in the same heritage. But linguistically the debt was expressed in a new manner. Whereas Roman words had formerly been taken over in French form, with all the modifications due to centuries of use, now the Latin vocabulary was plundered direct, at least to a much greater extent than before. Writers who knew some classical philology did not hesitate to adopt into English a number of forms unmodified except for a slightly Anglicized ending. Words like "armipotent," "obtestate," "maturity," "splendidous," "matutine," and "adjuvate" had not been in French popular use for centuries before reaching English; they were lifted directly out of classical texts with little change. Browne's *Religio Medici* furnishes many examples. Some writers went to such lengths that their language was crusted over with Latinisms.

The tendency had begun in the fifteenth century and went to absurd lengths in the sixteenth. Ben Jonson satirized it in his *Poetaster*, a play in which a character guilty of pretentious verbal concoctions is made to vomit them forth in a basin, in sight of all. The victim, named Crispinus, is supposed to stand for the playwright Marston who actually committed verbal atrocities of the sort. When the pill is administered Crispinus cries out:

CRISPINUS. Oh, I am sick—
HORACE.   A basin, a basin quickly, our physic works. Faint not, man.

CRISPINUS. Oh—*retrograde—reciprocal—incubus.*
CAESAR.   What's that, Horace?
HORACE.   *Retrograde,* and *reciprocal, incubus* are come up.
GALLUS.   Thanks be to Jupiter.
CRISPINUS. Oh—*glibbery—lubrical—defunct;* oh! . . .
TIBULLUS.   What's that?
HORACE.   Nothing, yet.
CRISPINUS. *Magnificate.*
MAECENAS.   *Magnificate?* That came up somewhat hard.

Among other words thus "brought up" are "inflate," "turgidous," "obla-
trant," "furibund," "fatuate," "prorumped," and "obstupefact." The ungentle
satire concludes with admonitions by Virgil to the exhausted Crispinus:
among other things

> You must not hunt for wild, outlandish terms,
> To stuff out a peculiar dialect;
> But let your *matter* run before your *words;*
> And if, at any time, you chance to meet
> Some Gallo-Belgic phrase, you shall not straight
> Rack your poor verse to give it entertainment,
> But let it pass. . . .

The critical attitude represented by Jonson was exaggerated in some
cases into a fanatical purism. There were some who leaned over backwards
in their attempts to avoid English neologisms out of Latin or Greek. If they
went too far it was because the "ink-horn" terms of "aureate" or gilded
English had become a kind of stylistic rash on the literary language. Still,
many of the conscious creations of this period filled a real need, and were
permanently adopted into standard speech.

Another consequence of the renewed, if not at all new, devotion to Latin
was the freshened awareness of the component parts of Latin words in
English. In the hands of gifted poets this resulted in a semantic rejuvenation
of words. . . . Even spelling was affected by this awareness. Words pronounced still in a French manner were given a Latinized orthography which
did not correspond to usage: thus "victuals" for ['vitlz] from French *vitaille.*

LATIN SYNTAX IN ENGLISH

Not only the English vocabulary was affected by the intensified devotion
to Latin. Many attempts were made to have syntax and sentence structure
conform too. There were attempts to implant long absolute constructions as
an imitation of the Latin ablative absolute, and to make the sentence a tissue

of intricately related clauses. The results were at times monstrous. This is one sentence committed by Sir Philip Sidney in the *Arcadia:*

> But then, Demagoras assuring himself, that now Parthenia was her own, she would never be his, and receiving as much by her own determinate answere, not more desiring his own happiness, envying Argalus, whom he saw with narrow eyes, even ready to enjoy the perfection of his desires; strengthening his conceite with all the mischievous counsels which disdained love, and envious pride could give unto him; the wicked wretch (taking a time that Argalus was gone to his country, to fetch some of his principal friends to honor the marriage, which Parthenia had most joyfully consented unto), the wicked Demagoras (I say) desiring to speak with her, with unmerciful force (her weak arms in vain resisting), rubbed all over her face a most horrible poison: the effect whereof was such that never leper looked more ugly than she did: which done, having his men and horses ready, departed away in spite of her servants, as ready to revenge as they could be, in such an unexpected mischief.

You can amuse yourself by counting up the numbers of times you are delayed in this sentence by participial constructions in *-ing* ("assuring," "desiring," "strengthening") just when you are waiting breathlessly for the main verb. The end of the sentence (after the last colon) starts with "which done," something as close as we can get to a passive absolute construction on Latin lines; and it omits a necessary pronoun subject to "departed," since Latin verbs do not normally need to express "he" or "she" or "it" as subjects. Moreover, a number of words are used by Sidney in their original Latin sense rather than the familiar English one: "perfection" means "accomplishment, completion" as *perficere, perfectus* had meant "to complete."

LATIN STYLE IN ENGLISH

Even those authors who tried to eschew an excessive Latin vocabulary sometimes followed Latin sentence structure and idiom very closely. Reginald Pecock begins one of his sentences thus:

> Even as grammar and divinity are 2 diverse faculties and cunnings, and therefore are unmeddled [distinct from each other], and each of them hath his proper to him bounds and marks, how far and no farther he shall stretch himself upon matters, truths, and conclusions. . . .

Every reader will notice how foreign-sounding is the expression "his proper-to-him bounds." Today we should consider it impossible to thrust a modifying phrase between "his" and the word it limits. But the phrase was so handled by Pecock, no doubt, because he was thinking of the Latin *fines sibi proprias*. The "how far" clause modifying "marks" has a Latin flavor also, recalling *quousque* clauses.

Notice too how Pecock creates new English idioms by translating literally certain Latin compounds. By "stretch himself upon," used in the non-physical sense, our author means "extend," from Latin *ex-tendere* "stretch out." In all self-conscious writers of the time there was a strong inclination to build elaborately balanced sentences, with clause counter-weighing clause, in the manner of Roman rhetoricians. Pecock did this too. In formal exposition there was great use of constructions to contrast ideas "on the one hand" —"and on the other hand. . . ." In belles-lettres these elaborate balancings, both great and small, were often underscored by alliteration, making an intricate pattern of sound to correspond to the pattern of sense:

> It happened this young imp to arrive at Naples, a *p*lace of more *p*leasure than *p*rofit, and yet of more *p*rofit than *p*iety, the very *w*alls and *w*indows whereof showed it rather to be the *t*abernacle of *V*enus than the *t*emple of *V*esta.

Thus John Lyly starts his hero Euphues on the artfully worded chronicle of his adventures. The italicized letters show how alliteration calls attention to the ideas put in antithesis. And once again we find illustration of Latin sentence structure used contrary to English idiom. It is not natural for us to say "It happened this young imp to arrive"—with "imp" presumably in an oblique (inflected) case as subject of the infinitive; nor was it probably a natural way of talking in Lyly's day. It is, however, a literal rendering of the Latin accusative with infinitive—*contigit iuvenem pervenīre*.

One more instance of non-English structure has persisted in limited scope into our day. It is the placement of adjectives after nouns on the model of both French and Latin—more particularly the former. Phrases like "lords appellants," "blood royal," "siege apostolic" are paralleled in contemporary use by surviving legal inversions: "notary public," "estates general," "body politic." Only the stereotyped inversions live on in ordinary speech, but poets avail themselves of the ability to create new ones when they are trying for an exalted effect. Thus Hart Crane, writing "wings imperious" and "junctions elegiac" is carrying on a minor Latin-Romance heritage of word order. In a phrase like "court martial" the unaccustomed inversion adds to the sense of ominous strangeness. Poets use this atmosphere to heighten desired effects deliberately.

UNSTANDARDIZED ELIZABETHAN GRAMMAR

Attempts to stretch English on the Procrustes bed of Latin grammar delayed the achievement of a generally accepted style of vigor and simplicity.

(Francis Bacon represented simplicity of a sort, but it was highly mannered.) Besides, English grammar was in a fairly unstable condition. There were conflicts of usage due to the heritage of archaisms from the Middle English period, and the competition of dialect forms from the regions outside of London, which persisted into the Elizabethan era.

The third singular present of the verb is a good example of this fluctuation. If Shakespeare, writing in London, had followed the London tradition in this he would have used the *-eth* ending always, and consistently set down "singeth, loveth, creepeth." But another ending, *-(e)s*, had been gaining popularity at the expense of *-eth*. Originally *-es* developed in the North country, but it spread southwards until in the sixteenth century it was becoming as acceptable as the native southern form. Shakespeare was able to use the two indifferently: "the bird of dawning *singeth* all night long" but "Tomorrow and tomorrow and tomorrow/*Creeps* in this petty pace from day to day."

Other matters of grammar were less rigidly established in Shakespeare's day than ours. There were still strong traces of grammatical gender in the use of "he" and "she" for inanimate objects where we should say "it." Pecock, it will be noticed, spoke of each faculty having "his" proper bounds, instead of "its." Shakespeare wrote, "The corn hath rotted ere *his* youth attained a beard," and spoke of the soul as "she," as when Hamlet says to Horatio:

> Since my dear soul was mistress of *her* choice
> And could of men distinguish, *her* election
> Hath seal'd thee for *herself.* . . .
>
> (*Hamlet,* III, ii)

The leveling of forms having proceeded with uneven tempo, there was considerable latitude of usage in inflected forms. Nominative and oblique cases of pronouns became somewhat confused; the newer usages have in many cases been approved by custom. The plays give us such forms as "My father hath no child *but I,*" "When *him* we serve's away," "And damned be *him* that first cries 'Hold, enough!'" and "*Who* does he accuse?" There are also examples of compound subjects and even straight plural subjects with singular verbs, singular verbs with plural subjects, plural pronouns like "they" referring to singular indefinites like "everyone," double comparatives like "more braver"—in short, most of the hair-raising mistakes which cost students bad marks today. In formal prose there was more rigid usage than this, but the drama, closer to current speech, reflects a wider tolerance. In addition there were commonly accepted formulas which we now feel to be quaint rather than wrong. We are accustomed to think of abstract qualities such as "honor," "truth," and "courtesy" as single indivisible units: an

Elizabethan, however, often made plural forms to indicate distributive use. His "Commend me to their loves," a very fair way of expressing things, simply appears odd to us, like the numerous words and phrases that have fallen into disuse: "I fain would know it," and so on.

THE AGE OF CLASSICISM AND FORMAL RULES

In the seventeenth and eighteenth centuries there was a strong reaction away from Elizabethan laxity and in favor of formal regularity of grammatical usage. Once more Latin exerted an influence, this time for the legislation of "rules": the intricate "do's" and "don'ts" to be observed if, as simple people often express it, one is to "talk grammar." The drive toward regularity and conformity in speech may be considered part and parcel of the general cultural manifestation known as "classicism," another term which we shall not attempt to define here. At least there is a certain appropriateness in the fact that grammatical relations were treated with a free and easy tolerance during an age of exploration, conquest, and colonization when plain piracy and robbery of land were being idealized; and that decorum and strict congruence were demanded as matters of taste (not only in grammar) when conquest had been organized into accepted, consolidated, and hence respectable empire. The parallelism may be worked out by students of culture in the large.

What we do know is that grammarians of the classical period set down fixed rules for the behavior of pronouns and verbs with a definiteness new in the history of English. A "good" writer could no longer put down "Between who?" even for the stage, if he intended it to be spoken by a prince like Hamlet. Such a locution was limited to low-class characters on the rare occasions when they were permitted to appear (for relief) in polite literature. When in doubt, the legislators of grammar appealed to Latin for authority. Was there some doubt about expressions such as "It is I," "It is me" or even "It am I"? The Latin rule about nominative cases as predicates after a finite form of "to be" decided the matter, and "It is I" was decreed despite a strong native tendency to say "It's me." In this period too, the fluctuating uses of "shall" and "will" were subjected to rules with complicated minor ramifications. Significantly enough, it was not a native Englishman but a French grammarian (George Mason) writing in 1622 for foreigners, who first tried to lay down the rules. In France as well as in England the dominant cultural tendencies favored regularity, probably for the same reasons. A Frenchman learning English would have been shocked at anything so chaotic as the "shall-will" conjugation, and it was natural for him, at that particular period, to try to give it a formal (if intricate) pattern.

Such an attitude affected the conservation of grammatical distinctions, too. While it regularized it also arrested leveling. For instance, the subjunctive in forms like "If I *were* you" or "If it *be* possible" had been giving way to the indicative, but a clear distinction was now reaffirmed in the precepts of eighteenth-century grammar. That codification has remained in force until our own times. Teaching has as usual had a conservative effect. If it were not for the careful preservation of these dying forms in school books, I should have begun this sentence with the words "If it was not. . . ." As it is, we tend to limit the few surviving subjunctives to formal discourse, printed or spoken.

In France an Academy had been established in order to give final, authoritative judgment on disputed questions of grammar and usage. Some writers in England advocated the establishment of a similar British Academy to legislate for the English language. It was felt in some quarters that refinement and formality should be made official. However, the project was never realized. Historians of English explain the resistance to it by citing the rugged independence of English character. This is no doubt true as far as it goes, but it is not a basic explanation. The rugged independence paradoxically manifested even in an age of conformity must itself be explained: perhaps by reference to the political interlude of the English Commonwealth, which effectively and permanently checked absolutism in government in the seventeenth century. It could not be successfully tried for any length of time after 1649. Any tendency towards absolutism in language was to some extent, therefore, checked by the changed political atmosphere resulting from the Commonwealth. Voltaire found this atmosphere to be very libertarian as compared with the French. Despite great similarities between French and English taste, there were great differences. France, lacking such a check as the experience of a republican government in the seventeenth century, showed the exaggerated effects of absolutism in both linguistic and cultural matters, down to 1789. The readjustment was the more drastic because it was so long delayed. The French Revolution, too, had its effect on the style and vocabulary of accepted speech—not only in France, but in England to a certain extent. The vogue of "simple" speech and rural dialects (one of the aspects of "romanticism") is connected with shifts in taste which heralded and accompanied the French Revolution.

IMPERIAL EXPANSION

Meanwhile the English language had been spread far and wide over the globe, following the course of imperial expansion. India, at first settled and claimed by the French as rival colonists, fell under exclusively English sway in the eighteenth century. In North America also French claims were forced to yield throughout the entire territory represented by Canada and the Thirteen Colonies. French survived as a language only in the Quebec region of Canada. English discoveries and settlements led to the claim over Australia and New Zealand. In the nineteenth century the greater part of the continent of Africa fell under English sway, both direct and indirect. The Dutch Colony of South Africa was taken over after the Boer War; large territories like the English Sudan became British dependencies in the form of colonies of "backward" peoples; and some countries like Egypt were in practice directed by British commercial and administrative interests while maintaining formal independent statehood. Not everywhere in this far-flung territory has English been adopted as the prevalent speech. The dominions use it, of course; but in some of the colonies there has been little attempt to disseminate it beyond the circle of resident administrators, and in certain quarters (in India, for instance) it has met with conscious opposition.

The linguistic results of imperial expansion were manifold. We have already noticed the influx of foreign loan words into English from all quarters of the globe. In addition, each colonial dialect separated from the mother country has developed its own special idiosyncrasies, so that English-speaking visitors to England can be labeled, by their pronunciation, as emanating from Canada, Australia, South Africa, or "the States."

The settlement of Englishmen in India was particularly momentous for the history of linguistic science. When the dust of battle died down somewhat and peaceful contacts became possible, administrators with the gift of intellectual curiosity began to be impressed with the character of the various Indian languages belonging to the Indo-European family. When some of the bolder spirits extended their inquiry so far as to undertake the study of ancient Sanskrit, the classical literary language, they were further impressed by its affinities with the known classical languages of Europe. Sir William Jones was able to draw the proper conclusion as early as 1786: he wrote that Sanskrit, when compared to Greek and Latin,

> bears a stronger affinity, both in the roots of verbs and in the forms of grammar, than could possibly have been produced by accident; so strong, indeed, that no philologer could examine them all three without believing them to have sprung from some common source, which, perhaps, no longer exists: there is a similar reason, though not quite so forcible, for supposing that both the Gothick and the Celtick, though blended with a very different idiom, had the same origin with the Sanskrit.

Sir William was quite right. His studies may be said to have opened the door on comparative philology, encouraged the work of Rask, Bopp, Grimm, Leskien, and the other pioneers who established family relations among languages in the nineteenth century.

CONTEMPORARY ENGLISH

In the recent past our language has shown no new tendencies of major importance. A great vowel shift has occurred since 1500, producing the modern sounds we associate with the printed symbols. The host of borrowed words is increasing daily, from all parts of the world. A supplementary list is being created from Latin and Greek roots to serve the purposes of scientific research. There is a revolt—within limits—against the rigid rules of classical grammarians. "Good" writers are again permitting themselves forms like these:

Those two, no matter who spoke, or whom was addressed, looked at each other.
(Dickens, *Our Mutual Friend*.)
It depends altogether on who I get.
(May Sinclair, *Mr. Waddington of Wick*.)
If I were her. . . .
(Middleton Murry, *The Things We Are*.)
Kitty and me were to spend the day there . . . (by the bye, Mrs. Forster and me are such friends!)
(Jane Austen, *Pride and Prejudice*.)
Her towards whom it made / Soonest had to go.
(Thomas Hardy, "In the Garden.")

Until very recently, histories of the English language usually ended with cheerful speculation on the outlook for it as a world language. There were several cogent arguments in favor of it. First, it was pointed out that it is a living language already spoken by a great number of persons all over the globe. Second, it has a comparatively simple grammar. It boasts of a rich and glorious literature which offers a strong inducement for any student to acquire mastery of it. It offers pleasure, in other words, as well as profit. And within the last few years a simplified form of it, Basic English, has been offered to beginners as a means of expediting communication through a vocabulary of 850 words, adequate for all practical purposes. By means of this list a student is able to express any ideas, and even achieve certain aesthetic values of simple poignancy, within a very short time. He learns to say "go in" for "penetrate" and "flow out" for "exude," and is thus able to meet any situation with an adequate periphrasis. (Whether he can understand the fluent replies of a native ignorant of Basic is a different question!) These are surely inducements towards the adoption of English. Mr. Ogden claimed too much when he stated that absence of an international language like Basic English is "the chief obstacle to international understanding, and consequently the chief underlying cause of war." Unhappily, much more will be needed than a single speech to end wars. Nevertheless, Basic has many supports from the point of view of pure reason. At a later date they may be discussed for practical application.

But in the present shock and roar of clashing empires, it would appear foolhardy to make any arguments or prophecies. The advantages of English, aside from its archaic spelling, still stand. But it may be some considerable time, longer than many of us had hoped, before these matters are decided by such mild individuals as professional philologists. The appeal to reason, the argument from simple practicality for all mankind, may have to wait upon history for a long time. And by then it may be that another candidate among the languages of the world may have achieved the position of outstanding advantage. We can only wait and see.

Vocabulary

amenities, tesselated, harry, incipient, coiffeur, prerogative, orthography, trochaic, dactylic, perennial, polyglot, juxtapose, poignant, cadence, rebuff, vernacular, mercantile, innovation, rejuvenation, decorum, congruence, codification, paradoxically, absolutism, libertarian, disseminate, affinities, philology, periphrasis, neologism

Review Questions

1. What examples of Roman cultural influence during the Roman occupation does Miss Schlauch find in Britain?
2. What was the predominant native language of Britain under Roman rule?
3. From what Germanic tribal dialects does English chiefly derive?
4. How did the members of these tribes happen to be in Britain?
5. What was the nature of the Latin influence upon Old English?
6. Under what conditions and in what ways did Danish influence Old English?
7. What are "strong" and "weak" verbs? Give two examples of each from modern English.
8. What is meant by "inflection"?
9. Identify Cynewulf, Caedmon, and the Venerable Bede.
10. Of what special importance is the date 1066 to the history of the English language?
11. Name two ways in which Middle English differs from Old English.
12. What is meant by "grammatical gender"?
13. Of what special importance is the date 1362 to the history of the English language?
14. How may the spelling of *ghost* and *ghastly* be accounted for?
15. Discuss some of the ways in which Latin influenced English during the period of the Renaissance.

16. What are "ink-horn" terms?

17. During what period of history did the "drive toward regularity and conformity in speech" first occur?

18. What were some of the linguistic results of British imperial expansion?

19. Why was the settlement of Englishmen in India "particularly momentous for the history of linguistic science"?

20. What, according to Miss Schlauch, gave some historians of the English language reason to believe that English might become a world language? What would be some of the problems encountered if English were officially adopted by all nations of the world?

21. Show how the development of Modern English has been "a drive toward simplicity."

Expository Technique

1. What basic principle of organization is employed by the author?

2. How would you formulate the controlling idea of this essay?

3. Headings indicate the various subdivisions of this essay. Would it be possible to group these subdivisions in larger units?

4. Find examples of coherence within and between paragraphs.

Exercises

1. The four passages below are versions of the parable of the Sower found in *The Gospel According to St. Mark* (4:1–20). The first is Old English of the tenth century; the second is Middle English of the fourteenth century. The third is from the King James *Authorized Version* of 1611; the last is from *The New English Bible* of 1961. Study these versions carefully and note the differences in spelling, vocabulary, grammar, and word order. (The Old English may seem difficult at first, but with more familiar versions of the same passage before you, you will be able to figure out many of the words with unfamiliar forms. For words which do not yield to informed guesses, consult J. R. Clarke Hall, *A Concise Anglo-Saxon Dictionary*, 4th ed., with Supplement by H. D. Meritt (Cambridge, Eng., 1960).

OLD ENGLISH

And eft hē ongan hī æt þǣre sǣ lǣran. And him wæs mycel menegu tō gegaderod, swā þæt hē on scip ēode, and on þǣre sǣ wæs; and eall sēo menegu ymbe þā sǣ wæs on lande. (2) And hē hī fela on bigspellum lǣrde, and him tō cwæð on his lāre, (3) Gehȳrað; Ūt ēode sē sǣdere his sǣd tō sāwenne. (4) And þā hē sēow, sum fēoll wið þone weg, and fugelas cōmon and hit frǣton. (5) Sum fēoll ofer stānscyligean, þār hit næfde mycele eorðan, and sōna ūp ēode; and for þām hit næfde eorðan þiccnesse, (6) þā hit ūp ēode, sēo sunne hit

forswǣlde, and hit forscranc, for þām hit wyrtruman nǣfde. (7) And sum fēoll
on þornas; þā stigon ða þornas and forðrysmodon þæt, and hit wæstm ne bær.
(8) And sum fēoll on gōd land, and hit sealde *ūppstīgendne* and *wexendne*
wæstm; and ān brōhte þrītigfealdne, sum syxtigfealdne, sum hundfealdne.
(9) And hē cwæð, Gehȳre, sē ðe ēaran hæbbe tō gehȳranne.

(10) And þā hē āna wæs, hine āxodon þæt bigspell þā twelfe þe mid him
wǣron. (11) And hē sǣde him, Ēow is geseald tō witanne Godes rīces gerȳnu;
þām þe ūte synt ealle þing on bigspellum gewurþað: (12) þæt hī geseonde
geseon, and nā ne geseon; and gehȳrende gehȳren, and ne ongyten; þē lǣs hī
hwǣnne sȳn gecyrrede, and him sīn hyra synna forgyfene. (13) Ðā sǣde hē
him, Gē nyton þis bigspell? and hū mage gē ealle bigspell witan? (14) Sē þe
sǣwð, word hē sǣwð. (15) Sōðlīce þā synt wið þone weg þar þæt word is
gesāwen; and þonne hī hit gehȳrað, sōna cymð Sātanas, and āfyrð þæt word
þe on heora heortan āsāwen ys. (16) And þā synt gelīce þe synt ofer þā
stānscyligean gesāwen; sōna þænne hī þæt word gehȳrað, and þæt mid blisse
onfōð; (17) and hī nabbað wyrtruman on him, ac bēoð unstaðolfæste; and
syþþan ūp cymð dēofles costnung and his ēhtnys for þām worde, [and hrædlīce
hī bēoð geuntrēowsode]. (18) Hī synd on þornum gesāwen, þæt synd þā ðe
þaet word gehȳrað; (19) and of yrmðe and swīcdōme *woroldwelena* and ōðra
gewilnunga þæt word ofþrysmiað, and synt būton wæstme gewordene. (20)
And þā ðe gesāwene synt ofer þæt gōde land, þā synd þe þæt word gehȳrað
and onfōð, and wæstm bringað, sum prītigfealdne, sum syxtigfealdne, and sum
hundfealdne.

MIDDLE ENGLISH

And eft Jhesus bigan to teche at the see; and myche puple was gaderid to hym,
so that he wente in to a boot, and sat in the see, and al the puple was aboute
the see on the loond. (2) And he taugte hem in parablis many thingis. And
he seide to hem in his techyng, (3) Here ge. Lo! a man sowynge goith out to
sowe. (4) And the while he sowith, summe seed felde aboute the weie, and
briddis of heuene camen, and eeten it. (5) Othere felde doun on stony places,
where it had not myche erthe; and anoon it spronge vp, for it had not depnesse
of erthe. (6) And whanne the sunne roos vp, it welewide for heete, and it
driede vp, for it hadde no roote. (7) And othere felde doun in to thornes, and
thornes sprongen vp, and strangliden it, and it gaf not fruyt. (8) And other
felde doun in to good loond, and gaf fruyt, springynge vp, and wexynge; and
oon brougte thretti foold, and oon sixti fold, and oon an hundrid fold. (9) And
he seide, He that hath eeris of heryng, here he. (10) And whanne he was bi
hym silf, tho twelue that weren with hym axiden hym to expowne the parable.
(11) And he seide to hem, To gou it is gouun to knowe the priuete of the
kyngdom of God. But to hem that ben with outforth, alle thingis be maad in
parablis, that thei seynge se, and se not, and thei herynge here and vnderstonde
not; lest sum tyme thei be conuertid, and synnes be forgouun to hem. (13)
And he seide to hem, Knowe not ge this parable? and hou ge schulen knowe
alle parablis? (14) He that sowith, sowith a word. (15) But these it ben that
ben aboute the weie, where the word is sowun; and whanne thei han herd,

anoon cometh Satanas, and takith awei the word that is sowun in her hertis.
(16) And in lijk maner ben these that ben sowun on stony placis, whiche
whanne thei han herd the word, anoon thei taken it with ioye; (17) and thei
han not roote in hem silf, but thei ben lastynge a litil tyme; aftirward whanne
tribulacioun risith, and persecucioun for the word, anoon thei ben sclaundrid.
(18) And ther ben othir that ben sowun in thornes; these it ben that heren the
word, (19) and disese of the world, and disseit of ritchessis, and othir charge
of coueytise entrith, and stranglith the word, and it is maad with out fruyt.
(20) And these it ben that ben sowun on good lond, whiche heren the word,
and taken, and maken fruyt, oon thritti fold, oon sixti fold, and oon an
hundrid fold.

KING JAMES BIBLE

And he began again to teach by the sea side: and there was gathered unto him
a great multitude, so that he entered into a ship, and sat in the sea; and the
whole multitude was by the sea on the land. (2) And he taught them many
things by parables, and said unto them in his doctrine, (3) Hearken; Behold,
there went out a sower to sow: (4) And it came to pass, as he sowed, some
fell by the way side, and the fowls of the air came and devoured it up. (5)
And some fell on stony ground, where it had not much earth; and immediately
it sprang up, because it had no depth of earth: (6) But when the sun was up,
it was scorched; and because it had no root, it withered away. (7) And some
fell among thorns, and the thorns grew up, and choked it, and it yielded no
fruit. (8) And other fell on good ground, and did yield fruit that sprang up
and increased; and brought forth, some thirty, and some sixty, and some an
hundred. (9) And he said unto them, He that hath ears to hear, let him hear.
(10) And when he was alone, they that were about him with the twelve asked
of him the parable. (11) And he said unto them, Unto you it is given to know
the mystery of the kingdom of God: but unto them that are without, all these
things are done in parables: (12) That seeing they may see, and not perceive;
and hearing they may hear, and not understand; lest at any time they should
be converted, and their sins should be forgiven them. (13) And he said unto
them, Know ye not this parable? and how then will ye know all parables?
(14) The sower soweth the word. (15) And these are they by the way side,
where the word is sown; but when they have heard, Satan cometh immediately,
and taketh away the word that was sown in their hearts. (16) And these are
they likewise which are sown on stony ground; who, when they have heard
the word, immediately receive it with gladness. (17) And they have no root
in themselves, and so endure but for a time: afterward, when affliction or
persecution ariseth for the word's sake, immediately they are offended. (18)
And these are they which are sown among thorns; such as hear the word,
(19) And the cares of this world, and the deceitfulness of riches, and the lusts
of other things entering in, choke the word, and it becometh unfruitful. (20)
And these are they which are sown on good ground; such as hear the word,
and receive it, and bring forth fruit, some thirtyfold, some sixty, and some an
hundred.

NEW ENGLISH BIBLE*

On another occasion he began to teach by the lake-side. The crowd that gathered round him was so large that he had to get into a boat on the lake, and there he sat, with the whole crowd on the beach right down to the water's edge. (2) And he taught them many things by parables.

As he taught he said:

(3) 'Listen! A sower went out to sow. (4) And it happened that as he sowed, some seed fell along the footpath; and the birds came and ate it up. (5) Some seed fell on rocky ground, where it had little soil, and it sprouted quickly because it had no depth of earth; (6) but when the sun rose the young corn was scorched, and as it had no proper root it withered away. (7) Some seed fell among thistles; but the thistles shot up and choked the corn, and it yielded no crop. (8) And some of the seed fell into good soil, where it came up and grew, and bore fruit; and the yield was thirtyfold, sixtyfold, even a hundredfold.' (9) He added, 'If you have ears to hear, then hear.'

(10) When he was alone, the Twelve and others who were round him questioned him about the parables. (11) He replied, 'To you the secret of the kingdom of God has been given; but to those who are outside everything comes by way of parables, (12) so that (as Scripture says) they may look and look, but see nothing; they may hear and hear, but understand nothing; otherwise they might turn to God and be forgiven.'

(13) So he said, 'You do not understand this parable? How then are you to understand any parable? (14) The sower sows the word. (15) Those along the footpath are people in whom the word is sown, but no sooner have they heard it than Satan comes and carries off the word which has been sown in them. (16) It is the same with those who receive the seed on rocky ground; as soon as they hear the word, they accept it with joy, (17) but it strikes no root in them; they have no staying-power; then, when there is trouble or persecution on account of the word, they fall away at once. (18) Others again receive the seed among thistles; they hear the word, (19) but worldly cares and the false glamour of wealth and all kinds of evil desire come in and choke the word, and it proves barren. (20) And there are those who receive the seed in good soil; they hear the word and welcome it; and they bear fruit thirtyfold, sixty-fold, or a hundredfold.'

2. The following passage is from Chaucer's General Prologue to *The Canterbury Tales*. You should be able to read the lines without much difficulty, but one of the modern translations of Chaucer, such as those by R. M. Lumiansky, Theodore Morrison, or Daniel Cook, may be helpful. Make a special study of the vocabulary of these lines. Using a standard reference work like the *OED* or C. T. Onions, *The Oxford Dictionary of English Etymology* (Oxford, 1966), determine what proportion of the words derive from French.

> Whan that Aprille with his shoures sote
> The droghte of Marche hath perced to the rote,

*From *The New English Bible, New Testament* © The Delegates of the Oxford University Press and the Syndics of the Cambridge University Press 1961. Reprinted by permission.

And bathed every veyne in swich licour,
Of which vertu engendred is the flour;
When Zephirus eek with his swete breeth
Inspired hath in every holt and heeth
The tendre croppes, and the yonge sonne
Hath in the Ram his halfe cours y-ronne,
And smale fowles maken melodye,
That slepen al the night with open yë
(So priketh hem nature in hir corages)   10
Than longen folk to goon on pilgrimages
And palmers for to seken straunge strondes)
To ferne halwes, couthe in sondry londes;
And specially, from every shires ende,
Of Englelond, to Caunterbury they wende,
The holy blisful martir for to seke,
Them hem hath holpen, whan that they were seke.

3. Read Pope's *Essay on Criticism, Essay on Man,* or *The Rape of the Lock.*
Assume that Pope is a careful poet whose rhymes are authentic; collect examples
of any couplets which would suggest pronunciations different from those of today.

4. Miss Schlauch's essay makes clear that great events leave their mark upon
language. Consult one of the standard histories of the English language, such as
those by A. C. Baugh, Stuart Robertson and Frederick G. Cassidy, or Margaret
Bryant, or if it is available in your library, Kenneth Cameron, *English Place-
Names* (London, 1961) and find examples of English place-names which reflect
the influence of other countries.

16.

R. C. SIMONINI, JR.

Word-Making
in Present-Day English

Words can be studied on all levels of English language teaching with reference to their *structure* (describing their morphemes) and their *etymology*
(describing their origin). Students can be highly motivated to notice English

From *English Journal* (September 1966). Reprinted with the permission of the
National Council of Teachers of English.

vocabulary if they have a technique for classifying words etymologically. Moreover, in focusing on the study of new words in our language, one can capitalize on the teenager's penchant for innovation and inspire him to collect interesting examples of his own from everyday speech and writing about him.

How do words in English originate? What processes of word-formation operate in the language? One may begin with a corpus of new words taken from dictionary addenda or from compilations of neologisms and then proceed inductively to make classifications (see my study, "Etymological Categories of Present-Day English and Their Productivity," in *Theory and Practice in English as a Foreign Language,* University of Michigan, 1963). Or if economy of time and presentation is important, one may begin with the established categories and then deductively find examples that are plentifully about us. In any case, one must either arrive at or work with precise definitions of etymological classes that are mutually exclusive. The subtleties of defining can be readily mastered with a little practice, and before long the average student will be able to classify accurately most words without reference to a dictionary.

There are three sources of Present-Day English vocabulary: native words, loan words, and new words or neologisms. Only loan words and neologisms, of course, produce additions to our current word stock, and of the latter there are 15 possible methods of making a new word.

One principal source of Present-Day English vocabulary is *native words* or words which can be traced back to the word stock of Old English. These will be, for the most part, the short, familiar words we use most often when we speak or write informally: articles (*a, an, the*), demonstratives (*this, that,* etc.), personal pronouns (*I, me, my, mine,* etc.), interrogatives (*who, what, where,* etc.), numerals (*one, once,* etc.), prepositions (*of, to,* etc.), conjunctions (*and, since,* etc.), adverbs of time and place (*then, there,* etc.), adjectives taking inflectional suffixes (*higher, highest,* etc.), strong verbs (*sell, think, sing,* etc.), modal auxiliaries (*must, shall,* etc.), helper verbs (*prefer, avoid, do,* etc.), and irregular verbs (*be, go*). About 20 percent of Modern English vocabulary can be traced to native words of Old English.

Loan words or *borrowings* are treated here separately because even though they are new words in the English language they had a previous independent existence in other languages. Borrowings from foreign languages make up about 80 percent of the total Modern English vocabulary, but loan words among new words of Present-Day English amount to less than 8 percent. This illustrates the great facility English had in the past in assimilating elements from other languages, although there is a significant tendency today—as was true of Old English—for the language to use its inner resources in word making. New loan words tend to preserve the foreign pronunciation, if not the foreign spelling, but may in the course of time undergo anglicization. Some examples of new loan words are *apartheid* (S. Afr. Dutch), *canasta* (Sp.), *montage* (Fr.), *pizza* (It)., *snorkel* (Ger.) *spelunker* (Latin), *kibitzer* (Yid). Most prevalently, however, new loan words in English are place names and proper names: *Vietnam, U Thant*.

Neologisms are new words or old words with new meanings. They can be assigned to the following classifications in order of productivity in Present-Day English:

1. *Idiomatic compounds* are highly productive in Present-Day English and account for one of the major difficulties a foreigner has in learning English. They are constructed of free base forms which, when compounded, are elliptical in meaning and must be learned in context instead of being taken literally. Some examples are *egghead, hairy dog story, atomic cocktail, top banana, brainwash*. These phrasal compounds involve distinctly new meanings and must be distinguished from self-explaining compounds which can be literally interpreted. Sometimes a phrase begins as a self-explaining compound (*iron curtain* meaning the curtain, now asbestos, that separated the stage from the orchestra in legitimate theatres), but when Winston Churchill used *iron curtain* in 1946 ("From Stettin in the Baltic to Trieste in the Adriatic, an *iron curtain* has descended across the Continent"), it immediately took on a distinctly new, figurative, and memorable meaning. Idiomatic compounds make up about 25 percent of new words in Present-Day English.

2. *Greek and Latin combining forms* are morphemes used to make modern scientific and technical vocabulary. These forms were originally bound bases in Greek and Latin, and some examples in Present-Day English are constructed of two bound bases: *astronaut, Anglophile, megapolis*. Some Greek and Latin bound bases have become free forms in Present-Day English and are combined with a bound form: *acrophobia, benthoscope, mononucleosis*. There are also examples of two free bases of Greek and Latin origin being used in combination: *psychoneurosis, homophone, audiometer*. It is also quite possible to combine a Greek or Latin form with an existing English form: *megaton, microgroove, teleprompter*. Greek and Latin combining forms are often used in what is called an "International Scientific Vocabulary," much as one would put together a chemical formula for descriptive purposes: *polyvinyl acetal, demography, pneumonoultramicroscopicsilicovolcanokoniosis* (a rare lung disease caused by inhalation of very small particles of volcanic dust). Greek and Latin combining forms are productive in Present Day English and make up about 16 percent of new words.

3. *Derivatives* come from stems to which familiar derivational affixes are added to make new words. Derivation may include the use of prefixes (*belittle, deplane, misconstrue*), suffixes (*finalize, inductee, eightish*), or both (*bizonal, unemployability, desalinization*). The vast majority of derivatives

are formed through suffixation. Derivatives make up about 13 percent of new words in Present-Day English.

4. *Semantic change words* originate from the addition of distinctly new meanings to words already existing in the language. Some people prefer to regard these as "new meanings" rather than as "new words," but this old creative process in English shows how the language can rely on its inner resources instead of borrowing from without. In Old English, for example, the meanings of the native words *speech* and *hoard* were extended to include the meanings of the words *treatise* and *responsibility* of French origin now used in the language to express these ideas. Important sources of semantic change words are place names and personal names. Some place names which have taken on distinctly new meanings are *bikini, cashmere, donnybrook, champagne, bologna.* Some personal names which have been generalized to describe products or processes are *Ford, mackintosh, sanforize, roentgen, Parkinson's disease.* Other examples of recent semantic change words are *bug* (microphone), *bird* (rocket), *rumble* (street fight), *gremlin* (beginning surfer), *tool* (dullard). The sources of most semantic change words are the slang of teenagers and the jargon of occupations. One should note that semantic change words are single words and that idiomatic compounds, which also show a distinct shift in meaning, are phrasal compounds. About 12 percent of new words in Present-Day English are semantic change words.

5. *Self-explaining compounds* are constructed of free base forms put together in phrasal compounds which can be interpreted literally. They differ from idiomatic compounds in that they explain themselves and from Greek and Latin combining forms in that they do not originate in classical words having special forms for combining purposes: *atomic bomb, supermarket, ballpoint pen, snow-grip tires, appointment book.* Self-explaining compounds account for about 8 percent of new words in Present-Day English.

6. *Acronyms* are formed by putting together the initial letters of a word group (*LP, TVA, VIP, GI, A-OK*) or the initial syllables of a word group (*Benelux, Texaco, Alcoa, Cominform, Comphibtralant*). The initial letters are pronounced and may be written as abbreviations (*A.M., D.D.T., Ph.D.*) or they may take the form of "cute spellings" (*emcee, teevee, veep, Esso, Seabee*). Acronyms may also form pronounceable syllables (*Nato, NASA, snafu, UNESCO, VEPCO*). Acronyms may have begun with the Romans' *SPQR* (Senatus Populusque Romanus) and exist today in foreign languages too: *Nazi* (Nazional-Socialist), *ONU* (Organization des Nations Unies), *FIAT* (Fabbrica Industriale Automobile di Torino). The first impetus to this kind of word-making in English came during World War I, and in World War II military bureaucracy peppered the language with shortenings of officialese. They are indeed evidence of what Henry L. Mencken called the U.S. talent for "reducing complex concepts to starkest abbreviations."

In Present-Day English, acronyms make up about 5 percent of new words, but one sometimes hears nonce expressions such as "Turn on the *AC* (air conditioning) while I get the *OJ* (orange juice)."

7. *Blends* are formed by combining the first part of one word with the second part of another. One of the elements is usually a fragment of a word, but the other elements may be either fragments or full words. The process involves both shortening and compounding. Blends are sometimes called *portmanteau* words after Humpty Dumpty's term in Carroll's *Through the Looking Glass*. "Jabberwocky" has provided us with a number of curious blends remembered by readers of Alice, the Jabberwock, and the Mad Hatter: *slithy* (lithe & slimy), *chortle* (chuckle & snort), *galumphing* (galloping & triumphing). Some examples from Present-Day English are *motel, twinight, smog, cafegymtorium, slanguage.* Some blends will by analogy inspire a series, such as the *Time* Magazine "cinema" blends (*cinemactress, cineman, cinemadoption, cinemonster, cinemasculated*) or the "sputnik" blends (*muttnik, lunik, protestnik, Uncle Samnik, beatnik*). Blends comprise only about 3 percent of new words in Present-Day English, but many others are used as "nonce words," being devised for a particular occasion or effect and not heard again, at least not often enough to be recorded in a dictionary.

8. *Functional change words* are shifts from one part of speech to another without form change. In making the change to a new syntactic class, a word may not change its base form or take derivational affixes—otherwise it would be a derivative—but it may take inflectional suffixes of its new part of speech: *premiere* (n. > v.), *know how* (v. > n.), *separates* (adj. = separate items of clothing > n.). Most examples of functional change today are shifts from noun to verb and are in accord with the rhetorical technique of seeking fresh and striking verbs. Some recent examples are "Another plane was *missiled* in North Vietnam today"; Radio Hong Kong *sourced* the item in Red China"; "One wonders why those careful scholars failed to *book* it." President Eisenhower, in deploring the 1965 racial violence in Los Angeles, made a noted functional change word: "the United States is being *atmosphered* in a policy of lawlessness." Functional change words comprise 2 percent of neologisms in Present-Day English, although many more are used as nonce words for stylistic effect.

9. *Pure root creations* or *coinages* are words formed from existing possible sounds and sound sequences natural to the structure of the language. The resulting word never existed as such before in English, but it will acquire meaning through repeated use in similar contexts. Some examples of pure root creations in recent English are *kodak, dacron, hep, zilch, schmoo.* Nonsense language, usually in the manner of Lewis Carroll, illustrates pure root creation: The *tilly zious veeps* were *dasking* the very *potest citer molently.* Reversals (pizza > *zappi*) and transpositions (kleenex >

neeklex) also make interesting coinages; and one may note that when these processes do not produce consonant clusters, syllables, and unstressed vowels normal to the English language, changes in phonemes will occur to make the new word pronounceable (*chewing* (gum) > *incha* /ɨnča/ rather than *ingchew* /iŋcuw/) Most slang expressions are pure root creations (*nerd, barf, dipley*), semantic change words (*fink, mouse, tool*), and idiomatic compounds (*zero cool, beard bag, huggy bear*). Coining a word which will be normal to English structure is really a highly technical process if the possibilities of phoneme combinations are analyzed. Benjamin Whorf has a formula for the phonemic combinations possible in a monosyllabic English word in John B. Carroll, editor, *Language, Thought, and Reality,* (Massachusetts Institute of Technology Press, 1956), page 223. Pure root creations are not an important source of new words, making up only about 2 percent of neologisms in Present-Day English. Other coinages may exist, however, as nonce words.

10. *Shortenings* or *clipped words* involve the omission of one or more syllables from a word with no shift in part of speech. In that there is no change in part of speech, shortenings must be distinguished from functional change words. Shortening may be accomplished in several ways. Sometimes syllables at the beginning of a word are dropped: *phone, bus, copter, scope, plane.* The shortening may come at the end of a word: *combo, props, bra, curio, pub.* The beginning and end of a word may also be clipped, leaving what is taken to be the base form without affixes: *still, flu.* Occasionally the shortening may involve only one of several derivational affixes: *complected.* Shortenings make up about 2 percent of new words in Present-Day English.

11. *Reduplications* are compounds which have recurrent syllables, a fixed consonant framework with a variant stressed vowel, or a variant consonant framework with a recurrent stressed or unstressed vowel. Some reduplications involving whole word repetition are *hush-hush, hubba-hubba, pooh-pooh.* Examples of stressed vowel variation are *shilly-shally, wishy-washy, chit-chat.* Consonant variations are illustrated in *huff-duff, willy-nilly, razzle-dazzle.* There are several hundred reduplications in Modern English vocabulary, but this type of word-making in Present-Day English produces only about 1 percent of new words.

12. *Echoisms, onomatopoetic words,* or *imitations* attempt to imitate the sound of the thing or activity named: *ack-ack, bebop, zipper, woofer-tweeter, zoomar. Time* Magazine recently used a combination of an echoism and eye dialect in a report on jokes about President Johnson: "Some are moderately sympathetic, such as the *yuk* that has one Texan saying to another: 'Ah think ouh President is absolutely fahn. He's the first President we've evah had who doesn't have an accent.'" Older echoisms in the language imitated animal cries (*cuckoo, meow, bobwhite, whippoorwill, hoot* owl), and at one time this method of word-making was considered important enough to be

made the basis for a theory of the origin of language known as the "bow wow" theory. This theory, however, accounts for relatively few words in a language, and in Present-Day English echoisms comprise less than 1 percent of new words.

13. *Back formations* are new words formed by the shortening of an existing word taken to its derivative. It amounts to reverse derivation in that derivational suffixes are dropped as one goes "back" to the base form. Unlike shortening, the process always involves a shift in part of speech. Some recent examples are *babysit* (< babysitter), *test drive* (< test driver), *grocery shop* (< grocery shopping), *shotgun marry* (< shotgun marriage), *fact find* (< fact finder). *Time* Magazine reported that the Sinatra yacht "*opted* to drop anchor at Hyannis Port." Older back formations, now well-established in the language, are *enthuse* (< enthusiasm), *emote, sculpt, edit, orate,* and *jell* (< jelly). Although back formations seem to occur often as nonce expressions, among the recorded new words of Present-Day English they make up only about 1 percent.

14. *Sound symbolism* employs in word formation a restricted group of morphemes which in certain contexts have acquired symbolic associations. The sound /ɨy/ has morpheme status in English as a derivational suffix when added to base forms to mean diminution or endearment: *Jimmy, tummy, hankie, sweetie, nightie.* Certain other initial and final sound clusters seem to have morpheme status in English. The initial consonant cluster /sn-/ suggests an association with the nose in *snore, sneeze, snout, sniffle, snarl,* and the final cluster /-əmp/ suggests a rounded protuberance in *bump, lump, dump, rump, hump.* Such morphemes, however, are not productive of many words, and in Present-Day English sound symbolism accounts for considerably less than 1 percent of new words.

15. *Mistaken -s singulars* are words formed through a special shortening process wherein an unusual -s singular form is mistaken for an inflectional suffix for plurality and is therefore dropped to make a base-form singular. They differ from shortenings in that mistaken -s singulars are limited to dropping the noun inflectional suffix for plurality, and they differ from back formations in that there is no change in part of speech. Some historical examples are *sherry* (< sherris), *cherry* (< cerise), *pea* (< pease). Examples from Present-Day English are rare and occur only in nonstandard speech: *Chinee, trapee, specie, aboriginee, len* (< lens), *pant* (< pants).

In Present-Day English, compounding—idiomatic, self-explaining, Greek and Latin combining forms, and blends—accounts for well over half the new words in written English. Derivatives and semantic change words are also productive categories and together with the various types of compounding account for about 80 percent of new words in the language. New loan words are of only average importance in the lexicon of Present-Day English. By using new combinations of existing words, by making old words accommodate new meanings, and by deriving new forms from existing words through a system of derivational affixes, we can readily adapt the English language to the communication needs of modern society.

This conclusion is not exactly in accord with what is said about word-making in some standard histories of the English language which emphasize the resourcefulness of Old English in using native elements in word-making and the facility of Modern English in borrowing words from other languages (see Albert C. Baugh, *A History of the English Language,* 2nd edition, Appleton-Century-Crofts, 1957, p. 75). Rather, the processes of compounding, derivation, and semantic change are highly productive of new words in both Old and Present-Day English, and if borrowing was insignificant in the ninth Century, it is of only average importance in the twentieth.

Vocabulary

etymology, penchant, corpus, addenda, anglization, elliptical, nonce words, onomatopoetic

Review Questions

1. What are the three sources of present-day English vocabulary?
2. Explain the meaning of *native words, loan words,* and *neologisms.*
3. List the principal classifications into processes by which new words or old words with new meanings add to Modern English vocabulary.
4. Explain and give examples of each of the following:

idiomatic compounds	pure root creations and coinages
Greek and Latin combining forms	shortenings
derivatives	reduplications
semantic change	echoisms
self-explaining compounds	back formations
acronyms	sound symbolism
blends	mistaken -s singulars
functional change words	

5. What distinction does Professor Simonini make between *idiomatic compounds* and *self-explaining compounds?*
6. How do *acronyms* differ from *blends?*
7. How do *echoisms* differ from *sound symbolisms?*

Expository Technique

1. Indicate the demarcations between beginning, middle, and end.
2. What is the controlling idea of the essay?

3. The essay is concerned with a number of processes by which vocabulary is increased in present-day English. It also incorporates other expository techniques. Identify some of them.

4. What principle of organization can you find in the middle of the essay? Are there any other possibilities which might be used to arrange the elements of the middle of essay?

Exercises

1. Consider the following list of words and attempt to identify the process by which they have entered the vocabulary:

NATO	astronaut	smog	buttercup
sizzle	bacchanalian	television	mob
steamboat	chortle	googol	lynch
goober	sputnik	sonar	Lilliputian
Thursday	murmur	whir	goon
clambake	sonar	ping	cab
kodak	jello	knife	bloomer
keel	beg	cyclotron	bikini
posh	tips	altar	ping

2. Select a Shakespearean sonnet and determine what proportion of its vocabulary is of foreign derivation.

3. Select ten terms from science or technology and explain their formation. Possible references:

Charles McLaughlin, *Space Age Dictionary* (Princeton, 1959).
George Mandlin and William Kessen, *The Language of Psychology* (New York, 1959).
Mario Pei, *Language of the Specialists* (New York, 1966).

4. Doublets, pairs of words which differ in form and meaning but which derive indirectly from a common source, are common in English. By consulting your dictionary determine the common source of each of the following doublets:

shirt–skirt   tavern–tabernacle
legal–loyal   gentle–jaunty
grammar–glamor   cattle–chattel
gallop–wallop   cipher–zero
disaster–constellation

5. Classify the following compounds in terms of the grammatical components and the grammatical forms which the compounds produce.

flagship	roughneck	whirlwind	touchdown
downpour	watertight	all-time	evergreen
kick-back	air-condition	All-American	walk-up

6. Consult Paul C. Berg, *A Dictionary of New Words in English* (London, 1953), or the supplementary pages of a dictionary which list recent vocabulary additions and select twenty or thirty new words and group them according to the categories of word-formation mentioned by Professor Simonini.

7. What derivations from the following roots can you think of:

> *cred*–(believe)   *cord*–(heart)
> *mort*–(death)   *cede* (give up, yield)
> *duce* (lead)

8. What words may be derived by adding suffixes to the following:

> code   ample   facile
> captive   drama   civil

9. What new examples of word formation can you produce by adding the following prefixes and suffixes to roots:

a. prefixes: *anti-, mini-, de-, tele-, self-, dis-*
b. suffixes: *-ish, -teria* (as in *cafeteria*), *-ee, -burger, -rama* (as in *Cinerama*), *-ite, -nik*

10. Study the earliest meanings for the following and note how present usage involves a metaphorical transfer of meaning:

> egregious   fret   petulant
> scruple   sullen   thrill

11. Consult S. V. Baum, "The Acronym, Pure and Impure," *American Speech*, XXXVII (February 1962), 48–50, and prepare an oral class report summarizing the views there expressed.

12. Words derived from proper names are fairly frequent in English. Investigate the etymology of some of the following words and briefly identify the person or place connected with them.

sandwich	bologna	hamburger	wiener	tantalize
meander	jovial	mercurial	saturnine	cashmere
port	cognac	bourbon	shetland	vandal
January	March	June	July	August
caesarean	Wednesday	Friday	pander	tuxedo
titanic	venereal	volcano	lawn	mesmerism
cereal	tawdry	brummagen	dollar	ohm
boycott	brougham	dunce	quixotic	maudlin
hector (*verb*)	chimera	bowdlerize	macadam	thrasonical
solon	stentorian	bedlam	volt	ampere
jeremiad	shrapnel	quisling	braggadoccio	Jezebel

13. Consult the *Dictionary of American Slang,* compiled by Harold Wentworth and Stuart Berg Flexner (New York, 1967), and list any examples of slang formation which are similar to the processes of word formation discussed by Professor Simonini.

17.

SIMEON POTTER

Etymology and Meaning

Few words have fixed significations like the pure numbers of mathematics
or the technical formulas of chemistry. The mathematical sign π denotes a
constant, namely, the ratio of the circumference of a circle to its diameter,
or 3.14159 . . . . The chemical formula NaCl denotes a substance, sodium
chloride, or salt, and it always means that substance and nothing else. These
symbols π and NaCl cannot vary with time or circumstance, nor do they
ever change with their contexts. Few expressions in daily use have such
simple and direct denotations as these. Even words like *mother* and *father,*
sun and *horse,* denoting primary human relationships or natural objects and
creatures, are not quite so definite. All four words occur in Old English and
their meanings have not changed in twelve centuries. But in such sayings
as 'Westminster is the mother of Parliaments', 'The child is father of the
man', 'He seeks a place in the sun', and 'He rides the high horse', the primary meanings of these words are manifestly transcended.

What is the *sun?* According to *The Oxford English Dictionary* it is
'the brightest (as seen from the earth) of the heavenly bodies, the luminary
or orb of day; the central body of the solar system, around which the earth
and other planets revolve, being kept in their orbits by its attraction and
supplied with light and heat by its radiation'. And what is the *horse?* It is
'a solid-hoofed perissodactyl quadruped (*Equus caballus*), having a flowing
mane and tail, whose voice is a neigh'. Now are these so-called 'dictionary
definitions' really definitions, or are they not descriptions? As long ago as
1891, when he was writing his magistral *Essai de Sémantique,* Michel Bréal
demonstrated that the cause of shifting meaning in so many words lay in
the impossibility of complete definition and in the varying complexity of
the word-thing relationship. 'Language', he wrote, 'designates things in an
incomplete and inaccurate manner: *incomplete,* since we have not exhausted
all that can be said of the sun when we have declared it to be shining, or
of the horse when we say that it trots: *inaccurate,* since we cannot say of

the sun that it shines when it has set, or of the horse that it trots when it is at rest, or when it is wounded or dead.'

Could the word or symbol *sun* ever alter its reference and come to mean 'moon', or 'star', or something else? That, surely, is inconceivable. *Sun* is an ancient word, indicating the same 'heavenly body' as its ancestral equivalent in Indo-European five thousand and more years ago. Day by day during those five thousand years, man has observed it 'coming forth as a bridegroom out of his chamber, and rejoicing as a giant to run his course'. Nevertheless, it has happened that ὕλ, the etymological equivalent of *sun* in Albanian (with *l*—instead of *n*—formative), has come to mean 'star'; whereas *súil*, its counterpart in Irish, has come to mean 'eye'. At some period in the history of each of these two languages that apparently simple and rigid relationship between word and thing, between *symbol* and *referend*, has been deflected and distorted. The meaning, we say, has been changed. The seemingly impossible has occurred and any notions that we may have entertained concerning the indissolubility of the links connecting *etymology* and *meaning* have been rudely dispelled. The shock is, to say the least, disconcerting. We should so much prefer to regard a 'speech-form as a relatively permanent object to which the meaning is attached as a kind of changeable satellite' (Leonard Bloomfield, *Language,* p. 426). The study of language would be so much easier for us if we could be assured that the etymology of a word is not only something *real* and *true* (as, indeed, the Greek *etymon* implies) but also that it is something permanent; and that the basic form or *root* of a word has some inherent connexion with the thing, quality or action denoted. Primitive peoples still believe that word has power over thing, that somehow the word participates of the nature of the thing. The word, in fact, is the symbol and it has no direct or immediate relation with the referend except through the image in the mind of the speaker. As Henri Delacroix once said (in *Le Langage et la Pensée*), 'All thought is symbolic. Thought first constructs symbols which it substitutes for things.' The symbol *sun* has no connexion with the celestial luminary other than through the thoughts or images in the mind of the speaker and the hearer. Unless these two images are identical, there can be no complete understanding.

Latin grammarians sometimes taught wrong etymologies long ago and more recent writers, who should have known better, have occasionally had recourse to fictitious etymologies in order to buttress a theory or to point a moral. Carylye liked to define *king* as 'he who can', associating the word with German *können* 'to be capable, to know how to'; and Ruskin found pleasure in reminding the married women in his audience that since *wife* meant 'she who weaves', their place was in the home. On the other hand, a speaker may knowingly or unwittingly ignore an etymology. He may refer to a 'dilapidated wooden shed', although *dilapidated* is strictly applicable only to a building of stone (Latin *lapis, lapidis*). He may say that 'the battalion was well equipped', although *to equip* (French *équiper*, from Old Norse *skipa*) means historically 'to fit out a ship'. He may say that 'the life-boat was manned by Wrens', 'the ocean liner sailed', and 'the cattle were shepherded into their stables'. A rediscovered etymology may be highly informative and may give pleasure. Those two attractive birds, the nuthatch and the redstart, have most interesting names. The nuthatch is that little creeping bird that breaks or *hacks* the nuts in order to feed on the kernel. For the alternation between final plosive and affricate in *hack* and *hatch*, you may like to compare *bake* and *batch, dike* and *ditch, lyke*wake and *lich*gate, *mickle* and *much, wake* and *watch*. The redstart is still called the fire-tail in some dialects and *start* 'tail' survives in *Start* Point 'tail-shaped promontory' and *stark*-naked, older *start*-naked. It is interesting to recall that a *governor* is etymologically a 'steersman', a *marshal* a 'horse-servant', and a *constable* a 'companion of the stable'. A *companion* is 'one who eats bread' with another, a *fellow* is 'one who lays down money', a *comrade* a 'chamber-fellow', and a *friend* 'one who loves'.

If the meanings of words are not fixed, if they are liable to flux and change, is there any way of predicting in which direction they are most likely to change? Do changes in meaning admit of empirical generalizations? It is the aim of students of *semantics* or *semasiology* to find the answers to these questions. So far there has been little coordination of semantic research and investigators have fallen into two groups according to their preoccupation with mental processes (Bronislaw Malinowski, C. K. Ogden, and I. A. Richards) or with mathematical symbols (Ludwig Wittgenstein, A. N. Whitehead, Bertrand Russell, and Rudolf Carnap). At present these two groups—the linguistic psychologists and the mathematical logicians—seem to be moving on different planes. The student of language sees many parallels, and he is able to distinguish certain semantic categories, but he inclines to the view that generalizations are dangerous and unprofitable.

The most obvious semantic category is that involving specialization or narrowing. When a speech-form is applied to a group of objects or ideas which resemble one another in some respect, it may naturally become restricted to just one object or idea, and if this particular restriction gains currency in a speech community, a specialized meaning prevails. *Meat*, as in *sweetmeat* and as in the archaic phrase 'meat and drink', meant any kind of food. It now means 'edible flesh', a sense formerly expressed by *flesh* and *flesh meat*. *Deer*, like Dutch *dier* and German *Tier*, used to mean 'animal' in general, as in Shakespeare's 'mice and rats and such small deer'. Latin *animal* and French *beast* have taken its place as the general words and *deer* now means 'wild ruminant of a particular (antlered) species'. *Fowl*, like Dutch and German *Vogel*, denoted 'bird in general as in Chaucer's 'Parlement of Foules' and Biblical 'fowls of the air' and as in modern names of larger kinds of birds used with a qualifying adjective, such as *sea fowl, water fowl,* and *wild fowl.* Otherwise, of course, *fowl* normally means a domestic cock or hen, especially when full grown. Hound formerly meant a dog of any breed and not, as now, a hunting-dog in particular. *Disease* was still conceived in Chaucer's day as being dis-ease 'absence of ease'. It might point to any kind of temporary discomfort and not, as now, to 'a morbid physical condition'. To *starve,* like Dutch *sterven* and German *sterben,* meant 'to die', not necessarily from lack of food. In modern Yorkshire dialect a body can still 'starve of cold'. A *wed* was a pledge of any kind. In conjunction with the suffix *-lock* forming nouns of action, it has come to be restricted to 'the marriage vow or obligation'. To the Elizabethans an *affection* was a feeling of any kind and both *lectures* and *lessons* were 'readings' of any kind. *Doctrine* was still teaching in general and *science* was still knowledge in general.

Sometimes a word has become restricted in use because a qualifier has been omitted. *Undertaker,* like French *entrepreneur* and German *Unternehmer,* used to mean 'contractor, one who *undertakes* to do a particular piece of work'. It is now used exclusively in the sense of *funeral undertaker,* although *mortician* has already superseded it in the cities and towns of America. In daily conversation *doctor* 'teacher' means 'medical doctor' and normally refers to a 'general practitioner'. Many words have both wider and narrower senses in the living language and many others have varying senses according to the persons addressed. *Pipe,* for example, evokes different images in the mind of the smoker, the plumber, the civil engineer, the geologist, the organist, and the boatswain. The *line* means a clothes-line to the laundrywoman, a fishing line to the fisherman, the equator to the seaman (as in Joseph Conrad's *Crossing the Line*), a communication wire to the telephonist, a succession of descent to the genealogist, and a particular kind of article to the man of business. To the geographer *cataract* means a cascade or waterfall, to the engineer a hydraulic controller, but a disease of the crystalline lens to the oculist.

The process of specialization and extension of meaning may take place in a language side by side. For instance, as we have just seen, *hound* has been restricted in the course of a thousand years from a dog in general to a hunting-dog in particular; contrariwise, *dog* . . . has been extended from 'a dog of ancient breed' to include any sort of dog, ranging from a formidable Alsatian to a puny and insignificant lap-dog. *Bird* meant 'young birdling', just as *pigeon* meant 'young dove' and *pig* 'young swine'. *Place* has had a remarkable history in English, where it has largely superseded the older words *stead* and *stow.* It derives from the feminine form of the Greek adjective meaning 'broad', as in *plateîa hodós* 'broad way'. In one of its senses it still means 'a group of houses in a town or city, now or formerly possessing some of the characters (positive or negative) of a square', like its well-known cognate in French, as in *Place de la Concorde,* or like Italian *piazza,* Spanish *plaza,* and German *Platz.* Now, however, it is also used in a hundred ways: 'Keep him in his place', 'It is not my place to inquire into that', 'The meeting will not take place', 'There is a place for everything', 'I have lost the place (in reading),' 'That remark was quite out of place (inappropriate, improper)', 'In the first, second place (first, secondly)'.

If we assume that the central meaning of *place* is still 'square' and that these other diverse uses *radiate* from that centre, we might equally well put it into our third semantic category: radiation, polysemia, or multiplication. Another excellent example is the word *paper.* It is the same as *papyrus,* the paper-reed of the Nile from the thin strips of which writing-sheets were first made as a substitute for parchment. The name was naturally transferred to paper made of cotton and thence to paper of linen and other fibres. To-day a paper may mean a document of any kind, for instance, a Government White Paper; an essay, dissertation or article on some particular topic, especially a communication read or sent to a learned society; a set of questions in an examination; a journal or a daily newspaper. *Power* 'ability to do, state of being able' may hold radiating meanings as diverse as 'capacity for mental or bodily action' (power of intellect, power of movement); 'mechanical or natural energy' (horse-power, candle-power, electric power-station); 'political or national strength' (the balance of power); 'possession of control or command over others, dominion, sway' (the power of the Cabinet); 'a political state' (the four great powers); and 'a mathematical conception' (5^4 or five to the fourth power). Because the *head* is that part of the human body containing the brain, it may be the top of anything, literally or metaphorically, whether it resembles the head in shape (the head of a nail, screw, pin, hammer, walking-stick, flower, or cabbage) or in position (the head of the page, the list, the bed, the table or the stairs); or it may signify the person who is the chief or leader (the head of the school, the business, the family, the house, the State, the Church). It may denote the head of a coin (that side of a coin bearing the sovereign's head); a headland or promontory (St Bees Head, Great Ormes Head, or Beachy Head, from tautologous Beau Chef Head); a single person or beast (lunch at five shillings a head, fifty head of cattle); or one of the main points or logical divisions of a subject or discourse (dealing with a theme under several heads). These and other senses do not derive from one another. They radiate from a common centre and are therefore mutually independent. Some of these senses will be translated by German *Kopf,* by French *tête,* by Spanish *cabeza* or by the ordinary word for *head* in other languages, but many senses will not permit of such direct translation. Each sense must be considered separately and, in the process of translating, our linguistic knowl-

edge may be severely put to the test. It is surprising that in ordinary conversation in English there is so little ambiguity.

It is surprising, too, that every day we use words in both literal and
metaphorical senses and that there is little danger of being misapprehended.
We may speak as we will of 'bright sunshine' or 'a bright boy'; 'a sharp
knife', 'a sharp frost' or 'a sharp rebuke'; 'a cold morning' or 'the cold war';
'the Black Country' or 'the black market'. A person who is slow-witted may
be described metaphorically as 'dull', 'obtuse', or 'dim', the latter term being
associated with the German *dumm* meaning 'stupid', although cognate with
our *dumb*. 'Dumb' in German is now *stumm,* which is related etymologically to our *stammer*. Many words are themselves old metaphors: *dependent*
'hanging from' (Latin *dē-pendens*); *egregious* 'selected from the herd'
(Latin *ē* for *ex+grex, gregis* 'herd'); *precocious* 'too early ripe' (Latin
praecox from *prae* 'before'+*coquere* 'to cook, ripen').

Our next category of semantic changes may be labelled concretization.
The naming of abstract qualities, such as *whiteness, beauty,* and *justice,*
comes late in the evolution of a language because it results from conscious
or unconscious comparison in the mind of man. Does *beauty* really exist
apart from beautiful things? On this question the medieval schoolmen
argued for centuries. No sooner are abstract nouns formed than men tend
to think of each appearance of a quality or action in the abstract as a separate entity and so, by concretization, they make abstractions tangible and
visible once more. *Youth,* 'youngness' in the abstract, becomes a 'young
man'. In the form *geogop* this word occurs eleven times in *Beowulf,* five
times with the abstract meaning 'youth', but six times with the concrete and
collective meaning 'young men'. In much the same way Latin *multitūdo*
'manyness, the quality of being many' came to signify 'a crowd' and *congregātio* 'flocking together' came to mean 'a body of people assembled'.
Barristers appointed counsel to the Crown are named *King's Counsel.* A
judge is addressed as *Your Honour* and an archbishop as *Your Grace.*
Health is the quality of being *hale* or *whole,* soundness of body and mind.
Modern man seeks diligently to maintain physical, mental, and social health.
It is Greek *hugíeia* (from the adjectival form of which comes our *hygiene*),
Latin *salūs,* French *la santé,* and German *die Gesundheit.* Clearly these are
all highly abstract forms. Nevertheless, even *health* becomes concrete in the
sense of a toast drunk—'Here's a health unto His Majesty!' *Wealth* was
primarily 'weal', 'welfare', or 'well-being', the state of being 'well'. In the
old assonantal formula 'health and wealth' the two abstract substantives were
practically synonymous. But side by side with this meaning of *wealth* the
concretized sense of 'worldly goods, riches, affluence' also developed. The
expression *wealth of nations,* denoting 'the collective riches of a people or
country', was certainly current before it was adopted by Adam Smith in

1776 as the title of his epoch-making book. 'Money', wrote John Stuart Mill in 1848, 'being the instrument of an important public and private purpose, is rightly regarded as wealth'. 'Let us substitute welfare for wealth as our governing purpose', said Edward Hallett Carr in 1948, exhorting us, in fact, to restore to the word *wealth* its older meaning. *Kindness, mercy, opportunity,* and *propriety* are historically abstractions, but to-day we speak of *kindnesses* in the plural in the sense of 'deeds of kindness', *mercies* as 'instances or manifestations of mercy', *opportunities* as 'favourable chances or occasions', and *proprieties* as 'proper forms of conduct'. Similarly *provision* 'foreseeing, foresight' has come to be applied in the plural to 'stores of food'.

Sometimes words, like men, 'fall away from their better selves' and show deterioration or catachresis. *Silly* once meant 'happy, blissful, holy', as in the 'sely child' of Chaucer's *Prioress's Tale*. Later it signified 'helpless, defenceless', becoming a conventional epithet in the 'silly sheep' of Milton, Cowper, and Matthew Arnold. Then it descended yet lower and came to imply 'foolish, feeble-minded, imbecile'. *Crafty* 'strong' and *cunning* 'knowing' were once attributes of unmingled praise. A crafty workman was one skilled in a handicraft; a cunning workman was one who knew his trade. *To counterfeit* meant simply 'to copy' reproduce', conveying no suggestion of fraud. 'What finde I here?' asked Bassanio, as he opened the leaden casket, 'Faire Portias counterfeit.' (*The Merchant of Venice*, III, ii, 115.) It was, in fact, no counterfeit in the modern sense, but a true and lifelike delineation that came 'so near creation'. A *villain* once meant 'a slave serving in a country-house or *villa'*, a man occupying a lowly station in life. Chaucer's *vileynye* already showed depreciation, for it connoted the opposite of *courteisye*, that comprehensive term for a noble and chivalrous way of life, implying high courtly elegance and politeness of manners. A *knave*, like German *ein Knabe*, was just 'a boy'; later, as in 'the kokes knave, thet wassheth the disshes' of the *Ancrene Riwle*, 'a boy or lad employed as a servant'; later still, 'a base and crafty rogue'. Like *rogue* and *rascal, knave* may still be used jocularly without seriously implying bad qualities. *Varlet,* a variant of *valet*, has shown an almost identical catachresis. *Nice* has become just a pleasant verbal counter: anything or everything may be nice. But *nescius,* its Latin antecedent, had the precise meaning 'ignorant, unaware', a meaning maintained in Chaucer side by side with that of 'foolish'. From 'foolish' it developed the sense 'foolishly particular about small things', and so 'fastidious, precise', as in 'nice in one's dress'. Later it was made to refer to actions or qualities, as in 'a nice discrimination' and 'a nice sense of honour'. Since then, as H. W. Fowler has sagaciously observed in *A Dictionary of Modern English Usage,* 'it has been too great a favourite with the ladies, who have charmed out of it all its individuality and converted it into a mere diffuser of vague and mild agreeableness'. It is a pleasant, lazy word which careful speakers are bound to avoid using in serious contexts. *Propaganda,* which now implies an organized and vicious distortion of facts for a particular purpose, has suffered sad depreciation in recent years. In 1622 Pope Gregory XV founded a special Committee or Congregation of Cardinals for the Propagation of the Faith, in Latin *Congregātio dē propāgandā fide.* That marked the beginning of the history of this word, which, you see, is the ablative singular feminine form of the gerundive of *propāgāre* 'to fasten or peg down slips of plants for growth, to multiply plants by layering'. Most appropriately the Latin metaphor is agricultural and botanical. *Propaganda* should mean, in its extended sense, the dissemination of news of any kind. Unfortunately, since the year 1880 the meaning of the word has been poisoned. Propaganda and trustworthy news are dissociated in our minds. We even hear of propaganda and counter-propaganda!

Now all these semantic categories—specialization, extension, radiation, metaphor, concretization, and deterioration—are very interesting. Others too might be added to show in yet greater detail how inconstant are the relationships between symbol, image, and referend (word, thought, and thing). Men have sometimes associated speech-forms wrongly and the meanings of words have thus been modified capriciously and unpredictably. Let us admit that there have been losses and gains. When we blunder and are forced to offer abject apologies, we talk of eating *humble pie* and not *umble pie,* one made of umbles or entrails. Vaguely and hazily we may associate the epithet with *humble bee,* which is the old *hummle bee,* the bee that continuously *hums.* Hazily and lazily we may associate an *insurance policy* with the Government's *foreign policy,* not pausing to recollect that these two *policies* are etymologically quite different words. We associate *touchy* with *to touch,* forgetting that *touchy, techy,* or *tetchy* derives from *tetch* 'a fit of petulance or anger, a tantrum'. We say *restive* 'refusing to move or budge' when we are half thinking of *restless.* Pardonably, perhaps, we connect *uproar* with *roar* and *outrage* with *rage.*

Certain expressions, like *comity* and *fruition,* are frequently 'used loosely', and, since they are correspondingly in danger of being 'understood loosely' too, careful speakers are almost compelled to refrain from using them. *Comity* means 'courtesy, urbanity', not 'company, assembly'. The *comity of nations* is 'the obligation recognized by civilized nations to respect one another's laws and customs'. *Fruition* signifies 'enjoyment', not 'bearing of fruit'. 'If we live by hope', said Bishop Hugh Latimer, 'let us desire the end and fruition of our hope'. Like Archbishop Thomas Cranmer in the Epiphany Collect, Latimer was here using the word correctly. Today we frequently hear of plans and projects 'coming, or being brought, to fruition'. *Definitive* 'having the quality or character of finality' should not be used as a more imposing form of *definite* 'clear, precise, unmistakable'. Our conception of the Middle Ages may be given a rosy tinge by an over-optimistic misinterpretation of the phrase 'merry England', echoed by Sir Walter Scott in the opening sentence of *Ivanhoe*. King Charles II was 'the merry monarch' and fun-fairs have their 'merry-go-rounds', but 'merry England' implied a pleasant and delightful countryside rather than a gay and carefree people. It was in the Northern *Cursor Mundi* that this epithet was first applied specifically to England. Later medieval poets repeated it and Spenser gave it wide currency in the First Book of *The Faerie Queene* (Canto X, Stanza 61) when he identified the Red Cross Knight with 'Saint George of mery England'. But Spenser's 'mery England' in the sixteenth century meant much the same as Blake's 'England's green and pleasant land' in the early nineteenth.

When Francis Bacon referred to various people in the course of his *Essays* as *indifferent, obnoxious,* and *officious,* he was describing them as 'impartial', 'submissive', and 'ready to serve'. When King James II observed that the new St Paul's Cathedral was *amusing, awful,* and *artificial,* he implied that Sir Christopher Wren's recent creation was 'pleasing, awe-inspiring, and skilfully achieved'. When Dr Johnson averred that Milton's *Lycidas* was *easy, vulgar,* and therefore *disgusting'*, he intended to say that it was 'effortless, popular, and therefore not in good taste'.

Men frequently find themselves at cross-purposes with one another because they persist in using words in different senses. Their long arguments emit more heat than light because their conceptions of the point at issue, whether Marxism, democracy, capitalism, the good life, western civilization, culture, art, internationalism, freedom of the individual, equality of opportunity, redistribution of wealth, social security, progress, or what not, are by no means identical. From heedlessness, sloth, or sheer lack of intelligence men do not trouble to clarify their conceptions. Symbols or counters remain unchanged, but as the argument proceeds images and referends (thoughts and things) vary without end. By the way, what do *you* mean by *progress?* To define your terms at every step may seem an intolerable burden, but it is a sobering and salutary discipline. It is, indeed, the only effective way to sharpen up a blunted word and restore its cutting edge.

Vocabulary

denoting, Indo-European, plosive, affricative

Review Questions

1. Identify Michel Bréal, Henri Delacroix, Thomas Carlyle, and John Ruskin.
2. Distinguish among symbol, image, and referend.

3. What kind of questions do students of semantics or semasiology attempt to answer?

4. Identify C. K. Ogden, I. A. Richards, and Bronislaw Malinowski; Ludwig Wittgenstein, A. N. Whitehead, Bertrand Russell, and Rudolph Carnap.

5. Explain each of the following types of semantic change and give two examples of each: specialization, extension, radiation, metaphor, concretization, and deterioration.

Expository Technique

1. How does the opening comparison between words and the symbolic vocabulary of science relate to the subject of this essay?

2. Is there a controlling idea in this essay? If so, where does it appear? If it is more implicit than explicit, attempt to formulate it in your own words.

3. If there is a central Controlling Idea, how does the discussion of various kinds of semantic change relate to it?

4. Does the essay have an "end"? If so, where does the end begin and how does it relate to the rest of the essay?

5. In the enumeration of the various processes of semantic change is there any discernible order or arrangement?

Exercises

1. Specialization and generalization, or "extension," are changes in the area of meaning attached to a word. Specialization narrows the application of a word to a limited meaning; generalization extends a word to a number of meanings. Consult the *OED* or *Webster's Third New International Dictionary* for any one group of the following words, study the meanings recorded there, and determine whether the process of meaning change represents specialization or generalization.

carol	tyrant	zest	engine
village	desert	disease	awful
virtue	meat	liquor	dainty
corn	tall	translate	picture
quarantine	butcher	injury	starve

2. Degeneration, or *pejoration,* is the process by which a word which originally conveyed a favorable meaning acquires an unfavorable one. Regeneration, or elevation or amelioration, is the process by which a word which originally conveyed an unfavorable meaning acquires a favorable one. Consult either the *OED* or the *Webster's Third New International Dictionary* and note the changes in meaning which the following words have undergone. Determine whether the change represents degeneration or elevation.

boor	churl	silly	wench	pioneer
boudoir	luxury	victuals	asylum	idiot
smug	hypocrite	courtesan	fascinate	sly
zealot	Quaker	Methodist	marshal	merchant
sophist	propaganda	fond	budge	coax
enthusiasm	knight	chivalry	imp	harlot
lewd	vice	minister	vulgar	amateur

3. Radiation is a process by which one word accumulates a number of significations which derive from a common central meaning but are mutually independent. The relation of the central to the radiated meanings is like that of the hub to the spokes of a wheel. Professor Potter illustrates this process with the meanings of *power* and *head*. Study the meanings for *pipe, heart, root,* or *hand* and be prepared to discuss the radiation of meanings from a central signification.

18.

HAROLD WHITEHALL

The Development of the English Dictionary

The evolution of the English dictionary is rooted in the general evolution of the English language. In this development the chief pressures were exerted by the steady increase in the word stock of English from the 50,000–60,000 words of Anglo-Saxon through the 100,000–125,000 words of the Middle-English vocabulary to the huge total of some 650,000 words which could theoretically be recorded in an exhaustive dictionary of contemporary English. Such an overall increase as this made the dictionary *necessary.* The pressure of vocabulary, however, has always been influenced and reinforced by the intellectual climate of each successive period of the language. A dictionary is not exactly a work of art, yet it bears as strongly as an artistic production the impress of the age that bore it. For that reason, the history of the dictionary is a fascinating chapter in the history of ideas.

The beginnings of dictionary history are neither national nor concerned with any of the national languages. They are concerned with the international language of medieval European civilization: Latin. Our first word books are lists of relatively difficult Latin terms, usually those of a Scriptural nature, accompanied by glosses in easier or more familiar Latin. Very early in the Anglo-Saxon period, however, we find glosses containing native English (i.e., Anglo-Saxon) equivalents for the hard Latin terms, and it may be that two of these—the *Leiden* and *Erfurt Glosses*—represent the earliest written English we possess. Such glosses, whether Latin-Latin or Latin-English, continued to be compiled during the entire Anglo-Saxon and most of the Middle-English period.

The next stage of development, attained in England around 1400, was the collection of the isolated glosses into what is called a *glossarium,* a kind of very early Latin-English dictionary. As it chances, our first example of the glossarium, the so-called *Medulla Grammatica* written in East Anglia around 1400, has never been printed; but two later redactions were among our earliest printed books, and one of these, the *Promptorium Parvulorum sive clericorum,* issued by Wynkyn de Worde in 1499, was the first work of a dictionary nature ever to be printed on English soil. Significantly enough, this version of the *Medulla* places the English term first and its Latin equivalent second.

The first onset of the Renaissance worked against rather than in favor of the native English dictionary. The breakdown of Latin as an international language and the rapid development of international trade led to an immediate demand for foreign-language dictionaries. The first of such works, Palsgrave's *Lesclaircissement de la Langue Francoyse* (1523), was rapidly followed by Salesbury's Welsh-English dictionary (1547), Percival's English-Spanish dictionary (1591), and finally, by the best known of all such works, Florio's Italian-English dictionary (1599). Meanwhile, the first great classical dictionary, Cooper's *Thesaurus* (1565), had already appeared. The history of dictionaries is larded with strange occurrences: we are not surprised, therefore, that the publication of Cooper's work was delayed five years because his wife, fearing that too much lexicography would kill her husband, burned the first manuscript of his magnum opus. It should be noted, in passing, that none of these various word books of the 16th century actually used the title *dictionary* or *dictionarium.* They were called by various kinds of fanciful or half-fanciful names, of which *hortus* "garden," and *thesaurus* "hoard" were particularly popular.

During the late 16th century, the full tide of the Renaissance had been sweeping a curious flotsam and jetsam into English literary harbors. Constant reading of Greek and Latin bred a race of Holofernes pedants who preferred the Latin or Greek term to the English term. Their principle in writing was to use Latino-Greek polysyllabics in a Latino-English syntax. Their strange vocabulary—studded with what some critics call "inkhorn" terms—eventually affected English so powerfully that no non-Latinate Englishman could ever hope to read many works in his own language unless he was provided with explanations of elements unfamiliar to him. The "Dictionary of Hard Words," the real predecessor of the modern dictionary, was developed to provide precisely such explanations. It is significant that the first English word book to use the name *dictionary*, Cokeram's *The English Dictionary* (1623), is subtitled "An Interpreter of Hard Words." Among those explained on its first few pages are *Abequitate, Bulbulcitate,* and *Sullevation*. In point of time, the first "dictionary of hard words" was Robert Cawdrey's *Table Alphabeticall of Hard Words* (1604). Of the various works of the same class appearing after this date may be mentioned John Bullokar's *English Expositor* (1616) and Edward Phillip's *New World of Words* (1658), both of which reveal a strong interest in the reform of spelling, Blount's *Glossographia* (1656) containing the first etymologies ever to appear in a printed English dictionary, and Thomas Kersey's *Dictionarium Anglo-Brittanicum* (1708), which also includes legal terms, provincialisms, and archaisms. If the 16th was the century of the foreign-language dictionary, the 17th was the century of the dictionary of hard words.

Between 1708 and 1721, hard-word dictionaries began to be replaced by word books giving ever-increasing attention to literary usage. The Latino-Greek borrowings of the earlier century had been either absorbed into the language or sloughed away. The French influence, from 1660 onwards, had replaced Renaissance stylistic ideas with notions of a simple elegance in syntax and a quiet effectiveness in vocabulary. These stylistic virtues were actually achieved in the works of Swift, Addison, Steele, and lesser writers. The literary mind of the early 18th century, therefore, was convinced that English had finally attained a standard of purity such as it had never previously known; it was also convinced that the brash outgrowth of mercantile expansionism, later to be reinforced by the infant Industrial Revolution, might very well destroy this hard-won standard of literary refinement. What more natural than that the standard should be enshrined in a dictionary for the admiration and guidance of posterity?

The first word book to embody the ideals of the age was Nathaniel Bailey's *Universal Etymological Dictionary of the English Language,* originally published in 1721, and then, in a beautiful folio volume with illustrations by Flaxman, in 1731. This, one of the most revolutionary dictionaries ever to appear, was the first to pay proper attention to current usage, the first to feature etymology, the first to give aid in syllabification, the first to give illustrative quotations (chiefly from proverbs), the first to include illustrations, and the first to indicate pronunciation. An interleaved copy of the 1731 folio edition was the basis of Samuel Johnson's *Dictionary* of 1755; through Johnson, it influenced all subsequent lexicographical practice. The position of dictionary pioneer, commonly granted to Johnson or to Noah

THE DEVELOPMENT OF THE ENGLISH DICTIONARY

Webster, belongs in reality to one of the few geniuses lexcography ever produced: Nathaniel Bailey.

Johnson's *Dictionary* (1755) enormously extends the techniques developed by Bailey. Johnson was able to revise Bailey's crude etymologies on the basis of Francis Junius' *Etymologicon Anglicanum* (first published in 1743), to make a systematic use of illustrative quotations, to fix the spelling of many disputed words, to develop a really discriminating system of definition, and to exhibit the vocabulary of English much more fully than had ever been attempted before. In his two-volume work, the age and following ages found their ideal word book. Indeed, a good deal of the importance of the book lies in its later influence. It dominated English letters for a full century after its appearance and, after various revisions, continued in common use until 1900. As late as the '90's, most Englishmen used the word *dictionary* as a mere synonym for Johnson's *Dictionary;* in 1880 a Bill was actually thrown out of Parliament because a word in it was not in "the Dictionary."

One of the tasks taken taken upon himself by Johnson was to remove "improprieties and absurdities" from the language. In short, he became a linguistic legislator attempting to perform for English those offices performed for French by the French Academy. From this facet of his activities we get the notion, still held by many dictionary users, and fostered by many dictionary publishers, that the dictionary is a "supreme authority" by which to arbitrate questions of "correctness" and "incorrectness." The dictionaries of the second half of the 18th century extended this notion particularly to the field of pronunciation. By 1750, the increasing wealth of the middle classes was making itself felt in the social and political worlds. Those who possessed it, speakers, for the most part, of a middle-class dialect, earnestly desired a key to the pronunciations accepted in polite society. To provide for their needs, various pronunciation experts—usually of Scottish or Irish extraction—edited a series of pronunciation dictionaries. Of these, the most important are James Buchanan's *New English Dictionary* (1769), William Kenrick's *New Dictionary of the English Language* (1773), Thomas Sheridan's *General Dictionary of the English Language* (1780), and, above all, John Walker's *Critical Pronouncing Dictionary and Expositor of the English Language* (1791). In such works, pronunciation was indicated by small superscript numbers referring to the "powers" of the various vowel sounds. Despite the legislative function exercised by the authors of almost all of these works, we must admit that they did indicate contemporary pronunciation with great accuracy, and when Walker's pronunciations were combined with Johnson's definitions the result was a dictionary which dominated the word-book field, both in England and the United States, until well after 1850.

If the chief contributions of the 18th century to dictionary making were

(1) authoritative recording of literary vocabulary and (2) accurate recording of pronunciation, those of the 19th were unmistakably (1) the recording of word history through dated quotations and (2) the development of encyclopedic word books. Already in 1755, Samuel Johnson had hinted in his preface that the sense of a word "may easily be collected entire from the examples." During the first twenty-five years of the century, the researches of R. K. Rask, J. L. C. Grimm, and F. Bopp clearly defined the historical principle in linguistics. It was only a question of time, therefore, before someone combined Johnson's perception with the findings of the new science of historical linguistics. That person was Charles Richardson, who, in this *New Dictionary of the English Language* (1836), produced a dictionary completely lacking definitions but one in which both the senses and the historical evolution of the senses were accurately indicated by dated defining quotations. Richardson's work leads directly to the great *New English Dictionary on Historical Principles,* first organized in 1858, begun under Sir James Murray in 1888, and completed under Sir William Craigie in 1928. With its supplement (1933), the *New English Dictionary* or *Oxford English Dictionary* (N.E.D. or O.E.D.) covers the vocabulary of English with a completeness of historical evidence and a discrimination of senses unparalleled in linguistic history. No other language has ever been recorded on anything approaching this scale, and no dictionary of English since the *New English Dictionary* was completed has failed to reveal a profound debt to this monumental work. As compared with the effort represented by the N.E.D., the attempt to record the technological vocabularies of the language as first seen in John W. Ogilvie's *Universal Dictionary of the English Language* (1850) seems to be of minor importance, although it has had great practical effect on subsequent American dictionaries.

Since the publication of the O.E.D., the only important British dictionary has been Henry Cecil Wyld's *Universal Dictionary of the English Language* (1932), a work of somewhat restricted vocabulary coverage but one which may well point the way to the dictionary of the future. Wyld has discarded the older logical definitions for definitions of a more functional nature; his examples delve deeply into idiom; his etymologies are of a completeness and modernity unparalleled until this present dictionary in any medium-sized word book. The failure of Wyld's book to achieve much popularity on this side of the Atlantic underlines the fact that the typical American dictionary of the English language is a work *differing in kind* from any of those so far mentioned. It differs because the conditions of American life and culture differ from those of English life and culture.

The modern American dictionary is typically a single compact volume published at a relatively modest price containing: (1) definitive American spellings, (2) pronunciations indicated by diacritical markings, (3) strictly limited etymologies, (4) numbered senses, (5) some illustrations, (6) selective treatment of synonyms and antonyms, (7) encyclopedic inclusion of scientific, technological, geographical, and biographical items. It owes its development, within the general framework of the evolution sketched above, to the presence of a large immigrant population in this country, to the elaborate American system of popular education, and to the vast commercial opportunities implicit in both of these.

The first American dictionaries were unpretentious little schoolbooks based chiefly on Johnson's *Dictionary* of 1755 by way of various English abridgments of that work. The earliest of these were Samuel Johnson Junior's *School Dictionary* (1798), Johnson and Elliott's *Selected Pronouncing and Accented Dictionary* (1800), and Caleb Alexander's *Columbian Dictionary* (1800). The most famous work of this class, Noah Webster's *Compendious Dictionary of the English Language* (1806) was an enlargement of Entick's *Spelling Dictionary* (London, 1764), distinguished from its predecessors chiefly by a few encyclopedic supplements and emphasis upon its (supposed) Americanism. The book was never popular and contributed little either to Webster's own reputation or to the development of the American dictionary in general.

The first important date in American lexicography is 1828. The work that makes it important is Noah Webster's *An American Dictionary of the English Language* in two volumes. Webster's book has many deficiencies— etymologies quite untouched by the linguistic science of the time, a rudimentary pronunciation system actually inferior to that used by Walker in 1791, etc.—but in its insistence upon American spellings, in definitions keyed to the American scene, and in its illustrative quotations from the Founding Fathers of the Republic, it provided the country with the first *native* dictionary comparable in scope with that of Dr. Johnson. It was not, as is often claimed, the real parent of the modern American dictionary; it was merely the foster-parent. Because of its two-volume format and its relatively high price it never achieved any great degree of popular acceptance in Webster's own lifetime. Probably its greatest contribution to succeeding American dictionaries was the style of definition writing—writing of a clarity and pithiness never approached before its day.

The first American lexicographer to hit upon the particular pattern that distinguishes the American dictionary was Webster's lifelong rival, Joseph E. Worcester. His *Comprehensive, Pronouncing, and Explanatory Dictionary of the English Language* (1830), actually a thoroughly revised abridgment of Webster's two-volume work of 1828, was characterized by the addition of new words, a more conservative spelling, brief, well-phrased definitions, full indication of pronunciation by means of diacritics, use of stress marks to divide syllables, and lists of synonyms. Because it was compact and low priced, it immediately became popular—far more popular, in fact, than any of Webster's own dictionaries in his own lifetime. As George P.

Krapp, in his *The English Language in America,* says: "If one balances the faults of the Webster of 1828 against the faults of the Worcester of 1830, the totals are greatly in the favor of Worcester." One might feel the same about its merits as compared with those of Webster's own revision of his *American Dictionary* (1841), which featured the inclusion of scientific terms compiled by Professor W. Tully. The first Webster dictionary to embody the typical American dictionary pattern was that of 1847, edited by Noah Webster's son-in-law, Chauncey A. Goodrich, and published by the Merriams.

Temperamentally the flamboyant Noah Webster and the cautious Joseph Worcester were natural rivals. Their rivalry, however, was as nothing compared with that which developed between the rival publishers of the Webster and Worcester dictionaries. By 1845, the great flood of immigration and the vast extension of the school system had suddenly lifted dictionary making into the realm of big business. In a "war of the dictionaries" that reflects the rudimentary business ethics of the period, the rival publishers used every device of advertisement and every stratagem of high-powered salesmanship to drive each other off the market. Unsavory as this war appears in retrospect, it certainly helped to force rapid improvement of the dictionaries that these publishers controlled. Worcester's initial advantages were surpassed in the Merriam-Webster of 1847; the innovations in Worcester's edition of 1860 were more than paralleled in the Merriam-Webster of 1864, one of the best dictionaries ever to appear, but one from which almost everything really characteristic of Noah Webster himself was deleted. The battle was finally decided in favor of the Webster dictionaries, chiefly because the popularity of Webster's "Little Blue Back Speller" had put their name in every household, partly because of the death of Joseph Worcester, and partly because of the merit of the Merriam product from 1864 onwards.

Since about 1870, the climate of American dictionary making has been much more peaceful. In the field of unabridged dictionaries, the most important accretion is the *Century Dictionary* (1889), edited by the great American linguist, William Dwight Whitney, and issued in six volumes. Unfortunately, this magnificent work, considered by many authorities to be basically the finest ever issued by a commercial publisher, has lost much of its popularity because of inadequate subsequent revision. The fact that it was not in a one-volume format undoubtedly also worked against its popular success. The only other new unabridged dictionaries that have appeared in the period are Webster's *Imperial Dictionary of the English Language* (1904), and Funk and Wagnalls *New Standard Dictionary* (1893). The first of these, the only unabridged dictionary ever published west of the Appalachians, was issued in Chicago by George W. Ogilvie, a publisher who carried on his own private guerrilla "war of the dictionaries" against the Merriam Company between 1904 and circa 1917. At the moment, the most important advances in lexicography are taking place in the field of the abridged collegiate-type dictionaries.

Meanwhile, the scholarly dictionary has not been neglected. Once the *New English Dictionary* was published, scholarly opinion realized the need to supplement it in the various periods of English and particularly in American English. The first of the proposed supplements, edited by Sir William Craigie and Professor J. R. Hulbert, is the *Dictionary of American English on Historical Principles,* completed in 1944. This was followed by a *Dictionary of Americanisms,* edited by Mitford M. Mathews and published in 1951. A *Middle English Dictionary,* a *Dictionary of the Older Scottish Tongue,* and a *Dictionary of Later Scottish* are in preparation, and work on the *American Dialect Dictionary* of the American Dialect Society is now finally under way.

Vocabulary

flotsam and jetsam, pedants, provincialism, archaisms, mercantile, facet, arbitrate, lexicography, stratagem, unsavory

Review Questions

1. Who was Holofernes and how is he appropriate to the discussion?
2. Explain "inkhorn" terms and "hard-word" dictionaries.
3. Why does the author speak of Nathaniel Bailey's *Dictionary* (1721) as "one of the most revolutionary dictionaries ever to appear"?
4. What were the chief contributions of the eighteenth century to dictionary making? Of the nineteenth century?
5. How might Henry Cecil Wyld's *Universal Dictionary* (1932) be said to "point the way to the dictionary of the future"?
6. Why is the year 1828 important in American lexicography?
7. What is "the typical American dictionary pattern"?
8. The author asserts that "the history of the dictionary is a fascinating chapter in the history of ideas." Give two examples from the essay which show this relationship.

Expository Technique

1. What is the most precise formulation of the controlling idea of this essay?
2. Show how the author carries out this idea in his essay.
3. The essay contains a considerable amount of information—names, dates, titles, and so forth. Discuss the organization principle(s) by which this information is ordered and made intelligible.

Writing Suggestions: Process

1. Using the specimen texts in Exercise 1, pages 250–253, and background information gained from Miss Schlauch's essay, pages 223–249, discuss the principal stages in the development from Old English to the present day.
2. Review the principal processes of word-making, discussed by Professor Simonini, pages 254–261, select two or three which you find most interesting, discuss, and illustrate by examples in current usage.
3. Examine the *Dictionary of American Slang,* compiled by Harold Wentworth and Stuart Berg Flexner (New York, 1967), and see what patterns you can discern in the formation of slang. On the basis of your investigation discuss some of the more interesting processes of slang formation.
4. Using the information gathered in Exercise 12, page 263, supplemented by other examples if you wish, discuss the process of conversion of proper names into general vocabulary words.
5. Using the information gathered in Exercise 2, pages 273–274, supplemented as necessary, discuss the semantic processes known as "degeneration" (or "pejoration") and "regeneration" ("elevation" or "amelioration").
6. Using the information gathered in Exercise 3, page 274, discuss the semantic process known as "radiation."
7. Using the information gathered in Exercise 1, page 273, supplemented as necessary, discuss the semantic processes known as "specialization" and "generalization."
8. Consult Walter W. Skeat, *Etymological Dictionary of the English Language,* 4th ed. (Oxford, 1910), or the similar work by Charles T. Onions and others (Oxford, 1966), and the *OED* and write a "biography" of the origin, changes in form, and changes in meaning of three or four words which interest you.
9. Investigate the process of name-giving in one of the following areas:
   personal names (perhaps in terms of certain national or ethnic practices)
   calendar names (days, months)
   place-names on the moon
   brand names for commercial products
   names of buildings on your campus
   stage-names for performers (motion picture stars, exotic dancers, comedians, etc.)
   street names in your city
10. Read pp. vii–xx, Vol. I, of the *OED.* Drawing upon the information found there, but using your own words, discuss the compilation of the material for this famous scholarly dictionary. (A similar discussion might be made of the compilation of two scholarly dictionaries of American English: *A Dictionary of American English on Historical Principles,* ed. Sir. William

Craigie, J. R. Hulbert, et al. [Chicago, 1936], and *A Dictionary of Americanisms,* ed. Mitford M. Mathews [Chicago, 1951].)

11. Read the Preface (many times reprinted) by Samuel Johnson to his famous *Dictionary of the English Language* (1755) and the discussion of this work in James Boswell's *Life of Samuel Johnson,* Modern Library edition (New York, 1931), pp. 105–109. Using information gathered from these sources, discuss the process by which Johnson produced his dictionary. (Additional information about Johnson's *Dictionary* can be found in Chapter IV of Joseph Wood Krutch, *Samuel Johnson* [New York, 1944].)

12. Discuss the process of selecting a good dictionary for purchase.

13. Write a directional process instructing a high school reader in the best way to use a dictionary.

14. Discuss a particular method of foreign language instruction (the Berlitz, for example, or one of the armed services language schools), or the operation of a language laboratory for instructional purposes.

15. Discuss the process of adding to one's vocabulary.

16. Discuss the process you would follow to estimate the number of words in the English language.

17. Discuss the process of teaching English as a foreign language. What problems would you expect to meet? How would you overcome them?

Analysis:
Division and Classification

ANALYSIS is the resolution of a subject into its component parts. It is an operation which we perform each day, for when we work out a study schedule or plan a budget, sort clothing to be sent either to the dry cleaners or to the laundry, or distinguish what we regard as the components of a friend's personality, we are analyzing. In expository writing, analysis serves to inform the reader about the composition of some subject. We have already seen that analysis is involved in explaining a process (see pages 207–211), for essential to that kind of expository writing is the division of the process into its significant steps or stages. But analysis is equally applicable to the discussion of subjects thought of as static, *e.g.,* an object, an idea, or an organization. Such subjects may be analyzed by one of two methods: division or classification. They may be distinguished by the subject to which each is applicable and by the results which each produces.

Analysis by division is applied to a subject thought of as a single entity. A sailboat, for example, may be divided into its hull, mast, rudder, and sail; or a play into acts and scenes; or a chemical compound such as sulphuric acid into its constituent elements: hydrogen, sulphur, and oxygen. As these examples indicate, the results of analysis by division are *parts* of the subject under analysis. Analysis by classification, on the other hand, is applied to a subject thought of as plural. Boats may be classified on the basis of their use as commercial, military, and private. Polonius, to the amusement of the court at Elsinore, classifies plays, according to their subject-matter, as "tragedy, comedy, history, pastoral, pastoral-comical, historical-pastoral, tragical-historical, tragical-comical-historical-pastoral." Inorganic compounds may be classified depending upon their behavior in aqueous solution as acids, salts, and bases. The results of analysis by classification are *wholes,* rather than *parts,* that is, lesser types of the larger subject which is being analyzed.

SPECIAL PROBLEMS IN ANALYSIS

A satisfactory analysis by either division or classification requires that the analysis be logical and, to the degree appropriate for the purpose of the analysis, thorough.

The first requirement for a logically sound analysis is that only one principle or basis of analysis be employed at any one time. The use of two or more principles of division or classification at the same time, sometimes designated as the fallacy of cross-reference, results in a meaningless analysis. Such an error would be committed by a catalogue librarian who classified books as general works, philosophy, religion, sociology, philology, natural science, useful arts, fine arts, literature, history, and quartos. The principle of classification here would seem to be that of subject matter, but the inclusion of "quartos" indicates that a second principle is also at work: classification by book size. The same kind of error would be involved if a college registrar analyzed the students at his college as veterans, nonveterans, philosophy majors, and juniors. Here the students are being classified by three different principles simultaneously: military experience, subject interest, and class membership. In addition to being meaningless, such illogical analyses are also confusing.

This is not to say that a subject may not be analyzed in more than one way. A college administrator may very well want to know how many veterans and nonveterans there are in the student body, how many majors in each discipline, and how many members in each class. But to supply such information would require three separate analyses, each conducted according to one principle.

A second requirement for a logical analysis is that the categories or parts into which the subject is analyzed be mutually exclusive. If, for example, the federal government were divided into the executive, judicial, legislative, and senatorial branches, the analysis would be faulty logically, because one of the elements is included in another: "senatorial" is a part of the legislative branch. A similar weakness would be found in an analysis which divided the personnel of a college into administration, faculty, Professor X, and students. Though most colleges, no doubt, have Professor X's who seem to demand or to deserve their own unique categories, such an analysis would be logically weak unless the writer were deliberately seeking a comic or witty effect, since Professor X would already be in the category of "faculty."

A third requirement for a logical analysis is that the members produced by each level of analysis be coordinate or comparable. Dean Y, faculty, and student body, as an analysis of the personnel of a college, does not satisfy this requirement. The items are not coordinate: "Dean Y" is more specific than "faculty" and "student body." The substitution of an individual for a group in this instance produces an analysis with conflicting levels. The division would logically be administration, faculty, and student body. One might then proceed to analyze each general group into its specific individuals.

In addition to being logical, a satisfactory analysis should be thorough. The degree of thoroughness in terms of the number of levels of analysis is relative to the individual's purpose. If a student in an elementary course in chemistry is given a solution containing four unknown elements which he is directed to identify, the success of his analysis of the solution will be judged by the number of unknowns which he correctly identifies. He probably would not be expected, however, to analyze the molecular structure of each of the four elements. In the same way, a student discussing the structure of the United Nations might wish merely to delineate the major components of this organization: the Secretariat, the Security Council, and the General Assembly. If his study were to be more detailed, however, he would then continue his analysis by indicating the components of each of these divisions. On any level, however, the analysis should be as thorough as possible.

When the structure of a subject is generally known or verifiable, it is fairly simple to evaluate the analysis offered. An informed reader would judge as deficient, for instance, a classification of the languages of the Indo-European family of languages which omitted mention of the Teutonic or Germanic branch, or an analysis of forms of government which omitted monarchies. However, there are many subjects whose components may not so easily be verified and whose analyses depend primarily on the judgment or interpretation of the individual making the analysis. In a well-known passage in his essay "Of Studies," Sir Francis Bacon imposed his own classification on books when he wrote:

> Some books are to be tasted, others to be swallowed, and some few to be chewed and digested; that is, some books are to be read only in parts; others to be read but not curiously; and some few to be read wholly, and with diligence and attention.

In an essay in the last section of this book, John Ciardi analyzes Robert Frost's poem "Stopping by Woods on a Snowy Evening" by dividing it into three "scenes." Other writers might add further categories to Bacon's three classes of books or make some other kind of division in analyzing Frost's poem. Though the criteria for judging such subjective analyses are not so definite as those pertaining to subjects which can be more objectively examined, the reader can expect that the analysis will not be superficial or casually impressionistic.

ORGANIZATION

It is frequently convenient in the first paragraph of an essay of analysis to state the subject and the principle by which it will be analyzed and to mention the components to be discussed. The organization of the main body of the composition is fairly simple, for the components established by the analysis are the subjects of the major sections of the essay. Each of these components should be discussed in sufficient detail to distinguish it from the others and to establish its relationship to the whole subject. The writer then needs merely to arrange the sections in the most effective order and to tie the parts together through transitional words and phrases.

AN EXAMPLE OF ANALYSIS

The following discussion utilizes both classification and division: classification as it categorizes the systems of communicational behavior, division as it breaks a category into its components.

SYSTEMS OF COMMUNICATION*

Communication is a specialization of symbolic behavior that exists conterminously with culture and society. Three systems may be used. One is vocalization, the making of various noises other than those of language proper. Another is the system of gestures and body movements, kinesics. The third and principal one is language.

Vocalizations include the noises that differentiate, on the basis of vocal quality, various emotional situations. Noises like laughing and crying are made by the newborn infant, but after about six weeks communication in terms of them begins. Crying is employed to signal distress, hunger and the like, and ceases when these are relieved; laughing is used in pleasurable situations. Other forms of vocalization include whispering, shouting, over-all nasalization and moaning. There are also vocal qualifiers: overloudness, oversoftness, over-high pitch, overlow pitch, drawl, clipping (shortened enunciation), singing (spreading of all pitch extremes), monotone (reduction of pitch differences), rasp, openness (opposite of rasp) and others. A third kind of vocalization is the use of verbal identifiers; in *uhuh* or *ahah* meaning affirmation, "yes," there is a smooth transition between the syllables, whereas in *uh-uh* or *ah-ah* meaning "no," there is a glottal closure.

* Reprinted by permission from *Encyclopaedia Britannica*, XIII, 669.

A system of kinesics involves units of body motion or gesture, such as an extended finger, a wink, a raising of an eyebrow, and patterns of units such as a shaking of the head accompanied by an admonitory finger and perhaps movement of the arms. Kinesic communication systems are more nearly alike in different parts of the world than are linguistic systems, but even within one area there may be clear differences.

In language, the principal and most complex communication system, there are systematically differentiated sounds, which are arranged into grammatically significant sequences, accompanied by elements of meaning from kinesics and vocalization.

Exercises on Analysis

1. Divide five objects into their constituent parts.
2. Classify five subjects, stating in each instance the principle of analysis you are using.
3. Analyze one subject by classification which will yield at least three categories each of which can be analyzed into subclasses.
4. Which of the items in each of the following series is inappropriate to the series in which it appears:
a. circle, triangle, square, rectangle
b. violin, piano, cello, viola
c. brick, stone, wood, slate
d. omelet, custard, soufflé
e. shark, tuna, whale, marlin
f. automobile, motorcycle, bus, airplane
g. oil, furnace, coal, gas
h. fry, bake, broil, chill
5. According to national origin into what categories may the following be analyzed:

| brioche | tamale | praline | pone | hominy |
| chowder | succotash | noodle | zwieback | sauerbraten |

6. How might you classify the following (add headings if you wish):

"The Fall of the House of Usher"	*Macbeth*	"Kubla Khan"	*Joseph Andrews*
	Babbitt	*Paradise Lost*	*Twelfth Night*
"To an Athlete Dying Young"	*The Rivals*	*Death of a Salesman*	"Dover Beach"
	Moby Dick	*Lord of the Flies*	"Young Goodman Brown"
"On First Looking into Chapman's Homer"	"Killers"	*The Alchemist*	
	Antigone	"The Canonization"	*Aeneid*
"The Solitary Reaper"	*Iliad*		

7. Classify the following words according to the word-making process they represent:

| brainwash | kindness | brunch | bus | phone | sizzle | deceive |
| gunsmoke | breakfast | smog | pub | radar | ping-pong | friendly |

Writing Suggestions: Analysis

1. The appeal of _____ (Johnny Carson, Joey Bishop, Jack Paar, the Smothers Brothers, Pat Paulsen, Judy Garland, Dean Martin, Jerry Lewis, Rowan and Martin, Lawrence Welk, Arthur Godfrey, Jean Shepherd)

2. The Comedy of _____ (Phyllis Diller, Totie Fields, Jackie Vernon, Professor Irwin Cory, Jerry Lewis, Pat Cooper, Mort Sahl, Victor Borge, Morey Amsterdam, Flip Wilson, Godfrey Cambridge, Nipsey Russell, Dick Gregory, Henry Morgan, Wally Cox, Don Knotts)

3. The Success of _____ (a Television Series, a Motion Picture, a Best-Seller)

4. The Problem of _____ (Racism, Student Disillusionment, Mass Transportation, Air-Traffic Control, Drunken Driving, Relief Payments, Occupational Discrimination by Race, Sex, or Age, Drugs and Narcotics, Educating the Culturally Deprived, Rising Medical Costs, Gun Control, National Strikes)

5. Analyze the appeal of some current best-seller like *Valley of the Dolls, Myra Breckinridge, Armies of the Night, Couples, In Cold Blood.*

6. Analyze the attraction of a hero or heroine like Eugene McCarthy, Martin Luther King, Jr., Robert F. Kennedy, George Wallace, James Bond, Jacqueline Onassis, Willie Mays, Mahamed Ali, Rap Brown, Stokely Carmichael, Adam Clayton Powell, Cesar Chavez.

7. Classify comedians, night-clubs, rock groups, ballad and folk groups, country-music groups, jazz trios, vocal groups, political leaders, cartoonists, styles of political oratory, types of advertising strategy, waiters, doctors, policemen, dates.

8. Analyze the advertising campaigns of Volkswagen, Avis, or anti-cigarette smoking, the commercials of Stan Freiberg, the appeal or strategy of a single advertisement.

9. Study a comic page of your paper carefully and make some classification of the various comic strips.

10. Study the "Letters to the Editor" section of some popular magazine like *Time, Newsweek, Life, Playboy,* or *Harper's.* Find some issue which has aroused considerable response from the readers and classify their letters concerning it.

(Additional writing suggestions on linguistic subjects are on pages 405–406).

The Sounds of English

19.

CHARLTON LAIRD

The Classification of Speech Sounds

Although speech is possible employing a stream of air which goes either in or out, and a few languages make some use of intaken breath, practically, speech relies upon an outward stream. The diaphragm thrusts upward, and the intercostal muscles contract the chest. The lungs, being compressed, expel air, which can escape only through the trachea, or windpipe. Obviously, several things can be done to this stream of air. It can be allowed to flow freely, or it can be disturbed. If disturbed, it can be disturbed in three ways: it can be stopped completely; it can be constricted; it can be made to vibrate as a column. Freely flowing air becomes normal breath; asthma and snoring, from a physical point of view, approach language, because they involve interference with the breath stream. True, snoring has little meaning, but some conversation has little meaning anyhow, so that if one wished to, he might call snoring a sort of subconscious sub-language.

The three means of disturbing the breath stream are the means by which we speak. These three are used in varying combinations, varying degrees, and are contrived by various instruments, but all speech is created by this vocal trinity. A speaker can stop the flow of air completely and then let it go, as in the letter *t*. He can constrict it so that it whistles, as in the letter *s*. He can make it vibrate while he relaxes, as in any pronunciation of the letter *a;* the pronunciation of this letter known as Italian *a* is so beloved of opera singers because it is made by the most uninhibited use of air for language. The singer has only to start his vibrating mechanism, relax, open his mouth, and having thus made himself into a sort of human saxophone, let himself go.

But how does one become a human saxophone? The key organ is the larynx, which is commonly known as the Adam's apple, just as though, deep in our subconscious, we were aware that the original sin was too much talking. This organ constitutes the upper end of the windpipe, and is made of various pieces of cartilage, elastic tissue, and mucous membrane called vocal cords, all so articulated that the membranes can be relaxed completely during normal breathing but can be contracted so that they will vibrate in pitch. The result of this vibration we call *voice*, and any sound made with the aid of these vocal cords is said to be *voiced*. You can feel the vibration by putting the tips of your fingers in the hollow of your throat and pronouncing any vowel.

Now to the sounds which we produce in speech. Roughly they may be divided into two sorts, *vowels*, in which the breath is but little constricted, and *consonants*, in which it is more emphatically constricted. Actually, there is no dividing line between the two. Some sounds are restricted so little that they cannot be very confidently called either a vowel or a consonant. For instance, of the various sounds indicated by the letter *r* in *rarer*, which are vowels and which consonants? The answer is not easy, but the distinction between consonants and vowels is traditional and familiar, and has enough reality to be useful in understanding what happens when we speak.

First, then, to the vowels. Since they are made with an almost unrestricted column of air, they must be voiced or somehow disturbed; otherwise we would not hear them. They all are voiced in English and in most other languages. Since the sound of the vowels depends upon a vibrating column of air, the differences in sound must depend upon the various ways in which the air can be made to vibrate. Here we should perhaps think of ourselves not as saxophones, but as instruments resembling a bagpipe, a slide trombone, a cornet, and a cat-tail fiddle. We can vary the stress by varying the pressure of air, as in a bagpipe. We can alter the center of vibration and the character of the vibrating column, as in a slide trombone. We can direct a column of air into different passages, as in a cornet. And we can alter the vibrations by changing the tension of the vibrating instrument, as in the cat-tail fiddle—the cat-tail fiddle being a somewhat legendary device said to have been played by grasping a tomcat by the neck and the tail, and sawing upon it as though it were a violin, increasing the tension on the tail to increase the pitch of the cat.

Of the methods of creating sounds, the most useful for our present discussion is that which permits shifting the point at which the vibration centers. In all true vowels, the vibration takes place in the mouth. If you will now pronounce slowly the words *sleek hawk*, you will notice that the vowel in *sleek* is made far forward and high up, about at the roots of the upper front teeth, and that the vowel in *hawk* is made so far back in the throat that you are almost in danger of swallowing it. Similarly, each of the

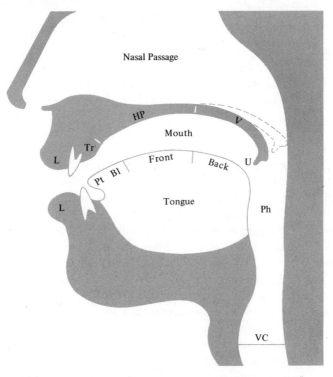

CONVENTIONALIZED DIAGRAM OF THE SPEECH ORGANS*

LL = lips. Pt = tongue point. Bl = tongue blade.
Tr = teethridge. HP = hard palate. V = velum (soft
  palate): black: lowered, or open; dotted: raised, or
  closed.
U = uvula. Ph = pharynx. VC = vocal cords.

other vowels has a distinctive place in the mouth at which the vibration centers. The resultant sound can be still further altered by the stress with which breath is expelled and by the shape of the oral cavity. This shape can be altered in many ways, but most noticeably by movements of the tongue, by rounding and unrounding the lips, and by the tenseness or slackness of the tongue and other muscles. Accordingly vowels can be described by the position of the vibration, the degree of stress, the degree of rounding, the degree of tenseness, and the action of the tongue.

At this point, we must become technical. Before we can go further in describing sounds, we must find out, one by one, how they are made. Fur-

* From *American Pronunciation,* by John S. Kenyon. 10th Ed. (Ann Arbor, 1951). Copyright, 1924, 1945, 1946, 1950, by John S. Kenyon. Reprinted by permission of George Wahr Publishing Co., Ann Arbor, Michigan.

thermore, we shall need a vocabulary with which we can talk about sounds, symbols which will permit me to know what I mean to say, and you to guess what I am trying to say. We cannot very well go on with me talking about "the sound of *a* in *aunt*." That is too clumsy, and there are a variety of ways of saying *aunt*. We need symbols for sounds, and then we need an understanding of how the sounds are made which are represented by the symbols.

Both are provided by what is known as IPA, the International Phonetic Alphabet. It runs to hundreds of symbols, and with it one can transcribe phonetically, at least roughly, any language on earth, and it is used by all serious students of language the world over. Fortunately, we shall need only a small part of it. After all, we are not transcribing a tonal language like Chinese or Zapotec. A few dozen symbols will represent most sounds in English, and learning to identify them can be quite a lot of fun.

Besides, doing so is economical. After all, you have been provided with an excellent linguistic laboratory, equipped with all instruments necessary for basic linguistic research, and if you insist on leaving this laboratory locked within you unused, you are guilty of shocking waste. At worst, you ought to run a few simple experiments, just to feel you are getting some return on your anatomical investment.

Seriously, a little attention to the manner in which sounds are made is likely to open vast new understandings of language. In the following discussion, you will do well to try each of the suggestions, using your own vocal laboratory, before you go on to read the discussion of it. For instance, if you are asked to say *cat* slowly, do so, before you find out why.

So now we are ready to begin our experiments. You will recall that a page or two back we pronounced the combination *sleek hawk,* and observed that the first vowel is pronounced just back of the upper teeth. It is tense; it cannot be pronounced without relatively strong tension in the tongue and the oral muscles. Try, for instance, to pronounce *eat* without some tenseness; it will inevitably become *it, et,* or *ut*. For this sound in *sleek,* the lips are unrounded. Therefore, we may describe it by calling it a high front tense unround vowel. The IPA symbol for it is [i], and you will find it appropriately placed in the diagram on the following page, which is intended to represent the oral cavity. The vowel in *hawk,* on the other hand, is a low back tense round vowel; the symbol for this sound is [ɔ]—the one my students nicknamed "the little shrimp." (To distinguish phonetic symbols from letters, they are put within brackets.)

Now try a few more sounds on your vocal laboratory. Repeat slowly the following words: *sought, sot, sat, set, sate, sit, seat*. If your pronunciation is roughly normal, you should produce a series of vowels that proceed in an orderly row along the lower side of your oral cavity, from [ɔ] to [i].

As you will observe in the diagram, the second of these vowels, the so-called Italian *a,* is written [ɑ]. The others follow in order [æ], [ɛ], [e], [ɪ], and [i]. Now pronounce consecutively, *foal, full,* and *fool.* This time you should produce a series of vowels that go upward along the back of your mouth; you will find them written as [o], [ʊ], and [u] in the diagram. Now say *cutaway.* In this word the first vowel is stressed, the second unstressed. As a result, the stressed sound appears a little higher than the unstressed sound, but the main difference between them is the difference in stress. They are written [ʌ] and [ə]; the latter is often called *schwa.* It is the most common sound in modern American speech, for all American unstressed vowels tend to become *schwa* or [ɪ].

This list completes the pure vowels that occur commonly in American speech. There are two groups of vowels which have peculiarities. For the first of these, pronounce the word *Herbert.* The first syllable is stressed and somewhat tense, the second unstressed and slack, but for both sounds the tongue flicks back a little; that is, these are called *retroflex* vowels. The first, the tense vowel, is written [ɝ]; the second, the slack vowel, [ə˞]. And now for the diphthongs. As their name indicates, they are composed of two sounds; in Greek the word *diphthong* means "two-sounds." To observe them, pronounce slowly the words, *white house,* several times, while you listen. In each of these words a keen ear will detect that the vowel starts out as one sound and shifts to another. Almost universally, the diphthong in *white* can be written with the two IPA symbols [ɑɪ]; the diphthong in *house* will appear in IPA symbols either as [ɑʊ] or [æʊ].

So much for the vowel. Later we shall need to observe that these vowels can be classified. They vary in stress, in tenseness, in position, and in the degree of their rounding, but let us pass that for the moment, and go on to the consonants.

Returning to our earlier analysis, we can observe that consonants can be made either by stopping the breath or by disturbing it, making it explode, or making it buzz or hum. Since stopping is simpler than disturbing, let us start with breath stoppages.

We have various instruments with which we can stop the breath, but let us start with the lips. Expel a column of air, stop it with the lips, and then let it go. If you have now done this, you have produced a sound like the first part of the word *putt* or the first part of the word *but.* These are the conventional sounds of *p* and *b* in English, and of [p] and [b] in IPA.

You must distinguish here between the name of the letter *p* in spelling and the sound of the symbol [p] in speaking. If I as writer could appear for even a few seconds before you as reader, I could make this sound [p], and thenceforth you would have no difficulty understanding what is meant by a phonetic symbol. But since obviously I cannot, you will have to make the sound. It is not anything I can describe, except that I can tell you how to make it. Purse your lips as though you were to say *put;* let some air pressure build up behind the lips. Then let the air go with a slight puff, but do not say any more of the word *put* except so much as is involved in the explosion when you suddenly open your lips. This much, and no more, is embodied in [p]. It is the transcription of a sound; it is not the name of a letter in spelling.

Now for the next sound, place your tongue against the roof of your mouth, just back of the upper teeth, stop the breath column with your tongue, and let the air go in a small explosion. You should have produced either the first part of the word *tub* or the first part of *dub,* that is, the sounds [t] or [d]. Now try raising your tongue in the back part of your mouth, stopping the air, and then releasing it. You will produce either [k] as in *kick,* or [g] as in *gig.* A little girl of my acquaintance would understand this explanation. She brought home the first report card on which she had received grades more explicit than *S* for *Satisfactory* and *U* for its opposite. Her mother praised her for her good grades, saying, "I know that reading is hard for you, but I see you got *G* in it."

"Oh, Mother," the little girl replied impatiently, "that's not *gee,* that's [g]."

Here we might pause to notice a curious detail. Is it not surprising that all of these stops occur in pairs, that wherever and however you make the stop, you get two? It is curious. It is more: it is significant, and if you will use your vocal laboratory you can find out why. Put the tips of your fingers on the hollow of your throat and make consecutively the sounds represented by the IPA symbols [p] and [b]. You ought to feel a vibration in your throat with [b] that you do not feel with [p]; if you feel this vibration with [p], it means that you are not pronouncing [p] only, but are following it with a vowel. Now try the same thing with the other stops, the sounds associated with [t] and [d], with [k] and [g]. You should have vibrations with [d] and [g], very little with [t] and [k]. Now pronounce any of the vowels, several of them. You should feel vibration similar to that in [b], [d], and [g]. But the vowels, you will remember, are all voiced. Now you will suspect—if you have not suspected it already—that certain of the consonants are voiced and others are unvoiced, and this causes the difference between them. A stoppage of the air by the lips produces [p] if the sound is voiceless, [b] if the sound is voiced; a stoppage of air with the tongue at the roots of the teeth produces [t] if the sound is voiceless, [d] if the sound is voiced; farther back in the oral cavity [k] is voiceless, [g] is voiced.

Those are the stops in English, all the sounds that are made by a complete and simple stoppage of the air. Now for the sounds made by obstructing the air; since they are made by friction of air, we may call them *frica-*

tives. First, direct a column of air straight at your middle upper front teeth. Your mouth should be nearly closed, and the air should be channeled through your tongue, but your tongue will probably take care of itself if you just try to make the air hit your two upper central front teeth. Let the air whistle past them. You have produced either the sound of *s* or the sound of *z*, in IPA [s] and [z] respectively. You will not need to be told why these sounds appear in a pair; [s] is voiceless, [z] is voiced. Now direct a column of air at the roof of your mouth just back of the upper teeth. You have produced the central sound in either *fresher* or *measure,* the first voiceless, the second voiced. Since these sounds are not well represented in European languages by one letter, we have special symbols in IPA for them, [ʃ] for the sound of *sh,* [ʒ] for the corresponding voiced sound. Now, barely touch your upper teeth to your lower lip, and constrict air as it passes through. You have produced either the sound associated with *f* or the sound associated with *v,* the first voiceless, the second voiced, and written [f] and [v]. Now, put your tongue against your upper teeth, and constrict the air. You have produced the first consonant in either *thing* or *this,* the first voiceless and written in IPA with the Greek theta [θ], the second voiced and written with the Anglo-Saxon crossed *d* [ð]. And these are all of the fricatives common in English.

There are, however, a few more consonants. Repeat the sentence, "The *judge* went to *church.*" A keen ear will detect that the consonants in *church* are neither exclusively tops nor fricatives. A very keen ear will detect that they are both, that the sounds begin with a [t], which shifts into a [ʃ]. That is, the word *church* sounds as though it should be written in English *tshurtsh,* and is written in IPA [tʃɝtʃ]. And as you will imagine, or find out by trying it on your vocal cords, the consonants in *judge* are only these same sounds voiced; that is, they sound like *dzh,* and are written [dʒ]. These sounds, which begin with a stop and continue with a fricative, are called *affricates.*

In the next set of consonants, you use your abilities as a cornet; that is, you stop your oral passage, and let the air out through your nose. Close your mouth completely, and make a sound through your nose. It was *m,* written [m]. Now stop the air by putting the forward part of your tongue against the roof of your mouth, and as before, make a sound in your nose. It was *n,* written [n]. Now stop the air farther back in your mouth, and again make a sound. It was the final consonant in *sing,* in IPA, [ŋ]. These are the common nasals in English. In French, there are more, but we manage with the three. All are made as a matter of course by voicing, and the sound you hear is the vibrating of the voiced column of air as it passes slowly through the nasal passages. This passage of air is so slow as to be almost imperceptible, but if you doubt that the air is moving, hold your nose, and then try to make the sound. If you tried it, you made no sound. This is, of course, the basis of the old joke about the man who delights in spring by saying, "Sprig is cub." His nose is stopped up, so that he cannot pronounce nasal sounds, and he makes the corresponding stops. These consonants are called *nasals,* or *nasal continuants,* or just *continuants.*

A few consonants will not be pinned down. For instance, say slowly the words *your, year,* and *loyal.* All the consonants here are said with so little restriction, that you may not be quite sure whether to call them vowels or consonants. You will probably notice, also, that they do not stay in one place in the mouth. There are many ways of pronouncing the sounds we indicate by the letter *y,* and perhaps even more ways of pronouncing the sounds indicated by *r* and *l,* but you will probably notice that they slip around, that they glide from one vowel to another, and, accordingly, they are called *glides.* They are sometimes called semivowels, also, because they resemble vowels. The sound of *y* is written [j]; *r* and *l,* [r] and [1]; the semivowel *w,* [w], is little more than a rounded vowel. The sound of *h,* [h], is a voiceless breath—it is sometimes called an *aspirate,* Greek for *breath*—with enough friction far back in the mouth to make it audible. This sound is combined with [w] in words like *when,* which are spelled *wh,* but in prevailing usage pronounced (*hw*). In IPA this combination is often represented by the letter *w* inverted [ʍ]. The simplified pronunciation [w] is now heard in increasing frequency.

We have now examined the commonest sounds in English and noticed roughly how each is made. We have found that they can be classified on the basis of their production. Since we shall need names for these sounds, we had best name them, also, from the manner in which they are produced. To do so, we shall need a few terms, not many, but if you do not know them you had better fix them in mind now. We have already used the word *vowel,* and have defined *voice, stop, fricative, affricate, nasal,* and *glide.* Now we need to define a few points in the oral cavity. The ridge just back of the upper teeth is called the *alveolar ridge.* Back of this, the roof of the mouth is called the *hard palate,* referred to in the adjective *palatal.* Back of the hard palate is the soft palate, or *velum,* referred to by the adjective *velar.* Back toward the throat is the *glottis,* and this area is identified as *glottal.* These words can be combined; for instance, *alveolopalatal* would mean that the sound could be made in the vicinity of either the alveolar ridge or the hard palate. *Lateral* refers to sounds which are spread out across the width of the tongue. Other words are more familiar; *labial* refers to the lips, and *bilabial* to both lips; *dental* to the teeth, *lingual* to the tongue, and *nasal* to the nose. *Retroflex* means turned back.

With these definitions we are ready to name sounds by describing the manner in which they are made. The following list is intended for reference.

VOWELS

[i]	as in *sleek*	High-front unround tense
[ɪ]	as in *ill*	Lower high-front unround slack
[e]	as in *ate*	Mid-front unround tense
[ɛ]	as in *tell*	Lower mid-front unround slack
[æ]	as in *cat*	Low-front unround slack
[ɑ]	as in *not*	Low-back unround tense
[ɔ]	as in *hawk*	Higher low-back round tense
[o]	as in *road*	Mid-back round tense
[ʊ]	as in *full*	Lower high-back round slack, lowered and retracted
[u]	as in *mood*	High-back round tense
[ʌ]	as in *hull*	Lower mid-back unround
[ɝ]	as in *bird*	Mid-central unround retroflex
[ə:]	as in 2nd syllable of Al*bert*	Mid-central unround retroflex slack
[ə]	as in 1st syllable of *a*bove	Mid-central unround slack

CONSONANTS

[p]	as in *papa*	Voiceless bilabial stop
[b]	as in *baby*	Voiced bilabial stop
[t]	as in *tat*	Voiceless alveolar stop
[d]	as in *did*	Voiced alveolar stop
[k]	as in *kick*	Voiceless palatal or velar stop
[g]	as in *gag*	Voiced palatal or velar stop
[f]	as in *fife*	Voiceless labiodental fricative
[v]	as in *vivid*	Voiced labiodental fricative
[s]	as in *sissy*	Voiceless alveolar fricative
[z]	as in *dizzy*	Voiced alveolar fricative
[θ]	as in *think*	Voiceless interdental fricative
[ð]	as in *this*	Voiced interdental fricative
[ʃ]	as in *she*	Voiceless alveolopalatal fricative
[ʒ]	as in *pleasure*	Voiced alveolopalatal fricative
[h]	as in *how*	Voiceless glottal fricative (also called aspirate)
[ʍ]	as in *when*	Voiceless glottal fricative followed by voiced labiovelar glide

[tʃ]	as in *church*	Voiceless alveolopalatal affricate
[dʒ]	as in *judge*	Voiced alveolopalatal affricate
[m]	as in *mama*	Voiced bilabial nasal continuant
[n]	as in *nanny*	Voiced alveolar nasal continuant
[ŋ]	as in *song*	Voiced velar nasal continuant
[l]	as in *lull*	Voiced alveolar lateral continuant
[w]	as in *water*	Voiced labiovelar glide
[r]	as in *roar*	Voiced retroflex tongue glide
[j]	as in *youth*	Voiced linguopalatal glide

Admittedly, the preceding discussion and this table are vastly simplified. . . . None of the characteristics mentioned here is a simple thing, and the characteristics are interreliant. Tenseness, for instance, is not one thing in all vowels which we have called tense; [i] is certainly more tense than [ɔ]. Tenseness itself is not a single thing. There is more tenseness in the tongue in [i], but perhaps more in some of the other muscles in [ɔ]. Similarly, tenseness tends to increase with stress. It tends to increase when the vowel is adjacent to certain consonants, before terminal stops, for instance. Note the difference between the vowels in *heat* and *stream*. Even the consonants are not so simple as we have made them seem. There is more than one sound for *t*, for instance, as you will see if you will say carefully, "take a step." The sound associated with the second *t* is made closer to the teeth than is the first; it uses a part of the tongue farther from the tip than does the first, and it has a little of the quality of a fricative. Even so, we should have to transcribe both sounds [t]. Similarly, the [z] in *freeze* is not identical with the [z] in *needs*. But for our purposes, the description here should be sufficiently detailed.

Vocabulary

diaphragm, intercostal, trachea, uninhibited, larynx

Review Questions

1. What are the three means of disturbing the breath stream?
2. Explain what "voiced" and "voiceless" mean.
3. Into what categories may vowels be classified?
4. What are "retroflex" vowels and what are "diphthongs"?
5. Explain the following terms as they relate to consonants: *stops, fricatives, affricates, nasal continuants, glides.*

6. List and identify the principal parts of the oral cavity used in the production of speech sounds.

Expository Technique

1. Is there a distinct tone to this piece of writing? If so, what is it and what produces it?

2. Make an outline of the discussion. Is there any demonstrable order in the presentation?

Exercises

1. Transcribe the following words using the appropriate IPA symbols.

speak	doubt	ached	shoemaker	further	salmon
stopped	castle	except	quart	nurture	psychology
rabbit	extinct	running	somewhat	colonel	knead
cupboard	accent	champagne	buckwheat	island	answer
seizure	church				

2. Read the following transcription aloud and then rewrite it using the English alphabet. The vertical marks indicate accent: (ˈ) for primary accent and (ˌ) for secondary; each is placed before the accented syllable. The [ɚ:], as in the second syllable of Albert, is represented in the transcription by [ɚ]

RIP VAN WINKLE*

ðə gret ˈɛrɚ ɪn rɪps ˌkampəˈzɪʃən wəz ən ɪnˈsiupərəbl̩ əˈvɝʒən
tu ɔl kaɪndz əv ˈprɑfɪtəbl̩ ˈlebɚ. ɪt ˈkudn̩t bi frəm ðə wɑnt əv
ˌæsəˈdɪuəti ɚ ˌpɝsəˈvɪrəns, fɚ i wəd sɪt ɑn ə wɛt rɑk, wɪð ə rɑd əz
lɔŋ ən ˈhɛvɪ əz ə ˈtɑrtɚz læns, ən fɪʃ ɔl de wɪðˈaut ə ˈmɝmɚ, ˈivən
ðo i ʃudn̩t bi ɪnˈkɝdʒd baɪ ə ˈsɪŋgl̩ ˈnɪbl̩. hid ˈkærɪ ə ˈfaulɪŋˌpis
ən ɪz ˈʃoldɚ fɚ aurz təˈgɛðɚ, ˈtrʌdʒɪŋ θru wudz n̩ swɔmps, ənd ʌp
hɪl ən daun del, tə ʃut ə fɪu skwɝlz ɚ waɪld ˈpɪdʒɪnz. hi wəd
ˈnɛvɚ rɪˈfiuz tu əˈsɪst ə ˈnebɚ, ˈivən ɪn ðə ˈrʌfɪst tɔɪl, ənd wəz ə
ˈforˌmost mæn ət ɔl ˈkʌntrɪ ˈfralɪks fɚ ˈhʌskɪŋ ˈɪndɪən kɔrn ɚ
ˈbɪldɪŋ ston ˈfɛnsɪz; ðə ˈwɪmɪn əv ðə ˈvɪlɪdʒ, tu, jus tu ɪmˈplɔɪ
ɪm tə rʌn ðɛr ˈɛrəndz, ən tə du sʌtʃ ˈlɪtl̩ ɑd dʒɑbz əz ðɛr les
əˈblaɪdʒɪŋ ˈhʌzbəndz ˈwudn̩t du fɔr ðəm. ɪn ə wɝd, rɪp wəz ˈrɛdɪ

---

* From *American Pronunciation*, by John S. Kenyon. 10th Ed. (Ann Arbor, 1951). Copyright, 1924, 1945, 1946, 1950, by John S. Kenyon. Reprinted by permission of George Wahr Publishing Co., Ann Arbor, Michigan.

tʊ əˈtɛnd tʊ ˈɛnɪˌbadɪz ˈbɪznɪs bət ɪz on; bət əz tə ˈduɪŋ ˈfæmlɪ
ˌdɪutɪ, ən ˈkipɪŋ ɪz farm ɪn ˈɔrdɚ, hi faʊnd ɪt ɪmˈpasəbḷ.

ɪn fækt, hi dɪˈklærd ɪt wəz əv no jus tə wɜk ən ɪz farm; ɪt wəz
ðə most ˈpɛstḷənt ˈlɪtḷ pis əv graʊnd ɪn ðə hol ˈkʌntrɪ; ˈɛvrɪˌθɪŋ
əˈbaʊt ɪt wɛnt rɔŋ, ənd ˈwʊd go rɔŋ, ɪn spaɪt av ɪm. hɪz ˈfɛnsɪz
wɚ kənˈtɪnjʊəlɪ ˈfɔlɪŋ tə ˈpisɪz; hɪz kaʊz wəd ˈiðɚ go əˈstre, ɚ gɛt
əˈmʌŋ ðə ˈkæbɪdʒɪz: hi ˈkʊdṇt ˈkipm̩ ət hom; wɪdz wɚ ʃʊr tə gro
ˈkwɪkɚ ɪn ˈhɪz fildz ðən ˈɛnɪ ˌhwær ɛls; ðə ren ˈɔlwɪz med ə
pɔɪnt əv ˈsɛtɪŋ ɪn dʒʌst əz i hæd səm ˈaʊt-əv-ˌdor wɜk tə du;
so ðət ðo ɪz ˌpætrəˈmonɪəl əˈstet əd ˈdwɪndḷd əˈwe ʌndɚ ɪz
ˈmænɪdʒmənt, ˈekɚ baɪ ˈekɚ, ənˈtɪl ðɚ wəz ˈlɪtḷ mor lɛft ðən ə
mɪr pætʃ əv ˈɪndɪən kɔrn ən pəˈtetʊz, jɛt ɪt wəz ðə ˈwɜst-kən-
ˈdɪʃənd farm ɪn ðə ˈnebɚˌhʊd.

3. The following is a transcription by Albert H. Marckwardt of Jacques'
speech on "The Seven Ages of Man" from *As You Like It*. Professor Marckwardt
attempts to suggest in this transcription how the language might have been pronounced in Shakespeare's time. Read it aloud, noting any differences in pronunciation between Elizabethan and contemporary English speech.

THE SEVEN AGES OF MAN†

ɔːl ðə wərldz ə stæːdʒ
ənd ɔːl ðə mɛn ənd wɪmən mɪrlɪ plæɪərz
ðæɪ əv ðər ɛgzɪts ənd ðər ɛntrənsɪz
ənd wʊn mæn ɪn ɪz təɪm plæɪz mɛnɪ pærts
ɪz ækts biɪŋ sɛvən æːdʒəz ət fərst ðɪ ɪnfənt
mjulɪŋ ən pjukɪŋ ɪn ðə nərsəz ærmz
ðɛn ðə hwəɪnɪŋ skulbɔɪ wɪð ɪz sætʃəl
ənd ʃaɪnɪŋ mɔrnɪŋ fæːs krɪpɪŋ ləɪk snæɪl
ʊnwɪlɪŋlɪ tə skul ən ðɛn ðə lʊvər
səɪŋ ləɪk fərnəs wɪð ə wofʊl bæləd
mæːd tu ɪz mɪstrɪs əɪbrəʊ ðɛn ðə soldʒər
fʊl əv stræːndʒ oðz ən berdəd lərk ðə pærd
dʒɛləs ɪn ɔnər sʊdn ən kwɪk ɪn kwærəl
sikɪŋ ðə bʊbl rɛpjutæːsjən
ɪn ðə kænənz məʊθ ən ðɛn ðə dʒʊstɪs
ɪn fæɪr rəʊnd bɛlɪ wɪð gʊd kæːpən ləɪnd
wɪð əɪz səvir ən berd əv fɔrməl kʊt
fʊl əv wəɪz sɔːz ənd mɔdərn ɪnstənsɪz
ən so i plæɪz ɪz pært ðə sɪksθ æːdʒ ʃɪfts
ɪntu ðə len ənd slɪpərd pæntəlun

† From *American English* by Albert H. Marckwardt. Copyright © 1968 by Oxford University Press, Inc. Reprinted by permission.

wɪð spɛktəklz ɔn noz ən pəutʃ ɔn səɪd
hɪz juθfʊl hoz wɛl sæ:vd ə wərld tu wəɪd
fər ɪz ʃruŋk ʃæŋk ənd ɪz bɪg mænlɪ vɔɪs
tərnɪŋ əgæɪn tɔrd tʃəɪldɪʃ trɛbl pəɪps
ənd hwɪslz ɪn ɪz səʊnd   læst sin əv ɔ:l
ðət ɛndz ðɪs stræ:ndʒ ɪvɛntfʊl hɪstərɪ
ɪz sɛkənd tʃəɪldɪʃnəs ən mɪr əblɪvjən
sænz tiθ sænz əɪz sænz tæ:st sænz ɛvrɪθɪŋ

4. Transcribe the following words and classify them according to whether the initial consonant is voiced or voiceless.

peek	four	thin	many	got
jury	chair	never	shoe	baby
then	top	dot	thought	there
see	king	zero	virtue	chick

5. Transcribe the following words and classify them according to the manner in which the initial consonant is formed.

paper	canary	merry	this	theme
chin	shove	barter	hoe	funny
never	watch	jam	zebra	tick
dip	gate	vender	soon	who

6. Transcribe the following words and classify them according to whether the vowel sound is pure, retroflex, or diphthong.

nice	fun	take	seat	louse
toy	fat	dove (*noun*)	take	white
all	mit	low	law	bird
earn	turn			

7. Transcribe the following as individual words and then as spoken utterances:

did you eat yet
let me do it
it sure is a pretty day
what do you know
hello
how much is it

good-bye
how should I know
pleased to meet you
did you go to the store
how are you doing

20.

MARIO PEI

The Problem of Spelling Reform

English spelling is the world's most awesome mess. The Chinese system of ideographs is quite logical, once you accept the premise that writing is to be divorced from sound and made to coincide with thought-concepts. The other languages of the West have, in varying degrees, coincidence between spoken sounds and written symbols. But the spelling of English reminds one of the crazy-quilt of ancient, narrow, winding streets in some of the world's major cities, through which modern automobile traffic must nevertheless in some way circulate.

In no other language is it possible to get seven different sounds out of a combination of written letters like *ough* (*dough, bought, bough, rough, through, thorough, hiccough*), or, conversely, spell a sound like that ordinarily represented by *sh* in fourteen different ways (*shoe, sugar, issue, mansion, mission, nation, suspicion, ocean, nauseous, conscious, chaperon, schism, fuchsia, pshaw*). In no other language would it be possible to write *phtholognyrrh* for *Turner* by using the *phth of phthisic*, the *olo* of *colonel*, the *gn* of *gnat* and the *yrrh* of *myrrh*. In no other language could a Hollander write, for the instruction of his fellow-countrymen wishing to learn English:

> Gear and tear, but wear and tear. . . .
> Meat and peat, but sweat and great
> (The last word rhymes with freight and weight);
> Quite different again is height
> Which sounds like bite, indict and light. . . .
> Crew and blew and few, but sew,
> Cow and row, but sow and row. . . .

and so on for many, many lines.

It is quite simple to say that the *p* of *pneumonia* and the silent *k*'s of *knickknack* were sounded when Caxton's printers began to codify the written language, and offer that as an excuse for their presence today. We can even point with pride to the abandonment of medieval spellings like *housbonde, mynde* and *ygone*, and account for the irrational spelling of *delight* (once *delite*) by saying that it became confused with *night* and *light*. The fact remains that our spelling is more than irrational—it is inhuman, and forms the bane not merely of foreigners, but of our own younger generations, compelled to devote interminable hours to learning a system which is the soul and essence of anarchy. It is hardly surprising that one of America's leading linguists suggests that we stop teaching spelling altogether for a few years, at the end of which time a new system based on the sounds of the spoken language will have perforce evolved.

A glaring example of the inadequacies of English spelling appeared in a test given to sixty-four graduate students of journalism at Columbia University. The average was twenty-five misspellings out of seventy-eight words. Typical words used in the test were *analogous, dissension, harassed, siege, canoeist, ecstasy, restaurateur, vilification, dietitian, guerrilla, supersede,* and, appropriately, *misspell.* Foreign students did better than the native-born, pointing up the advantages of bilingualism.

It is somewhat surprising, on the other hand, that a high school survey should reveal that the words most frequently misspelled are not the hard ones one would suspect. Instead, they are relatively simple and much in use, like *develop, cordially, proceed, meant, absence, decide, receive, athletic, sincerely, practical, volume, argument, finally.* The list also includes *February, whether* and *secretary*, but here it is probable that the ear deceives the eye (pronunciations like *Febuary, wether* and *seketary* are current). *Principal* is confused with *principle, scene* with *seen*, while *foreign* has a *gn* that is in conflict with our high-frequency *ng*.

Another school test revealed eighteen spellings for *Appalachian*, including *Appelation, Appleachean* and *Appliciation. Alleghany* was much misspelled also, but in extenuation of this it must be remarked that there are correct local variants, such as *Allegheny* and *Allegany*. Variant spellings, so common in the days of the early printers, are often permissible today (*comptroller* and *controller*, or *gray* and *grey;* though for the latter pair a vague distinction of meaning is said to exist). Historically, we find *segar* as a current mid-nineteenth-century spelling for *cigar, travail* used for *travel* in British railroad instruction-books of a century ago and, if we go further back, the spelling *parliament* from Medieval Latin *parliamentum* while the pronunciation stems from Old French *parlement,* as well as the *h* of *Magna Charta,* recently abolished, from a late Latin *chartula* probably already influenced by French *charte.*

Two spelling-pronunciation curios are worth mentioning. One, recently pointed out in the daily press, is that in the English pronunciation of *Circe* every letter, without exception, has a different value from what it had in the Greek original. The other is that a learned foreign colleague of the writer regularly pronounces *shepherd* as *sheferd,* on the ground that *ph* in English has the sound of *f;* and no one can cure him of this habit.

When did spelling first become a conscious problem with English speakers? The *Ormulum,** composed about 1200, shows a doubling of consonants after short vowels, which would indicate an attempt to reflect pronunciation. There are rumors of an early thirteenth-century attempt to regularize spelling, but the details are vague. The sixteenth century marks the real beginning of the reform movement. This was the period when a gardening treatise uses indifferently *Zodiac, Zodiack and Zodyacke,* and places an *-yng* ending on *tillyng* and *sowyng, -ynge* on *speakynge,* and *-ying* on *buyldying.* The problem of "right writing" was uppermost in the minds of the sixteenth-century grammarians, one of whom is rumored to have devised a phonetic alphabet of no less than 450 characters. Cheke, Hart, Bullokar and Mulcaster vied in "improving" the quality of the written language, and if we are tempted to belittle their efforts, let us at least give thanks that they left us generally with a single irrational spelling for words that had previously had half a dozen equally irrational variants.

Samuel Johnson, who endeavored to put a premium on "correct" spelling, was himself torn asunder by the conflicting forces of analogy, etymology and pronunciation. To him and his followers we owe in large part the inconsistency of *deceit* vs. *receipt, deign* vs. *disdain,* the *b* of *debt* and *doubt,* the progression of *gn* from *reign* to *sovereign* to *foreign,* one of the words, be it noted, that disturb our present-day high school spellers. He suggested a *k* for *critick* and *musick,* on the ground that "truly English spelling should always have a Saxon *k,*" and this, remarks Robertson with tongue in cheek, is Johnson's own personal contribution to the Anglo-Saxon alphabet.

Benjamin Franklin and Noah Webster were America's pioneers in the realm of spelling reform, but while the former limited himself to the vague advocacy of a new alphabet, the latter made distinct contributions that color the written American language of today. To his *American Dictionary* of 1828 we owe the use of *-or* vs. the British *-our* (*labor, labour*), *-er* vs. *-re* (*theater, theatre*), the single *l* of *traveled,* the *k* of *mask* (*masque*), the *ck* of *check* (*cheque*), the *f* of *draft* (*draught*), the *-se* of *defense* (*defence*), the *w* of *plow* (*plough*). He pulled his punches on several of the drastic reforms he had advocated in 1789 (*helth, breth, frend, beleeve, receeve, yeer, rong, ritten, tung, munth, iz, lauf, touf, korus, mashine, wimmen*).

It was Webster also who gave a fillip to the spelling bee, which he said was "good for the articulation," and for which Franklin had laid down the rules in 1750. For over a century the spelling bee cast a magnetic spell over

---

* [A verse paraphrase of the Gospels composed by Orm (fl. 1200?), an Augustinian monk, or his disciples—*Eds.*]

America (four thousand people crowded the Philadelphia Academy of Music in 1875 to see eighty competitors spelled down), and the vogue is far from dead. The spelling bee proved fairly conclusively that women are better spellers than men, possibly because they are more conscious of appearance, in words as well as clothes.

In 1837 Isaac Pitman devised his method of stenography, which opened the eyes of many scholars to the deficiencies of English spelling and the advantages of phonetization. Coupled with the filtration into learned milieus of the earlier versions of the International Phonetic Alphabet, this led to the first serious attempts at phonetic spelling reform. In England, G. B. Shaw fought for a standard phonetic alphabet that would enable him to transfer to the printed page the full tang of "coster English," the "grave music of good Scotch," and the "exquisite diphthong with which a New Yorker pronounces such words as *world* and *bird*." For want of such an alphabet, he complained, he had to do with such makeshifts as "a cup of cowcow" and "bless yr awt, y' cawnt be a pawrit naradys."

On this side of the ocean, we have had a Simplified Spelling Board since 1906; but even the support of Theodore Roosevelt could not arouse the American people to the importance of the problem. Senator Robert Owen's attempt to create a "Global Alphabet" elicited from a distinguished kinswoman of the reform-loving Theodore, Mrs. Eleanor Roosevelt, the comment that "it seems quite difficult to learn."

And there the matter rests. With the exception of some popular innovations, mostly of commercial origin (*thru, tho, alright, Starlite, nite* and *nitery, donut, burlesk, thanx, sox*), the great spelling problem of the English language is still unsolved.

It is not that there are no organizations and individuals interested in spelling reform. Quite the contrary. On both sides of the Atlantic we find swarms of would-be reformers. There are the Simplified Spelling Society of England and the Simpler Spelling Association of America, which advance a composite method whereby *may* is spelled *mai* or *mae, who* becomes *huu* or *hoo, there* appears as *dhaer* or *thair*. There is an American Phonetic League, which would bring in new symbols and suprascripts (*bilō* for *below, fφlz* for *falls, sum* for *some*). There is a Georgia organization which seems to stem directly from the Websterian tradition (*agen, hipnosis, wurld, gras, enuf, vois, vizit, stopt*).

A British Labour M.P. (Mont Fosdick) would abolish C, Q and X, and represent vowel-sounds by their normal continental equivalents ("*Sins Sheikspiers taim dher haz bien ei greiter oltereishun in dhu Inglish languij dhan Ai am propozing nau*"). Samuel Seegay, a printing teacher in a Brooklyn high school, who claims the chances against a student spelling *thermometer* correctly are six hundred million to one, advocates a system very similar to that whereby Webster's Dictionary gives the pronunciation of words. Our Simplified Spelling Board, which began operations forty-five years ago, offers a form as follows: *"Forskor and sevn yeers agoe our faadherz braut forth on dhis kontinent a nue naeshun."* Most moderate among native reformers are the *Chicago Tribune* and the *Washington Times-Herald,* which limit themselves to eliminating a few unpronounced letters and using *f* for *ph* (*burocracy, demagog, ameba, bagatel, thorobred, midrif, lexicografer*).

With all due respect for the hard labors and excellent intentions of the reformers, there are two major criticisms of their efforts that may be advanced at this point. One is purely technical and deals with their proce- dure. If we are to go through the throes of a major linguistic transformation, why not do a complete job? The sounds of spoken English, whether British or American, are limited in number; for each of them there exists a precise symbol in the International Phonetic Alphabet. Adoption of these IPA symbols, or a modification of them to simplify the printing problem, is perfectly possible, and thereafter we should have a completely phonetic written language.

The other criticism is concerned with the praiseworthy but erroneous ideology displayed by the majority of the reformers. For some incompre- hensible reason, they choose to link their activities with the two largely unrelated problems of the adoption of English as an international language and the preservation of world peace. "Simplify English spelling," many of them say, "and you will abolish the major obstacle to the adoption of English as world tongue; then, when we have an international language, and this language is English, there will be no more quarrels among the nations, and no more wars." One spelling reformer goes so far as to assert that we could make several major political concessions to the Soviet Union in return for their acceptance of phonetized English.

One might say that this logical sequence is so illogical that one should take no notice of it. Yet it is widespread. The three desiderata (phonetiza- tion of English, adoption of a universal tongue, and world peace) are each of them such worthy causes that it is a pity to see them thrown together in a stew-pot of confusion. It goes without saying that the adoption of an international language will not, all by itself, halt wars. It also remains to be proved (and no foreign government has been heard from on this score) that if we reform our evil spelling ways other nations will adopt our tongue. The reform of English spelling is such an urgent internal problem that it can and should be discussed on a purely internal basis rather than an interna- tional one. Is it a worth-while project so far as we, the speakers of English, are concerned? If it is, let us proceed to discuss it, in our own selfish interests and without too much regard for what foreign nations may think or do about it. Other countries never asked our permission in connection with their own language changes. The Turks switched from the Arabic to the

Roman alphabet, the Russians revised their Cyrillic spelling, the speakers of Portuguese and Norwegian go through periodic spelling revisions, and all without consulting anyone outside their own countries. Surely our children and children's children, who have to go through the drastic spelling-learning process we went through, should be enough of a consideration with us to warrant our careful study of the question, regardless of the possible and very hypothetical future actions of other nations.

It is often asserted that the only thing that keeps us from reforming our spelling and going over to a simpler system is the dead hand of tradition, or, to put it another way, our national perversity. Clark, for example, states: "English-speaking peoples, particularly American, take a perverted pride in the intricate and mysterious anomalies of the spelling of their language; it makes them feel superior to foreigners." This is a splendid wise-crack, but it hardly corresponds to the linguistic reality. Robertson has neatly summarized the advantages and disadvantages of spelling reform. The former, according to him, are: a saving in education, printing, typing, an improvement in pronunciation, an aid in the Americanization of foreigners and a contribution to the acceptance of English as an international language. The disadvantages (and we should note them carefully) are: the loss of etymological values, the falling together of homophones, the impossibility of keeping related words together in the dictionary, and a loss in the esthetic quality of the language. An additional difficulty, cited from Samuel Johnson, is that the reformers would be taking "that for a model which is changing while they apply it," which means in effect that the process of phonetization would have to be repeated every fifty or a hundred years to keep pace with spoken-language changes.

To each of these arguments there is a reply, to be sure. The "loss of etymological values" means that whereas a few of us now know at a glance what the derivation of *phthisic* is, we would no longer know once the word was spelled *tisic* or something similar. Other languages have been through this particular mill, with no apparent ill effects. Italian *tisico* has no trace of Greek *phth*, but the Italians seem to be able to struggle along. Homophones like *pear, pair, pare* would fall together in spelling if the reform were adopted; this would not be a new situation; we already have it in *Pole* and *pole*, and, without even benefit of capitals, in words like *post, toll* and *bat*. But there are even corresponding advantages in the distinction that would arise between *tear* [ti:r] and *tear* [te:r], *read* [ri:d] and *read* [red]. Context and word-order, as Chinese teaches us, are great aids to comprehension. More serious is the dictionary divorcement of *zeal* and *zealous, nation* and *national,* but cross-references could be created by titillating the ingenuity of our lexicographers. As for the esthetic factor, that seems to coincide largely with traditionalism. We think that is beautiful which is familiar. The changing phonetics of the English language could be taken care of by a periodical revision, as in Portuguese, and we ought not to forget that a truly phonetic writing-system would act as a powerful deterrent to pronunciation changes which are now largely arbitrary because the pronunciation is not supported by the writing.

Robertson, it would seem, has overlooked what is undoubtedly the principal valid objection to spelling reform, an objection that was dramatically brought into the limelight when a commission of American educators urged the Japanese to use Roman characters instead of their ideographs and *kanas*. "What shall we do with all our present printed works?" asked the Japanese. "Scrap them and reprint them in Roman, at infinite cost of money, time and labor? Or allow them to remain in our libraries, side by side with the new works in Roman alphabet, which will mean that our growing generations will have to learn both systems, the old and the new?"

Orthographic reform is relatively simple where the majority of the population is illiterate, as was the case in Kemal's Turkey. It becomes a terrific problem where the majority is literate, as in Japan, Britain or America. The older generations must learn all over again, while the younger cannot be separated at one blow from the previous tradition, save by the well-nigh impossible expedient of burning all past records and creating them anew.

Robertson makes the observation that phonetic spelling is not necessary if only the letters are associated by habit with the word. It is not the sole function of writing, he holds, to symbolize the spoken language's sounds. We too have ideographic elements in our capitals and punctuation, not to mention our spelling of homophones like *so, sow, sew*. But then ought we not to go over to a frankly ideographic system, like the Chinese? What is galling about our English spelling is that it is neither phonetic nor ideographic, but attempts to combine both elements.

In an impassioned and lengthy letter to the *New York Times* Charles Funk once protested against the full phonetization of English. His major argument was the difference between British and American pronunciation, which he claimed was such as to compel both British and Americans to use glossaries to read phonetic transcriptions of each other's spoken tongue.

This, of course, is another major stumbling-block in the path of spelling reform. It seems to point, indeed, to a need for reform in speech rather than writing. . . .

Before leaving this question of spelling reform, however, let us summarize what a phonetic spelling could do for us, not on the international plane, by making our language easier for foreigners to swallow, but on the isolationistic, national level.

English spelling is at times confusing to those who know it well, and leads to frequent trips to the dictionary to discover not the meaning, but the form of words. But to our younger native learners of English, those descendants concerning whom so many fine words flow, it is distressing and difficult. How much of the school child's time is spent on the purely mechanical memorization of spelling? If all those hours were added up and multiplied by the number of learners, the sum-product would be astronomical. If those hours were devoted, as they are in most other western countries, to the acquisition of factual knowledge, what might we not expect in the way of educational improvement?

This consideration alone ought to give us pause and make us reflect on what might be the advantages and disadvantages of a true phonetization of our written language. The body of material knowledge at our disposal is increasing at an astounding rate. Already it is difficult, not to say impossible, to achieve that well-rounded education that used to be the boast of earlier centuries, and this is not because we have become intellectually duller, but simply because there is so much more to learn, so many fields of which our ancestors, even our parents, had no conception, but with which the educated man of today must have some familiarity. If, under the circumstances, we were to unburden ourselves of one of the unnecessary burdens our grandparents carried so easily in their stride, would we not be doing the intelligent thing? Must a twentieth-century soldier, in addition to his modern equipment, continue to carry a nineteenth-century knapsack and a twenty-pound musket?

Vocabulary

ideograph, phthisic, myrrh, analogous, restaurateur, vilification, bilingualism, extenuation, curio, advocacy, fillip, phonetization, diphthong composite, suprascript, ideology, desiderata, perversity, homophones, titillating, ingenuity, orthography, expedient

Review Questions

1. What conditions in the system of English spelling make spelling reform seem desirable?
2. What contribution did Noah Webster make to spelling reform?
3. Why does the problem of spelling remain unsolved?
4. Pei offers two major criticisms of the efforts of spelling reformers. What are they?
5. Even if a more accurately phonetic spelling system were adopted, why would revisions have to be made every fifty or a hundred years?
6. Why is orthographic reform "relatively simple where the majority of the population is illiterate"?
7. Comment on the validity of Pei's comparison of "outmoded" spelling to nineteenth-century military equipment.

8. What examples of analysis can you find in Pei's essay?

Expository Technique

1. Into what smaller units does Pei divide "the problem of spelling reform"?
2. Attempt to formulate a minor thematic idea for each of these components.

Exercises

1. The sound *e* [i] as in *me* is represented in a number of ways in English spelling. List as many of these ways as you can. Do the same for *a* [e] as in *bake*.

2. Pei notes that *ough* is pronounced in several ways. Compile a list in which *ea* appears and in each case is pronounced differently.

3. Because a sound may be represented by a number of different symbols, Pei suggests *phtholognyrrh* as a possible spelling for *Turner*. How might *ghoti* be justified as a spelling for *fish*, *phrheagh* for *free*? What "logical" spellings can you suggest for the following words: *circle, enough, peel, psychology,* and *Shakespeare?*

4. Compile a list of ten English words which, like *island*, contain letters that are silent in ordinary pronunciation.

5. If spelling in Modern English has not regularly conformed to pronunciation, it has occasionally made pronunciation conform to it. Whether from a reverence for the printed word as a standard from which spoken English has degenerated or from a lack of acquaintance with more traditional pronunciations, people have striven to introduce, or reintroduce, written spelling pronunciations, which have occasionally displaced the more traditional ones. Transcribe the following words as you are accustomed to hearing them and then as their spelling dictates. Consult a standard contemporary desk dictionary to see which pronunciations have currency.

clothes	vehicle	often	arctic	nephew
separate	forehead	extraordinary	almond	every
coxswain	chocolate	salmon	subtle	forward
government	waistcoat	Edinburgh	Greenwich	Concord
Cirencester	Leicester	Chelmsford	Thames	Hampshire

6. Homonyms, words with the same pronunciation but with different meanings and spellings, such as *to* and *two*, are sometimes a source of confusion to those attempting to spell conventionally. Compile a list of ten pairs of homonyms.

7. Some find the jingle below helpful as an aid to the conventional spelling of words containing *ie* or *ei*, as in *believe* and *receive*.

I before *e*
Except after *c*

Or when sounded as *a*,
As in *neighbor* and *weigh*.

How accurate is this rule? What exceptions to it can you find? A brief, but detailed, discussion of this rule is that of Donald W. Lee, "The 'ei and ie' Rule," *College English*, VI (December 1944), 156–159.

8. The regular plural inflection of English nouns has three phonetic forms. Using IPA symbols indicate the sounds represented by the conventional spelling of the plural in the following words:

| pick | gag | pot | tab | tip | ring | church |
| rose | fad | dish | pun | ham | mash | rafter |

The inflectional endings for the past tense of *walk* and *answer* are spelled the same. Are they pronounced the same?

9. The addition of suffixes sometimes modifies the pronunciation of the consonant to which they are added. Using the IPA indicate the change in pronunciation of the final base consonant in each of the following series:

a. logic, logicity, logician
b. electric, electricity, electrician
c. physic, physician
d. beast, beastly
e. moist, moisture, moisten
f. right, righteous
g. grand, grandeur
h. Christ, Christmas
i. worth, worthy

10. An interesting debate concerning the desirability of spelling reform was conducted a few years ago by Helen Bowyer and Louis Foley. Read their essays, listed below, and prepare a summary of the two writers' views.

Helen Boyer, "It's Not Johnny!" *Phi Delta Kappan*, XL (June 1959), 378–380.
———— "Upsetting the Alphabet-Cart," *Word Study*, XXXVI (December 1960), 4–6.
Louis Foley, "Upsetting the Alphabet-Cart," *Word Study*, XXXV (April 1960), 1–5.
———— "The Alphabet-Cart Jogs On," *Word Study*, XXXVI (February 1961), 5–6.
———— "Doctor of Letters," *Phi Delta Kappan*, XLII (April 1961), 316–321.

11. In a brief essay Frederick S. Wingfield classifies and gives examples of some of the more serious proposals for reforming English spelling. Read his essay in *American Speech*, VII (October 1931), 54–57, and prepare an oral report on it.

12. Some modifications of the alphabet which would facilitate teaching children to read have received considerable attention during the sixties. Consult the *Reader's Guide* for 1960–1965 and investigate some of the articles cited there. Prepare a report on the results of your research.

13. Investigate and analyze George Bernard Shaw's proposals for spelling reform.

21.

ARTHUR BRONSTEIN

Sound Changes

. . . The spoken language is never at rest. It is constantly changing, although these changes are never really obvious at any given time. Many of these changes are resisted or delayed, while some are obviated by other strong influences. This chapter analyzes and classifies the more obvious sound changes present in our language. Through a study of the forms of these changes we are able to understand the phonemic relationships between different forms of the same words.

Since these changes are often due to the influence of adjacent sounds, shifts in stress, analogy, or the ease of speech, our discussion must consider the sounds of speech in context with other sounds. Some of these phonetic changes are obvious, others are not. Some are easily explained, while others are seemingly unexplainable. Some changes take place fairly rapidly, while others are slow to take place. Nor is there a point at which we can say that a sound change is about to take place. We can observe change only after it has taken place, or, if enough evidence is available, while it is taking place.

Do not expect to find complete consistency. Sounds surrounded by the same stress and sound patterns will change in certain words, but not in others. The influences that cause phonetic change can be counter-balanced by such other factors as analogy, the psychological barrier of "acceptability," and the spelled form. You will see many such "inconsistencies" in the lists of words demonstrating the different sound changes throughout this chapter.

The matter of "acceptability" deserves special mention here. Certain changed forms have become part of the standard pattern, while others have not. The category of the type of change is not a criterion of acceptability. *Nature* as [neɪtʃʊɚ] and *did you* as [dɪdʒə] reflect the same type of sound change. Your acceptance of one and not the other is only one illustration of the fact that the criterion of acceptability is not dependent on the category of change. It *is* dependent on the extent to which the speech habit is current in educated speech. Widespread use of a changed form will be the sanction it needs for acceptability. If enough students stood and acknowledged a teacher's presence each time he entered the classroom, and if this form of acknowledgement became habitual over a considerable period of time, it would become the *accepted* form of behavior in such situations. Acceptability of the spoken form works very much the same way.

It is also important to keep in mind that sound changes are slow to begin and slow to evolve. Many go on without our being consciously aware of them. And so many have taken place over the period of time during which English has been spoken, that unless we seek them out, we are not aware how different earlier English speaking habits were. No language in use is static. Its grammar, vocabulary, meanings of words, and its phonology are continually being modified. Sound change is probably the most dramatic of these modifications.

Our concern in this chapter does not lead us into a study of the historical changes which have taken place over the history of our language. These are the concern of *historical* or *diachronic linguistics*. Such study accounts for our knowledge of earlier English forms, tracing and explaining such phenomena as the earlier pronunciations of *house* as [hus], of *wife* as [wif], of *point* as [paɪnt], of *father* as [fæðər]. . . . And such study in turn leads to the analysis of sounds in related languages, and their comparative development *(comparative linguistics)*, explaining English *day* and German *Tag*; English *three*, Dutch *drie*, and Danish *tre*; French *mère*, Spanish or Italian *madre*, and Portuguese *mãe*. The essential concern of this chapter . . . is current speech, the study of fairly recent sound changes—those quite recently completed or still going on. Such analysis is a part of *synchronic linguistics* and is separated in intent from the historical approach. Although some diachronic illustrations of sound change may appear, our predominant concern remains synchronic—with the language we use and hear around us.

SOUND CHANGE DUE TO ASSIMILATION

It has long been known that the sounds of a language tend to become similar to, or identical with, a following sound. Latin *ad* and *tenuo* led to the present *attend, sit down* may be heard as [sɪdːaʊn] and the two /k/ sounds in *cool* and *key* are influenced by the different positions of the following vowels. These changes result from anticipating the following sound: the *d* of *ad-tenuo* was devoiced in anticipation of the following voiceless /t/; the /k/ sound in *cool* is made farther back in the mouth than the /k/ of *key*, because the tongue anticipates the position of /u/ or /i/ in each word; and the /t/ of *sit* is assimilated into the following /d/ of *down*. These sound changes are the most common in our language. They are known as *anticipatory* or *regressive* changes, because the influence is backwards in the word or phrase, and the speaker anticipates the following sound by changing the preceding one to become more like it. A change in the opposite direction may be noticed in our pronunciation of the word *calls*. The plural form *s* is pronounced as a /z/, while the plural *s* of *cats* remains voiceless. In the former word /s/ > /z/ because of the influence of the voiced *l* before it, while in the latter word, the plural form already follows a voiceless sound. The same kind of a change occurs in *open*, when it is pronounced as [opm̩], where an alveolar /n/ becomes a bilabial /m/ because of the influence of the preceding bilabial /p/. These changes are forward in the word and are known as *forward* or *progressive* assimilations. They are not as common as the anticipatory changes mentioned above.

Any characteristic of a sound may change in the assimilative process. A non-nasal vowel sound may be emitted nasally in *man*: [mæ̃n]. A velar nasal sound, /ŋ/, may be shifted to an interdental position when before a /θ/ sound, as in *length*: [lɛn̪θ]. A voiceless sound may be voiced, as occurs when the /θ/ of *worth* becomes a /ð/ in *worthy*. And a voiced sound may become voiceless, as does the final sound of *walked*.

When one sound is changed *into* a neighboring sound, as in the pronunciation of *horseshoe* as [hɔɚʃu], (s > ʃ), or *cupboard* as [kʌbɚd], (p > b), the assimilation is called a *full* or *complete assimilation*. When a sound is changed *in the direction of* a neighboring sound, as results in the formation of the two /k/ sounds in *key* and *cool*, or when the /n/ of *hand* becomes an /ŋ/ in *handkerchief*, [hæŋkɚtʃɪf], the result is known as a *partial* or *incomplete assimilation*.

An assimilation occurs when a sound becomes more like its neighboring sound. It may become similar to or identical with the sound influencing the change.

Following are a number of assimilations that have already taken place. Some are a normal part of your speech pattern, found in everyday, standard, colloquial usage. Others are not commonly found in educated usage, according to current sources. The failure to use normal assimilated forms may make the speech sound "old-fashioned," "pedantic," or "affected." Widespread use of questionable forms makes the speech sound "careless."

Note each of the following assimilated forms. Those that are considered currently acceptable appear in the first part of each group of words. Those in the second part are either commonly associated with less-educated speech or those for which acceptability is not clearly established.

EXAMPLES OF ANTICIPATORY ASSIMILATIONS

WORD OR PHRASE	ASSIMILATED FORMS FOUND IN COLLOQUIAL-EDUCATED SPEECH	CHANGE
comfort	[kʌɱfɚt	[m > ɱ

income tax	ɪŋkəm tæks	n > ŋ
pumpkin	pʌŋkɪn	m > n
congress	kɑŋgrəs	n > ŋ
handkerchief	hæŋkɚtʃɪf	n > ŋ
pancake	pæŋkeɪk	n > ŋ
comptroller	kəntrolɚ	m > n
have to	hæf tu	v > f
used to	justu	z > s
grandpa	græmpɑ	n > m
grandma	græm:ɑ	n > m
on the top	ɑn̪ ðə tɑp	n > n̪
in the box	ɪn̪ ðə bɑks	n > n̪
at the beach	æt̪ ðə bitʃ	t > t̪
newspaper	n(j)uspeɪpɚ	z > s
with time	wɪθ taɪm	ð > θ
horseshoe	hɔɚʃ:u	s > ʃ
don't believe it	dom(p) bəlivɪt]	n > m]

ASSIMILATED FORMS ASSOCIATED
WITH LESS-EDUCATED SPEECH

strength	[strɛn̪θ	[ŋ > n
in contact with	ɪŋkɑntækt wɪð	n > ŋ
I can go	aɪ kɪŋgo	n > ŋ
inbred	ɪmbrɛd	n > m
goodbye	gʊbaɪ	d > b
let me	lɛmi]	t > m]

FORWARD OR PROGRESSIVE ASSIMILATIONS

WORD OR PHRASE	ASSIMILATED FORMS FOUND IN COLLOQUIAL-EDUCATED SPEECH	CHANGE
open the door	[opm̩ ðə dɔɚ	[n > m
it happens	ɪt hæpm̩z	n > m
wagon train	wægŋ treɪn	n > ŋ
bacon	beɪkŋ]	n > ŋ]

	ASSIMILATED FORMS ASSOCIATED WITH LESS-EDUCATED SPEECH	
ribbon	[rɪbm̩	[n > m
captain	kæpm̩	tn > m
candidates	kænɪdeɪts	d > n
something	sʌmpm̩	ŋ > m
twenty	twɛni]	t > n]

Reciprocal Assimilations

Reciprocal assimilations occur when both anticipatory and forward assimilations seem to take place simultaneously. Such words as *nature, virtue, picture, mission,* and *vision,* pronounced during the eighteenth century as though spelled "natyure, virtyue, pictyure," and so on, developed palatalized forms with [ʃ] and [ʒ] due to the influence of the /t, s, or z/ and /j/ sounds upon each other. Today, the older forms have disappeared, leaving only the assimilated [neɪtʃɚ, vɝtʃu, pɪktʃɚ, mɪʃən, vɪʒən]. Similar pronunciations, both assimilated and nonassimilated, were heard for such words as *gradual, graduate, usury, assiduous,* and *verdure,* with a favoring of the assimilated form and a gradual discontinuance of the older, non-assimilated form. The use of such pronunciations as [neɪtjʊɚ, grædjʊəl, əprɪsɪeɪt] in current, educated-colloquial speech is rare and unexpected. However, *duteous* and *beauteous* are unassimilated, [bjutɪəs, djutɪəs], while such words as *educate, maturation,* and *nausea* are heard both as [ɛdjʊkeɪt, mætjʊreɪʃən, nɔzɪə (nɔsɪə)] and [ɛdʒʊkeɪt (ɛdʒɚ-), mætʃʊreɪʃən, nɔʒɚ (nɔʒɪə), nɔʃə (nɔʃɪə)]. The use of nonassimilated [ɪsju] for *issue* is chiefly British as is the assimilated [ʃɛjul] for *schedule*.

WORD OR PHRASE	ASSIMILATED FORMS ASSOCIATED WITH LESS-EDUCATED SPEECH	CHANGE
tune	[tʃun	[tj > tʃ
Indian	ɪndʒən	dj > dʒ
duty	dʒuti	dj > dʒ
he has your coat	hi hæʒjɚ koʊt	zj > ʒ
was your car there	wɑʒɚ kɑɚ ðɛɚ]	zj > ʒ]

VOICING ASSIMILATIONS*

WORD OR PHRASE	ASSIMILATED FORMS FOUND IN COLLOQUIAL-EDUCATED SPEECH	CHANGE
letter	lɛtɚ †	t > t̬
butter	bʌtɚ †	t > t̬
thirty	θɝti †	t > t̬
seventy	sɛvn̩ti †	t > t̬
forty	fɔɚti †	t > t̬

WORD OR PHRASE	ASSIMILATED FORMS FOUND IN COLLOQUIAL-EDUCATED SPEECH	CHANGE
gosling (from goose)	[gɑzlɪŋ	[s > z
husband (from house)	hʌzbənd	s > z
usurp	juzɝp	s > z
absolve	æbzɑlv	s > z
absurd	æbzɝd	s > z
absorb	æbzɔɚb]	s > z]

	ASSIMILATED FORMS ASSOCIATED WITH LESS-EDUCATED SPEECH	
got to	[gɑdə	[t > d
notice	noʊdɪs]	t > d]

* The addition of voice to a voiceless consonant due to the influence of a neighboring voiced sound.

† The [t] in these words may occur as a weakly aspirated voiceless stop or as a voiced tap.

DEVOICING‡

WORD OR PHRASE	ASSIMILATED FORMS FOUND IN EDUCATED SPEECH	CHANGE
twenty	[twɛnti	[w > ʍ
quiet	kʍaɪət	w > ʍ
quick	kʍɪk	w > ʍ
twice	tʍaɪs	w > ʍ
absorption (absorb)	æbsɔɚpʃən	b > p
resorption (resorb)	rɪsɔɚpʃən	b > p
subscription (subscribe)	səbskrɪpʃən	b > p
prescription (prescribe)	prɪskrɪpʃən]	b > p]

	ASSIMILATED FORMS ASSOCIATED WITH LESS-EDUCATED SPEECH	
because	[bɪkɔs	[z > s
a good cause	ə gʊd kɔs	z > s
the river flows	ðə rɪvɚ flous	z > s
bags	bægs]	z > s]

These last four examples are probably more accurately represented by the use of a voiceless *z* [z̥]: [bɪkɔz̥, kɔz̥, flouz̥, bægz̥]. In normal usage, final *z*, before a pause, off-glides from the voiced sound to a voiceless sound before the silence: *cause* > [kɔzz̥].

DISSIMILATION

An assimilative change, in which one sound is altered to become *more* like its neighbor, is the most common form of sound change. Less common, but equally dramatic, are those changes which occur when one of two recurring sounds is altered to become *less* like its neighbor. In these instances, one of the two repeated sounds is dropped, or it is changed into a different sound. This type of sound-change is known as a *dissimilation*.

You have probably heard the pronunciations [laɪbɛri] for *library*, [gʌvɚmənt] for *government*. Dissimilations occur in both instances when the first of the recurring /r/ and /n/ sounds are dropped. A historical dissimilation exists in the word *pilgrim* (derived from the Latin *peregrinum*—note our word *peregrinate*), where an /l/ replaced the first /r/. The word *marble* has an interesting history of dissimilation. The Latin *marmorem*

---

‡ The removal of voice from a voiced consonant due to the influence of a neighboring voiceless sound or to the pause following the end of the word.

changed in French to *marbre*, the excrescent /b/ acting as a means of separating the two /r/ sounds. Middle English borrowed the French word and showed two forms of it: *marbre* and *marbel*. Our choice today is the dissimilated form [mɑɚbəl]. Some other examples of this type of change are shown below.

WORD	DISSIMILATED FORMS FOUND IN COLLOQUIAL-EDUCATED SPEECH	REPEATED OR SIMILAR SOUNDS
government	[gʌvəˑmənt	[n — m
surprise	səpraɪz	ɚ — r
northerner	nɔðənɚ	ɚ — ɚ
library	laɪbɛri	r — r
secretary	sɛkətɛri	r — r
governor	gʌvənɚ	ɚ — ɚ
charivari	ʃɪvəri]	r — r]

	DISSIMILATED FORMS ASSOCIATED WITH LESS-EDUCATED SPEECH	
chimney	[tʃɪmli	[m — n
environment	ɪnvaɪrəmənt]	n — m]

METATHESIS AND HAPLOLOGY SOUND CHANGES

Two rather peculiar sound changes take place in the pronunciation of certain sounds in context. The first is a reversal of the order of sounds, for example, [æsk] into [æks] for *ask*. This reversal of sounds is known as *metathesis*. The second is the deletion of duplicate elements or syllables, a form of dissimilation known as *haplology*. These sound changes are uncommon. A few of the more common ones are listed below. They are not commonly found in the speech of cultivated speakers.

METATHESIS		HAPLOLOGY	
relevant	> [rɛvələnt]	Mississippi	> [mɪsɪpi]
irrelevant	> [ɪrɛvələnt]	Mrs. Smith	> [mɪs smɪθ]
I asked him	> [aɪ ækst ɪm]	probably	> [prɑbli]
perspire	> [prəspaɪɚ]	particularly	> [pɚtɪkjəli]
perspiration	> [prɛspɚreɪʃn]	similarly	> [sɪməli]
pronounce	> [pɚnaʊns]		
tragedy	> [trædədʒi]		
elevate	> [ɛvəleɪt]		
rejuvenate	> [rɪdʒunəveɪt]		
hundred	> [hʌndɚd]		

OTHER COMMON SOUND CHANGES

A few other changes of sounds in context occur. . . . They are: (1) the nasalization of sounds and (2) the lengthening and shortening of sounds.

Nasalization

Any vowel in the language can be nasalized. The tendency to do so is greatest when there is a nasal sound adjacent to the vowel. Completely assimilated nasality exists for certain vowels in French, where the nasal vowel represents a formerly spelled vowel plus a nasal sound, pronounced as a single nasal vowel at present. If you are a student of French, you know that a nasal consonant, as we know it, does not exist in any of the following words (the nasality has been completely assimilated into the vowel); *faim* [fɛ̃], *Jean* [ʒɑ̃], *bon* [bɔ̃], and *un* [œ̃].[2] In our language, such complete assimilation of the nasal sound does not take place. Some degree of it how- ever, is almost unavoidable when we pronounce such words as *man, many, candy, mean,* and *none.* Such nasalization of the vowels results from the failure of the soft palate to shut off the nasal passage. When nasalization of vowels is excessive, it is considered faulty usage. It results in the kind of speech often labeled as a "nasal twang." Some slight degree of nasality may occur even to *consonants* adjacent to nasal sounds, as in "have more," "He gave Ned . . ." [ṽ]; "with Mary" [ð̃]; "has many" [z̃]; and so on. Although all speakers are likely to possess some degree of nasality, excessive nasaliza- tion is not found in cultivated speech.

The Lengthening and Shortening of Sounds

The lengthening and shortening of sounds is a common occurrence. These concepts too have been discussed previously. They are included here, however, for they are another aspect of sound change. Lengthening and shortening of vowel sounds are closely associated with the stressing and unstressing of syllables. Stressed syllables normally contain longer vowels, while unstressed syllables possess shorter vowels. Thus the syllable *man* in *dairyman* or *postman* is shortened and weakened to [-mən]. The vowels in the words *have, has,* and *were* are similarly shortened and weakened to [ə]

---

[2] [œ̃] is a rounded [ɛ] sound found in such French words as *chauffeur, soeur,* and *coiffeur.*

forms when unstressed in such phrases as "I have come," "He has come," and "They were here."

Identical consonants in two syllables are blended into one long consonant in such phrases as *hit Tom, big goose, will Lucy,* and *one night:* [hɪt:ɑm], [bɪg:us], and so on. The three nasals [m], [n], and [ŋ] and the [l] sound are lengthened, normally, when they are in stressed syllables before other voiced consonants, or when final in the phrase. Long vowels tend to break or diphthongize in our language, accounting for the historical change from [hus] to [haʊs], from [wif] to [waɪf], the current pronunciations of *too* and *blue* as [tɪu] and [blɪu], and *candy* and *ask* as [kæ˞əndi] and [æ˞əsk]. The deletion of a post-vowel *r*, in such words as *lark* and *part*, may lead to a compensatory lengthening of the vowel /ɑ/: [lɑːk], [pɑːk].

All these examples of lengthening and shortening of sounds are actually slight variations of the sounds. They are normally disregarded in broad phonetic transcription. They do account, however, for some of the changes of sounds in our language. Further examples of these changes are found below.

The unstressing of a formerly stressed syllable may lead to a change in its phonetic structure. This change is manifested by a change in the vowel toward a shortened form (*man* in *postman* is unstressed and short), the substitution of a syllabic consonant or one vowel for another (*beetle* and *event* become [bitl̩] and [ɪvɛnt], or the deletion of one or more sounds in the unstressed syllable (*and* may become [n̩d] or [n̩]). The change in a vowel from a stressed form to a lesser stressed or unstressed vowel occurs as a syllable becomes less prominent in the word or phrase. The reverse may occur also—an unstressed vowel may change into a stressed and lengthened form, or into another stressed vowel as the syllable gains prominence. Both of these changes are known as *vowel gradation*. Some examples of each will be found in the lists below.

In certain words the stress-shifts result in the change of a normally unstressed or weaker vowel to a stressed full vowel, as the word assumes a somewhat different form or meaning. The word *the,* in this very sentence, normally contains the unstressed, weak vowel /ə/. When stressed, as in the sentence "This is *the* school," meaning a particular or special school, the phonetic value of the vowel normally changes to /i/. Similar changes of unstressed vowels to other vowels may be heard in the final syllables of each of the following nouns or adjectives as they assume verbal functions: *address, record, separate*; and in the indicated unstressed syllables as the following words assume different forms: *anim̆ate—anim̆ated*; *vŏcal—vŏcalic*; *Cæ̆sar—Cæ̆sarian.*

LENGTHENED FORMS

WORD	PRONUNCIATION WITH LENGTHENED FORM
card	[kɑːd
farther	fɑːðə
third	θɜːd
burn	bɜːn
candy	kæəndi
glass	glæəs
sings	sɪŋːz
field	fɪlːd
take care	teɪkːɛ˞
set two places	sɛtːuː—]

SHORTENED FORMS AS SYLLABLE LOSES PROMINENCE

WORD	SHORTENED FORM	PHRASE
he	[i or ɪ	Is he here?
her	ə, ə˞, hə, or hə˞	I see her.
she	ʃɪ	Is she coming?
him	ɪm, əm	Give it to him.
them	ðəm, əm	I saw them.
their	ðə˞	It's their own fault.
you	jə	I saw you there.
from	frəm]	Take it from him.
and	[ṇd, ṇ	He and John.
could	kəd	I could touch it.
were	wə˞, wə	We were here.
the	ðə	The boy and the girl.
would	wəd	She would see.
was	wəz	He was here yesterday.
there	ðə˞	There aren't any.
shall	ʃəl	We shall come at nine.
can	kən	When can you come?
as	əz	She's as small as he is.
at	ət	He came at once.
does	dəz	What does she do?
had	əd	She had four dresses.
than	ðən	No bigger than a mouse.
what	hwət	I found what I lost.
some	səm	Some other time.
must	məst]	We must go now.

STRESSED FORMS AS SYLLABLE GAINS PROMINENCE
COMPARED WITH UNSTRESSED SOURCE

SOURCE WITH UNSTRESSED FORM	SOURCE WITH STRESSED FORM	SOUND CHANGE	
a	I'll take *a* plum, not two	[ə	> eɪ
the	Show her *the* dress	ðə	> ði
refer	reference	rɪ	> rɛf
associate (adj.)	associate (verb)	ət	> eɪt
molecule	molecular	lə	> lɛk
spectacle	spectacular	tə	> tæk
equal	equality	kwəl	> kwɑl
subject (verb)	subject (noun)	səb	> sʌb
excellent	excel	sə	> sɛl
college	collegiate	lədʒ	> li
moment	momentous	mənt	> mɛnt
history	historic	tə	> tɑr
personal	personality	nəl	> næl]

ANALOGY

The change of one sound into another because of the analogy of a similar word has long been with us. Some of these analogic changes seem reasonable, others seem strange. We do know that analogic change does not occur easily in commonly-used words. When it does occur, it can often be explained by the lack of such conserving forces as common usage or the spelled form. It is difficult too to explain why analogy will affect one word, but not another just like it.

Our pronunciations of *wife—wives* and *life—lives* should lead us to expect *hoof—hooves* and *roof—rooves*. The pronunciation [huvz] is rare, although our dictionaries do list it. [hufs (or hʊfs)] is the more common form. The plural of *roof* followed the analogy of adding an *s* to the singular form, rather than following the pronunciation with a plural [vz] as in *wives*. The amusing [potɑto] for *potato* results from a mistaken belief that it is pronounced that way by Britishers or New Englanders, by analogy with *tomato* which does possess the [ɑ] in the medial syllable. A popular song appeared out of Hollywood in the thirties, with the words: "You say *tomato* [təmeɪto] and I say *tomato* [təmɑto]; you say *potato* [pəteɪto] and I say *potato* [pətɑto]." Did the lyricist assume that if a Britisher said [təmɑto], he could be sure that he would also say [pətɑto]?

The word *fancy* has an "affected" form. By analogy with such words as *dance, prance, enhance,* and *glance,* which in the Received Pronunciation of British English (or in certain sections of eastern United States) may be heard with [ɑ], *fancy* may appear as [fɑnsi], a created pronunciation of affected speech, since this is not one of the so-called "broad *a*" words. Our pronunciation of *February* as [fɛbjuɛri], possibly explained as an "*r*-dissimilation," can be categorized more readily as a modification of the pronunciation with both "*r*'s," following the analogy of *January* with [-juɛri]. In the earlier discussion of post-vocalic *r* (as in *idea-r* or *law-r-*) you noticed how these "added-*r*" words occurred as a result of analogy with other similar final-*r* words: *fear* was heard as [fɪə], *idea* as [aɪdɪə]; *fear of* as [fɪərəv] led to the analogic *idea-r of* [aɪdɪərəv].

A very interesting use of analogy affecting pronunciation appears in some of our medial "ng" words in English. Have you ever wondered about the confusing use of [ŋ] and [ŋg] in *singer—stronger, youngish—younger?* *Singer* and *youngish* are pronounced with [ŋ], *younger* and *stronger* with [ŋg]. We know that earlier "ng" was always [ŋg] and that the [g] was dropped when it appeared in the unaccented syllables, as in *walking,* and later whenever final, as in *sing.* The medial "ng" was retained as [ŋg], heard in *finger* and *mingle* and *younger.* But analogy with the [ŋ] of *sing* led to *singer* as [sɪŋɚ], and with *young* to *youngish* as [jʌŋɪʃ], with no velar stops following the [ŋ]. A conflict between analogy and "phonetic law" developed. As a result, we have a confusing use of [ŋg] in *stronger,* but of [ŋ] in *strongly.* *Clangor,* earlier [klæŋgɚ], and still so heard today, has quite recently added the pronunciation [klæŋɚ], by analogy with other "ng" words with suffixed forms. Earlier [hæŋgɑɚ] for *hangar* (the pronunciation during the First World War and thereafter) has given way to [hæŋɚ] so that *hangar* is now a homonym of *hanger.* The pronunciation with the [ŋg] for *hangar* is generally avoided as a "mispronunciation," despite its inclusion in the dictionaries as an educated pronunciation. . . .

CONCLUSION

As you can see, sound changes represent one of the most interesting of linguistic phenomena. It was not until fairly recently (the nineteenth century) that the analysis and classification of sound changes were begun. Once uniform phonetic similarities were noticed in the changes taking place, methods for their detection and explanation were presented. Some of these changes seem accidental, failing to fall into a special category. But with the knowledge we now have of the types of change and the phonetic reasons therefore, we are able to appreciate the seeming inconsistencies we sometimes hear around us. With an understanding of sound change, our varying language should make more sense to you than it may have before.

CARNOY, Albert J., "The Real Nature of Dissimilation," *Transactions* of the American Philological Association, Vol. 49 (1918), pp. 101–113. An older but still excellent account of dissimilation.

FRANCIS, W. Nelson, *The Structure of American English* (New York, Ronald, 1958), pp. 208–220. A short, good review of current (synchronic) sound changes.

HEFFNER, R-M S., *General Phonetics* (Madison, University of Wisconsin Press, 1950), "Speech Sounds in Context," pp. 163–212. A detailed and advanced study of vowel and consonant adaptations, with examples from English and other languages.

KANTNER, Claude E., and WEST, Robert W., *Phonetics* rev. ed. (New York, Harper, 1960), pp. 223–279. Detailing of acoustic and physiologic changes with an especially good discussion on sound incompatibilities on pp. 258–263.

KENT, Roland G., "Assimilation and Dissimilation," *Language,* Vol. 12 (October, 1936), pp. 245–258.

KENYON, John S., *American Pronunciation,* 10th ed. (Ann Arbor, George Wahr Publishing Co., 1951), pp. 76–80. Excellent discussion of assimilation in American English. *r*-dissimilations are illustrated on p. 165; many examples of vowel gradation appear on pp. 96–101.

READ, Allen Walker, "Basis of Correctness in the Pronunciation of Place-Names," *American Speech,* Vol. 8 (February, 1933), pp. 422–426.

SIMONINI, R. C., Jr., "Phonemic Analysis and Analogic Lapses in Radio and Television Speech," *American Speech,* Vol. 31 (December, 1956), pp. 252–263. Analysis of some hilarious contemporary "fluffs" and "bloopers" heard over radio and TV.

STURTEVANT, Edgar H., *An Introduction to Linguistic Science* (New Haven, Yale University Press, 1947), "Assimilation and Dissimilation," Ch. 9, pp. 85–95. Innumerable examples from many languages of these two phenomena.

THOMAS, Charles K., *The Phonetics of American English,* 2nd ed. (New York, Ronald, 1958), pp. 169–190. One of the most readable accounts of the common phonetic changes in American English, with many examples.

WISE, Claude M., *Applied Phonetics* (Englewood Cliffs, N. J., Prentice-Hall, 1957), "Sound Change," Ch. 5, pp. 146–168. A lengthy discussion of sound changes and their causes.

Vocabulary

analogy, criterion, sanction, habitual, evolve, phonology

Review Questions

1. On what does the criterion of "acceptability" depend?
2. With what kind of subject-matter is each of the following concerned: diachronic linguistics, comparative linguistics, synchronic linguistics?
3. Explain and give an example or two of each of the following: assimilation, dissimilation, metathesis, haplology, analogy.

4. When is the tendency to nasalize a vowel sound greatest?

5. Show how lengthening and shortening of vowel sounds are closely associated with the stressing and unstressing of syllables.

Expository Technique

1. Show how this essay utilizes analysis.

2. Reread paragraph two and comment on the sources of coherence within it.

3. Do you think the author succeeds through specific examples in making the various concepts of sound change clear?

Exercises

1. In terms of Professor Bronstein's discussion account for the following pronunciations, some of which are not regarded as part of standard, educated usage:

was	[wəz	red top	[rɛt:ɑp
twice	tʌaɪs	going to	gɔnə
envelope	ɛmvəloup	Hogan's here	hougŋz hɪɚ
want to	wɑnə	seventy	sɛvn̩di
had to	hætu	aren't	eɪnt
has she	hæʒʃi	hit you	hɪtʃu
was sure	wəʒʃʊɚ	would you	wʊdʒə
nice shave	naɪʃʃeɪv	this year	ðɪʃjɪɚ
last show	læʃᵗ ʃou	notice	noṭɪs
call the boy	kɔlðə bɔɪ	shut up	ʃʌdʌp
pretty	pəti	children	tʃɪldɚn]
oatmeal	oupmil]		

2. Named for the Reverend W. A. Spooner (1844–1930)—a man famous for his phonological mishaps—*spoonerism* is an unintentional interchange of sounds in two or more words. Some illustrations are the following: "It is kistumary to cuss the bride"; "Ladies and Gentlemen, the President of the United States, the Honorable Hoobert Heever"; and "Is the bean dizzy?" for "Is the dean busy?" What other spoonerisms can you recall or devise?

The Structure of English

22.

W. NELSON FRANCIS

Revolution in Grammar

I

A long overdue revolution is at present taking place in the study of English grammar—a revolution as sweeping in its consequences as the Darwinian revolution in biology. It is the result of the application to English of methods of descriptive analysis originally developed for use with languages of primitive peoples. To anyone at all interested in language, it is challenging; to those concerned with the teaching of English (including parents), it presents the necessity of radically revising both the substance and the methods of their teaching.

A curious paradox exists in regard to grammar. On the one hand it is felt to be the dullest and driest of academic subjects, fit only for those in whose veins the red blood of life has long since turned to ink. On the other, it is a subject upon which people who would scorn to be professional grammarians hold very dogmatic opinions, which they will defend with considerable emotion. Much of this prejudice stems from the usual sources of prejudice—ignorance and confusion. Even highly educated people seldom have a clear idea of what grammarians do, and there is an unfortunate confusion about the meaning of the term "grammar" itself.

Hence it would be well to begin with definitions. What do people mean when they use the word "grammar"? Actually the word is used to refer to three different things, and much of the emotional thinking about matters grammatical arises from confusion among these different meanings.

The first thing we mean by "grammar" is "the set of formal patterns

From *Quarterly Journal of Speech,* XL (October 1954), 299–312. Reprinted by permission of the Speech Association of America and the author.

in which the words of a language are arranged in order to convey larger meanings." It is not necessary that we be able to discuss these patterns self-consciously in order to be able to use them. In fact, all speakers of a language above the age of five or six know how to use its complex forms of organization with considerable skill; in this sense of the word—call it "Grammar 1"—they are thoroughly familiar with its grammar.

The second meaning of "grammar"—call it "Grammar 2"—is "the branch of linguistic science which is concerned with the description, analysis, and formulization of formal language patterns." Just as gravity was in full operation before Newton's apple fell, so grammar in the first sense was in full operation before anyone formulated the first rule that began the history of grammar as a study.

The third sense in which people use the word "grammar" is "linguistic etiquette." This we may call "Grammar 3." The word in this sense is often coupled with a derogatory adjective: we say that the expression "he ain't here" is "bad grammar." What we mean is that such an expression is bad linguistic manners in certain circles. From the point of view of "Grammar 1" it is faultless; it conforms just as completely to the structural patterns of English as does "he isn't here." The trouble with it is like the trouble with Prince Hal in Shakespeare's play—it is "bad," not in itself, but in the company it keeps.

As has already been suggested, much confusion arises from mixing these meanings. One hears a good deal of criticism of teachers of English couched in such terms as "they don't teach grammar any more." Criticism of this sort is based on the wholly unproved assumption that teaching Grammar 2 will increase the student's proficiency in Grammar 1 or improve his manners in Grammar 3. Actually, the form of Grammar 2 which is usually taught is a very inaccurate and misleading analysis of the facts of Grammar 1; and it therefore is of highly questionable value in improving a person's ability to handle the structural patterns of his language. It is hardly reasonable to expect that teaching a person some inaccurate grammatical analysis will either improve the effectiveness of his assertions or teach him what expressions are acceptable to use in a given social context.

These, then, are the three meanings of "grammar": Grammar 1, a form of behavior; Grammar 2, a field of study, a science; and Grammar 3, a branch of etiquette.

II

Grammarians have arrived at some basic principles of their science, three of which are fundamental to this discussion. The first is that a language constitutes a set of behavior patterns common to the members of a given community. It is a part of what the anthropologists call the culture of the community. Actually it has complex and intimate relationships with other phases of culture such as myth and ritual. But for purposes of study it may be dealt with as a separate set of phenomena that can be objectively described and analyzed like any other universe of facts. Specifically, its phenomena can be observed, recorded, classified, and compared; and general laws of their behavior can be made by the same inductive process that is used to produce the "laws" of physics, chemistry, and the other sciences.

A second important principle of linguistic science is that each language or dialect has its own unique system of behavior patterns. Parts of this system may show similarities to parts of the systems of other languages, particularly if those languages are genetically related. But different languages solve the problems of expression and communication in different ways, just as the problems of movement through water are solved in different ways by lobsters, fish, seals, and penguins. A couple of corollaries of this principle are important. The first is that there is no such thing as "universal grammar," or at least if there is, it is so general and abstract as to be of little use. The second corollary is that the grammar of each language must be made up on the basis of a study of that particular language—a study that is free from preconceived notions of what a language should contain and how it should operate. The marine biologist does not criticize the octopus for using jet-propulsion to get him through the water instead of the methods of a self-respecting fish. Neither does the linguistic scientist express alarm or distress when he finds a language that seems to get along quite well without any words that correspond to what in English we call verbs.

A third principle on which linguistic science is based is that the analysis and description of a given language must conform to the requirements laid down for any satisfactory scientific theory. These are (1) simplicity, (2) consistency, (3) completeness, and (4) usefulness for predicting the behavior of phenomena not brought under immediate observation when the theory was formed. Linguistic scientists who have recently turned their attention to English have found that, judged by these criteria, the traditional grammar of English is unsatisfactory. It falls down badly on the first two requirements, being unduly complex and glaringly inconsistent within itself. It can be made to work, just as the Ptolemaic earth-centered astronomy can be, but at the cost of great elaboration and complication. The new grammar, like the Copernican sun-centered astronomy, solves the same problems with greater elegance, which is the scientist's word for the simplicity, compactness, and tidiness that characterize a satisfactory theory.

III

A brief look at the history of the traditional grammar of English will make apparent the reasons for its inadequacy. The study of English grammar is actually an outgrowth of the linguistic interest of the Renaissance. It was during the later Middle Ages and early Renaissance that the various vernacular languages of Europe came into their own. They began to be used for many kinds of writing which had previously always been done in Latin. As the vernaculars, in the hands of great writers like Dante and Chaucer, came of age as members of the linguistic family, a concomitant interest in their grammars arose. The earliest important English grammar was written by Shakespeare's contemporary, Ben Jonson.

It is important to observe that not only Ben Jonson himself but also those who followed him in the study of English grammar were men deeply learned in Latin and sometimes in Greek. For all their interest in English, they were conditioned from earliest school days to conceive of the classical languages as superior to the vernaculars. We still sometimes call the elementary school the "grammar school"; historically the term means the school where Latin grammar was taught. By the time the Renaissance or eighteenth-century scholar took his university degree, he was accustomed to use Latin as the normal means of communication with his fellow scholars. Dr. Samuel Johnson, for instance, who had only three years at the university and did not take a degree, wrote poetry in both Latin and Greek. Hence it was natural for these men to take Latin grammar as the norm, and to analyze English in terms of Latin. The grammarians of the seventeenth and eighteenth centuries who formulated the traditional grammar of English looked for the devices and distinctions of Latin grammar in English, and where they did not actually find them they imagined or created them. Of course, since English is a member of the Indo-European family of languages, to which Latin and Greek also belong, it did have many grammatical elements in common with them. But many of these had been obscured or wholly lost as a result of the extensive changes that had taken place in English—changes that the early grammarians inevitably conceived of as degeneration. They felt that it was their function to resist further change, if not to repair the damage already done. So preoccupied were they with the grammar of Latin as the ideal that they overlooked in large part the exceedingly complex and delicate system that English had substituted for the Indo-European grammar it had abandoned. Instead they stretched unhappy English on the Procrustean bed of Latin. It is no wonder that we commonly hear people say, "I didn't really understand grammar until I began to study Latin." This is eloquent testimony to the fact that the grammar "rules" of our present-day textbooks are largely an inheritance from the Latin-based grammar of the eighteenth century.

Meanwhile the extension of linguistic study beyond the Indo-European and Semitic families began to reveal that there are many different ways in which linguistic phenomena are organized—in other words, many different kinds of grammar. The tone-languages of the Orient and of North America, and the complex agglutinative languages of Africa, among others, forced grammarians to abandon the idea of a universal or ideal grammar and to direct their attention more closely to the individual systems employed by the multifarious languages of mankind. With the growth and refinement of the scientific method and its application to the field of anthropology, language came under more rigorous scientific scrutiny. As with anthropology in general, linguistic science at first concerned itself with the primitive. Finally, again following the lead of anthropology, linguistics began to apply its techniques to the old familiar tongues, among them English. Accelerated by the practical need during World War II of teaching languages, including English, to large numbers in a short time, research into the nature of English grammar has moved rapidly in the last fifteen years. The definitive grammar of English is yet to be written, but the results so far achieved are spectacular. It is now as unrealistic to teach "traditional" grammar of English as it is to teach "traditional" (i.e. pre-Darwinian) biology or "traditional" (i.e. four-element) chemistry. Yet nearly all certified teachers of English on all levels are doing so. Here is a cultural lag of major proportions.

IV

Before we can proceed to a sketch of what the new grammar of English looks like, we must take account of a few more of the premises of linguistic science. They must be understood and accepted by anyone who wishes to understand the new grammar.

First, the spoken language is primary, at least for the original study of a language. In many of the primitive languages,[1] of course, where writing is unknown, the spoken language is the *only* form. This is in many ways an advantage to the linguist, because the written language may use conventions that obscure its basic structure. The reason for the primary importance of the spoken language is that language originates as speech, and most of the changes and innovations that occur in the history of a given language begin in the spoken tongue.

Secondly, we must take account of the concept of dialect. I suppose most laymen would define a dialect as "a corrupt form of a language spoken in a given region by people who don't know any better." This introduces moral judgments which are repulsive to the linguistic scholar. Let us approach the definition of a dialect from the more objective end, through the

---

[1] "Primitive languages" here is really an abbreviated statement for "languages used by peoples of relatively primitive culture"; it is not to be taken as implying anything simple or rudimentary about the languages themselves. Many languages included under the term, such as native languages of Africa and Mexico, exhibit grammatical complexities unknown to more "civilized" languages.

notion of a speech community. A speech community is merely a group of people who are in pretty constant intercommunication. There are various types of speech communities: local ones, like "the people who live in Tidewater Virginia"; class ones, like "the white-collar class"; occupational ones, like "doctors, nurses, and other people who work in hospitals"; social ones, like "clubwomen." In a sense, each of these has its own dialect. Each family may be said to have its own dialect; in fact, in so far as each of us has his own vocabulary and particular quirks of speech, each individual has his own dialect. Also, of course, in so far as he is a member of many speech communities, each individual is more or less master of many dialects and shifts easily and almost unconsciously from one to another as he shifts from one social environment to another.

In the light of this concept of dialects, a language can be defined as a group of dialects which have enough of their sound-system, vocabulary, and grammar (Grammar 1, that is) in common to permit their speakers to be mutually intelligible in the ordinary affairs of life. It usually happens that one of the many dialects that make up a language comes to have more prestige than the others; in modern times it has usually been the dialect of the middle-class residents of the capital, like Parisian French and London English, which is so distinguished. This comes to be thought of as the standard dialect; in fact, its speakers become snobbish and succeed in establishing the belief that it is not a dialect at all, but the only proper form of the language. This causes the speakers of other dialects to become self-conscious and ashamed of their speech, or else aggressive and jingoistic about it—either of which is an acknowledgment of their feelings of inferiority. Thus one of the duties of the educational system comes to be that of teaching the standard dialect to all so as to relieve them of feelings of inferiority, and thus relieve society of linguistic neurotics. This is where Grammar 3, linguistic etiquette, comes into the picture.

A third premise arising from the two just discussed is that the difference between the way educated people talk and the way they write is a dialectical difference. The spread between these two dialects may be very narrow, as in present-day America, or very wide, as in Norway, where people often speak local Norwegian dialects but write in the Dano-Norwegian *Riksmaal*. The extreme is the use by writers of an entirely different language, or at least an ancient and no longer spoken form of the language—like Sanskrit in northern India or Latin in western Europe during the later Middle Ages. A corollary of this premise is that anyone setting out to write a grammar must know and make clear whether he is dealing with the spoken or the written dialect. Virtually all current English grammars deal with the written language only; evidence for this is that their rules for the plurals of nouns, for instance, are really spelling rules, which say nothing about pronunciation.

This is not the place to go into any sort of detail about the methods of analysis the linguistic scientist uses. Suffice it to say that he begins by breaking up the flow of speech into minimum sound-units, or phones, which he then groups into families called phonemes, the minimum significant sound-units. Most languages have from twenty to sixty of these. American English has forty-one: nine vowels, twenty-four consonants, four degrees of stress, and four levels of pitch. These phonemes group themselves into minimum meaningful units, called morphemes. These fall into two groups: free morphemes, those that can enter freely into many combinations with other free morphemes to make phrases and sentences; and bound morphemes, which are always found tied in a close and often indissoluble relationship with other bound or free morphemes. An example of a free morpheme is "dog"; an example of a bound morpheme is "un-" or "ex-". The linguist usually avoids talking about "words" because the term is very inexact. Is "instead of," for instance, to be considered one, two, or three words? This is purely a matter of opinion; but it is a matter of fact that it is made up of three morphemes.

In any case, our analysis has now brought the linguist to the point where he has some notion of the word-stock (he would call it the "lexicon") of his language. He must then go into the question of how the morphemes are grouped into meaningful utterances, which is the field of grammar proper. At this point in the analysis of English, as of many other languages, it becomes apparent that there are three bases upon which classification and analysis may be built: form, function, and meaning. For illustration let us take the word "boys" in the utterance "the boys are here." From the point of view of form, "boys" is a noun with the plural ending "s" (pronounced like "z"), preceded by the noun-determiner "the," and tied by concord to the verb "are," which it precedes. From the point of view of function, "boys" is the subject of the verb "are" and of the sentence. From point of view of meaning, "boys" points out or names more than one of the male young of the human species, about whom an assertion is being made.

Of these three bases of classification, the one most amenable to objective description and analysis of a rigorously scientific sort is form. In fact, many conclusions about form can be drawn by a person unable to understand or speak the language. Next comes function. But except as it is revealed by form, function is dependent on knowing the meaning. In a telegraphic sentence like "ship sails today"[2] no one can say whether "ship" is the subject of "sails" or an imperative verb with "sails" as its object until he knows what the sentence means. Most shaky of all bases for grammatical analysis is meaning. Attempts have been made to reduce the phenomena of meaning to objective description, but so far they have not succeeded very well. Mean-

---

[2] This example is taken from C. C. Fries, *The Structure of English* (New York, 1952), p. 62. This important book will be discussed below.

ing is such a subjective quality that it is usually omitted entirely from scientific description. The botanist can describe the forms of plants and the functions of their various parts, but he refuses to concern himself with their meaning. It is left to the poet to find symbolic meaning in roses, violets, and lilies.

At this point it is interesting to note that the traditional grammar of English bases some of its key concepts and definitions on this very subjective and shaky foundation of meaning. A recent English grammar defines a sentence as "a group of words which expresses a complete thought through the use of a verb, called its predicate, and a subject, consisting of a noun or pronoun about which the verb has something to say."[3] But what is a complete thought? Actually we do not identify sentences this way at all. If someone says, "I don't know what to do," dropping his voice at the end, and pauses, the hearer will know that it is quite safe for him to make a comment without running the risk of interrupting an unfinished sentence. But if the speaker says the same words and maintains a level pitch at the end, the polite listener will wait for him to finish his sentence. The words are the same, the meaning is the same; the only difference is a slight one in the pitch of the final syllable—a purely formal distinction, which signals that the first utterance is complete, a sentence, while the second is incomplete. In writing we would translate these signals into punctuation: a period or exclamation point at the end of the first, a comma or dash at the end of the second. It is the form of the utterance, not the completeness of the thought, that tells us whether it is a whole sentence or only part of one.

Another favorite definition of the traditional grammar, also based on meaning, is that of "noun" as "the name of a person, place, or thing"; or, as the grammar just quoted has it, "the name of anybody or anything, with or without life, and with or without substance or form."[4] Yet we identify nouns, not by asking if they name something, but by their positions in expressions and by the formal marks they carry. In the sentence, "The slithy toves did gyre and gimble in the wabe," any speaker of English knows that "toves" and "wabe" are nouns, though he cannot tell what they name, if indeed they name anything. How does he know? Actually because they have certain formal marks, like their position in relation to "the" as well as the whole arrangement of the sentence. We know from our practical knowledge of English grammar (Grammar 1), which we have had since before we went to school, that if we were to put meaningful words into this sentence, we would have to put nouns in place of "toves" and "wabe," giving something like "The slithy snakes did gyre and gimble in the wood." The pat-

[3] Ralph B. Allen, *English Grammar* (New York, 1950), p. 187.
[4] *Ibid.*, p. 1.

tern of the sentence simply will not allow us to say "The slithy arounds did gyre and gimble in the wooden."

One trouble with the traditional grammar, then, is that it relies heavily on the most subjective element in language, meaning. Another is that it shifts the ground of its classification and produces the elementary logical error of cross-division. A zoologist who divided animals into invertebrates, mammals, and beasts of burden would not get very far before running into trouble. Yet the traditional grammar is guilty of the same error when it defines three parts of speech on the basis of meaning (noun, verb, and interjection), four more on the basis of function (adjective, adverb, pronoun, conjunction), and one partly on function and partly on form (preposition). The result is that in such an expression as "a dog's life" there can be endless futile argument about whether "dog's" is a noun or an adjective. It is, of course, a noun from the point of view of form and an adjective from the point of view of function, and hence falls into both classes, just as a horse is both a mammal and a beast of burden. No wonder students are bewildered in their attempts to master the traditional grammar. Their natural clearness of mind tells them that it is a crazy patchwork violating the elementary principles of logical thought.

V

If the traditional grammar is so bad, what does the new grammar offer in its place?

It offers a description, analysis, and set of definitions and formulas—rules, if you will—based firmly and consistently on the easiest, or at least the most objective, aspect of language, form. Experts can quibble over whether "dog's" in "a dog's life" is a noun or an adjective, but anyone can see that it is spelled with " 's" and hear that it ends with a "z" sound; likewise anyone can tell that it comes in the middle between "a" and "life." Furthermore he can tell that something important has happened if the expression is changed to "the dog's alive," "the live dogs," or "the dogs lived," even if he doesn't know what the words mean and has never heard of such functions as modifier, subject, or attributive genitive. He cannot, of course, get very far into his analysis without either a knowledge of the language or access to someone with such knowledge. He will also need a minimum technical vocabulary describing grammatical functions. Just so the anatomist is better off for knowing physiology. But the grammarian, like the anatomist, must beware of allowing his preconceived notions to lead him into the error of interpreting before he describes—an error which often results in his finding only what he is looking for.

When the grammarian looks at English objectively, he finds that it conveys its meanings by two broad devices: the denotations and connotations of words separately considered, which the linguist calls "lexical meaning," and the significance of word-forms, word-groups, and arrangements apart from the lexical meanings of the words, which the linguist calls "structural meaning." The first of these is the domain of the lexicographer and the semanticist, and hence is not our present concern. The second, the structural meaning, is the business of the structural linguist, or grammarian. The importance of this second kind of meaning must be emphasized because it is often overlooked. The man in the street tends to think of the meaning of a sentence as being the aggregate of the dictionary meanings of the words that make it up; hence the widespread fallacy of literal translation—the feeling that if you take a French sentence and a French-English dictionary and write down the English equivalent of each French word you will come out with an intelligible English sentence. How ludicrous the results can be, anyone knows who is familiar with Mark Twain's retranslation from the French of his jumping frog story. One sentence reads, "Eh bien! I no saw not that that frog has nothing of better than each frog." Upon which Mark's comment is, "if that isn't grammar gone to seed, then I count myself no judge."[5]

The second point brought out by a formal analysis of English is that it uses four principal devices of form to signal structural meanings:

1. Word order—the sequence in which words and word-groups are arranged.
2. Function-words—words devoid of lexical meaning which indicate relationships among the meaningful words with which they appear.
3. Inflections—alterations in the forms of words themselves to signal changes in meaning and relationship.
4. Formal contrasts—contrasts in the forms of words signaling greater differences in function and meaning. These could also be considered inflections, but it is more convenient for both the lexicographer and the grammarian to consider them separately.

Usually several of these are present in any utterance, but they can be separately illustrated by means of contrasting expressions involving minimum variation—the kind of controlled experiment used in the scientific laboratory.

To illustrate the structural meaning of word order, let us compare the

---

[5] Mark Twain, "The Jumping Frog; the Original Story in English; the Retranslation Clawed Back from the French, into a Civilized Language Once More, by Patient and Unremunerated Toil," *1601 . . . and Sketches Old and New* (n.p., 1933), p. 50.

two sentences "man bites dog" and "dog bites man." The words are identical in lexical meaning and in form; the only difference is in sequence. It is interesting to note that Latin expresses the difference between these two by changes in the form of the words, without necessarily altering the order: "homo canem mordet" or "hominem canis mordet." Latin grammar is worse than useless in understanding this point of English grammar.

Next, compare the sentences "the dog is the friend of man" and "any dog is a friend of that man." Here the words having lexical meaning are "dog," "is," "friend," and "man," which appear in the same form and the same order in both sentences. The formal differences between them are in the substitution of "any" and "a" for "the," and in the insertion of "that." These little words are function-words; they make quite a difference in the meanings of the two sentences, though it is virtually impossible to say what they mean in isolation.

Third, compare the sentences "the dog loves the man" and "the dogs loved the men." Here the words are the same, in the same order, with the same function-words in the same positions. But the forms of the three words having lexical meaning have been changed: "dog" to "dogs," "loves" to "loved," and "man" to "men." These changes are inflections. English has very few of them as compared with Greek, Latin, Russian, or even German. But it still uses them; about one word in four in an ordinary English sentence is inflected.

Fourth, consider the difference between "the dog's friend arrived" and "the dog's friendly arrival." Here the difference lies in the change of "friend" to "friendly," a formal alteration signaling a change of function from subject to modifier, and the change of "arrived" to "arrival," signaling a change of function from predicate to head-word in a noun-modifier group. These changes are of the same formal nature as inflections, but because they produce words of different lexical meaning, classifiable as different parts of speech, it is better to call them formal contrasts than inflections. In other words, it is logically quite defensible to consider "love," "loves," "loving," and "loved" as the same word in differing aspects and to consider "friend," "friendly," "friendliness," "friendship," and "befriend" as different words related by formal and semantic similarities. But this is only a matter of convenience of analysis, which permits a more accurate description of English structure. In another language we might find that this kind of distinction is unnecessary but that some other distinction, unnecessary in English, is required. The categories of grammatical description are not sacrosanct; they are as much a part of man's organization of his observations as they are of the nature of things.

If we are considering the spoken variety of English, we must add a fifth device for indicating structural meaning—the various musical and rhythmic patterns which the linguist classifies under juncture, stress, and intonation. Consider the following pair of sentences:

Alfred, the alligator is sick!
Alfred the alligator is sick.

These are identical in the four respects discussed above—word order, function-words, inflections, and word-form. Yet they have markedly different meanings, as would be revealed by the intonation if they were spoken aloud. These differences in intonation are to a certain extent indicated in the written language by punctuation—that is, in fact, the primary function of punctuation.

VI

The examples so far given were chosen to illustrate in isolation the various kinds of structural devices in English grammar. Much more commonly the structural meaning of a given sentence is indicated by a combination of two or more of these devices: a sort of margin of safety which permits some of the devices to be missed or done away with without obscuring the structural meaning of the sentence, as indeed anyone knows who has ever written a telegram or a newspaper headline. On the other hand, sentences which do not have enough of these formal devices are inevitably ambiguous. Take the example already given, Fries's "ship sails today." This is ambiguous because there is nothing to indicate which of the first two words is performing a noun function and which a verb function. If we mark the noun by putting the noun-determining function-word "the" in front of it, the ambiguity disappears; we have either "the ship sails today" or "ship the sails today." The ambiguity could just as well be resolved by using other devices: consider "ship sailed today," "ship to sail today," "ship sail today," "shipping sails today," "shipment of sails today," and so on. It is simply a question of having enough formal devices in the sentence to indicate its structural meaning clearly.

How powerful the structural meanings of English are is illustrated by so-called "nonsense." In English, nonsense as a literary form often consists of utterances that have a clear structural meaning but use words that either have no lexical meaning, or whose lexical meanings are inconsistent one with another. This will become apparent if we subject a rather famous bit of English nonsense to formal grammatical analysis:

All mimsy were the borogoves
And the mome raths outgrabe.

This passage consists of ten words, five of them words that should have lexical meaning but don't, one standard verb, and four function-words. In so far as it is possible to indicate its abstract structure, it would be this:

All ....y were the ....s
And the ... ...s ....

Although this is a relatively simple formal organization, it signals some rather complicated meanings. The first thing we observe is that the first line presents a conflict: word order seems to signal one thing, and inflections and function-words something else. Specifically, "mimsy" is in the position normally occupied by the subject, but we know that it is not the subject and that "borogoves" is. We know this because there is an inflectional tie between the form "were" and the "s" ending of "borogoves," because there is the noun-determiner "the" before it, and because the alternative candidate for subject, "mimsy," lacks both of these. It is true that "mimsy" does have the function-word "all" before it, which may indicate a noun; but when it does, the noun is either plural (in which case "mimsy" would most likely end in "s"), or else the noun is what grammarians call a mass-word (like "sugar," "coal," "snow"), in which case the verb would have to be "was," not "were." All these formal considerations are sufficient to counteract the effect of word order and show that the sentence is of the type that may be represented thus:

All gloomy were the Democrats.

Actually there is one other possibility. If "mimsy" belongs to the small group of nouns which don't use "s" to make the plural, and if "borogoves" has been so implied (but not specifically mentioned) in the context as to justify its appearing with the determiner "the," the sentence would then belong to the following type:

[In the campaign for funds] all alumni were the canvassers.
[In the drought last summer] all cattle were the sufferers.

But the odds are so much against this that most of us would be prepared to fight for our belief that "borogoves" are things that can be named, and that at the time referred to they were in a complete state of "mimsyness."

Moving on to the second line, "And the mome raths outgrabe," the first thing we note is that the "And" signals another parallel assertion to follow. We are thus prepared to recognize from the noun-determiner "the," the plural inflection "s," and the particular positions of "mome" and "outgrabe," as well as the continuing influence of the "were" of the preceding line, that we are dealing with a sentence of this pattern:

> And the lone rats agreed.

The influence of the "were" is particularly important here; it guides us in selecting among several interpretations of the sentence. Specifically, it requires us to identify "outgrabe" as a verb in the past tense, and thus a "strong" or "irregular" verb, since it lacks the characteristic past-tense ending "d" or "ed." We do this in spite of the fact that there is another strong candidate for the position of verb: that is, "raths," which bears a regular verb inflection and could be tied with "mome" as its subject in the normal noun-verb relationship. In such a case we should have to recognize "outgrabe" as either an adverb of the kind not marked by the form-contrast ending "ly," an adjective, or the past participle of a strong verb. The sentence would then belong to one of the following types:

> And the moon shines above.
> And the man stays aloof.
> And the fool seems outdone.

But we reject all of these—probably they don't even occur to us—because they all have verbs in the present tense, whereas the "were" of the first line combines with the "And" at the beginning of the second to set the whole in the past.

We might recognize one further possibility for the structural meaning of this second line, particularly in the verse context, since we are used to certain patterns in verse that do not often appear in speech or prose. The "were" of the first line could be understood as doing double duty, its ghost or echo appearing between "raths" and "outgrabe." Then we would have something like this:

> All gloomy were the Democrats
> And the home folks outraged.

But again the odds are pretty heavy against this. I for one am so sure that "outgrabe" is the past tense of a strong verb that I can give its present. In my dialect, at least, it is "outgribe."

The reader may not realize it, but in the last four paragraphs I have been discussing grammar from a purely formal point of view. I have not once called a word a noun because it names something (that is, I have not once resorted to meaning), nor have I called any word an adjective because it modifies a noun (that is, resorted to function). Instead I have been working in the opposite direction, from form toward function and meaning. I have used only criteria which are objectively observable, and I have assumed only a working knowledge of certain structural patterns and devices known to all speakers of English over the age of six. I did use some technical terms like "noun," "verb," and "tense," but only to save time; I could have got along without them.

If one clears his mind of the inconsistencies of the traditional grammar (not so easy a process as it might be), he can proceed with a similarly rigorous formal analysis of a sufficient number of representative utterances in English and come out with a descriptive grammar. This is just what Professor Fries did in gathering and studying the material for the analysis he presents in the remarkable book to which I have already referred, *The Structure of English*. What he actually did was to put a tape recorder into action and record about fifty hours of telephone conversation among the good citizens of Ann Arbor, Michigan. When this material was transcribed, it constituted about a quarter of a million words of perfectly natural speech by educated middle-class Americans. The details of his conclusions cannot be presented here, but they are sufficiently different from the usual grammar to be revolutionary. For instance, he recognizes only four parts of speech among the words with lexical meaning, roughly corresponding to what the traditional grammar calls substantives, verbs, adjectives, and adverbs, though to avoid preconceived notions from the traditional grammar Fries calls them Class 1, Class 2, Class 3, and Class 4 words. To these he adds a relatively small group of function-words, 154 in his materials, which he divides into fifteen groups. These must be memorized by anyone learning the language; they are not subject to the same kind of general rules that govern the four parts of speech. Undoubtedly his conclusions will be developed and modified by himself and by other linguistic scholars, but for the present his book remains the most complete treatment extant of English grammar from the point of view of linguistic science.

VII

Two vital questions are raised by this revolution in grammar. The first is, "What is the value of this new system?" In the minds of many who ask it, the implication of this question is, "We have been getting along all these years with traditional grammar, so it can't be so very bad. Why should we go through the painful process of unlearning and relearning grammar just because linguistic scientists have concocted some new theories?"

The first answer to this question is the bravest and most honest. It is that the superseding of vague and sloppy thinking by clear and precise thinking is an exciting experience in and for itself. To acquire insight into the workings of a language, and to recognize the infinitely delicate system of relationship, balance, and interplay that constitutes its grammar, is to become closely acquainted with one of man's most miraculous creations, not unworthy to be set beside the equally beautiful organization of the physical universe. And to find that its most complex effects are produced by the multi-layered organization of relatively simple materials is to bring our thinking about language into accord with modern thought in other fields, which is more and more coming to emphasize the importance of organization—the fact that an organized whole is truly greater than the sum of all its parts.

There are other answers, more practical if less philosophically valid. It is too early to tell, but it seems probable that a realistic, scientific grammar should vastly facilitate the teaching of English, especially as a foreign language. Already results are showing here; it has been found that if intonation contours and other structural patterns are taught quite early, the student has a confidence that allows him to attempt to speak the language much sooner than he otherwise would.

The new grammar can also be of use in improving the native speaker's proficiency in handling the structural devices of his own language. In other words, Grammar 2, if it is accurate and consistent, *can* be of use in improving skill in Grammar 1. An illustration is that famous bugaboo, the dangling participle. Consider a specific instance of it, which once appeared on a college freshman's theme, to the mingled delight and despair of the instructor:

Having eaten our lunch, the steamboat departed.

What is the trouble with this sentence? Clearly there must be something wrong with it, because it makes people laugh, although it was not the intent of the writer to make them laugh. In other words, it produces a completely wrong response, resulting in total breakdown of communication. It is, in fact, "bad grammar" in a much more serious way than are mere dialectal divergences like "he ain't here" or "he never seen none," which produce social reactions but communicate effectively. In the light of the new grammar, the trouble with our dangling participle is that the form, instead of leading to the meaning, is in conflict with it. Into the position which, in this pattern, is reserved for the word naming the eater of the lunch, the writer has inserted the word "steamboat." The resulting tug-of-war between form and meaning is only momentary; meaning quickly wins out, simply because our common sense tells us that steamboats don't eat lunches. But if the pull of the lexical meaning is not given a good deal of help from common sense, the form will conquer the meaning, or the two will remain in ambiguous equilibrium—as, for instance, in "Having eaten our lunch, the passengers boarded the steamboat." Writers will find it easier to avoid such troubles if they know about the forms of English and are taught to use the form to convey the meaning, instead of setting up tensions between form and meaning. This, of course, is what English teachers are already trying to do. The new grammar should be a better weapon in their arsenal than the traditional grammar, since it is based on a clear understanding of the realities.

The second and more difficult question is, "How can the change from one grammar to the other be effected?" Here we face obstacles of a formidable nature. When we remember the controversies attending on revolutionary changes in biology and astronomy, we realize what a tenacious hold the race can maintain on anything it has once learned, and the resistance it can offer to new ideas. And remember that neither astronomy nor biology was taught in the elementary schools. They were, in fact, rather specialized subjects in advanced education. How then change grammar, which is taught to everybody, from the fifth grade up through college? The vested interest represented by thousands upon thousands of English and Speech teachers who have learned the traditional grammar and taught it for many years is a conservative force comparable to those which keep us still using the chaotic system of English spelling and the unwieldy measuring system of inches and feet, pounds and ounces, quarts, bushels, and acres. Moreover, this army is constantly receiving new recruits. It is possible in my state to become certified to teach English in high school if one has had eighteen credit hours of college English—let us say two semesters of freshman composition (almost all of which is taught by people unfamiliar with the new grammar), two semesters of a survey course in English literature, one semester of Shakespeare, and one semester of the contemporary novel. And since hard-pressed school administrators feel that anyone who can speak English can in a pinch teach it, the result is that many people are called upon to teach grammar whose knowledge of the subject is totally inadequate.

There is, in other words, a battle ahead of the new grammar. It will have to fight not only the apathy of the general public but the ignorance and inertia of those who count themselves competent in the field of grammar. The battle is already on, in fact. Those who try to get the concepts of the new grammar introduced into the curriculum are tagged as "liberal" grammarians—the implication being, I suppose, that one has a free choice between "liberal" and "conservative" grammar, and that the liberals are a bit dangerous, perhaps even a touch subversive. They are accused of undermining standards, of holding that "any way of saying something is just as good as any other," of not teaching the fundamentals of good English. I trust that the readers of this article will see how unfounded these charges are. But the smear campaign is on. So far as I know, neither religion nor patriotism has yet been brought into it. When they are, Professor Fries will have to say to Socrates, Galileo, Darwin, Freud, and other members of the honorable fraternity of the misunderstood, "Move over, gentlemen, and make room for me."

Vocabulary

paradox, dogmatic, couched, anthropologists, corollary, concomitant, agglutinative, multifarious, cultural lag, jingoistic, neurotics, ludicrous, sacrosanct, concocted, tenacious, vested

Review Questions

1. Professor Francis begins his essay with three definitions of *grammar*. How are these definitions themselves a kind of analysis?

2. In the first sentence of Section II, Francis refers to grammar as a science. To what extent is this true? In what particular ways is it not true?

3. Identify Ptolemy, Copernicus, Ben Jonson, Procrustean bed.

4. Why does the author believe that in the original study of a language its spoken form is more important than its written form?

5. Using "the *boys* are here" as an example, compose three sentences and analyze three other words according to form, function, and meaning.

6. What specific faults does Francis find in grammar as it is traditionally taught?

7. What is meant by *structural meaning?*

8. Name and cite your own examples of the five devices for indicating structural meaning.

9. What is the primary purpose of punctuation?

10. What are the advantages of teaching grammar structurally rather than traditionally? What are the disadvantages?

11. Do you feel that it is reasonable to class C. C. Fries, one of the fathers of structural grammar, with other intellectual rebels like Socrates, Galileo, Darwin, and Freud? Why?

Expository Technique

1. Comment on the function of the first paragraph.

2. What is the controlling idea of this essay?

3. Show how this main idea controls the selection of material and unifies the essay.

4. Comment on the skill with which the essay is brought to a conclusion.

5. Professor Francis indicates the principal stages in the development of his essay by Roman numerals. Comment on the organization apparent *within* each of these sections. Is any attempt made to tie the sections' internal divisions into the context of the whole essay? Can you find purposive arrangement of these components?

6. This essay is a small anthology of expository techniques. Identify as many expository patterns as you can in this essay.

Exercises

1. Francis makes the point that because English is a comparatively noninflectional language, meaning is frequently determined by word order. Show the validity of this statement by placing the word *only* before each word in the following sentence and show how the meaning of the entire sentence changes with each different placement.

She asked him to love her.

2. Show how each of the following pairs of sentences exemplifies one or more of the devices of form which signal structural meaning.

a. The gloops gleep.   The gloop gleeps.
b. Glooping reebs are blearious.   Glooping reebs is blearious.
c. The gloop is brunter.   The gloop is a brunter.
d. The gloops are brunter.   The gloops are brunters.
e. Blipy gloops gleep.   Bliply gloops gleep.
f. There are many pretty old churches in this city.
  There are many pretty, old churches in this city.
g. She married nobody.   She married a nobody.
h. The child likes the woman very much.
  The children liked the women very much.
i. Take the flowers into the green house.
  Take the flowers into the greenhouse.
j. My father watches stocks.   My father stocks watches.
k. Shirley Jones is arriving in town today.
  The Shirley Jones is arriving in town today.
l. The soldier's fear departed.   The soldiers fearfully departed.

3. Each of the following sentences contains problems of interpretation because of structural ambiguity. In each case discuss the source of the ambiguity and revise the sentence to make its meaning clear.

a. His employer asked him to submit more pertinent comments on the building project before next Friday.
b. Charging elephants can be dangerous.
c. The smoking room is ruined.
d. More serious-minded students entered the course.
e. The shooting of the soldiers was deliberate.
f. We were surprised to learn that the French teacher was also a fashion designer in her spare time.
g. The blond looked harder than the brunette.
h. The prime minister frequently gave in to compromise.
i. The swimming pool was open to men only on Mondays and Wednesdays.
j. He bought a young man's coat.
k. The dean approved a modern language laboratory.
l. Your parents are entertaining guests.

4. Brevity of statement in newspaper captions occasionally produces ambiguities like "Ship sails today." Be alert for this phenomenon and try to collect examples of it in your local newspaper and on street signs, such as *SLOW/ Children/ Crossing.*

5. Each of the following groups of morphemes is a jumble of a short poem or witty statement. Analyze the morphemes and, in accordance with the principles by which English structures statements and signals meaning, attempt to reconstruct the original.

a. A familiar rhyming couplet
breast, is, man, the, hope, never, blest, to, human, in, be, eternal, spring, but, always, -s

b. A quatrain by Coleridge beginning, "Sir, I admit your general rule"
rule, not, every, poet, is, that, it, to, that, fool, serve, every, general, is, but, a, poet, your, show, your, -self, a, admit, fool, sir, you, I, may

c. A quatrain, one line reading "Will never rise to fight again"
away, day, he, will, slain, again, but, will, that, never, he, live, in, is, battle, the, fight, rise, to, run, -s, that, fight, -s, and, fight, to, another

d. A quatrain by the Earl of Rochester on Charles II
king, on, thing, one, the, relies, fool, wise, -ish, a, did, ever, nor, a, said, man, lord, sovereign, lies, here, our, word, whose, no, never, who

e. A quip
age, the, has, perpetual, lie, -s, her, she, youth, dis-, of, cover, -ed, about, she, secret

f. A quotation from Sir Winston Churchill
subject, a, the, and, fanatic, won't, can change, is, change, one, '-t, who, mind, his

6. *Time* (November 9, 1953)* reports the following test based on the structural aspects of an artificial language which was given to candidates for appointment to West Point. Read the structural characteristics of this language carefully and try to translate the passage at the end of the section into English.

Plurals end in *-s.*
Numerals must follow nouns.
Bal is one; *bals* is ten; *balsebal* is eleven, etc.
Verbs are conjugated in the following manner: *binob*—I am; *binol*—you are; *binom*—he is; *binof*—she is; *binos*—it is; *binobs*—we are; *binols*—you are; *binoms*—they are.
Gender is indicated as follows: *jeval*—horse; *omjeval*—stallion; *jijeval*—mare.
Adjectives are formed by adding *-ik* to noun stems.
Ordinal numbers are formed as follows: *balid*—first; *balsid*—tenth.
Sample vocabulary:

at—this	*kim*—who	*ol*—you
buk—book	*kima*—whose	*penob*—I write
dom—house	*kime*—to whom	*tel*—two
dlinob—I drink	*kimi*—whom	*tidel*—teacher
e—and	*labob*—I have	*ut*—one who
fol—four	*lautel*—author	*vin*—wine
in—in	*lodob*—I live	*vom*—woman
julel—scholar	*man*—man	
kel—that	*ob*—I	

* Reprinted by permission of *Time.*

Translate:

Vom dlinof vini. Buk at binom olik. Tidel obsik labom julelis telsefol.
Man ut kel lodom in dome binom lautel e penom bukis.

In what ways is the structure of English the same as this artificial language?
In what ways is it different?

7. Investigate one of the proposals for a world language, such as Esperanto, Ido, Volapük, Novial, Interlingua, Pikto, or Basic English. Prepare a class report explaining the system of the language you choose.

8. The *Encyclopaedia Britannica* offers a good introduction to Pidgin, a variety of speech which has grown out of contact between English and other languages. Investigate this interesting language and prepare a class report on its system of communication.

9. Try to devise an artificial language. It might help to limit the occasion or area of concern which the language will serve.

10. As Professor Francis notes, English has forty-one phonemes—four degrees of pitch, four degrees of stress, nine vowels, and twenty-four consonants. From these phonemes is formed the staggeringly large English vocabulary. Inevitably, two or more morphemes which have identical, or nearly identical, phonemes but distinctly different meanings are occasionally produced. Such a linguistic occurrence makes possible the pun, a venerable figure of speech which plays upon a similarity of sound and a disparity of meaning. Much esteemed by Shakespeare and his contemporaries as a form of wit, the pun appears today as part of the comedian's act or as a stylistic ornament for journalists (*e.g., Newsweek's* "Soviet Czechmate" or "Klannishness"). Skim through several issues of *Time, Newsweek, Variety,* or the newspaper sports section and collect examples which will test your classmates' "respunsiveness." In addition, Richard Armour's *Twisted Tales from Shakespeare* (New York, 1957) offers many examples of the pun.

23.

PAUL ROBERTS

Intonation

Besides the thirty-three vowels and consonants, English has a series of phonemes of an entirely different kind—or rather of three different kinds. These are the features called **stress, pitch,** and **juncture.** Taken together, stress, pitch, and juncture make up what we call **intonation.** Every time we

From *Patterns of English,* by Paul Roberts. ©, 1956, by Harcourt, Brace & World, Inc. and reprinted with their permission.

utter a sentence, we use some kind of intonation, and the meaning of our sentences changes according to the intonation we use.

The whole story of English intonation is a very complicated matter, and we won't try to explain all the details here. But it is easy to see some of the contrasts of intonation and to realize that we react accurately to them whenever we hear English.

STRESS

Probably the simplest feature of intonation to understand is stress. Stress is simply the loudness or softness with which we utter the different syllables in the speech stream. We make use of stress all the time in forming our sentence patterns. For instance, if we use the word *subject* as a noun, we pronounce the *sub* louder than the *ject:*

What's the súbject?

But if we use it as a verb, we pronounce the *ject* part louder:

We'll subjéct him to an examination.

We have the same contrast in *íncrease* and *incréase, prótest* and *protést, réfuse* and *refúse,* and many other pairs.

But that's by no means all there is to stress in English. Each speaker of English makes use of four different stresses—four degrees of loudness —when he speaks his sentences. The names and symbols for them are these:

Primary, the loudest degree / ´ /
Secondary, the next to loudest / ^ /
Tertiary, the third from loudest / ` /
Weak, the softest / ˘ /

Here's a sentence that has all of them:

The White House is a white house.

If you'll pronounce the sentence naturally, you'll see that you don't say "White House" quite as you say "white house." The difference is mainly in the stress.

Stress usually distinguishes adjectives modifying nouns from nouns modifying nouns. [In the] ambiguous sentence "He's a sweet salesman," you can't tell whether the salesman is sweet or sells candy. But this is ambiguous in writing only. In speech, *sweet* will have secondary stress if it's an adjective but primary stress if it's a noun.

He's a sweet sálesman. (The salesman is sweet.)

He's a sweet sàlesman. (He sells candy.)

Stress is so important that if the speaker gets the stresses mixed up the result is likely to be nonsense. You might not be surprised to get a "wríting dèsk" for Christmas. But you would probably be very much surprised if you got a "writing désk."

PITCH

The second feature of intonation is pitch. **Pitch** is caused by the vibration of the sounds as they come from our mouths. If they vibrate fast—say 800 times a second—we get what we call **high pitch.** If they vibrate slowly—say 200 times a second—we get **low pitch.**

We are all familiar with pitch, because we know, for example, that women's voices are generally higher than men's and that adults' voices are lower than children's. What most people don't realize, however, is that each of us—whether his voice is generally high or generally low—makes use of four contrasting pitch points or pitch phonemes. We give these numbers, not names. The highest pitch phoneme is /4/; the next to highest is /3/; the next to lowest is /2/; the lowest is /1/.

We can also indicate them by drawing lines above and below the letters. A line just over the letters means pitch /3/; a line well above the letters means pitch /4/; a line just under the letters means pitch /2/; and a line well below the letters means pitch /1/.

For instance, suppose we want to mark the pitch on the sentence "What are you doing?" This could be said in several ways, but the most common way would be to begin on pitch /2/, to stay on that until the stressed syllable is reached, to rise to /3/ on the stressed syllable, and then to fall to /1/. Like this:

What are you | do | ing?

We use pitch for many purposes in our sentences. It is closely bound up with the structural patterns of our sentences. But we also use it to express such meanings as surprise, indignation, insistence, panic, boredom, and many others. For example, one could put a note of panic into the question "What are you doing?" by rising to the fourth pitch instead of the third:

What are you | do | ing?

Or if one is just sort of exasperated with the other person and what he's doing, he might say:

What | are | you | do | ing?

Often we make jokes by deliberately using the wrong pitch. Here's one:

What did you put in the | sa | lad? Alice?

In place of:

What did you put in the | sa | lad, Alice?

JUNCTURE

The third part of intonation is juncture. **Juncture** is a way of breaking or stopping the speech flow. English intonation seems to go in fours, and there are four junctures just as there are four stresses and four pitches; the first one, however, is quite different from the other three. Junctures are named after the symbols used to indicate them.

The first juncture is called **plus juncture** because it is marked with a plus sign: /+/.

The second juncture is called **single bar juncture.** It is marked with one upright line or bar: /|/.

The third juncture is called **double bar juncture.** It is marked with two upright lines: /||/.

The last juncture is called **double cross juncture.** It is marked with two crossing lines: /#/.

Plus juncture is a special kind of break between phonemes. It is the difference between *I scream* and *ice cream*. In *I scream* we have plus juncture before the /s/ phoneme: /ay+skriym/. In *ice cream* the plus juncture comes after the /s/ phoneme: /ays+kriym/. The reason that the two sounds are different is that in *I scream* we have the kind of /s/ that comes at the beginning of a word and the kind of /k/ that comes after /s/; but in *ice cream* we have the kind of /s/ that comes at the end of a word and the kind of /k/ that comes at the beginning. This is what plus juncture does;

it breaks up the phonemic flow and makes words, although the phonemic words are not always identical with the ones we commonly write.

The other junctures come at the end of groups of words. These junctures are closely tied up with stress and pitch. If a sentence has only one primary (loudest) stress, then we won't have any junctures inside the sentence. But if we have two primary stresses, then we will have a single bar or double bar juncture between them.

For instance, we can say the sentence "The man on your right is her brother" with just one primary stress; then there is no juncture inside the sentence:

The man on your right is her bróther.

Or we can say it with two primary stresses; then there will be a single bar juncture after the first primary stress:

The man on your ríght | is her bróther.

If there are three primary stresses, there will be two single bar junctures:

The mán | on your ríght | is her bróther.

This would be a very slow and emphatic way of saying the sentence.

The difference between single bar, double bar, and double cross juncture is a matter of what happens to the pitch. If the pitch stays the same, we have single bar; if it goes up a little (but not to the next pitch level) we have double bar; if it goes down a little, we have double cross.

The sentence "The man digging in the garden is Mr. Jones" might have one or two single bar junctures, depending on the number of primary stresses; or it might have none at all:

The mán | digging in the gárden | is Mr. Jónes.
The man digging in the gárden | is Mr. Jónes.
The man digging in the garden is Mr. Jónes.

But the sentence "Mr. Jones, digging in his garden, found a worm" would be pronounced quite differently. There would be three primary stresses with double bar junctures separating them:

Mr. Jónes || digging in his gárden || found a wórm.

That is, the pitch would rise slightly after *Jones* and after *garden*. The pitch would be something like this:

Mr. | Jon | es, digging in his | gar | den, found a | wo | rm.

Double bar juncture corresponds more or less to a comma in writing.

Double cross juncture is a slight drop in pitch. Notice in the last example that a slight drop is shown at the very end, after *worm*. This is a double cross juncture, in its usual place at the end of a sentence:

Mr. Jones || digging in his garden || found a worm #

By and large, double cross junctures in speech correspond to semicolons and periods in writing.

Here are a few more examples showing primary stresses and the different junctures. There would be other ways of saying some of these of course:

Where are you góing #

Where aré | you góing #

Running into the hóuse || Agnes told us the néws #

We invited Ál || who had a cár #

Ál || who had a cár || offered to take ús #

Al had a cár # therefore we had to invíte him #

Al had a cár # he wouldn't || howevér || let us úse it #

People who own cars are pretty lúcky #

People who own cárs | are pretty lúcky #

Review Questions

1. What is a phoneme?
2. Define stress, pitch, and juncture.
3. What are the degrees of stress? of pitch?
4. What are the designations for the four junctures?

Exercises*

1. Intonation is hard to study because it is so difficult to say something and listen to it at the same time. We won't try to identify all the stresses, pitches, and

---

* Exercises 1–6 are from *Patterns of English,* by Paul Roberts, ©, 1956, by Harcourt, Brace & World, Inc. and reprinted with their permission.

junctures as they occur in our sentences. All we need to do is develop a general awareness of some of the contrasts and notice how they affect sentence meaning. Say the following groups of sentences as naturally as you can. Can you detect a difference in stress? On what words do the primary stresses fall?

a. He's a good salesman.   He's a car salesman.
b. That's a blackbird.   That's a black bird.
c. He looks like his mother (not his father).
   He looks like his mother (but acts like his father).
   He looks like his mother (but his sister doesn't).

2. Frequently we shift the primary stress to get a different emphasis or to express a different feeling. Pronounce the following sentences observing the different locations of the primary stress. What changes in meaning or feeling are indicated?

a. Where are you góing?   d. Where are yóu going?

b. Whére are you going?   e. Where áre you goíng?

c. Where áre you going?

3. Pronounce the following pairs of sentences as naturally as possible. Where does the pitch rise and fall? How do the sentences in each pair differ in meaning?

a. Was he mad?   Was he mad!
b. Are you reading Shakespeare?   Are you reading, Shakespeare?
c. Why are you washing, Alice?   Why are you washing Alice?
d. Watch this rock skip.   Watch this rock, Skip.
e. What are you eating, Charlie?   What are you eating? Charlie?

4. The phonemes in *yellow drug* and *yellowed rug* are the same: /yelowdrəg/. What is the difference in the pronunciation? Spell each expression in phonemic spelling, this time putting in the plus juncture. Do the same for these pairs.

a. a name—an aim   /əneym/
b. flight wrap—fly trap   /flaytræp/
c. needed rain—need a drain   /niydədreyn/

5. Pronounce each of the following sentences three times—first with one primary stress, then with two, then with three. When you put in two primary stresses, you will have one single bar juncture. Where? With three primary stresses you will have two junctures. Where?

a. The fellow in the office needs a shave.
b. The child petting the skunk is my kid brother.
c. My mother peels potatoes with a soup spoon.

6. The following sentences contain double bar and double cross junctures. Where do they come and which are they? Say the sentences aloud and try to hear the short rises (double bar) and the short falls (double cross).

a. My Aunt Flora, who lives in Albany, owns seven goats.
b. My kid brother, looking guilty, tried to sneak away.
c. We all wanted to help him; however, there was nothing we could do.
d. We all wanted to help him. There was nothing, however, that we could do.
e. Sam wanted the car badly, but he didn't have enough money. In fact, he didn't have any money at all.

7. The following sentences are ambiguous. How might the ambiguity be removed through intonation?

a. My friends who saw the picture frequently praised it.

b. He often returns to the park he liked so much in the summertime.

c. Disturbing people can be unpleasant.

d. The girl who just entered noisily spoke to the waiter.

e. George threw his smoking jacket out the window.

f. We hope to see you before the autumn leaves.

8. The *Saturday Review* records the following word-game devised by Mr. Harry Kruis. Called "Transitional Logic and the Atrocious Pun," the game produces the following syllogism to prove that a sheet of paper is a lazy dog:

> A sheet of paper is an ink-lined plane;
> an inclined plane is a slope up;
> therefore, a sheet of paper is a lazy dog.

What feature of intonation is illustrated in this syllogism? Can you work out other examples like this?

9. By varying the pitch and degree of stress, how many meanings can you communicate in uttering the word *yes?* In regard to this exercise you might consult Daniel Jones, *The Pronunciation of English* (Cambridge, Eng., 1950) for the method by which he graphs pitch configurations.

10. Intonation is a very important part of an actor's performance on stage. He can give a character certain qualities simply by the way in which he speaks the written words. Consider the following passages from Shakespeare and indicate for the italicized phrases the various interpretations which can be produced by different intonations.

a. MACBETH. If we should fail?

   LADY MACBETH. *We fail?*
   But screw your courage to the sticking-place,
   And we'll not fail.

b. POLONIUS. What do you read, my lord?

   HAMLET. *Words, words, words.*

c. OPHELIA. Good my lord,
   How does your Honor for this many a day?

   HAMLET. I humbly thank you—*well, well, well.*

11. One writer has reported that in Stanislavsky's Moscow Art Theatre aspiring actors were asked to convey forty different meanings by reflecting different emotional situations in speaking the phrase *this evening.* How many meanings can you communicate without and with recourse to facial expressions or gestures?

12. In addition to the linguistic system, vocalization is an important means of communication. As indicated earlier, vocalization includes (*a*) nonlinguistic noises such as crying, laughing, whispering, shouting, and moaning, (*b*) vocal qualifiers such as overloudness, oversoftness, overhigh pitch, and overlow pitch, and (*c*) verbal identifiers like *ummmmm, uh-huh,* and *aha.* Using one or two types of vocalization, qualify the meaning of the statement "Look at the window."

13. What are some other verbal qualifiers with which you are familiar? Are

some characteristic of particular situations? Do any have special relationship to ethnic, racial, or national backgrounds? In this regard you might wish to consult the somewhat technical, but interesting study by William M. Austin, "Some Social Aspects of Paralanguage," *Canadian Journal of Linguistics,* XI (Fall 1965), 31–39.

14. A recent study of vocalization is that of David Crystal and Randolph Quirk, *Systems of Prosodic and Paralinguistic Features in English* (London, 1964). Prepare an oral class report on one of its chapters.

24.

OWEN THOMAS

Generative Grammar: *Toward Unification and Simplification*

The grammatical theories of Noam Chomsky, Morris Halle, and their followers are widely discussed but only rarely, if at all, are they applied to the teaching of English grammar in secondary schools. The reasons for this lack of application are many, varied, and complex, and even the primary reasons make an almost overwhelming list:

1. Chomsky, the generally acknowledged leader of the group, published the original statement of the theory less than ten years ago and, consequently, the development of the theory is still in its early stages.

2. The explications of his theory have been directed more toward linguists, psychologists, and mathematicians than toward teachers of English grammar.[1]

3. The criticisms of his theory by other linguists have generated more heat than light, and most secondary school teachers—who, after all, neither are nor need be linguists—have prudently rejected the opportunity to be burned.

4. The secondary school teacher, even if he should be curious, has no

From *English Journal,* LI (February 1962), 94–99. Reprinted with the permission of the National Council of Teachers of English and Owen Thomas.

[1] Chomsky's pertinent publications include the following: "Systems of Syntactic Analysis," *J. of Symbolic Logic* (18.242–56, 1953); *Transformational Analysis,* Ph.D. Dissertation, U. of Penna. (1955); "Three Models for the Description of Language," *I.R.E. Transactions on Information Theory,* v. IT-2 (Sept., 1956); *Syntactic Structures* ('S-Gravenhage, 1957); and a review of B. F. Skinner, *Verbal Behavior,* in *Language* (35.26–58, 1959).

effective way of satisfying his curiosity since, almost without exception (according to the two-score catalogues I checked), departments of English offer no courses in comparative grammar.

Unfortunately, these reasons (and I have idealistically ignored the inertia of school boards and the conservatism of traditionally trained parents) have caused many teachers of English to assume that generative grammar —though perhaps "correct" in some mathematical sense—is pedagogically unadaptable to the needs of a secondary school curriculum.[2] Such an assumption, I feel, is false.

This personal feeling is based largely upon the response to a course, "English Grammar for Teachers," that I conducted in the summer of 1961 at Indiana University. The thirty students in the class were of widely varying backgrounds and experience. Some had just completed their second year of college work; others had been teaching for more than twenty years. All of them, however, although they didn't know it until the end of the eight-week session, were subjects in an experiment that the liberal administration of Indiana University permitted me to conduct. Briefly, and this is something of an over-simplification, we hoped to answer one question: what do secondary school teachers—not professional linguists—think of generative grammar?

The answer proved the validity of the question. Without exception, the students were convinced that certain deductions from the theories of Chomsky could be applied systematically to the teaching of grammar, not only in the secondary school but with equal effectiveness in the elementary school.

Because of the unanimity of class opinion, it seems worthwhile to examine the structure of the course. Purposely, no text was assigned for general use during the first four weeks. Purposely also, the initial lectures were devoted to the history of the language and to the development of grammatical studies during the eighteenth and nineteenth centuries. The course, in short, was made to appear as non-controversial as possible. As a supplement to the lectures, the students were given daily assignments: "memorize the eight parts of speech, the four kinds of sentences, the six kinds of pronouns, and the four kinds of adjectives; diagram ten sentences; conjugate three verbs." Every Friday was given over to an informal clinic where we discussed the work of the preceding week. For the students, the initial clinic was a nearly shattering experience. Controversy forced its way into the syllabus.

---

[2] The terms "transformational grammar" and "generative grammar" are sometimes used interchangeably. The latter term, however, seems to be supplanting the former. This trend was particularly noticeable at the recent (summer 1961) meeting of the Commission on English which debated some of the questions considered in this article.

TRADITIONAL GRAMMAR EXAMINED

Since no single text was assigned, the students had necessarily sought their definitions and diagraming rules in different books; without exception, these books were "traditional." The marked lack of agreement among these books (many of which were texts currently being used in various school systems) was surprising and, for most students, disconcerting. Some texts defined eight parts of speech; others admitted only seven (dismissing or ignoring the interjection). Some presented purely semantic definitions ("A noun is the name of a person, place, or thing"); others made a half-hearted blow toward structural definitions ("A noun is a word that names something"); and still others tried to combine the two types ("A noun is a word used to name a person, place, or thing"). Some listed four kinds of pronouns; others, six; and one, bravely, twelve. Some diagraming rules (which a few texts quietly ignored) called for left-slanting lines, some for right-slanting lines, some for perpendicular lines, and some for dashed lines. The students soon concluded that the traditionalists were not united, even on basic definitions, that—in fact—there was no single traditional grammar.

The second two weeks of the course were spent in determining why this lack of agreement existed. The lectures continued to be historical, although somewhat more controversial, and emphasized the contributions of Otto Jespersen, Holger Pedersen, Edward Sapir, and Leonard Bloomfield.[3] Meanwhile, the students were consulting the initial chapters (those generally devoted to debunking the traditionalists) in works by structural linguists such as Charles C. Fries, James Sledd, and Harold Whitehall.[4] These analyses, particularly Sledd's concise discussion, convinced the students that the inconsistencies of traditional grammar were fundamental. But curiously, the Friday clinic revealed that their initial dissatisfaction with the traditionalists was somewhat tempered, and they agreed (with Sledd) that traditional grammar—although Latinate and essentially inadequate to describe English —provides at least a useful terminology.

Probably the most important conclusion reached by the class during this period was that "form underlies meaning."[5]

---

[3] Jespersen, *Language: Its Nature, Development and Origin* (1923); Pedersen, *Linguistic Science in the Nineteenth Century* (trans. by Spargo, 1931); Sapir, *Language* (1921); Bloomfield, *Language* (1933). For an introductory discussion on the contributions of these authors, see C. C. Fries, "Advances in Linguistics," *College English,* vol. 23, no. 1 (Oct., 1961). pp. 30–37.

[4] Fries, *Structure of English* (1952); Sledd, *A Short Introduction to English Grammar* (1959); Whitehall, *Structural Essentials of English* (1951).

[5] This is one of the major points of disagreement between the structuralists and the traditionalists and probably stems (as Fries notes in *The Structure of English,* p. 7)

At this point, and building on this axiom, we began a detailed study of Fries's method, which we supplemented from time to time with definitions taken from Sledd. The class was eager and excited; they expected to find, as they later revealed, a simple, self-consistent system to replace traditional grammar. They had no difficulty in accepting the essentials of Sledd's definitions since they were not aware that "mixing levels" is supposedly the unpardonable sin among structuralists. (They balked slightly, however, when Sledd introduced pitch and stress levels into some of his definitions.) They admitted, in theory, that Fries was right in emphasizing patterns and functions, but they rebelled, in fact, when we came to a sentence analysis such as the following:[6]

$$\text{D} \quad 3 \quad 3 \quad 1^a \quad \text{f} \quad \text{D} \quad 1^b \quad 4 \quad 2 \quad \text{D} \quad 3 \quad 1^c \quad \text{f} \quad \text{D} \quad 1^d \quad \text{f} \quad 2 \quad \text{f} \quad 1^e$$
$$- \text{F} \quad\quad - \quad\quad - \quad\quad\quad\quad\quad - \text{F} \quad + \text{J} + \text{F}—$$
$$\quad\; \text{it} \quad\quad\; \text{it} \quad\quad\quad \text{it} \quad\quad\quad\quad\quad \text{he} \;\text{he} \quad\quad \text{it}$$

As one student said at a Friday clinic, "The high school pupil who understands *that* doesn't have to study grammar." They felt, in brief, that the cure was worse than the disease.

Thus halfway through the course, the students were wandering through two worlds, "powerless to be born." While in this uncomfortable state, they investigated—during the third two-weeks—the pertinent literature in *College English, Educational Forum,* the *English Journal,* and the *NEA Journal.* They found the attacks, counter-attacks, and counter-counter-attacks of the traditionalists and the structuralists. (They found very little on Chomsky.) These investigations convinced them that they were not alone in their confusion and that the structuralists were as divided as the traditionalists, perhaps even more so.

At this point, then, most of the class felt that they could not conscientiously teach traditional grammar: the inconsistencies were too widespread and too basic. But they also felt that structural grammar—even assuming that the disagreements could be resolved—was far too complex to be readily adapted to the needs of secondary school pupils. Furthermore, they were antagonistic toward the emphasis by the structuralists on stress, pitch, and juncture, particularly as incorporated in "immediate constituent analysis" which splits the sentence, as one student said, "into a hodge of podges." They were, in short, ready for any theory that would justify traditional

from Jespersen: "But in syntax meaning is everything." Curiously, no traditionalist has noted that William Cobbett—as staunch a traditionalist as ever conjugated a verb—anticipated the structuralists in "Letter XII" of his *Grammar of the English Language* (originally published in 1818 and reprinted by Ward, Lock, & Bowden, Limited, London, n.d.) when he said: "the sense in which a word is used . . . determines what is the part of speech to which it belongs."

[6] Fries, *Structure of English,* p. 268.

grammar or simplify structural grammar, particularly (in the latter case) if the theory redirected the emphasis toward the sentence as the most significant part of grammar.

With this attitude, they began their study of generative grammar, using the same text for the first time in the course: Chomsky's *Syntactic Structures*. Within one week they were agreed that his theory provided the necessary simplification of structural grammar (or rather, that his theory was simpler to understand than that of the structuralists) and that the resultant grammar could be adapted readily to the needs of secondary school students. During the final week of the course, the class experimented—both in and out of class—with applications of Chomsky's theory.

What, then, is the theory? And how can his theory be applied to the teaching of grammar? Before answering these questions, we must consider his definition of grammar: a grammar is a device for generating the sentences of a language. Thus (to belabor the point), if a student understands the grammar of a language, he can construct grammatically correct sentences in that language. No grammar, however, can tell a student which of two grammatically correct sentences is *stylistically* better. Such judgments are outside the realm of grammar; they are solely matters of taste and must be taught accordingly.

"KERNEL" SENTENCES

After having defined the limits of his theory, Chomsky introduces a basic concept: that of a group of "kernel" sentences. A kernel sentence is "simple, active, declarative," and Chomsky feels that "all other sentences" are derived from kernel sentences by means of "transformations." Roughly, a "transformation" is a rule that either introduces new elements into kernel sentences (e.g., adjectives, negatives), or rearranges the elements of a kernel sentence (e.g., to produce an interrogative sentence), or both (e.g., to produce a passive sentence). Chomsky implies, therefore, that passive, interrogative, and negative sentences, and sentences containing, for example, adjectives, adverbs, and conjunctions, are all more complex or "sophisticated" than kernel sentences.

Not surprisingly, Chomsky's "kernel sentence" bears a strong resemblance to the simple "subject-verb-complement" sentence of traditional grammar. He states that a kernel sentence is composed of a "noun phrase plus a verb phrase." A "noun phrase" (symbol: NP) consists simply of an article (T) plus a noun (N), and the presence of the article is optional.[7] A "verb

---

[7] More properly, I feel, the "article" should be called a "determiner" according to a definition such as that of Sledd in *A Short Introduction to English Grammar*, p. 207.

phrase" (VP) consists of an auxiliary (Aux) plus a main verb (V) plus a noun phrase (and this last "noun phrase" is, of course, similar to the traditional "complement"); the noun phrase contained within the verb phrase is also optional. This may seem confusing at first reading, but the symbolic representation is straightforward and easy to understand:[8]

Sentence → NP + VP
   (where the arrow means "rewrite," i.e., "rewrite Sentence as NP plus VP")
NP → T + N
VP → Aux + V + NP

Thus, the following are "noun phrases":

John, the boy, a dog, the men

And the following are "verb phrases":

reads, eats the apple, may bury a bone, have bought the farm

Therefore, the following are "kernel sentences":

John reads.
The boy eats the apple.
A dog may bury a bone.
The men have bought the farm.

Chomsky thus simplifies the descriptions of English (such as that from Fries, quoted above) by limiting these descriptions to a relatively small number of simple sentences. All other sentences are "generated from" (i.e., built upon) these kernel sentences by applying certain constant and *invariable* transformations, and the constancy of the transformation is, for most teachers of English, a major feature of Chomsky's theory.

    Thus, given a kernel sentence (e.g., "The men have bought the farm"), we may generate a passive sentence ("The farm has been bought by the men"), a negative sentence ("The men haven't bought the farm"), a "yes-or-no" interrogative sentence ("Have the men bought the farm?"), two "wh?" interrogative sentences ("What have the men bought?" and "Who has bought the farm?"), and even combinations of these sentences (e.g., a negative-passive: "The farm hasn't been bought by the men"). Furthermore, with still other transformations we may introduce adverbs, adjectives, and

---

[8] This is the simplest possible presentation. Copyright laws being what they are, we cannot duplicate the presentation, and it must suffice to say that those rules, for example, pertaining to "noun phrase singular" (NP^s) are equally explicit, self-consistent, and easy to understand.

prepositional phrases into any or all of these sentences ("Who has finally bought the old farm on the hill?").[9]

These transformations, it is worth repeating, are invariable. Given a kernel sentence of a particular form (and Chomsky defines the required form precisely), then any and all related non-kernel sentences can be generated by applying the appropriate (and quite simple) transformation. One specific example will serve to illustrate these remarks. The "passive transformation" may be given in the following form:

To derive a passive sentence, we first need a kernel "string," containing the following elements: a noun phrase (NP), an auxiliary (Aux), a verb (V), and a second noun phrase (NP). These might be represented as follows:

$$[NP_1] + [Aux] + [V] + [NP_2]$$

To transform this string into a "passive string," the four basic elements are rearranged and three other elements are (invariably) added, as follows:

$$[NP_2] + [Aux] + be + en + [V] + by + [NP_1]$$

(The "en" which is added is the so-called "past participle morpheme.")
Finally, the resultant string is converted into an English sentence by inserting appropriate parts of speech into the string.
Thus, given the kernel sentence:

$$[The\ man] + [has] + [eaten] + [the\ apple]$$

we may apply the transformation to produce:

$$[The\ apple] + [has] + be + en + [eaten] + by + [the\ man]$$

This, of course, reduces to:

$$"The\ apple\ has\ been\ eaten\ by\ the\ man."[10]$$

Such is the nature of Chomsky's major contribution toward the simplification of grammar. In addition, he makes another, quite important contribution: he divides all of grammar into three parts. The first part presents

[9] There is quite obviously a relationship between Chomsky's kernel sentences and simple traditional diagraming, and even between those transformations which add adjectives and phrases to the kernel and those diagrams which indicate the subordinate position of adjectives and phrases. Transformations, however, indicate the exact nature of subordination; more importantly, they indicate the exact nature of the relationship between a kernel sentence and the associated passive, negative, and interrogative sentences.

[10] For purposes of illustration, the transformation, as given, is somewhat simplified as the reader may see for himself by substituting, for example, a plural subject or object into the kernel. Such refinements, however, are easily and systematically handled through certain so-called "obligatory" transformations. The principle, at any rate, is invariable.

those rules that pertain to kernel sentences ("phrase structure"), and here his theory will certainly draw upon the work of the structuralists. The second part presents rules that generate non-kernel sentences ("transformational structure"). And the third part presents the rules that are necessary to account for such irregular forms as "child, children" and "buy, bought" ("morphological structure"), and this part of his theory will probably draw upon the work of the historical grammarians (e.g., Jespersen).

The theory, then, is not too difficult for an adult to understand. And most persons acquainted with Chomsky's work, including the members of my class, feel that his theories provide the only logical explanation currently available for the intuitive sense which most native speakers have of a relationship between active and passive, or positive and negative, or declarative and interrogative sentences. But we may legitimately ask whether transformations can be taught to secondary school pupils. This is essentially the same question we asked above: "How can Chomsky's theory be applied to the teaching of grammar?" To answer this question completely would be to write a text, or at least a syllabus, for a course on methods of teaching grammar. Obviously, nothing of that sort is being attempted here. But during the final meetings of my class, we reached agreement on a number of points that will probably be included in any text that is written.

APPLICATION TO SENTENCE STRUCTURE

We agreed, for example, that the study of grammar has one primary function: to enable a student to construct grammatically correct sentences. The most significant advance that an understanding of Chomsky's theory permits is the organization of this study according to increasing ("graduated") levels of sophistication in sentence construction. Thus, we should first teach the use of the kernel sentence (terminology is unimportant and should be subordinate to an understanding of the kernel form, i.e., to an understanding of a sentence that is "simple, declarative, active, with no complex verb or noun phrases"). The following sentences are typical kernel sentences:

1. The boy hit the ball.
2. The girl bought the dress.
3. The teacher ate the apple.
4. John loves Mary.

Conversely, the following sentences are *not* kernel sentences:

5. The ball was hit by the boy.
6. The girl didn't buy the dress.

7. Did the teacher eat an apple?
8. Who loves Mary?

Secondary school pupils, the class agreed, could construct kernel sentences of their own. Next they could be taught to construct passive sentences from their kernels; then, negative sentences, "yes-or-no" interrogative sentence, and "wh-" interrogative sentences. At each step, the teacher can point out the recurring elements of the resultant sentences (i.e., the underlying form). The repetition would familiarize the student—unconsciously, perhaps, but nonetheless effectively—with the basic form, and the ordering of the exercises—in gradually increasing levels of complexity—would enable the student to build his confidence systematically.

Students may then combine their sentences, for example the passive and the negative (and the teacher may note that the passive is formed before the negative is added). After (and sometimes during) exercises of this type, the teacher may introduce adjectives, adverbs, and prepositional phrases, noting that any of these may appear in any sentence form.[11]

Of course, in any presentation, certain definitions are required, but the definitions should be introduced only when they are necessary, that is, only when a student needs a "label" to discuss the elements he is, in fact, using. Thus, "noun" and "verb" should be defined when the students are being taught the form of the kernel sentence. (I feel Sledd's definitions are quite appropriate.) In this way, those parts of speech that are simplest to define (and for the student to understand) are taught first, and the hard-to-define (and to understand) parts of speech, such as the "preposition" and the "conjunction," are postponed until the student has developed familiarity and confidence with the simpler and more important forms.

There are still other benefits to be derived from an understanding of Chomsky's theories. Transformations *per se,* as we have noted, probably cannot be taught to pre-college students; but from *any* transformation a teacher can deduce several invariable rules. For example, from the passive transformation we can deduce such rules as the following (and the list is by no means exhaustive):

1. There can be no passive voice unless a kernel sentence contains a subject and its object.
2. There can be no passive voice without an auxiliary verb or verbs. (If there is only one auxiliary, it must be a form of *to be.*)
3. The subject of the kernel sentence invariably follows the verb in the related passive sentence and is invariably introduced with the word "by."

---

[11] A method such as that advocated by D. M. Wolfe ("Grammatical Autobiography," *English Journal,* XLIX, 1 (January 1960), pp. 16-21) would be quite suitable for this kind of study.

4. The main verb in a passive sentence is invariably in the past participial form.

Similar rules, it is worth repeating, can be derived from any transformation, and the form of the transformation guarantees that there are no exceptions to these rules.

In brief, then, Chomsky's theories are not difficult to understand. They are, in fact, a means of systematizing the almost countless "rules" of both traditional and structural grammarians. And most importantly, an understanding of Chomsky's theories permits a teacher to select and arrange grammatical elements in the most logical order and to build effectively upon preceding material. As teachers, we can hardly ask more of any theory.

Vocabulary

inertia, pedagogically, unanimity, syllabus, disconcerting, debunking, concise, axiom, interrogative, auxiliary verb, intuitive, subordinate

Review Questions

1. What explains, according to Professor Thomas, the lack of application of grammatical theory of men like Chomsky and Halle to the teaching of grammar in secondary schools?
2. What justification does Thomas offer for concluding that there is "no single traditional grammar"?
3. Explain what is meant by the statement "form underlies meaning."
4. What do the linguistic terms *stress, pitch,* and *juncture* mean?
5. What is Chomsky's definition of grammar?
6. Does a knowledge of grammar, according to Chomsky, make it possible for the student to choose on a stylistic basis from several grammatically correct sentences?
7. What does Chomsky mean by a "kernel sentence" and "transformations"?
8. Translate the following:

$$Sentence \rightarrow NP + VP$$
$$NP \rightarrow T + N$$
$$VP \rightarrow Aux + V + NP$$

9. Give your own examples of a "noun phrase," a "verb phrase," and a kernel sentence.
10. What are some of the more sophisticated sentences which can be generated from the following kernel sentence:

A boy ate the candy.

11. Into what components does Chomsky divide grammar?
12. What are some of the benefits of understanding Chomsky's theories?

Expository Technique

1. What example of enumeration can you find?
2. What value does the fairly lengthy report of Thomas's course at Indiana University have? Might the space better have been devoted to further elucidation of generative grammar?
3. Into what stages may the work of Thomas's course be divided?
4. What are the principal divisions of the essay?
5. Into what components does Thomas analyze generative grammar?
6. Comment on the function of the final paragraph.

Exercises

1. Replace the symbols in the following formulae with appropriate words:

$$S \rightarrow NP + VP$$
$$N \rightarrow T + N$$
$$VP \rightarrow Aux + V$$
$$[NP_1] + [Aux] + [V] + [NP_2]$$

2. Which of the following sentences are kernels and which are transformations?

a. She is a mother.
b. A loud noise sounded.
c. The people are enjoying the weather.
d. Dogs bark.
e. They are enjoying the warm weather.
f. The beautiful girl smiled.
g. A pitcher can't win every game.
h. The student can solve the problem.
i. The salesman has sold the old house.
j. A professor purchased the house.
k. Why did he do it?
l. The pistol was sold to Roger.
m. What is it for?
n. She answered with a sweet voice.
o. Did Alice call?

3. Consider the examples of kernel sentences which Professor Thomas gives in his essay. Can you think of other varieties of kernel, or basic, sentences?

4. From the kernel sentence "The girl read the book" generate a passive sentence according to the passive transformation rule:

$$[NP_2] + [Aux] + be + en + [V] + by + [NP_1]$$

5. Transform the sentence "The car has been purchased by the Smiths" into a kernel sentence represented by the following rule:

$$[NP_1] + [Aux] + [V] + [NP_2].$$

6. Consider the following pairs of sentences:

KERNELS	TRANSFORMATIONS
The men bought the farm.	Have the men bought the farm?
The people elected a presdent.	Have the people elected a president?
The women sold the chances.	Have the women sold the chances?

Can you devise a *yes-or-no* Interrogative Transformation Rule covering the above transformations? Will it apply to the following:

John eats the apple.	Has John eaten the apple?

7. Give the kernel sentences for the following transforms:

Does John read?	The toy was not taken by the boy.
Who bought the car?	The girl did not eat the cake.

8. From the kernel sentence "The students introduced their parents" generate the following kinds of statements:

a passive sentence	a *who-* interrogative
a negative sentence	a negative passive
a *yes-or-note* interrogative	a negative *yes-or-no* interrogative

9. Generate negative sentences for each of the following:

The boys like cookies.	She is eating the candy.
Joan writes a letter.	We are the winners.
We will drink the punch.	

What difficulties would you encounter in attempting to write a Transformation Rule which would generate such negative sentences?

25.

DONALD J. LLOYD
HARRY R. WARFEL

Meaning—
Structural and Otherwise

An aspect of language that is very hard to grasp and harder even to accept is the evasiveness of meaning. We hear a person speak and we understand him; his utterance has meaning. He says, "Coke?" We say, "Sure." He says, "Snack Bar?" We say, "No time." And we walk off together, both knowing that we are going to the machine in the basement, which is closer and faster. But if a man from Mars, wrapped in his invisibility suit, were to overhear us and try to find the meaning in the expressions we have used, he would be baffled. The meaning isn't in the expressions alone, of course; it is in the situation. A large part of the situation is the fact that two members of the same speech-community are standing on familiar ground and talking about familiar things.

The meaning here is in the system of signals only as the signaling-system is part of a larger complex of common and repeated actions. The making of the signals is a set of actions related to other actions that we perform and propose to perform with our bodies; they sound cryptic to an outsider because they are economical. In speech we tend to say what we have to say to make ourselves clear, and no more. A person who says more than he needs to say is a bore, and we don't like to be bores. In the act of communication, writing has less than speech of this situational support to which we can apply the general term *context*.

Context in the broadest sense is all of the human acts that bear on a specific act of communication; in its narrowest sense it is the words that come immediately before and after any single word in the communication. The richest contexts are shared by members of one speech-community in constant face-to-face contact with each other; therefore, their actual speech can be a sketchy kind of oral shorthand. The skimpiest contexts exist between a writer and reader who are strangers to each other when the writer is trying to explain something that is new and outside the reader's experience. In a relationship where the contexts are many and rich, the actual burden of expression that falls on the communication itself is very light; but in a relationship where the contexts are skimpy and remote the communication has to contain within itself all that is necessary to its understanding.

One of the problems always facing a speaker or writer is the problem of guessing how much context—how much mutual understanding—exists between himself and his audience before he launches on the actual communication. Much depends on what the audience knows about the subject to begin with. Much depends on the overlap there is between the signals habitually used by the person trying to express his meaning and the person trying to grasp the meaning. The speaker or writer must guess: he has to feel his way; but the speaker is better off than the writer because his audience is in a position to let him know as soon as they cannot understand. The writer's audience may never get a chance or may never bother to tell him. Any act of writing is in this respect a blind flight into the unknown, but there is one precaution that the writer can take—he can risk getting too much in rather than too little.

Even within the utterance or sentence—assuming that it is complete in all that is necessary to understanding—meaning is still evasive. It seems to reside everywhere—and nowhere. We can break the utterance down into the signals that compose it, right down to the phonemes; but we find that specific phonemes taken alone mean nothing in particular, the morphemes mean nothing in particular, the words mean nothing in particular, and the structural patterns mean nothing in particular. Take the utterance as a whole, and it has meaning; take it part by part, and you do not arrive at parts of the meaning in little capsules. The meaning of an utterance is held in solution until the speaker indicates that the utterance is done. The meaning of a sentence is held in solution until the writer indicates that the sentence is done.

> He made a little bow—a short, sharp thing—to the ladies.
> He made a little bow—a short, sharp thing—for his boat.

Nothing is the same in those two sentences, but you don't know it until you reach the final word-group. *He* in the one is a person out in society; *he* in the other is a person building a boat. *Made* in the one sentence is the performance of an act; in the other it is the construction of a thing. *Bow* in the one is a movement of the body; in the other, *bow* is a part of a boat. The important thing is that you don't know any of this until all the evidence is in, and if you try to jump the evidence you go wrong.

It is really hard to believe that a word has no meaning except in context, but if we once get the idea we have a key that unlocks language. A word has meaning only in a complete utterance as a part of the total meaning of the whole utterance. A word is not a thing, but a complicated set of acts, a fast and integrated set of motions of the organs of speech. Before it is spoken, a word is merely a set of potential, well-worn grooves of nerve impulse and muscle action, more like a swimming stroke or a golf swing that comes into existence only when we are in the water or addressing a golf ball. Writing a word is a set of finger motions, pushing a pencil or hitting a key. The sound or the written letters are only the product of the act, comparable to the swimmer's progress through the water or the golfer's drive down the fairway. We should not be confused that we write a "word" with spaces before and after or that we can say or write the word alone without any other words. That is not communication.

We can understand the way a clock works by taking it apart, but we cannot find time in it. Time does not reside in the clock; it can't be divided among the gears. Lay the works out on a table—the spring, the gears, the hands, the balance wheel—and you don't have little bits of time—seconds in this gear, minutes in that, hours in the spring. You have intricately formed bits of metal; they could be put to work doing many kinds of things. Such a spring is used to scoot a toy across the floor, arm a mine to sink a ship, or drive the mechanism of a movie camera. Assembled and adjusted to each other, the parts of the clock tell time; spread out on a cloth, they mean nothing. So it is with the parts of an utterance: individually they mean nothing; engaged with each other in the total utterance, they mean what the utterance means.

This conclusion is a hard one to accept; it runs counter to what we feel to be our experience, and it contradicts ordinary notions about language. We have a habit of depending on dictionaries to tell us the "real" meanings of words. But the dictionary, useful as it is, can only tell us what seems to be the part of the total meaning of a sentence associated with the word in question; the dictionary record is constructed out of an examination of whole sentences written in the past and, therefore, finished as acts. It is a kind of history; and history, as we well know, is a record of what has been done, not a promise of what we are about to do. It is not an essay in prediction. *The Oxford English Dictionary* records over 14,500 "meanings" for the two hundred most common "words." What kind of a jungle is that for us to hunt in for "real meanings"?

Let us consider the word *man*—surely a common word. Almost anyone feels that he can define it: "an adult male human being." Try it in a few sentences:

Man the boats.
Man has lived on this earth for fifty thousand years.

Man has never been able to get along with woman.
She wore a man-tailored suit.
He tipped the chess-board, dumping the men to the floor.
The visitor sent his man for the luggage.
When the factory closed, the men went home, but the staff stayed to take
   inventory.

We have not repeated a single meaning of the word *man* in these
sentences, nor have we run the range of the meanings recorded for it. What,
then, is its meaning: "take your places in," "mankind," "the male half of
the human race," "according to the tailoring standards of men's clothing,"
"a counter used in chess," "a servant," "an employee"? Is it really a verb as
in the first sentence; really an adverb as in the fourth; or really a noun as
in the others? In each sentence it really means what it means in that sentence, and nothing else. Its meaning is the product of its interaction with
all the other structural signals in the sentence.

Let us examine the meaning of a couple of structure-words, *the* and *a*.
These are noun-markers; they commonly begin noun phrases: *the books;
a book; the morning; the bright morning; a clear, bright morning.* They
are among the most often repeated words in our language, so often repeated
that they seldom bear any stress in utterances. Any native speaker uses them
unconsciously and negligently; if he feels that he has any problem with his
language, you can be sure that it does not involve these. Yet their use has
never been adequately described. A foreigner is likely to make all sorts of
mistakes with these words, but a native cannot tell him what is wrong. The
native can set him right but cannot explain the difference between acceptable
and unacceptable usage. If the foreigner has a sharp ear and a flair for imitation, he soon smooths out his trouble; but when he begins to use these
words our way, he is no more prepared than we are to describe what changes
he has made in his employment of them. Here is a little exercise in variations:

At the time of the day when the bell rings, we go home.
At a time of the day when a bell rings, we go home.
At a time of a day when the bell rings, we go home.

There are differences between the meanings of these sentences, but what
are they? Each answers the question, "When do we go home?" We can
cut the problem by saying, *When a bell rings, we go home* or *When the
bell rings, we go home.* Both leave out something. Whether *the* or *a* means
"a certain instance" of the noun or "any instance" of the noun must be
decided more broadly than by examining these words: we have to look at
the whole utterance. Their meaning is the product of their interaction with
all the other structural signals in the sentence.

Or we can consider one of the sound changes—one of the morphemes—added to nouns, the one written *-s*, as in *cat, cats*. This is a very common signal: *book, books; dog, dogs; board, boards*. We might try to say that the noun without the *-s* signifies one instance of the noun, and with it more than one.

The paper is on the table.
The papers are on the table.

But try this:

The wheat is in the bin.
The wheats are in the bin.

The oat is in the bin.
The oats are in the bin.

Or this:

The worm crawled into the wood.
The worm crawled into the woods.

He made good time on the way to the party,
    and good times for everybody after he got there.

The meaning of this signal is the product of its interaction with all the other structural signals in the sentence.

Words, stresses, junctures, pitches, inflectional changes—all taken by themselves—are empty. Each, taken by itself, means no more than a slot punched in an IBM card. We have all seen the checks, registration cards, employee records, file cards, and so on, punched with a pattern of little oblong slots. The slots mean nothing in themselves. They mean what the person who uses the machine wants them to mean. As part of a situation outside the machine, they have meaning. In themselves they merely trigger the mechanism. And so with all the separate elements of language. Each in itself means nothing; it merely triggers the mechanism of the utterance.

We have seen that such a word as *man*, taken by itself outside all sentences, has so many possibilities of meaning that it has no meaning. It has two kinds of possibilities, old and new. *Man* can fit again into such utterances as it has been found in through history, and it can fit into new utterances of a kind in which it has never appeared before. The first is more likely, but we can make no greater error about language than to rule out the second, for language is constantly alive with first utterances—combinations of signals that have never been made before. The user of language does not know from moment to moment when he will blunder into a new

EXPOSITORY TYPE: ANALYSIS

experience, make or find a new thing, think a new thought. Yet the continuity of language rests in its repetition of old combinations, in its saying again what has been said before.

In such a word as *man* there is a range of potential meanings, and each word that might be combined with *man* has its own range. A word, then, is a generalization; and a sentence is a fitting together of generalizations. Let us take a list of words arranged in alphabetical order: *at, beats, corner, his, man, mild, seems, the, very, who, wife, young. Beats* is "repeated striking" or "winning"; *corner* is "any coming together of two sides"; *mild* could be "soft, gentle, not sharp to the tongue"; *wife* is "any woman linked in marriage to a man"; and *young* refers to "that stage in life between birth and maturity, as of a flower, a man, or a planet." Taken as a list these words mean nothing. They are only capable of meaning.

Let us make a sentence of them:

The young man at the corner who seems very mild beats his wife.

Here we have a statement, something specific, something as definite as the list of words taken separately is indefinite. What turns the trick? We can see what relates the words to each other by removing the nouns, verb, and adjective from the sentence, leaving this:

The ——— ——— at the ——— who seems very ——— ———s his ———.

And we can fill this framework with other words:

The old soldier at the front who seems very frightened risks his life.
The shrewd salesman at the market who seems very gullible cheats his customers.
The tired boy at the counter who seems very hungry eats his lunch.

The other words give a different total meaning. It is clear that the pattern sets up relationships that allow the meaning to become specific. We have to come at the problem of meaning in a different way.

Let us choose one word, *man*, as our key word. We can strip the sentence to its very core and come out with this: *Man beats wife.* We are in a sort of intermediate stage between the very general potentialities of the alphabetical list—*at, beats, corner, his, man, mild, seems, the, very, who, wife, young*—and the specific sentence: *The young man at the corner who seems very mild beats his wife.*

Beginning with *man*, let us use a circle to indicate all the possible meanings of *man* in all potential utterances:

We will take *the* as pointing out one instance of *man*—whatever *man* means. We put a dot in the circle to stand for this one instance.

The word *young*—whatever it means—has the force of cutting out of consideration all meanings of *man* that cannot accept the description *young*.

The group *at the corner* cuts out of consideration all meanings of *man* that cannot be located in that bit of space:

The group *who seems very mild* cuts out all *young men* who do not *seem mild*:

The word *beats* cuts out all such men who *do not beat*—whatever *beat* means.

The group *his wife* limits *beats* and by doing so puts a further limitation on *man*. It excludes all other objects of beating, such as *dogs, opponents,* or *rugs*.

The force of the pattern is to cut away meanings not intended, and the pattern works on *soldier* or *salesman* or *boy* the same way. Each word or word-group removes from consideration all instances of the key word that do not accept the qualification expressed in the word or in the group. The utterance reveals a successive removal from attention of the instances of the key word that are not affirmed by the successive elements in the sentence. It cuts a large and unmanageable area of meaning down to size. The whole sentence becomes the equivalent of what has traditionally been called a proper noun: a noun "used to designate a specific individual, place, etc." It is a marvelous operation.

Vocabulary

cryptic, morpheme, flair

Review Questions

1. Distinguish between social and linguistic context. Give examples of both.

2. Why do Lloyd and Warfel think that a speaker has an advantage over a writer in successfully "guessing how much context . . . exists between himself and his audience"?

3. Lloyd and Warfel believe that dictionaries do not give the "real" meanings of words. What, then, do they think is the function of the lexicographer? Do you think Hall and Pulgram would agree with them?

4. The authors mention that the *-s* ending is employed to indicate plurality of nouns. Are there any other ways in which nouns form their plurals? If so, does this fact strengthen or weaken the argument of Lloyd and Warfel?

5. Comment on the statement "A word, then, is a generalization."

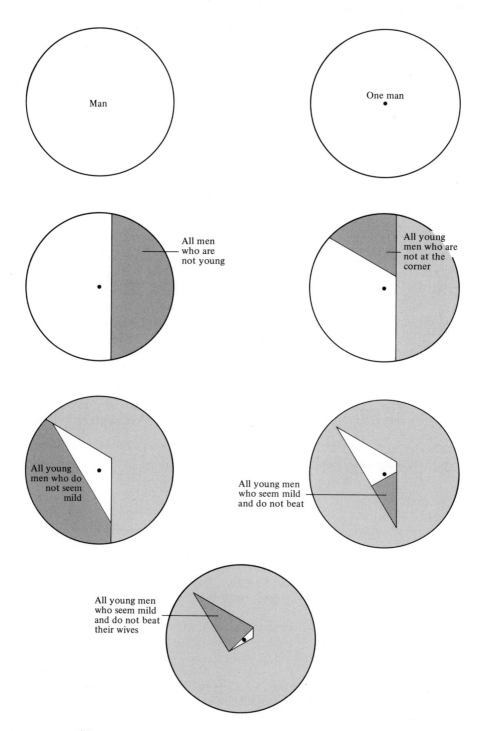

Man

One man

All men
who are
not young

All young
men who are
not at the
corner

All young
men who do
not seem
mild

All young men
who seem mild
and do not beat

All young men
who seem mild
and do not beat
their wives

Expository Technique

1. What is the controlling idea of this essay?
2. What examples of definition, analogy, illustration, and analysis does this essay contain?
3. Discuss the first paragraph as an introductory paragraph.

Exercises

1. Consider the use of *hand* in each of the sentences below. Show how its *meaning* is dependent upon the context in which it appears.
a. His experience in playing bridge enabled him to recognize a good *hand* immediately.
b. Her father was furious because she had eloped with a hired *hand*.
c. He received a good *hand* for his rendition of the *Moonlight Sonata*.
d. Her letters are always written in a neat, legible *hand*.
e. The horse that won the race stood fifteen *hands* high.
f. All his relatives were on *hand* for his speech.
g. Robert's *hand* is bandaged because he cut it on a broken milk bottle this morning.
h. As I passed him he asked me to give him a *hand* with his flat tire.
i. Yesterday, John formally asked Mr. Spencer for the *hand* of his daughter in marriage.
j. You have to *hand* it to John; he certainly gets the work done.
k. The teacher instructed Philip to *hand* in his work promptly.
l. Owning an automobile is certainly convenient; on the other *hand*, it is certainly expensive.
2. Devise several sentences, like those above, for each of the following words which will illustrate the fact that meaning depends upon context: *strike, air, pool, pipe, play, key, grass, trip*.
3. Compose two sentences and show, as Lloyd and Warfel do on pages 376–378, how "the utterance reveals a successive removal from attention of the instances of the key word [the subject] that are not affirmed by the successive elements in the sentence."
4. A fascinating and important system of communication is kinesics, the study of nonverbal body motions, such as gestures and facial expressions, which convey meaning in their own right or as part of the context for verbal messages. Kinesics is of interest to the anthropologist, who finds that different cultures employ different gestures or attach different meanings to the same gesture; to psychiatrists and physicians, who explore these forms of behavior as manifestations of mental or physical ills; and to linguists, who find that a command of the kinesics of a given language is important for effective use of that language. Kinesics is an important part of the rich context which, as Lloyd and Warfel explain, facilitates spoken communication.

a. To gain some awareness of the part kinesics plays in communication, turn on your television set but turn the volume off. Note the contortions, the grimaces, movements, and so on which a singer uses in singing about love. You might try to define love on the basis of the pantomime of such television performers.

b. If you have had the opportunity to see Marcel Marceau or another good pantomimist, attempt to generalize about the kinesics of grief or joy.

c. Analyze a comic strip or a series of cartoons. How does the artist suggest attitude and mood? If you wish to make a serious study of such a subject, see W. LaBarre, "The Apperception of Attitudes with Reference to '*The Lonely Ones*' of William Steig," *American Imago,* VI (1949), 3–43.

d. Ask two of your classmates to strike and hold poses which communicate surprise, joy, or rage. Analyze the kinesics involved here. Do the two individuals agree in essentials about what expressions, posture, and gestures suggest these emotions?

e. Kinesics is involved in the game of charades. Agree with other members of your class on a few conventional gestures to communicate such things as punctuation, the end of a word, keep guessing, and so on, and attempt to act out familiar advertising slogans without any verbalization.

5. Read one of the following works and prepare an oral class report on it:

Ray L. Birdwhistell, "Background to Kinesics," *ETC,* XIII (1955), 10–18.

———, *Introduction to Kinesics* (Foreign Service Institute, Washington, D.C., 1952.)

MacDonald Critchley, *The Language of Gesture* (New York, 1939).

Edward T. Hall, *The Silent Language* (New York, 1959).

Jurgen Ruesch and Weldon Kees, *Nonverbal Communication* (New York, 1956).

Thomas Sebeok and others, *Approaches to Semiotics* (New York, 1964).

6. Do you think kinesics differ noticeably among cultures, racial or ethnic groups, age groups, or sexes?

7. A context of mutual understanding plays an important part in certain forms of literary wit. As Bergen and Cornelia Evans note in discussing the cliché (pages 98–99), wits often turn an ancient cliché to witty purposes by minor revisions. Oscar Wilde observed, for example, "Punctuality is the thief of time"; Ambrose Bierce, "A man is known by the company he organizes"; Tallulah Bankhead (concerning one of Maeterlinck's plays), "There is less here than meets the eye"; and James Thurber, "Early to rise and early to bed makes a male healthy and wealthy and dead." All of these revitalized clichés rely on the audience's familiarity with and expectation of the usual wording.

a. Collect additional examples of the rewritten cliché from humorists like Wilde, Shaw, Bierce, Thurber, Benchley, and Perelman.

b. Try to rewrite some trite proverbial expressions in the manner exemplified above.

8. Forms of literary satire like parody, mock epic, and travesty demand a context of common understanding in order to communicate their message. Parody makes amusing or ridiculous another writer's style by imitating its special

features to an exaggerated degree or by applying that style to some trivial or clearly inappropriate subject. In "For Whom the Gong Sounds" Cornelia Otis Skinner parodies Hemingway's style in *For Whom the Bell Tolls*. For example:

> The mouth of the cave was camouflaged by a curtain of saddleblankets, matadores' capes and the soles of old espadrilles. Inside it smelt of man-sweat, acrid and brown . . . horse-sweat sweet and magenta. There was a leathery smell of leather and the coppery smell of copper and borne in on the clear night air came the distant smell of skunk.

And when the old Spanish gypsy Pilar is introduced to Robert Jordan, the following dialogue occurs in Miss Skinner's parody:

> "This is the Inglés of the street car. He of the boardwalk to come soon."
> "I obscenity in the unprintable of the milk of all street cars."
> The woman was stirring the steaming mess with the horns of a Mura bull. She stared at Robert Jordan then smiled. "Obscenity, obscenity, obscenity," she said, not unkindly.

a. Consult a collection of parodies and select a brief example which you can share with the class. Be prepared to comment on the context required to appreciate the parody as parody. References:

Robert P. Falk, *American Literature in Parody* (New York, 1955).
Dwight MacDonald, *Parodies* (New York, 1960).
Joel Wells, *Grim Fairy Tales for Adults* (New York, 1967).

b. Mock epic applies the lofty style appropriate to great heroic enterprises to a trivial subject. The incongruity makes for comedy and lowers the importance of the subject and persons whom it seems to raise. The best example in English is Pope's *The Rape of the Lock*. Read this poem or Swift's *Battle of the Books* or Chaucer's *Nun's Priest's Tale* and be prepared to explain the context required to understand the mock epic quality of the work.

c. Travesty makes fun of a specific work by treating its subject in a low or crude manner, making, as Boileau said, Dido and Aeneas speak "like fishwives and ruffians." Amusing examples of travesty are recordings of Andy Griffith's *Romeo and Juliet* and Anna Russell's *Hamletto*. Find an example of travesty which you can share with the class and make clear the context required for its enjoyment.

The Classification
of Languages and Dialects

26.

GEORGE PHILIP KRAPP

The Classification of Languages

One of the important results of the modern study of language has been the classification of the various languages of the world into groups according to their relationships. Although the science of language has not been able to confirm the Scriptural story of the original creation of language, nor, as yet, even to arrive at any altogether satisfactory theory of the beginnings of speech, it nevertheless has done a great deal in discovering lines of evolution and development in those languages of which we have record. It has discovered that there has been a continual change and growth in language, that the languages of modern times are each of them a historic product which developed slowly and regularly out of preceding stages. Moreover, it has shown that many apparently dissimilar languages are really closely related and are the descendants of some single original stock. It has thus divided languages into families.

THE INDO-EUROPEAN FAMILY OF LANGUAGES

One of the largest and most carefully studied groups or families of languages is that known as the Indo-European or Indo-Germanic family. This group comprises certain of the languages of Asia and practically all the languages of Europe. The original unified Indo-European language from which they are all theoretically derived is no longer in existence. Its former

Reprinted from *Modern English: Its Growth and Present Use,* by George Philip Krapp.

382

existence is inferred, however, from the comparative study of the various Indo-European languages, since no theory serves so well to explain the many similarities which exist among them as the theory of a common origin. It should not be forgotten, however, that the theory of a common original language from which the various Indo-European languages were derived does not carry with it the theory of a common and single racial ancestry of all the Indo-European peoples. In the course of its development the primitive Indo-European speech undoubtedly imposed itself upon peoples of widely different race, very much as the branch languages, French or English, have done in later periods. We accept, therefore, a common speech ancestry for the Indo-European peoples, but not necessarily a common race ancestry. The period and the place in which this common original language was spoken are matters of very uncertain inference, and, indeed, are matters of comparatively slight importance. It concerns us much more to know the history, the changes and developments which have brought about the differentiation of the various languages of which we have specific knowledge. These languages have been carefully studied, so that now we are enabled to classify them according to their branches and subdivisions in an orderly fashion. The following is a list of the main members of the family, beginning with the languages farthest east in Asia and proceeding thence in order to the languages of western Europe:

1. Indo-Iranian. This branch is subdivided into (a) the Indian languages, including Sanskrit, the ancient literary language of India, and Prakrit and Pali, the modern native dialects of India; and (b) the Iranian languages, including Persian and Avestan in their various periods, besides several other languages of the tablelands of Central Asia.

2. Armenian, spoken in parts of Asia Minor.

3. Greek, which may be subdivided into the various Greek dialects, Ionic, Attic, Doric, etc.

4. Albanian, spoken in the limited region of Albania, north of Greece.

5. Italic. The main language of this branch is Latin, from which are derived the modern Romance languages, French, Spanish, Italian, Portuguese, and Provençal, and several other less known languages besides.

6. Celtic. This branch may be subdivided into Gallic, the language of the people of ancient Gaul, of which little is known; British, the language of the original inhabitants of Britain; Welsh, the language of Wales; and Gaelic, including the language of the Scotch Highlands, Irish, and Manx.

7. Teutonic or Germanic. This branch, the one we are particularly interested in, falls into three main subdivisions, as follows:

a. East Germanic, the main dialect of which is Gothic, known chiefly from fragments of a translation of the Bible, made in the fourth century by Ulfilas, the bishop of the West Goths.

b. North Germanic, including Icelandic, Norse, Swedish, and Danish.

c. West Germanic, including the following languages:

    i. English, in its various periods of Anglo-Saxon, or Old English, Middle English, and Modern English.

    ii. Frisian, in the two periods of Old and Modern Frisian.

    iii. Franconian, the chief modern representatives of which are the languages of Holland and Flanders.

    iv. Low German, the modern representative of which is Plattdeutsch.

    v. High German, in its three periods of Old High German, Middle High German, and New High German, the language of modern Germany.

    8. Balto-Slavonic. This branch falls into two main divisions (*a*) the Baltic languages, including Old Prussian, Lithuanian, and Lettic; and (*b*) the Slavonic languages, including Russian, Bulgarian, Illyrian, Bohemian, and Polish.

THE PRINCIPLES OF CLASSIFICATION OF LANGUAGES

The question arises, How do we know that these languages are related? What are the points of difference and resemblance which justify us in holding together the languages of the Indo-European family in a single group, and at the same time in dividing this group into the eight branches indicated above, with their further subdivisions? In answering the question, it should be noted, first, that the Indo-European family is constituted a group apart from the other languages of the world by certain features which all the languages of the family have in common, but which are unknown to languages outside the group. Thus, first of all, the languages of the Indo-European family are all inflectional in structure, that is, they indicate the relations which words bear to each other in the sentence by the use of case, gender, number, tense, voice, and other endings. This seems to those whose native speech is inflectional such a natural characteristic of language that it is often supposed that all languages make use of this device. Such is not the case, however, and there are certain languages, like the Chinese, which have no inflection at all, and others, like the Turkish, which have a kind of inflection that is so different from our kind of inflection that it has to be put into an entirely separate class from it.

In the second place, it has been found that the languages of the Indo-European family have a considerable number of words in common that are not found in other languages, and the number and the character of these words are so significant as to lead one almost necessarily to the inference that they are a common inheritance from a common original stock. The study of the languages of the Indo-European family from the point of view of their sounds and of their syntax confirms the results of the study of vocabulary and inflection, and makes unavoidable the conclusion that we have in them a group of closely and mutually related languages.

The method by which the division of the family into its branches has been obtained is similar to that which determined the classification of the family as a whole. It has been found that, although all the branches of the family have certain characteristics in common, which hold them together as a family, at the same time each branch has its own individual character-istics, due to the special development it has followed and the special influ-ences to which it has been subjected. It would carry us too far at present to attempt to show all the special characteristics of each branch, for example, how Greek differs from Latin and how Celtic differs from both; all we can do is to point out the main characteristics which distinguish the Teutonic or Germanic branch, the one in which our special interest lies.

THE TEUTONIC LANGUAGES

The main characteristics which the Teutonic languages have in common as features distinguishing them from the other Indo-European languages are four: (*a*) a regular shifting or change of consonants, known as Grimm's Law; (*b*) the Teutonic classification of the verb as strong and weak (or irregular and regular); (*c*) the twofold declension of the adjective as strong and weak; (*d*) the Teutonic system of word-accent. The last three of these characteristics need only a word of explanation, but the importance of Grimm's Law makes it deserving of a more extended discussion, and we shall therefore leave it to the last.

A comparison of the Modern English verb, which is representative of the Teutonic verb in general, with the Latin as representative of the original Indo-European verb, will show the distinguishing features of the Teutonic verbal system. The English verb consists of two classes, the weak, or regular verb, which forms its past tense by adding *d,* or *ed* (sometimes assimilated to *t*) to the present or infinitive stem, as for example, *walk, walked, walked;* and second, the strong, or irregular verb, which forms its tenses by an inter-nal change of the radical vowel of the word, as in the verb *sing, sang, sung.* The Latin verb, on the other hand, falls into a number of different classes, dependent to be sure on the formation of the principal parts, but in which can be found no such simple principle of tense formation as that which distinguishes the English verb.

The twofold declension of the adjective has been lost in Modern English, inasmuch as the declension of the adjective (except for comparison) has been lost altogether. In the Old English period of the language, how-ever, the full declension of the adjective was still maintained, as it is in New High German to this day. The simple principle of it is this—that when the adjective is preceded by a demonstrative pronoun or a definite article, it is declined in one way, called weak, and when not preceded by a demonstra-tive pronoun or a definite article, it is declined in another way, called strong.

Thus the phrase *These young boys* would take the weak form of the adjective in Old English, *þas geongan cnapan;* but the phrase *Young boys* would take the strong form, *Geonge cnapan*. Latin, like Modern English, would take the same form of the adjective in both phrases.

The Teutonic system of word-accent is sufficiently illustrated by Modern English usage. The rule there is that words of native origin usually take the stress on the root syllable, and this root syllable, except in the case of prepositional compounds, is almost always the first syllable of a word. Moreover, the accent of English words is *fixed,* that is, a noun has the same accent, no matter what its case may be, and a verb keeps the same accent through all its various inflections. Latin, on the contrary, which is again representative of the Indo-European accent, has what is called a *free* or *variable* accent, changing with the various forms of a word. Thus the nominative is stressed *imperátor,* but the accusative is *imperatórem*. The English derivative word, "emperor," has a fixed accent on the first syllable.

GRIMM'S LAW

This law is named Grimm's Law because it has become generally known through its formulation in the year 1822, by the German scholar, Jacob Grimm, who was not only the writer of the famous fairy tales, but was also a philologist of great industry and learning. It is called a law, but it is purely an empirical law. That is to say, by observation the discovery was made that a definite set of linguistic phenomena operated in a certain regular way, and the generalization drawn from this observation was formulated as the law, or rule, of the phenomena. This kind of law does not imply that the phenomena *must* act in a certain way, that there is a compelling law-giver or power back of the law which controls its action. It simply states what does happen, or what appears to our observation to happen. The ultimate explanation of the cause of the series of phenomena known as Grimm's Law is one that, so far, has escaped the scientific students of language. The facts as they are we accept because we observe them, but no satisfactory theory in explanation of these facts has yet been brought forward.

The phenomena which are the facts upon which Grimm's Law is based are certain regular changes in sounds. It was observed that where Indo-European words (as represented say by Greek or Latin) appeared with certain consonants, the same word in the Teutonic languages appeared with different consonants, always, however, according to a regular scheme of equivalents. Thus Indo-European *p* became regularly Germanic *f*, and *d* became regularly *t;* the relation of English *foot* to Greek ποδ-ος (pod-os) is therefore obvious. Other illustrations of the change of *p* to *f* are Latin *pater,* English *father;* Latin *pellis,* English *fell*. The change of Indo-European *d* to *t* is further illustrated by English *tooth*, Latin *dent-is;* English *ten* (Old English *tigon*), Latin *decem*. Another regular change, which has been illustrated by the word-pairs English *father*, Latin *pater*, and English *tooth*, Latin *dent-is*, is that of Indo-European *t* to Teutonic *th*. Further illustrations are Latin *tres*, English *three;* Latin *tenuis*, English *thin;* Latin *tu*, English *thou*. Another regular change is that from Indo-European *c* to Teutonic *h*, as in Latin *corn-us*, English *horn;* Latin *coll-is*, English *hill*. Illustrations of these changes might be increased indefinitely. Instead of adding others, however, it will suffice to make a general statement of all the consonants affected by the law and their correspondences. They may be grouped as follows:

The Indo-European labial consonants, *bh*, *b*, *p* became respectively the Teutonic consonants *b*, *p*, *f*.

The Indo-European dental consonants, *dh*, *d*, *t* became respectively the Teutonic consonants, *d*, *t*, *th*.

The Indo-European palatal and gutteral consonants *gh*, *g*, *ķ* (*c*), became respectively the Teutonic consonants *g*, *ķ*, *h*.

It should be understood, of course, that this is a very general statement of Grimm's Law, and that, as thus expressed, it is open to numerous exceptions and to the qualifications of some important sub-laws. Moreover, it should be remembered in tracing back English words to their cognates in the other Indo-European languages which are not subject to this shifting of consonants, as for example, Latin, that these other languages may also have had each its own peculiar development in its consonant system which may serve to obscure the simple operation of the law. It is also apparent that only those English words which are of native origin, that is, only that half of our bilingual language which is Teutonic and not late borrowed Romance, can be subject to Grimm's Law. Despite its various restrictions and qualifications, however, Grimm's Law is one of the most valuable linguistic principles which we possess. It enables us not only to group the Teutonic languages together, but also often to determine the history and etymology of the vocabularies of the various Teutonic languages, to tell what words are native and what are foreign. Moreover, the study of Grimm's Law has carried in its wake the discovery of many other linguistic laws and principles which are of the greatest interest and importance, but which cannot be entered into at present.

ENGLISH AND GERMAN

The exact relation between Modern English and Modern German should be clearly understood. Of course one is not derived from the other, as is so frequently the popular belief. The number of words in the German language which were directly borrowed from English is comparatively small, most of them having been taken over of recent years, and the same is true of the German words in the English language. The two languages are, however, of the same stock, and they resemble each other because they, like the other Teutonic languages, are derived from some common original Teutonic mother speech, which is no longer in existence and which has left no written records, but the existence of which we infer from the comparative study of the various Teutonic languages, just as we infer the former existence of a parent Indo-European speech for all the different Indo-European languages. German and English, therefore, have much in common because they inherit their language from a common ancestral speech. They differ, on the other hand, from each other, because throughout centuries of development each has followed its own course and has been subject to its own special influences. The most important special development of German, which differentiates it from English, is what is known as the second shifting of consonants. English and German alike are subject to Grimm's Law, or the first shifting of consonants, but the German consonants which resulted from the operation of Grimm's Law have undergone a further change, a shifting which is peculiar to that language, and which is one of the things which justify the linguist in setting off that language as a special subdivision of the Teutonic language. Thus where English has *p*, German usually has *f* or *pf* in cognate words, as in English *help*, German *helfen*; English *ship*, German *schiff*; English *sleep*, German *schlafen*; English *sheep*, German *schaf*; English *sap*, German *sapf*. Likewise where English has *d* German usually has *t*, as in the following pairs of words: *dead, tot* (formerly spelled *todt*); *deaf, taub*; *deal, theil* (the *h* being silent in pronunciation); *do, thun*; *cold, kalt*; *hold, halten*; and so with many others. English *t* frequently appears as German *z* or *tz*, as in *to, zu*; *tin, zinn*; *tooth, zahn*; *tongue, zunge*; *write, ritzen*; *cat, katz*; *sit, sitzen*. English *v* appears in cognate German words as *b*, as in *over, ober*; *leave*, (*er-*) *lauben*; *grave, grab*; *shove, schieben*; *love, liebe*; *knave, knabe*.

PERIODS OF ENGLISH

From the seventh century, the earliest period of which we have any knowledge of recorded forms of English, the language has been subject to constant change. In this it merely partakes of the nature of language in general, for speech, so long as it is living in actual unconstrained use, is continually growing and developing. It is only in the so-called "dead" languages that language can be drawn up into a system once and for all. From the earliest Indo-European times, therefore, down to the present day, it is safe to say that the language which we now know as English has been ceaselessly, though often imperceptibly, dropping old and assuming new forms. Since this process has been unbroken from the beginning, it is in a way illogical to divide the history of the language into periods. There have been, however, certain times at which changes took place more rapidly than at others, owing to special attendant circumstances, and provided we keep always in mind that the dates by which we divide a language into periods are more or less arbitrarily chosen, they will serve the convenient purpose of indicating roughly the large general divisions in the development of the language. In this way we may indicate three great divisions in the history of English:

I. The Old English, or Anglo-Saxon period, beginning with the coming of the Angles, Jutes, and Saxons to England and ending with the Norman Conquest in 1066, or better, about 1100.

II. The Middle English period, extending from 1100 to about 1500.

III. The Modern English period, extending from 1500 to the present time.

The language in each of these periods is distinguished by developments which are to a large extent characteristic of the respective periods. These developments affect all the various sides of the language—sounds, inflections, words, and syntax. . . .

Review Questions

1. That there once existed an Indo-European language is only an hypothesis. Why is it, however, a reasonable one?

2. What features do the languages belonging to the Indo-European family have in common?

3. What are the principal characteristics which Teutonic languages have in common?

4. What is Grimm's Law?

5. To what part of the English vocabulary does Grimm's Law pertain?

6. Why do Modern English and Modern German resemble each other? Why do they differ?

7. What are the three major periods in the historical development of English? What periods of time does each cover?

Exercises

1. One feature which distinguishes languages in the Indo-European system from those in other systems is that they are inflectional, that is, as Krapp explains,

"they indicate the relations which words bear to each other in the sentence by the use of case, gender, number, tense, voice, and other endings." Consult an elementary textbook of the languages indicated below and complete the table of pronouns.

ENGLISH	OLD ENGLISH	GERMAN	DUTCH	DANISH	SWEDISH
I	ic				
my, mine	mīn				
me	mē, mec				
thou	þu				
thy	þīn				
thee	þē, þec				
he	hē				
his	his				
him	hine				
she	hēo				
her	hiere				
her	hīe				
it	hit				
its	his				

2. Conjugate the verb *speak* or *drink* and consult an elementary textbook of German for the corresponding German verb and its conjugation. How are the conjugations similar?

3. The declension of *stān* (stone) in Old English is as follows:

	SINGULAR	PLURAL
Nom.	stān	stān-as
Gen.	stān-es	stān-a
Dat.	stān-e	stān-um
Acc.	stān	stān-as

What are the declensional endings for *stone* in Modern German?

4. Krapp notes that the considerable number of words which the languages of the Indo-European family have in common suggests that these languages have developed from a common language. Complete the table of cognate words below.

ENGLISH	OLD ENGLISH	DUTCH	GERMAN	DANISH	SWEDISH
mother	mōdor				
bread	brēad				
sleep	slǣp				
end	ende				
house	hūs				
twelve	twelf				

5. Complete the following table showing similarities in vocabulary between English and some other Indo-European languages:

ENGLISH	LATIN	GREEK	SANSKRIT
arm			irmas
cow			gaus
mother			matar
mouse			muš
star			star
three			travas

6. Complete the table below showing similarities in the ordinal numbers of Romance languages:

LATIN	FRENCH	SPANISH	ITALIAN
unum			
duo			
tres			
quattuor			
quinque			
sex			
septem			
octo			
novem			
decem			

7. From Miss Schlauch's discussion of the development of English (pages 223–249) we have seen that many words in the vocabulary of English have been borrowed from other languages (e.g., *fraternal* from Latin *fraternalis; candle* from Latin *candela*). It is important to distinguish, however, such borrowings, or loan words, from cognate words. Cognate words are words in different languages which have developed from a common origin. The appearance of *Buch* in German and *book* in English does not mean that one language borrowed the word from the other. Rather, the words are simply different forms of a word shared by the two languages. Consider the words listed below and indicate how Grimm's Law helps us to see that the Latin and English words in each of the pairs are cognates.

piscis—fish	*nepos*—nephew
tres—three	*gelu*—cold
mater—mother	*tenuis*—thin
canis—hound	*duo*—two
decem—ten	*ager*—acre

8. Krapp notes that certain German consonants underwent a shift which did not occur in English. This shift took place during the sixth through the eighth

centuries. As a result, the German consonants affected by this development differed from their English equivalents as indicated in the table below.

ENGLISH	GERMAN
p	f, pf
d	t
t	z, s, tz
v	b
th	d

Consider the following pairs of words and indicate how the recognition of this consonant shift enables us to see that the English and German words in each pair are cognates.

water—*Wasser*	deer—*Tier*
pipe—*Pfeife*	day—*Tag*
liver—*Leber*	pepper—*Pfeffer*
brother—*Bruder*	heath—*Heide*
ten—*zehn*	that—*das*

9. The following texts* are versions of the Lord's Prayer (Matthew 6:9–13) in various early Germanic languages. Study each carefully. Which seems the most similar to Modern English? Can you find similarities among these texts which would support the view that these languages are all related?

GOTHIC

Atta unsar þu in himinam, weihnai namo þein. Qimai þiudinassus þeins. Wairþai wilja þeins, swe in himina jah ana airþai. Hlaif unsarana þana sinteinan gif uns himma daga. Jah aflet uns þatei skulans sijaima, swaswe jah weis afletam þam skulam unsaraim. Jah ni briggais uns in fraistubnjai, ak lausei uns af þamma ubilin.

OLD NORSE

Faþer várr, sá þū ert ī(ā) hifne (himnum), helgesk nafn þitt. Til kome þitt rīke. Verþe þinn vile, suā ā iorþ sem ā hifne. Gef oss ī dag várt dagligt brauþ. Ok fyrerlāt oss ossar skulder, suā sem vēr fyrerlātom ossom skuldonautom. Ok inn leiþ oss eige ī freistne. Heldr frels þū oss af illo.

WEST SAXON

Fæder ūre þū þe eart on heofonum, sī þīn nama gehālgōd. Tōbecume þīn rīce. Geweorþe þīn willa on eorþan swā swā on heofonum. Ūrne gedæghwāmlīcan hlāf syle ūs tō dæg. And forgyf ūs ūre gyltas, swā swā wē forgyfaþ ūrum gyltendum. And ne gelæd þū ūs on costnunge, ac ālȳs ūs of yfele.

HELIAND

Fadar ūsa, thu bist an them himila rīkea. Geuuīhid sī thīn namo. Cuma thīn rīki. Uuertha thīn uuilleo, sō sama an ertho, sō an them himilo rīkea. Gef ūs dago gehuuilikes rād, endi ālāt ūs managoro mēnsculdio, al sō uuē ōthrum

---

* From *A Comparative Germanic Grammar* by Friedrich Prokosch. Reprinted by permission of the Linguistic Society of America.

mannum dōan. Ne lāt ūs farlēdean lētha uuihti, ac help ūs uuithar allun ubilon dādiun.

WEISSENBURGER KATECHISMUS

Fater unsēr, thu in himilon bist, giuuīhit sī namo thīn, quaeme rīchi thīn. Uuerdhe uuilleo thīn, sama sō in himile endi in erdhu. Broot unseraz emezzīgaz gib uns hiutu. Endi farlāz uns sculdhi unsero, sama sō uuir farlāzzēm scolōm unserēm. Endi ni gileidi unsih in costunga, auh arlōsi unsih fona ubile.

TATIAN

Fater unser, thū thār bist in himile, sī giheilagōt thīn namo, queme thīn rīhhi, sī thīn uuillo, sō her in himile ist, sō sī her in erdu. Unsar brōt tagalihhaz gib uns hiutu, inti furlāz uns unsara sculdi, sō uuir furlāzemēs unsarēn sculdīgōn, inti ni gileitēst unsih in costunga, ūzouh arlōsi unsih fon ubile.

SANKT GALLER PATERNOSTER

Fater unseer, thū pist in himile, uuīhi namun dīnan, qhueme rīhhi dīn, uuerde uuillo dīn, sō in himile, sōsa in erdu. Prooth unseer emezzihic kip uns hiutu, oblāz uns sculdi unseero, sō uuir oblāzēm uns sculdīkēm, enti ni unsih firleiti in khorunka, ūzzer lōsi unsih fona ubile.

FREISINGER PATERNOSTER

Fater unsēr, dū pist in himilum, kauuīhit sī namo dīn. Piqhueme rīhhi dīn. Uuesa dīn uuillo, sama sō in himile ist, sama in erdu. Pilipī unsraz emizzīgaz kip uns eogauuanna. Enti flāz uns unsro sculdi, sama sō uuir flāzzamēs unsrēm scolōm. Enti ni princ unsih in chorunka, ūzzan kaneri unsih fora allēm suntōn.

27.
JEAN MALMSTROM
ANNABEL ASHLEY

The Main
Dialect Areas of the U.S.A.

INTRODUCTION

The most important single contribution of Atlas research to our knowledge of present-day American English is Professor Hans Kurath's definition of the three major dialect areas of the eastern U. S. A. This definition was first published in his *A Word Geography of the Eastern United States* in 1949. This book was based on the atlases of New England, and the Middle and South Atlantic States.

By means of strong dialect boundaries—closely knit bundles of isoglosses—showing consistent pronunciations, vocabulary, and grammar, Kurath described the Northern, the Midland, and the Southern dialect areas. Later research for the other regional atlases has shown that these same dialect divisions can be traced across the continent to the Pacific Coast. The farther west we go, the more overlapping and mingling of dialects we find. However, with sufficient knowledge of the history of our country, its geography, and dialect field work, the areas can be interestingly charted.

In this essay, these three major dialect areas will be discussed. For each in turn, first its geographic extent will be stated, and then its typical dialect characteristics will be defined in terms of pronunciation, vocabulary, and grammar.

THE NORTHERN DIALECT AREA

On the Atlantic Seaboard, the Northern dialect area includes New England, the Hudson Valley, upstate New York, the northernmost strip of

Pennsylvania, and Greater New York City. Moving westward into the area covered by the Atlas of the North-Central States, we find the inland Northern area which includes Michigan, Wisconsin, the northern counties of Ohio, Indiana, Illinois, and Iowa. Still farther west, in the Upper Midwest Atlas area, the Northern dialect appears in Minnesota, North Dakota, the northern third of Iowa, and the northeastern half of South Dakota. In this area, there is some mingling of dialect forms so that the lines of separation between Northern and Midland are harder to draw. Apparently, in the Upper Midwest, the Northern dialect is contracting and the Midland is expanding. Farther west, in the Rocky Mountain States, only Colorado has been thoroughly studied. Here Denver and Gunnison are "islands" of Northern dialect. There is other evidence, too, of Northern forms in Colorado. However, overlapping of Northern and Midland dialects is the rule in this state. Utah generally shows a preference for Northern terms although the southern part of that state shows some Midland usage. Western Montana shows a Northern-Midland mixture. In the Pacific Northwest, Washington and northern and eastern Idaho are predominantly Northern in dialect. Preliminary editing of the California material shows that many words from Northern dialect areas in the East and Great Lakes region occur in California.

Typical Northern pronunciation items are:
Contrast between /o/ and /ɔ/ in the pairs:[1]
  mourning and *morning* I, II, III.
  hoarse and *horse* I, II, III.
  fourteen and *forty* I, II, III.
/ɨ/ in the unstressed syllable of *haunted* and *careless* I, II, III.
/ð/ regularly in *with* I, II, III.
/s/ in *grease* (verb) and *greasy* (adjective) I, II, III.
/bɨkəz/ *because* I, II, III.

Typical Northern vocabulary items are:
  pail (Midland and Southern *bucket*) I, II, III.
  clapboards 'finished siding' (Midland and Southern *weather-boards* and *weatherboarding*) I, II, III.
  brook 'small stream' I, II, III.
  cherry pit 'cherry seed' I, II, III.
  angleworm 'earthworm' I, II, III.
  johnnycake 'cornbread' I, II, III.

[1] The Roman numerals after each item state the type of informants who characteristically use the term:
  I. Old fashioned, rustic speakers of eighth-grade education
  II. Younger, more modern speakers of high-school education
  III. Cultured speakers of college education
When these Roman numerals are enclosed in brackets, less currency in that group is indicated.

eaves trough 'gutter on roof' I, II, [III].
spider 'frying pan' I, II.

Typical Northern grammar items are:
dove as past tense of *dive* I, II, III.
sick to the stomach I, II, [III].
he isn't to home 'he isn't at home' I, II.
hadn't ought 'oughtn't' I, II.
clim as past tense of *climb* I, II.
be as a finite verb (*How be you?* for 'How are you?') I.
scairt 'scared' I, II.

THE MIDLAND DIALECT AREA

On the Atlantic Seaboard, the Midland dialect area includes central and southern Pennsylvania, northern Delaware, and the areas of Pennsylvania settlement on the Delaware, Susquehanna, and upper Ohio Rivers. It extends south into the Shenandoah Valley, the southern Appalachians, and the upper Piedmont of North and South Carolina. Moving westward to the North-Central States area, we find North Midland forms (and Midland forms) in central Ohio, central and northern Indiana, and central Illinois. South Midland forms (and Midland forms) occur in Kentucky and the areas settled by Kentuckians in southern Ohio, southern Indiana, and southern Illinois. Furthermore, because of migrations north on the Mississippi River, South Midland forms are found also in the mining regions of northwestern Illinois, southwestern Wisconsin, and southern Iowa.

The Upper Midwest also shares in this expansion north of the Midland dialect. Midland forms are found in all the states of the Upper Midwest Atlas area and South Midland forms in all except North Dakota. Farther west, in Colorado, we find competition between the Midland and the Northern dialects. Probably, however, Midland is Colorado's basic usage. Upon this early and continuing base, apparently, certain Northern features have been superimposed. In the Pacific Northwest, Oregon and western and southern Idaho show a preference for Midland forms, though there is a great and confusing overlapping which has not yet been completely analyzed. In California, Midland terms are as frequent and as widely distributed as Northern forms are.

In Texas the vocabulary is predominantly Midland and Southern, with purely Southern terms in a minority. Apparently Texas pronunciation, as far as it has been studied, shows definitely South Midland characteristics in the northern and western parts of the state.

In the Inland South, Midland and South Midland vocabulary items seem to form a distribution pattern which vaguely resembles a T. The top of the T goes along the northern borders of Tennessee, Arkansas, and Oklahoma, and expands southward into these states and into northern Mississippi and northwestern Georgia. The stem of the T goes south through Alabama to the Gulf of Mexico, bounded by the Chattahoochie River on the east and the Tombigbee River on the west. On the other hand, certain features of pronunciation suggest that the basic Midland-Southern dialect boundary across Alabama may lie just north of Montgomery. Until field interviews are conducted and furnish more evidence on the dialect situation in the Inland South, these two types of evidence are both of great interest to the student of dialect geography.

Typical Midland pronunciation items are:
/r/ kept after vowels I, II, III.
/ɔ/ in *on;* /ɔh/ in *wash* and *wasp;* /ɔw/ in *hog, frog,* and *fog* I, II, III.
[ɛ] in *Mary* and *dairy* I, II, III.
/ə/ in the unstressed syllable of *haunted* and *careless* I, II, III.
/θ/ regularly in *with* I, II, III.
/r/ frequently intruding in *wash* and *Washington* I, II.

Typical Midland vocabulary items are:
a little piece 'a short distance' I, II, III.
blinds 'window shades' I, II, III.
skillet 'frying pan' I, II, III.
snake feeder 'dragon fly' I, II, [III].
poke 'paper sack' I, II, [III].
green beans 'string beans' I, II, III.
to hull beans 'to shell beans' I, II, [III].
spouts, spouting 'eaves troughs' I, II, [III].

Typical Midland grammar items are:
all the further 'as far as' I, II.
I'll wait on you 'I'll wait for you' I, II, [III].
I want off 'I want to get off' I, II, [III].
quarter till eleven I, II, III.

THE SOUTHERN DIALECT AREA

On the Atlantic Seaboard, the Southern dialect area includes Delmarvia (the Eastern Shore of Maryland and Virginia, and southern Delaware). It extends southward into the Virginia Piedmont, northeastern North Carolina, eastern South Carolina, Georgia, and Florida. Along the Gulf Coast, Southern forms appear in central and southern Mississippi and throughout Louisiana and Texas. In *The Regional Vocabulary of Texas,* Professor Atwood says, "I have no hesitation in classing virtually all of Texas and an indeterminate portion of the surrounding states as a major branch of General Southern, which I will label *Southwestern*." It contains Southern, Midland, and Southwestern words. In the North-Central States, only Kentucky shows Southern forms—especially western Kentucky—since that state has always been somewhat dependent culturally on Tidewater and Piedmont Virginia. Southern forms are relatively rare in California and practically absent in the Pacific Northwest as well as in other Northern dialect areas.

Typical Southern pronunciation items are:
/r/ lost except before vowels I, II, III.
/ey/ in *Mary* I, II, III.
/ɨ/ in unstressed syllables of *haunted* and *careless* I, II, III.
/ɨl/ in *towel* and *funnel;* /ɨn/ in *mountain* I, II, [III].
/z/ in *Mrs.* [I], II, III.

Typical Southern vocabulary items are:
low 'moo' I, II, III.
carry 'escort, take' I, II, [III].
snap beans, snaps 'string beans' I, II, III.
harp, mouth harp 'harmonica' I, II, III.
turn of wood 'armload of wood' I, II, [III].
fritters I, II, III.

Typical Southern grammar items are:
it wan't me I, II, [III].
he belongs to be careful I, II.
he fell outn the bed I.
all two, all both 'both' I, [II].
on account of 'because' I, [II].

SUMMARY

Although much more work has to be done to finish mapping the dialects of the United States, enough is now known so that we can make certain broad generalizations about our country's speech. The most important of these generalizations is that three different dialect bands extend from east to west across the U. S. A. These dialects are named Northern, Midland, and Southern. They are defined by means of differences in pronunciation, vocabulary, and grammar. On the Atlantic Seaboard, they reflect the patterns of original settlement. Farther inland, they reflect later migrations of people. The more recently settled the area, the less clearly defined are its patterns of dialect distribution.

These important conclusions wipe out earlier notions that something called "General American" speech exists. This supposed speech type is usually defined as extending from New Jersey on the Atlantic Coast through

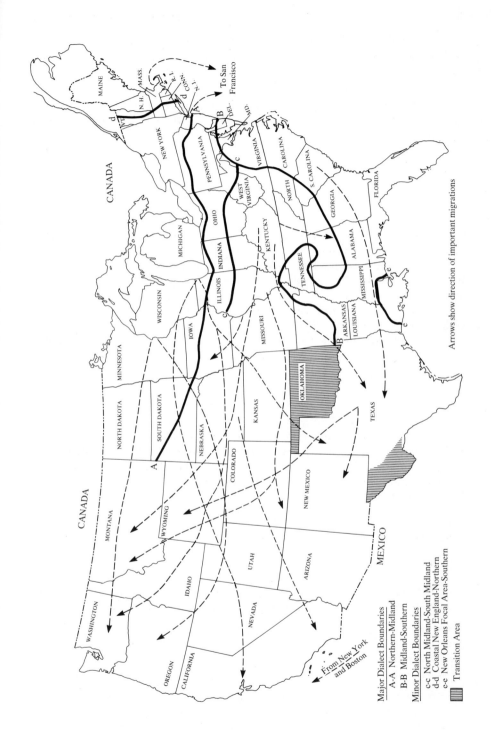

Arrows show direction of important migrations

Major Dialect Boundaries
A-A Northern-Midland
B-B Midland-Southern

Minor Dialect Boundaries
c-c North Midland-South Midland
d-d Coastal New England-Northern
e-e New Orleans Focal Area-Southern
▦ Transition Area

From New York and Boston

To San Francisco

CANADA

CANADA

MEXICO

MAINE
N. H.
MASS.
VT.
R. I.
CONN.
N. J.
NEW YORK
PENNSYLVANIA
DEL.
MD.
OHIO
WEST VIRGINIA
VIRGINIA
NORTH CAROLINA
S. CAROLINA
MICHIGAN
INDIANA
KENTUCKY
TENNESSEE
GEORGIA
FLORIDA
ALABAMA
WISCONSIN
ILLINOIS
MISSISSIPPI
IOWA
MISSOURI
ARKANSAS
LOUISIANA
MINNESOTA
NORTH DAKOTA
SOUTH DAKOTA
NEBRASKA
KANSAS
OKLAHOMA
TEXAS
COLORADO
NEW MEXICO
MONTANA
WYOMING
UTAH
ARIZONA
IDAHO
NEVADA
WASHINGTON
OREGON
CALIFORNIA

the Middle West and the entire Pacific Coast. Nor does a Midwestern dialect as such exist. Clearly, such descriptions of dialects in the U. S. A. are vastly oversimplified.

Another interesting fact revealed by the Atlas investigations is that dialect areas do not match up with state lines. Indeed, dialects show practically no respect for man-made boundaries. They are deeper and stronger than such divisions.

Review Questions

1. What important contributions has Professor Hans Kurath's *A Word Geography of the Eastern United States* made to the study of our language?

2. What are the geographical boundaries of the three major dialectal areas of the United States? What are the distinguishing dialectal characteristics of each area?

3. Why do we find increasing evidence of the overlapping and mingling of dialects as we trace their distribution westward?

4. Is there any significant relationship between state and dialect boundaries?

Exercises

1. The words and phrases listed below are in general use in the Eastern United States. Consult Hans Kurath's *A Word Geography of the Eastern United States* (Ann Arbor, 1949) and determine what regional variants exist for each of these expressions. Be prepared to tell the class the approximate geographic limits for each of the variants.

dragon fly	wheel the baby	string bean
doughnut	pancake	corn bread
creek	seesaw	kindling wood
baby carriage	hay stack	play hookey

2. According to Kurath's *Word Geography* in what areas are the following expressions most prevalent? What is the meaning of each?

snack	groomsman	chivaree
hooked jack	Christmas gift!	smearcase
breakfast meat	you'ns	lucky-bone
clabber	piazza	blinds

3. Consult *The Pronunciation of English in the Atlantic States* (Ann Arbor, 1961) by Hans Kurath and Raven I. McDavid, Jr., and prepare a brief summary of the various pronunciations of the following words in the Atlantic states.

barn	merry	marsh
worry	Mary	room
calf	marry	log
soot	tomato	drought
Tuesday	greasy	diphtheria

4. Read aloud each of the sentences printed below and record in IPA symbols your pronunciation of each of the italicized words. Ask two or three fellow-students, each from a different section of the country, to read the same sentences aloud. Again transcribe in IPA symbols the pronunciations you hear of each italicized word. Summarize the results of your investigation for the class.

a. I am going to visit my *aunt* in August.
b. He asked to *borrow* a book.
c. *Mary* stopped by to wish us a *Merry* Christmas.
d. We were *about* to leave when the bell sounded.
e. The *girl* in the blue dress is my sister.
f. We asked him *again* to submit his report.
g. The old Smith *house* was sold recently.
h. A *third* doctor was asked to give his opinion.
i. My *father* was unable to attend my *brother's* wedding.

5. What differences in vocabulary, pronunciation, and syntax have you noticed between your speech and that of a student on your campus who is a native of some area of the United States other than your own?

6. Following is a list of vocabulary items* which you may expect to vary in certain parts of the Northern, Midland, and Southern dialect areas. Make a survey of your class, fraternity, or dormitory by asking your friends to give a response to each item in column one with the synonym which first comes to mind. Record all answers and compare them with those synonyms cited in the checklist for the appropriate geographical area. Report your findings to the class. With students from which areas is the list most accurate? Least accurate?

ITEM	NORTHERN	MIDLAND	SOUTHERN
To put room in order		redd up ridd up	
Paper container	bag	sack	sack
[*Water outlet*] *on outside of house*	faucet	spigot spicket hydrant	spigot spicket hydrant
Container	pail	bucket	bucket
Metal utensil (frying pan *common everywhere*)	spider	skillet	skillet

* Materials for Exercises 6 and 7 are from *Discovering American Dialects*, by Roger W. Shuy. Reprinted with the permission of the National Council of Teachers of English and Roger W. Shuy.

ITEM	NORTHERN	MIDLAND	SOUTHERN
[*Water outlet*] *over a sink*	faucet	spigot spicket	spigot spicket
Boards (siding *common everywhere*)	clapboards	weatherboards	
Devices at roof	gutters (*ENE*) eaves spouts eavestroughs	gutters spouting spouts	gutters
Baby moves	creeps	crawls	crawls
Animal	skunk	skunk polecat woodspussy woodpussy	polecat
Animal (*note: for some people,* chipmunk *and* ground squirrel *are two different animals*)	chipmunk	ground squirrel	ground squirrel
Worm	angleworm	fish(ing) worm	fish(ing) worm
Insect	firefly (*urban*) lightning bug (*rural*)	lightning bug fire bug	lightning bug
Insect	(devil's) darning needle sewing bug dragon fly	snake feeder snake doctor dragon fly	snake feeder snake doctor dragon fly mosquito hawk
Cherry	pit stone	seed stone	seed stone
Peach	pit stone	seed stone	seed stone
Dish	dessert sauce fruit	dessert fruit	dessert fruit
Corn	corn-on-the-cob green corn sweet corn	corn-on-the-cob sweet corn roasting ears	roasting ears sweet corn
Tops		greens	greens salad salat
Cheese (cottage cheese *common everywhere*)	dutch cheese pot cheese	smear-case	clabber cheese curds

ITEM	NORTHERN	MIDLAND	SOUTHERN
Confection	doughnut fried cake	doughnut	doughnut
Bread	johnny cake corn bread	corn bread	corn bread corn pone
To carry	armful	armload	armload
Quarter ———	to of	till	till to
Become ill	get sick	take sick	take sick
With a cold	catch a cold	take a cold	take a cold
Sick ——— (at his stomach *common* *everywhere*)	to his stomach	on his stomach in his stomach	

7. Regional differences of grammatical choice are not as clearly marked as phonological or vocabulary differences. The following sentences have, however, proven helpful to field workers in determining the geographical distribution of different kinds of syntax. Ask several friends from different parts of the country to complete the sentences with one of the words or phrases suggested in parentheses. Record their answers and prepare a brief report on your conclusions.[1]

a. *Prepositions*

Trouble comes all ———— (to=N, at) once.
It's half ———— (past, after) six.
It's quarter ———— (of, to=N, till=M, before, until) four.
It's ———— (behind, hindside, in back of, back of) the door.
He isn't ———— (at home, to home, home).
It's coming right ———— (at, toward, towards) you.
Guess who I ran ———— (into, onto, up against, upon, up with, against, again, afoul of=NE, across).
They named the baby ———— (after, for, at, from) him.
I fell ———— (off, off of, offen, off from, from) the horse.
I wonder what he died ———— (of, with, from, for).
He's sick ———— (to=N, at=M,S of, on=M, in=M, with) his stomach.
He came over ———— (to, for to=SM,S for=S) tell me.
I want this ———— (instead, stead, in room, in place) of that.
We're waiting ———— (on=M, for) John.
The old man passed ———— (away, on, out, φ).
He did it ———— (on, a, for, φ) purpose.
I want ———— (off=M, to get off) the bus.
He was ———— (singing, a-singing) and ———— (laughing, a-laughing).
How big ———— (a, of a) house is it?

[1] Whenever φ appears, it signifies that nothing is added to the statement. N stands for Northern, M for Midland, S for Southern and NE for New England. For a map of these dialect areas see page 399.

b. *Matters of agreement*

Here _____ (is, are) your pencils.

The oats _____ (is=M, are=N) thrashed.

These cabbages _____ (is, are) for sale.

c. *Plural formations*

I have two _____ (pair=N, S, pairs=M) of shoes.

They had forty _____ (bushel=N, bushels=M) of apples.

He has two _____ (pound=S, pounds=M) of butter.

The fence has twenty _____ (posts, post, postis, poss).

He likes to play _____ (horseshoe, horseshoes).

Put your feet in the _____ (stirrup, stirrups).

Let's spray for _____ (moth, moths, mothis).

I bought two _____ (head, heads) of lettuce.

That's a long _____ (way=N, ways=M).

That's a short _____ (way=N, ways=M).

It's nine _____ (foot, feet) high.

We have three _____ (desks, desk, deskis, desses, dess).

d. *Pronouns*

It wasn't _____ (me, I).

This is _____ (yours, yourn).

This is _____ (theirs, theirn).

Are _____ (*pl.*) (you, youse, yuz, youns, you-all) coming over?

_____ (Those, them, them there) boys are all bad.

He's the man _____ (that, who, what, which, as, φ) owns the car.

He's the boy _____ (whose, that his, that the, his) father is rich.

"I'm not going!" "_____." (Me either, Me neither, Neither am I, Nor I either, Nor I neither)

It is _____ (I, me).

It is _____ (he, him).

He's going to do it _____ (himself, hisself).

Let them do it _____ (themselves, themself, theirselves, theirself).

I'll go with _____ (φ, you).

e. *Adjectives*

The oranges are all _____ (φ, gone).

Some berries are _____ (poison, poisonous).

f. *Adverbs*

You can find these almost _____ (anywhere, anywheres, anyplace).

This is _____ (as far as, as fur as, all the farther, all the further, the farthest, the furthest, the fartherest, the furtherest) I go.

g. *Conjunctions*

It seems _____ (as though, like, as if) we'll never win.

I won't go _____ (unless, without, lessen, thouten, douten, less, else) he does.

I like him _____ (because, cause, on account of, count, owing to) he's funny.

Do this _____ (while, whiles, whilst) I eat lunch.

This is not _____ (as, so) long as that one.

h. *Articles*

John is _____ (in, in the) university.
She is _____ (in, in the) hospital.
I have _____ (a, an) apple.
John has _____ (flu, the flu).
Do you have _____ (mumps, the mumps)?

i. *Verbs*

Past tense forms:

began, begun, begin   learned, learnt, larnt, larnd
blew, blowed   lay, laid
climbed, clim (*N*), clum (*M*)   rode, rid
came, come, comed   ran, run
could, might could (*SM, S*)   saw, seen (*M*), seed (*M*), see (*N*)
dived, dove (*N*)   sat, set
drank, drunk, drinked   spoiled, spoilt
did, done   swam, swim
drowned, drownded   threw, throwed
ate, et, eat   wore, weared
gave, give (*M*)   wrote, writ
grew, growed

Past participles:
tore up, torn up
wore out, worn out
rode (*M*), ridden
drank, drunk
bit, bitten

Negative:
hadn't ought (*N*), ought not, oughtn't, didn't ought

Writing Suggestions: Analysis

LINGUISTIC SUBJECTS

1. Unfamiliar Sounds for Americans in _____ (German, French, Spanish, or Another Foreign Language)
2. An Analysis of _____ (Anglic, Hunter's "Foenetik Sistem," or Another Alphabet and Spelling Reform)
3. _____ (George Bernard Shaw, Noah Webster) as a Spelling Reformer
4. The Initial Teaching Alphabet in Reading Instruction
5. Phonics as a Way of Teaching Reading
6. Our National Mania for "Correctness" in Spelling
7. Orm on Spelling
8. Pronunciation by Spelling
9. The Spelling Problems of the Freshman Class at My College

10. Leave Your Spelling Alone
11. Ways of Improving One's Spelling
12. The Runes
13. The Ogam Alphabet
14. The Elocution Teacher Battles Assimilation
15. The Heritage of the Reverend W. A. Spooner
16. Sound Changes in Noun (or Verb) Compounds
17. An Analysis of _____ (Esperanto, Ido, Volapük, Novial, Inter-lingua, Pikto, Basic English)
18. The Need for a World Language
19. The Language of Some Secret Society
20. The Grammar of Pidgin
21. _____ (Leibnitz, Bacon, Descartes) and a Universal Language
22. Translation Machines
23. Computers and the Study of a Language
24. Devising a Written Language for Emerging African Nations
25. It's Not What You Say, But the Way You Say It: Intonation and Meaning in English
26. The Relation of Intonation in English to Punctuation
27. When You Say That, You Better Smile
28. Intonation and Prosody
29. The Semantics of Verbal Identifiers
30. Kinesics and Psychiatry
31. Teenage Verbal Identifiers
32. Sacred and Profane Gestures
33. Gestures of Grief in Another Society
34. In Japan, Nod Your Head If You Mean *No*
35. The Gestures of _____ (Some National, Ethnic, Racial, or Social Group)
36. The Eloquence of Dance
37. What Modern Popular Dances are Saying
38. Male and Female Dialect Differences
39. Dialect and Social Status
40. Linguistic Regionalism in _____ (Joel Chandler Harris, James Russell Lowell, Mark Twain, William Faulkner, Damon Runyon)
41. The Dialects of *Huckleberry Finn*
42. Problems in the Study of American Dialects

Cause and Effect

WHEN ONE EVENT follows another and the two are closely related in time and space, we tend to regard the first as the cause of the second and the second as the effect of the first. We more firmly believe that the two events are causally related if they always occur together and are always absent together. By *cause* we usually mean, as the English philosopher John Locke (1632–1704) put it, "that which makes any other thing . . . begin to be"; and by *effect,* "that which has its beginning from some other thing." Noting, for example, that heat is always present when lead melts and that lead does not melt when heat is absent, or that moisture is always present when iron rusts and that the rust does not appear in the absence of moisture, we say that heat *causes* lead to melt and moisture *causes* iron to rust. Inasmuch as a cause is always followed by its effect, provided that the necessary conditions are present, we can often use our knowledge of causal relationships to bring about desired effects or to deter the occurrence of undesirable ones. In order to pour lead into a mold, we first apply heat to melt it; to prevent iron from rusting, we coat it with oil or paint.

This concept, which is so essential in imposing order upon our lives and environment, is utilized in expository writing to explain a wide range of subjects. Discussion of such varied topics as the reason for the poor performance of a football team, the influence of one writer on another, the impact of tax legislation on the national economy, or the effects of radioactive fallout on human life involves in each instance the familiar notion of cause and effect. Although the concept is familiar, it is not in essence a simple one, as the technical discussions by philosophers concerning its meaning and

409

validity well demonstrate.[1] Such discussions are too involved to consider here; we are concerned only with the common-sense idea of cause and effect. Yet some further comment about this idea and certain problems in its application in expository writing is necessary.

When we say that a thing, force, or event *causes* something else, that is, "makes any other thing . . . begin to be," we are in reality simplifying what is frequently a complex relationship. We usually single out as a *cause* one factor which is conspicuous among several, but in reality, these several together are often required to produce the effect. Even in carefully controlled laboratory experiments, causes and effects do not occur as isolated phenomena: they appear under conditions or circumstances, some of which may be purely incidental while others are absolutely essential to the occurrence of the effect. In lighting a match, for example, more is involved than the physical act of striking the match. For one thing, the match must be dry and there must be a surface against which to strike it which will provide the proper friction. In addition, some combustible material and oxygen to support its combustion are essential. Although our common sense would identify the *cause* of the flame with the act of striking the match, we can see from this example something of the real importance of the conditions required in order for this cause to produce its effect. Frequently, writers treating such complex subjects as the causes of a military victory or an economic depression will devote much of their attention to a discussion of the conditions which produced these effects.

A further complexity in the idea of cause and effect appears when we realize that what we identify as a cause will frequently depend upon the point of view or the kind of interest concerning the causal situation. In order to illustrate this point, let us assume that on leaving a friend's house one evening and turning a corner, we come upon two men in a violent argument. To our horror, one man takes a pistol from his pocket and kills the other. Notice the possible ways in which the cause of the man's death might be viewed. Police summoned to the scene will seek to apprehend the man who caused the other's death. In his report the coroner will indicate that the cause of death was the penetration of the victim's heart by a .38 caliber bullet fired at close range. A psychologist might find that a state of mental derangement caused the assailant to kill. The assailant's attorney might argue that the victim caused his own death by threatening his client, who was then forced to shoot in self-defense. All of these would seem to be legitimate and possibly valid approaches to a study of this cause-and-effect situation, which suggests that the cause of an effect may be defined in a number of ways. What is important to note is the degree to which our attitude toward the cause of an effect can be qualified by our particular interest.

---

[1] See, for example, L. S. Stebbing, *A Modern Introduction to Logic,* 2nd ed. (New York, 1933), Chapters XIII–XXI.

Precision in employing cause-and-effect analysis might, therefore, be said to require (1) that we take into account the significant circumstances in which the causal relationship occurs and (2) that we be conscious of our own interests in investigating and interpreting a particular causal situation. Keeping these two points in mind will help prevent gross oversimplifications and will remind us that complex causes may have many *effects* and that complex effects may frequently be viewed as the product of many *causes*.

SPECIAL PROBLEMS IN CAUSE AND EFFECT

Some of the problems involved in the use of causal thinking have been mentioned above; others requiring careful consideration follow.

1. A common error is mistaking a simple sequence of events for a causal relationship. Upon this error, known as the fallacy of *post hoc ergo propter hoc* ("after this therefore because of this"), are based many superstitions. Merely because sometime prior to a misfortune a black cat crossed our path does not entitle us to say that the encounter with the cat *caused* our misfortune. Similarly, an increase in national employment during the first year a particular administration is in office does not necessarily mean that that administration *caused* higher employment.

2. The fallacy of *post hoc ergo propter hoc* is a form of hasty generalization which may take other forms in causal analysis. In our eagerness to establish a causal relationship we may neglect to consider thoroughly all the possibly relevant factors. For example, discovering that potato salad was common to the diets of some picnickers who became ill from food poisoning, we might identify the salad as the cause of the illness, neglecting to take into account that each of the ailing picnickers had also eaten some innocuous-looking cream puffs. In our haste to reach a conclusion, we can also easily overlook instances in which the supposed cause did not produce its expected effect: in the preceding example, the picnickers who had eaten the same salad but who had *not* become ill.

3. In attempting to apply a conclusion about a causal relationship to various situations, it is important to consider what essential conditions may be missing or may be modified in any new situation. At one time in the history of the United States high tariff barriers may have contributed to the prosperity of certain industries without harming other domestic industries. International economic conditions may be such now, however, that high protective tariffs may not be imposed without damaging reprisals by other nations.

4. Finally, the explanation of a causal relationship requires more than mere assertion. A writer is expected to offer some support for his contention that a particular relationship is in fact a causal one. It would not be very

convincing for a writer simply to assert that a novelist's experiences as a sailor influenced his novels. The reader would rightly expect some proof for this contention: some rather thorough discussion, for example, indicating that the novelist's works reflect a knowledge of the sea and life aboard ship which he could have acquired only from practical experience; or the citation from the novelist's letters and diaries of passages which describe in detail certain of his shipmates who could clearly be identified with some of his fictional characters.

ORGANIZATION

It is difficult to generalize about the organization appropriate to an essay which is largely concerned with cause and effect, for the uses of this method of explanation and the kinds of emphases given it are subject to great variation. If the essay is primarily concerned with the operation of a single cause and effect, the cause of hail, for example, a time factor will be involved as the writer explains how the effect—hail—occurs. Thus, a chronological pattern would be employed. If the writer, however, is identifying causes—influences, forces, contributive factors—of some effect, or the effects—results, consequences—of some cause, the organizational problem will be similar to that of an essay of classification or division: several elements to be arranged in the most effective way possible.

EXAMPLES OF CAUSE AND EFFECT

The following passage from Alexis de Tocqueville's *Democracy in America* discusses the effect of democracy on the American language.

The principle of equality necessarily introduces several other changes into language. In aristocratic ages, when each nation tends to stand aloof from all others and likes to have distinct characteristics of its own, it often happens that several peoples which have a common origin become nevertheless estranged from each other, so that, without ceasing to understand the same language, they no longer all speak it in the same manner. In these ages each nation is divided into a certain number of classes, which see but little of each other, and do not intermingle. Each of these classes contracts, and invariably retains, habits of mind peculiar to itself, and adopts by choice certain words and certain terms, which afterwards pass from generation to generation, like their estates. The same idiom then comprises a language of the poor and a language of the rich—a language of the citizen and a language of the nobility—a learned language and a vulgar one. The deeper the divisions, and the more impassable the barriers of society become, the more must this be the case. I would lay a wager, that amongst the castes of India there are amazing variations of language, and that there is almost as much difference between the language of the pariah and that of the Brahmin as there is in their dress. When, on the contrary, men, being no longer restrained by ranks, meet on terms of constant intercourse—when castes are destroyed, and the classes of society are recruited and intermixed with each other, all the words of a language are mingled. Those which are unsuitable to the greater number perish; the remainder form a common store, whence everyone chooses pretty nearly at random. Almost all the different dialects which divided the idioms of European nations are manifestly declining; there is no *patois* in the New World, and it is disappearing every day from the old countries.

The influence of this revolution in social conditions is as much felt in style as it is in phraseology. Not only does everyone use the same words, but a habit springs up of using them without discrimination. The rules which style had set up are almost abolished: the line ceases to be drawn between expressions which seem by their very nature vulgar, and others which appear to be refined. Persons springing from different ranks of society carry the terms and expressions they are accustomed to use with them, into whatever circumstances they may pass; thus the origin of words is lost like the origin of individuals, and there is as much confusion in language as there is in society.

I am aware that in the classification of words there are rules which do not belong to one form of society any more than to another, but which are derived from the nature of things. Some expressions and phrases are vulgar, because the ideas they are meant to express are low in themselves; others are of a higher character, because the objects they are intended to designate are naturally elevated. No intermixture of ranks will ever efface these differences. But the principle of equality cannot fail to root out whatever is merely conventional and arbitrary in the forms of thought. Perhaps the necessary classification which I pointed out in the last sentence will always be less respected by a democratic people than by any other, because amongst such a people there are no men who are permanently disposed by education, culture, and leisure to study the natural laws of language, and who cause those laws to be respected by their own observance of them.

The following paragraph by Professor Albert C. Baugh* also provides a good illustration of cause and effect.

In the introduction and popularizing of new words journalism has been a factor of steadily increasing importance. The newspaper and the more popular type of magazine not only play a large part in spreading new locutions among the people but are themselves fertile producers of new words. The reporter necessarily writes under pressure and has not long to search for the right word. In the heat of the moment he is as likely as not to strike off a new expression or wrench the language to fit his idea (*pacifist, socialize*). In his effort to be interesting and racy he adopts an informal and colloquial style, and many of the colloquialisms current in popular speech find their way into writing first in the magazine and the newspaper. In this way we have come to *back* a horse or a candidate, to *boost* our community, *comb* the woods for a criminal, *hop* the Atlantic, *oust* a politician, and *spike* a rumor, and we speak of a *probe,* a *cleanup,* a business *deal,* a *go-between,* a political *slate.* Most of these expressions are still limited to the newspaper and colloquial speech and are properly classed as journalistic. The sports writer is often hard pressed to avoid monotony in his description of similar contests day after day, and in his desire to be picturesque seldom feels any scruple about introducing the latest slang in his particular field of interest. Many an expression originating in the sporting page has found its way into general use. We owe *crestfallen, fight shy,* and *show the white feather* to cockfighting, *neck and neck* and *out of the running* to the race track, and *sidestep, down and out, straight from the shoulder,* and many other expressions to boxing. In America we owe *caught napping* and *off one's base* to baseball. If some of these locutions are older than the newspaper, there can be no question but that today much similar slang is given currency through this medium. One of our popular news magazines makes the use of verbal novelties a feature of its style. In the pages of this weekly we no longer read of a 'captain of industry' but of a *tycoon.* So too we find *newshawk* for reporter, *jeerworthy, pulp magazine, nobelity* (winners of a Nobel prize), and many other examples of the search for novelty. We must recognize that in the nineteenth century a new force affecting language arose, and that among the many ways in which it affects the language not the least important are its tendency constantly to renew the vocabulary and its ability to bring about the adoption of new words.

Exercises

1. Find three or four superstitions which involve the fallacy of *post hoc ergo propter hoc.*

2. Consult newspapers for statements which reflect hasty generalization in assigning causes and effects. (Pronouncements by political figures and representatives in labor-management disputes frequently provide good examples.)

3. Work out with other members of your class the possible and likely consequences of some significant action in your college community (e.g., the institution of an honor system or of co-educational dormitories).

4. Find two or three examples from contemporary comment of failure to make allowances for changing conditions in assigning causes or predicting consequences.

5. Find some recent and significant event and work out with your classmates the *conditions* and *cause(s)* which brought it about. What distinction is there between a "condition" and a "cause"?

6. What causes, if any, can be inferred from the following effects:

a. More people commit suicide in June than in any other month.

b. Men have contributed more to the arts and sciences than women.

c. Winners of beauty pageants have a divorce rate 4.2 times higher than that of the rest of the American female population.

d. Since 1963 major crimes such as murder, rape, arson, burglary, and aggravated assault have been increasing in the United States at the rate of 6–9 percent annually.

e. The cost of living has been rising at the following rate:

1961—0.6 percent	1964—1.1 percent	1967—3.2 percent
1962—1.2 percent	1965—2.0 percent	1968—4.0 percent
1963—1.7 percent	1966—3.3 percent	(first half of year)

Writing Suggestions: Cause and Effect

1. Why I _____ (Smoke, Drink, Protest, Sit-In, Diet, Won't or Will Fight, Left or Joined the Church)

2. Why I _____ (Hate, Love, Admire, Follow) Some Prominent Figure

3. The Cause(s) of _____ (Juvenile Delinquency, Academic Failure, Racial Prejudice, Unemployment, Poverty, Divorce, Strikes, Misunderstandings between Parents and Children, Mental Retardation, Violence, the Decline in School Spirit, Faculty Indifference)

4. The Effect(s) of _____ (Smoking, Alcoholism, Narcotics, Pornography, Television Violence, Censorship, Military Service, Wire-tapping, an Assassination, Advertising, Bigotry, a Death in the Family, Third Parties in American Politics)

5. What Makes for Success in _____ (Motion Pictures, Investment, Real Estate Speculation, Politics, Medicine, Law, Lobbying, the Military, Business)

6. How _____ (Rackets, Illegal Betting, the Mafia, Shylocking, the Dope Market, Police Corruption) Operate(s)

7. Why Young People _____ (Rebel, Don't Trust Adults, Cop Out, Leave Home, Become Drug Addicts, Turn On or Off, Drop Out of College)

(Additional writing suggestions for linguistic subjects are on page 462.)

Influences on
the American Language

28.

FALK JOHNSON

How We Got Our Dialects

I

Despite a general uniformity of language in the United States, a newcomer in many regions can be spotted at once by the way he talks. He may say *car* if he is from the Midwest, *cah* if from New England, and *ca* if from the South—all of them variations on the pronunciation of the single letter *r*. Aside from his quirks in pronouncing individual letters, he may give himself away by peculiarities of elision, slurring, stress, intonation or rate of speech.

Then if he talks long enough, he is bound to come up with unfamiliar words. If he is a Georgian, it may be *bodacious* for "bold and audacious." If a Rhode Islander, he may speak of a see-saw as a *dandle*. Or if he is an Arizonan, he may refer to a prank as a *ranikaboo*.

These peculiarities of vocabulary and pronunciation raise several questions about our language. How did local differences get started? What effect are they now having upon our language? Will they decrease, making our language more uniform? Or will they increase, eventually developing several new languages and dividing America into linguistic compartments like those of Europe?

These questions have fascinated American linguists for a long time. As early as the eighteenth century some enthusiastic scholars started to gather data on regional variations in our speech. Until 1889 these men usually worked sporadically and alone. In that year they formed a cooperative orga-

From *American Mercury*, LXIV (January 1947), 66–70. Reprinted by permission of *American Mercury* and the author.

nization, the American Dialect Society, and later began a nationwide campaign for volunteers to help collect localisms.

In recent years, grants from philanthropic foundations have enabled our linguists to set out with paid and well-equipped staffs to explore the speech of the land scientifically. The most ambitious of these research programs is one which plans to map the geography of speech peculiarities in all North America. Begun in 1931 and still in process, this study is sponsored by the American Council of Learned Societies and several universities. It is at work on a mammoth *Linguistic Atlas of the United States and Canada,* and a series of supplementary studies based on a continental survey. Headed by Dr. Hans Kurath of Michigan University, the staff has already published the section of the *Atlas* for New England, and has completed survey of the Atlantic Seaboard and portions of the Great Lakes region.

Only professional philologists are sent into the field. Those who gathered material on New England and the South, for example, were trained scholars who had consulted with European linguistic geographers and made several trial surveys to perfect the special techniques required for this work.

In the field, these experts interview only a small percentage of the local residents, but the residents are selected as meticulously as those interviewed in the Gallup Poll. They are chosen to represent in the correct ratio such differences in location, age, education and ancestry as are likely to affect language. In order to encourage natural speech, the interviews are held in homes, fields, stores and offices; and the questions are so arranged that they seem to be merely key points in a series of friendly talks. These conversations are guided by a worksheet with 807 questions. The field worker may talk as long as twenty hours with an individual, and in addition prepare a phonograph recording of characteristic pronunciations.

After records and worksheets are sent in from the field, the editors of the *Atlas* subject each individual's pronunciation and vocabulary to a thorough laboratory analysis, breaking them down into their component parts. They try to detect the slightest variations in language from individual to individual, from age group to age group, and from district to district.

From such investigations, answers to the fundamental questions about our dialects have begun to emerge. For one thing, we have begun to learn how we got our local speech differences.

II

The origin of our dialects is partly illustrated by the story of *angledog,* a New England word for "earthworm."

Field workers for the *Atlas* found that not many New Englanders use the word; it is common in only a few communities, and it is used only by older people. An 81-year-old farmer told the field worker, *"Angledog* was the only term I heard until I was grown up." A housewife of 74 said, "We often call 'em *angledogs;* my mother always did." And a spinster somewhere between 70 and 80 declared, "My father always said *angledog.* I don't know why."

From this information it began to look as if *angledog* were a relic, a word that stuck in one locality after disappearing from the surrounding areas. And it seemed to be disappearing here, too. Only persons more than 70 years old reported it, and they recalled it chiefly as a holdover from childhood. Certainly the word had disappeared from or had never reached most New England communities. Interviewers for the *Atlas* went from the New York state line to the northern tip of Maine, but they found the usage of *angledog* concentrated in one small area—the lower valley of the Connecticut River. Only rarely did they find the word anywhere else.

Why? Why was *angledog* used chiefly in communities of one district? And why did it sometimes pop up in a few places widely separated from this district?

Members of the *Atlas* staff studied the histories of all the communities in which the word was found. They traced back the histories of the families in which it was used. And they discovered that wherever they found the word there had been at least a few settlers from Windsor, Connecticut, or nearby towns. It looked, therefore, as if *angledog* had come from Windsor. But why had the word previously been used only in the vicinity of Windsor?

Again the investigators went through town and family histories, and again they discovered a common origin for many of the settlers—the southwestern part of England, somewhere around Devonshire. The next step was to consult the *English Dialect Dictionary,* a huge work based on literally tons of reports gathered by volunteer collectors. It was found that *angledog* had been reported from only one region in England—Devonshire. It was obvious that the word had been brought to Windsor by colonists from Devonshire, that this Connecticut localism was without question an imported English localism.

The theory that many American dialects began as transplanted British dialects is not new. Scholars in the last century suggested it and gathered a good deal of evidence to support their suggestions. But only in recent years, as investigators have traced back to England innumerable words like *angledog,* has the theory become generally accepted.

But our language has received dialectal transfusions from other sources. From the Indians, for example, the Southerners got *pone,* meaning "cornbread." From European countries immigrants have brought hundreds of words which are now localisms. An instance of this is *smearcase,* a word meaning a soft cheese, which is found in several areas settled largely by Germanic people and is seldom understood elsewhere. *Smearcase,* incidentally, is a partly-anglicized word which shows how pronunciation may change when two dialects or languages are spoken in the same place. The German word is *Schmierkäse,* and a complete anglicization would be *smear-cheese* or *smear cheese.* Thus *smearcase* is about halfway between the original and anglicized forms.

Transplanting from British dialects and from native and European languages is only a part of the story of how we got our dialects. Many local words—like the Southerner's telescoping of "bold and audacious"—cannot be traced back to any other dialect or language. They are our own creations.

Take *slab,* for instance. It is used in some parts of the West and Midwest to designate a concrete highway, but in this sense it has not been reported in any other American or British dialect. It is local and original—a dialectal innovation. No doubt *slab,* which is short and picturesque, arose partly because "concrete highway" is a cumbersome and unimaginative expression—one lacking in bodacity. It came into use to fill a gap in our language.

So did *you-all.* It came into the language to supply a badly needed separate form for the plural of *you.* H. L. Mencken has pointed out that in the South "the true plural is commonly indicated by *you-all,* which despite a Northern belief to the contrary, is seldom used in the singular save by the most ignorant."

As a matter of fact, the uneducated Southerner's feeling for the plurality of the expression is so strong that he sometimes says *you-alls. The Dictionary of American English,* one of the major subsidized studies of our language, has extracted an example from a magazine published in 1869: "During the war we all heard enough of 'we-uns' and 'you-uns,' but 'you-alls' was to me something fresh."

This need for a plural form of *you* has led, not only to *you-all,* but also to such innovations as *youse guys, you folks,* and *you people;* and it has caused many languages, including French and German, to provide plural forms for *you.*

At the same time that innovations are coming into the language, relics are leaving it. This fluctuating gain and loss of words is a process going on constantly in every area. In some regions it tends to create new dialects; in others it tends to bring about greater uniformity of speech.

Why these opposite results?

The answer involves an understanding of differentiation and standardization. The two forces are always working against each other in the shaping of language, differentiation tending to tear it into smaller and smaller pieces while standardization unifies it.

III

Consider differentiation first. If natural barriers or inadequate transportation cut off a place from the outside, then transplanting is stopped, innovations cannot be spread, and words which disappear on the inside may not disappear on the outside. As a result, the speech in the two places becomes more and more diverse and finally divides into two languages.

A few thousand years ago differentiation divided the Indo-European language into Latin, Greek, German and more than a half-dozen other tongues. Then it divided Latin into Portuguese, Spanish, French, Italian and Rumanian; and it divided Old German into Icelandic, English, Norwegian, Swedish, Danish, Dutch and Modern German. After the Renaissance, printing lessened the linguistic isolation of many communities and limited the effectiveness with which differentiation worked.

Nevertheless, the force is not obsolete; it has divided modern British English into 42 dialects—3 in Ireland, 9 in Scotland, and 30 in England and Wales. And it has made some of these dialects so dissimilar that a Lincolnshire farmer has difficulty understanding a Lancashire miner.

As a sample of these multiplying localisms, look at what differentiation has done throughout New England to a common word, *earthworm*. It has made more than a score of words out of it, some of them unintelligible to an outsider:

dirtworm, mudworm, muckworm, groundworm, angleworm, angling worm, angler, angledog, fishworm, fishing worm, easworm, eastworm, easterworm, eelworm, rainworm, redworm, simplex worm, nightwalker, nightcrawler, nightprowler, crawler and bait.

This force of differentiation, which for thousands of years has been tearing languages into smaller and smaller pieces, has diminished recently, though it is not yet spent. Standardization, however, has become the dominant force in our language. It is the tendency which gradually makes the Southerner, after he has been in the North a while, feel self-conscious whenever he says *you-all*. Later it makes him avoid the expression.

Today, of course, the forces contributing to standardized speech are more powerful than ever before. Mass entertainment by radio and motion pictures, mass education, mass reading of national publications and mass traveling—all tend to build up uniform speaking habits. As a result, some of our many minor dialects—like that of the Gullah Negroes living on islands off the coast of South Carolina—have started to disappear, and our major dialects are few. For example, Dr. Kurath in his *A Word Geography of the Eastern States,* shows only three major speech regions along the Coast —the New England, Middle Atlantic and South Atlantic. Preliminary studies indicate that the Middle West and West are even more uniform.

Now it is possible for a person to go anywhere in the United States and be understood immediately—though he may evoke a few smiles now and then. Sometimes it is possible for a person to be a thousand miles from home and still not be recognized as an outsider.

The forces for standardization are so strong that only a cataclysm of the first magnitude—something like an atomic war, pulverizing our mass society and making men live in small detached groups—can halt this trend toward uniformity.

Vocabulary

elision, sporadically, philanthropic, meticulous, relic, anglicize, subsidize, cataclysm

Review Questions

1. In the third paragraph of his essay, Johnson poses four questions raised by "peculiarities of vocabulary and pronunciation." How and where in the essay does he answer each of these questions?
2. What relevance to his essay does Johnson's discussion of the work of Hans Kurath and his staff have?
3. What is meant by "differentiation and standardization" as forces shaping our language?
4. What word does Johnson use to illustrate the force of differentiation?
5. What influences does Johnson note as contributing to standardization?

Expository Technique

1. By the use of Roman numerals the author indicates that his essay is divided into three parts. How is each a unit in the essay? Is there any reason for arranging these units in their present order?
2. How does the series of questions posed in the third paragraph relate to the organization of the essay?

29.

ALBERT C. BAUGH

Noah Webster and
the American Language

The Declaration of Independence and the years during which the colonies were fighting to establish their freedom from England produced an important change in American psychology. Accustomed for generations to dependence upon the mother country, the people settled in America imported most of their books and many of their ideas from Europe. It was a natural and entirely just recognition of the superior civilization of the Old World and the greatness of English literature and learning. But with political independence achieved, many of the colonists began to manifest a distaste for anything that seemed to perpetuate the former dependence. An ardent, sometimes belligerent patriotism sprang up, and among many people it became the order of the day to demand an American civilization as distinctive from that of Europe as were the political and social ideals which were being established in the new world.

No one expressed this attitude more vigorously than Noah Webster (1758–1843). Born on the outskirts of Hartford, Conn., he received at Yale such an education as universities in the country then offered, and later undertook the practice of law. But business in the legal profession was slow, and he was forced for a livelihood to turn to teaching. The change determined his whole subsequent career. The available English schoolbooks were unsatisfactory, and the war diminished the supply of such as there were. Webster accordingly set about compiling three elementary books on English, a spelling book, a grammar, and a reader. These he published in 1783, 1784, and 1785 under the high-sounding title *A Grammatical Institute of the English Language*. They were the first books of their kind to be published in this country. The success of the first part was unexpectedly great. It was soon reissued under the title *The American Spelling Book,* and in this form went through edition after edition. It is estimated that in a hundred years

From A HISTORY OF THE ENGLISH LANGUAGE, Second Edition, by Albert C. Baugh. Copyright © 1957 by Appleton-Century-Crofts, Inc. Reprinted by permission of the publishers.

more than 80,000,000 copies of the book were sold. From a profit of less than
a cent a copy Webster derived most of his income throughout his life. The
influence of the little book was enormous and will be discussed below. Here
it is sufficient to note that it had the effect of turning its author's attention
to questions of language and enabled him to devote himself to a number of
projects of a linguistic kind. In 1789 he published a volume of *Dissertations
on the English Language, with Notes Historical and Critical*. In 1806 he
brought out a small *Dictionary*, the prelude to his greatest work. This was
An American Dictionary of the English Language, published in 1828 in
two quarto volumes. In all of these works and in numerous smaller writings
he was animated by a persistent purpose: to show that the English language
in this country was a distinctly American thing, developing along its own
lines, and deserving to be considered from an independent, American point
of view.

In the preface to the first part of the *Grammatical Institute* he says:
"The author wishes to promote the honour and prosperity of the confed-
erated republics of America; and cheerfully throws his mite into the common treasure of patriotic exertions. This country must in some future time,
be as distinguished by the superiority of her literary improvements, as she is
already by the liberality of her civil and ecclesiastical constitutions. Europe is
grown old in folly, corruption and tyranny . . . For America in her infancy
to adopt the present maxims of the old world, would be to stamp the wrinkles
of decrepit age upon the bloom of youth and to plant the seeds of decay in
a vigorous constitution." Six years later, in his *Dissertations on the English
Language,* he went much further. "As an independent nation," he says, "our
honor requires us to have a system of our own, in language as well as government. Great Britain, whose children we are, should no longer be *our* standard; for the taste of her writers is already corrupted, and her language on
the decline. But if it were not so, she is at too great a distance to be our
model, and to instruct us in the principles of our own tongue." But independence of England was not the only factor that colored men's thinking
in the new nation. A capital problem in 1789 was that of welding the thirteen
colonies into a unified nation, and this is also reflected in Webster's ideas. In
urging certain reforms of spelling in the United States he argues that one of
the advantages would be that it would make a difference between the English
orthography and the American, and "that such an event is an object of vast
political consequence." A "national language," he says, "is a band of national
union. Every engine should be employed to render the people of this country
national; to call their attachments home to their own country; and to inspire
them with the pride of national character." Culturally they are still too dependent upon England. "However they may boast of Independence, and the
freedom of their government, yet their *opinions* are not sufficiently independent; an astonishing respect for the arts and literature of their parent

country, and a blind imitation of its manners, are still prevalent among the Americans." It is an idea that he often returns to. In his *Letter to Pickering* (1817) he says, "There is nothing which, in my opinion, so debases the genius and character of my countrymen, as the implicit confidence they place in English authors, and their unhesitating submission to their *opinions,* their *derision,* and their *frowns.* But I trust the time will come, when the English will be convinced that the intellectual faculties of their descendants have not degenerated in America; and that we can contend with them in *letters,* with as much success, as upon the *ocean."* This was written after the War of 1812. So far as the language is concerned, he has no doubt of its ultimate differentiation. He is sure that "numerous local causes, such as a new country, new associations of people, new combinations of ideas in arts and science, and some intercourse with tribes wholly unknown in Europe, will introduce new words into the American tongue. These causes will produce, in a course of time, a language in North America, as different from the future language of England, as the Modern Dutch, Danish, and Swedish are from the German, or from one another."

The culmination of his efforts to promote the idea of an American language was the publication of his *American Dictionary* in 1828. Residence for a year in England had somewhat tempered his opinion, but it is still fundamentally the same. In the preface to that work he gave final expression to his conviction: "It is not only important, but, in a degree necessary, that the people of this country, should have an *American Dictionary* of the English Language; for, although the body of the language is the same as in England, and it is desirable to perpetuate that sameness, yet some differences must exist. Language is the expression of ideas; and if the people of our country cannot preserve an identity of ideas, they cannot retain an identity of language. Now an identity of ideas depends materially upon a sameness of things or objects with which the people of the two countries are conversant. But in no two portions of the earth, remote from each other, can such identity be found. Even physical objects must be different. But the principal differences between the people of this country and of all others, arise from different forms of government, different laws, institutions and customs . . . the institutions in this country which are new and peculiar, give rise to new terms, unknown to the people of England . . . No person in this country will be satisfied with the English definitions of the words *congress, senate* and *assembly, court,* &c. for although these are words used in England, yet they are applied in this country to express ideas which they do not express in that country." It is not possible to dismiss this statement as an advertisement calculated to promote the sale of his book in competition with the English dictionaries of Johnson and others. He had held such a view long before the idea of a dictionary had taken shape in his mind. Webster was a patriot who carried his sentiment from questions of political and social organization over into matters of language. By stressing American usage and American pronunciation, by adopting a number of distinctive spellings, and especially by introducing quotations from American authors alongside of those from English literature, he contrived in large measure to justify the title of his work. If, after a hundred years, some are inclined to doubt the existence of anything so distinctive as an American language, his efforts, nevertheless, have left a permanent mark on the language of this country.

HIS INFLUENCE ON AMERICAN SPELLING

It is a matter of common observation that American spelling often differs in small ways from that customary in England.[1] We write *honor, color,* and a score of words without the *u* of English *honour, colour,* etc. We sometimes employ one consonant where the English write two: *traveler—traveller, wagon—waggon,* etc. We write *er* instead of *re* in a number of words like *fiber, center, theater.* We prefer an *s* in words like *defense, offense,* and write *ax, plow, tire, story, czar, jail, medieval,* etc., for *axe, plough, tyre, storey, tsar, gaol,* and *mediaeval.* The differences often pass unnoticed, partly because a number of English spellings are still current in America, partly because some of the American innovations are now common in England, and in general because certain alternatives are permissible in both countries. Although some of the differences have grown up since Webster's day, the majority of the distinctively American spellings are due to his advocacy of them and the incorporation of them in his dictionary.

Spelling reform was one of the innumerable things that Franklin took an interest in. In 1768 he devised *A Scheme for a New Alphabet and a Reformed Mode of Spelling* and went so far as to have a special font of type cut for the purpose of putting it into effect. Years later he tried to interest Webster in his plan, but without success. According to the latter, "Dr. Franklin never pretended to be a man of erudition—he was self-educated; and he wished to reform the orthography of our language, by introducing new characters. He invited me to Philadelphia to aid in the work; but I differed from him in opinion. I think the introduction of new characters neither practicable, necessary nor expedient."[2] Indeed, Webster was not in the beginning sympathetic to spelling reform. At the time he brought out

[1] For an excellent discussion of English and American spellings see H. L. Mencken, *The American Language,* Chap. VIII.

[2] *Letter to Pickering* (1817), p. 32. Franklin's letter to Webster on the subject was written June 18, 1786, and indicates that Webster had already devised an alphabet of his own (*Writings of Benjamin Franklin,* ed. A. H. Smyth, IX, 518, 527; for Franklin's *Scheme,* V, 169–78).

the first part of his *Grammatical Institute* (1783) he wrote: "There seems to be an inclination in some writers to alter the spelling of words, by expunging the superfluous letters. This appears to arise from the same pedantic fondness for singularity that prompts new fashions of pronunciation. Thus they write the words *favour, honour,* &c. without *u* . . . Thus *e* is omitted in *judgment;* which is the most necessary letter in the word . . . Into these and many other absurdities are people led by a rage for singularity . . . We may better labour to speak our language with propriety and elegance, as we have it, than to attempt a reformation without advantage or probability of success." But by 1789 Franklin's influence had begun to have its effect. In the *Dissertations on the English Language,* published in that year, Webster admitted: "I once believed that a reformation of our orthography would be unnecessary and impracticable. This opinion was hasty; being the result of a slight examination of the subject. I now believe with Dr. Franklin that such a reformation is practicable and highly necessary." As an appendix to that volume he published *An Essay on the Necessity, Advantages and Practicability of the Mode of Spelling, and of Rendering the Orthography of Words Correspondent to the Pronunciation.* In this he urged the omission of all superfluous or silent letters, such as the *a* in *bread* and the *e* in *give,* the substitution of *ee* for the vowels in *mean, speak, grieve, key,* etc., the use of *ƙ* for *ch* in such words as had a *ƙ*-sound (*character, chorus*), and a few other "inconsiderable alterations." The next year he exemplified his reform in *A Collection of Essays and Fugitive Writings,* from which a few sentences in the preface may be quoted by way of illustration:

> In the essays, ritten within the last yeer, a considerable change of spelling iz introduced by way of experiment. This liberty waz taken by the writers before the age of queen Elizabeth, and to this we are indeted for the preference of modern spelling over that of Gower and Chaucer. The man who admits that the change of *housbonde, mynde, ygone, moneth* into *husband, mind, gone, month,* iz an improovment, must acknowlege also the riting of *helth, breth, rong, tung, munth,* to be an improovment. There iz no alternativ. Every possible reezon that could ever be offered for altering the spelling of wurds, stil exists in full force; and if a gradual reform should not be made in our language, it wil proov that we are less under the influence of reezon than our ancestors.

This is neither consistent nor adequate. The changes here proposed met with so much opposition that he abandoned most of them in favor of a more moderate proposal.

By 1806 when he published his first small dictionary[3] he had come to

---

[3] *A Compendious Dictionary of the English Language. In which Five Thousand Words are added to the number found in the best English compends. The Orthography is, in some instances, corrected,* etc. By Noah Webster (Hartford, 1806).

hold that "it would be useless to attempt any change, even if practicable, in those anomalies which form whole classes of words, and in which, change would rather perplex than ease the learner." The most important modifications which he introduces are that he prints *music, physic, logic,* etc., without a final *k; scepter, theater, meter,* and the like with *er* instead of *re; honor, favor,* etc., without the *u; check, mask, risk,* etc., for *cheque, masque, risque; defense, pretense, recompense,* and similar words with an *s;* and *determin, examin, doctrin, medicin,* etc., without a final *e.* In all except the last of these innovations he has been followed generally in American usage. He was not always consistent. He spelled *traffick, almanack, frolick,* and *havock* with a final *k* where his own rule and modern practice call for its omission. But on the whole the principles here adopted were carried over, with some modifications and additions,[4] into his *American Dictionary* of 1828 and from this they have come into our present use.[5]

It has been thought well to trace in some detail the evolution of Webster's ideas on the subject of spelling, since it is to him that we owe the most characteristic differences between English and American practice today. Some of his innovations have been adopted in England, and it may be said in general that his later views were on the whole moderate and sensible.

HIS INFLUENCE ON AMERICAN PRONUNCIATION

Though the influence is more difficult to prove, there can be no doubt that to Webster are to be attributed some of the characteristics of American pronunciation, especially its uniformity and the disposition to give fuller value to the unaccented syllables of words. Certainly he was interested in the improvement of American pronunciation and intended that his books should serve that purpose. In the first part of his *Grammatical Institute,* which became the *American Spelling Book,* he says that the system "is designed to introduce uniformity and accuracy of pronunciation into com-

---

[4] E.g., he restored the *e* in *determine, examine,* stated the rule for not doubling the consonant in words like *traveler, traveling,* etc.

[5] "Webster inculcated his views on orthography and pronunciation upon all occasions. He wrote, he lectured, he pressed home his doctrines upon persons and assemblies. . . . The present printer [1881] of 'Webster's Dictionary' remembers that when he was a boy of thirteen, working at the case in Burlington, Vermont, a little pale-faced man came into the office and handed him a printed slip, saying, 'My lad, when you use these words, please oblige me by spelling them as here: *theater, center,* etc.' It was Noah Webster traveling about among the printing-offices, and persuading people to spell as he did: a better illustration could not be found of the reformer's sagacity, and his patient method of effecting his purpose." (Horace E. Scudder, *Noah Webster* [Boston, 1882], pp. 213–214.)

mon schools." That it was not without effect can, in one case at least, be shown. In the preface to that work he says, *"Angel, ancient,* the English pronounce *anegel, anecient,* contrary to every good principle." Now James Fenimore Cooper, in his *Notions of the Americans,* tells how as a boy he was sent off to a school in Connecticut, and when he came home for a vacation he was pronouncing the first syllable of *angel* like the article *an,* and *beard* as *berd* or *baird* (another Websterian pronunciation). He was only laughed out of the absurdity by the rest of his family. But he adds: "I think . . . a great deal of the peculiarity of New England pronunciation is to be ascribed to the intelligence of its inhabitants. This may appear a paradox; but it can easily be explained. They all read and write; but the New Englandman, at home, is a man of exceedingly domestic habits. He has a theoretical knowledge of the language, without its practice. . . . It is vain to tell a man who has his book before him, that *cham* spells *chame,* as in *chamber,* or *an, ane* as in *angel;* or *dan, dane,* as in *danger.* He replies by asking what sound is produced by *an, dan,* and *cham.* I believe it would be found, on pursuing the inquiry, that a great number of their peculiar sounds are introduced through their spelling books, and yet there are some, certainly, that cannot be thus explained."[6]

In this case the effect was fortunately temporary. But the use to which the Webster *Spelling Book* was put in thousands of schools renders it very likely that some of its other effects were more lasting. In the reminiscences of his early life, Joseph T. Buckingham, a newspaper publisher of some prominence in New England, gives an interesting account of the village school at the close of the eighteenth century:

It was the custom for all such pupils [those who were sufficiently advanced to pronounce distinctly words of more than one syllable] to stand together as one class, and with *one voice* to read a column or two of the tables for spelling. The master gave the signal to begin, and all united to read, letter by letter, pronouncing each syllable by itself, and adding to it the preceding one till the word was complete. Thus a-d *ad,* m-i *mi, admi,* r-a *ra, admira,* t-i-o-n *shun, admiration.* This mode of reading was exceedingly useful; as it required and taught deliberate and distinct articulation. . . . When the lesson had been thus read, the books were closed, and the words given out for spelling. If one was misspelt, it passed on to the next, and the next pupil in order, and so on till it was spelt correctly. Then the pupil who had spelt correctly went up in the class *above* the one who had misspelt. . . . Another of our customs was to choose sides to spell once or twice a week. . . . [The losing side] had to sweep the room and build the fires the next morning. These customs, prevalent sixty and seventy years ago, excited emulation, and emulation produced improvement.[7]

[6] Cooper, *Notions of the Americans* (London, 1828), II, 172–74.

[7] Letter to Henry Barnard, December 10, 1860, printed in Barnard's *American Journal of Education,* XIII (1863), 129–32.

No. 107.—CVII.

WORDS OF FOUR SYLLABLES, ACCENTED ON THE THIRD.

pub li ca′ tion	lit i gā tion	dis til lā tion
rep li ea tion	mit i gā tion	per eo lā tion
im pli ea tion	in sti gā tion	vī o lā tion
eom pli ea tion	nav i gā tion	im mo lā tion
ap pli ea tion	pro mul gā tion	des o lā tion
sup pli ea tion	pro lon gā tion	eon so lā tion
ex pli ea tion	ab ro gā tion	eon tem plā tion
rep ro bā tion	sub ju gā tion	leġ is lā tion
ap pro bā tion	fas çi nā tion	trib ū lā tion
per tur bā tion	me di ā tion	pee ū lā tion
in eu bā tion	pal li ā tion	spee ū lā tion
ab di ea tion	ex pi ā tion	eal eu lā tion
ded i ea tion	va ri ā tion	cīr eu lā tion
med i tā tion	de vi ā tion	mod ū lā tion
in di ea tion	ex ha lā tion	reg ū lā tion
vin di ea tion	eon ġe lā tion	gran ū lā tion
del e gā tion	mu ti lā tion	stip ū lā tion
ob li gā tion	in stạl lā tion	pop ù lā tion
al le gā tion	ap pel lā tion	grat ū lā tion
ir ri gā tion	eon stel lā tion	re tar dā tion

Legislation is the enacting of laws, and a legislator is one who
makes laws.

God is the divine legislator. He proclaimed his ten commandments from mount Sinai.

In free governments the people choose their legislators.

We have legislators for each State, who make laws for the
State where they live. The town in which they meet to
legislate, is called the seat of government. These legislators, when they are assembled to make laws, are called the
legislature.

The people should choose their best and wisest men for their
legislators.

It is the duty of every good man to inspect the moral conduct

A page from *The Elementary Spelling-Book*
of Noah Webster

Webster quotes Sheridan* with approval to the effect that "A good articulation consists in giving every letter in a syllable its due proportion of sound, according to the most approved custom of pronouncing it; and in making such a distinction, between syllables, of which words are composed, that the ear shall without difficulty acknowledge their number." And he adds the specific injunction, "Let words be divided as they ought to be pronounced *clus-ter, hab-it, nos-tril, bish-op,* and the smallest child cannot mistake a just pronunciation." In the light of such precept and evidence of its practice, and considering the popularity of spelling bees among those of a former generation, it seems certain that not a little influence on American pronunciation is to be traced to the old blue-backed spelling book.

Vocabulary

ardent, belligerent, conversant, advocacy, erudition, expedient, expunging, superfluous, anomalies, emulation

Review Questions

1. What important change in American psychology did the Declaration of Independence and the struggle of the colonies against England produce?
2. What was nationalistic in Webster's thought about the language of America?
3. Baugh states that Webster's efforts "left a permanent mark on the language of this country." How does he support this view?

Exercise

Linguistic nationalism can generate such intensity of feelings that riots and disturbances are among its results. See what you can find out about the difficulties generated by language loyalties in the recent history of one of the following: Wales, Ireland, India, Belgium, Canada, Ceylon, Israel. You might consult, in this regard, Jacob Ornstein and W. W. Gage, *The ABC's of Language and Linguistics* (New York, 1964).

* [Thomas Sheridan (1719–1788), a rhetorician and the father of the dramatist. —*Eds.*]

30.

THOMAS PYLES

The Influence of
the Frontier on American English

For some years after the Revolution, there was no national literature worthy
of the name, and in language British fashion continued to hold sway. A
genuinely indigenous American spirit was not to make itself manifest until
well into the nineteenth century—not, in fact, until the reverberations of
the amazing westward thrust began to be heard in the land. This new spirit,
completely uncolonial, self-confident, daring, pushing, uncouth, obsessed
with the notions of greatness and strength, was quite unlike anything that
had been known before. Its incarnation was a new folk hero, Andrew Jackson, compared to whom such men as Washington, Adams, and Jefferson
must have seemed as moonlight unto sunlight and as water unto wine. He
was the pioneer *par excellence,* the Bayard of the backwoods, the rough
diamond, the epitome of the noble, free soul. For a new America had indeed
come into being beyond the Alleghenies, an America of wilderness, mountains, rivers, plains, and mining camps—an America whose voice was strident
and whose words were wild and whirling. Vulgar it was, perhaps, but it
was at least vigorous and virile.

Rodomontade and turgidity, born of a new expansiveness of spirit and
nourished by backwoods braggadocio, were rampant in the American speech
of the first half of the nineteenth century, particularly in what was then
called our West, the area south of the Ohio River and west of the Allegheny
Mountains—the "dark and bloody hunting ground" of American romance.
Although the "tall talk" was somewhat toned down after the Civil War, it
remains a minor characteristic of American English to this day, and the
leaping, shouting, boastingly rhapsodical backwoodsman, the self-styled
"half hoss, half alligator, and a touch of the airthquake," the "yaller flower
of the forest," who spoke it—or is supposed to have done so, for one suspects,
despite ample evidence of his reality, that he was to some extent a literary

convention—is still popularly regarded as having been a sort of beau ideal of American manhood.

The heroes who pushed the frontier constantly westward were rough men, with gargantuan appetites and little refinement, men who did prodigiously hard physical labor. They are epitomized in such folk characters as Paul Bunyan, Ben Hardin (Davy Crockett's mythical companion who had taken mermaids for concubines), and Mike Fink. Their idea of play was the rough-and-tumble brawl, in which they brought to perfection the manly arts of biting, butting, scratching, and gouging. Their ways of life were indeed not modest; neither were their opinions of themselves; neither was their language. "I can lick my weight in wildcats" was a favorite boast—and the expression has become a part of the national speech. They were proud to boast of animal ancestry or upbringing: "I'm a child of the snapping-turtle"; "I was raised with the alligators and weaned on panther's milk." They could "wrastle a buffalo and chaw the ear off a grizzly" or "outrun, outjump, outshoot, throw down, drag out, and lick" any other man in the country. Cooper's Paul Hover in *The Prairie* (1827) is such a one. "If a bear crosses my path," he brags, "he is soon a mere ghost of Bruin. . . . As for the buffalo, I have killed more beef . . . than the largest butcher in all Kentuck." In answer to the question "Is your hand true and your look quick?" this preposterous ass, whom the reader is expected to regard as a noble fellow and a true-blue American, replies: "The first is like a steel trap, and the last nimbler than buckshot. I wish it was hot noon now . . . and that there was an acre or two of your white swans or of black feathered ducks going south, over our heads; you or Ellen here might have set your heart on the finest in the flock, and my character against a horn of powder, that the bird would be hanging head downwards in five minutes and that too with a single ball." Cooper had not, it is obvious, mastered the grammatical minutiae of frontier speech, but the spirit is there. Davy Crockett tells in his *Life* of a "smart, active young fellow of the steamboat and alligator breed" of whom Crockett inquired (the question was of a sort which caused no surprise at the time and place) "whether he was a rhinoceros or a hyena." "Neither the one nor the t'other, Colonel," said this remarkable person, "but a whole menagerie in myself. I'm shaggy as a bear, wolfish about the head, active as a cougar, and can grin like a hyena, until the bark will curl off a gum log. There's a sprinkling of all sorts in me, from the lion down to the skunk [a sprinkling of the skunk?]; and before the war is over, you'll pronounce me an entire zoölogical institute, or I miss a figure in my calculation. I promise to swallow Santa Anna without gagging, if you will only skewer back his ears, and grease his head a little." Such exuberance could hardly be confined to language; this amazing, if somewhat nauseating, breed of "roaring boys" had a whole repertoire of physical stunts: they crowed, they neighed, they roared, they made prodigious leaps and cracked their heels together in mid-air. It is indeed a wonder that any sensible person ever took them seriously. That they were admired is, however, obvious, and to this day Dan'l Boone, Davy Crockett, and "Old Hickory" Jackson are far more sympathetic characters to most Americans than the Adamses, the Lees, or even the self-made Franklin.

The race of putative supermen who inhabited the West were reported to use an almost incredible lingo. Whether their talk was actually as represented by literary observers I shall not attempt to answer. But enough of the "tall" words have at any rate survived—for instance, *rapscallionly, rambunctious, to hornswoggle, cahoots, to cavort,* and such elegant expressions as *to go the whole hog, root hog or die, slick as goose grease, to pick a crow with someone, to kick the bucket*—to lead one to believe that at least some of the others—for instance, *conbobberation, helliferocious, mollagausauger, to puckerstopple,* and *peedoddles*—were actually in use and seem unbelievably outlandish today only because of their unfamiliarity. And there can be no doubt that the rough-hewn, stout-hearted, straight-shooting characters in buckskin who gave utterance to these verbal delicacies were regarded, perhaps somewhat wishfully, by merchants and their bookkeepers in the East as typical of the American spirit. The Revolutionary worthies must have seemed an altogether different breed, anemic by comparison, and only a few degrees above Englishmen. Even today some of these "tall" words, words like *bodacious, to absquatulate, cattywampus, slantindicular, grandiferous, ring-tailed roarer, to exflunctify, to exflunctificate, to hornswoggle, to honeyfogle, bustiferous, monstracious, monstropolous, to obflisticate, sockdologer, to sumtotalize,* and *teetotaciously* are popularly regarded as picturesque and admirably American.

The "tall talk" of the backwoods, moving ever westward with the frontier, left unmistakable traces in the writings of Mark Twain, John Hay, Bret Harte, and a good many smaller fry. Strangely, there is really very little of it in Walt Whitman, who expressed his admiration for what he called "strong and beautiful words . . . tangible and clean-lived, all having texture and beauty," although he neither tells us what words he had in mind nor does he make much use of "tall" words in his poetry; there are, of course, some individual novelties, but these must be considered Whitmanisms rather than Americanisms. In general his diction, unlike his subject matter, hardly differs from that of the salon coteries for which he professed such wholesome American contempt. In his "American Primer," which was not published until 1904, when it appeared in the April issue of the *Atlantic Monthly,* he declared that "the appetite of the people of These States, in popular speeches and writings, is for unhemmed latitude, coarseness, directness, live epithets, expletives, words of opprobrium, resistance," informing us that "I have pleasure in the use, on fit occasions, of—*traitor, coward, liar, shyster, skulk, doughface, trickster, mean cuss, backslider, thief, impotent, lickspittle,*" a number of which are, it will be noted, standard English words. His own coinages are usually epicine affairs, linguistic cream puffs like *to eclaircise, to imperturbe, to effuse, affetuoso,* and *civilizee.* As far as literary men of the nineteenth century other than those mentioned are concerned, "tall talk" seems to have had little effect; but the psychology which gave birth to this somewhat naïve love of orotund exaggeration has had a continuous life.

There can be little doubt that the political and patriotic oratory which thrived between the War of 1812 and the Civil War was a development in part of the talk of the frontier. There is little flamboyant boasting in the speeches or the writings of the founding fathers of the Republic, whose models in prose were Addison, Pope, Swift, Goldsmith, Hume, and to some extent Johnson, and whose thinking was colored by the rationalism of eighteenth-century Enlightenment. We have Webster's word for it that the common people of the period of the Revolution, and for a long time thereafter, read the Bible and volumes of elevating sermons—at least in Connecticut.

After the War of 1812, unbridled eloquence, expansiveness, a fine flux of words, particularly long, mouth-filling words, came to be passionately admired in all parts of the country save perhaps the Sodoms and Gomorrahs of the Atlantic coast. Inasmuch as everything about America was felt to be on a grand (or "grandiferous") scale, overstatement became the rule. This inflated verbosity was defended, or at least explained, by Daniel Drake (*Discourse on the History, Character, and Prospects of the West,* 1834) who felt that there was a definite connection between the declamatory style, as he called it, and political freedom. Moreover, according to him, "a people who have fresh and lively feelings will always relish oratory." That the flamboyant style was a Western development is evident from the fact that Timothy Flint, writing as late as 1830 in the *Western Monthly Review,* could still characterize the oratory of the East as "sober, passionless, condensed, metaphysical," whereas that of the West was "free, lofty, agitating, grand, impassioned." All the same, the American eagle was often made to scream and the British lion to roar with pain even in staid New England, particularly by Fourth of July orators; one commentator remarked in 1846 that "the bird of America has so often been made to take flight that his shadow may be said to have worn a trail across the basin of the Mississippi." As for the British lion, said the same observer, "the poor lord of the beasts has become so familiar with the point of a hickory pole and of an ash splinter, that he has slunk away to his lair." There can be no doubt that this frontier grandiloquence has lingered on into our own day, particularly in the more backward parts of the country. Lincoln's Gettysburg Address was not an altogether fatal blow to it, nor were F.D.R.'s studiedly informal "fireside chats." Many a citizen remains impressed by an impassioned gush of roaring words. So recently as March 6, 1950, *Time* made reference to "the treasury of the vehement, sonorous and shamelessly corny phrasing which is the tribal language of U.S. politics," by way of illustration quoting a Southern congressman as expressing his disapproval of a certain bill by declaring that it was "conceived in iniquity and nurtured with the milk of corruption," along with other fine flowers of rhetoric. Readers of the *Congressional Record* will not consider the language exceptional, and it is altogether likely that the congressman's constituents consider him to be in the line of Demosthenes, Burke, Clay, and William Jennings Bryan.

Vocabulary

indigenous, reverberations, uncouth, *par excellence,* epitome, strident, rodomontade, turgidity, braggadocio, rampant, beau ideal, gargantuan, prodigiously, concubine, minutiae, exuberance, repertoire, putative, lingo, coteries, epithets, expletives, opprobrium, epicene, orotund, flamboyant, staid, grandiloquence, iniquity

Review Questions

1. When did a "generally indigenous American spirit" begin to influence American language and literature? What accounts for its appearance at this particular time?

2. In what ways was this American spirit a totally new force?

3. What does Pyles mean by "tall talk"? How has it affected our language?

4. How did Walt Whitman describe the American appetite for popular speeches and writings?

5. What support does the author give for his statement that the "love of orotund exaggeration has had a continuous life"?

6. Do you agree with the author's contention that there is a connection between bombastic, inflated language and political freedom?

7. What is meant by "the line of Demosthenes, Burke, Clay, and William Jennings Bryan"?

Expository Technique

1. Study the first paragraph of this selection and comment on its coherence. In particular, how does the author use grammatical structure to strengthen coherence?

2. This essay's third paragraph is skillful and effective writing. What is particularly forceful about its diction?

3. Comment on the success with which you think the author establishes the influence of the Frontier on American language.

Exercises

1. In some issues of the *Congressional Record* and, perhaps, some newspaper reports containing political addresses look for recent examples of what *Time* Magazine has called "the vehement, sonorous and shamelessly corny phrasing which is the tribal language of U.S. politics."

2. A good example of tall talk is the "Raft Passage" in Mark Twain's *Life on the Mississippi* (chapter III, beginning with paragraph 7). Read this selection and prepare a class report on its unusual diction.

3. Find out what you can about the career of one of the Frontier heroes such as Davy Crockett or Mike Fink. A good place to begin is Constance Rourke's *American Humor*. Prepare a class report on the exploits and language of the figure you select.

4. What manifestations of the Frontier do you find in the language of television westerns? Is there a consistent effort to develop characters through qualities of speech?

5. In our times Jimmy Durante has kept alive the tall-talk tradition with such expressions as *discompooperated* and *giganticolossoloscious*. What other tall-talk terms and inflated language used for comic purposes can you find in Durante's performances or in those of other comedians?

31.

ALBERT H. MARCKWARDT

The Genteel Tradition and the Glorification of the Commonplace

Pervasive as the influence of the frontier may have been in early America, it was by no means all of one piece. Throughout most of the nineteenth century, settlement proceeded in stages. At the very time that the restless woodsman and trapper was making his initial foray into that portion of the wilderness farthest in advance of the march of civilization, the territory one or two hundred miles behind him was already taking on the aspects of permanent settlement. Farms were established in the oak openings or on the prairie; shipping points became the nuclei from which villages developed; local government, schools, churches, and even libraries soon took on at least a rudimentary form of organization. Even the theater and the lyceum course were seldom far behind the woodsman's axe. According to Constance Rourke:

> On rafts, in broadhorns, [theatrical] companies traveled down the Ohio and the Mississippi, stopping at the larger cities, often playing in small villages. Some went on by wagon into the hills of Kentucky, where the roads were so steep that they were obliged to unload their properties and carry them . . . Everywhere they found theaters or theaters were improvised for them; everyone came, black and white, children and their elders.

Certainly the reflection of frontier life and institutions, the absence of certain restraints associated with more permanent types of civilization, the ingenuity born of sheer necessity are all evident in the language. But there is more to the story than just this. Other ramifications of pioneer civilization and indeed certain counter-movements or reactions against it must be taken into consideration as well if we are to comprehend the development of American English in its totality.

One important factor in our early national life which had a profound effect on our language may appropriately be termed the glorification of the commonplace. It had its roots, perhaps, in two aspects of pioneer culture. First of all it must be realized that life in these primitive communities beyond the Appalachians was both hard and dull. Days were long; the work seemed endless. There were few comforts, and at times life must have seemed a continual struggle against cold and hunger. At the same time, many of the early pioneers had known other kinds of life. They had come from cities and towns which had acquired stability and certain cultural accoutrements. Small wonder, then, that the settlers permitted their imaginations to clothe their drab and commonplace surroundings with the salient features of the life they had known before.

One striking illustration of this tendency may be found in the peculiarly American development of the word *saloon*, the equivalent of British English *public house*. This word was originally an early eighteenth-century adaptation of French *salon*, and at the time it was borrowed signified just what it has continued to mean in French, namely, a drawing room. Not long after its adoption it came to be applied to drawing rooms which were particularly large and elegant, often those of a public character. This association with elegance and fashion has remained unchanged in British English—witness the coinage *saloon car* for an automobile with an enclosed body.

Moreover, late in the eighteenth or early in the nineteenth century there seems to have been some confusion in the terminology relative to establishments where liquor was sold at retail or by the glass. *Tavern*, which in England came to denote a drinking place but one which had no sleeping accommodations in connection, seems to have been used in America to designate a hotel or inn. *Public house*, apparently used in America as early as 1704 or at least in British legislation affecting American colonies, had become somewhat disreputable by including brothels within the scope of its meaning. It was only natural, therefore, that Americans should cast about for a new term which could be respectably applied to a drinking establishment which was not a hotel.

Their first coinage was *bar-room*, which is recorded by a British traveler as early as 1809. Indirect evidence suggests that the new term was insufficiently elegant to be wholly satisfactory, nor did *groggery*, which appeared just a little later, seem to constitute an acceptable improvement. About three decades later we find *saloon* appearing first on the eastern seaboard and then spreading westward with amazing rapidity. Whether this was direct adaptation of the term in America, or whether its use was first suggested by the English *saloon bar*—the most elegant of the three types of bars in a public house, the other two being the private and the public bar—cannot be determined from the evidence currently available. The important thing, however, is that a word previously associated with fashion, elegance, and politeness came to be used in connection with a kind of establishment which was often fairly mean and dingy. Consequently the word suffered in status, underwent pejoration.

As the agitation against the sale and use of alcohol increased, the Anti-Saloon League was organized, and the saloon became a symbol of corruption and evil influence. One of the principal aims of the Prohibition movement was to wipe out the saloon, and although it failed after a decade and a half, and liquor eventually came back, Mencken's comment that, "So far as I know, there is not a simple undisguised saloon in the United States today," is still essentially correct. Nor is the owner of such an establishment any longer content to refer to himself as a saloonkeeper. The bartender, too, has attempted to cloak his occupation with a new word, but the campaign, instituted in 1901 by the *Police Gazette,* to substitute *bar clerk* or *mixologist* as an occupational term had no success.

In all this, however, what is significant is the attempt to lend dignity and attractiveness through the use of a new and somewhat elegant word—more elegant, perhaps, than the situation would reasonably permit.

A similar development occurred in connection with the term *opera house,* but unfortunately little factual information concerning its use is available in the usual lexicographical sources. Nevertheless, throughout the nineteenth century and continuing on into the twentieth, it seems to have been customary in many small towns to use this word for the theater or auditorium which served the community. Some notion of its possible range of applica-

tion may be obtained from Schlesinger and Fox's *History of American Life;*
the time to which the quotation refers is 1870:

> Behind the courthouse grounds, around the corner from the Y.M.C.A. quar-
> ters and the Gazette office, stood the only other civic building—a barnlike brick
> structure sheltering the jail, the mayor's office, and an auditorium and stage.
> The "op'ry house" it was called by official decree.

Needless to say, most of the opera houses scattered throughout the length
and breadth of the land seldom witnessed any performance even remotely
resembling an opera, except possibly for an occasional venture into Gilbert
and Sullivan by the local high school. The Lynds in their cultural analysis of
Middletown [Muncie, Indiana] list the following as opera-house sensations
of the 'nineties: *The Telephone Girl, Over the Garden Wall, East Lynne,
Guilty Without Crime, The Black Crook,* and the inevitable *Uncle Tom's
Cabin.* It would seem, therefore, that *opera house* as a term for the small-
town American theater represents precisely the same tendencies, cultural
and semantic, that were behind the adoption of *saloon* for a drinking establishment: a desire to make the ordinary seem somewhat grander than it
actually was, coupled perhaps with the hope that some day the structure
might come to justify the name given it.

Another manifestation of the same tendency is to be observed in connection with our terms for educational institutions and various types of
training schools. In fact, there is if anything a double impulse here. The first
is to be found in the tendency to dignify academic institutions of all kinds
with a name that is a degree above, or at best somewhat more impressive
than, that which they would merit in England. This has already been dealt
with in part in connection with the generalization of the word *college.* A
telling illustration of how this tendency operates is furnished by the state of
Michigan where, in the decade of the 1930's, all but one of the normal schools
in the state officially became Colleges of Education and in the 'fifties dropped
the modifying phrase. This change was officially justified by the establishment in each of them of a liberal arts curriculum leading to the bachelor's
degree, but the fact remains that *college* clearly seemed to the educational
authorities a more desirable and respectable term than *school.* That *university*
underwent a similar extension for much the same reason is evident from
the exultant statement of a misguided patriot of the 1870's quoted by
Schlesinger and Fox: "There are two universities in England, four in France,
ten in Prussia, and thirty-seven in Ohio." Even *high school,* the American
use of which dates from 1824, is seldom used for a secondary school in England, and in Europe it regularly denotes an institution of college or university rank. Here, however, American usage may have had its roots in Scotland.

The secondary tendency is to apply to trade schools and other establishments devoted to the training of artisans the same labels which have in the

past been reserved for academic institutions. Again evidence is scanty, but *business college* as a term for a stenographic and secretarial training venture, is to be found as early as 1865. The dictionaries are strangely silent on *barber college,* but it was current in parts of the United States early in the twentieth century. Its sister institutions, the schools and colleges of cosmetology, devoted to initiating the beginner into the mysteries of the permanent wave, probably do not go back beyond the 1920's.

Occupational terminology in America has undergone a series of changes quite similar to those which have already been observed in connection with the educational institutions: old terms have been extended in application; new ones have been created. The words *doctor* and *professor* are obvious instances of extensions in application. Both of these are carefully restricted in their use in England, where surgeons are *Mr.* even if they do hold the M.D. degree, and professorships are naturally much less numerous than in the United States. In America, dentists, osteopaths, chiropractors, optometrists, chiropodists, and veterinarians are all doctors, and in addition the tremendous extension of the doctorate in American graduate schools, and the lavish manner in which American colleges and universities distribute honorary degrees add to the number of doctors on other levels as well. Even so, this does not take into account such jocular applications, either in full form or the clipped *Doc,* which, as the *Dictionary of Americanisms* indicates, was extended to logging camp cooks late in the nineteenth century.

Professor has developed in much the same directions; in fact, it may have begun earlier and gone farther. We find an enterprising bookseller styling himself a Professor of Book Auctioneering as early as 1774, and virtually every attempt at a glossary of Americanisms during the nineteenth century mentions the extension of the title to such groups as dancing teachers, magicians, and phrenologists. Certainly in most small towns the title was regularly applied not only to superintendents of schools and principals but even to male grade-school teachers as well. The inevitable result of this wholesale doctoring and professoring is, of course, an avoidance of the titles by those who are normally entitled to them, an outcome suggested by the mock-serious society organized at the University of Virginia "for the encouragement of the use of *mister* to all men, professional or otherwise."

Academic usage in the north of the United States as contrasted with the south also offers a striking illustration of the operation of what might be called scarcity values. In the colleges and universities of the North there are many holders of the doctorate who have not yet attained professorial rank in a teaching faculty. Consequently, one who is both a professor and a doctor is customarily addressed as *professor.* In the South, on the other hand, until quite recently many college faculty members of professorial rank did not possess a doctor's degree. In this part of the country one who has both the rank and the degree is normally addressed as *doctor.*

In a sense the extension of the use of both *professor* and *doctor* is closely related to the American passion for honorifics, but a further discussion of these must be postponed until we take a hasty glance at the creation of other so-called professional titles and occupational terms. *Mortician,* frequently thought of in this connection, appears to have been created about 1895 on the convenient analogy of *physician,* and the same process of derivation has given us *beautician, loctician,* and six or eight others, all somewhat bizarre. It is possible that *mortician* may owe its creation quite as much to the age-old and constant search for euphemisms for terms connected with death and burial as to the desire for professional status. There is, after all, a somewhat gruesome pun in the word *undertaker,* and though it has served the English from 1698 on, they do at times soften the effect by substituting *funeral furnisher.*

Realtor, another oft-cited instance of the American creation of pseudo-professional terms, could be excused by the generously inclined on the ground that it permitted a single word to replace the somewhat cumbersome *real-estate agent,* but there is probably more truth than fiction in the statement expressed by Sinclair Lewis's Babbitt to the effect that, "We ought to insist that folks call us 'realtors' and not 'real-estate men.' Sounds more like a reg'lar profession." Though the Lewis citation comes from the early 'twenties, the term itself dates from 1915.

American regard for technology is shown by the overwhelming popularity of the word *engineer,* used in strange and numerous combinations. Our early use of the term in connection with railroading was a portent of things to come; the English in general content themselves with the somewhat more humdrum sounding *engine driver.* But since that time we have employed the word in an astounding number of combinations, running to well over 2000. H. L. Mencken reported that the Extermination Engineers, namely the rat and roach eradicators, have had a national association for some thirty years. Such further terms as *patent engineer, recreation engineer, erosion engineer,* and *casement window engineer* illustrate the variety of uses to which the term has been put.

The proposal of a Janitor's Institute, held at Mt. Pleasant, Michigan, in 1939, to the effect that janitors henceforth be called *engineer-custodians* reveals as well the temporary nature of the satisfaction to be derived from verbal glorification, for historically *janitor* represents quite the same state of mind that gave rise to *realtor* and *mortician.* Derived somewhat artificially from the mythological character Janus, it was first used for a doorkeeper or porter, and its application to the sweeper of floors and builder of fires has been confined primarily to the United States; in England *caretaker* is the common term. As is evident from the action of the institute, even twenty years ago the word had become sufficiently tarnished that *engineer, custodian,* or both, sounded more attractive. One of the amusing sequels of the shift in terminology from *janitor* to *custodian* in one American university was that the title of the head of a research library had, in turn, to be changed from *Custodian* to *Director,* since there was some danger of confusing him with the janitor of the place.

Nor was the tendency to glorify the commonplace limited to the professional and work-a-day world. The American household bears some marks of this, even today. For example, the Lynds in their study *Middletown in Transition* find occasion to quote this very revealing excerpt from a current newspaper:

> The time will easily be remembered when masculine and juvenile members of a household received glaring looks punctuated by lifted eyebrows when they forgot in the presence of guests and referred to the evening meal as "supper." But time has changed that. Smart folks are having buffet suppers, and many . . .

Disregarding for the moment the recently regained prestige of a certain type of supper, we may conclude that in the 'twenties and 'thirties it was considered proper, particularly by women, to refer to the evening meal as *dinner* and presumably to the midday meal as *luncheon,* and that this terminology had quite recently replaced *dinner* as the term for the noon meal and *supper* for the evening meal.

This shift is a slightly delayed reflection of the changed eating habits of many American families which developed from the increased urbanization and industrialization of American life, and has, of course, some justification in fact. For the farming and small-town families at the beginning of the present century, the heaviest meal of the day was served at noon, and the evening repast was considerably lighter. Thus for that time, *dinner* and *supper* were accurate descriptions. The present tendency toward lighter meals at noon, frequently consumed away from the home by the male members of the family and by the children, has resulted in the heavier meal being served at home in the evening, with a resultant change in terminology and a prestige-loss for *supper.*

In this connection it is interesting to observe that *supper* not only continued in common use in America some sixty or seventy years longer than in England, but that this was a matter for comment by at least two mid-nineteenth century British travelers. In 1859, Gosse in a series of letters from Alabama wrote, "The meal which we are accustomed to call 'tea' is by Americans, universally, I believe, called 'supper,' and it is the final meal, there being but three in the day." Five years later we find C. Geithe reporting, "I chatted . . . till tea, or as they called it, supper."

As American domestic architecture has changed, so too have the names given to the various rooms. The principal phenomenon over the past century has been the disappearance of a "best room," rarely occupied on weekdays, and used only to entertain guests and for holidays or festive occasions. In American usage this was the *parlor*. This in itself was a shift from British English, for there the term *parlor* was applied to a rather small intimate chamber, whereas the more pretentious one was called the *drawing room,* a term which never caught on with the Americans. In the United States, as long as the parlor was an institution, the room which was ordinarily used by the family circle was the *sitting room,* but as the parlor disappeared, the sitting room became the *living room,* and the former term came to be felt as somewhat rustic and old-fashioned.

It may be noted that only in America was the term *cuspidor*—an importation from Portuguese through Dutch—adopted for what was at one time a not uncommon accessory in the home, to say nothing of clubrooms and legislative halls. This somewhat delicate word was also introduced in England as early as 1781 but never gained any real currency.

Finally, the tendencies toward verbal elegance and sentimentality appear to have combined to produce a more extensive use of *home* in America than in England. At the close of the last century, George Warrington Steevens commented, "As to the home, the American talks about it a great deal. He never builds himself a house; he builds himself a home." Consequently, contractors for domestic dwellings are *home builders,* the householder is a *homeowner,* vacuum sweepers, dishwashing machines, ironers, and the other manifold mechanical appurtenances of the American household are *home appliances.* School instruction in cooking and sewing has become *homemaking,* and when exalted to a more learned level, *home economics.* Even the housewife became a *homemaker* by formal resolution of the Long Island Federation of Women's Clubs, as Mencken has pointed out. Moreover, the institutions of refuge for the needy and those of detention for troublesome juveniles are quite regularly *homes,* to say nothing of the *funeral home,* which now customarily serves as the setting for final rites.

Travelers to America, almost from its very beginning as an independent country, have taken great delight in pointing out what seemed to them a fundamental inconsistency between the theory of equality upon which the government of the country is based and the fondness of the American people for titles of honor. Although Crèvecœur, reflecting on his pre-Revolutionary experience, stoutly insisted that *lawyer, merchant,* and *farmer* were the fairest titles our country at that time afforded, observers from the 1840's on have a quite different story to tell. As late as 1896, George Warrington Steevens inquired somewhat petulantly in describing the American, "Why does he cling all his life to the title of some rank or office he held twenty years ago?" Two answers to the question were offered some years before Steevens phrased it, and without question there is some truth in each. In 1849 the Scotsman Alexander Mackay defended the Americans on the ground that, "the fondness for titles which they display is but a manifestation of the fondness for distinction natural to the human mind." A somewhat different opinion was voiced a decade later by Thomas Colley Grattan, who concluded, "Were a well-established national self-reliance felt among the leading men in the United States, there would be none of the melancholy parodies of 'High Life,' none of the yearnings after aristocratical distinctions which are now so flagrant."

When American honorifics are examined in a dispassioned light, it must be said that they are still a far cry from Teutonic usage, for example. They are notable chiefly for some extension of such bogus military titles as *Colonel,* the retention of legislative and judicial titles, as noted by Steevens, beyond the period of service, and the somewhat comic extension of the word *Honorable* itself. Judged by either general European or Latin American standards in these matters, the English-speaking American becomes almost a shrinking violet. It is only in the light of English practice that our use of honorifics seems somewhat overweighted, and even the English have their silly periods, as anyone who witnessed the furor over the proper application and meaning of *Esquire* which raged in the autumn of 1953 can well testify.

In this connection it is well to remember that the United States came into being as the result of a political rather than a social revolution. The latter frequently does result in a highly conscious effort to do away with artificial titular distinctions; witness the adoption of *Citizen* in the French Revolution and that of *Comrade* in post-revolutionary Russia. This did not occur in the United States, for there was no nobility to displace, no class of governing officials to turn out of office. If anything, some offices and distinctions had to be created, and even the title to be given to the chief executive of the country was for a time a moot question.

In consequence of H. L. Mencken's picturesque and entertaining assault upon *Honorable,* little remains to be said except to point out the problem posed by the vastness of the country and the complexities of its governmental machinery. To begin with, we have the President and the members of his cabinet and the justices of the Supreme Court. No one would be inclined to doubt that any one of these merits the term. But if the executive and judicial branches of our government are thus entitled to the distinction, and so far we have imaginarily conferred it upon no more than thirty individuals, our very concept of the equality of all three branches of our government demands that all members of the Senate and the House of Representatives receive it as well. Thus at a single stroke we have added some 550 *Honorables.* Going back to the executive and judicial branches, we must now ask whether we stop with Supreme Court justices and cabinet secretaries. What about appellate and district judges, to say nothing of undersecretaries and assistant secretaries? There is the whole diplomatic corps in addition, and officials in special governmental agencies not represented in the cabinet.

Leaving the national government and pursuing the same problem on the state level, we must now multiply by forty-eight the possibly 2000 *Honorables* we have already conferred. Nor can we stop here, for surely a metropolitan mayor has a position equal in dignity and responsibility to the governor of one of our smaller states. Ultimately we arrive at the township justice and the village fire marshal. Moreover, many of these offices are no longer than a biennium in duration, and once a man has acquired the title he is not likely to relinquish it. The wonder is that anyone at all escapes the term, or perhaps that we have not attempted to create distinctions within it, that is to say, degrees and classifications of honorability.

A further sector of the American vocabulary which scarcely has a counterpart in British life comprises the wide variety of names given to fraternal orders. The last two decades of the nineteenth century gave rise to an almost unbelievable number of these, very nearly 500, in fact. Schlesinger and Fox, in commenting upon this gaudy variety, among which are included such choice items as the American Order of Druids, the Prudent Patricians of Pompeii, and the Concatenated Order of Hoo-Hoo, make the very sound observation that "the nomenclature of fraternalism will someday offer interesting material for the student of suppressed desires and wishful thinking." Although they do not develop the point, there can be little question that the motivating force behind these is of a class with what we have just observed.

Euphemism, verbal prudery or the avoidance of the unpleasant word, is another somewhat indirect product of the frontier which, from a semantic and lexical point of view at least, is often closely allied to verbal glorification. In fact, it is often difficult to decide whether the motive behind such a substitution as that of *casket* for *coffin* was primarily that of suggesting something more elegant or that of avoiding a term connected with death and burial. Much of the verbal prudery, however, for which we became notorious in the nineteenth century, may be traced to two factors; the position of woman in American society and the predominantly middle-class character of American culture.

The second of these points is so obvious as not to require extensive elaboration. Within the history of modern societies it has always been the middle class which has manifested a greater and more anxious concern for the properties than either the lower class, which has tended toward indifference, or the upper, which has been protected by a thick coat of self-assurance. Among the properties thus affected, that of language has usually assumed a prominent position. It was the English middle class, or at least the upper sector of it, which created the demand that led to the excessive schoolmastering of the language in eighteenth-century England. That the Puritan settlers of New England—also predominantly middle class—were intensely concerned with linguistic propriety is indicated by the amount of colonial legislation directed against profanity. Noah Webster interested himself in expurgating the Bible, and considered this one of his important works.

There is ample evidence in a dozen sociological studies that most Americans today are prone to think of themselves as belonging to the middle class. Consequently, there is every reason to expect from American English a typical middle-class delicacy, expressed in a multitude of linguistic taboos. The record, as we shall see, in no way dispels our expectations.

This verbal delicacy received a strong reinforcement from the position which women enjoyed in our frontier society. In his *Society of Thought in Early America,* Harvey Wish points out that:

> . . . their relative scarcity and economic opportunities made them more diffi-
> cult to please in courtship. While the South enjoyed a latter-day chivalry with
> roots deep in feudal times, the North, too, had its ritual of courtesies due to
> women. Everywhere seduction and breach of promise suits were apt to be
> prejudiced in the woman's favor. Here one addressed a mixed audience as
> "Ladies and Gentlemen" instead of the traditional "Gentlemen and Ladies."
> Women travelled alone without losing caste, and their daughters dispensed
> with chaperones (even if they belonged to the well-to-do class). While the
> Industrial Revolution was emancipating western European women as well as
> their American sisters, the American woman was definitely ahead in status.*

Because of this scarcity value, American women seem to have been in a position to foster an extreme sensitivity in linguistic matters. Calhoun in his study of the American family cites one letter written a few years before 1850 which asserts, "Women can alter the dialect, change the manners, dictate the dress and habits of life, and control the morals of every community." Captain Frederick Marryatt's comments on this point have furnished what is often considered the classic example of verbal delicacy. He tells first of how he offended an American woman by saying *legs* instead of limbs and then goes on to the account of the girls' seminary where the piano "limbs" were "dressed in modest little trousers with frills at the bottom of them." That the veracity of the latter story has been questioned is of little importance; it is true in spirit to the segment of American life it purported to reflect. Nor was this cult of super-refinement one of short duration only. The Lynds in their study of Middletown cite a commencement essay at the local high school as late as 1891 bearing the title, "Woman is Most Perfect When Most Womanly."

The first and most prominent linguistic effect of female dominance and middle-class morality was an extreme reticence on matters directly or even remotely connected with sex. Again the Lynd's *Middletown in Transition* furnishes corroborative evidence from a society studied less than two decades ago:

> Sex is one of the things Middletown has long been taught to fear. Its institu-
> tions—with the important exception of the movies and some of the periodicals

* Reprinted by courtesy of Longmans, Green & Co. and David McKay Company, Inc.

it reads, both imported from the outside culture—operate to keep the subject out of sight and out of mind as much as possible.

In language, of course, questionable subjects are kept out of sight and mind, ostensibly if not actually, by developing new and less-shocking terms to replace those which have taken on taboo characteristics. All languages do this to some extent. It is the degree to which these euphemistic tendencies have operated in American English that is of particular interest.

One outlet for verbal delicacy of this nature was the creation of a host of more or less thinly disguised terms for houses of prostitution. *Assignation house* is cited by the *Dictionary of Americanisms* for 1854; *house of assignation* preceded this by twenty years. *Sporting house,* which in England meant first merely a house frequented by sportsmen and later a gambling house, was finally applied to a brothel in America in 1894 in a book which bore the somewhat disconcerting title, *If Christ Came to Chicago.* None of the dictionaries, however, seem to record the related use of *sport* for a prostitute, which was current about the same time. *Crib* also reflects the same transition from a gaming house to one of prostitution, though somewhat earlier, and such terms as *cat house, fancy house, cow bag,* and *call house* were all in use at one time or another; and on a somewhat more dignified level *disorderly house* and *house of ill fame. Cadet* as a euphemism for procurer seems to have flourished from the first to the third decades of the twentieth century. There was also an equal reticence with respect to naming specific venereal diseases, but this has been generally overcome within the past twenty years.

Another object which has particularly invited euphemistic terminology is what the English call a *water closet* and the Americans a *toilet.* Commenting on the use of *toilet,* the *Oxford English Dictionary* says, "In the U.S. especially a dressing room furnished with bathing facilities; in a restricted sense, a bathroom, a lavatory," but it is difficult to fix the time the precise application to the water closet itself occurred. The first citation which may be so interpreted with reasonable certainty bears the date 1909, though it must have had this meaning considerably earlier. *Rest room* (1909) and *comfort station* (1904) were also concocted during the first decade of the century, and Mencken credits *powder room* to the speakeasies of the Prohibition era. The American use of *washroom* in the same sense goes back to 1853.

It is to be expected that during a period of extreme verbal delicacy there will be many taboos for various parts of the body, particularly those which have any connection with sex or with the excretive functions. Mid-nineteenth-century America was no exception. This topic, however, has been so fully treated by Mencken and by Pyles that it will be necessary only to point out one or two matters which seem to have been overlooked.

For example, despite Captain Marryatt's oft-quoted stories of the woman who was offended at the mention of *limb,* it should not be forgotten that this word acquired the meaning of "leg" not in America but in England as early as 1400. *Oxford English Dictionary* citations show that it was in constant use in England from the beginning of the fifteenth century until 1837. Marryatt's account of his American experience bears the date 1839, and from that time until 1924 all the citations are American. What we have here then is the continuation of a British euphemism rather than an American invention.

The taboo against *leg* was extended to fowl prepared for the table, as is frequently pointed out, but *drumstick,* one of the euphemisms which appeared on the scene as a substitute, is clearly of British origin, and on the basis of dictionary evidence, at least, was as much used in Britain as in the United States. The extension of *joint* from its British use in connection with such meats as beef, mutton, and venison, to roast fowl seems clearly to have originated in America, and so too the further distinction between a first joint and a second. An English traveler in America in 1845 reported himself as being "requested by a lady, at a public dinner table, to furnish her with the first and second joint." The presumed indecency of the word *leg,* coupled with an almost equally strong taboo against *breast,* gave rise to another pair of American euphemisms used in this connection. Thomas C. Grattan, in his *Civilized America* (1859) explained that, "some . . . would scarcely hesitate, though almost all call it the 'white meat,' in contradistinction to the 'dark meat' as all ladies and gentlemen designate the legs of poultry." *White meat* as a term had previously existed in England, but was limited in its meaning to milk, cheese, and other dairy products, literally white food.

Undergarments for both men and women likewise offered a fertile field for mid-nineteenth-century ingenuity. *Unmentionables,* which refers at times to trousers and at others to drawers, is cited as early as 1839; *sub-trousers* as late as 1890. Between these dates a wide variety of terms appeared, though it should be noted that *inexpressibles,* sometimes classed with American euphemisms of this type, is actually British in origin and seems to have been used in England throughout the greater part of the century.

Death, dying, and burial constitute another area of the lexicon in which most languages develop a large number of euphemisms. America was no exception, and Professor Louise Pound has dealt with this subject most exhaustively. Of the American terms which developed in this way, I have already mentioned one of the best known and most widely used today: *casket,* which serves as a delicate substitute for *coffin.* It seems to have entered the language by way of the compound *burial casket,* which along with *burial case* was coined in the 'fifties and 'sixties of the last century. It must have caught on very rapidly, for by 1870 a British news correspondent in

New York was able to make the flat statement, "In America a coffin is called a casket." That the term did not immediately win universal favor is shown by Nathaniel Hawthorne's comment in *Our Old Home* (1863): " 'Caskets!' —a vile modern phrase which compels a person . . . to shrink . . . from the idea of being buried at all." The perfumed practices of the modern mortician have, of course, resulted in a host of evasive expressions, against which Evelyn Waugh trained the shafts of his wit in the novel *The Loved One*.

The Puritan prohibition of profanity has already been mentioned, and although the number of violations of the laws clearly indicates that this was more often honored in the breach than in the observance, yet the fact that the laws should have existed at all, as well as the length of time they remained on the books, offers satisfactory evidence of an active taboo against profanity in the Puritan conscience. As a consequence of this, it would seem, American English has developed a whole lexicon of near-swearing, including *darn, drat, doggone, blasted, Sam Hill, gee whittaker, gee whiz,* and their progeny of sixty or seventy others, most of them still bearing more or less phonetic resemblance to the particular morsel for which they have been substituted.

Darn offers a fairly satisfactory example of the way one of these terms developed. We need not concern ourselves here with the debate which went on some years ago over whether *derne,* the Middle English word for "secret," was its real progenitor, or whether it emanated from an aphetic form of *eternal,* with *er* pronounced as in British *clerk (clark)*. The facts are simply that we do have *darnation* used as an adjective as early as 1798, and a quarter of a century later as an interjection. The earliest examples indicate use by, or with reference to, coastal New Englanders. If we assume that by this time post-vocalic *r* was either weakened or had disappeared entirely, and that the coastal New England *a* before *r* was a low central vowel with something of the quality of present-day Bostonian *park* [pa:k], the close resemblance of this to the ordinary pronunciation of *damnation* is clear enough. They are virtually the same except for the medial *m*. *Darn* appears by itself a decade or so later. A contemporary but very shrewd and accurate analysis of the whole situation was given in 1832 by J. T. Buckingham, writing in the *New England Magazine:* "We have 'Gaul darn you' for 'G— d— you' . . . and other like creations of the union of wrath and principle."

Nor is it merely the nineteenth century and the standards of propriety peculiar to it which give the impetus to usages designed to soften the harsh facts of life. We have at hand at least one twentieth-century phenomenon which has fostered a similar development—present-day American educational practices. The extension of elementary and secondary education to virtually all of the youth population, coupled with the determination on the part of educational psychologists to avoid injury to budding juvenile or adolescent personalities, no matter how academically inept, has resulted on the one hand in almost a total abandonment of the practice of failing a student, thus causing him to repeat a grade or unit of work, and on the other, in the creation of a host of special courses designed for those who are clearly unfitted for even the watered-down academic regimen of the present era. Consequently the practice of advancing the academic failures has become known as *social promotion* in some quarters, and high-school curricula now include courses which bear such strange labels as *Social English* and *Social Mathematics*. Moreover, the "exceptional" child may mean one of less than normal intelligence.

It is important to recognize that taboos and the resulting euphemisms have always operated in language. We have had them in English from the time that some Anglo-Saxon monk with an over-keen sense of propriety, coupled with a distinctly worldly knowledge of what went on in harbor resorts, coined the term *port-cwene* (port woman) to translate "harlot" in the parable of the Prodigal Son, up to the present era when one of our recent governmental administrations was careful to characterize a slight economic depression as a *recession*. The interesting aspect of the mid-nineteenth-century development of euphemisms in America lies in the peculiar combination of cultural circumstances which brought it about, the lavish scale upon which it operated, and the extremes which it often attained.

Every movement has its counter-force, and the genteel tradition of the past was no exception. Nineteenth-century America was not without those individuals who not only accepted their lack of culture and refinement as an established fact but who gloried in it, and indeed, flaunted it. The "I don't know anything about art but I know what I like" cliché—and the attitude it portrays—is a patent instance of this resistance to culture with a capital *C*. There is a good deal of this, for example, in Mark Twain, some of it undoubtedly sincere and some clearly with tongue in cheek. The extreme of such an attitude has at times been called the "mucker pose," one which certain politicians and others dependent upon large-scale popular support have at time found it profitable to adopt. Linguistically the mucker pose is frequently manifested by the conscious employment of features of substandard English. A case in point was the thoroughly cultured millionaire candidate for the presidential nomination recently, who rarely made a speech or television appearance without using *ain't* at least once. Currently this is scarcely a potent factor on the linguistic scene, but it is present to some extent, and its existence cannot be overlooked.

Vocabulary

nuclei, rudimentary, lyceum, ramifications, accoutrements, exultant, artisans, jocular, phrenologists, bizarre, bogus, moot, biennium, expurgating, corroborative, aphetic

Review Questions

1. Marckwardt is mainly concerned with two forces which exert influence upon American English: the glorification of the commonplace and verbal prudery. Briefly summarize the effects of these two forces upon our language. What examples, in addition to those cited by the author, can you give of these effects?

2. What reasons does the author give for the desire to glorify the commonplace? Is this desire in evidence today? If so, what examples of it can you cite?

3. Identify Janus and Crèvecœur.

4. Marckwardt believes that the American Revolution was political rather than social. What effect does he suggest this kind of revolution had on our attitudes and practices with regard to titles?

5. What two causes does the author cite for the rise of verbal prudery in America?

6. What is a euphemism? What is its purpose? Comment upon its relation to verbal taboo. In what social areas is verbal taboo most frequently applied?

7. Marckwardt notes that euphemism has always operated in language. What does he think was especially interesting, however, about the development of euphemisms in mid-nineteenth-century America?

8. What twentieth-century social and linguistic effects have resulted from the desire "to soften the harsh facts of life"?

9. Comment on the effectiveness of what Marckwardt calls the "mucker pose" in language and society. How influential do you think it really is?

Expository Technique

1. Comment on the function of the first two paragraphs. How does the first prepare for the introduction of the essay's controlling idea?

2. What is the controlling idea?

3. In developing the controlling idea Professor Marckwardt discusses two factors which affected the American language. What are these factors, and how do they constitute the principal structural elements of the essay?

4. Show how the author indicates the divisions within the essay.

5. How does the author establish causal relationships?

Exercises

1. In chapter VI of H. L. Mencken's *The American Language* (New York, 1948) read the section "Euphemisms" and report to the class some of the examples of the glorification of the commonplace recorded there. What examples can you add from your own observation?

2. In the same chapter of *The American Language* read the section "Forbid-

den Words" and report to the class on the examples of verbal prudery recorded there.

3. In "Verbal Taboo in a College Community" (*American Speech,* XIII [1938], 96–107), E. B. Hunter and B. E. Gaines report on a survey of reactions by college students to a list of expressions. Prepare a similar list, perhaps incorporating more current expressions, and circulate it among your class members. Summarize their reactions in an oral class report. You will probably want to have the replies made anonymously, but it might be interesting to code the replies by sex to see if there is any appreciable difference between sexes in attitudes toward verbal taboos.

4. For those who are inclined to swear but fearful of doing so, American English, as Professor Marckwardt points out, provides "a whole lexicon of near-swearing," expressions like *darn, heck,* and *Sam Hill,* happy linguistic compromises. What other examples of such innocuous profanity can you cite. In this regard, consult Ashley Montague, *The Anatomy of Swearing* (New York, 1967), chapter 12, "Swearing in the Nineteenth Century," for discussion and examples.

5. In an article entitled "American Euphemisms for Dying, Death, and Burial" (*American Speech,* XI [1936], 195–202), Louise Pound lists over two hundred euphemisms for and about death, among them "called to his reward" and "taken his last cue from life's stage." Read the article and report to the class on those which you find most interesting.

6. In *The American Way of Death* (New York, 1963) Jessica Mitford lists some of the euphemisms employed by morticians today in the conduct of their business. Read the appropriate sections of the book and report your findings to the class.

7. Like euphemism, circumlocution seeks to employ language that will avoid unacceptable words or ideas. While a euphemism is usually a single word or at most a phrase, a circumlocution, literally, attempts to "talk around" a subject. The following anecdote which Senator Everett Dirksen shared with his Senate colleagues, illustrates a circumlocution:

> I am reminded of the man who filled in an application for an insurance policy. One of the questions he had to answer was "How old was your father when he died and of what did he die?" Well, his father had been hanged, but he did not like to put that in his application. He puzzled over it for quite a while. He finally wrote, "My father was 65 when he died. He came to his end while participating in a public function when the platform gave way.

Find examples of circumlocutions in magazine and newspaper advertisements and advertising circulars for funeral services, grave markers, cemeteries, or life insurance policies. Or find in other areas expressions which are intended to soften or to hide the unpleasant realities under discussion.

8. An attempt counter to euphemism is *dysphemism,* which is, literally, *a speaking ill.* Where a euphemism is deliberately mild, a dysphemism is deliberately crude and offensive. A euphemism for *die* might be *pass away;* a dysphemism for the same word might be *kick the bucket* or *push up daisies.* Prepare a list of euphemisms (or circumlocutions) and dysphemisms for *stomach, unintel-*

ligent, wed, and *becoming nauseated, drunk,* and *pregnant.* See *Dictionary of American Slang,* compiled by Harold Wentworth and Stuart Berg Flexner (New York, 1967) for some suggestions.

9. Comment on the function of profanity, obscenity, or dysphemistic expressions in one of the following:

a. The writing of Norman Mailer, James Jones, Allan Ginsberg, Edward Albee, or LeRoi Jones.

b. Student demonstrations, newspapers, or literary magazines.

c. Graffiti.

32.

ALBERT C. BAUGH

Some Cultural Influences on Modern English

The events of the nineteenth century and of the early twentieth affecting the English-speaking countries were of great political and social importance, but in their effect on the language they were not of a revolutionary character. The success of the British on the sea in the course of the Napoleonic Wars, culminating in Nelson's famous victory at Trafalgar in 1805, left England in a position of undisputed naval supremacy and gave her control over most of the world's commerce. The war against Russia in the Crimea (1854–56) and the contests with native princes in India had the effect of again turning English attention to the East. The great reform measures—the reorganization of parliament, the revision of the penal code and the poor laws, the restrictions placed on child labor, and the other industrial reforms—were important factors in establishing English society on a more democratic basis. They lessened the distance between the upper and the lower classes and greatly increased the opportunities for the mass of the population to share in the economic and cultural advantages that became available in the course of the century. The establishment of the first cheap newspaper (1816) and of cheap postage (1840), and the improved means of travel and communication

From A HISTORY OF THE ENGLISH LANGUAGE, Second Edition, by Albert C. Baugh. Copyright © 1957 by Appleton-Century-Crofts, Inc. Reprinted by permission of the publishers.

brought about by the railroad, the steamboat, and the telegraph had the effect of uniting more closely the different parts of England and of spreading the influence of the standard speech. At the same time the growth in importance of some of England's larger colonies, their steady trend towards autonomy, and the rapid development of the United States have given increased significance to the forms of English spoken in these territories and have led the populations of them to the belief that their use of the language is as much entitled to be considered a standard as that of the mother country.

Some of these events and changes are reflected in the English vocabulary. But more influential in this respect are the great developments in science and the rapid progress that has been made in every field of intellectual activity in the last hundred years. Periods of great enterprise and activity seem generally to be accompanied by a corresponding increase in new words. This is the more true when all classes of the people participate in such activity, both in work and play, and share in its benefits. Accordingly, the great developments in industry, the increased public interest in sports and amusements, and the many improvements in the mode of living, in which even the humblest worker has shared, have all contributed to the vocabulary. Among recent circumstances affecting the life of almost every one have been the world wars and the troubled periods following them. We shall find them also leaving their mark on the language. The last hundred years offer an excellent opportunity to observe the relation between a civilization and the language which is an expression of it.

THE GROWTH OF SCIENCE

The most striking thing about our present-day civilization is probably the part which science has played in bringing it to pass. We have only to think of the progress which has been made in medicine and the sciences auxiliary to it, such as bacteriology, biochemistry, and the like, to realize the difference that marks off our own day from that of only a few generations ago in everything that has to do with the diagnosis, treatment, prevention, and cure of disease. Of we may pause to reflect upon the relatively short period that separates Franklin, flying his kite in a thunderstorm, or Faraday, deflecting a magnetic needle with an electric current, from Bell and Edison and Westinghouse, from telephones and electric refrigerators and hydroelectric power plants. In every field of science, pure and applied, there has been need in the last hundred years for thousands of new terms. The great majority of these are technical words known only to the specialist, but a certain number of them in time become familiar to the layman and pass into general use.

Thus, in the field of medicine this is particularly apparent. We speak familiarly of *acidosis, anaemia, appendicitis, arteriosclerosis,* difficult as the word is, of *bronchitis, diphtheria,* and numerous other diseases and ailments. We use with some sense of their meaning words like *homeopathic, osteopathy, bacteriology, immunology, orthodontia.* We maintain *clinics,* administer an *antitoxin* or an *anesthetic,* and *vaccinate* for smallpox. We have learned the names of new drugs like *aspirin, iodine, insulin, morphine, strychnine,* and we acquire without effort the names of antibiotics and so-called 'wonder drugs', such as *penicillin, streptomycin,* and a whole family of *sulfa* compounds. We speak of *adenoids, endocrine glands,* and *hormones,* and know the uses of the *stethoscope* and the *bronchoscope.* We refer to the combustion of food in the body as *metabolism,* distinguish between *proteins* and *carbohydrates,* know that a dog can digest bones because he has certain *enzymes* or digestive fluids in his stomach, or say that a person who has the idiosyncrasy of being made ill by certain foods has an *allergy.* All of these words have come into use during the nineteenth, and in some cases, the twentieth century.

In almost every other field of science the same story could be told. In the field of electricity words like *dynamo, commutator, alternating current, arc light* have been in the language since about 1870. Physics has made us familiar with terms like *calorie, electron, ionization, ultraviolet rays,* the *quantum theory,* and *relativity,* though we don't always have a very exact idea of what they mean. More recently *atomic energy, radioactive, hydrogen bomb, chain reaction,* and on a more colloquial level *atom smasher* have come into common use. Chemistry has contributed so many common words that it is difficult to make a selection—*alkali, benzine, cyanide, creasote, formaldehyde, nitroglycerine, radium,* to say nothing of such terms as *biochemical, petrochemical,* and the like. Originally scientific words and expressions such as *ozone, natural selection, stratosphere* have become familiar through the popularity of certain books or the scientific reports in magazines and newspapers. The psychologist has taught us to speak of *apperception, egocentric, extravert* and *introvert, behaviorism, inhibition, inferiority complex,* and *psychoanalysis.* Consciously or unconsciously we have become scientifically minded in the last few generations, and our vocabularies reflect this extension of our consciousness and interest.

AUTOMOBILE, MOVING PICTURE, RADIO

Scientific discoveries and inventions do not always influence the language in proportion to their importance. It is doubtful whether the radio and the moving picture are more important than the telegraph and the telephone, but they have brought more new words into general use. Such additions to the vocabulary depend more upon the degree to which the discovery or invention enters into the life of the community. This can be seen admirably exemplified in the many new words or new uses of old words that have resulted from the popularity of the automobile and the numerous activities associated with it. Many an old word is now used in a special sense. Thus we *park* a car, and the verb *to park* scarcely suggests to the average man anything except leaving his car along the side of a street or road or in a *parking space*. But the word is an old one, used as a military term (*to park cannon*) and later of carriages. The word *automobile* and the more common word in England, *motor car*, are new, but such words as *sedan, coach, coupé, runabout* are terms adapted from earlier types of vehicle. The American *truck* is the English *lorry* to which we may attach a *trailer*. We have learned new words or new meanings in *carburetor, spark plug, choke, clutch, gear shift, piston rings, throttle, differential, universal, steering wheel, self-starter, shock absorber, radiator, hood* (English *bonnet*), *windshield* (in England *wind screen*), *bumper, chassis, hubcap,* and *automatic transmission*. We go into *high* and *low*, have a *blowout* or a *flat*, use *tubeless tires*, carry a *spare*, drive a *convertible* or *station-wagon*, and put the car in a *garage*. We may *tune up* the engine or *stall* it, it may *knock* or *backfire*, or we may *skid, cut in, side swipe* another car, and be fined for *speeding* or passing a *traffic signal*. Of late we have heard a good bit about *safety glass, knee-action, power steering*, while *service stations* and *motor courts* are everywhere along the road and the *superhighway*. We must buy *gas* in America and *petrol* in England. Many more examples could be added of terms familiar to every motorist, but they would only further illustrate what is sufficiently clear, the way in which a new thing which becomes genuinely popular makes demands upon and extends the resources of the language.

The same principle might be illustrated by the moving picture and the radio. The words *cinema* and *moving picture* date from 1899, while the alternative *motion picture* is somewhat later. *Screen, reel, newsreel, film, scenario, projector, close-up, fade-out, feature picture, animated cartoon,* are now common. While *radiogram* goes back to 1905, it is only with the spread of popular interest in wireless transmission that the vocabulary has been expanded from this source. The word *radio* in the sense of a receiving set dates from about 1925. From the circumstance that in the beginning many amateurs built their own sets, a good many technical terms came to be widely used, words like *variable condenser, radio-frequency transformer, input, inductance, impedance, superheterodyne, kilocycle*. Even now when any one can turn the dials of a factory-built set we are familiar with such expressions as *listen in, stand by, hook-up, selectivity, loudspeaker, aerial, antenna, lead-in,* and *FM* or *frequency modulation*. Words like *announcer, broadcast, reception, microphone,* and *tone control* have acquired special meanings sometimes commoner than their more general senses.

THE WORLD WARS

As a further example of how great developments or events leave their mark upon language we may observe some of the words that came into English between 1914 and 1918 as a direct consequence of the war then being waged. Some of these were military terms representing new methods of warfare, such as *air raid, battleplane, antiaircraft gun, tank, whippet* (a small tank), and *blimp* (a small dirigible). *Gas mask* and *liaison officer* were new combinations with a military significance. *Camouflage* was borrowed from French, where it had formerly been a term of the scene-painter's craft, but it caught the popular fancy and was soon used half facetiously for various forms of disguise or misrepresentation. Old words were in some cases adapted to new uses. *Sector* was used in the sense of a specific portion of the fighting line; *barrage,* originally an artificial barrier like a dam in a river, designated a protective screen of heavy artillery or machine-gun fire; *dud,* a general word for any counterfeit thing, was specifically to a shell that did not explode; and *ace* acquired the meaning of a crack airman, especially one who had brought down five of the enemy's machines. In a number of cases a word which had had but a limited circulation in the language now came into general use. Thus *hand grenade* goes back to 1661, but attained new currency during the war. Other expressions already in the language but popularized by the war were *dugout, machine gun, periscope, no man's land,* and even the popular designation of an American soldier, *doughboy,* which was in colloquial use in the United States as early as 1867. *Blighty* was a popular bit of British army slang, derived from India and signifying England or home, and was often applied to a wound that sent a man back to England. Other expressions such as *slacker, trench foot, cootie, war bride,* and the like were either struck off in the heat of the moment or acquired a poignant significance from the circumstances under which they were used. Many of these words will doubtless prove a permanent part of the vocabulary.

It would seem that World War II was less productive of memorable words, as it was of memorable songs. Nevertheless it made its contribution to the language in the form of certain new words, new meanings, or an increased currency for expressions which had been used before. In connection with the *air raid,* so prominent a feature of the war, we have the words *alert* (air-raid warning), *blackout, blitz* (German *Blitzkrieg,* literally lightning war), *blockbuster, dive-bombing, evacuate,* air-raid *shelter.* The words *beachhead, parachutist, paratroop, landing strip, crash landing, roadblock, jeep, fox hole* (as a shelter for one or two men), *bulldozer* (an American word used in a new sense), *decontamination, task force* (a military or naval unit assigned to the carrying out of a particular operation), *resistance movement,* and *radar* are not in the *Oxford Dictionary* or its 1933

Supplement. *To spearhead* an attack, *to mop up,* and *to appease* were new verbs or old verbs with a new military or political significance. The colloquial *flattop* is shorter and more convenient than *aircraft carrier. Flack* (antiaircraft fire) was taken over from German, where it is an abbreviation of *Fliegerabwehrkanone,* antiaircraft gun. *Commando,* a word which goes back to the Boer War, acquired a new and specialized meaning. Some words which were either new or enjoyed great currency during the war—*priority, tooling up, bottleneck, ceiling* (upper limit), *backlog, stockpile*—have become a part of the vocabulary of civilian life, while *lendlease* has passed into history. The aftermath of the war has given us such expressions as *iron curtain, cold war, fellow traveler, front organization, police state,* all with a very special connotation.

LANGUAGE AS A MIRROR OF PROGRESS

Words, being but symbols by which a man expresses his ideas, are an accurate measure of the range of his thought at any given time. They obviously designate the things he knows, and just as obviously the vocabulary of a language must keep pace with the advance of his knowledge. The date when a new word enters the language is in general the date when the object, experience, observation, or whatever it is that calls it forth has entered his consciousness. Thus with a work like the *Oxford Dictionary,* which furnishes us with dated quotations showing when the different meanings of every word have arisen and when new words first appear in the language, we could almost write the history of civilization merely from linguistic evidence. When in the early part of the nineteenth century we find growing up a word like *horsepower* or *lithograph* we may depend upon it that some form of mechanical power which needs to be measured in familiar terms or a new process of engraving has been devised. The appearance in the language of words like *railway, locomotive, turntable* about 1835 tells us that steam railways were then coming in. In 1839 the words *photograph* and *photography* first appear, and a beginning is made towards a considerable vocabulary of special words or senses of words such as *camera, Kodak* (still a trade-mark), *film, enlargement, emulsion, focus, shutter, light meter. Concrete* in the sense of a mixture of crushed stone and cement dates from 1834, but *reinforced concrete* is an expression called forth only in the twentieth century. The word *cable* occurs but a few years before the laying of the first Atlantic cable in 1857–58. *Refrigerator* is first found in English in an American quotation of 1841. The words *emancipation* and *abolitionist* have for every American specific meanings connected with the efforts to abolish slavery, efforts which culminated in the Civil War. In the last quarter of the nineteenth century an interesting story of progress is told by new words or new meanings such as *typewriter, telephone, apartment house, twist drill, drop-forging, blueprint, oilfield, motorcycle, feminist, fundamentalist, marathon* (introduced in 1896 as a result of the revival of the Olympic games at Athens in that year), *battery* and *bunt,* the last two indicating the growing popularity of professional baseball in America.

The twentieth century permits us to see the process of vocabulary growth going on under our eyes, sometimes, it would seem, at an accelerated rate. At the turn of the century we get the word *questionnaire* and in 1904 the first hint of *television.* In 1906 the British launched a particular battleship named the *Dreadnaught,* and the word *dreadnaught* passed into popular use for any warship of the same class. A year later we got the word *raincoat* and about the same time *Thermos bottle.* This is the period when many of the terms of aviation that have since become so familiar first came in—*airplane, aircraft, airman, monoplane, biplane, hydroplane, dirigible,* and even *autogiro. Nose-dive* belongs to the period of the war. About 1910 we began talking about the *futurist* and the *postimpressionist* in art. *Intelligentsia* as a desig-nation for the class to which superior culture is attributed, and *bolshevik* for a holder of revolutionary political views were originally applied at the time of the First World War to groups in Russia. At this time *profiteer* and in America *prohibition* arose with specialized meanings. Meanwhile *foot-fault, fairway, plus fours, fox trot, auction bridge,* and *contract* were indicative of popular interest in certain games and pastimes. The 1933 supplement to the *Oxford Dictionary* records *Cellophane* (1921), *Celanese* (1923), and *rayon* (1924), but it does not yet know the *Mazda lamp. Mazda* is a trade-mark which few people probably realize is derived from the name of the Zoroas-trian god of the light-giving firmament. Only yesterday witnessed the birth of *crooner, nudist, air-conditioned, plastic* (the noun), *nylon* (originally a trade name), *transistor, Deepfreeze, record changer, tape recorder, automa-tion, prefabricated,* and such popular American expressions as *coffee break* and *baby sitter.* Tomorrow will witness others as the exigencies of the hour call them into being. . . .

Vocabulary

autonomy, currency, accelerated, exigencies

Review Questions

1. Professor Baugh holds that the past hundred years or so offer good exam-ples of the relation between a civilization and its language. What principal devel-opments in modern civilization support this view?

2. What evidence does the author provide to show the influence that historical events and developments have had upon English?

Exercises

1. The following subjects have received special attention during the last decade or so. Select one of them for study and compile a list of words or expressions pertaining to that subject and see how many of them have been included in recent dictionaries.

nuclear energy	professional basketball	social legislation	motion pictures
cold war	television	civil rights	recording
professional football	Vietnam	dope traffic	computers

2. The assimilation of members of various national and racial groups has been a marked feature of the culture of the United States, and American English has been strongly affected by such groups as the Indians, French, Dutch, Spanish, and Germans. Select one of these nationalities, learn as much as you can about its influence on American English, and report your findings to the class. The following works will be of use in obtaining information for your report:

Albert H. Marckwardt, *American English* (New York, 1958).
Mitford Mathews, *American Words* (New York, 1959).
H. L. Mencken, *The American Language,* 4th ed. (New York, 1949).
John Nist, *A Structural History of English* (New York, 1966).
Thomas Pyles, *Words and Ways of American English* (New York, 1952).

3. Notably responsive to influences from other languages, British and American English have also had an impact on other national tongues. Read and prepare an oral class report on one of the following:

Morton Benson, "English Loan Words in Russian Sport Terminology," *American Speech, XXXIII* (1958), 252–259.
Britta M. Charleston, "The English Linguistic Invasion of Switzerland," *English Studies,* XL (1959), 271–282.
Jacek Fiziak, "English Sports Terms in Modern Polish," *English Studies,* XLV (1964), 230–236.
P. F. Gang, "Some English Loanwords in Germany," *Modern Language Review,* XLIX (1954), 478–483.
Watson Kirkconnell, *Common English Loanwords in Eastern European Languages.* Slavistica No. 14. Winnipeg, Canada, The Ukrainian Free Academy of Science, 1952.
Paul G. Krauss, "The Anglo-American Influence on German," *American Speech* XXXVIII (1963), 257–269. See other studies of Krausson English influence on German in *German Quarterly,* XXI (1958), 272–286; *American,* XXXVI (1961), 41–47, XXXVII (1962), 123–129, and XLI (1966), 28–38.
Ralph H. Lane, "English into Dutch," *Germanic Review,* XXXIV (1959), 235–241.
C. E. Schorer, "English Loan Words in Puerto Rico," *American Speech,* XXVIII (1953), 22–25.

Aasta Stene, *English Loan-words in Modern Norwegian: a Study of Linguistic Borrowing in the Process* (London, 1945).

Donald C. Swanson, "English Loanwords in Modern Greek," *Word,* XIV (1958), 26–46.

Stephen Ullmann, "Anglicisms in French—Notes on their Chronology, Range, and Reception," *PMLA,* LXII (1947), 1153–1177.

Writing Suggestions: Cause and Effect

LINGUISTIC SUBJECTS

1. The Causes of Dialects
2. The Effect of Geographical Barriers on Dialect
3. Forces Making for ＿＿＿＿＿ (Standardization, Differentiation) in American English
4. The Social or Political Consequences of ＿＿＿＿＿ (Dialect, Substandard English, Foreign Accent)
5. Nationalism in American Language and Literature
6. The Causes or Effects of Linguistic Nationalism in ＿＿＿＿＿ (Wales, Ireland, Belgium, India, Ceylon)
7. Why Black Americans Study Swahili
8. The Effect of Language on Morality
9. Why We ＿＿＿＿＿ (Swear, Euphemize, Dysphemize)
10. The Consequences of Verbal Prudery
11. The Effect of ＿＿＿＿＿ (Wars, Computers, Space Exploration, Nuclear Research, Journalism, Sports, Politics, Business) on American English
12. The Influence of ＿＿＿＿＿ (the Bible, an Author, the Classics, Dictionaries) on American English
13. Influences ＿＿＿＿＿ (Bible, Classics, Nationalities) on ＿＿＿＿＿ (Place Names, Personal Names)

Comparison and Contrast

THE USE of comparison and contrast always involves a treatment of a subject by reference to something else; *A* is thus placed beside *B* for the purpose of establishing similarities and differences between the two. If a writer wants to point out *similarities* between *A* and *B*, he will use comparison. If, on the other hand, his purpose is to show *differences* between them, he will use contrast. We increase our store of knowledge daily by using comparison and contrast. Are the Yankees a better team than the Dodgers? Is Harvard's medical school as good as Yale's? Do Fords use as much gasoline as Chevrolets? Is the United States losing the space race? Is the cost of living rising? The answers to these questions and others like them must be based upon an assessment of similarities and differences between *A* and *B*.

As expository devices, comparison and contrast have two major purposes: (1) to explain the unfamiliar; (2) to examine two or more ideas or objects in order to find similarities and dissimilarities between them. First, if we wish to treat a subject with which the reader is unfamiliar, we can compare and contrast it with some subject with which he is acquainted. An effective way of explaining the English game of cricket to an American, for instance, would be to compare it to baseball and to note that like baseball it is a team sport in which a ball and bat are employed, but that unlike baseball a cricket team is composed of eleven men, the ball is bowled rather than pitched, and the bat is shaped something like a paddle. In this situation we are using the reader's knowledge of baseball as a point of reference in order to explain the unfamiliar. Secondly, comparison and contrast can be used for the purpose of analysis and critical appraisal to discuss two subjects

465

which are equally well known to the reader. We could, for instance, compare and contrast the social attitudes of two novelists, the marking habits of two college professors, or the advantages of different political systems or ways of life.

SPECIAL PROBLEMS IN COMPARISON
AND CONTRAST

Any subject can be effectively treated by means of comparison and contrast, but the development of the topic deserves careful consideration. Regardless of the topic we must be confident that whatever we select to compare and contrast with it is similar (or dissimilar) enough to make such treatment fruitful. Although it is true that the poetic imagination can find a basis for comparison and contrast in any two things (e.g., Shakespeare compares the world to a stage, Emily Dickinson contrasts a frigate and a book), it is usually best for inexperienced writers to avoid such figurative analysis and to restrict their use of comparison and contrast to members of the same general class. Thus, for example, revolutions should be compared and contrasted with other revolutions, languages with other languages, cities with other cities.

It should also be noted that an essay will usually be more effective if both comparison and contrast are used. Unless the express purpose of an essay were to present *only* likenesses or differences, the use of one of the techniques to the exclusion of the other would probably present a false impression of the relationship between the two ideas or objects under consideration. To discuss only the similarities between a cat and a tiger would be to overlook the obvious differences between them and to leave the reader with the idea that they are much more alike than nature has made them.

ORGANIZATION

Organization is of special importance in the use of comparison and contrast because unity is difficult to maintain unless a definite method of development has been decided upon in advance. First, to be significant and useful, the comparison and contrast of two or more subjects must not be haphazard, but purposeful and systematic. A mere listing of the characteristics of two subjects does not constitute a comparison or contrast of the two. For this it is necessary that the two subjects be treated according to some discernible pattern or set of principles. Two colleges may be compared and contrasted by the caliber of their student bodies, the size of their libraries, the excellence of their faculties, and the extent of their laboratory facilities. These four points then become the set of principles upon which the comparison and contrast is based, thus giving a logical, coherent structure to the essay.

Secondly, organization is important because in this expository type there are two possible means of developing the subject, each effective under different circumstances. If we were comparing and contrasting College A with College B, we might do it in either of the following ways: In Plan I College A is completely examined in terms of the predetermined set of four principles, then College B is examined in the same manner. In Plan II *both* colleges are compared and contrasted on the first of the four principles, then the second, and so on. Plan I is most effective when the subject is fairly simple and when the reader will be able to remember all of what he read about College A when he begins reading about College B. Plan II is superior

PLAN I	PLAN II
College A	*Caliber of student body*
Caliber of student body	College A
Size of library	College B
Excellence of faculty	*Size of library*
Extent of laboratory facilities	College A
College B	College B
Caliber of student body	*Excellence of faculty*
Size of library	College A
Excellence of faculty	College B
Extent of laboratory facilities	*Extent of laboratory facilities*
	College A
	College B

to Plan I, however, when the subject is somewhat complex and when there is a significant amount of detailed material, such as statistics or dates, in the essay. Plan II requires that fewer details be remembered by the reader as he reads from one part of the essay to another, and for this reason it will usually result in a more effective use of comparison and contrast in most college writing situations.

AN EXAMPLE OF COMPARISON AND CONTRAST

In reading the following selection by Henry Sweet, notice how he has employed comparison and contrast in his treatment of the parts of speech, and try to determine how his technique is particularly adaptable to his topic.

*THE PARTS OF SPEECH**

As regards their function in the sentence, words fall under certain classes called **parts of speech,** all the members of each of these classes having certain formal characteristics in common which distinguish them from the members of the other classes. Each of these classes has a name of its own—noun, adjective, verb, etc.

Thus, if we compare nouns, such as *snow, tree, man,* with adjectives, such as *big, white, green,* and verbs, such as *melt, grow, speak,* we shall find that all nouns whose meaning admits of it agree in having plural inflections—generally formed by adding *s* (*trees*); that adjectives have no plural inflections, but have degrees of comparison (*big, bigger, biggest*)—which nouns and verbs have not; that verbs have inflections of their own distinct from those of the other parts of speech (*I grow, he grows, grown*); that each part of speech has special form-words associated with it (*a tree, the tree; to grow, is growing, has grown*); and that each part of speech has a more or less definite position in the sentence with regard to other parts of speech (*white snow, the snow melts, the green tree, the tree is green*).

If we examine the **functions** of these three classes, we see at once that all verbs are predicative words—that they state something about a subject-word, which is generally a noun (*the snow melts*); that adjectives are often used as assumptive words (*white snow*), and so on.

If we examine the **meanings** of the words belonging to the different parts of speech, we shall find that such nouns as *tree, snow, man,* are all substance-words, while the adjectives and verbs given above are all attribute-words, the adjectives expressing permanent attributes, the verbs changing attributes or phenomena. We can easily see that there is a natural connection between the functions and meanings of these parts of speech. We see that the most natural way of speaking of a substance is to imply or state some attribute about it (*white snow, the snow melts*); and that permanent attributes, such as "whiteness," can often be taken for granted, while phenomena, such as "melting," being often sudden and unexpected, require to be stated explicitly.

But this connection, though natural, is not necessary. In language it is often necessary to state, as well as imply, permanent attributes (*the tree is green*), and it is sometimes convenient to make statements about attributes as well as substances. Thus, instead of using the word *white* as a means of implying something about *snow* or any other substance, we may wish to state or imply something about the attribute itself, as when we say *whiteness is an attribute of snow,* or talk of *the dazzling whiteness of the snow.* It is easy to see that there is no difference of meaning between *whiteness is an attribute of snow* and *snow is white:* the difference between *white* and the noun *whiteness* is purely formal and functional—grammatical, not logical.

* Reprinted from *New English Grammar, Logical and Historical* by Henry Sweet.

Exercises on Comparison and Contrast

1. Consult the catalogues of two colleges or universities and, by employing the criteria and organization described on page 467, compare them with your own.

2. How is secondary school similar to college? How is it different? Formulate a set of principles upon which the two may be profitably compared and contrasted, and show how you would develop the ideas suggested by your plan into a coherent essay.

3. Which actresses and actors might best portray the following roles in motion pictures?

Eve	Juliet	Huckleberry Finn	Job
Lady Macbeth	Becky Sharp	Holden Caulfield	Don Juan

In each case name those you considered but did not select. Give the reasons for your choice in each case.

4. Indicate how you would develop one of the following sentences into a theme on the two major American political parties:

a. For all practical purposes, America has a one-party system, for there is no significant difference between the political, moral, economic, or philosophical beliefs of the Democrats and Republicans.

b. America's political system works because it allows the electorate to choose its President from two parties whose philosophies differ markedly and who present very different solutions to such problems as foreign policy, civil unrest, inflation, and states rights.

Writing Suggestions: Comparison and Contrast

1. America Through Foreign Eyes
2. Capitalism and Communism: Two Ways of Life
3. American Critics of America
4. Urban and Rural Living
5. Traditional and Progressive Jazz
6. Man—The Superior Sex
7. Woman—The Superior Sex
8. What Military Service Did for (or to) Me
9. You Can't Go Home Again
10. Drama on Stage and Television
11. Religious and Scientific Truth
12. Good and Bad _____ (Music, Literature, Art, Courses, Investments, Hobbies, Bosses, Roommates, Dates, Parents)
13. The New and the Old _____ (Parents, Children, Army, Navy, Grocery Store, Drug Store, Salesman, Dentist, Doctor, Fisherman)
14. Compare and/or contrast two novels, dramas, fictional characters, pianists, conductors, newspapers, magazines, television personalities, television programs, political platforms; or do the same for a novel or play and its film version.

(Additional writing suggestions on linguistic subjects are on page 497.)

British and American Usage

33.

MARGARET NICHOLSON

The Unity of English

Some thirty years ago a professor of English at the University of California introduced his students to Fowler's *Dictionary of Modern English Usage*. That was in 1926 or 1927. I wish I could remember which, because it would be interesting to know that, without the fanfare of today's publicity, a scholarly reference book published in England could have found immediate enthusiasts in California that first spring of its publication. But I can't remember. Nor can I remember, I am ashamed to say, which of my English professors made the introduction. I do know that he spent the full hour that day reading snatches from it, and that I, for one, was an immediate convert. I stopped in at Sather Gate Book Shop that noon and bought a copy, and from that day on "MEU" has been my delight and mentor.

I never in those days felt that Fowler was particularly British or difficult. During the three years I taught high-school English MEU was always on the classroom reference shelf and to the best of my memory it was used, even by suburban California teen-agers of the "roaring twenties." I can't remember any complaints about its being un-American.

It wasn't till several years later, after I had abandoned teaching and was working at the Oxford University Press in New York, that I became aware of the battle between American-English and English-English. Oxford was militantly British at the time and the staff was virtuously conscious of representing one of the last outposts of British civilization. We addressed letters to our authors "John Doe Esq."—*Mr.* was allowed only for printers, paper men, and unpaid accounts. Posted above each desk was a list of English

From *Atlantic Monthly*, CIC (May 1957), 71–73, originally entitled "What Is Good English?" Copyright, 1957, by Margaret Nicholson and reprinted by her permission.

spellings to be rigorously adhered to in all correspondence: *analyse* with an
s, judgement with an *e, pyjamas* with a *y*—though in what context *pyjamas*
would appear in our daily correspondence I can't imagine. It became almost
natural for me to speak of my *holiday,* rather than my vacation; *in the
circumstances* (not *under*—though I should have remembered Fowler's
remarks on that bit of foolishness), of course, I should need new *luggage.*
I even remember once saying unblushingly that I should leave *Wednesday
fortnight.* If my friends suspected me of snobbism (which they probably in
their ignorance called snobbishness) it is hardly surprising. Today it all
seems like a foreshadowing of "U. and Non-U."* under the guise of "Brit.
and Non-Brit.":

BRITISH	NON-BRITISH (OR "CHIEFLY U.S.")
tin	can
biscuit	cracker
chemist	druggist
packet	package or pack
ill	sick
shop	store
braces	suspenders
I fancy	I think (or worse, *I guess*)
increase (of wages)	rise (in salary) or lamentably, a *raise*
lodger	roomer
sweets	candy

And so on. Fortunately, before very long Oxford New York changed its
policy. American spelling became the standard, our mimeographed lists
were tossed into the basket, I graduated (a good Americanism) into editorial work, and the war of Brit. and Non-Brit. was forgotten. *Modern
English Usage* remained on my desk, an indispensable help in editing both
English and American manuscripts. But it was then that I began wondering
about the possibility of a slightly simplified Fowler with American variations.
Some fifteen years later, to my delight and apprehension, I was invited to
undertake the task of preparing one.

Of course there is an English idiom and an American idiom, but in
scholarly or serious speech and writing, as opposed to informal talk and
fiction, the difference is not as evident as many of us believe. In books that
do not contain dialogue, and that have not been deliberately edited for the
American reader, our first clue that the writer is British is the spelling; in
speeches that seem typically British, it is chiefly the accent that gives this
impression; read in the newspaper there is often little that would not be
the natural expression of any literate American. I consciously watched for

---

* [U. and Non-U: Upper-class and Non-Upper-class—*Eds.*]

expressions and constructions that one could label peculiarly English or peculiarly American in all my reading during the five years or so that I was working on the "American Fowler" and found many times that I could read chapters in succession without finding any example that could be cited as one or the other without qualification.

The other day I decided to make a random test of my theory in a book I was reading for pleasure (and what a pleasure it is to be able to give one's whole mind to the meaning rather than reserving at least half of it for spotting idiomatic usage and construction!). I found nothing in the first hundred pages, and rather desperately stopped on page 108 when I came to "Here we are back *full circle* to theories long familiar to philosophers." There is nothing in that that an American could not have written, but I suspected that "full circle" so used would come perhaps more natural to an Englishman. But very soon after that I found "A novelist who disregards major public events is either *a footler* or a plain idiot." A footler? If I had not consciously been watching for Briticisms I should have passed this over without noticing, but having stopped I realized I had no reliable idea of what a footler is; I reached for my dictionaries. Both *Webster's Collegiate* and *The American College Dictionary* give *footle,* n., "twaddle, drivel," and label it slang, but whether British or American slang they do not say. *The Concise Oxford Dictionary* gives *footle,* v., "to trifle, play the fool," and n., "twaddle, folly"—also both slang. I am no authority on slang, so I gave up, but my feeling is that as current slang *footler* is chiefly Brit., not U.S. Then I found a term that I felt would justify me in stamping the writer British (if I had not already known he was): "Civilization can lift itself up by its *boot-tags.*" *Boot-straps* is the American for that; no American would write *boot-tags* unless he was deliberately affecting familiarity with British idiom. Our man is English. I wish I had closed the book before I read the last sentence on the same page: "An electoral system *gerrymandered* in the interest of the moneyed class." Gerrymandered? What is our man now?

To be fair, I must admit that as I read on into the more specific chapters of the book I came across many individual words and phrases that would identify it as English rather than American: *motor-cars, tinned food, the greengrocer,* "old maids biking to Holy Communion through the mists of the Autumn morning," "posh tailor-made clothes." (*Webster's Collegiate* doesn't even list *posh; The Concise Oxford* defines it "smart, tip-top," and labels it slang. What about *tip-top?*)

And what about the reverse of the picture? What is it that tells the English reader "this book was written by an American"? First, of course, as with us, the spelling. We wantonly omit hyphens when they are needed and insert them when they are unnecessary; we use *z* when *s* is called for and discard the *u* in *-our* endings; we do not realize (or realise) that *wor-shiped* and *kidnaped,* without doubling the penultimate consonants, are not only wrong but invite flagrant mispronunciation. So let us forget the spelling. Wanting to have something more than a theoretical opinion, I asked some English friends how they identified a nonfiction book as American. "By its illiteracies," one of them retorted immediately. And what are the peculiarly American illiteracies? I insisted. Although it is rather unfair, since this was an informal, off-the-record conversation, I am going to give his list in the order in which it was presented.

Improper use of *will* for *shall,* first person future. This delighted me. It is true that the distinction between *will* and *shall* is less and less observed in America, even by good speakers and writers. Those of us who were brought up on traditional English still observe it instinctively; we are a minority. But is *will* for *shall* in this usage peculiarly American and indisputably an illiteracy? Sir Ernest Gowers, in his *ABC of Plain Words,* published in England for English writers in 1951, does not agree. He points out that "I will go" has always been the plain future for the Celts, that Americans have followed their practice, and that "the English have taken to imitating the Americans." "If we go by practice rather than precept," he continues, "we can no longer say dogmatically that 'I will go' for the plain future is wrong." Fowler would not like this. In his article on *will* (MEU) he says: "Of the English of the English *shall & will* are the shibboleth . . . and endow his speech with a delicate precision that could not be attained without it." Opposite views by two men to the manner born. Americans may choose whichever they will.

In back of for *behind.* "All Americans say it," according to my friends. Well, a great many Americans do. Certainly it slips easily from the tongue of many who should know better. I do not remember having come across it in print, and I cannot believe that a serious writer would be guilty of it. I agree that it is an illiteracy. Of *back of* for *behind* (the *in* is completely otiose) Fowler says gently, "An American, not an English idiom."

The omission of the preposition in such phrases as "I'll see you Tuesday," "He works nights," "I'll write you as soon as I know." These are all standard American usage now; the Englishman, however, would say *on Tuesday, at night,* and *to you.* In recording *write you* when there is direct object, *The Oxford English Dictionary* says, "freq. c. 1790–c. 1865" and gives several examples.

He aimed to (*be*) rather than *at* (*being*). Whatever the purists may say, this is now standard American usage, although it is no longer condoned in England. OED lists it as obsolete, *Webster's Collegiate* without qualification, and ACD as "U.S.," contrasting it with the English *at* plus the gerund.

Different than instead of *different from.* How long this battle has been going on! It was in full swing in my own schooldays, and quite recently when I was discussing Americanisms with a college professor she exclaimed in horror, "I hope you're not going to allow *different than!*" Allow it? We have it, whether we like it or not. Again I turn for comfort to OED: "The usual construction is now with *from*. . . . The construction with *than* is found in Fuller, Addison, Steele, DeFoe, Richardson, Goldsmith, Miss Burney, Coleridge, Southey, DeQuincey, Carlyle, Thackeray, Newman, Trench, and Dasent, among others"—the others, I am afraid, including two thirds of the American public.

So much for peculiarly American illiteracies. We have them, yes. But I was happy that my friend selected the examples he did.

Apart from so-called illiteracies, there are some words that have different meanings on the two sides of the Atlantic. For example, *faculty* is used on the *campuses* (so used only in America) of both English and American colleges, but as applied to the whole body of teachers and perhaps administrative officers (*A faculty meeting was called for Wednesday night*) it is "U.S. only." *Sabbatical* is used in England in its religious sense but not for an academic *sabbatical leave. The Humane Society* in England rescues the drowning and has nothing to do with the prevention of cruelty to animals.

Differences of this kind can be misleading, and it is well not to have too sanguine an acceptance of dictionary definitions. Even in the most recent edition of *The Concise Oxford Dictionary*, which helpfully uses an asterisk to indicate words and meanings "chiefly or originally American," one discovers some surprising things. "*Faucet* (chiefly U.S.), tap for a barrel." "*Filibuster* . . . obstructionist in legislative assembly." "*Barn-dance* (orig. U.S.), dance in which partners advance side by side & then dance a schottische step." "*Bat*, v. (U.S. & dial.), to wink (*never batted an eyelid = did not sleep a wink*)." "*Beauty Parlour* (orig. U.S.), establishment in which the art or trade of face massage, face lifting, applying cosmetics, &c. is carried on." A *bouncer*, U.S. slang, is a *chucker out. Call down*, U.S. colloq., means *challenge*.

There are of course many words that we—and the British—now use without being conscious of the fact that they are Americanisms: a *blanket* ruling, a blood *donor*, the Red Cross *drive*, to be *through* one's work, to *grill* the prisoner, to meet the *deadline*. Most of these were at one time slang or colloquial, but are now standard, at least in informal use.

Understandably it is in slang and colloquialisms that the differences between British and American are greatest and most apparent. Even in one country there is difference in regional, occupational, and social slang. If slang has color, if it expresses some idea or feeling with an economy not found in standard English, it may pass its own boundaries and even become part of the permanent language. No one thinks now of *mob, bus,* or *cab* as slang. It is my belief that *gangster, hold-up,* and *hoodlum* are also in the language to stay (although it is regrettable that they reflect so unsavory an element of American life). The R.A.F. *gremlins* are much at home in the United States as they are in England and may live to rival pixies and elves. Americans *grouse* (British slang) about their troubles and the British have little sympathy with *grouches* (U.S. slang).

Fowler says, speak as your neighbor speaks. True, the advice comes from his article on pronunciation, but it is as applicable to the use of English-English and American-English idiom. Personally I am unable to go the whole way and concede that if a large enough number of my neighbors say or write a thing in a given way, that way is right—or at least not until enough time has elapsed to give its blessing to the usage in question. To me *adviser* is so spelled, no matter how many times I see *advisor* in print, even in scholarly books. I prefer *John's going to Boston amazed me* to *John going to Boston* . . . even though I am assured that the gerund in America is dead. Speak as your neighbor speaks—but today our neighbor is the English-speaking world. If we have an idea to give to our neighbor, whether it is a commercial product or a global (U.S. vogue word) philosophy, we are inefficient if we allow disputed constructions or local peculiarities in our language to distract his attention. English-English and American-English are coming closer together, not growing farther apart. Two world wars, our publications, motion pictures, radio, television, and even the UN are seeing to that.

My feeling is that good English is good English, whatever the nationality of the writer. In every community there are local meanings, terms, and constructions, arising from the circumstances and environment of that particular locality. Some of these should be treasured, some should be eschewed in formal speech and writing. There is no essentially American-English or English-English. There are only not-too-important regional variations.

Vocabulary

otiose, sanguine, eschewed

Expository Technique

1. Miss Nicholson frequently introduces contrasts between British and American English by use of firsthand experience, for example, her work at Oxford University Press and her reading of a book. What is the purpose of this technique?

2. What conclusion does the author reach? How is it prepared for by the fact that both *booth-tags* and *gerrymandered* appeared in the book she was reading?

3. Outline the plan of comparison and contrast used in this essay.

Review Questions

1. As a result of Miss Nicholson's research for *A Dictionary of American-English Usage* (New York, 1957), what did she learn about the differences between British and American English?

2. On what levels are the differences between British and American usage greatest?

3. According to Miss Nicholson, English-English and American-English are coming closer together, not growing apart. What forces does she think account for this growing unity? If you agree with her, what other forces might be seen as contributing to this development?

(Exercises relating to Essays 33 and 34 are on pages 480–482.)

34.

THOMAS PYLES

American and British Differences in Pronunciation

Some of the phonetic differentiae of British and American English remaining to be discussed are on the whole less significant as national characteristics than those attitudes toward language which have been discussed previously; for, as has been pointed out, the "American accent" and the "British accent" cannot be explained merely by pointing out variations in the pronunciation of words—that is, differences in syllable stress and the articulation of individual speech sounds. These are as a rule what the observer first notices: they are obvious and more or less superficial.

In the treatment of postvocalic *r*, and of *a* in words of the *after, answer, path, grass* type, the usage of the great majority of Americans stands in sharp contrast to that of speakers of standard British English. The use of broad *a* by Americans who do not have it by tradition is fraught with dangers for the unwary, for it is not invariable in standard British English in words of the type under discussion: it occurs, for instance, in *dance* but not in *romance;* in *plaster* but not in *plastic;* in *class* but not in *crass;* in *can't* but not in *cant;* in *master* but not in *mascot.* The British reduction or loss of the penultimate syllable of words in *-ary, -ery, -ory* is not to be heard in any normal American speech save occasionally in *stationery* (perhaps to distinguish it from the adjective *stationary*), *primary, cemetery,* and *confectionery;* it may be heard in *dictionary* as an affectation, but those who affect it do not say *ordin'ry, territ'ry, necess'ry,* etc. British and eastern New England speech are alike in their use of a rounded or partially rounded vowel for short *ŏ* in words of the *got, odd, stop, clock* type. British English pronounces the *-ile* ending in *agile, docile, reptile, servile, tactile,* and the like to rime with *file.* American English usually preserves an older pronunciation of these words with reduced vowel or syllabic *l. Mobile* "movable" has two pronunciations in American English: it may rime with *noble* or it may be pronounced *mobeel* exactly like the totally unrelated Choctaw word which is the name of the city and the river in Alabama. Both these pronunciations of *mobile,* incidentally, are current in British English as variants of the somewhat more frequent pronunciation with *ī* in the final syllable. The American pronunciation of *fragile* occurs very occasionally as a British variant. The so-called long *ī* occurs in American English in *crocodile* and *gentile,* usually in *infantile,* and often in *juvenile, mercantile,* and *textile.*

There are other differences less sweeping in nature. Standard British English usually stresses the second syllable in *doctrinal, laboratory,* and *centenary,* these syllables being pronounced *try, bore,* and *tee* or *ten,* though *dóctrinal, láboratory,* and *céntenary* (the last two with characteristic British loss or reduction of the vowel in the penultimate syllable) occur as variants. *Advertisement* is always stressed on the second syllable in standard British English, but this stressing is also widely current in educated American English nowadays.

There are actually very few supposedly American pronunciations of individual words which do not occur as variants in British English. Daniel Jones, who in his *English Pronouncing Dictionary* is concerned only with what he calls Received Pronunciation, that is, standard British English, records as occurring in this type of speech a good many pronunciations usually thought of as characteristic of American English. The British, it is true, usually pronounce the past tense of the verb *to eat* as *et* (current but substandard in American English); however, the only pronunciation current in educated American use, riming with *late,* does occur in standard British English as a variant. *Been, either, neither, again,* and *against* are usually *bean, eyether, nyether, agayn,* and *agaynst* in standard British English; but Jones lists *bin, eether, neether, agen,* and *agenst,* the usual American pronunciations, as variants. *Trait* is in England usually pronounced *tray,* but the American pronunciation without suppression of the *-t* is also current; *nephew* with medial *-f-* is somewhat less usual than with *-v-,* but it is perfectly "standard." *Progress* (noun) and *process* usually have long *ō* in their first syllables, but Jones lists pronunciation with short *ŏ* as occurring, though rarely. Some American speakers use the long vowel in *process,* but not in *progress.*

Many, perhaps most, British speakers use long *ē* (as in *eve*) in the first syllable of *evolution, economic, equable, epoch,* and *predecessor,* but short *ĕ* as in *get* is also to be heard in all these words save the two last named. Of these words, *equable* frequently has *ē* in American English, and so has *economic,* but never *evolution.* Long *ē* in *epoch* and *predecessor* would be decidedly unusual in American English, but such pronunciations are occasionally heard; probably they are affected. *Patriot* and its derivatives *patriotic* and *patriotism* usually have *pat-* for their first syllable in British English, though pronunciations with *pate-* occur as variants; only the latter are current in normal American English. British English has *pate-* in *patron* and *patroness,* with *pat-* as a variant, but only *pat-* in *patronage* and *patronize;* American English usually has *pate-* in all these words, though *pat-* occurs as a variant in *patroness* and *patronage.*

Much, undoubtedly too much, has been made of supposed distinctively British pronunciations of such words as *profile* (riming with *no feel*), *tryst* (riming with *iced*), *zenith* (riming with *Kenneth*), *primer* "book" (riming with *timer*), *venison* (as *venzn*), *quandary* (with penultimate stress), *marital* (with stressed *i* in the penultimate, as in *recital*), and *aristocrat* (with stress on the first syllable, as also occasionally in American English). These words occur in most lists purporting to set forth differences between British and American pronunciation. It is quite true that the British pronunciations indicated within the parentheses are, except for *aristocrat,* never heard from American speakers. It is even more striking, however, that every one of these words—and a number of similar instances might be cited—has in British English a variant pronunciation identical with that most widely current in American English. The possibility must be admitted that some of the variants recorded by Daniel Jones are somewhat rarer in British English than he seems to indicate, for he specifically disclaims including any forms which can be considered rare without the use of some qualifying term such as *rarely* or *old-fashioned.* Not one of the variants cited above is so labeled, however, and Jones's observation and judgment are usually to be trusted in such matters. The usual American pronunciations of *quinine, corollary, tomato, figure, frontier, premier, squirrel, dynasty, chagrin, suave, miscellany, clerk, vase,* and *schedule* are not current in Standard British English, in which they are pronounced respectively *quinéen* (with short, unstressed *i* in the first syllable), *coróllary, tomahto, figger, fróntyer, prémyer* (with short *ĕ* in the first syllable), *squearel, dinnasty, shágrin* or *shagréen, swayve, miscéllany, clark* (so pronounced also in our Southern Highlands), *vahz,* and *shedule. Leisure* rimes with *pleasure* in British English, a pronunciation recorded in American dictionaries but seldom heard, the usual American pronunciation riming with *seizure.* But except for such general tendencies as have been discussed earlier, sporadic differences between British and American pronunciation are on the whole insignificant. The list of words having strikingly different pronunciations in the two great English-speaking nations might have been expanded somewhat, but not really very much.

Vocabulary

postvocalic, fraught, penultimate, purporting

Expository Technique

1. Compare and contrast Pyles's style with that of Margaret Nicholson in the preceding essay.
2. Into what subdivisions does Pyles divide the subject of pronunciation for the purposes of developing his essay?

Review Questions

1. What differences does Pyles cite between British and American pronunciation? Does he conclude that these differences are of a major or minor nature?
2. How do you account for the fact that Britons and eastern New Englanders pronounce in the same way a rounded or partially rounded vowel sound in words such as *got, odd, stop,* and *clock?*

Exercises

1. Consult a standard desk dictionary and list the American equivalent for each of the following Briticisims:

perambulator	bobby	barrister
lift (*noun*)	geyser	treacle
chemist	tram	fortnight
dust bin	petrol	exchequer
biscuit	ironmonger	chips
tin	queue	mucker

2. George Bernard Shaw once remarked that England and the United States were "two countries separated by the same language." How might an American and Englishman interpret the italicized words in the sentences below?

a. The little boy was very proud because he was wearing *braces* like his father's.

b. The lessons learned on the playing fields of the *public schools* served him well in later life.

c. Every time he visits his relatives he is sure to lose a few *pounds*.

d. I'm *mad* about my *flat*.

e. The sign outside the building read, "No *Solicitors* Allowed."

f. He was a *bloody* fighter.

g. The new *bonnet* was damaged in the accident.

3. Indicate the British spelling for the following:

rumor	aluminum	tire	connection
jail	check (*noun*)	pajamas	defense
vial	meter	pigmy	glycerin

4. Consult *An English Pronouncing Dictionary,* compiled by Daniel Jones (London, 1925), and determine the British pronunciation of the following:

Berkeley	epoch	neither	St. Clair
clerk	evolution	rather	tomato
derby	Magdalene	Shropshire	waistcoat

5. The following quotations have been selected respectively from advertisements for a resort, a school, and a car tire manufacturer in a British publication. Which linguistic usages are uniquely British?

a. On Holiday? Run down to Saunton. Just a day's drive from town but a different world. Time-honoured natural beauty in a modern setting. Every amenity—tennis, squash, putting, driving nets, billiards, library, dancing— The Lot! A fortnight at Saunton will do you and your wife a world of good and you'll benefit from out-of-season terms.

b. Recognised preparatory coaching school, South Coast will have two places next term for boys preferably aged from nine to eleven on joining. Eight boys to each group, no form orders.

c. A point not often realised about our tyres is that they are braced with cords of supple steel to give them a safe grip on the road. The general run of radials rely on textile to achieve the same result. But driving in the wet is a particular condition, and this is when you need reliability most. See your local dealer straight away for details.

6. Compare the vocabulary and spelling used in an article or editorial in the London *Times* or the *Manchester Guardian* with one in the *New York Times* or your own city newspaper. Prepare a brief report of your findings.

7. Do you think it true that the lower the level of writing in terms of Pooley's categories, the greater the difference between British and American English? In this connection, consult *A Dictionary of Slang and Unconventional English*, compiled by Eric Partridge (New York, 1950), and collect twenty British expressions and their meanings which are unfamiliar to you or which would be unfamiliar to most Americans.

8. What evidence of mutual influence of British and American English can you find? Consult chapter VI of H. L. Mencken's *Supplement I* (New York, 1948) to *The American Language.*

9. In addition to differences in American and British English, other variations of the mother tongue can be fruitfully studied. Summarize one of the following articles for a class report.

CANADIAN ENGLISH

Harold B. Allen, "Canadian-American Speech Differences Along the Middle Border," *Journal of the Canadian Linguistic Association,* V (1959), 17–24.

Walter S. Avis, "Canadian English Merits a Dictionary," *Culture,* XVIII (1957), 245–256.

———, "Linguistica Canadiana: Canadian English," *Journal of the Canadian Linguistic Association,* II (1956), 82.

———, "Speech Differences Along the Ontario-United States Border," *Journal of the Canadian Linguistic Association* I (1954), 13–19.

Christopher Dean, "Is There a Distinctive Literary Canadian English?" *American Speech,* XXXVIII (1963), 278–282.

AUSTRALIAN ENGLISH

Sidney John Baker, "Australian English," *The Australian Encyclopedia,* ed. A. H. Chisholm, Vol. I (1958).

JAMAICAN ENGLISH

Frederic G. Cassidy, *Jamaica Talk: Three Hundred Years of the English Language in Jamaica* (1961).

NEWFOUNDLAND ENGLISH

Bernard H. Porter, "A Newfoundland Vocabulary," *American Speech,* XXXVIII (1963), 297–301.

G. M. Story, "Research in the Language and Place-Names of Newfoundland," *Journal of the Canadian Linguistic Association,* III (1957), 47–55.

J. D. A. Widdowson, "Some Items of a Central Newfoundland Dialect," *Canadian Journal of Linguistics,* X (1964), 37–46.

SOUTH AFRICAN ENGLISH

G. Knowles-Williams and others, "English in South Africa, 1960," *English Studies in Africa* IV, (1961), 63–98.

Semantics

35.

IRVING J. LEE

The Useful Use of Words

THE WORK OF WORDS

Though widely differing in statement, much agreement may be found about what it is that words are supposed to do for us. Some typical definitions:

> A sign or expression may concern or designate or describe something, or, rather, he who uses the expression may intend to refer to something by it, e.g., to an object, or a property, or a state of affairs.[1]

> Words are vocal sounds or letter combinations which symbolize or signify something. They . . . have no other function except to direct attention. The words now being read by the reader for instance are directing his attention to something; to the fact that words are attention directors. . . . Thus the word gold directs attention to a yellow, incorrodible, dense metal of atomic weight 197, and the word vertebrate to a class of animals having a spinal column.[2]

> Words may be thought of as signs which *name* that for which they are signs: "*table* is the name of an object, *red* of a quality, *run* of an activity, *over* of a relation."[3]

Pp. 15–22 in LANGUAGE HABITS IN HUMAN AFFAIRS by Irving J. Lee. Copyright 1941 by Harper & Row, Publishers, Incorporated. Reprinted by permission of Harper & Row, Publishers.

[1] Rudolf Carnap, *Foundations of Logic and Mathematics* (Chicago: The University of Chicago Press, 1939), p. 4.

[2] James MacKaye, *The Logic of Language* (Hanover, N. H.: Dartmouth College Publications, 1939), p. 21.

[3] Gustaf Stern, *Meaning and Change of Meaning* (Goteborg, Elanders Boktryckeri Aktiebolag, 1931), p. 19.

Thus, words may be considered as *pointers, indicators, forms of representation,* which are intended to correspond to anything whatsoever that may exist, that may be experienced, or that anyone might want to talk about. Or put another way, words may be used for the almost *endless naming* of the inexhaustible electronic events, objects, persons, situations, relations, etc., observed in the world outside-our-skins, along with the sensations, feelings, beliefs, opinions, values, tensions, affective states, etc., experienced inside-our-skins.

NOTE THE TWO MEDIA

Such an analysis of the work of words makes one point inevitable: the phenomenon of language is different from the non-verbal phenomena which we represent by it. We live in two worlds which must not be confused, a world of words, and a world of not-words. If a word is not what it represents, then whatever you might say about anything will not be *it.* If in doubt, you might try eating the word *steak* when hungry, or wearing the word *coat* when cold. In short, the universe of discourse *is not* the universe of our direct experience.

If a word *were* what it used to stand for, that is, a "complete reproduction," it would then be no word, but one more non-verbal fact. For words have aspects and functions quite different from the non-verbal facts which they may represent. William James once remarked that words should be taken as "summaries of things to look for," and not, it should

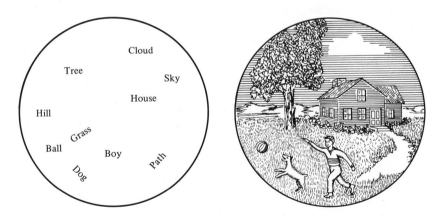

be added, as the actual existent "things." A book on astronomy is not the heavenly bodies, distances, and movements which make up the stellar universe, and the calculations and hypotheses which result from studying the stars clearly are not the phenomena in space. And the names and addresses on envelopes are not the human beings who receive them.

There exists, then, a world of words which must be sharply distinguished from a world of not-words about which talk occurs, even though frequently we tend to identify them.

FITTING THE TWO

Language will have maximum usefulness when it properly corresponds to what it is supposed to represent. We need to know what constitutes adequate representation. This may be illustrated in reverse. Suppose that a thermometer registered at freezing point when the liquid in which it was placed boiled furiously; a speedometer recorded only a thousand miles when the auto had been driven from New York to Denver; a roadmarker showed the arrow pointing to the left, while the actual road turned to the right. One can say that each of these symbolic recording devices was "wrong," "inaccurate," "erroneous," "misleading," etc. Such evaluations, however, though understandable, do not in themselves account for the wrongness. We get that in the suggestion that the recording did not *fit* the facts.

But what of words? When are they "adequate" and "useful"? Korzybski has said, "If we reflect upon our languages, we find that at best they must be considered *only as maps*." And further, "A language, to be useful, should be similar in its structure to the structure of the events which it is supposed to represent."[4]

An example may help. Suppose you receive a book entitled *Guide to Beautiful Bali,* which you read carefully. Never having been there, how can you know that such a place exists, and that what is said is correct to fact? A friend who has been there asserts that the book can be read with confidence. He argues further that if passage be taken to Bali, the directions followed, and the places visited, the book will be found to correspond to what is seen. If the trip is taken, and if the book is verified—that is, if the descriptions of Bali parallel the experienced Bali—then we can say that the language of the book was an accurate representation of the non-verbal facts. In the normal run of affairs we cannot personally corroborate what we read. But whenever we do, this notion of correspondence of words with facts will become clear.

Korzybski's famous analogy makes the point even more graphically, so that the notion of "usefulness" becomes readily apparent.

[4] Alfred Korzybski, *Science and Sanity: An Introduction to Non-Aristotelian Systems and General Semantics* (Lancaster, Pa.: The Science Press Printing Co., 1933), pp. 58, 412.

Let us take some actual territory in which cities appear in the following order: San Francisco, Chicago, New York, when taken from the West to the East. If we were to build a *map* of this territory and place San Francisco *between* Chicago and New York thus:

	* _____ * _____ *
Actual territory	San Francisco Chicago New York
	* _____ * _____ *
Map	Chicago San Francisco New York

we should say that the map was wrong, or that it was an incorrect map, or that the map has a *different structure* from the territory. If, speaking roughly, we should try, in our travels, to orient ourselves by such a map, we should find it misleading. It would lead us astray, and we might waste a great deal of unnecessary effort. In some cases, even, a map of wrong structure would bring actual suffering and disaster, as, for instance, in a war, or in the case of an urgent call for a physician.[5]

WITH WORDS ALONE

Even though language can be made to fit life facts, it is essential that another point be clearly understood, that words can be manipulated independently without corresponding to any non-verbal facts.

Just as it is easy to make a map without bothering to survey the terrain, or address letters to imaginary people, so one can indulge in verbalism, using words at random. No inner necessity governs the use of words in their relationship to things, feelings, and circumstances. Stories of people may be manufactured, nonexistent places may be talked about, situations may be verbally distorted beyond recognition, and denials and affirmations may be made regardless of what happens. Nothing *in the nature of language* could have prevented Bismarck from altering the Ems telegram, could have stopped the writing of the letter which helped convict Alfred Dreyfus, or hindered Mencken's hoax about the first American bathtub.

If in 1938 Adolf Hitler could say that he "wants no more land in Europe," even as his armies mobilized for invasion; and if astrologers can assert that those born under Libra should have musical talent, while a researcher finds that the birth dates of 1498 musicians show that almost "fewer are born under Libra than under any sign except Scorpio"[6]—if these things can be said, it should begin to be clear that words *may be used according to the whim of the user*. Without checking and testing with life it is impossible by merely looking at statements to know whether or not they

---

[5] *Ibid.*, p. 58.   [6] *Time* (Jan. 27, 1941), p. 38.

represent some existing territory in the world of happenings. Without an "inner check" one may turn out a false war communiqué, forge the "Protocols of the Elders of Zion," concoct nonverifiable racist dogmas, maintain the prophetic virtues of crystal-gazing, tell a yarn in contest for the "Liars' Championship," and on occasion provide pleasant diversion:

> Two of Joe Cook's favorite "gags" in *Why I Will Not Imitate Four Hawaiians* are a note reading "See frontispiece" and another "See page 226," the frontispiece being totally irrelevant to the matter in question, and the book having only 64 pages. Josh Billings had a similar gag. At the bottom of the card advertising his lecture on milk—in which, moreover, the subject of milk was never mentioned—he printed the word *over* in large type, and the other side was blank.[7]

John Locke argued that "in inquiries after philosophical knowledge . . . names must be conformable to things."[8] More recently Bridgman agreed that language "owes whatever success it attains to its ability to set up and maintain certain correspondences with experience."[9] However, one who uses words does not have to be governed by such demands. By itself language cannot force a user to seek that correspondence with actual facts. Indeed, there is a certain convenience in avoiding it. As Vilfredo Pareto says,

> It is much easier to talk about antipodes than to go out and see if they are really there. To discuss the implication of a "principle of fire" or "damp" is much more expeditious than to prosecute all the field studies that have made up the science of geology. To ruminate on "natural law" is a much more comfortable profession than to dig out the legal codes of the various countries in various periods of history. To prattle about "value" and ask when and under what circumstances it is said that "a thing has value" is much less difficult than to discover and comprehend the laws of economic equilibrium.[10]

Relevant here is a story of the small Austrian village under attack from hostile forces. To preserve the priceless possession of the community, a bell in the tower of the *Rathaus,* three of the elders rowed with it to the center of a nearby lake. To remember the place where it was dropped overboard, a deep mark was cut on the side of the boat.

Just as that boat mark can be moved, unrelated to its object, so, too, can

---

[7] Max Eastman, *The Enjoyment of Laughter* (New York: Simon & Schuster, 1936), p. 55.

[8] John Locke, *Essay Concerning Human Understanding* (Boston: Cummings and Hilliard and J. T. Buckingham, 1813), II, 51.

[9] P. W. Bridgman, *The Nature of Physical Theory* (Princeton, N. J.: Princeton University Press, 1936), p. 19.

[10] Vilfredo Pareto, *The Mind and Society,* ed. by Arthur Livingston (New York: Harcourt, Brace & World, Inc., 1935), I, 58.

words be handled and bandied about without regard to what they are supposed to represent.

ON ADJUSTMENT

Mr. George had never given a speech to youngsters. But the Principal assured him that they would listen quietly and eagerly and that it was as easy to talk to them as to adults. Mr. George was satisfied and looked forward to the occasion. For the first three minutes the children paid careful attention. Then a few up in front began to wiggle. Then the group burst into laughter at something he thought not at all funny. When a door at the other end of the corridor slammed, they all turned in that direction. And after that they began to whisper. . . . In the next five minutes the confusion increased, and Mr. George, much distraught, mumbled a "Thank you" and sat down.

That the speaker lost control is not too surprising. He was led to expect simplicity and found complexity. His adjustment was affected when the circumstances ran counter to what he expected. The verbal assurances given him had low predictability value.

This suggests a general principle: Our adjustment (and ultimately, survival) is correlated with our expectations, that is, our ability to predict happenings accurately. This is a way of saying that the correctness of our expectations depends upon the similarity of structure of the language used and the happenings represented. If the statements by means of which we are oriented are not adequate representations, it will be difficult to prepare for what is to be met in the world of direct experience.

But a nice problem thus emerges. If it becomes necessary to check everything anyone says with our own personal experience of the life facts, we should have time for little else. In this highly technical and minutely specialized civilization much must be taken on "faith," on the say-so of those who are supposed to know and expected to be responsible. One of the great sources of confusion in our time, however, lies in the fact that many find it profitable and expedient to betray this faith by making "maps" which do not fit the facts. This may be readily documented by reference to the findings of the Better Business Bureaus, the Food and Drug Administration, the Department of Weights and Measures, the Underwriters' Laboratory, the Bureau of Investigation of the American Medical Association, the Federal Trade Commission, Consumers Union, Federal Bureau of Investigation, Senate Investigating Committees, etc. In one form or another these organizations serve as reminders that *complete* faith in what is said, and expectations based on that faith, too often end in disappointment and disaster.

Awareness, then, of the different characteristics of words (map) and what they stand for (territory) should lead to the understanding that all utterance is to be neither blindly rejected nor blindly accepted. To know that language can be false to fact should make for more searching consideration of the nature of language. Those who argue that *all* public statements must be discounted suffer in their cynicism from delusions no less harmful than those who insist that if important men and official statements say so, then it must be so. What is urged here is something quite different: that men and women should be conscious of the *possibility* of structural dissimilarity between words and "things," and further, that a large step is taken toward proper evaluation, predictability, and adjustment, when they begin to ask whether or not the map fits the territory.

IN SHORT

A map is not the territory. To be most useful, statements must fit, must be similar in structure to the life facts being represented. Words can be

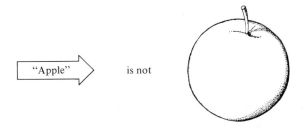

manipulated independently of what they represent, and so made false to fact both consciously and unconsciously. In either case their reliability and our predictability are impaired.

The basic question: not, What did he say? but, Did what he said fit the life facts?

Vocabulary

stellar, corroborate, astrologers, protocol, correlated

Expository Technique

1. What different reasons for italicization of words are in evidence in the first and second paragraphs of this essay?

2. This essay contrasts the "worlds of words" and "not-words," of "maps" and "territories." On what basis is the contrast made?

3. Is the final paragraph effective? Does it serve as an effective conclusion? How?

Review Questions

1. What does the author believe are the main function of words?

2. Comment on the notion that the "world of words" and "world of not-words" must be sharply distinguished.

3. When does Lee think language will have its maximum usefulness?

4. How effective is Lee's use of comparison and contrast?

5. What does the idea of map and territory illustrate?

6. Give some examples from your own experience of situations in which the "map" did not adequately fit the "territory."

Exercises

1. Show how each of the following ideas is or can be a "map" which improperly describes a "territory."

Santa Claus

Easter Bunny

the Stork

a stereotype of any religious
  or racial group

wealth brings happiness

one word has one meaning

New Yorkers are unfriendly

marriage will solve all problems

two can live as cheaply as one

marital bliss will come to you if you
  use a certain toothpaste, face cream,
  or deodorant

2. The theme of illusion and reality, embodied in many works of literature, is a form of the problem Lee has discussed as "maps and territories." Read one of the following works and prepare a short class report on the treatment of the theme of illusion and reality by its author.

Sophocles, *Oedipus Rex*

Shakespeare, *Othello, King Lear*

Henry Fielding, *Joseph Andrews*

Gustave Flaubert, *Madame Bovary*

George Orwell, *1984*

Tennessee Williams, *The Glass Menagerie*

Arthur Miller, *The Crucible*

J. D. Salinger, *The Catcher in the Rye*

3. Try to prepare reliable "maps" for the following "territories." Comment on the difficulty encountered in each case: Which is the hardest? the easiest?

Communist   Paris   truth   one mile   water

4. In the light of "The Useful Use of Words" what might Lee's attitude be toward each of the following?

a. A man who would not permit the name of Franklin D. Roosevelt to be spoken in his presence.
b. A parent who complained to a high school principal because the word *syphilis* was used in her daughter's hygiene course.
c. A college president who thought it unpatriotic to teach Russian in his college.
d. An individual who agitated against the performance of Wagnerian opera in the United States during World War I.

36.

S. I. HAYAKAWA

Extensional and Intensional Meaning

. . . Briefly explained, the extensional meaning of an utterance is that which it *points to* or denotes in the extensional world. . . . That is to say, the extensional meaning is something that *cannot be expressed in words,* because it is that which words stand for. An easy way to remember this is to put your hand over your mouth and point whenever you are asked to give an extensional meaning.

The *intensional meaning* of a word or expression, on the other hand, is that which is *suggested* (connoted) inside one's head. Roughly speaking,

whenever we express the meaning of words by uttering more words, we are giving intensional meaning, or connotations. To remember this, put your hand over your eyes and let the words spin around in your head.

Utterances may have, of course, both extensional and intensional meaning. If they have no intensional meaning at all—that is, if they start no notions whatever spinning about in our heads—they are meaningless noises,

like foreign languages that we do not understand. On the other hand, it is possible for utterances to have no extensional meaning at all, in spite of the fact that they may start many notions spinning about in our heads. The statement, "Angels watch over my bed at night," is one that has intensional but no extensional meaning. This does not mean that there are no angels watching over my bed at night. When we say that the statement has no extensional meaning, we are merely saying that we cannot see, touch, photograph, or in any scientific manner detect the presence of angels. The result is that, if an argument begins on the subject whether or not angels watch over my bed, *there is no way of ending the argument to the satisfaction of all disputants,* the Christians and the non-Christians, the pious and the agnostic, the mystical and the scientific. Therefore, whether we believe in angels or not, knowing in advance that any argument on the subject will be both endless and futile, we can avoid getting into fights about it.

When, on the other hand, statements have extensional content, as when we say, "This room is fifteen feet long," arguments can come to a close. No matter how many guesses there are about the length of the room, all discussion ceases when someone produces a tape measure. This, then, is the important difference between extensional and intensional meanings: namely, when utterances have extensional meanings, discussion can be ended and agreement reached; when utterances have intensional meanings only and no extensional meanings, arguments may, and often do, go on indefinitely. Such arguments can result only in irreconcilable conflict. Among individuals, they may result in the breaking up of friendships; in society, they often split organizations into bitterly opposed groups; among nations they may aggravate existing tensions so seriously as to become real obstacles to the peaceful settling of disputes.

Arguments of this kind may be termed "non-sense arguments," because they are based on utterances about which no sense data can be collected. Needless to say, there are occasions when the hyphen may be omitted—that depends on one's feelings toward the particular argument under consideration. The reader is requested to provide his own examples of "non-sense arguments." Even the foregoing example of the angels may give offense to some people, in spite of the fact that no attempt is made to deny or affirm the existence of angels. He can imagine, therefore, the uproar that might result from giving a number of examples from theology, politics, law, economics, literary criticism, and other fields in which it is not customary to distinguish clearly sense from non-sense.

. . . In addition to tone of voice and rhythm, another extremely important affective element in language is the aura of feelings, pleasant or unpleasant, that surrounds practically all words. It will be recalled that . . . a distinction was made between denotations (or extensional meaning) pointing to things, and connotations (or intensional meaning) "ideas," "notions," "concepts," and feelings suggested in the mind. These connotations can be divided into two kinds, the *informative* and the *affective*.

INFORMATIVE CONNOTATIONS

The informative connotations of a word are its socially agreed upon, "impersonal" meanings, *insofar as meanings can be given at all by additional words*. For example, if we talk about a "pig," we cannot readily give the extensional meaning (denotation) of the word unless there happens to be an actual pig around for us to point at; but we can give the informative connotations: "mammalian domestic quadruped of the kind generally raised by farmers to be made into pork, bacon, ham, lard . . ."—which are connotations upon which everybody can agree. Sometimes, however, the informative connotations of words used in everyday life differ so much from place to place and from individual to individual that a special substitute terminology with more fixed informative connotations has to be used when special accuracy is desired. The scientific names for plants and animals are an example of terminology with such carefully established informative connotations.

AFFECTIVE CONNOTATIONS

The affective connotations of a word, on the other hand, are the aura of personal feelings it arouses, as, for example, "pig": "Ugh! Dirty, evil-smelling creatures, wallowing in filthy sties," and so on. While there is no necessary agreement about these feelings—some people like pigs and others don't—it is the existence of these feelings that enables us to use words, under certain circumstances, *for their affective connotations alone,* without regard to their informative connotations. That is to say, when we are strongly moved, we express our feelings by uttering words with the affective connotations appropriate to our feelings, without paying any attention to the informative connotations they may have. We angrily call people "reptiles," "wolves," "old bears," "skunks," or lovingly call them "honey," "sugar," "duck," and "apple dumpling." Indeed, all verbal expressions of feeling make use to some extent of the affective connotations or words.

All words have, according to the uses to which they are put, some affective character. There are many words that exist more for their affective value than for their informative value; for example, we can refer to "that man" as "that gentleman," "that individual," "that person," "that gent," "that guy," "that hombre," "that bird," or "that bozo"—and while the person referred to may be the same in all these cases, each of these terms reveals a difference in our feelings toward him. Dealers in knick-knacks frequently write "Gyfte Shoppe" over the door, hoping that such a spelling carries, even if their merchandise does not, the flavor of antiquity. Affective connotations suggestive of England and Scotland are often sought in the choice of brand names for men's suits and overcoats: "Glenmoor," "Regent Park," "Bond Street." Sellers of perfume choose names for their products that suggest France—"Mon Désir," "Indiscret," "Evening in Paris"—and expensive brands always come in "flacons," never in bottles. Consider, too, the differences among the following expressions:

> I have the honor to inform Your Excellency . . .
> This is to advise you . . .
> I should like to tell you, sir . . .
> I'm telling you, Mister . . .
> Cheez, boss, git a load of dis . . .

The parallel columns below also illustrate how affective connotations can be changed while extensional meanings remain the same.

Finest quality filet mignon.	First-class piece of dead cow.
Cubs trounce Giants 5-3.	Score: Cubs 5, Giants 3.
McCormick Bill steam-rollered through Senate.	Senate passes McCormick Bill over strong opposition.
She has her husband under her thumb.	She is deeply interested in her husband's affairs.

French armies in rapid retreat! The retirement of the French forces to previously prepared positions in the rear was accomplished briskly and efficiently.

The governor appeared to be gravely concerned and said that a statement would be issued in a few days after careful examination of the facts.

The governor was on the spot.

The story is told that, during the Boer War, the Boers were described in the British press as "sneaking and skulking behind rocks and bushes." The British forces, when they finally learned from the Boers how to employ tactics suitable to veldt warfare, were described as "cleverly taking advantage of cover."

Vocabulary

agnostic, irreconcilable, aura, wallowing, sties, Boers, veldt

Review Questions

1. Explain briefly what you understand Hayakawa to mean by the terms *extensional* and *intensional meaning*.
2. What is the only time the author believes that disputes can be settled? Do you agree with him?
3. What are "informative" and "affective" connotations of words? Give two examples of each.
4. Comment on the statement, "Indeed, all verbal expressions of feeling make use to some extent of the affective connotations of words."

Expository Technique

How does Hayakawa relate the first part of his essay (the contrast between extensional and intensional meaning) to the second (the contrast between informative and affective connotations)?

Exercises

1. Each of the following pairs of words may have similar extensional meaning; but the words of each pair differ in their connotational or intensional meanings. Define the connotational differences.

cheap—inexpensive	house—home
retreat—withdraw	persuade—brainwash
inn—hotel	civil war—revolution
gamble—invest	drunk—alcoholic
sanitary engineer—plumber	tie—cravat
depression—recession	educate—indoctrinate
trailer—mobile home	war—police action
abortion—termination of pregnancy	rug—carpeting
psychiatrist—headshrinker	tavern—gin mill
assistant—stooge	thrifty—penurious
Negro—black	egghead—intellectual
Negro—Afro-Asian	outside agitator—civil rights worker
insurrectionist—freedom fighter	

2. Which of the words in the series below would you most readily associate with the italicized word? Why? How might such a word-association test reveal a great deal about your personality?

Sunday: church, comics, double-header, chicken, boredom
doctor: pain, white, fear, confidence
mother: kitchen, country, earth, tears, Mary
father: office, money, punishment, priest, God
king: throne, ritual, England, ermine, God
green: spring, go, inexperienced, money

3. Because of their affective connotations, the names of animals are frequently applied to humans. What is suggested when a human is described by each of the following? Can you think of any others?

wolf	fox	lion	tiger	shark	snake	dove
horse	pig	chicken	goat	cat	cow	hawk

4. Examine carefully the implications of the controversial term *black power.* Why is its meaning so debated? Is its definition more extensional or intensional? Can you think of any similar sociopolitical terms?
5. The utterance of certain words and phrases (e.g., "I pronounce thee man and wife," "abracadabra") is believed by many to have certain magical qualities, to bring the speaker good or bad fortune, or to endow the listener with special privileges or powers. Name as many such words or phrases as you can.
6. Consider two writers' views of *conformity:*
a. Conformity implies blind and unreasoning obedience to authority, a passive acceptance of things-as-they-are, and submission to intellectual inertia. It is a hard taskmaster, subjugating the individual to the will of the majority with sometimes subtle but always tyrannical pressure.
b. Conformity is the force which insures social cohesion and allows change and individual initiative to take place within an orderly framework. It must also be given credit for assuring social stability by presenting an accepted system of values and practices, without which anarchy would reign.

Are these writers talking about the same thing? Which view is closer to your own? Why? Try to write similar pairs of paragraphs on the following words: *freedom, idealism, emotionalism, revolution, isolationism, socialism.*

Writing Suggestions: Comparison and Contrast

LINGUISTIC SUBJECTS

1. Differing Attitudes Toward Correctness in English
2. Differences in British and American _____ (Vocabulary, Pronunciation, Spelling, or Punctuation
3. American and _____ (Canadian, Australian) English
4. British Imitators of American English
5. American Imitators of British English
6. Speaking and Writing
7. Levels of Usage: or Proper Dress for Various Occasions
8. The English of _____ (Chaucer, Shakespeare, or Milton) and That of Today
9. Lindley Murray and Robert A. Hall, Jr.: Two Students of English
10. Contrast the attitudes of two literary critics, essayists, novelists, or grammarians toward the "respectability" of American English.
11. Compare and contrast any two English dictionaries in terms of purpose, scope, approach and lexical apparatus.
12. The Traditionalists, Structuralists, and the Transformationalists
13. Class Dialects
14. Formal and Informal Style
15. Personal and Impersonal Style

Illustration

ILLUSTRATION IS one of the most effective methods by which a writer can clarify his meaning and support his assertions. Two of the more useful kinds of illustration are example and analogy. In example, the general is explained or supported by a particular and typical instance. In analogy, the unfamiliar is explained by comparing it to something more familiar. Both example and analogy take advantage of the mind's attraction to the concrete and its ability to assimilate the specific more readily than the general or abstract.

In the following paragraph from *On Liberty*, note the effective use John Stuart Mill makes of examples to illustrate the general statements made in the second and last sentences of the paragraph:

But, indeed, the dictum that truth always triumphs over persecution, is one of those pleasant falsehoods which men repeat after one another till they pass into commonplaces, but which all experience refutes. History teems with instances of truth put down by persecution. If not suppressed for ever, it may be thrown back for centuries. To speak only of religious opinions: the Reformation broke out at least twenty times before Luther, and was put down. Arnold of Brescia was put down. Fra Dolcino was put down. Savonarola was put down. The Albigeois were put down. The Vaudois were put down. The Lollards were put down. The Hussites were put down. Even after the era of Luther, wherever persecution was persisted in, it was successful. In Spain, Italy, Flanders, the Austrian empire, Protestantism was rooted out; and most likely, would have been so in England, had Queen Mary lived, or Queen Elizabeth died. Persecution has always succeeded, save where the heretics were too strong a party to be effectually persecuted.

501

The examples in this passage make clear what Mill means by "instances of truth put down by persecution."

In addition to clarifying a writer's meaning, examples can often convince the reader of the truth of the writer's assertions. It should be remembered, however, that the citation of examples does not necessarily establish the truth of a generalization. Upon careful consideration or investigation one might discover that the examples cited by a writer are not quite as representative as he claims or that they are not accurately treated and that examples might be cited contradictory to those mentioned by the writer.

Analogy, like example, is a means of clarification; but analogy illuminates the unfamiliar idea or object by comparing it with other ideas or objects which are more familiar and with which it shares significant similarities. In order, for instance, to explain the concept of latitude and longitude to a person unfamiliar with navigation, one might compare the lines of latitude and longitude circling the earth to streets and avenues, and point out that just as the location of a residence may be indicated by the house number on a particular street, so the ship's position, its "address," may be expressed in degrees, minutes, and seconds of north or south latitude and east or west longitude.

The following passage from "A Liberal Education" by Thomas Huxley affords a good example of an analogy worked out in detail:

> Yet it is a very plain and elementary truth that the life, the fortune, and the happiness of every one of us, and more or less, of those who are connected with us, do depend upon our knowing something of the rules of a game infinitely more difficult and complicated than chess. It is a game which has been played for untold ages, every man and woman being one of the two players in a game of his or her own. The chessboard is the world, the pieces are the phenomena of the universe, the rules are what we call the laws of Nature. The player on the other side is hidden from us. We know that his play is always fair, just, and patient. But we also know, to our cost, that he never overlooks a mistake, or makes the smallest allowance for ignorance. To the man who plays well, the highest stakes are paid, with that sort of overflowing generosity with which the strong shows delight in strength. And one who plays ill is checkmated—without haste but without remorse.

Analogies may be very brief, like a simile—"My love is like a red, red rose"—or the implied comparison of a metaphor—"Life is a tale told by an idiot." On the other hand, they may be worked out in greater detail, as is Huxley's, or developed at greater length in the form of a fable, anecdote, or parable. Regardless of the form, however, the illumination of the unknown by the light of the known should always be the purpose of the analogy.

SPECIAL PROBLEMS IN ILLUSTRATION

Some of the most important considerations in the use of illustration in exposition are the following:

1. Be sure that illustrations are pertinent and functional. They should be thought of as subordinate to the subject to which they pertain. An illustration may be clever, amusing or emotionally forceful; but none of these attributes alone makes a good illustration or necessarily justifies its use. The primary essentials of a good illustration are its relevance and its power to clarify the subject under discussion.

2. If you attempt a longer type of illustration, try to select a subject which you understand well and can write about clearly. Confused or highly complex illustrations do not enlighten the reader; they make him wish for an illustration to clarify the illustration.

3. Strive to avoid the trite and hackneyed analogies, for example, *quick as a flash, hard as a rock, dead as a doornail.*

4. Select examples and analogies which are appropriate to the tone and the level of usage employed in the essay as a whole.

ORGANIZATION

The organization of the essay of illustration will usually be built around a movement either from the general to the particular or from the particular to the general. Since the purpose of this expository technique is to support, to reinforce, and to clarify, examples and analogies should lead either *from* or *to* the topic sentences of paragraphs. A chronological organization is appropriate for extended illustrations such as the fable or parable, whereas some kind of spatial organization might be appropriate in analogies drawn between objects.

AN EXAMPLE OF ILLUSTRATION

In the following selection Ossie Davis uses illustration to explain his views concerning the relationship between two words and the things they represent.

THE ENGLISH LANGUAGE IS MY ENEMY*

A superficial examination of *Roget's Thesaurus of the English Language* reveals the following facts: the word WHITENESS has 134 synonyms: 44 of

* Reprinted by permission of the Association for the Study of Negro Life and History, Washington, D.C. from *The Negro History Bulletin*, XXX (April 1967), 18.

which are favorable and pleasing to contemplate, i.e. purity, cleanness, immaculateness, bright, shining, ivory, fair, blonde, stainless, clean, clear, chaste, unblemished, unsullied, innocent, honorable, upright, just, straight-forward, fair, genuine, trustworthy, (a white man colloquialism). Only ten synonyms for WHITENESS appear to me to have negative implications—and these only in the mildest sense: gloss over, whitewash, gray, wan, pale, ashen, etc.

The work BLACKNESS has 120 synonyms, 60 of which are distinctly unfavorable, and none of them even mildly positive. Among the offending 60 were such words as: blot, blotch, smut, smudge, sully, begrime, soot, becloud, obscure, dingy, murky, low-toned, threatening, frowning, foreboding, forbidden, sinister, baneful, dismal, thundery, evil, wicked, malignant, deadly, unclean, dirty, unwashed, foul, etc. . . . not to mention 20 synonyms directly related to race, such as: Negro, Negress, nigger, darky, blackamoor, etc.

When you consider the fact that *thinking* itself is sub-vocal speech—in other words, one must use *words* in order to think at all—you will appreciate the enormous heritage of racial prejudgement that lies in wait for any child born into the English Language. Any teacher good or bad, white or black, Jew or Gentile, who uses the English Language as a medium of communication is forced, willy-nilly, to teach the Negro child 60 ways to despise himself, and the white child 60 ways to aid and abet him in the crime.

Who speaks to me in my Mother Tongue damns me indeed! . . . the English Language—in which I cannot conceive my self as a black man without, at the same time, debasing myself . . . my enemy, with which to survive at all I must continually be at war.

Exercises on Illustration

1. Each of the following statements contains a generality. Develop each into a paragraph by supporting its idea with a series of concrete examples:
   a. The Supreme Court has gone too far in weakening the law enforcement agencies in their fight against crime.
   b. The surest way to become President of the United States is to become a victorious general and then run for election.
   c. Boxing isn't what it used to be.
   d. The more things change, the more they remain the same.
   e. Around the world no food is served in as many different guises as wheat.

2. Read one of the following parables, fables, or allegories. Be prepared to comment in class on the effectiveness of the author's use of illustration to support, develop, and clarify his main idea.

Geoffrey Chaucer, "The Pardoner's Tale," "The Nun's Priest Tale."
George Orwell, *Animal Farm.*
Plato, "The Allegory of the Cave."
The Biblical parable of the Good Samaritan, the Prodigal Son, the House Built on Sand, or the Sower.
Aesop's fable of the Fox and the Grapes.

3. Comment on the effectiveness, relevance, and precision of the illustrations in the following passages, each of which was written by an acknowledged master of English prose:

a. Pity is not natural to man. Children are always cruel. Savages are always cruel. Pity is acquired and improved by the cultivation of reason. We may have uneasy sensations from seeing a creature in distress, without pity; for we have not pity unless we wish to relieve them. When I am on my way to dine with a friend, and finding it late, have bid the coachman make haste, if I happen to attend when he whips the horses, I may feel unpleasantly that the animals are put to pain, but I do not wish him to desist. No, Sir, I wish him to drive on.

(Samuel Johnson, quoted in Boswell's *Life of Johnson*)

b. No body can be healthful without exercise, neither natural body nor politic; and, certainly, to a kingdom, or estate, a just and honorable war is the true exercise. A civil war, indeed, is like the heat of a fever; but a foreign war is like the heat of exercise, and serveth to keep the body in health; for in slothful peace, both courages will effeminate and manners corrupt.

(Francis Bacon, *The True Greatness of Kingdoms*)

c. Time is but the stream I go a-fishing in. I drink at it; but while I drink I see the sandy bottom and detect how shallow it is. Its thin current slides away, but eternity remains. I would drink deeper; fish in the sky, whose bottom is pebbly with stars. I cannot count one. I know not the first letter of the alphabet. I have always been regretting that I was not as wise as the day I was born. The intellect is a cleaver; it discerns and rifts its way into the secret of things. I do not wish to be any more busy with my hands than is necessary. My head is hands and feet. I feel all my best faculties concentrated in it. My instinct tells me that my head is an organ for burrowing, as some creatures use their snout and fore-paws, and with it I would mine and burrow my way through these hills. I think that the richest vein is somewhere hereabouts; so by the divining-rod and thin rising vapors I judge; and here I will begin to mine.

(Henry David Thoreau, *Walden*)

Writing Suggestions: Illustration

1. The Attractions of Suburbia
2. The Best Things in Life Are Free
3. _____ (Courage, Sportsmanship, Faith, Integrity, Determination, Sacrifice): A Good Illustration
4. The Vast Wasteland of Television
5. British and American Humor
6. The Evils of (Nepotism, Racial Discrimination, Dope Addiction, Alcoholism, the Draft)
7. Good and Bad Movies
8. New Commercial Values for Old Masterpieces

9. Three Attitudes toward _____ (Jazz, Abstract Painting, Modern Architecture)

10. The Westernization of Japan

11. Women in a Man's World

12. The Parable of _____ (the Prodigal Son, the Wise and Foolish Virgins, Sower, A House Built Upon Sand) in a Modern Setting

13. Better Things for Better Living Through Chemistry

14. The Superiority of _____ (Men, Women)

15. The Case _____ (for, against) Fraternities

(Additional writing suggestions on linguistic subjects are on pages 533–534.)

Language and Bias

37.

S. I. HAYAKAWA

A Semantic Parable

Once upon a time (said the Professor), there were two small communities, spiritually as well as geographically situated at a considerable distance from each other. They had, however, these problems in common: Both were hard hit by a depression, so that in each of the towns there were about one hundred heads of families unemployed. There was, to be sure, enough food, enough clothing, enough materials for housing, but these families simply did not have money to procure these necessities.

The city fathers of A-town, the first community, were substantial businessmen, moderately well educated, good to their families, kindhearted, and sound-thinking. The unemployed tried hard, as unemployed people usually do, to find jobs; but the situation did not improve. The city fathers, as well as the unemployed themselves, had been brought up to believe that there is always enough work for everyone, if you only look for it hard enough. Comforting themselves with this doctrine, the city fathers could have shrugged their shoulders and turned their backs on the problem, except for the fact that they were genuinely kindhearted men. They could not bear to see the unemployed men and their wives and children starving. In order to prevent starvation, they felt that they had to provide these people with some means of sustenance. Their principles told them, nevertheless, that if people were given something for nothing, it would demoralize their character. Naturally this made the city fathers even more unhappy, because they were faced with the horrible choice of (1) letting the unemployed starve, or (2) destroying their moral character.

507

The solution they finally hit upon, after much debate and soul-searching, was this. They decided to give the unemployed families relief of fifty dollars a month; but to insure against the pauperization of the recipients, they decided that this fifty dollars was to be accompanied by a moral lesson, to wit: the obtaining of the assistance would be made so difficult, humiliating, and disagreeable that there would be no temptation for anyone to go through the process unless it was absolutely necessary; the moral disapproval of the community would be turned upon the recipients of the money at all times in such a way that they would try hard to get off relief and regain their self-respect. Some even proposed that people on relief be denied the vote, so that the moral lesson would be more deeply impressed upon them. Others suggested that their names be published at regular intervals in the newspapers, so that there would be a strong incentive to get off relief. The city fathers had enough faith in the goodness of human nature to expect that the recipients would be grateful, since they were getting something for nothing, something which they hadn't worked for.

When the plan was put into operation, however, the recipients of the relief checks proved to be an ungrateful, ugly bunch. They seemed to resent the cross-examinations and inspections at the hands of the relief investigators, who, they said, took advantage of a man's misery to snoop into every detail of his private life. In spite of uplifting editorials in A-town *Tribune* telling them how grateful they ought to be, the recipients of the relief refused to learn any moral lessons, declaring that they were "just as good as anybody else." When, for example, they permitted themselves the rare luxury of a movie or an evening of bingo, their neighbors looked at them sourly as if to say, "I work hard and pay my taxes just in order to support loafers like you in idleness and pleasure." This attitude, which was fairly characteristic of those members of the community who still had jobs, further embittered the relief recipients, so that they showed even less gratitude as time went on and were constantly on the lookout for insults, real or imaginary, from people who might think that they weren't as good as anybody else. A number of them took to moping all day long, to thinking that their lives had been failures; one or two even committed suicide. Others found that it was hard to look their wives and kiddies in the face, because they had failed to provide. They all found it difficult to maintain their club and fraternal relationships, since they could not help feeling their fellow citizens despised them for having sunk so low. Their wives, too, were unhappy for the same reasons and gave up their social activities. Children whose parents were on relief felt inferior to classmates whose parents were not public charges. Some of these children developed inferiority complexes which affected not only their grades at school, but their careers after graduation. Several other relief recipients, finally, felt they could stand their loss of self-respect no longer and decided, after many efforts to gain honest jobs, to earn money by their own efforts, even if they had to go in for robbery. They did so and were caught and sent to the state penitentiary.

The depression, therefore, hit A-town very hard. The relief policy had averted starvation, no doubt, but suicide, personal quarrels, unhappy homes, the weakening of social organizations, the maladjustment of children, and, finally, crime, had resulted. The town was divided in two, the "haves" and the "have-nots," so that there was class hatred. People shook their heads sadly and declared that it all went to prove over again what they had known from the beginning, that giving people something for nothing inevitably demoralizes their character. The citizens of A-town gloomily waited for prosperity to return, with less and less hope as time went on.

The story of the other community, B-ville, was entirely different. B-ville was a relatively isolated town, too far out of the way to be reached by Rotary Club speakers and university extension services. One of the aldermen, however, who was something of an economist, explained to his fellow aldermen that unemployment, like sickness, accident, fire, tornado, or death, hits unexpectedly in modern society, irrespective of the victim's merits or deserts. He went on to say that B-ville's homes, parks, streets, industries, and everything else B-ville was proud of had been built in part by the work of these same people who were now unemployed. He then proposed to apply a principle of insurance: If the work these unemployed people had previously done for the community could be regarded as a form of premium paid to the community against a time of misfortune, payments now made to them to prevent their starvation could be regarded as insurance claims. He therefore proposed that all men of good repute who had worked in the community in whatever line of useful endeavor, whether as machinists, clerks, or bank managers, be regarded as citizen policyholders, having claims against the city in the case of unemployment for fifty dollars a month until such time as they might again be employed. Naturally, he had to talk very slowly and patiently, since the idea was entirely new to his fellow aldermen. But he described his plan as a "straight business proposition," and finally they were persuaded. They worked out the details as to the conditions under which citizens should be regarded as policyholders in the city's social insurance plan to everybody's satisfaction and decided to give checks for fifty dollars a month to the heads of each of B-ville's indigent families.

B-ville's claim adjusters, whose duty it was to investigate the claims of the citizen policyholders, had a much better time than A-town's relief investigators. While the latter had been resentfully regarded as snoopers, the former, having no moral lesson to teach but simply a business transaction to carry out, treated their clients with businesslike courtesy and got the same amount of information as the relief investigators with considerably less difficulty. There were no hard feelings. It further happened, fortunately, that news of B-ville's plans reached a liberal newspaper editor in the big city at the other end of the state. This writer described the plan in a leading feature story headed "B-VILLE LOOKS AHEAD. Great Adventure in Social Pioneering Launched by Upper Valley Community." As a result of this publicity, inquiries about the plan began to come to the city hall even before the first checks were mailed out. This led, naturally, to a considerable feeling of pride on the part of the aldermen, who, being boosters, felt that this was a wonderful opportunity to put B-ville on the map.

Accordingly, the aldermen decided that instead of simply mailing out the checks as they had originally intended, they would publicly present the first checks at a monster civic ceremony. They invited the governor of the state, who was glad to come to bolster his none-too-enthusiastic support in that locality, the president of the state university, the senator from their district, and other functionaries. They decorated the National Guard armory with flags and got out the American Legion Fife and Drum Corps, the Boy Scouts, and other civic organizations. At the big celebration, each family to receive a social insurance check was marched up to the platform to receive it, and the governor and the mayor shook hands with each of them as they came trooping up in their best clothes. Fine speeches were made; there was much cheering and shouting; pictures of the event showing the recipients of the checks shaking hands with the mayor, and the governor patting the heads of the children, were published not only in the local papers but also in several metropolitan picture sections.

Every recipient of these insurance checks had a feeling, therefore, that he had been personally honored, that he lived in a wonderful little town, and that he could face his unemployment with greater courage and assurance, since his community was back of him. The men and women found themselves being kidded in a friendly way by their acquaintances for having been "up there with the big shots," shaking hands with the governor, and so on. The children at school found themselves envied for having had their pictures in the papers. All in all, B-ville's unemployed did not commit suicide, were not haunted by a sense of failure, did not turn to crime, did not get personal maladjustments, did not develop class hatred, as the result of their fifty dollars a month. . . .

At the conclusion of the Professor's story, the discussion began:

"That just goes to show," said the Advertising Man, who was known among his friends as a realistic thinker, "what good promotional work can do. B-ville's city council had real advertising sense, and that civic ceremony was a masterpiece . . . made everyone happy . . . put over the scheme in a big way. Reminds me of the way we do things in our business: as soon as we called horse-mackerel tuna-fish, we developed a big market for it. I suppose if you called relief 'insurance,' you could actually get people to like it, couldn't you?"

"What do you mean, 'calling' it insurance?" asked the Social Worker. "B-ville's scheme wasn't relief at all. It *was* insurance. That's what all such payments should be. What gets me is the stupidity of A-town's city council and all people like them in not realizing that what they call 'relief' is simply the payment of just claims which those unemployed have on a community in a complex interdependent industrial society."

"Good grief, man! Do you realize what you're saying?" cried the Advertising Man in surprise. "Are you implying that those people had any *right* to that money? All I said was that it's a good idea to *disguise* relief as insurance if it's going to make people any happier. But it's still relief, no matter what you *call* it. It's all right to kid the public along the reduce discontent, but we don't need to kid ourselves as well!"

"But they *do* have a right to that money! They're not getting something for nothing. It's insurance. They did something for the community, and that's their prem—"

"Say, are you crazy?"

"Who's crazy?"

"You're crazy. Relief is relief, isn't it? If you'd only call things by their right names . . ."

"But, confound it, insurance is insurance, isn't it?"

(Since the gentlemen are obviously losing their tempers, it will be best to leave them. The Professor has already sneaked out. When last heard of, not only had the quarrelers stopped speaking to each other, but so had their wives—and the Advertising Man was threatening to disinherit his son if he didn't break off his engagement with the Social Worker's daughter.)

This story has been told not to advance arguments in favor of "social insurance" or "relief" or for any other political and economic arrangement, but simply to show a fairly characteristic sample of language in action. Do the words we use make as much difference in our lives as the story of A-town and B-ville seems to indicate? We often talk about "choosing the right words to express our thoughts," as if thinking were a process entirely independent of the words we think in. But is thinking such an independent process? Do the words we utter arise as a result of the thoughts we have, or are the thoughts we have determined by the linguistic systems we happen to have been taught? The Advertising Man and the Social Worker seem to be agreed that the results of B-ville's program were good, so that we can assume that their notions of what is socially desirable are similar. Nevertheless, they *cannot agree.*

Alfred Korzybski, in his preface to *Science and Sanity* (which discusses many problems similar to those discussed in this book), asks the reader to imagine what the state of technology would be if all lubricants contained emery dust, the presence of which had never been detected. Machines would be short-lived and expensive; the machine age would be a dream of the distant future. If, however, someone were to discover the presence of the emery, we should at once know *in what direction to proceed* in order to release the potentialities of machine power.

Why do people disagree? It isn't a matter of education or intelligence, because quarreling, bitterness, conflict, and breakdown are just as common among the educated as the uneducated, among the clever as the stupid. Human relations are no better among the privileged than the underprivileged. Indeed, well-educated people are often the cleverest in proving that insurance is *really* insurance and that relief is *really* relief—and being well educated they often have such high principles that nothing will make them modify their position in the slightest. Are disagreements then the inevitable results of the nature of human problems and the nature of man? Possibly so—but if we give this answer, we are confessing to being licked before we have even started our investigations.

The student of language observes, however, that it is an extremely rare quarrel that does not involve some kind of *talking*. Almost invariably, before noses are punched or shooting begins, *words are exchanged*—sometimes only a few, sometimes millions. We shall, therefore, look for the "previously undetected emery dust" (or whatever it is that heats up and stops our intellectual machinery) in *language*—that is to say, *our linguistic habits* (how we talk and think and listen) and *our unconscious attitudes toward language*. If we are even partially successful in our search, we may get an inkling of the *direction in which to proceed* in order to release the now imperfectly realized potentialities of human co-operation.

P.S. Those who have concluded that the point of the story is that the Social Worker and the Advertising Man were "only arguing about different names for the same thing," are asked to reread the story and explain what they mean by (1) "only" and (2) "the same thing."

(Exercises relating to Essays 37 and 38 are on pages 520–521.)

38.

F. A. PHILBRICK

Bias Words

There are three classes into which all the women past seventy that ever I knew were to be divided:
1. That dear old soul; 2. That old woman; 3. That old witch.
Samuel Taylor Coleridge

NEUTRAL, FAVORABLE, AND UNFAVORABLE WORDS

Languages differ in the extent to which they allow a writer a choice of different words with the same referent. In Spanish this variation can often be achieved by different endings, such as *-ico, -ito, -uelo, -on, -azo,* or *-acho.* For example, the Spanish words for "dog" include *perro, perrazo, perrillo, perrito, perrezno,* and *perrico,* each with a different reference. The first is the plain neutral word; the second implies large size and grotesqueness ("ugly" or "hulking"); the third, small size and pity ("poor little wretch"); the fourth, small size and fondness ("darling little"); the fifth, immaturity ("puppy"); and the sixth, what the dictionary, with rare candor, calls "sprightly humor impossible to characterize." The twist given by these endings to a neutral word, such as *perro,* is different for each word and is so subtle that all the manuals on the Spanish language advise the foreigner to be cautious in using such terminations or even not to use them at all. If he neglects this advice, a foreigner is apt to make awkward mistakes, and when wishing to compliment a Spanish lady on her "dear little baby," he may inadvertently suggest that the infant is undersized, contemptible, and of a disagreeable shape.

In English the possibilities are more limited, and the writer often has to chose from such a set as *dog, cur,* and *hound.* With fewer words available, each has to cover a wider range, so that while *cur* is always derogatory, *hound* sometimes implies grandeur ("majestic hound," "The Hound of the

From *Understanding English,* by F. A. Philbrick. Reprinted by permission of Mrs. Sybil Philbrick. Published by The Macmillan Company, 1942.

Baskervilles," "The Hound of Heaven") but sometimes the opposite ("mean hound," "wretched hound"). This variability does not make the word less effective, and "The Dog of the Baskervilles" or "The Dog of Heaven" are plainly less satisfactory than the actual titles. It is true that *hound,* like *perrazo,* implies large size, but even "The Large Dog of the Baskervilles" fails to come quite up to original.

Words such as *cur* and *hound,* which have the same referent, but different references expressing different attitudes on the part of the user, will here be called *bias words.* Matthew Arnold called them words "touched by emotion," and Coleridge, calling them "watch-words," warned his readers against them, recommending "the beneficial after-effects of verbal precision in the preclusion of fanaticism, which masters the feelings more especially by indistinct watch-words."[1] In one of the most amusing scenes in Wycherley's *The Plain Dealer* (Act II, Sc. 1) Lord Plausible and Olivia describe the same people in different terms, Lord Plausible using nothing but commendatory phrases and Olivia nothing but scornful ones. And it may be remembered that Françoise in Proust's *A la Recherche du Temps Perdu* readily believed that Germans were murderers, but thought the suggestion that they were *boches* too shocking to be true.

SOME BIAS WORDS EXAMINED

While it must never be forgotten that a word owes much of its meaning to its setting, yet it is still possible to estimate the kind of bias that certain words have acquired. The writer's attitude can also be expressed by phrases. "John did not come" and "John failed to come" refer to the same fact, but the second phrase suggests, without clearly saying so, that John was at fault. Writers use such phrases because of the possibility of hinting at a meaning without committing themselves.

As a first example of a pair of bias words *liberty* and *license* may be considered in the phrase "liberty not license." In the referents of the two words there is no difference; each word suggests the absence of restrictions on the doing of something, but *license* implies the liberty to do something of which the writer does not approve. Thus, writers wishing to restrict someone else's liberty often refer to that liberty as *license,* and sometimes draw attention to their own use of bias words as a substitute for reasoning by quoting the phrase itself. To call liberty *license* is not to advance an argument against it, but simply to say that we do not like it, and it tells the reader nothing about the thing referred to except that it is unwelcome to the writer. Again, the word *fad* may refer to any belief or practice that the

---

[1] *Biographia Literaria,* Ch. 22.

writer disapproves of, with the implications that the person adhering to it (called the *faddist*) attaches too much importance to it, and that few others share his opinions. *Crank* is similar to *faddist,* with perhaps a deeper tinge of dislike and contempt.

Politics, as one of the great fields of controversy, is an abundant source of bias words. *Statesman* and *statesmanlike* are favorable words, *politician* and *political* often unfavorable. Here are two extracts from a recent account of the political situation in Washington:

> Last week he was a great President, or a potentially great President, working in his study on great affairs of state. But all around him in the White House could be heard the ratlike sounds of politics, the scurrying and whispers . . . .
>
> Some of the truth about the incredibly tangled situation leaked out from Washington last week in little whiffs of rumor, in planted "true stories" circulated by each interested faction.[2]

The force of these sentences is chiefly derived from the bias words used in them . . .; *affairs of state* and *politics* are favorable and unfavorable words respectively, though with similar referents. *Faction* is also a bias word (compare the stronger word *pressure group*) and has no favorable word with the same referent; *party* is more nearly neutral, but in some settings is unfavorable, as in "And the party gave up what was meant for mankind." The quotation marks around *true stories* are to suggest that the stories were not true. *Whiff* is one of several words in the *odor* group; it has an unfavorable bias. Still more unfavorable words in the same group are the words *stink* and *stench; odor* and *smell* have a wide range of bias according to setting, but the middle of this range is perhaps almost neutral; *savor, aroma, perfume,* and *bouquet* (of wines) are all favorable. (Thus, an advertisement for cigars will refer to the *aroma* of the smoke, not to its *odor* or *smell,* still less to its *stench* or *stink.*) Finally, to revert to the quoted passages from *Time, scurrying* is an unfavorable word, and so are *rat* and *ratlike.* Zoological metaphors, as applied to people, are deservedly popular as being obvious and usually insulting. *Brute, animal,* and *creature* are unfavorable. *Lion, eagle,* and sometimes *tiger* are usually favorable; whereas unfavorable attitudes are suggested by *pig, donkey, mule, jackass, rat, monkey, ape, vulture, cat, bitch, fox, vixen, jackal, hyena, snake, reptile, worm, toad, skunk,* and *polecat.*

Metaphors and bias words drawn from family life are all favorable. To speak of *Mother Nature* is to emphasize the pleasanter features of our environment; consider too *alma mater* or *the father of his people.* To call a man *a son of Texas* (or South Dakota or any other place) is always to refer favorably to him—"one of Missouri's most loyal sons." Machine metaphors as applied to a person are also usually favorable, as in *dynamo, steam engine,* or *steam roller,* but *machine politics* and *sausage machine* are unfavorable.

Our study of the language of persuasion may now be continued in tabular form, though a complete list would fill a small dictionary. Political words will be found near the beginning.

FAVORABLE	NEUTRAL	UNFAVORABLE
leader of the people tribune of the people	party leader	demagogue ringmaster rabble-rouser political boss

strong man
  (*e.g.,* "the strong man
  of Ruritania")
	absolute ruler	dictator

community	people	mob [3] the many-headed
patriot [4]	nationalist	jingo chauvinist
rights [5]		privileges
	socialist communist	red
	liberal	pink
social reformer		revolutionary
	conservative (*adj.*)	reactionary backward
with reference to the Spanish War:		
loyalist	supporter of the Spanish republic	red
anti-red	supporter of General Franco	rebel

to develop the
  resources of
		to exploit the
		  resources of

a go-getter
  salesman
	an energetic
	  salesman
		a high-pressure
		  salesman

[3] "Democracy dissolves communities into individuals and collects them again into mobs." Dean Inge, *Outspoken Essays, First Series* (Longmans, Green & Co., Inc.).

[4] "The controversy quickly got into the newspapers, and was carried on for months, with American patriots on one side and Englishmen and Anglomaniacs on the other." H. L. Mencken, *The American Language* (New York, 1936).

[5] We are apt to contrast our own rights with other people's privileges.

FAVORABLE	NEUTRAL	UNFAVORABLE
time-tested old-established well-tried	old (has wide range)	out-of-date, outmoded, obsolete, antiquated, old-fashioned, (has wide range)
up-to-date progressive advanced	new modern (has wide range)	newfangled cranky crackpot
thinking men	those who agree with me	
right-minded		wrong-headed
devout		bigoted
freethinker *esprit fort*	atheist unbeliever	infidel pagan heathen
	to compel	to dragoon
A modern theory would suggest that	I think	
confidence		complacency
self-confidence		conceit, arrogance

Many of the words in this list, and other words like them, are a valuable part of the English language, but a writer who uses them, or a reader who encounters them in the writing of others, should understand what is being done. Instead of giving information about the referent, these words give information about the writer; they express his attitudes and feelings and are chosen by him to convey, if possible, these attitudes and feelings to the reader. Such words are dangerous if they lead the writer or the reader to confuse the exposure of an attitude with the statement of an argument.

OTHER METHODS OF INDICATING BIAS

Direct statements of opinion, the selection of material, and the use of bias words by no means exhaust the means available to the writer who wishes to communicate his prejudices. The exploitation of words with multiple meaning is not a very common device, because it requires more skill than plain lying or calling names, but it is dangerous because less easily detected. *Progressive* is a word with multiple meaning, and as applied to a school it may mean either of two things—namely, that the school is devoted to certain theories of education, most concisely described as those of Dewey, Froebel, and Montessori, or alternatively, that the school makes progress along the scale from bad to good. Everybody must approve of progress of this second kind, because each person can put his own interpretation on *good* and *bad,* but it is not everyone who thinks that schools of the "progressive school" type are the best. Since many people are by no means well informed about multiple meaning, and believe, in a muddled kind of way, that things with the same name must be the same thing, it is possible for a dishonest writer (and easy for a speaker) to use the word *progressive* in two senses in the same passage, thereby convincing the thoughtless that a school "progressive" in one way must be "progressive" in the other.

The suggestion of inferences is a favorite method of persuasion, because readers are likely to hold more tenaciously to opinions supposedly their own than to those handed them ready-made by the author. Rhetorical questions— "Should the American people entrust its destiny to unscrupulous politicians?"—are crude exploitations of the same theory, for it is supposed that the mental effort of discovering the answer will make the reader familiar with the line of reasoning employed, thereby convincing him that the conclusion must be true. But to achieve more lasting impressions the writer must use a less direct approach. "The scandal of Bishop X's connection with the Organ Fund," we read, "is now a thing of the past." The incautious reader will conclude, as is intended, that Bishop X stole the money out of the Organ Fund, or perhaps just borrowed it without meaning to pay it back. Yet this is nowhere asserted by the writer, and if he were accused of suggesting it, he would reply that the scandal arose because the bishop refused to have anything to do with the Organ Fund and wanted the money to be devoted to foreign missions instead.

Bias can quite as well be suggested by an omission as by a statement. Here is a beautiful example from Swift's *Directions to Servants:*

> To grow old in the office of a footman, is the highest of all indignities; therefore, when you find years coming on, without hopes of a place at court, a command in the army, a succession to the stewardship, an employment in the revenue (which two last you cannot obtain without reading and writing) . . . .

Bias words are fine material for irony. Most people feel that the weakness of irony is a tendency to be obvious, commonplace, and cheap—that it is pre-eminently the rhetorical weapon of the immature. Some of the obviousness of directly inverted statements can be avoided, however, by the use of bias words—the favorable one for the unfavorable one, or more rarely, the other way around. Thus, a writer may use the word *aroma* or *perfume* in referring to a bad smell, or describe some disastrous political error as *states-*

manlike. Abbreviation is another method of indicating disrespect; "Musso" and "Mrs. B." are examples. More often the intention is facetious, as in "the B. of A." for Shakespeare (the Bard of Avon), or "rooted to the *s*" (P. G. Wodehouse).

Certain words, of which *real, true, genuine,* and *good* are examples, are used in conjunction with bias words as intensifiers, or as appeals to the reader not to ignore the bias intended by the writer. "No Real Sportsman"[6] means "No sportsman (as I understand the word)," and "All really modern theories" means "All theories now current that I approve of." When so used, these words are mere admissions of failure by the writer.

BIAS AND SETTING

The writer who uses bias words will do well to consider what readers his work is likely to find, because the references of these words may change in different times and places. *Socialist* is almost a term of abuse in some circles but a term of praise in others. Again, *Uncle Sam* is a term sure of a favorable reception in the United States (except perhaps in penitentiaries), and a political cartoon would miss its mark if it showed this figure doing anything base, but in some foreign countries the opposite is true, and an allusion to Uncle Sam would likely to arouse feelings of anger and dislike.

Vocabulary

candor, derogatory, tenaciously, irony, facetious, allusion

Review Questions

1. What does Philbrick mean by "bias words"?
2. Do you agree with the author that words frequently give more information about the writer than they do about the referent? What terms or expressions can you add to the author's table of Unfavorable, Neutral, and Favorable bias words?
3. Identify Dewey, Froebel, Montessori.
4. What methods, other than the use of words of multiple meaning, are there of indicating bias?

[6] "No Real Sportsman Takes Black Salmon"—headline in *The Boston Herald,* April 24, 1941.

Exercises

1. The following words are in Philbrick's terminology "neutral" words. For each, list two synonyms, one which communicates a favorable, the other an unfavorable bias.

horse	car	teacher	worker	lawyer
girl	dance	kill	speak	write

2. In *Straight and Crooked Thinking* (New York, 1932), Robert H. Thouless quotes a well-known saying "declining" the word *firm* as follows: "I am firm, thou art obstinate, he is pig-headed." Decline the following words in a similar manner: *hungry, overweight, prudent, sleepy.*

3. Read the following paragraph which might have appeared in a newspaper in sympathy with racial segregation. Comment on any examples of connotational meaning or bias words which you note.

Senator Puffwell's ill-advised effort to railroad civil rights legislation through this session of Congress encountered courageous opposition from a small but determined group of Southern senators in Washington today. Representing Northern big city interests, Puffwell resorted to the basest kind of shyster tactics when he and his clique of demagogues sought to tack onto the Bullhorn-Snortwell Bill a rider which would withhold Federal funds from all segregated schools. Senator Trueheart of Virginia jumped to his feet, forced Puffwell to yield the floor, and quoting pertinent sacred words of our Constitution decried Puffwell's rider as a Machiavellian attempt to blackjack the South into submission without regard for its God-given rights to liberty and self-determination. The gallery cheered wildly as Trueheart and three other senators spoke at length against the rider, warning the Senate against the tyranny of the majority and sinister attempts to undermine a way of life centuries old.

4. Rewrite the above paragraph as a reporter for a newspaper militantly opposed to racial segregation might fashion it.

5. Write two paragraphs describing the same event. In the first employ words which will produce a generally favorable impression; in the second employ words which will produce an unfavorable impression.

6. An opponent of the Administration's foreign aid program, Oregon Senator Wayne Morse, was severely criticized by Washington columnist Joseph Alsop in 1963 for "know-nothingism" and obstructionism. Morse replied on the floor of Congress with the following speech. Examine it carefully for examples of bias words:

Mr. President, in this morning's *Washington Post,* an alleged newspaperman by the name of Joseph Alsop has published a scathing criticism of the Senate opponents of the wasteful, inefficient, and corruption-producing foreign aid program of the administration and the Foreign Relations Committee.

This is the Alsop who is the well-known lackey of the Pentagon Building and the State Department. His war-mongering columns for a long time past have demonstrated his disregard for, and presumably his ignorance of, the checks and balances system provided by our constitutional fathers and indelibly written into the Constitution itself.

His writings give the impression that he would be happier if the President of the United States were given dictatorial powers similar to those of many of the Fascist leaders of the world whose regimes Alsop seems to admire so much.

He gives the impression that he would like to be an intellectual snob, but lacks the intellect to be snobbish about.

I am very proud of my enemies, particularly the members of the yellow press; and I am highly complimented to have this gutter journalist confess his enmity to me in his irrational, White House bootlicking column of this morning.

I ask unanimous consent that his column entitled, "The New Know-Nothings," be printed in the Record, inasmuch as it is such devastating proof of his own know-nothingism.

(*Congressional Record,* CIX [Nov. 15, 1963], 20843–20844)

39.

GORDON ALLPORT

Linguistic Factors in Prejudice

Without words we should scarcely be able to form categories at all. A dog perhaps forms rudimentary generalizations, such as small-boys-are-to-be-avoided—but this concept runs its course on the conditioned reflex level, and does not become the object of thought as such. In order to hold a generalization in mind for reflection and recall, for identification and for action, we need to fix it in words. Without words our world would be, as William James said, an "empirical sand-heap."

NOUNS THAT CUT SLICES

In the empirical world of human beings there are some two and a half billion grains of sand corresponding to our category "the human race." We

From Gordon Allport, *The Nature of Prejudice,* 1954, Addison-Wesley, Reading, Mass. Reprinted by permission.

cannot possibly deal with so many separate entities in our thought, nor can we individualize even among the hundreds whom we encounter in our daily round. We must group them, form clusters. We welcome, therefore, the names that help us to perform the clustering.

The most important property of a noun is that it brings many grains of sand into a single pail, disregarding the fact that the same grains might have fitted just as appropriately into another pail. To state the matter technically, a noun *abstracts* from a concrete reality some one feature and assembles different concrete realities only with respect to this one feature. The very act of classifying forces us to overlook all other features, many of which might offer a sounder basis than the rubric we select. Irving Lee gives the following example:

> I knew a man who had lost the use of both eyes. He was called a "blind man." He could also be called an expert typist, a conscientious worker, a good student, a careful listener, a man who wanted a job. But he couldn't get a job in the department store order room where employees sat and typed orders which came over the telephone. The personnel man was impatient to get the interview over. "But you're a blind man," he kept saying, and one could almost feel his silent assumption that somehow the incapacity in one aspect made the man incapable in every other. So blinded by the label was the interviewer that he could not be persuaded to look beyond it.[1]

Some labels, such as "blind man," are exceedingly salient and powerful. They tend to prevent alternative classification, or even cross-classification. Ethnic labels are often of this type, particularly if they refer to some highly visible feature, e.g., Negro, Oriental. They resemble the labels that point to some outstanding incapacity—*feeble-minded, cripple, blind man*. Let us call such symbols "labels of primary potency." These symbols act like shrieking sirens, deafening us to all finer discriminations that we might otherwise perceive. Even though the blindness of one man and the darkness of pigmentation of another may be defining attributes for some purposes, they are irrelevant and "noisy" for others.

Most people are unaware of this basic law of language—that every label applied to a given person refers properly only to one aspect of his nature. You may correctly say that a certain man is *human, a philanthropist, a Chinese, a physician, an athlete*. A given person may be all of these; but the chances are that *Chinese* stands out in your mind as the symbol of primary potency. Yet neither this nor any other classificatory label can refer to the whole of a man's nature. (Only his proper name can do so.)

Thus each label we use, especially those of primary potency, distracts

---

[1] I. J. Lee, "How do you talk about people?" *Freedom Pamphlet* (New York, Anti-Defamation League, 1950), p. 15.

our attention from concrete reality. The living, breathing, complex individual—the ultimate unit of human nature—is lost to sight. As in Fig. 1,

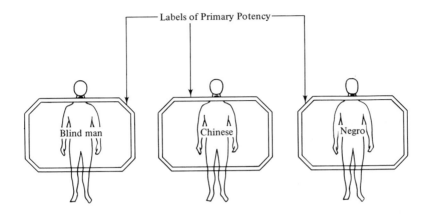

the label magnifies one attribute out of all proportion to its true significance, and masks other important attributes of the individual. . . .

A category, once formed with the aid of a symbol of primary potency, tends to attract more attributes than it should. The category labeled *Chinese* comes to signify not only ethnic membership but also reticence, impassivity, poverty, treachery. To be sure, . . . there may be genuine ethnic-linked traits, making for a certain *probability* that the member of an ethnic stock may have these attributes. But our cognitive process is not cautious. The labeled category, as we have seen, includes indiscriminately the defining attribute, probable attributes, and wholly fanciful, nonexistent attributes.

Even proper names—which ought to invite us to look at the individual person—may act like symbols of primary potency, especially if they arouse ethnic associations. Mr. Greenberg is a person, but since his name is Jewish, it activates in the hearer his entire category of Jews-as-a-whole. An ingenious experiment performed by Razran shows this point clearly, and at the same time demonstrates how a proper name, acting like an ethnic symbol, may bring with it an avalanche of stereotypes.[2]

Thirty photographs of college girls were shown on a screen to 150 students. The subjects rated the girls on a scale from one to five for *beauty, intelligence, character, ambition, general likability.* Two months later the same subjects were asked to rate the same photographs (and fifteen additional ones introduced to complicate the memory factor). This time five of the original photographs were given Jewish surnames (Cohen, Kantor, etc.), five Italian (Valenti, etc.), and

[2] G. Razran, "Ethnic dislike and stereotypes: a laboratory study," *Journal of Abnormal and Social Psychology*, XLV (1950), 7–27.

five Irish (O'Brien, etc.); and the remaining girls were given names chosen
from the signers of the Declaration of Independence and from the Social
Register (Davis, Adams, Clark, etc.).

When Jewish names were attached to photographs there occurred the following changes in ratings:

> decrease in liking
> decrease in character
> decrease in beauty
> increase in intelligence
> increase in ambition

For those photographs given Italian names there occurred:

> decrease in liking
> decrease in character
> decrease in beauty
> decrease in intelligence

Thus a mere proper name leads to prejudgments of personal attributes. The
individual is fitted to the prejudiced ethnic category, and not judged in his own
right.

While the Irish names also brought about depreciated judgment, the depreciation was not as great as in the case of the Jews and Italians. The falling of
likability of the "Jewish girls" was twice as great as for "Italians" and five
times as great as for "Irish." We note, however, that the "Jewish" photographs
caused higher ratings in *intelligence* and in *ambition*. Not all stereotypes of
out-groups are unfavorable.

The anthropologist, Margaret Mead, has suggested that labels of primary potency lose some of their force when they are changed from nouns
into adjectives. To speak of a Negro soldier, a Catholic teacher, or a Jewish
artist calls attention to the fact that some other group classifications are just
as legitimate as the racial or religious. If George Johnson is spoken of not
only as a Negro but also as a *soldier,* we have at least two attributes to know
him by, and two are more accurate than one. To depict him truly as an
individual, of course, we should have to name many more attributes. It is a
useful suggestion that we designate ethnic and religious membership where
possible with *adjectives* rather than with *nouns*.

EMOTIONALLY TONED LABELS

Many categories have two kinds of labels—one less emotional and one
more emotional. Ask yourself how you feel, and what thoughts you have,
when you read the words *school teacher,* and then *school marm*. Certainly
the second phrase calls up something more strict, more ridiculous, more
disagreeable than the former. Here are four innocent letters: m-a-r-m. But

they make us shudder a bit, laugh a bit, and scorn a bit. They call up an image of a spare, humorless, irritable old maid. They do not tell us that she is an individual human being with sorrows and troubles of her own. They force her instantly into a rejective category.

In the ethnic sphere even plain labels such as Negro, Italian, Jew, Catholic, Irish-American, French-Canadian may have emotional tone for a reason that we shall soon explain. But they all have their higher key equivalents: nigger, wop, kike, papist, harp, cannuck. When these labels are employed we can be almost certain that the speaker *intends* not only to characterize the person's membership, but also to disparage and reject him.

Quite apart from the insulting intent that lies behind the use of certain labels, there is also an inherent ("physiognomic") handicap in many terms designating ethnic membership. For example, the proper names character-istic of certain ethnic memberships strike us as absurd. (We compare them, of course, with what is familiar and therefore "right.") Chinese names are short and silly; Polish names intrinsically difficult and outlandish. Un-familiar dialects strike us as ludicrous. Foreign dress (which, of course, is a visual ethnic symbol) seems unnecessarily queer.

But of all these "physiognomic" handicaps the reference to color, clearly implied in certain symbols, is the greatest. The word Negro comes from the Latin *niger*, meaning black. In point of fact, no Negro has a black com-plexion, but by comparison with other blonder stocks, he has come to be known as a "black man." Unfortunately *black* in the English language is a word having a preponderance of sinister connotations: the outlook is black, blackball, blackguard, blackhearted, black death, blacklist, blackmail, Black Hand. In his novel *Moby Dick*, Herman Melville considers at length the remarkably morbid connotations of black and the remarkably virtuous con-notations of white.

Nor is the ominous flavor of black confined to the English language. A cross-cultural study reveals that the semantic significance of black is more or less universally the same. Among certain Siberian tribes, members of a privileged clan call themselves "white bones," and refer to all others as "black bones." Even among Uganda Negroes there is some evidence for a white god at the apex of the theocratic hierarchy; certain it is that a white cloth, signifying purity, is used to ward off evil spirits and disease.[3]

There is thus an implied value-judgment in the very concept of *white race* and *black race*. One might also study the numerous unpleasant con-notations of *yellow*, and their possible bearing on our conception of the people of the Orient.

Such reasoning should not be carried too far, since there are undoubt-edly, in various contexts, pleasant associations with both black and yellow. Black velvet is agreeable, so too are chocolate and coffee. Yellow tulips are

[3] C. E. Osgood, "The nature and measurement of meaning," *Psychological Bulletin*, XLIX (1952), 226.

well liked; the sun and moon are radiantly yellow. Yet it is true that "color" words are used with chauvinistic overtones more than most people realize. There is certainly condescension indicated in many familiar phrases: dark as a nigger's pocket, darktown strutters, white hope (a term originated when a white contender was sought against the Negro heavyweight champion, Jack Johnson), the white man's burden, the yellow peril, black boy. Scores of everyday phrases are stamped with the flavor of prejudice, whether the user knows it or not.[4]

We spoke of the fact that even the most proper and sedate labels for minority groups sometimes seem to exude a negative flavor. In many contexts and situations the very terms *French-Canadian, Mexican,* or *Jew,* correct and nonmalicious though they are, sound a bit opprobrious. The reason is that they are labels of social deviants. Especially in a culture where uniformity is prized, the name of *any* deviant carries with it *ipso facto* a negative value-judgment. Words like *insane, alcoholic, pervert* are presumably neutral designations of a human condition, but they are more: they are finger-pointings at deviance. Minority groups are deviants, and for this reason, from the very outset, the most innocent labels in many situations imply a shading of disrepute. When we wish to highlight the deviance and denigrate it still further we use words of a higher emotional key: crackpot, soak, pansy, greaser, Okie, nigger, harp, kike.

Members of minority groups are often understandably sensitive to names given them. Not only do they object to deliberately insulting epithets, but sometimes see evil intent where none exists. Often the word Negro is spelled with a small *n,* occasionally as a studied insult, more often from ignorance. (The term is not cognate with white, which is not capitalized, but rather with Caucasian, which is.) Terms like "mulatto," or "octoroon" cause hard feeling because of the condescension with which they have often been used in the past. Sex differentiations are objectionable, since they seem doubly to emphasize ethnic difference: why speak of Jewess and not of Protestantess, or of Negress and not of whitess? Similar overemphasis is implied in the terms like Chinamen or Scotchman; why not American man? Grounds for misunderstanding lie in the fact that minority group members are sensitive to such shadings, while majority members may employ them unthinkingly.

THE COMMUNIST LABEL

Until we label an out-group it does not clearly exist in our minds. Take the curiously vague situation that we often meet when a person wishes to

---

[4] L. L. Brown, "Words and White Chauvinism," *Masses and Mainstream,* III (1950), 3–11. See also: *Prejudice Won't Hide! A Guide for Developing a Language of Equality* (San Francisco, California Federation for Civic Unity, 1950).

locate responsibility on the shoulders of some out-group whose nature he cannot specify. In such a case he usually employs the pronoun "they" without an antecedent. "Why don't they make these sidewalks wider?" "I hear they are going to build a factory in this town and hire a lot of foreigners." "I won't pay this tax bill; they can just whistle for their money." If asked "who?" the speaker is likely to grow confused and embarrassed. The common use of the orphaned pronoun *they* teaches us that people often want and need to designate out-groups (usually for the purpose of venting hostility) even when they have no clear conception of the out-group in question. And so long as the target of wrath remains vague and ill-defined specific prejudice cannot crystallize around it. To have enemies we need labels.

Until relatively recently—strange as it may seem—there was no agreed-upon symbol for *communist*. The word, of course, existed but it had no special emotional connotation, and did not designate a public enemy. Even when, after World War I, there was a growing feeling of economic and social menace in this country, there was no agreement as to the actual source of the menace.

A content analysis of the *Boston Herald* for the year 1920 turned up the following list of labels. Each was used in a context implying some threat. Hysteria had overspread the country, as it did after World War II. Someone must be responsible for the postwar malaise, rising prices, uncertainty. There must be a villain. But in 1920 the villain was impartially designated by reporters and editorial writers with the following symbols:

alien, agitator, anarchist, apostle of bomb and torch, Bolshevik, communist, communist laborite, conspirator, emissary of false promise, extremist, foreigner, hyphenated-American, incendiary, IWW, parlor anarchist, parlor pink, parlor socialist, plotter, radical, red, revolutionary, Russian agitator, socialist, Soviet, syndicalist, traitor, undesirable.

From this excited array we note that the *need* for an enemy (someone to serve as a focus for discontent and jitters) was considerably more apparent than the precise *identity* of the enemy. At any rate, there was no clearly agreed upon label. Perhaps partly for this reason the hysteria abated. Since no clear category of "communism" existed there was no true focus for the hostility.

But following World War II this collection of vaguely interchangeable labels became fewer in number and more commonly agreed upon. The out-group menace came to be designated almost always as *communist* or *red*. In 1920 the threat, lacking a clear label, was vague; after 1945 both symbol and thing became more definite. Not that people knew precisely what they meant when they said "communist," but with the aid of the term they were at least able to point consistently to *something* that inspired fear. The term developed the power of signifying menace and led to various repressive measures against anyone to whom the label was rightly or wrongly attached.

Logically, the label should apply to specifiable defining attributes, such as members of the Communist Party, or people whose allegiance is with the Russian system, or followers, historically, of Karl Marx. But the label came in for far more extensive use.

What seems to have happened is approximately as follows. Having suffered through a period of war and being acutely aware of devastating revolutions abroad, it is natural that most people should be upset, dreading to lose their possessions, annoyed by high taxes, seeing customary moral and religious values threatened, and dreading worse disasters to come. Seeking an explanation for this unrest, a single identifiable enemy is wanted. It is not enough to designate "Russia" or some other distant land. Nor is it satisfactory to fix blame on "changing social conditions." What is needed is a human agent near at hand: someone in Washington, someone in our schools, in our factories, in our neighborhood. If we *feel* an immediate threat, we reason, there must be a near-lying danger. It is, we conclude, communism, not only in Russia but also in America, at our doorstep, in our government, in our churches, in our colleges, in our neighborhood.

Are we saying that hostility toward communism is prejudice? Not necessarily. There are certainly phases of the dispute wherein realistic social conflict is involved. American values (e.g., respect for the person) and totalitarian values as represented in Soviet practice are intrinsically at odds. A realistic opposition in some form will occur. Prejudice enters only when the defining attributes of "communist" grow imprecise, when anyone who favors any form of social change is called a communist. People who fear social change are the ones most likely to affix the label to any persons or practices that seem to them threatening.

For them the category is undifferentiated. It includes books, movies, preachers, teachers who utter what for them are uncongenial thoughts. If evil befalls—perhaps forest fires or a factory explosion—it is due to communist saboteurs. The category becomes monopolistic, covering almost anything that is uncongenial. On the floor of the House of Representatives in 1946, Representative Rankin called James Roosevelt a communist. Congressman Outland replied with psychological acumen, "Apparently everyone who disagrees with Mr. Rankin is a communist."

When differentiated thinking is at a low ebb—as it is in times of social crises—there is a magnification of two-valued logic. Things are perceived as either inside or outside a moral order. What is outside is likely to be called "communist." Correspondingly—and here is where damage is done —whatever is called communist (however erroneously) is immediately cast outside the moral order.

This associative mechanism places enormous power in the hands of a demagogue. For several years Senator McCarthy managed to discredit many citizens who thought differently from himself by the simple device of calling them communist. Few people were able to see through this trick and many reputations were ruined. But the famous senator has no monopoly on the device. As reported in the *Boston Herald* on November 1, 1946, Representative Joseph Martin, Republican leader in the House, ended his election campaign against his Democratic opponent by saying, "The people will vote tomorrow between chaos, confusion, bankruptcy, state socialism or communism, and the preservation of our Americal life, with all its freedom and its opportunities." Such an array of emotional labels placed his opponent outside the accepted moral order. Martin was re-elected. . . .

Not everyone, of course, is taken in. Demagogy, when it goes too far, meets with ridicule. Elizabeth Dilling's book, *The Red Network,* was so exaggerated in its two-valued logic that it was shrugged off by many people with a smile. One reader remarked, "Apparently if you step off the sidewalk with your left foot you're a communist." But it is not easy in times of social strain and hysteria to keep one's balance, and to resist the tendency of a verbal symbol to manufacture large and fanciful categories of prejudiced thinking.

VERBAL REALISM AND SYMBOL PHOBIA

Most individuals rebel at being labeled, especially if the label is uncomplimentary. Very few are willing to be called *fascistic, socialistic,* or *anti-Semitic.* Unsavory labels may apply to others; but not to us.

An illustration of the craving that people have to attach favorable symbols to themselves is seen in the community where white people banded together to force out a Negro family that had moved in. They called themselves "Neighborly Endeavor" and chose as their motto the Golden Rule. One of the first acts of this symbol-sanctified band was to sue the man who sold property to Negroes. They then flooded the house which another Negro couple planned to occupy. Such were the acts performed under the banner of the Golden Rule.

Studies made by Stagner[5] and by Hartmann[6] show that a person's political attitudes may in fact entitle him to be called a fascist or a social-

[5] R. Stagner, "Fascist attitudes: an exploratory study," *Journal of Social Psychology,* VII (1936), 309–319; "Fascist attitudes: their determining conditions," *ibid.,* 438–454.

[6] G. Hartmann, "The contradiction between the feeling-tone of political party names and public response to their platforms," *Journal of Social Psychology,* VII (1936), 336–357.

ist, and yet he will emphatically repudiate the unsavory label, and fail to endorse any movement or candidate that overtly accepts them. In short, there is a *symbol phobia* that corresponds to *symbol realism*. We are more inclined to the former when we ourselves are concerned, though we are much less critical when epithets of "fascist," "communist," "blind man," "school marm" are applied to others.

When symbols provoke strong emotions they are sometimes regarded no longer as symbols, but as actual things. The expressions "son of a bitch" and "liar" are in our culture frequently regarded as "fighting words." Softer and more subtle expressions of contempt may be accepted. But in these particular cases, the epithet itself must be "taken back." We certainly do not change our opponent's attitude by making him take back a word, but it seems somehow important that the word itself be eradicated.

Such verbal realism may reach extreme length.

The City Council of Cambridge, Massachusetts, unanimously passed a resolution (December, 1939) making it illegal "to possess, harbor, sequester, introduce or transport, within the city limits, any book, map, magazine, newspaper, pamphlet, handbill or circular containing the words Lenin or Leningrad.[7]

Such naïveté in confusing language with reality is hard to comprehend unless we recall that word-magic plays an appreciable part in human thinking. The following examples, like the one preceding, are taken from Hayakawa.

The Malagasy soldier must eschew kidneys, because in the Malagasy language the word for kidney is the same as that for "shot"; so shot he would certainly be if he ate a kidney.

In May, 1937, a state senator of New York bitterly opposed a bill for the control of syphilis because "the innocence of children might be corrupted by a widespread use of the term. . . . This particular word creates a shudder in every decent woman and decent man."

This tendency to reify words underscores the close cohesion that exists between category and symbol. Just the mention of "communist," "Negro," "Jew," "England," "Democrats," will send some people into a panic of fear or a frenzy of anger. Who can say whether it is the word or the thing that annoys them? The label is an intrinsic part of any monopolistic category. Hence to liberate a person from ethnic or political prejudice it is necessary at the same time to liberate him from word fetishism. This fact is well known to students of general semantics who tell us that prejudice is due in large part to verbal realism and to symbol phobia. Therefore any program

[7] S. I. Hayakawa, *Language in Action* (New York: Harcourt, Brace & World, Inc., 1941), p. 29.

for the reduction of prejudice must include a large measure of semantic therapy.

Vocabulary

conditioned reflex, empirical, rubric, salient, ethnic, reticence, impassivity, cognitive, stereotypes, out-groups, ludicrous, apex, theocratic, chauvinistic, condescension, exude, opprobrious, *ipso facto,* denigrate, epithets, malaise, array, abated, intrinsically, acumen, ebb, demagogue, unsavory, repudiate, phobia, naiveté, eschew, reify, fetishism

Review Questions

1. According to the author what is the advantage of nouns which classify groups of people in "clusters"? What is the disadvantage?
2. What is the significance of the "name-face" experiment described in this essay?
3. Are all stereotypes of out-group members unfavorable? Give examples.
4. Why does professor Allport suggest that labels of primary potency lose some of their force when changed from nouns to adjectives?
5. Is it true that the unfamiliar is frequently odd or humorous to us? What examples can you cite from your own experience?
6. When does an out-group begin to exist as an entity in our minds?
7. What examples of confusion of words and things does Allport cite?

Expository Technique

1. Why is the quotation from I. J. Lee on page 522 a good illustration of the shortcomings of classifying? What other kinds of illustration can you find in this essay?
2. In addition to illustration, this essay uses the six other expository devices discussed and exemplified in this book. Examine this essay carefully and point out how Allport utilizes first one type and then another to his best advantage.

Exercises

1. Read one of the following recent books and report on the prejudice described therein to the class. Show how linguistic factors and stereotypes contribute to the bias presented in the book.

Hal Borland, *When the Legends Die* (Philadelphia, 1963).
Claude Brown, *Manchild in the Promised Land* (New York, 1965).

Dick Gregory and R. Lipsyte, *Nigger* (New York, 1964).
John H. Griffin, *Black Like Me* (Boston, 1961).
Alfred Kazin, *A Walker in the City* (New York, 1951).
C. L. Mayerson, *Two Blocks Apart* (New York, 1965).
Charles E. Silberman, *Crisis in Black and White* (New York, 1964).
Piri Thomas, *Down These Mean Streets* (New York, 1967).

2. Allport points out that in a series of categories to which a man belongs, we tend to remember labels of primary potency, such as Chinese, blind man, Negro. Test this assertion by composing a list of fifteen adjectives which describe a person of your acquaintance, only one of which is a label of primary potency. Read this list once to your roommate, relatives, and friends, asking that they recite all fifteen items back to you. If Allport is correct, the label of primary potency should be remembered most often. Report your findings to the class.

3. A recent study by two psychologists into the nature of religious and national stereotypes showed that the following groups and adjectives were most frequently associated:

Germans: scientifically minded, industrious, stolid
Italians: artistic, impulsive, passionate
English: sportsmanlike, intelligent, conventional
Jews: shrewd, mercenary, industrious
Americans: industrious, intelligent, materialistic
Negroes: superstitious, lazy, happy-go-lucky
Irish: pugnacious, quick-tempered, witty
Chinese: superstitious, sly, conservative
Japanese: intelligent, industrious, progressive
Turks: cruel, very religious, treacherous

Apply the appropriate stereotypes to three people you know well. Do they fit? Report your findings to the class. What do your results reveal to you about the nature of stereotypes?

4. An experiment described in 1946 by Eugene L. Hartley was designed to determine the attitudes of American college students toward various nationalities. The students were instructed to indicate the degree of social intimacy they would allow each of the following national groups: American, Canadian, Chinese, English, German, Italian, Japanese, Negro, Russian. Their responses were to be recorded on a scale from 1–8 as follows:

1: would exclude from my country.
2: would allow as visitors only to my country.
3: would admit to citizenship in my country.
4: would admit to employment in my occupation.
5: would allow to enrol in my school as classmates.
6: would allow to live on my street as neighbors.
7: would allow to join my club as personal chums.
8: would admit to close kinship by marriage.

Hartley scored each of the groups by figuring the median of the positions assigned it by the subjects taking the test. Thus, a median of four would entitle the group to employment in the occupation of the students taking the test; 7 would allow them into private clubs and fraternities. A selection of the results is as follows:

	BENNINGTON	HOWARD	CCNY
American	8.0	5.9	8.0
Canadian	8.0	3.9	7.4
Chinese	5.1	2.6	5.3
English	8.0	3.9	7.8
German	8.0	2.1	7.6
Italian	6.6	2.7	7.1
Japanese	3.9	2.3	3.6
Negro	5.4	8.0	5.5
Russian	7.0	2.9	6.8

Conduct a similar experiment in your dormitory, fraternity, or home. Add other groups such as *Communist, Hippy,* and *liberal* to the list. Bring your results to class and compare them with those of your fellow students.

5. What is your image of the religion to which you belong? Of your national origin? How do nonmembers view these groups? How do you account for the difference?

6. "National, religious, and ethnic labels and classifications have always tended to drive men farther apart rather than closer together." Comment.

7. " 'Anti-Semitism' is strongest in the Northeast and Middlewest where Jews are found in greatest concentration, and weakest in the South and West; stronger in urban populations, particularly large cities, than in rural populations; stronger in upper-income brackets than in lower-income brackets; stronger among whites than among Negroes; and stronger among men than among women." (S. H. Flowerman and M. Jahoda, "Polls on Anti-Semitism: How Much Do They Tell Us?" *Commentary,* I [1946], 83). What do these facts tell us about the nature of prejudice?

Writing Suggestions: Illustration

LINGUISTIC SUBJECTS

1. Old Folks or Senior Citizens (Government Hand-outs or Government Assistance, Culturally Deprived or Slum Ruffians, Young Punks or Improperly Motivated Children, Bums or Derelicts)

2. The Meaning of (a) Color

3. What _____ (Being Black, Italian, Polish, Mexican, Puerto Rican, Catholic, Jewish, a Conscientious Objector, a Pacifist) Has Done to Me

4. The Use and Abuse of Words in _____ (Political Oratory, United Nations Debates, Advertising, Commencement Addresses)

5. What _____ (Bias Words, Gestures, Vocal Inflections, Posture) Communicate(s)

6. It's Not What You Say But the Way That You Say It

7. The Language of _____ (Science, Diplomacy, Politics) and Every-day

8. Analyze a political speech; note the use of bias words and give examples of terms with potent connotational force.

9. Illustrate the different impressions a reader can gain from different reports of the same event. Consider, for example, the versions of Soviet intervention in Czechoslovakia given in the New York *Times* and *Pravda,* or some topic treated in *The National Review* and *The New Republic.*

10. Language and _____ (Emotions, Psychology, Religion, Labor Disputes, Racial Strife, Riots, Fluctuation of the Stock Market, Political Success, Political Leadership)

11. Foreign Words Have Connotations, Too: or, Short Semantic Parables for American Tourists

12. _____ (Occupational, Ethnic, Political, Religious, National, Age-group) Stereotypes

13. The Language of Prejudice

14. Read the following sets of words to ten friends asking them if they have different reactions (favorable, unfavorable, neutral) to the words in each pair. Compile your results and write a short essay in which you state your conclusions.

Catholic—Catholic President	Jew—Jewish soldier
Italian—Italian composer	Negro—Negro doctor

part three

SPECIAL PROBLEMS IN LANGUAGE STUDY

FOR THE MOST PART, we have studied language as something abstracted from the ordinary concerns of man, as something to be observed, analyzed, classified, or defined. Part Three deals with language as it enters into certain spheres of man's life. W. H. Werkmeister and Henryk Skolimowski study the potent persuasive effects of language in propaganda and advertising. Henry J. Abraham briefly reviews the history, bases, and kinds of censorship imposed by society on language considered too profane, obscene, or politically suspect to be tolerated. Clement Wood and Charles Child Walcutt discuss language as it becomes a medium for literary expression. The final group of essays present studies of language and logic. Richard D. Altick and Max Black, respectively, discuss deductive and inductive reasoning; Robert H. Thouless analyzes the pitfalls inherent in reasoning by analogy; Daniel J. Sullivan concludes Part Three with a discussion of the various kinds of linguistic fallacies.

Language and Persuasion

40.

W. H. WERKMEISTER

Propaganda Devices

. . . The list of nine devices given below is not meant to be exhaustive, but it includes the most commonly used tricks and techniques of propagandists. A clear understanding of these devices is in practically all cases sufficient to determine whether or not a given item actually is propaganda.

1. *Name Calling and the Use of Invectives*	**[Inv]**
2. *Glittering Generalities*	**[Glit]**
3. *Tabloid Thinking*	**[Tab]**
4. *Testimonials*	**[Test]**
5. *Bifurcation*	**[Bi]**
6. *Association*	**[Assoc]**
7. *Identification*	**[Ident]**
8. *Band Wagon*	**[Band]**
9. *Card Stacking*	**[Card]**

In the analyses of examples the bracketed abbreviations of the devices will be used to indicate in the body of the text which device is employed. The part of the item under analysis which indicates the employment of the propaganda device will be underlined.

1. NAME CALLING AND THE USE
OF INVECTIVES [Inv]

The propagandist appeals to prejudices, fears, and hates by using emotionally colored words which reinforce biases and negative attitudes. He employs question-begging epithets for the purpose of determining the course of people's thinking, and he tries to lead them into forming negative judgments without examining the evidence upon which such judgments should be based. He indulges in "name calling" and denounces persons, causes, and ideas by the use of derogatory adjectives and of verbs which carry emotionally negative overtones. He resorts to "snarl" words which imply disapproval or condemnation, but he does not take the trouble to justify the use of such words. He attempts to carry people along emotionally in an attitude of negativity, without presenting any actual evidence which would justify a negative decision.

Example: "For fifteen years we were the irresolute and helpless object [Inv] of international exploitation [Inv] which, in the name of democratic ideals of humanity, belabored [Inv] our people with the whip [Inv] of sadistic egoism [Inv]."   (Adolf Hitler, 1940)

Example: "Mr. Roosevelt—cold [Inv], calculating [Inv], self-seeking [Inv] politician [Inv] that he is—has catered [Inv] to the communists on every occasion but one."
(Col. Robert R. McCormick, publisher of the *Chicago Tribune,* April 18, 1944.)

Example: "Jimmy Byrnes, the American Secretary of State and sharp little lawyer [Inv] with a cold smile [Inv] and a hard mind [Inv], ran the proceedings of the Security Council with the contemptuous [Inv] assurance of a county political boss [Inv]."
(Report on the U. N. Security Council Meeting, *New Masses,* April 9, 1946.)

When confronted with items involving this propaganda device, it is necessary to ask: What is the real meaning of the "snarl" words or invectives, of the emotionally colored verbs and "names"? Does this meaning have any justifiable connection with the ideas, causes, or persons referred to? Is there any evidence which justifies the employment of these words in the case at hand? Disregarding the invectives, what are the merits of the ideas presented? What is the purpose behind them? Who will profit from this propaganda? What is my interest in the issue? How will the outcome affect society as a whole? Complete answers to these questions should go far toward protecting people from an unwarranted propagandistic play upon their emotions by the use of such obvious devices as name calling and the employment of invectives.

2. *GLITTERING GENERALITIES* [Glit]

The propagandist employs this device when he appeals to a person's "idealism"; to his love, religion, patriotism, or generosity; to his sense of justice, pride, hope, courage, and the like; when he wants to call forth in people an emotional response of approval. He employs "purr" words or words charged with emotionally positive overtones, words which suggest or imply positive and affirmative attitudes. He uses undefined and abstract terms—"glittering generalities,"—with a high emotional appeal; terms, such as "truth," "freedom," "honor," "progress," "Americanism," "democratic way of life," which mean different things to different people, and he never specifies in which particular sense he is using them. He deliberately refrains from being specific, for he hopes that every one of his listeners or readers will provide his own interpretation of the "glittering generalities" and will thus assume that the propagandist means the same thing; that he and the propagandist are in complete agreement; that they approve the same ideas, the same cause, the same course of action. In other words, the propagandist hopes that his listeners or readers will be "taken in" by the emotional appeal of the undefined words; that they will not ask for evidence or concretely defined particulars, but that their emotions will be assuaged and their reason satisfied by the suggestive force of the emotionally positive words.

Example: "Let the sanctity [Glit] of human rights [Glit] be preferred to the sanctity [Glit] of property or financial rights [Glit], and let the Government's chief concern [Glit] be toward the poor [Glit]."

(Father Coughlin, February 26, 1939.)

Example: "The Socialist Party—like most Americans—wants the earliest peace that will last [Glit], wants the preservation [Glit] and increase [Glit] of democracy [Glit], and wants complete victory [Glit] over poverty and unemployment."

(Norman Thomas, "The Socialist Party in 1944," *Liberty,* October 28, 1944).

Example: "Our policy is a positive policy [Glit]. This policy is to protect [Glit], to defend [Glit] and to perpetuate [Glit] our free [Glit], constitutional form of government, our free enterprise system [Glit] of economy, our system of free society [Glit]. This is a real American policy [Glit], and it is broad enough [Glit] to be embraced by men and women of every party."

(Representative J. W. Martin of Massachusetts, June 27, 1944.)

Example: "Militant liberalism [Glit] is our passion and our faith. We want to lead in the struggle for true freedom [Glit] and for lasting peace [Glit]. We believe that true freedom [Glit] requires effective democratic government [Glit] able to provide the opportunity for a full life [Glit]. . . . We believe in the Four Freedoms [Glit] and in One World [Glit]. . . . We will do everything within our power [Glit] to create from the liberal spirit [Glit] of our people a liberal movement [Glit], organized for political action [Glit] and conscious of its responsibility [Glit] to the world [Glit]."

(From "A Statement of Faith," *New Republic,* April 15, 1946.)

When the device of "glittering generalities" is employed by a propagandist, it is well to ask: What do these words usually mean? In what sense does the propagandist use them? Does he define them in any way at all? What connection do the words have with the ideas which the propagandist presents? Disregarding the "glittering generalities," what is the merit or demerit of the ideas presented? Who will benefit from them? How will they affect organized society?

It is quite possible that after a careful analysis of all factors and facts involved we find ourselves in complete agreement with the aims and intentions of the propagandist; that we are willing to give him our full support. But we should approve of and support his aims only because of their merit and not because of the persuasiveness of the propaganda; because of their "rightness," not because of the "purr" words. Whatever our decision, it should be arrived at on the basis of facts and indisputable evidence, uninfluenced by the suggestiveness of undefined terms which are emotionally "loaded" so that they tend to persuade the reason by satisfying the affections.

3. TABLOID THINKING [Tab]

. . . In the field of propaganda the employment of hasty generalizations in settling a dispute or an argument leads to "tabloid thinking."

"Every man has his price"; "It's human nature for men to fight"; "You can't change human nature"; "All gangsters are foreigners"; "Once a disrupter, always a disrupter"; "We did it before; we can do it again"—generalized and dogmatically asserted propositions such as these are the earmarks of "tabloid thinking." The propagandist makes effective use of them, for they fit in with man's tendency to simplify; they provide focal points for beliefs and prejudices. "Generalizations" such as these are, as a rule. widely accepted even before the propagandist uses them, and they possess the suggestiveness of so-called "*a priori* truths," implying a finality which brings reasoning to an end.

Example: "Those who earnestly think that the 'brave new world' will differ from the world that is gone forever, forget that human nature is unchangeable [**Tab**]."

(*The Steuben News,* March, 1946.)
Example: "The United States never lost a war and never won a conference [**Tab**]. Under Mr. Roosevelt it is still true, only the conferences are becoming more and more expensive."

(From an editorial in the *Brattleboro Reformer,* September 18, 1944.)
Example: "Let the ruling classes tremble at a Communistic revolution. The proletarians have nothing to lose but their chains [**Tab**]."

(From the *Communist Manifesto.*)
A special form of tabloid thinking is the use of "slogans": "Make the

world safe for Democracy!"; "America first!"; "Buy American!"; "Down with Capitalism!"; "Vote the bureaucrats out of office!"; "Clean house in Washington!"; "Let us restore honest government!"; "Let's keep Nebraska the White Spot of the Nation!"; "Workers of the world, unite!"—The suggestive force of slogans must not be underestimated. Like tabloids, they put an end to thinking. They are designed to carry people along on the strength of their emotional appeal.

When confronted with slogans or tabloids, one should ask: What is the intention of the propagandist? What does he want me to do? Who will benefit from my action? What will be the effect upon society as a whole? In other words, when confronted with slogans and tabloids, one should refuse to yield to the emotional appeal and make a factual analysis of all sides of the issue.

4. TESTIMONIALS [Test]

This device is employed by the propagandist to "sell" anything from patent medicine to a suburban home, from a magazine subscription to a panacea for the economic ills of the nation, from a vacation trip to an ideology. It consists in using some "authority," some person, party, document, or institution, in support of the idea which is to be "sold."

. . . the reference to "authority" is legitimate under certain conditions of competence, authenticity, verifiability, and general trustworthiness. The propagandist, however, does not, as a rule, use "authorities" in this legitimate sense. He has recourse to untrustworthy sources and quotes incompetent or biased "authorities," *i.e.,* he commits the fallacy of *argumentum ad verecundiam*. Moreover, he misquotes or distorts the facts or opinions derived from reliable sources. He attributes facts and opinions to some competent authority which do not come from that source and, in general, he selects and manipulates the "testimonials" to suit his own purpose.

Example: "The White House is rather cautious in making declarations concerning the American program for future domination of the world. The American papers which are not directly influenced by the White House show absolutely no delicacy when speaking of their British Allies. The *Chicago Tribune* [**Test**], for instance, publishes an article by Colonel McCormick [**Test**] who thinks that it would be opportune to incorporate the countries of the British Empire into the United States of America." (Radio Rome, April, 1943, Axis-controlled.)—The purpose of this propaganda item obviously was to make the English people suspicious of American peace aims. The ideas were so presented as to give the impression that the real aims of America, the desires of her people, were not at all identical with the professed foreign policy of the Roosevelt administration, and that

Colonel McCormick represented the overwhelming sentiment of the American people. Colonel McCormick and the *Chicago Tribune,* however, can hardly be regarded as competent or unbiased spokesmen for America.

Example: "Secret reports [**Test**] of those days (spring, 1919) made accessible [**Test**] only now, speak of the frightening possibility that the two defeated powers, Russia and Germany, might unite themselves overnight and force the exhausted allied armies to fresh battles." (Emil Ludwig, *Stalin,* p. 207.)—Whenever "testimonials" of this type, giving only a vague reference to some source, are encountered, one should ask: Who or what is quoted? Why should this source be regarded as competent, as having trustworthy information or expert knowledge concerning the matter at issue? Is it possible to verify the facts or opinions in this case through some other channels?

Example: "I quote again: 'December 7, 1941, found the Army Air Forces equipped with plans but not planes.' Did that come from Goebbels? That statement was made in an official report [**Test**] on January 4 of this year by H. H. Arnold [**Test**], commanding General of the Army Air Forces of the United States of America." (Thomas E. Dewey, October 16, 1944.)— In this statement Mr. Dewey, the Republican candidate for president, charged Franklin D. Roosevelt, who was a candidate for re-election, with having neglected to prepare America for war. The report referred to by Mr. Dewey actually stated: "Dec. 7, 1941 (Dec. 8, Hawaiian time) found the Army Air Forces equipped with plans but not with planes. . . . The entire year 1941 was one of acceleration, in building bases and training facilities, teaching air crews and ground crews, establishing supply depots and supply lines, strengthening our continental defenses, expanding our aircraft and engine factories, furnishing friendly nations with more planes and equipment than we could spare, and getting ready for war. When the Japanese attacked on Dec. 7, 1941, we may not have had a powerful air force but we knew that we soon would have one. We had the plans, and our organization was growing every hour. We knew that we had done everything permitted us by a peace-loving nation to prepare and defend that nation against cruel and cunning foes. . . . The resourcefulness and energy of our people would have been of little avail against our enemies if the Army Air Forces had not begun preparations for war long before Pearl Harbor. By Dec. 7, 1941, we were in low gear and were shifting into second. That we were rapidly building up our strength at that time has been erased from the minds of many people by succeeding events. But due in large part to the initiative of our Commander in Chief [Franklin D. Roosevelt], we did not start this war from scratch."—By quoting only one sentence and by neglecting completely its context in the official report, Mr. Dewey distorted the facts in the case and betrayed his propaganda aim. He attributed to a competent "authority" an idea which, in essence, that "authority" never held—a common trick or device of many propagandists.

Another trick of propaganda agencies is to "plant" an idea—in the form of a "news item," "editorial," or "feature article"—in some newspaper or magazine and then to quote that newspaper or magazine as the "source" of the idea. This is, of course, only another variation of the "testimonial."

5. BIFURCATION [Bi]

The propagandist frequently employs this device in order to drive home his point by contrast. He speaks of "we" and "they," of the "rich" and the "poor," the "good" and the "bad," the "haves" and the "have-nots," dividing persons, things, ideas, groups, parties, or countries into two mutually exclusive groups which are "for" or "against" us, leaving no room for intermediate groups, positions, attitudes, or points of view. He carries out a strict "bifurcation" and proceeds to argue his case from this simplified position of "either-or" when actually there may exist one or more additional alternatives mediating between the extremes.

Example: "The German is a destroyer or a creator [Bi]. His soul moves between two polarities [Bi]. He is either very very good, or very very bad. [Bi]. He is either, like Nietzsche, the Iconoclast, or, like Kant, the creator of an ideal system [Bi]."
(Dorothy Thompson, *Listen, Hans,* propaganda broadcasts to Nazi Germany.)

Example: "If you want to destroy private enterprise, if you want to turn our country over to those who openly admit they hate everything American, if you want to open the gates to all the people of the earth and destroy our immigration laws, if you want to destroy our Republic, if you want every heartbeat controlled from Washington, vote for this bill [the anti-poll-tax bill]. On the other hand [Bi], if you still believe in the principles of States' rights, if you still believe that our country is the greatest Nation on earth, if you still believe a republic is the best form of government, vote against this bill."
(Congressman Manasco of Alabama, May 24, 1943, in the House of Representatives.)

Example: "This, then, is what America faces in the historic November elections. On one side [Bi] is the Roosevelt-led Democratic Party, bent on the most effective prosecution of the war, close to the people, aligned with and backed by the great labor and progressive movement. On the other side [Bi] is a party whose candidate can now be, at best, the mouthpiece of Herbert Hoover. Its victory would enhance enormously the power within the country of the most reactionary, pro-fascist, appeaser elements in America."

(The Daily Worker, April 18, 1944.)

These examples suffice to illustrate the device in question and to indicate its wide use. To counteract its effectiveness one must ask: What is the evidence upon which the bifurcation is based? What additional alternatives are available? What bearing do they have upon the point at issue? What does the propagandist want me to do? What are the merits and demerits of his program? Who benefits from it? How does it affect me personally? What effect has it upon society as a whole?

If one remembers that all contrary terms—i.e., terms such as "good-bad," "conservative-radical," "civilized-uncivilized," "normal-abnormal," "public interest-private interest"—indicate only extremes on a continuous scale of values, permitting various degrees of intermediacy, one has gained a first step in the defense against propaganda based upon bifurcation.

6. *ASSOCIATION* [Assoc]

This is a device by means of which the propagandist tries to establish a connection, a psychological association, between the idea he presents and some object, person, party, cause, or idea which people respect, revere, or cherish, or which they fear, condemn, or repudiate. If the association is established, the propagandist hopes that his hearers or readers will transfer their attitude from the thing, cause, or person cherished (or feared, as the case may be) to the idea, cause, or person he wants them to cherish (or fear).

Example: "My friends, this is the most important crusade [**Assoc**] which we have ever undertaken. Its result will be financial democracy [**Glit**] or [**Bi**] slavery [**Inv**]. It is a contest between Christ [**Assoc**] and chaos [**Bi**]. . . . Under the symbol of His cross [**Assoc**] are we organized to be our brother's keeper. That is why I ask each one of you to carry about in your pockets or in your purses this symbol of redemption [**Assoc**] from slavery [**Inv**] both here and hereafter; this symbol of brotherly love [**Assoc**]. There is a crucifix in my office for you for the asking if you will address a letter to me this week. You are with us or against us [**Bi**]. You can't be indifferent [**Tab**]. This crucifix [**Assoc**] is a symbol of credits for all [**Glit**], justice for all [**Glit**] and love for all [**Glit**]."
(Father Coughlin, February 25, 1934, announcing a new financial credit scheme.)

Example: "Frankly, I don't like the name Free Enterprise [**Glit**] for the system under which this country has grown great. I'd rather call it American [**Assoc**] Enterprise, because it's the most American thing [**Assoc**] we have. It really *is* America [**Assoc**]. Let's *keep* it."

(From an advertisement of Republic Steel.)

Example: "There are two kinds of speakers, one appeals to your emotions, the other to reason [**Bi**]. Roosevelt is the kind that works your emotions, the same as does Hitler [**Assoc**], and the masses blindly follow to the bitter end."

(Omaha World-Herald, October 8, 1944.)

The examples given speak for themselves. In each case the purpose of the propagandist is evident. In order to guard against his machinations one must ask: Does the alleged connection actually exist? What evidence, if any, is there to prove it? Who wants me to believe in this association? Who benefits from it? If the suggested association is disregarded, what is the merit of the ideas presented? What is the cause to be served?—If all of these questions are answered competently and in accordance with the facts, it is unlikely that anyone can be victimized by the propaganda trick of establishing associations.

7. *IDENTIFICATION* [Ident]

In order to win the confidence and approval of the persons addressed, the propagandist identifies himself with them and their interests. He becomes "one of the boys." This device is used by all who want to "sell" themselves to an audience. It is used by politicians, labor leaders, and agitators of various sorts. It is used by candidates for public office who are "just plain folks," and by the businessman or the banker, the doctor or the lawyer, who wants to be considered "one of us."

Example: "The fact that my American forebears [**Ident**] have for so many generations played their part in the life of the United States and that here I am, an Englishman, welcomed in your midst makes this experience one of the most moving and thrilling in my life, which is already long and has not been entirely uneventful. I wish indeed that my mother whose memory I cherish across the veil of years, could have been here to see me. By the way, I cannot help reflecting that if my father had been American and my mother British, instead of the other way round, I might have got here on my own [**Ident**]. In that case, this would not have been the first time you would have heard my voice [**Ident**]. In that case I would not have needed any invitation [**Ident**], but if I had it is hardly likely that it would have been unanimous. So, perhaps things are better as they are. I may confess, however, that I do not feel quite like a fish out of water in a legislative assembly where English is spoken [**Ident**]. I am a child of the House of Commons. I was brought up in my father's house to believe in democracy [**Ident**]; trust the people, that was his message. I used to see him cheered at meetings and in the streets by crowds of workingmen way back in those aristocratic Victorian days when Disraeli said, 'The world was for the few and for the

very few.' Therefore, I have been in full harmony with the tides which have flowed on both sides of the Atlantic [**Ident**] against privileges and monopoly and I have steered confidently towards the Gettysburg ideal [**Ident**] of government of the people, by the people, for the people."
(Winston Churchill in an address before Congress, December 26, 1941.)

The device of identification is always used to win trust and confidence. In order to counteract it, one must remember that any idea, plan, scheme, proposition, or article, must in itself merit consideration if it is to be accepted. The charming manner and the "I'm-just-one-of-you" attitude of the salesman, the politician, or the propagandist are insufficient proof of the merit of any proposition. Whenever the device of identification is employed, one may be certain that a propagandist is at work, and the wise course of action is to be especially wary and skeptical.

8. *BAND WAGON* [Band]

This device is calculated to make people "follow the crowd." "Everybody is doing it"; "Everybody is using it"; "Don't throw your vote away; vote for Mr. Blank; he is sure to win!"—phrases and expressions such as these characterize the band wagon device. Parades, music, crowds, the whole scale of the dramatic arts may be employed to catch and hold attention, to "sweep people off their feet." From medicine shows to political rallies, the technique is the same.

The band wagon device is encountered quite frequently, although in less conspicuous form, in campaign speeches, articles, reports, broadcast commentaries, and political tracts designed to win votes or increase the support of a party or cause.

Example: "Since I was last here in June, a great campaign has gained force daily [**Band**] to restore honesty and competence to our government. All over the country [**Band**] that movement has taken hold until now it has become an irresistible tide [**Band**], sweeping on [**Band**] toward victory for a free America in November. The strength of that movement [**Band**] does not lie in any individual. It springs from an urgent conviction in the minds of our people [**Band**]."
(Thomas E. Dewey, Republican candidate for president, October 25, 1944.)

Example: "For many years I have been writing and lecturing that the people have been losing four-fifths of everything they earn through the interest collecting swindle [**Inv**]. Now most everybody [**Band**] except the financiers and their touts [**Inv**] who get a rake-off [**Inv**] are saying 'Lawson is right.' No doubt, eighty per cent of the people [**Band**] of the United States of America will welcome this program of justice for everybody [**Glit**] that harms nobody [**Glit**] as fast as it is brought to their attention."
(Alfred Lawson in *The Benefactor,* Vol. I, No. 26.)

Whenever band wagon tactics are employed, it is necessary to ask: What is the program which the propagandist tries to "put across"? What are its merits? What evidence is there for or against it? How will it affect me? How will it affect society as a whole? Who will benefit from it? Against whom is it directed? Any program deserving support must be defensible on rational and empirical grounds without the claptrap and theatricals of a band wagon campaign.

In some cases of worthwhile programs, however, the "beating of drums" may be necessary to overcome the natural lethargy of the people; and there is no danger in "following the crowd" so long as a person's decision to do so is reached on the basis of actual evidence and is consistent with the true merits of the issues involved. Only when one follows the crowd blindly, when one is "swept off one's feet" and no longer examines the merits and demerits of the case, does the band wagon device become a vicious and dangerous propaganda trick. Its use, however, always earmarks propaganda for what it is: an appeal to the emotions rather than to reason, an attempt to influence a person's behavior by suggestion rather than by rational persuasion, a means for breaking down all resistance by implying that the cause sponsored by the propagandist is what everybody really wants and works for, and that anyone who does not follow the crowd is an isolated individual whose judgment and opinion do not count.

9. CARD STACKING [Card]

This is one of the most vicious of all propaganda devices, for it depends upon distortions, exaggerations, false evidence, forgeries, mis-statements of facts, outright lies, and deceptions of all kinds. Sham and hypocrisy characterize its devotees. It is so prominent a device in so-called "bad" propaganda that many people identify it with propaganda itself, failing to see that propaganda ends may be accomplished through other devices as well.

It is difficult to detect some forms of card stacking, for not all relevant facts are readily accessible for a careful check-up on a suspected item. If definite proof cannot be produced at once, it is best to suspend judgment until more facts are available or until the purpose of the propagandist becomes evident.

A useful criterion is that of *consistency*. Is the suspected item consistent within itself? Is it consistent with other reports on the same subject? Is it consistent with well-established facts, laws, and principles? If a significant inconsistency is discovered, particular caution is in order.

Example: When the campaign to "keep Nebraska the White Spot of the Nation" was at its height, the sponsors of the campaign told the people of Nebraska that their intention was to bring new industries into the state. But if this was the real intention, why was the campaign carried on with especial intensity in the State of Nebraska itself? Here was an inconsistency between the declared intention and the actual procedure—an inconsistency which should have aroused the suspicion of the people of Nebraska. Had they analyzed the situation objectively, they would have discovered much sooner than they did that the whole campaign was meant to perpetuate the inequitable tax system which existed in the state at that time.

Some forms of card stacking can be detected from the internal evidence of a suspected item. For example:

(*a*) The card stacker may employ the simple device of *complex question*. By the use of such questions the propagandist leads his listener or reader into assuming the real point at issue while presenting "evidence" which is irrelevant to that point. It is not difficult, however, to spot complex questions and thus to discover the trick of the propagandist.

Example: "The question is sometimes asked, 'How are the public utilities of the United States developed on such a sound foundation that they excel those of all other countries [**Card**]? Managers of these companies, early in the growth of industry, began to realize that success lay in square dealing [**Glit**] and a full public understanding [**Glit**] of their affairs. Today these great industrial organizations stand for democracy in business [**Glit**]. There is no secrecy [**Inv**] or official pomp [**Inv**] surrounding them [**Card**]. They are natural monopolies [**Card**], and their rates and services are subject to public regulations [**Card**]. Their stocks and bonds are owned by millions of American citizens [**Card**]. The lowest man on the pay roll has as good a chance to become president of the company, if he has the ability, as the president's son [**Card**]. Efficiency [**Glit**] and service [**Glit**] are the watchwords [**Card**] of these institutions [**Assoc**]."

(Editorial supplied by the *Hofer and Sons Service* to nearly thirteen
  thousand American newspapers. *Hofer and Sons Service* was at that
  time subsidized by the utility companies.)

The "editorial" just quoted was published in connection with the controversy between publicly owned and privately owned utilities in the 1920's. The propagandist adroitly side-stepped the real issue by asking a complex question which simply assumed that the privately owned utilities of the United States have been developed on a sound basis and that they do excel those of all other countries. He then proceeded to answer his own misleading question by giving his readers glittering generalities and by stacking the cards through the use of misleading statements and half-truths. At that time American utility companies were largely controlled by absentee holding companies. The stock-market crash of 1929 disclosed a shockingly unsound basis for many of America's privately owned utilities.

(*b*) Card stacking may also be achieved by the use of ambiguous words or phrases which tend to confuse the issue, or by the use of undefined terms which assume the point to be proved. In all such cases of card stacking it is necessary to ask: What do these words really mean? What do they assume or imply? When properly defined, what actual situation do they describe? Is there any evidence which justifies their employment?

Example: "It is conceded [**Card**] that both Doctors Marx and Hitler, together with their assistants, were more or less accurate [**Card**] in discovering the nature of the disease which afflicted Russia and Germany. Their diagnosis is very applicable to America [**Card**], but it is my belief that America, sick as she is [**Card**], is reluctant to swallow [**Card**] either the red pill of Communism or the brown pill of Nazism." (Father Coughlin, February 26, 1939.)—If one asks, What do the words and phrases marked by "Card" in this item mean?, one soon discovers that their meaning is far from clear, and that it is the very ambiguity of these words and phrases upon which the propagandist relies in stacking the cards. "It is conceded"—by whom? When? Where? "More or less accurate"—just what does that mean? "Is very applicable to America"—in what respects? "Sick as she is"—is she? Who diagnosed the case? In what respects is she sick? What is meant here by "sick"? "Reluctant to swallow"—does this mean "passive resistance" or does it mean "an active campaign of 'extermination' "?

(*c*) The propagandist may also accomplish his card stacking by presenting distorted facts and figures and by arguing from them to establish his point.

Example: "Reviewing briefly the history of Russia from the time of the last war, Sir Bernard Pares pointed to 'the filthy, sexual beast [**Inv**] Rasputin' as the reason for the revolutionary movement against the church in Russia [**Card**]. The movement was against a church headed by such a person as Rasputin [**Card**], 'it had nothing to do with Christianity' [**Card**], he said." (*Montreal Gazette,* December 8, 1943.)—It so happens that Rasputin was not an ordained priest, that he did not "head" the Russian church, and that he was murdered before the Soviet regime came into power. Furthermore, Marxist opposition to religion antedates the period of Rasputin's influence, for it was none other than Marx himself who spoke of religion as an "opiate for the people."

(*d*) Card stacking is also accomplished when the emphasis is placed upon unimportant or irrelevant aspects instead of the central issue.

Example: In February, 1946, the New York City tugboat workers went on strike. Because of the fuel emergency which resulted from the strike, Mayor O'Dwyer virtually closed down the entire city. On February 12, the New York *World-Telegram* devoted its entire front page to a report on the strike situation. The headlines across all 8 columns of that page read:

SHUTDOWN STILLS ENTIRE CITY
US Calls on Strikers to Return

On page 5 of the same issue was printed the following item: "The striking UM division of the ILA (AFL) sought increased pay and shorter hours, but, under the urging of its leaders, voted unanimously yesterday to submit the demands to arbitration. The operators—some 92 NY tugboat companies —balked, holding that they needed increased rates to take care of the salary increases they would be called on to pay." There was not even a hint at these facts on the whole front page. A reader who did not turn to page 5 was left with the impression that the workers were still stubbornly staying away from work. The treatment of the strike situation reveals a pronounced anti-labor bias of the *World-Telegram.*

(*e*) Various forms of card stacking frequently are used in the same item.

Example: "The abolition of the poll tax is an extension of democracy to 10,000,000 Americans [**Card**]. The abolition of the poll tax is a re-assertion and re-affirmation of the Constitution [**Card**] and of the very principles upon which our Government rests. It is extending democracy within the boundaries of our own land. It is a blow at fascism [**Card**] against which Americans are fighting everywhere in the world. The fundamental issue involved in this bill [the anti-poll-tax bill] today is democracy [**Glit**]. The contest is between those who want a government of the rich, the few, and the well-born and those of us [**Bi**] who believe in a government of the people [**Card**]. It is an issue of whether or not the principles of equality shall live everywhere in America [**Card**]. That is the issue. It is not an issue monopolized by any groups; it is not an issue monopolized by any political party; it is an issue in which every believer in American democracy [**Glit**] stands up against [**Bi**] bias and prejudice [**Inv**], against tyranny [**Inv**] and domestic fascism [**Inv**], and once again in the Congress of the United States re-affirms the proposition of the Declaration of Independence, that all men are created equal and, like a true patriot [**Glit**], refuses to bow and kneel before the false god of race or color supremacy [**Card**]."
(Congressman Marcantonio of New York, May 25, 1943, in the House
of Representatives.)

The card stacking in this speech can be discovered only if it is kept in mind that the poll tax is a property qualification for voting and does not discriminate against Negroes any more than against white Americans. Actually it affects 4,000,000 Negroes and 6,000,000 whites. It must also be remembered that passage of the anti-poll-tax bill will not give franchise to the 4,000,000 Negroes, for numerous other qualification requirements are in force in the Southern states which effectively bar the Negro even if he pays the poll tax. Lastly, it must not be forgotten that Congress may regulate only the conditions under which candidates for federal offices are elected. State elections are under the exclusive control of the states themselves.[1]

---

[1] The merits or demerits of the issue involved in the item quoted above are unaffected by pointing out the propaganda elements in Mr. Marcantonio's speech.

MIXED USE OF PROPAGANDA DEVICES

The examples of propaganda given in the preceding section were selected specifically to provide illustrations of the various devices employed by the propagandist. Even so it was apparent in some cases that various devices were employed in one and the same item. In actual practice, such simultaneous employment of different devices is the general rule. A good propagandist will overlook no trick to put his ideas across.

The discovery of one propaganda device in a suspected item should be taken as a hint that others may also be present; and the more tricks and devices are discovered in any given item, the more certain it is that the item is "nothing but" propaganda.

Example: "Ours must be a moral platform [**Glit**] from which there is preached [**Assoc**] a positive policy [**Glit**] based upon the principles of religion [**Assoc; Glit**] and of patriotism [**Glit**]. For God [**Assoc**] and country [**Assoc; Glit**], for Christ [**Assoc**] and the flag [**Assoc**]—that is our motto as we prepare for action [**Card**], for Christian American action [**Glit**], which is neither anti-German, anti-Italian, nor anti-Semitic [**Card**]. Any negative policy [**Inv**] is destined to failure. Only a positive policy [**Glit**] can hope to succeed. Unified action on a common program [**Glit**] for God [**Assoc**] and country [**Assoc; Glit**] is more necessary now than at any other period in the history of our civilization [**Card**]."

(Father Coughlin, February 26, 1939.)

Second example: "The red-baiters [**Inv**], in their black hatred [**Inv**] for communism, have condemned recklessly [**Inv**] the whole Russian people [**Card**]. The American communists, by their absurdly unbalanced [**Inv**] and erratic [**Inv**] espousal of what they assume [**Card**] to be Russia's foreign and domestic policies have done the Russian cause [**Glit**] even more harm [**Card**] than the red-baiters [**Inv**] and have contributed enormously [**Card**] toward the confusion of the public mind. The truth is [**Card**] that the American communists are and always have been a Trotzkyite [**Inv**] party [**Card**], advocating international revolution, and I doubt [**Card**] whether there has been any communication [**Card**] between them and the Kremlin since Trotzky was driven out of Russia by Stalin. Certainly [**Card**], it is abundantly evident [**Card**] from their dizzy [**Inv**] record of shifting positions that they never have any advance information [**Card**] concerning the moves Stalin makes. . . . The tight shoe [**Inv**] of German-born Marxian [**Inv**] communism did not fit the big and vigorous foot [**Glit; Card**] of Russia and adjustments [**Card**] have been going on ever since, away from government by the state [**Inv; Card**] toward government by the people [**Glit; Card**]."

(Louis Bromfield, *A Voice from the Country,* April 23, 1944.)

Exercises

1. Read each of the following selections carefully noting the presence of any of the nine propaganda devices discussed by Werkmeister.

a. I know not what course others may take, but as for me, give me liberty or give me death.

b. Fifty million Frenchmen can't be wrong.

c. By order of President Truman, General MacArthur was dismissed as top commander in the Far East. Yesterday's chief commander of the interventionist forces in Korea, the "uncrowned emperor" of Japan as he was called by the American bourgeoisie press, appeared to be out of the picture.

(*Pravda,* April 18, 1951)

d. United we stand, divided we fall.

e. We are justly proud that ours is a government of free thinking, free acting, free speaking citizens.

f. Germans by nature love only three things: beer, music, and war.

g. But where, say some, is the King of America? I'll tell you, Friend; he reigns above and doth not make havoc of mankind like the Royal brute of Great Britain.   (Thomas Paine, *Common Sense*)

h. We cannot successfully fight Communism by being negative. We will not be satisfied to destroy Communism at the expense of accepting Nazism. We must be positive, first, by recognizing the social injustices which gave rise to Communism and Nazism; and second, by uniting our forces behind a sound program of reform which is in harmony with our Constitution and our Christianity. Millions of American citizens, now followers either of the Communistic or Nazi cause, once this program is presented, will abandon the red flag and the swastika as soon as they can discover an active, sound program, in harmony with the Stars and Stripes and the Cross of Christ, a program which, if reduced to action, will liquidate the social, the industrial, the political, and the financial abuses which are responsible for national misery. (Rev. Charles E. Coughlin, in a radio address delivered February 26, 1939)

i. Workers, you must look upon me as your guarantor. I was born a son of the people; I have spent all my life struggling for the German people, and when this hardest struggle of my life is over, there will be new tasks for the German people. We have already projected great plans. All of our plans have but one aim: to develop still further the great German state, to make that great German nation more and more conscious of its existence and, at the same time, to give it everything which makes life worth living. We have decided to break down to an ever-increasing degree the barriers preventing individuals from developing their faculties and from attaining their just due. We are firmly determined to build up a social state which must and shall be a model of perfection in every sphere of life.

(Adolf Hitler, in a speech delivered December 10, 1940)

2. Find an example of a contemporary piece of propaganda and identify and comment upon the devices of propaganda it contains. Comments by leaders in

racial disputes, political key-note addresses, acceptance speeches, and sermons usually provide good examples.

3. Advertising copywriters sometimes attempt to form favorable opinions concerning their products by highly selective quotations from users and critics. Examine the abbreviated comments supposedly made by critics which are used in advertising a play, musical, motion picture, or book in newspapers and magazines. If you can, find the original statement by the critic and compare it with the quotation. Do you find any instance in which the quotation distorts or qualifies the critic's opinion so that the subject is given a more favorable presentation?

4. Quoting "out of context," that is, quoting a statement without including the verbal (and perhaps situational) context in which it appeared, is a favorite resource of propagandists. As an experiment, ask a friend to write down his views on some controversial subject. Then by selecting a statement from his comments and giving it a different context distort his meaning so that he appears to contradict his original statement.

41.

HENRYK SKOLIMOWSKI

The Semantic Environment in the Age of Advertising

I

David Ogilvy is a very successful advertising man. In addition, Mr. Ogilvy has turned out to be a successful writer. His book, *Confessions of an Advertising Man,* was a best-seller in 1965. His confessions are in fact intimate whisperings of one adman to another. These whisperings, however, turned out to be interesting enough to make his book one of the most readable and lucid stories of advertising ever written. What is so fascinating about this book is not the amount of linguistic contortions which he advocates, but the amount of truth which is expressed there incidentally. There is nothing more comforting than to find truth accidentally expressed by

Reprinted by permission from *ETC: A Review of General Semantics,* Vol. XXV, No. 1; copyright 1968, by the International Society for General Semantics.

one's adversary. *Confessions of an Advertising Man* provides a wealth of such truths.

Mr. Ogilvy tells us that "the most powerful words you can use in a headline are FREE and NEW. You can seldom use FREE," he continues, "but you can always use NEW—if you try hard enough." It is an empirical fact that these two words have a most powerful influence upon us. This fact has been established by scientific research. Whenever these words appear, they are used deliberately—in order to lull and seduce us.

The word FREE is especially seductive. Whether we are aware of this or not, it has an almost hypnotic effect on us. Although we all know "nothing is for nothing," whenever the word FREE appears, it acts on us as the light of a candle acts on a moth. This is one of the mysteries of our language. And these mysteries are very skillfully exploited by advertising men.

Apart from the words FREE and NEW, other words and phrases "which make wonders," as Mr. Ogilvy's research has established, are: "HOW TO, SUDDENLY, NOW, ANNOUNCING, INTRODUCING, IMPORTANT, DEVELOPMENT, AMAZ-ING, SENSATIONAL, REVOLUTIONARY, STARTLING, MIRACLE, OFFER, QUICK, EASY, WANTED, CHALLENGE, ADVICE TO, THE TRUTH ABOUT, COMPARE, BARGAIN, HURRY, LAST CHANCE." Should we not be grateful to Mr. Ogilvy for such a splendid collection? Should we not learn these "miraculous" phrases by heart in order to know which particular ones drive us to the marketplace? To this collec-tion I should like to add some of the phrases which I found: SIMPLE, SAVE, CONVENIENT, COMFORT, LUXURY, SPECIAL OFFER, DISTINCTIVE, DIFFERENT, RARE.

II

Having provided his collection, Ogilvy comments upon these words that make wonders (and this comment is most revealing): "Don't turn up your nose at these clichés. They may be shopworn, but they work." Alas! They work on us. What can we do about their merciless grip? Nothing. Language and its workings cannot be controlled or altered through an act of our will. The cumulative process of the development of language used as the instru-ment of tyranny or as the bridge to God through prayers; as a recorder of everyday trivia or as a clarion trumpet announcing new epochs in human history; as an expression of private feelings of single individuals or as a transmitter of slogans to the masses—this process has endowed some words with incredible subtleties and others with irresistible power. The only thing we can do about the influence of language on us is to become aware of it. This awareness may diminish the grip language has on us.

It is very gratifying to know that nowadays advertising is so punctilious, so systematic, and so scientific in its approach to the customer. Mr. Ogilvy in *Confessions* relentlessly repeats that "research has shown" so and so, "research shows" this and that, "research suggests" that, "research has established" that, etc. This constant reference to research is not an advertising humbug. It is through systematic research that we are "hooked" more and more thoroughly. With perfect innocence Ogilvy informs us that "Another profitable gambit is to give the reader helpful advice or service. It hooks about [was this a slip of the tongue, or intentional, plain description?] 75 per cent more readers than copy which deals entirely with the product."

Madison Avenue has, above all, established that through words we may be compelled to perform certain acts—acts of buying. This conclusion is not to be found in Ogilvy. Whether it is an historical accident or not, it is a rather striking fact that, independent of semanticists and logicians and linguistic philosophers, advertising men have made some important discoveries about language. And they have utilized these discoveries with amazing success. They are probably not aware of the theoretical significance of their discoveries and are no doubt little interested in such matters.

III

J. L. Austin, one of the most prominent linguistic philosophers at Oxford during the 1950's, developed a theory of what he called *performative utterances*. He observed that language is systematically employed not only for stating and describing but also for performing actions. Such utterances as "I warn you to . . ." or "I promise you x" are performances rather than descriptions. They function not only on a verbal level, but also as deeds, as concrete performances through words. The discovery and classification of performative utterances is an important extention of ordinary logic—that is, logic concerned with declarative utterances. On the other hand, it is an important finding of the hidden force of language in shaping our social and individual relationships.

Quite independently, advertising men have developed and successfully applied their own theory of performative utterances. They may be oblivious to the logical subtleties involved; however, they are not oblivious to the power of their medium—that is, the verbal utterances through which they induce our acts of buying. Again, there is very little we can do about it. This is the way language works. We can only recognize this fact. But once we recognize it, we acquire some immunity.

Now, we all know that advertising messages are conveyed in words. Usually, there are not only words, but pictures and images which suggest appropriate associations to the person reading the words. The images are projected to be psychologically appealing. Psychologically appealing images are those which appeal to our seven deadly sins: sexual urges, vanity, snobbery, gluttony, greed, etc.

Many analyses of advertising have shown the mechanism of psychological associations built into the ad message. In particular they showed that the level of most of these appeals is that of sheer brutes, of ultimate half-wits whose only desire is to satisfy their most rudimentary biological urges. However, not many analyses of advertising, if any at all, show how frail the link is between the picture set to evoke emotional reactions and the linguistic utterance which, in the final analysis, is the message of the ad. We must remember that it is the verbal message which ultimately draws us to the marketplace. The analysis of this verbal or linguistic level of the ad is our main concern here.

IV

Language is, of course, basically a medium of communication. To be an adequate medium, language must be flexible. But to be flexible is one thing; to be entirely elastic and malleable is another. These other two characteristics, extreme elasticity and malleability, are required from the language which is set to infiltrate people's minds and contaminate their mental habits. It is in this latter capacity that admen want to employ language. And consequently, they do everything conceivable, and sometimes inconceivable, to make language infinitely flexible and as malleable as plasticene.

The point is very simple. If language is made a plasticene, the meaning of concepts is so stretched that words are deprived of their original sense and end up with whatever sense the wild imagination of the admen equips them. Since the language of ads often departs radically from ordinary language, advertisements could in one sense be regarded as pieces of poetry.[1]

A piece of poetry should have a nice ring to its words, pleasant or extraordinary association of ideas, unusual combinations of meanings. The factual content is not important. For communication, as I shall use the term here, the factual content is most important. It is the content that we wish to communicate, and this is conveyed in messages. Consequently, messages must contain factual information. If there is no factual information in the message, the message does not communicate anything. Usually the actual content of the message may be expressed in many different ways. What is important is the content, not the manner of expression. If the manner of expressing a message is more important than its content, then the message does not serve the purpose of communication. It may serve many other purposes, but it does not serve the purpose of conveying factual information.

---

[1] The idea that advertising is a kind of bad poetry was first forcibly and tellingly expressed by E. E. Cummings in his "Poem, or Beauty Hurts Mr. Vinal" (1926). See also "Poetry and Advertising," Chapter XV of Hayakawa's *Language in Thought and Action* (rev. ed., 1964).

And this is exactly the case with advertising. The advertising messages are pseudo-messages, not genuine messages. They do not contain factual information. At any rate, this is not their main purpose. Their main purpose is not to inform but to force us to buy. It is clear that if the content of advertising were of any importance, then the same message worded differently would serve the same function; namely, of informing us. This is obviously not the case with advertising: the overwhelming majority of ads would have little effect, if any, if they were phrased differently.

In art, our emotional involvement is the source of our delight. It is the uniqueness of the form that inspires our thoughts and arouses our emotions. The meaning and significance of the work of art hinge upon the uniqueness of its form. Once the form is destroyed or altered, the work of art does not exist any more. If the validity of advertisements depends on preserving their form intact, then they pretend to be pieces of art, but not the carriers of factual information. The trouble is that they *do* pretend to give factual and objective information—but in a rather peculiar way: in such a way that the "information" would force us to acquire the product which is the substance of the message.

V

Communication is for humans. It is the mark of a rational man to grasp the content of a message irrespective of the form of its presentation—that is, irrespective of its linguistic expression. The nature of any communication in which the actual information conveyed is less significant than the manner of its presentation is, to say the least, illogical. The illogical man is what advertising is after. This is why advertising is so anti-rational; this is why it aims at uprooting not only the rationality of man but his common sense; this is why it indulges in exuberant but deplorable linguistic orgies.

Distortion of language, violation of logic, and corruption of values are about the most common devices through which advertising operates. This is particularly striking in endless perversions of the word FREE. Since this word has such a powerful impact on us, there is no limit to its abuse. In his novel *1984,* George Orwell showed that what is required for establishing a "perfect" dictatorship is perhaps no more than a systematic reform of language. The condition is, however, that the reform must be thorough and complete. "Doubletalk" as a possible reality has, since Orwell's novel, been viewed with horror, but not with incredulity. The question is whether doubletalk has not already become part of our reality, has not already been diffused in our blood stream through means different from those Orwell conceived of. Isn't it true that advertising has become a perfect Orwellian institution?

Nowadays there is in operation a doubletalk concept of freedom according to which protecting the public from fraud and deceit and warning people about dangers to their health is but "an erosion of freedom." This concept of freedom is, needless to say, advocated and defended by advertising agencies. In the opinion of admen, "freedom" for people means protecting people from their common sense and ability to think. For many admen "freedom" means freedom to advertise in whatsoever manner is profitable, freedom to force you to buy, freedom to penetrate your subconscious, freedom to dupe you, to hook you, to make a sucker of you, freedom to take away your freedom. Anything else is for them but an "erosion of freedom." Hail Mr. Orwell! Hail doubletalk!

VI

Now to turn to some concrete illustrations:

Mustang! A Car To Make Weak Men Strong, Strong Men Invincible.

Do not say that we do not believe such obvious blusterings. We do. It seems that the art of magicians—according to which some incantations evoke events, bring rain, heal wounds; some amulets bring good luck, prevent bad luck or illness—has been re-established by contemporary advertising. Motor cars in particular are the amulets of the atomic age. They possess all the miraculous qualities you wish them to possess—from being a substitute for a sweetheart (or mistress, if you prefer) to being a soothing balm to a crushed ego. Dictionaries usually define an automobile as a self-propelled vehicle for the transportation of people or goods. The car industry and car dealers are of a quite different opinion. Perhaps lexicographers are outdated in their conception of "automobile."

Roughly speaking, motor cars are advertised to be amulets of two kinds. The first casts spells on us and makes us happy, or builds up our personality, or adds to our strength, or makes us invincible if we are already strong; the second casts spells on others and, while we drive this magic vehicle, makes other people see us as more important, more influential, more irresistible. As yet, there are no cars which, being driven by us, would bring punishment upon our enemies. Perhaps one day this will come to pass. The question is how many of us can really resist the incantations of car dealers and remain impervious to the "magical" qualities allegedly embodied in the modern automobile. How many of us can remain uninfluenced by the continuous flow of messages, in spite of our ability to see the nonsense of each one individually?

Our civilization has often been called the motor-car civilization. But in no less degree, it is the drug civilization; it is also the detergent civilization. Each of these elements is apparently essential to the well-being of our society. But it is by no means only detergents, cars, or drugs that offer us full happiness "at a reasonable price." Nowadays, practically any product can give you happiness.

HAPPINESS IS TO GET (OR GIVE) A BULOVA

The only problem is to believe it. Whether Bulova is a yellow canary, a black watch, or a green giraffe, it unfortunately takes a bit more to achieve happiness than getting or giving a Bulova. But of course the counter-argument can go, "happiness" in this ad was not meant literally but only figuratively. Admen today are like poets; we must allow them poetic license. But must we? And how figuratively would they really like to be taken? It seems that they (and the producers of the products they advertise) would be very unhappy if we took all their messages figuratively. On the contrary, they want their messages to be taken as literally as possible. It is precisely their business to convince us about the "loveliness" of soaps, "happiness" in Bulovas, and "delights" of a cigarette puff. The poetic language they use is meant to break our resistance, to produce desirable associations which we usually associate with poetry.

VII

The sad part of the story is that in the process of serving advertising, poetry has gone down the drain. Poetic expressions are poetic so long as they are in the context of poetry; so long as they evoke unusual emotional reactions, serve as a substance of an esthetic experience—the experience of delight. In its exuberant development, advertising has debased almost the entire poetic vocabulary. And advertising seems to be responsible for a decline of the poetic taste and for a considerable indifference, if not hostility, of American youth toward poetry.

The nausea which one experiences on being bombarded by the pseudo-poetry of advertising may recur when one approaches genuine poetry, unless one has developed love for poetry *before* becoming aware of advertising— which is impossible for young people nowadays. It is quite natural that such a reaction would develop. We are not likely to seek nausea deliberately, and so we would rather avoid whatever reminds us of it. It seems that if the process of debasing and abusing language by advertising is carried further, we may discover a new value in absolute simplicity of language. Perhaps one day, when the traditional poetry is completely ruined, we shall count as poetry some simple and concrete descriptions like this: "There is a table in the room. The table is brown. There are three chairs at the table. A man is sitting on one of the chairs."[2]

The main point is more significant. By applying highly charged emotional terms like "lovely" to soaps, and "bold" and "proud" to automobiles, advertising pushes us to consider objects as if they were human beings. Through the language of advertising, we participate in the process of constant personification of objects which we should "love," be "enchanted by," be "delighted with," and "be happy with." Unconsciously we have developed emotional attachments to objects surrounding us. We have become worshippers of objects. Advertising has been a powerful force in this process.

VIII

My thesis is that the semantic environment has a more profound influence on our behavior and our attitudes than we are aware. If this thesis is correct, it may throw some light on the phenomenon which we usually attribute to the population explosion and the mechanization of our lives; namely, the depersonalization of human relations. I should like to suggest that perhaps a transfer of attitudes through the change of the semantic environment has taken place. Previously, highly emotional expressions were applied to human beings. Nowadays, they are constantly and massively applied by the admen to objects. We have thus developed loving fondness for objects which we worship. Dehumanizing of human relations seems to be the other part of this process. It is quite natural that when we become more and more emotionally involved with objects, we tend to be less and less involved with people. As a consequence, attitudes traditionally reserved for objects are now displayed toward people. In love, in friendship, and in the multitude of other human relations, detachment, lack of interest, and coldness seem to prevail. Human beings are treated like objects.

To summarize, the success of advertising and our failure to defend ourselves against it result mainly from our obliviousness to some of the functions of language. We think that language is a tool, an indifferent piece of gadgetry which simply serves the process of communication and that the only relation we have to language is that *we use language*. We do indeed use it. But this is only part of the story. The other part, which is usually overlooked, is that *language uses us*—by forming our personal and emo-

[2] Perhaps some poets have discovered this principle already. [See] "The Red Wheelbarrow" by William Carlos Williams. (*Collected Poems 1921–1931*, Objectivist Press, 1934.)

tional habits, by forming our attitudes. Language is thus not only our servant; it is also our master. No one knows this better than the adman!

The relation between language and us is more complicated than we usually are prepared to admit. To escape the tyranny of language, we have to recognize the double role of language in human relations, (1) as a carrier of messages we send, and (2) as a shaper of the content of human relations. We cannot reduce or nullify the influence of language on us by simply denying the existence of this influence. The only reasonable thing we can do is to recognize the force of language: its strength, the way it works, its theater of operations. By identifying the traps of language, by identifying the linguistic strategies of the admen and other propagandists, we shall be able to cope with the semantic environment much more effectively than we have done hitherto.

Exercises

1. Attempting to create favorable attitudes toward products, writers of advertising copy make considerable use of connotational meaning and appeal of words. Read the following advertisements and comment on any examples of affective connotation you note.

a. Royal Secret Luxury Mist.* A cloud of fragrance at a finger's touch—brilliant finale to the luxury of a Royal Secret Beauty Bath. Slim golden aerosol robes you in a heartlifting fragrance that clings for hours with sweet persistence.

b. "For my fair love . . . a timeless talisman." Through the eyes of love, a man beholds in his beloved a rare, stirring radiance, reads in her glance a message just for him of tenderness and faith. To tell his joy, to pledge his devotion, he gives to her a lovely talisman, their engagement diamond. This magic light, earth-born for them, will ever recall the delights of the engagement time, hold close through all their life the first bright meaning of their love. To mark your engagement, your ringstone may be modest in size, but it should be chosen with care, for it will be cherished always, by you and all who follow you, as long as there's a world. A diamond is forever.

c. Salem refreshes your taste—*"air-softens"* every puff. As you smoke a Salem cigarette, your taste is refreshed by a springtime softness . . . so fresh and so flavorful is Salem. Smoke refreshed . . . smoke Salem! Menthol fresh. Rich tobacco taste. Modern filter, too.

d. Get the Friendlier Feeling of Full-Taste Beer. People who have fun . . . have Schmidt's! It's the *full-taste beer* that turns people into friends . . . a get-together into a real party. Schmidt's is brewed naturally . . . with *full-taste* pleasure in every friendly drop. All over the East you'll find folks enjoying the friendlier feeling of *full-taste* Schmidt's of Philadelphia. How about you?

* A registered trademark of Germaine Monteil Cosmetiques Corporation.

WHEREVER PEOPLE HAVE FUN, PEOPLE HAVE SCHMIDT'S. BEER AS BEER SHOULD BE.

e. This cologne swaggers. As robust as a buccaneer chanty. Yet as refreshing as dusk at sea. St. Johns West Indian Lime Cologne is blended of the essence of true West Indian limes with tropical woody spices added. Eight ounces, seven dollars and fifty cents; four ounces, four dollars and fifty cents. Plus tax. Each bottle has a handwoven jacket of palm frond. Imported only to fine shops from the Virgin Islands.

f. See Spain! Jet overnight to Madrid. Then take 2 leisurely weeks and let the pageant of Spain unfold before you like a rose. There are still castles in Spain, and guitars and castanets, and now they await you, now in the bullfight season, in the time of Spain at its best, of Spain in full bloom. The fabled cities of Andalucia await you. Their names evoke the spell of a legendary land: Algeciras, Cadiz, Cordoba, Granada, Seville, Malaga, . . . enjoy not merely a taste but a full banquet of the land which is Europe's most memorable travel experience—Spain.

2. The concern of the business world that the names of its products possess the proper connotations was interestingly demonstrated a few years ago when The Ford Motor Company retained the services of a prominent American poetess to assist in the selection of a name for a new line of automobile. What model names, such as *Impala* and *Rocket 88,* for American automobiles can you think of? What connotations does each name possess? What examples of the utilization of favorable connotations can you cite in the naming of streets, housing developments, motion picture stars, perfumes, shaving lotions, beers, liquors?

3. Select a full-page advertisement in a well-known magazine. Try to analyze the appeal which the advertisement seeks to make through its pictorial and verbal qualities and the means by which this appeal is (or is not) realized.

4. Certain advertising campaigns, such as those for Avis or Volkswagen, have been highly successful. Select such a campaign and analyze its strategy.

5. To change the "image" of a product requires thought, imagination, and money. Marlboro cigarettes at one time were treated as suitably mild for women. Later, a masculine appeal was sought. Find out what you can about the changing strategy of the Marlboro advertisements.

6. The appeal of sex is one which advertisers attempt to utilize in behalf of a wide range of products. Find examples of the association of sex with products which strike you as completely unrelated to it.

7. Select an advertisement which is obviously directed toward some specific social group (elder citizens, a minority group, one sex) and attempt to revise it so that it will appeal to a different group.

8. Certain figures in advertisements become as indelibly impressed on our minds as fictional characters or people we actually know. Name five or six individuals whom you know from advertising and give a brief character sketch of each.

Language and Morality

42.

HENRY J. ABRAHAM

Censorship

Censorship is essentially a "policy of restricting the public expression of ideas, opinions, conceptions and impulses which have or are believed to have the capacity to undermine the governing authority or the social and moral order which that authority considers itself bound to protect" (Lasswell 1930, p. 290). Censorship usually takes two forms: prior, which refers to advance suppression; and *post facto,* which involves suppression after publication or pronouncement has taken place. Although it is more frequently practiced under autocratic regimes, it is also present, in varied forms, in those states normally viewed as Western liberal democracies; and its execution is as variegated as are the states and governments involved. Broadly speaking, however, those who favor and those who oppose censorship normally bracket themselves with one of two approaches to society as represented by great names of the past. The former agree with Plato, St. Augustine, and Machiavelli that those who are qualified to identify evil should be empowered to prevent its dissemination. The latter, siding with Aristotle, Oliver Wendell Holmes, Jr., and John Dewey, maintain that a man is free only so long as he is empowered to make his own choices.

In its contemporary form, censorship is exercised both by public and by private authorities. Although it is still predominantly associated with governmental (public) action, its exercise by private groups—with religious as well as secular interests—is becoming more common. In the United States, since the end of World War II, the rise of private vigilante groups in a number of areas of everyday life clearly indicates this trend. The erstwhile dichotomy (Lasswell 1930, p. 291) of either political or religious censorship no longer suffices. Today, censorship, both public and private, may be generally grouped into four categories: political censorship; religious censorship; censorship against obscenity, i.e., censorship of morals; and censorship affecting academic freedom. It is important to remember, however, that these are merely categories of convenience and that a given act of censorship may, of course, embrace more than one category. Thus, the Tridentine Rules (formulated at the Council of Trent in 1564 under the guidance of Pope Pius IV) were religious in origin, but to some extent they were involved with obscenity; their enforcement was political; and there was then no academic freedom as we know it today. The investigations of alleged subversive influences in American schools, colleges, and universities in the years following World War II had political, as well as educational, overtones.

HISTORY

The history of censorship, so closely linked with a basic sense of insecurity, represents a continuum of the battle between the individual and society and can be sketched only briefly here. Turning first to the Bible (Jer. 36.1–26), we find that the prophet Jeremiah encountered censorship when the book he had dictated to Baruch was mutilated by King Jehoiakim. During classical antiquity, censorship was sporadically applied. In the fifth century B.C., Sparta placed a ban on certain forms of poetry, music, and dance, because its rulers believed, or wished to believe, that these cultural activities tended to induce effeminacy and licentiousness. For their liberal thoughts on religious matters, Aeschylus, Euripides, and Aristophanes felt the censor's sting. Republican Rome considered itself devoted to virtue and assumed the right to censor any citizen who did not embrace that concept in the cultural realm. The theater was banned by the censor, except on the occasion of certain games (where tradition bestowed upon dramatic art a degree of license in both gesture and speech). Although there is no conclusive evidence of literary censorship either in Rome or Greece, the famed poet Ovid was banished to the Black Sea area by Emperor Augustus, allegedly because of his "licentiousness" but more likely because of his political views.

In the era of the Christian church, the earliest and most extreme manifestation of censorship is found in the Apostolic Constitutions, said to have been written in A.D. 95 by St. Clement of Rome at the dictates of the apostles. The constitutions forbade Christians to read any books of the gentiles, since it was thought that the Scriptures were all a *true* believer need read. There then followed a long series of prohibitions issued by the early church fathers, among them the death penalty edicts of the Council of Nicaea and the

Emperor Constantine against the pens of Arius and Porphyry in 325; the decree of 399 by the Council of Alexandria under Bishop Theophilus, forbidding the Origens to read and own books; the stern punitive measures, akin to the book-burning days of the Hitler era, by Pope Leo I in 446; and the first papal Index, which made its appearance in 499 under Pope Gelasius. The concept of the Index, which was formalized by the amended Tridentine Rules, embracing a list of proscribed books for Roman Catholics, is still in existence today (see Gardiner 1958, pp. 51–54).

During the Middle Ages a new version of prior censorship commenced: the submission of manuscripts by writers to their superiors, both as a matter of courtesy and as a prophylactic against subsequent censure. But with the advent of printing and with steady cultural growth, the ecclesiastic authorities insisted upon formal, organized censorship. In 1501 Pope Alexander VI issued his famous bull against printing of books, which was designed to protect the vast domain of the Church of Rome against heresy. Even more drastic measures were taken by the Scottish Estates in 1551. By 1586, all books printed in England had to be read and approved by the Archbishop of Canterbury or the Bishop of London prior to publication. But the written word was not all that felt the censor's power in England; it was extended to drama by the public authorities, once religious drama, always under the control of the church, had become obsolete.

In 1693, England substituted *punitive* for *prior* censorship of printing. This form essentially exists in many lands now and is generally much preferred to prior censorship, if there must be censorship. Probably the best-known illustration of this type of censorship is the John Peter Zenger case in 1735, often referred to as the birth of freedom of the press; for New York Governor William Cosby was unsuccessful in his gross attempt to silence and punish the courageous printer (see Zenger 1957, pp. 3–131).

It should be noted here that the triumph of Protestantism, and the subsequent rise of the nation-state, had brought about a significant switch in emphasis in the employment of censorship. Practically speaking, the monarchs became separated from the church, and to a considerable extent their interests in censorship no longer coincided. Thus, the compelling force necessary to sustain censorship was no longer concerned with religious beliefs. In those instances in which a state still guarded against blasphemy or heresy, it was from the conviction that these were often antecedent steps to sedition and treason, especially where the authority for the monarch's position came from the doctrine of the divine right of kings. Censorship was still aimed at beliefs and facts, but the orientation had switched from the religious to the political arena.

The seventeenth and eighteenth centuries were the transition years in the development of the freedoms and rights of men, which we value so much. Here the first voices began to ring out for the rights of the individual against the state, so that by 1695 the last formal governmental restraint upon literature in England had been withdrawn. Among the voices who made themselves heard in those centuries were Milton, Spinoza, Voltaire, and Locke.

Prior to this transition period, sundry intriguing devices had been employed to look after the interests of the monarch. King Henry VIII had entrusted the control of books to the infamous Court of Star Chamber. Queen Elizabeth maintained control by giving the Stationers' Company a monopoly on printing, for which they reciprocated by hunting out all undesirable books. Coincident with this she granted powers of suppression to the archbishops of Canterbury and York.

The Stuarts brought with their rule even more severe censorship, allowing their bishops control over the importation of books. The first breakthrough for free thought came in 1640 when the Long Parliament abolished the Court of Star Chamber. This brief respite lasted until 1643, when Parliament reintroduced licensing. This was the specific act that resulted in Milton's eloquent plea for free speech, his *Areopagitica*. In this work, he exposes the many absurdities, anomalies, and tyrannies inherent in literary censorship. During the Restoration, the devices of censorship employed by the former monarchs were maintained with the passage of the Licensing Act of 1662, which was aimed at "heretical, seditious, schismatical or offensive books or pamphlets."

The move toward individual rights being generated in England at this time reached its culmination in 1695, when the Licensing Act was not renewed, and governmental censorship temporarily disappeared from the English scene. Although the English had gained their freedom, in those nations where Catholicism still held sway, there was very little freedom to express ideas that would offend the church. This tradition has lasted even into the modern era in such nations as Spain.

The eighteenth century is conspicuous in historical perspective because of the freedom of expression that it attained. Even in the colonies, with the spread of the Great Awakening (dating from about 1740), the growth of freedom from the chains of Puritan control was evident. By 1789, the freedoms of the bill of rights were accepted as the natural heritage of all men. The remarkable feature of this phenomenon, both in England and America, was that it was a reality, not just an idea on a piece of paper.

It is in the field of morals—the area of censorship commonly classified as that of obscenity—that not the most widespread but the most extreme forms of censorship and attempted censorship have transpired during the past two or three centuries. This censorship has been both on a public and private level, the former chiefly by virtue of a host of defense-against-obscenity statutes and ordinances, the latter by pressure groups, chief among them the Catholic church, whose emphasis in the realm of censorship has perceptibly changed from the old preoccupation with heresy to one that emphasizes morals, although the religious overtones are understandably present. But public and private aims and designs again merge here.

Although in certain types of censorship the political authority is concerned with defending the *status quo* and its position in it, this is not true of censorship of morals. More often than not, state action is not in defense of itself but in the form of a service to some influential members of the polity, in ridding the society of certain ideas that are considered offensive by these influential members. The common method of achieving these ends is the formation of watchdog groups that comb the arts and letters and upon finding works—books, plays, movies, etc.—that they consider obscene strive either for their official suppression or for private boycotts. The first of these societies, the English Society for the Suppression of Vice, appeared in London in 1802. It was to be the forebear of such American vigilante groups as Anthony Comstock's New York Society for the Suppression of Vice and the New England Watch and Ward Society (Craig 1962, pp. 138–139).

The effectiveness of these groups in the United States is evidenced by the vast amount of obscenity legislation that has been passed in the last century. Beginning with the clause in the Tariff Act of 1842 that barred the importation of obscene matter, American legislatures have produced a multitude of statutes designed to protect the minds and morals of both children and adults in our society. The 1920s through the 1940s marked the height of this moralistic legislation.

In England, the single most important piece of censorship legislation was the famous Campbell Act of 1857 (the Obscene Publications Act of 1857), named for its proponent, who was the lord chief justice. There was a great cry against it in Parliament, because in Campbell's attempt to strike down the sale of obvious hard-core pornography from the shelves of the bookstores of Holywell Street in London, he had left few safeguards to defend against similar attacks upon all literature that dealt with sex. The act was finally passed when Campbell defined an obscene work as written for the single purpose of corrupting the morals of youth, and of a nature calculated to shock the common feelings of decency in any well-regulated mind.

However, his successor, Lord Cockburn, in the grasp of the Victorians, did not so limit the obscene. In the famous Hicklin case he said, "the test of obscenity is this, whether the tendency of the matter charged as obscenity is to deprave and corrupt those whose minds are open to such immoral influences, and into whose hands a publication of this sort may fall" (L.R3/QB/371, 1868). Using standards such as this, the Comstocks on both sides of the Atlantic—indeed throughout the world—infiltrated various boards of censorship, and by the turn of the century succeeded in reducing "acceptable" literature to that fit for reading by children. At that time, more than one author was endangering his chances of publication if he referred to a leg as a "leg," rather than calling it a "limb." Starting in the late 1920s, however, American federal courts have been instrumental in salvaging some semblance of reasonableness in these matters.

In a series of opinions, the most important of which were the combined 1957 cases *Roth* v. *U.S.* and *Alberts* v. *California* (354 U.S. 476), the Supreme Court both defined the obscene and detailed the protections to which literature accused of being obscene was entitled. Associate Justice William Brennan, in his opinion, made clear that "obscenity is not within the area of constitutionally protected speech or press," because it is "utterly without redeeming social importance" (354 U.S. 484, 485). However, he cautioned that "sex and obscenity are not synonymous," and the portrayal of sex, for example, in art, literature, and scientific works, "is entitled to constitutional protection as long as it is not obscene." But his judicial test is not entirely helpful: Material is obscene when "to the average person, applying contemporary community standards, the dominant theme of the material taken as a whole appeals to prurient interest" (354 U.S. 487). This standard, and its later application by the courts to specific works, seems to indicate that the Supreme Court's view of what literature is obscene in modern America is limited to that genre of literature generally known as hard-core pornography. But the need to define hard-core pornography reintroduced the basic dilemma of drawing lines.

A categorized, comprehensive list of works censored in the United States was compiled in 1940 by Morris Ernst, one of the foremost crusaders against censorship. It includes some of the world's greatest classics, for example, works by Homer, Shakespeare, Whitman, and Darwin (Ernst & Lindey 1940, pp. 228–230).

The history of censorship in France and the other European nations has an amazing historical similarity to that of America. The giants of French literature, such as Baudelaire, Hugo, Verlaine, and Zola, have felt the same stings of censors as their counterparts in English. The modern laws regarding obscenity in France, Italy, Belgium, Germany, and the Netherlands, roughly parallel those of America; whereas those of the Scandinavian nations are a little more lenient. This is probably a reflection of the different attitudes toward sex prevailing in those nations.

Censorship in the world of dictatorships must be viewed from a different perspective, of course. Essentially, the rights of individuals in these nations are at a pre-Renaissance level in terms of the Western world. Consequently, censorship there is designed to propagandize as well as to forbid. This has been especially true in the totalitarian dictatorships, where complete control of the mind is a prerequisite for complete control of the society.

CRITIQUE

In its most general form, censorship is involved with the realm of ideas, ideas that naturally must take the form of something written or spoken in order to be censorable. Censorship implies that certain ideas are not only invalid, but that they should not be presented; that they constitute a genuine danger. In Lasswell's terms of "who gets what, why and how," censorship is thus concerned with controlling "dangerous" expression of ideas. It follows, then, that those who have been most successful in controlling ideas that endanger their interests are those who already possess authority. Hence, the most successful practitioners of censorship through the ages have been the authority figures themselves—church, monarchs, dictators. Those in non-public positions, who desire the suppression of certain ideas but do not of themselves have the necessary official authority to do so, will thus endeavor to enlist the aid of whatever authority may be promising. Because this is often difficult, if not impossible, private groups in today's Western democracies then resort to personal pressure tactics, designed to intimidate those who have influence over, or who are in command of, channels of communication. A pertinent illustration of this technique, very successfully employed in the United States since the 1940s and 1950s (particularly during the McCarthy era), has been the so-called blacklisting of controversial literary figures as well as performing artists, thus blocking their employment in certain media of communication, notably and the movies, radio, and television—the live stage having more successfully resisted that type of pressure (see Cogley 1956, *passim*).

Far less successful, especially in the United States, however, have been attempts to censor the press, which has enjoyed a unique position of communication freedom, even more so than in traditionally censorship-leery Britain. Although press censorship has continued in many lands even in the 1960s, not excluding certain Western democracies (France, for example), the Supreme Court of the United States again made quite clear in 1964 that the press is not only not censorable by way of prior restraint but that it cannot even be sued for allegedly libelous statements unless deliberate malice is proved conclusively in a court of law (*The New York Times Co.* v. *Sullivan,* decided March 9, 1964, 84 U.S. Sup. Ct. 710).

The bases of censorship are themselves largely repugnant to the ideas of Western liberal tradition, yet even the West must comprehend the three possible rationalizations that seem to exist for censorship.

The first rationalization is that ideas presented, or about to be presented, are "false" and/or "dangerous" by the standards of the authorities in power and that they must hence be suppressed or punished.

Related to this is the second rationale for censorship, equally obnoxious to Western traditions, that of elitism, the justification of which goes back to Plato and the *Republic*. Here, the belief is that the minds of those who would be subjected to the ideas to be censored are not capable of seeing the "falsity" and would hence be led astray. Western political tradition rejects this notion, but many a private pressure group in the West does not, as the persistent attempts by them, and at times by public authorities, to censor school textbooks demonstrate to this day. Yet any historical investigation will quickly prove that those who have set themselves up as being uniquely qualified to ferret out the truth have been no more capable of doing so than their adversaries.

The third rationale for censorship seems to be the one that stands on strongest grounds. Ideas that lead to "antisocial action"—for example, hard-core pornography—may be censored. Here, however, a crucial distinction enters: We are no longer so much in the realm of ideas as in the realm of overt action, and it is here that even the West may wish to, indeed may have to, draw a line between the cherished freedom of expression and the right of society to establish a modicum of standards of overt behavior. How, where, and by whom such a line is to be drawn is the peculiar dilemma of those who love and cherish the precious tradition of ordered liberty.

BIBLIOGRAPHY

CHAFEE, ZECHARIAH, JR. 1941 *Free Speech in the United States*. Cambridge, Mass.: Harvard Univ. Press.   Supersedes Chafee's *Freedom of Speech*, 1920.

CLYDE, WILLIAM M. 1934 *The Struggle for the Freedom of the Press From Caxton to Cromwell*. St. Andrews University Publications, No. 37. Oxford Univ. Press.

COGLEY, JOHN 1956 *Report on Blacklisting*. 2 vols. New York: Fund for the Republic.

CRAIG, ALEC (1962) 1963 *Suppressed Books: A History of the Conception of Literary Obscenity*. New York: World.   First published as *The Banned Books of England and Other Countries: A Study of the Conception of Literary Obscenity*.

ERNST, MORRIS L.; and LINDEY, ALEXANDER 1940 *The Censor Marches On: Recent Milestones in the Administration of the Obscenity Law in the United States*. New York: Doubleday.   Still a classic.

FAULK, J. HENRY 1964 *Fear on Trial*. New York: Simon & Schuster.

GARDINER, HAROLD, S. J. (1958) 1961 *Catholic Viewpoint on Censorship*. Rev. ed. Garden City, N.Y.: Doubleday.

GELLHORN, WALTER 1956 *Individual Freedom and Governmental Restraints*. Baton Rouge: Louisiana State Univ. Press.

HANEY, ROBERT W. 1960 *Comstockery in America: Patterns of Censorship and*

Control. Boston: Beacon.   Superb analysis of America's privately engendered drive for "morality" and "purity" in social action.

HART, H. L. A. 1963 *Law, Liberty and Morality.* Stanford Univ. Press.

KILPATRICK, JAMES J. 1960 *The Smut Peddlers.* Garden City, N.Y.: Doubleday.

LASSWELL, HAROLD 1930 Censorship. Volume 3, pages 290–294 in *Encyclopaedia of the Social Sciences.* New York: Macmillan.

LEVY, LEONARD W. 1960 *Legacy of Suppression: Freedom of Speech and Press in Early American History.* Cambridge, Mass.: Belknap Press.

MCCORMICK, JOHN; and MACINNES, MAIRI (editors). 1962 *Versions of Censorship: An Anthology.* Chicago, Ill.: Aldine.

MACIVER, ROBERT M. 1955 *Academic Freedom in Our Time.* New York: Columbia Univ. Press.

PAUL, JAMES C. N.; and SCHWARTZ, MURRAY L. 1961 *Federal Censorship: Obscenity in the Mail.* New York: Free Press.

SWAYZE, HAROLD 1962 *Political Control of Literature in the USSR, 1946–1959.* Russian Research Center Studies, No. 44. Cambridge, Mass.: Harvard Univ. Press.

WIGGINS, JAMES R. (1956) 1964 *Freedom or Secrecy.* Rev. ed. New York: Oxford Univ. Press.

ZENGER, JOHN PETER 1957 *The Trial of Peter Zenger.* Edited and with introduction and notes by Vincent Buranelli. New York Univ. Press.   Trial in the Supreme Court of Judicature of the province of New York in 1735 for the offense of printing and publishing a libel against the government.

ZENGER, JOHN PETER 1963 *A Brief Narrative of the Case and Trial of John Peter Zenger, Printer of the New York Weekly Journal,* by James Alexander. Edited by Stanley N. Katz. Cambridge, Mass.: Belknap Press.

Exercises

1. Classic statements concerning freedom of expression occur in Plato's *Republic* (Books II and X), John Milton's *Areopagitica,* and John Stuart Mill's *On Liberty.* Prepare an oral class report on the views presented in one of these works.

2. The following is the First Amendment to the Constitution of the United States:

> Congress shall make no law respecting an establishment of religion, or prohibiting the free exercise thereof; or abridging the freedom of speech, or of the press; or the right of the people peaceably to assemble, and to petition the Government for a redress of grievances.

In an important decision relating to obscenity, the United States Supreme Court in 1957 upheld the conviction of a man for selling obscene literature (*Roth* v. *United States,* 354 U.S. 476). The majority of the Court held that "obscenity is

not within the area of constitutionally protected freedom of speech or press." In
Justice Brennan's words, the Court maintained

> All ideas having even the slightest redeeming social importance—unorthodox
> ideas, controversial ideas, even ideas hateful to the prevailing climate of opin-
> ion—have the full protection of the guarantee, unless excludable because they
> encroach upon the limited area of more important interests; but implicit in the
> history of the First Amendment is the rejection of obscenity as utterly without
> redeeming social importance.

Defining "obscene material" as that "which deals with sex in a manner appealing to prurient interest—i.e., material having a tendency to excite lustful
thoughts," the Court invoked as a standard for judging the obscene "whether, to
the average person, applying contemporary community standards, the dominant
theme of the material, taken as a whole, appeals to prurient interest."

In a 1966 case (*Ginzburg* v. *United States,* 383 U.S. 463) Justice Black summarized the criteria established in the Roth case which must pertain before a
work can be called obscene: "(1) the material must appeal to the prurient interest, (2) it must be patently offensive, and (3) it must have no redeeming social
value. All three must coalesce before it is obscene."

There were dissenting opinions in both the Roth and the Ginzburg cases.
Relating to the first, Justice Douglas wrote:

> I would give the broad sweep of the First Amendment full support. I have
> the same confidence in the ability of our people to reject noxious literature as
> I have in their capacity to sort out the true from the false in theology, eco-
> nomics, politics, or any other field.

Justice Black wrote concerning the Ginzburg decision:

> . . . I believe the Federal Government is without any power whatever under
> the Constitution to put any type of burden on speech and expression of ideas
> of any kind (as distinguished from conduct) . . . the First Amendment allows
> all ideas to be expressed—whether orthodox, popular, offbeat, or repulsive. I do
> not think it permissible to draw lines between the "good" and the "bad" and
> defer to the constitutional mandate to let all ideas alone. . . . The theory is
> that people are mature enough to pick and choose, to recognize trash when
> they see it, to be attracted to the literature that satisfies their deepest need, and,
> hopefully, to move from plateau to plateau and finally reach the world of
> enduring ideas.

Concerning the Ginzburg case, Justice Stewart wrote:

> Censorship reflects a society's lack of confidence in itself. It is a hallmark
> of an authoritarian regime. Long ago those who wrote our First Amendment
> charted a different course. They believed a society can be truly strong only
> when it is truly free. In the realm of expression they put their faith, for better

or for worse, in the enlightened choice of the people, free from the interference of a policeman's intrusive thumb or a judge's heavy hand. So it is that the Constitution protects coarse expressions as well as refined, and vulgarity no less than elegance. A book worthless to me may convey something of value to my neighbor. In this free society to which our Constitution has committed us, it is for each to choose for himself.

What is *your* reaction to the difficult question of censorship? Do you think censorship should ever be imposed? If so, when, where, and why? If not, why not? What dangers lie in the imposition of censorship? In removing all restraint on freedom of expression? In deciding what is censorable?

3. Professor Abraham writes that censorship today is exercised by both public and private agencies. Select one of those listed below and find out as much about its powers, activities, and standards as you can and prepare an oral class report on your findings:

Public: Federal Communication Commission, U.S. Postal Department, state and community film boards

Private: National Organization for Decent Literature, Protestant Churchmen's Committee for Decent Publications, Citizens for Decent Literature, National Catholic Office for Motion Pictures, Watch and Ward Society of Boston

4. Public school and community libraries sometimes become involved in censorship controversies. Some citizens object to the circulation of materials which they regard as pornographic, communistic, or racially repugnant. Prepare an oral class report on one of the following articles, each of which gives an interesting view of this kind of controversy.

Blanche Collins, "Ordeal at Long Beach," *Library Journal* (June 1, 1965), 2486–2490, 2494.

Charles Crosthwait, "Censorship and the School Library," *Wilson Library Bulletin,* XXXIX (April 1965), 671–672.

Joseph A. King, "Books and Banners: A Case History," *Saturday Review,* XLVI (November 9, 1963), 28–29, 66.

5. Find out what sort of control is exercised and by whom in the selection of books for your college or community library.

6. A particularly interesting case of censorship arose in California following the publication of *The Dictionary of American Slang,* a selection from which is reprinted on pages 152–167. One citizens' group complained that it was "a practicing handbook of sexual perversion" and that it contained "shocking sexual and homosexual definitions, the terms to use in acquiring narcotics, the defamatory names for minority, ethnic groups and anti-religious definitions." Investigate this controversy and report your findings to the class. *The Reader's Guide* will supply you with references, but the following may here be cited:

Library Journal (July 12, 1963), 2657.

Newsweek (July 29, 1963), 69.

Publisher's Weekly (July 15, 1963), 65–66.

7. The following is a partial list of works involved in censorship controversy in recent years. Choose one and find out what you can about it in terms of censorship; report your findings to the class.

Mark Twain, *Huckleberry Finn*

Rolf Hochhuth, *The Deputy*

J. D. Salinger, *The Catcher in the Rye*

James Baldwin, *Another Country*

Henry Miller, *Tropic of Cancer*

Harold Robbins, *The Carpetbaggers*

Hubert Selby, Jr., *Last Exit to Brooklyn*

D. H. Lawrence, *Lady Chatterley's Lover*

John Cleland, *Memoirs of a Woman of Pleasure*

William Burroughs, *Naked Lunch*

Terry Southern and Mason Hoffenberg, *Candy*

Interesting material relating to some of these works and to the problem of literary censorship can be found in Charles Rembar, *The End of Obscenity* (New York, 1968) and *Literary Censorship,* ed. Kingsley and Eleanor Widmer (San Francisco, 1961).

8. The questions so far posed relate to the written word, but the question of censorship is, of course, relevant to other areas—television, radio, motion pictures, drama. What views do you have concerning censorship in one of these areas? Does the public need to be protected in what it sees and hears? If so, who should be the censors? According to what (and whose) definitions of the undesirable should these media be regulated?

Language and Literature

43.

Figurative Language

Figurative language is as much at home in prose as in poetry. The essence of most figurative language is likening one thing to another. To see such a resemblance, the mind has to make a generalization, or recognition of kinship between two or more things; and the power of generalization, Lester Ward says, is the highest power that the intellect displays. Man's method toward mental comprehension of truth is the method of generalization: seeing what resemblances exist in things apparently remote and different. As when Newton observed an apple falling, and deduced from it that the same force that pulled the apple down toward the earth (and, in small, the earth upward toward the apple) functioned throughout the solar system and the universes, and explained their positions and movements. Such generalizations appeal to the esthetic or the mental emotions; but these are strong, too, and need the rousing effect of generalizations and figurative language in poetry. Poetry without them tends to be dull, flat, and two-dimensional. Only figurative language at times can afford the effect of three- or more dimensional existences.

The simpler figures, as applied to poetry, will be indicated here.

1. A *simile* is an expressed comparison.

> As idle *as* a painted ship
> Upon a painted ocean. . . . .
>
> I pass, *like* night, from land to land.
> *The Rime of the Ancient Mariner,* Coleridge

From POETS' HANDBOOK by Clement Wood. Copyright © 1940 by Chilton Company. Used with permission of Chilton Book Company, Phila. and New York.

The presence of the *as* and the *like* make these similes.

2. A *metaphor* is an unexpressed or implied comparison.

> Blossomed the lovely stars, the forget-me-nots of the angels.
> *Evangeline,* Henry Wadsworth Longfellow

> (Pelican fishing), feathered plunging thunderbolt.
> *Pelicans Fishing,* Clement Wood

Many metaphors use the verbs to imply the comparison:

> The ship *ploughs* the sea. (As if it were a plough.)
> The very deep *did rot.* (As if the ocean could rot.)

At times the implicit comparison is in the adjective:

> A marble brow (that is, a brow like marble).
> A copper sky.

It can appear in some use of the noun:

> A volley of oaths.
> The realms of gold.

The danger here is in mixing inharmonious metaphors. Yet we have the classic example from *Hamlet,*

> Or to take arms against a sea of troubles.

3. An *allegory* is a presentation of a meaning implied, but not expressly stated. It is in essence a prolonged metaphor, in which actions symbolize other actions, and often the characters are types or personifications. Bunyan's *Pilgrim's Progress* and Spenser's *Faerie Queene* are famous examples. *Fables* belong to this group, since the acts and words attributed to animals or inanimate objects symbolize human beings or human relationships.

4. *Personification* is that form of metaphor in which life and human attributes are attributed to inanimate objects, plants and animals, and forces of nature.

> Love took up the glass of Time, and turned it in his glowing hands.
> *Locksley Hall,* Alfred Tennyson

Apostrophe is that form of personification in which the personified object (or, a dead or absent person) is directly addressed:

> Milton, thou shouldst be living at this hour!
>
> William Wordsworth

> O Death, where is thy sting.

> Lafayette, we are here!

5. *Metonomy* is the use of one word for another that it suggests; as, the effect for the cause, the cause for the effect, the sign for the thing signified, the container for the thing contained, and the like. A hackneyed instance can lose all force:

> The kettle is boiling.

Here we accept without thought that the meaning is that the water in the kettle is boiling. Common examples of metonomy are:

> The pen is mightier than the sword.

> To tend the homely slighted shepherd's trade.
>
> *Lycidas,* John Milton

The shepherd's trade here, of course, refers to poetry. *Synechdoche* is an instance of metonomy in which the part is named for the whole, or the whole for the part: *heads* of cattle, factory *hands,* a fleet of ten *sail,* I like to read *Keats,* a man's own *roof.*

6. *Irony* is saying one thing and meaning its opposite. Examples,

> For Brutus is an honorable man.
>
> *Julius Caesar,* William Shakespeare

> My, what a George Washington *you* turned out to be!

7. *Euphemism* is a figure of enlargement, meaning literally "speaking well of a thing." Thus the Greeks called the Furies the "Eumenides" or well-wishers, in an effort to earn their good will. Similarly, Christians refer to the devil as "the old Nick," "the old gentleman," "old Scratch," and use other placating terms. A different motive appears in calling a spade "an agricultural implement," in an effort to elegantize the language. The use of such euphemisms as "daughters of joy," "street-walkers," "girls on the turf" and the like, for prostitutes, showed the same tendency, in some cases coupled with the same Mrs. Grundyism that calls syphilis and gonorrhea "social diseases." Euphemisms for death are common, from "passed on," "departed," "went west," "in Abraham's bosom," "is with the angels," "is in his final sleep," to the more humorous "kicked the bucket" or "croaked."

8. Another figure of enlargement is *hyperbole*—exaggeration for the purpose of emphasis. Poetry is full of examples:

> Two of the fairest stars in all the heaven,
> Having some business, do entreat her eyes
> To twinkle in their spheres till they return.
> What if her eyes were there, they in her head?
> The brightness of her cheek would shame those stars,
> As daylight doth a lamp; her eyes in heaven
> Would through the airy regions stream so bright
> That birds would sing, and think it were not night.
>
> *Romeo and Juliet,* William Shakespeare

> Here's the smell of the blood still: all the perfumes
>   of Arabia will not sweeten this little hand. . . .
>
> Will all great Neptune's ocean wash this blood
> Clean from my hand? No; this my hand will rather
> The multitudinous seas incarnadine,
> Making the green one red.
>
> *Macbeth,* William Shakespeare

Here we have frantic poetic exaggeration at its greatest. The height of the poetry achieved is often measured by the leap above reality that the hyperbole takes.

9. *Climax* is a figure of arrangement, by which words, phrases, clauses, sentences, or longer divisions of composition, are so arranged that the thought mounts continuously in intensity to its close.

> Many a time and oft
> Have you climb'd up to walls and battlements,
> To towers and windows, yea, to chimney-tops,
> Your infants in your arms, and there have sat
> The live-long day, with patient expectation,
> To see great Pompey pass the streets of Rome. . . .
> And do you now put on your best attire?
> And do you now cull out a holiday?
> And do you now strew flowers in his way
> That comes in triumph over Pompey's blood?
> Be gone!
>
> *Julius Caesar,* William Shakespeare

Anti-climax is the same figure, with the concluding statement made weak in intensity, often to the point of ridiculousness. Samuel Hoffenstein, in *Poems in Praise of Practically Nothing,* arrives at his anti-climax when desired, even if the course leading to it has digressions:

> Your life's a wreck; you're tired of living,
> Of lending, spending, borrowing, giving;
> Of doubt and fear, of hope and question,
> Of women, children, and digestion;
> There isn't a single dream you cherish—
> You simply pine and pray to perish.
> You haven't the nerve to take bichloride,
> But you stay up nights till you're gaunt and sore-eyed;
> You don't eat greens, as the doctors tell you,
> And you drink the very worst they sell you;
> You've earned, at least, let's say, cirrhosis—
> And what do you get for it? Halitosis!

A more consistent example, in prose, would be:

> This man robbed as a child, stole from his parents, became a gangster, murdered hundreds of men, and always played golf on Sunday.

10. Rhetorical questions are classed as a figure of speech, under the name of *Interrogation*. They are questions in which the speaker implies an answer, often in the negative; and in which no answer at all is really expected. Examples are found throughout Mark Anthony's funeral oration in *Julius Caesar:*

> Did this in Caesar seem ambitious?

and as the refrain line to many ballades, as Villon's most famous one:

> Where are the snows of yesteryear?

Poetry requires the illumination of apt and original figurative language, to waken its maximum emotional response. Another effective device is, in place of the direct statement, an *allusiveness,* which implies figurative language. Here is Elinor Wylie's *The Crooked Stick:*

FIRST TRAVELER. It's the sort of crooked stick that shepherds know.
SECOND TRAVELER.   Some one's loss.
FIRST TRAVELER. Bend it, you make of it a bow. Break it, a cross.
SECOND TRAVELER.   But it's all grown over with moss!

Here the implications—the shepherd's crook, the bow, the Christian cross, and the moss indicating disuse, broaden the simple wording immeasurably. She achieves the same effect at the end of *A Crowded Trolley Car:*

> One man stands as free men stand,
> As if his soul might be

> Brave, unspoken; see his hand
> Nailed to an oaken tree.

She does not mean any physical nailing: only the allusion to the Christ story, as if the man had suffered similar spiritual martyrdom, as the price of standing like a free man. Again,

> I was, being human, born alone;
> I am, being woman, hard beset;
> I live by squeezing from a stone
> The little nourishment I get.

The allusion here is to the unspoken, "And if a man ask for bread, will you give him a stone?" Or Robinson's magnificent evocation, at the end of *Eros Turannos,* of an embroidered version of the story of the Gadarenean swine:

> Meanwhile, we do no harm; for they
>   That with a god have striven,
> Not hearing much of what we say,
>   Take what the god has given;
> Though like waves breaking it may be,
> Or like a changed familiar tree,
> Or like a stairway to the sea
>   Where down the blind are driven.

Take the allusion to *Midsummer Night's Dream* in *Ben Jonson Entertains a Man from Stratford:*

> Shakespeare, who alone of us
> Will put an ass's head in Fairyland
> As he would add a shilling to more shillings,
> All most harmonious,

or the more dreadful passage in *Cassandra,*

> And though your very flesh and blood
>   Be what your Eagle eats and drinks,
> You'll praise him for the best of birds,
>   Not knowing what the Eagle thinks.

Samuel A. DeWitt uses a device as strong, in the historical allusion in *To Thaddeus C. Sweet,* dealing with the ousting of Socialist assemblymen from the New York State legislature:

> For what you did and what you said
> Farmers dropped their scythes and bled;

> And for the puppets in round rows
> Bare feet tracked the olden snows—
> Feet that wrote for tyrant George
> A bloody print at Valley Forge;
> And you forget that there are men
> Glad to march that way again.

A hint, a fugitive reference, may be all that is needed to open the reader's mind and heart to a resemblance that emphasizes the spoken message of poem or verses immeasurably. It is devices like this that give wings to your words.

WORD MUSIC IN POETRY

The most intangible trait which great verse and poetry must possess has been left to the last; and no critic ever improved on Pope's wording of it:

> True ease in writing comes from art, not chance,
> As those move easiest who have learned to dance.
> 'Tis not enough no harshness gives offense;
> The sound must seem an echo to the sense.
> *An Essay on Criticism*

This last line should be calligraphed in letters of gold, and used as the poet's constant wall-motto: "The sound must seem an echo to the sense." But to explain how this must be done throughout your verse is not easy.

The practice of the masters aids us. Here Pope's very use of the word *harshness* illustrates the whole thesis; the word is as harsh as its meaning. He proceeds,

> Soft is the strain when Zephyr gently blows,
> And the smooth stream in smoother numbers flows;

and then, a sudden change—

> But when loud surges lash the sounding shore,
> The hoarse rough verse should like the torrent roar.

He proceeds with words tense and panting with muscular strain:

> When Ajax strives some rock's vast weight to throw,
> The line too labours, and the words move slow.

The shrewd use of spondees here supplements the use of such harsh knotty words as *Ajax, rock's, vast*. This alters swiftly to the gracility and speed of winged beauty:

> Not so when swift Camilla scours the plain,
> Flies o'er the unbending corn, and skims along the main.

The word *Camilla* dances as surely as *Ajax* retards and strains. The sound must seem an echo to the sense. . . .

We find the spirit of this sung more lightly in the first song of Prince Nanki-Poo, in W. S. Gilbert's *The Mikado*. To demonstrate how differing word-usage and tone-music may be used to express differing emotions, the minstrel prince—and he speaks for each one of us—calls upon the inner evocatory qualities and overtones in the words themselves, to evoke the desired mood in the hearer and reader. Here all the repetition devices in sounds are called upon, including one not hitherto considered: the repetition of familiar groups of words, to evoke emotions they have already stored up in previous usage. In delicious light verse, the Mikado's son proceeds to establish this:

> A wandering minstrel I—
> A thing of shreds and patches,
> Of ballads, songs and snatches,
> And dreamy lullaby!
> My catalogue is long,
> Through every passion ranging,
> And to your humors changing,
> I tune my simple song!

First we have a dolorous strain that Ophelia might have moaned, while dirging her way to her watery grave:

> Are you in sentimental mood?
> I'll sigh with you,
> Oh, willow, willow!
> On maiden's coldness do you brood?
> I'll do so, too—
> Oh, willow, willow!

From this he snaps into jingoistic patriotism:

> But if patriotic sentiment is wanted,
> I've patriotic ballads cut and dried;
> For where'er our country's banner may be planted,
> All other local banners are defied!

Suddenly his mood goes chantey:

> And if you call for a song of the sea,
>   We'll heave the capstan round,
> With a yeo heave-ho, for the wind is free,
> Her anchor's a-trip and her helm's a-lee,
>   Hurrah for the homeward bound!
>   Yeo-ho—heave-ho,
>   Hurrah for the homeward bound!

The sound, as an echo to the sense. . . . The onomatopoetic theory of the origin of much of our language—that the word imitates a sound in nature —is clearly illustrated in many words:

> coo, hiss, hum, drone, bump, thud, smash, buzz, tingle, chatter, bicker, squeak, murmur, scream, shriek, bubble, gargle, growl, howl, roar, slash, lash, crash.

These are mainly words denoting sound; but the list is infinitely longer, and involves many derivatives from all languages, where the original sound-echoing nature of the word has veered immensely in meaning, although still with overtones of the original sound. Classic poetry furnishes two famous lines illustrating this: Homer's line describing a heavy stone rolling down a mountainside, and Vergil's description of a horse's hoofs galloping over a hard plain. Far more informative are Pope's lines, such as the one describing the immense labor of Sisiphus,

> Up the high hill he heaves a huge round stone,

and that giving the crashing debacle:

> Thunders impetuous down, and smokes along the ground.

A far greater poet, Shakespeare, in the third line of dying Hamlet's charge to his friend Horatio, clogs the word-sounds artificially so that they must be pronounced to fit the meaning:

> If ever thou didst hold me in thy heart,
> Absent thee from felicity awhile,
> And in this harsh world draw thy breath in pain
> To tell my story.

Milton caught the spirit of this, when he had the gates of Paradise swing welcomingly:

> Heaven opened wide
> Her ever-during gates, harmonious sound
> On golden hinges turning,

contrasted with this entrance to the gates of Hell:

> On a sudden open fly,
> With impetuous recoil and jarring sound,
> The infernal doors; and on their hinges grate
> Harsh thunder.

This use of the word *harsh* in Pope, Shakespeare and now Milton is no accident; the word's tone-music sets the key for the desired emotional response. The harshest line in English verse, deliberately so written, is Browning's famous thought-demanding puzzler:

> Irks care the crop-full bird, frets doubt the maw-crammed beast?

To the extreme contrary is Swinburne's lilting line from one of the choruses to *Atalanta in Calydon:*

> With lisp of leaves and ripple of rain.

Between these two extremes lie most of the rest of English poetry and verse. It is the writer's task to choose, in each instance, in preference, the words whose precise sounds convey the mood and idea he seeks to evoke.

As Sidney Lanier points out in *The Science of English Verse,* obviously *lal lal lal* is easy to pronounce; *bag bag bag* is much more difficult and retarding; while such a line as—

> Thou, stalwart, shouldst stiffest stand

cannot be said rapidly at all. These successive *st* sounds require in each instance an entirely new adjustment of the vocal organs, and necessitate a perceptible interval of time between one *st* and the next. The poet has the whole gamut of consonantal and vowel sounds, flowing and retarding, to choose from. For ordinary purposes, he will choose sounds that melt flowingly into one another. For especial purposes, he will utilize the eruptive and retarding sounds.

A few examples of sounds which perfectly echo the sense they convey may aid. All of *Kubla Khan* illustrates Coleridge's mastery of this evocatory word-magic:

> Through caverns measureless to man
> Down to a sunless sea. . . .

Five miles meandering with a mazy motion. . . .

A damsel with a dulcimer
In a vision once I saw. . . .

Weave a circle round him thrice,
And close your eyes with holy dread;
For he on honey-dew hath fed,
And drunk the milk of Paradise.

Keats became an enduring master of the same magnificent evocation of the music in words:

Season of mists and mellow fruitfulness!
Close bosom-friend of the maturing sun.

To Autumn

O what can ail thee, knight-at-arms,
Alone and palely loitering?
The sedge has wither'd from the lake,
And no birds sing.

Ballad: La Belle Dame Sans Merci

St. Agnes Eve—ah, bitter chill it was!
The owl, for all his feathers, was a-cold;
The hare limp'd trembling through the frozen grass. . . .

With jellies soother than the creamy curd,
And lucent syrops, tinct with cinnamon;
Manna and dates, in argosy transferr'd
From Fez; and spicéd dainties, every one,
From silken Samarcand to cedared Lebanon.

The Eve of St. Agnes

Swinburne, for all of his soporific quality from its overuse, is one of the masters of the language in evoking from words all of the music innate in them:

Where beyond the extreme sea-wall, and between the remote sea-gates,
Waste water washes, and tall ships founder, and deep death waits;
Where, mighty with deepening tides, clad about with the sea as with wings,
And impelled of invisible tides, and fulfilled of unspeakable things,
White-eyed and poisonous-finned, sharp-toothed and serpentine-curled,
Rolls, under the whitening wind of the future, the wave of the world.

Hymn to Proserpine

By the ravenous teeth that have smitten
Through the kisses that blossom and bud,

By the lips intertwisted and bitten
　　Till the foam has a savor of blood,
By the pulse as it rises and falters,
　　By the hands as they slacken and strain,
I adjure thee, respond from thine altars,
　　　　Our Lady of Pain.
                                                    Dolores

Tennyson is repeatedly as magical—often throughout the pastel tapestry of
The Idylls of the King, the tense ballad *The Revenge,* and most of all in
The Princess and its songs:

Sweet and low, sweet and low,
　　Wind of the western sea,
Low, low, breathe and blow,
　　Wind of the western sea!
Over the rolling waters go,
Come from the dying moon, and blow,
　　Blow him again to me;
While my little one, while my pretty one, sleeps. . . .

Ah, sad and strange as in dark summer dawns
The earliest pipe of half-awaken'd birds
To dying ears, when unto dying eyes
The casement slowly grows a glimmering square;
So sad, so strange, the days that are no more. . . .

Myriads of rivulets hurrying thro' the lawn,
The moan of doves in immemorial elms,
The murmuring of innumerable bees.

G. K. Chesterton is full of the same appropriate wedding of sound to sense:

And men brake out of the northern lands,
　　Enormous lands alone,
Where a spell is laid upon life and lust
And the rain is changed to a silver dust
　　And the sea to a great green stone.
                                          The Ballad of the White Horse

For every tiny town or place
　　God made the stars especially;
Babies look up with owlish face
　　And see them tangled in a tree. . . .

Likelier across these flats afar,
　　These sulky levels smooth and free,
The drums shall crash a waltz of war
　　And Death shall dance with Liberty.

> Likelier the barricades shall blare
> Slaughter below and smoke above,
> And death and hate and hell declare
> That men have found a thing to love.
> *Dedication to The Napoleon of Notting Hill*

> Dim drums throbbing, in the hills half heard,
> Where only on a nameless throne a crownless prince has stirred,

and all the magical rest of *Lepanto*. There was never a more distinguished user of the evocation of the latent tone music in words, to set the key of the mood, than Edgar A. Poe:

> And the Raven, never flitting, still is sitting, still is sitting,
> On the pallid bust of Pallas just above my chamber door;
> And his eyes have all the seeming of a demon's that is dreaming,
> And the lamplight o'er him streaming casts his shadow on the floor;
> And my soul from out that shadow that lies floating on the floor
> Shall be lifted—nevermore.
> *The Raven*

What these masters did, every versifier must strive to do, to evoke from his words the full magic of which they are the sealed containers. This calls for careful critical analysis, once the verses have been written, of the mood sought to be conveyed throughout; and a careful excision of offending and jarring elements, and a substitution of those words whose tone and overtones evoke the mood desired. For moods come from the emotions; and, where the object is to awaken emotions in a certain direction, are of far more importance than mere mental accuracy. Sooner or later, the mind's best accuracy is discovered to be inaccurate. The emotion's accuracy does not alter.

The extremest instances of letting the sound echo the sense are found in the direction of light verse. Of this kinship is Poe's *The Bells*:

> Hear the sledges with their bells—
> Silver bells!
> What a world of merriment their melody foretells!
> How they tinkle, tinkle, tinkle
> In the icy air of night,
> While the stars, that oversprinkle
> All the heavens, seem to twinkle
> With a crystalline delight!

Or Southey's tour-de-force, *How the Water Comes Down at Lodore,*

> And thumping and plumping, and bumping and jumping,
> And dashing and flashing, and splashing and clashing,

> And so never ending,
> And always descending,
> Sounds and motions for ever and ever are blending,
> All at once and all o'er
> With a mighty uproar,
> And this way the water comes down at Lodore.

Much of the appeal of Vachel Lindsay was based upon a use of this device
that became exaggerated at times, as in this effort to catch the sound of automobile horns, somewhat as Gershwin did in *An American in Paris:*

> Hark to the calm-horn, balm-horn, psalm-horn,
> Hark to the faint-horn, quaint-horn, saint-horn. . . .
>
> Hark to the pace-horn, chase-horn, race-horn. . . .
> They tour from Memphis, Atlanta, Savanna,
> Tallahassee and Texarkana. . . .
> Cars from Concord, Niagara, Boston,
> Cars from Topeka, Empiria, and Austin. . . .
>   *The Santa Fé Trail*

> Oh, the longhorns from Texas,
> The jay hawks from Kansas,
> The plop-eyed bungaroo and giant giassicus,
> The varmint, chipmunk, bugaboo,
> The horned toad, prairie-dog and ballyhoo,
> From all the newborn states arow,
> Bidding the eagles of the west fly on,
> Bidding the eagles of the west fly on.
>   *Bryan, Bryan, Bryan, Bryan*

> He would trade engender for the red bartender,
> He would homage render to the red bartender,
> And in ultimate surrender to the red bartender,
> He died of the tremens, as crazy as a loon. . . .
> The moral, the conclusion, the verdict now you know,
> The saloon must go!
> The saloon must go!
> The saloon, the saloon, the saloon must go!
>   [*The Drunkard's Funeral*]

Here at last art is replaced with ineffective artlessness.

But the lesson does not escape us. All verse, all poetry, gain by an actual
welding of sound and overtone to the emotions intended to be evoked by
the message sought to be conveyed. Poetry requires it, used with shrewd
reticence; light verse can gain by a direct and aggressive use of mimetic
sounds, or noises imitating the actual noises of things. So it is that the sound
echoes truly the sense.

Exercises

1. The connotational force of words is important in poetry, for it enables the poet to communicate a richness of meaning in a concentrated way. The careful selection of words bearing connotations appropriate to the poet's purposes is one of those specific acts of choice which distinguishes good poetry from bad.

John Keats, unable to read the Homeric poems in their original Greek, expresses in the famous sonnet below the sense of discovery he experienced in reading a translation by George Chapman (1559?–1634) of the works of the great epic poet. Read the poem carefully and be prepared to discuss the connotational values of the italicized words and to indicate how each is a better choice than any of the alternates listed below the poem.

ON FIRST LOOKING INTO CHAPMAN'S HOMER

Much have I travelled in the *realms* of *gold,*
And many *goodly* states and *kingdoms* seen;
Round many western islands have I been
Which *bards* in *fealty* to Apollo hold.
Oft of one wide expanse had I been told
That deep-browed Homer ruled as his *demesne;*
Yet did I never breathe its pure serene
Till I heard Chapman speak out loud and *bold;*
Then felt I like some *watcher* of the skies
When a new *planet* swims into his *ken;*   10
Or like stout Cortez when with *eagle* eyes
He stared at the Pacific—and all his men
Looked at each other with a *wild surmise—*
Silent, upon a peak in Darien.

1 *realms:* territories, lands, areas	8 *bold:* forcefully, clearly
gold: silver, worth	9 *watcher:* observer, gazer
2 *goodly:* splendid, impressive	10 *planet:* star
kingdoms: countries	*ken:* sight
4 *bards:* poets, writers	11 *eagle:* hawk, keen
fealty: allegiance	13 *wild:* excited, surprised
6 *demesne:* land, estate, domain	*surmise:* conjecture, guess

2. Read the following sonnet by Shakespeare and comment on any words or expressions which you think have special pertinence to the poem because of their connotational values.

SONNET 73

That time of year thou mayst in me behold
When yellow leaves, or none, or few, do hang

Upon those boughs which shake against the cold,
Bare ruined choirs where late the sweet birds sang.
In me thou seest the twilight of such day
As after sunset fadeth in the west,
Which by and by black night doth take away,
Death's second self, that seals up all in rest.
In me thou seest the glowing of such fire
That on the ashes of his youth doth lie,   10
As the death-bed whereon it must expire,
Consumed with that which it was nourished by.
    This thou perceiv'st, which makes thy love more strong
    To love that well which thou must leave ere long.

3. What examples of the figures of speech which Wood defines and illustrates
can you find in the following poems?

LORD RANDALL

Anonymous

"O where hae ye been, Lord Randall, my son?
O where hae ye been, my handsome young man?"
"I hae been to the wild wood; mother, make my bed soon,
For I'm weary wi hunting, and fain wald lie down."

"Where gat ye your dinner, Lord Randall, my son?
Where gat ye your dinner, my handsome young man?"
"I dined wi my true-love; mother, make my bed soon,
For I'm weary wi hunting, and fain wald lie down."

"What gat ye to your dinner, Lord Randall, my son?
What gat ye to your dinner, my handsome young man?"   10
"I gat eels boiled in broo; mother, make my bed soon,
For I'm weary wi hunting, and fain wald lie down."

"What became of your bloodhounds, Lord Randall, my son?
What became of your bloodhounds, my handsome young man?"
"O they swelld and they died; mother, make my bed soon,
For I'm weary wi hunting, and fain wald lie down."

"O I fear ye are poisond, Lord Randall, my son!
O I fear ye are poisond, my handsome young man!"
"O yes! I am poisond; mother, make my bed soon,
For I'm sick at the heart, and I fain wald lie down."   20

SINCE THERE'S NO HELP

Michael Drayton

Since there's no help, come let us kiss and part;
Nay, I have done, you get no more of me,

And I am glad, yea glad with all my heart
That thus so cleanly I myself can free;
Shake hands forever, cancel all our vows,
And when we meet at any time again,
Be it not seen in either of our brows
That we one jot of former love retain.
Now at the last gasp of love's latest breath,
When, his pulse failing, passion speechless lies,   10
When faith is kneeling by his bed of death,
And innocence is closing up his eyes,
   Now if thou wouldst, when all have given him over,
   From death to life thou mightst him yet recover.

DEATH, BE NOT PROUD

John Donne

Death, be not proud, though some have callèd thee
Mighty and dreadful, for thou art not so;
For those whom thou think'st thou dost overthrow
Die not, poor death, nor yet canst thou kill me.
From rest and sleep, which but thy pictures be,
Much pleasure—then, from thee much more must flow;
And soonest our best men with thee do go,
Rest of their bones and soul's delivery.
Thou art slave to fate, chance, kings, and desperate men,
And dost with poison, war, and sickness dwell;   10
And poppy or charms can make us sleep as well,
And better than thy stroke. Why swell'st thou then?
One short sleep passed, we wake eternally,
And death shall be no more; death, thou shalt die.

A DIRGE

James Shirley

The glories of our blood and state
   Are shadows, not substantial things;
There is no armor against fate;
   Death lays his icy hand on kings:
      Scepter and crown
      Must tumble down,
And in the dust be equal made
With the poor crooked scythe and spade.

Some men with swords may reap the field,
   And plant fresh laurels where they kill;   10
But their strong nerves at last must yield;

They tame but one another still:
  Early or late
  They stoop to fate,
And must give up their murmuring breath
When they, pale captives, creep to death.

The garlands wither on your brow;
  Then boast no more your mighty deeds;
Upon Death's purple altar now
  See where the victor-victim bleeds: 20

  Your heads must come
  To the cold tomb;
Only the actions of the just
Smell sweet, and blossom in their dust.

I WANDERED LONELY AS A CLOUD

William Wordsworth

I wandered lonely as a cloud
That floats on high o'er vales and hills,
When all at once I saw a crowd,
A host, of golden daffodils,
Beside the lake, beneath the trees,
Fluttering and dancing in the breeze.

Continuous as the stars that shine
And twinkle on the milky way,
They stretched in never-ending line
Along the margin of a bay;   10
Ten thousand saw I at a glance,
Tossing their heads in sprightly dance.

The waves beside them danced, but they
Outdid the sparkling waves in glee;
A poet could not but be gay,
In such a jocund company;
I gazed—and gazed—but little thought
What wealth the show to me had brought:

For oft, when on my couch I lie
In vacant or in pensive mood,   20
They flash upon that inward eye
Which is the bliss of solitude;
And then my heart with pleasure fills,
And dances with the daffodils.

THE LATEST DECALOGUE

Arthur Hugh Clough

Thou shalt have one God only; who
Would be at the expense of two?
No graven images may be
Worshiped, except the currency.
Swear not at all; for, for thy curse
Thine enemy is none the worse.
At church on Sunday to attend
Will serve to keep the world thy friend.
Honor thy parents; that is, all
From whom advancement may befall.   10
Thou shalt not kill; but need'st not strive
Officiously to keep alive.
Do not adultery commit;
Advantage rarely comes of it.
Thou shalt not steal; an empty feat,
When it's so lucrative to cheat.
Bear not false witness; let the lie
Have time on its own wings to fly.
Thou shalt not covet, but tradition
Approves all forms of competition.   20
The sum of all is, thou shalt love,
If anybody, God above:
At any rate shall never labor
More than thyself to love thy neighbor.

TO AUTUMN

John Keats

Season of mists and mellow fruitfulness,
    Close bosom-friend of the maturing sun;
Conspiring with him how to load and bless
    With fruit the vines that round the thatch-eves run;
To bend with apples the mossed cottage-trees,
    And fill all fruit with ripeness to the core;
        To swell the gourd, and plump the hazel shells
With a sweet kernel; to set budding more,
    And still more, later flowers for the bees,
    Until they think warm days will never cease,   10
        For Summer has o'er-brimmed their clammy cells.

Who hath not seen thee oft amid thy store?
    Sometimes whoever seeks abroad may find

Thee sitting careless on a granary floor,
  Thy hair soft-lifted by the winnowing wind;
Or on a half-reaped furrow sound asleep,
  Drowsed with the fume of poppies, while thy hook
    Spares the next swath and all its twinèd flowers:
And sometimes like a gleaner thou dost keep
  Steady thy laden head across a brook;   20
  Or by a cider-press, with patient look,
    Thou watchest the last oozings hours by hours.

Where are the songs of Spring? Ay, where are they?
  Think not of them, thou hast thy music too,—
While barrèd clouds bloom the soft-dying day,
  And touch the stubble-plains with rosy hue;
Then in a wailful choir the small gnats mourn
  Among the river sallows, borne aloft
    Or sinking as the light wind lives or dies;
And full-grown lambs loud bleat from hilly bourn;   30
  Hedge-crickets sing; and now with treble soft
  The red-breast whistles from a garden-croft;
    And gathering swallows twitter in the skies.

OZYMANDIAS

Percy Bysshe Shelley

I met a traveler from an antique land
Who said: "Two vast and trunkless legs of stone
Stand in the desert. Near them, on the sand,
Half sunk, a shattered visage lies, whose frown,
And wrinkled lip, and sneer of cold command,
Tell that its sculptor well those passions read
Which yet survive, stamped on these lifeless things,
The hand that mocked them, and the heart that fed:
And on the pedestal these words appear:
'My name is Ozymandias, king of kings: 10
Look on my works, ye Mighty, and despair!'
Nothing beside remains. Round the decay
Of that colossal wreck, boundless and bare
The lone and level sands stretch far away."

CARGOES*

John Masefield

Quinquireme of Nineveh from distant Ophir
Rowing home to haven in sunny Palestine,

---

* Reprinted with permission of The Macmillan Company from *Poems* by John Masefield. Copyright 1912 by the Macmillan Company; renewed 1940 by John Masefield.

With a cargo of ivory,
And apes and peacocks,
Sandalwood, cedarwood, and sweet wine.

Stately Spanish galleon coming from the Isthmus,
Dipping through the Tropics by the palm-green shores,
With a cargo of diamonds,
Emeralds, amethysts,
Topazes, and cinnamon, and gold moidores.   10

Dirty British coaster with a salt-caked smoke-stack
Butting through the Channel in the mad March days,
With a cargo of Tyne coal,
Road-rail, pig-lead,
Firewood, iron-ware, and cheap tin trays.

4. What devices of "word-music" can you find in the following poems?

THE SUN RISING

John Donne

Busy old fool, unruly sun,
Why dost thou thus
Through windows and through curtains call on us?
Must to thy motions lovers' seasons run?
Saucy pedantic wretch, go chide
Late schoolboys and sour prentices,
Go tell court-huntsmen that the king will ride,
Call country ants to harvest offices;
Love, all alike, no season knows, nor clime,
Nor hours, days, months, which are the rags of time.   10

Thy beams, so reverend, and strong
Why shouldst thou think?
I could eclipse and cloud them with a wink,
But that I would not lose her sight so long;
If her eyes have not blinded thine,
Look, and tomorrow late tell me
Whether both the Indias of spice and mine
Be where thou left'st them, or lie here with me.
Ask for those kings whom thou saw'st yesterday,
And thou shalt hear, all here in one bed lay.   20

She is all states, and all princes I;
Nothing else is.
Princes do but play us; compared to this,
All honor's mimic, all wealth alchemy.
Thou, sun, art half as happy as we,
In that the world's contracted thus;

Thine age asks ease, and since thy duties be
To warm the world, that's done in warming us.
Shine here to us, and thou art everywhere;
This bed thy center is, these walls thy sphere.   30

THE CANONIZATION

John Donne

For God's sake hold your tongue, and let me love!
    Or chide my palsy, or my gout,
My five gray hairs, or ruin'd fortune flout,
        With wealth your state, your mind with arts improve,
            Take you a course, get you a place,
            Observe his Honor, or his Grace,
    Or the king's real, or his stampèd face
        Contemplate, what you will, approve,
        So you will let me love.

Alas, alas, who's injur'd by my love?   10
    What merchant's ships have my sighs drown'd?
Who says my tears have overflowed his ground?
        When did my colds a forward spring remove?
            When did the heats which my veins fill
            Add one man to the plaguy bill?
Soldiers find wars, and lawyers find out still
    Litigious men, which quarrels move,
        Though she and I do love.

Call us what you will, we are made such by love;   20
    Call her one, me another fly,
We're tapers too, and at our own cost die.
        And we in us find th' eagle and the dove.
            The phoenix riddle hath more wit
            By us; we two being one, are it.
So to one neutral thing both sexes fit,
    We die and rise the same, and prove
        Mysterious by this love.

We can die by it, if not live by love,
    And if unfit for tombs and hearse
Our legend be, it will be fit for verse;   30
        And if no piece of chronicle we prove,
            We'll build in sonnets pretty rooms;
            As well a well-wrought urn becomes
The greatest ashes, as half-acre tombs
        And by these hymns, all shall approve
        Us canoniz'd for love.

And thus invoke us: "You whom reverent love
   Made one another's hermitage;
You, to whom love was peace, that now is rage;
   Who did the whole world's soul contract, and drove   40
     Into the glasses of your eyes
     (So made such mirrors, and such spies,
That they did all to you epitomize)
   Countries, towns, courts: Beg from above
   A pattern of your love!"

THE COLLAR

George Herbert

I struck the board and cried, No more!
      I will abroad.
What? Shall I ever sigh and pine?
My lines and life are free, free as the road,
   Loose as the wind, as large as store.
      Shall I be still in suit?
   Have I no harvest but a thorn
   To let me blood, and not restore
What I have lost with cordial fruit?
      Sure there was wine   10
Before my sighs did dry it; there was corn
     Before my tears did drown it.
Is the year only lost to me?
     Have I no bays to crown it?
No flowers, no garlands gay? All blasted?
      All wasted?
Not so, my heart! But there is fruit,
     And thou hast hands.
     Recover all thy sigh-blown age
On double pleasures. Leave thy cold dispute   20
Of what is fit and not. Forsake thy cage,
     Thy rope of sands,
Which petty thoughts have made, and made to thee
   Good cable, to enforce and draw,
     And be thy law,
   While thou didst wink and wouldst not see.
      Away! Take heed!
      I will abroad.
Call in thy death's head there. Tie up thy fears.
      He that forbears   30
    To suit and serve his need
     Deserves his load.

But as I raved and grew more fierce and wild
    At every word,
Me thoughts I heard one calling, Child!
    And I replied, My lord.

ON THE LATE MASSACRE IN PIEMONT

John Milton

Avenge, O Lord, thy slaughtered Saints, whose bones
Lie scattered on the Alpine mountains cold;
Even them who kept thy truth so pure of old,
When all our fathers worshiped stocks and stones,
Forget not: in thy book record their groans
Who were thy sheep, and in their ancient fold
Slain by the bloody Piemontese, that rolled
Mother with infant down the rocks. Their moans
The vales redoubled to the hills, and they
To heaven. Their martyred blood and ashes sow   10
O'er all the Italian fields, where still doth sway
The triple Tyrant; that from these may grow
A hundredfold, who, having learnt thy way,
Early may fly the Babylonian woe.

TO HIS COY MISTRESS

Andrew Marvell

Had we but world enough, and time,
This coyness, Lady, were no crime.
We would sit down and think which way
To walk, and pass our long love's day.
Thou by the Indian Ganges' side
Should'st rubies find; I by the tide
Of Humber would complain. I would
Love you ten years before the Flood;
And you should, if you please, refuse
Till the conversion of the Jews.   10
My vegetable love should grow
Vaster than empires, and more slow.
An hundred years should go to praise
Thine eyes, and on thy forehead gaze;
Two hundred to adore each breast;
But thirty thousand to the rest.
An age at least to every part;
And the last age should show your heart.
For, Lady, you deserve this state;
Nor would I love at lower rate.   20

But at my back I always hear
Time's wingèd chariot hurrying near;
And yonder all before us lie
Deserts of vast eternity.
Thy beauty shall no more be found;
Nor, in thy marble vault, shall sound
My echoing song; then worms shall try
That long-preserved virginity,
And your quaint honor turn to dust,
And into ashes all my lust.   30
The grave's a fine and private place;
But none, I think, do there embrace.
   Now therefore, while the youthful hue
Sits on thy skin like morning dew,
And while thy willing soul transpires
At every pore with instant fires,
Now let us sport us while we may,
And now, like amorous birds of prey,
Rather at once our time devour
Than languish in his slow-chapt power.   40
Let us roll all our strength and all
Our sweetness up into one ball,
And tear our pleasures with rough strife
Through the iron gates of life:
Thus, though we cannot make our sun
Stand still, yet we will make him run.

DOVER BEACH

Matthew Arnold

The sea is calm to-night.
The tide is full, the moon lies fair
Upon the straits;—on the French coast, the light
Gleams, and is gone; the cliffs of England stand,
Glimmering and vast, out in the tranquil bay.
Come to the window, sweet is the night air!
Only, from the lone line of spray
Where the sea meets the moon-blanch'd land,
Listen! you hear the grating roar
Of pebbles which the waves draw back, and fling,   10
At their return, up the high strand,
Begin, and cease, and then again begin,
With tremulous cadence slow, and bring
The eternal note of sadness in.

Sophocles long ago
Heard it on the Ægæan, and it brought

Into his mind the turbid ebb and flow
Of human misery; we
Find also in the sound a thought,
Hearing it by this distant northern sea.   20

The Sea of Faith
Was once, too, at the full, and round earth's shore
Lay like the folds of a bright girdle furl'd.
But now I only hear
Its melancholy, long, withdrawing roar,
Retreating, to the breath
Of the night-wind down the vast edges drear
And naked shingles of the world.

Ah, love, let us be true
To one another! for the world, which seems   30
To lie before us like a land of dreams,
So various, so beautiful, so new,
Hath really neither joy, nor love, nor light,
Nor certitude, nor peace, nor help for pain;
And we are here as on a darkling plain
Swept with confused alarms of struggle and flight,
Where ignorant armies clash by night.

THE MAJOR-GENERAL'S SONG

W. S. Gilbert
Arthur Sullivan

I am the very model of a modern Major-General,
I've information vegetable, animal, and mineral,
I know the kings of England, and I quote the fights historical,
From Marathon to Waterloo, in order categorical;
I'm very well acquainted too with matters mathematical,
I understand equations, both the simple and quadratical,
About binomial theorem I'm teeming with a lot o' news—
With many cheerful facts about the square of the hypotenuse.

I'm very good at integral and differential calculus,
I know the scientific names of beings animalculous;   10
In short, in matters vegetable, animal, and mineral,
I am the very model of a modern Major-General.

I know our mythic history, King Arthur's and Sir Caradoc's,
I answer hard acrostics, I've a pretty taste for paradox,
I quote in elegiacs all the crimes of Heliogabalus,
In conics I can floor peculiarities parabolous.
I can tell undoubted Raphaels from Gerard Dows and Zoffanies,
I know the croaking chorus from the *Frogs* of Aristophanes,

Then I can hum a fugue of which I've heard the music's din afore,
And whistle all the airs from that infernal nonsense *Pinafore*.   20

Then I can write a washing bill in Babylonic cuneiform,
And tell you every detail of Caractacus's uniform;
In short, in matters vegetable, animal, and mineral,
I am the very model of a modern Major-General.

In fact, when I know what is meant by "mamelon" and "ravelin,"
When I can tell at sight a chassepôt rifle from a javelin,
When such affairs as sorties and surprises I'm more wary at,
And when I know precisely what is meant by "commissariat,"
When I have learnt what progress has been made in modern gunnery,
When I know more of tactics than a novice in a nunnery: 30
In short, when I've a smattering of elemental strategy,
You'll say a better Major-General has never sat a gee—

For my military knowledge, though I'm plucky and adventury,
Has only been brought down to the beginning of the century:
But still in matters vegetable, animal, and mineral,
I am the very model of a modern Major-General.

THE SNAKE*

Emily Dickinson

A narrow Fellow in the Grass
Occasionally rides—
You may have met Him—did you not
His notice sudden is—

The Grass divides as with a Comb—
A spotted shaft is seen—
And then it closes at your feet
And opens further on—

He likes a Boggy Acre
A Floor too cool for Corn—   10
Yet when a Boy, and Barefoot—
I more than once at Noon

Have passed, I thought, a Whip lash
Unbraiding in the Sun
When stooping to secure it
It wrinkled, and was gone—

Several of Nature's People
I know, and they know me—
I feel for them a transport
Of cordiality—   20

But never met this Fellow
Attended, or alone
Without a tighter breathing
And Zero at the Bone—

5. Wood defines *allegory* as "a presentation of a meaning implied but not expressly stated. It is in essence a prolonged metaphor, in which actions symbolize other actions and often the characters are types or personifications." Discuss Nathaniel Hawthorne's "Young Goodman Brown" in terms of this quotation.

YOUNG GOODMAN BROWN

Young Goodman Brown came forth at sunset into the street at Salem village; but put his head back, after crossing the threshold, to exchange a parting kiss with his young wife. And Faith, as the wife was aptly named, thrust her own pretty head into the street, letting the wind play with the pink ribbons of her cap while she called to Goodman Brown.

"Dearest heart," whispered she, softly and rather sadly, when her lips were close to his ear, "prithee put off your journey until sunrise and sleep in your own bed to-night. A lone woman is troubled with such dreams and such thoughts that she's afeard of herself sometimes. Pray tarry with me this night, dear husband, of all nights in the year."

"My love and my Faith," replied young Goodman Brown, "of all nights in the year, this one night must I tarry away from thee. My journey, as thou callest it, forth and back again, must needs be done 'twixt now and sunrise. What, my sweet, pretty wife, dost thou doubt me already, and we but three months married?"

"Then God bless you!" said Faith, with the pink ribbons; "and may you find all well when you come back."

"Amen!" cried Goodman Brown. "Say thy prayers, dear Faith, and go to bed at dusk, and no harm will come to thee."

So they parted; and the young man pursued his way until, being about to turn the corner by the meeting-house, he looked back and saw the head of Faith still peeping after him with a melancholy air, in spite of her pink ribbons.

"Poor little Faith!" thought he, for his heart smote him. "What a wretch am I to leave her on such an errand! She talks of dreams, too. Methought as she spoke there was trouble in her face, as if a dream had warned her what work is to be done to-night. But no, no; 'twould kill her to think it. Well, she's a blessed angel on earth; and after this one night I'll cling to her skirts and follow her to heaven."

With this excellent resolve for the future, Goodman Brown felt himself justified in making more haste on his present evil purpose. He had taken a dreary road, darkened by all the gloomiest trees of the forest, which barely stood aside to let the narrow path creep through, and closed immediately behind. It was all as lonely as could be; and there is this peculiarity in such a solitude, that the traveller knows not who may be concealed by the innumerable trunks and the thick boughs overhead; so that with lonely foot-steps he may yet be passing through an unseen multitude.

"There may be a devilish Indian behind every tree," said Goodman Brown to himself; and he glanced fearfully behind him as he added, "What if the devil himself should be at my very elbow!"

His head being turned back, he passed a crook of the road, and, looking forward again, beheld the figure of a man, in grave and decent attire, seated at the foot of an old tree. He arose at Goodman Brown's approach and walked onward side by side with him.

"You are late, Goodman Brown," said he. "The clock of the Old South was striking as I came through Boston, and that is full fifteen minutes agone."

"Faith kept me back a while," replied the young man, with a tremor in his voice, caused by the sudden appearance of his companion, though not wholly unexpected.

It was now deep dusk in the forest, and deepest in that part of it where these two were journeying. As nearly as could be discerned, the second traveller was about fifty years old, apparently in the same rank of life as Goodman Brown, and bearing a considerable resemblance to him, though perhaps more in ex-pression than features. Still they might have been taken for father and son. And yet, though the elder person was as simply clad as the younger, and as simple in manner too, he had an indescribable air of one who knew the world, and who would not have felt abashed at the governor's dinner table or in King William's court, were it possible that his affairs should call him thither. But the only thing about him that could be fixed upon as remarkable was his staff, which bore the likeness of a great black snake, so curiously wrought that it might almost be seen to twist and wriggle itself like a living serpent. This, of course, must have been an ocular deception, assisted by the uncertain light.

"Come, Goodman Brown," cried his fellow-traveller, "this is a dull place for the beginning of a journey. Take my staff, if you are so soon weary."

"Friend," said the other, exchanging his slow pace for a full stop, "having kept covenant by meeting thee here, it is my purpose now to return whence I came. I have scruples touching the matter thou wot'st of."

"Sayest thou so?" replied he of the serpent, smiling apart. "Let us walk on, nevertheless, reasoning as we go; and if I convince thee not thou shalt turn back. We are but a little way in the forest yet."

"Too far! too far!" exclaimed the goodman, unconsciously resuming his walk. "My father never went into the woods on such an errand, nor his father before him. We have been a race of honest men and good Christians since the days of the martyrs; and shall I be the first of the name of Brown that ever took this path and kept"—

"Such company, thou wouldst say," observed the elder person, interpreting his pause. "Well said, Goodman Brown! I have been as well acquainted with your family as with ever a one among the Puritans; and that's no trifle to say. I helped your grandfather, the constable, when he lashed the Quaker woman so smartly through the streets of Salem; and it was I that brought your father a pitch-pine knot, kindled at my own hearth, to set fire to an Indian village, in King Philip's war. They were my good friends, both; and many a pleasant walk have we had along this path, and returned merrily after midnight. I would fain be friends with you for their sake."

"If it be as thou sayest," replied Goodman Brown, "I marvel they never spoke of these matters; or, verily, I marvel not, seeing that the least rumor of the sort would have driven them from New England. We are a people of prayer, and good works to boot, and abide no such wickedness."

"Wickedness or not," said the traveller with the twisted staff, "I have a very general acquaintance here in New England. The deacons of many a church have drunk the communion wine with me; the selectmen of divers towns make me their chairman; and a majority of the Great and General Court are firm supporters of my interest. The governor and I, too—But these are state secrets."

"Can this be so?" cried Goodman Brown, with a stare of amazement at his undisturbed companion. "Howbeit, I have nothing to do with the governor and council; they have their own ways, and are no rule for a simple husband-man like me. But, were I to go on with thee, how should I meet the eye of that good old man, our minister, at Salem village? Oh, his voice would make me tremble both Sabbath day and lecture day."

Thus far the elder traveller had listened with due gravity; but now burst into a fit of irrepressible mirth, shaking himself so violently that his snake-like staff actually seemed to wriggle in sympathy.

"Ha! ha! ha!" shouted he again and again; then composing himself, "Well, go on, Goodman Brown, go on; but, prithee, don't kill me with laughing."

"Well, then, to end the matter at once," said Goodman Brown, considerably nettled, "there is my wife, Faith. It would break her dear little heart; and I'd rather break my own."

"Nay, if that be the case," answered the other, "e'en go thy ways, Goodman Brown. I would not for twenty old women like the one hobbling before us that Faith should come to any harm."

As he spoke he pointed his staff at a female figure on the path, in whom Goodman Brown recognized a very pious and exemplary dame, who had taught him his catechism in youth, and was still his moral and spiritual ad-viser, jointly with the minister and Deacon Gookin.

"A marvel, truly, that Goody Cloyse should be so far in the wilderness at nightfall," said he. "But with your leave, friend, I shall take a cut through the woods until we have left this Christian woman behind. Being a stranger to you, she might ask whom I was consorting with and whither I was going."

"Be it so," said his fellow-traveller. "Betake you to the woods, and let me keep the path."

Accordingly the young man turned aside, but took care to watch his com-panion, who advanced softly along the road until he had come within a staff's length of the old dame. She, meanwhile, was making the best of her way, with singular speed for so aged a woman, and mumbling some indistinct words—a prayer, doubtless—as she went. The traveller put forth his staff and touched her withered neck with what seemed the serpent's tail.

"The devil!" screamed the pious old lady.

"Then Goody Cloyse knows her old friend?" observed the traveller, confronting her and leaning on his writhing stick.

"Ah, forsooth, and is it your worship indeed?" cried the good dame. "Yea, truly is it, and in the very image of my old gossip, Goodman Brown, the grandfather of the silly fellow that now is. But—would your worship believe it?—my broomstick hath strangely disappeared, stolen, as I suspect, by that unhanged witch, Goody Cory, and that, too, when I was all anointed with the juice of smallage, and cinquefoil, and wolf's bane"—

"Mingled with fine wheat and the fat of a new-born babe," said the shape of old Goodman Brown.

"Ah, your worship knows the recipe," cried the old lady, cackling aloud. "So, as I was saying, being all ready for the meeting, and no horse to ride on, I made up my mind to foot it; for they tell me there is a nice young man to be taken into communion tonight. But now your good worship will lend me your arm, and we shall be there in a twinkling."

"That can hardly be," answered her friend. "I may not spare you my arm, Goody Cloyse; but here is my staff, if you will."

So saying, he threw it down at her feet, where, perhaps, it assumed life, being one of the rods which its owner had formerly lent to the Egyptian magi. Of this fact, however, Goodman Brown could not take cognizance. He had cast up his eyes in astonishment, and, looking down again, beheld neither Goody Cloyse nor the serpentine staff, but his fellow-traveller alone, who waited for him as calmly as if nothing had happened.

"That old woman taught me my catechism," said the young man; and there was a world of meaning in this simple comment.

They continued to walk onward, while the elder traveller exhorted his companion to make good speed and persevere in the path, discoursing so aptly that his arguments seemed rather to spring up in the bosom of his auditor than to be suggested by himself. As they went, he plucked a branch of maple to serve for a walking stick, and began to strip it of the twigs and little boughs, which were wet with evening dew. The moment his fingers touched them they became strangely withered and dried up as with a week's sunshine. Thus the pair proceeded, at a good free pace, until suddenly, in a gloomy hollow of the road, Goodman Brown sat himself down on the stump of a tree and refused to go any farther.

"Friend," said he, stubbornly, "my mind is made up. Not another step will I budge on this errand. What if a wretched old woman do choose to go to the devil when I thought she was going to heaven: is that any reason why I should quit my dear Faith and go after her?"

"You will think better of this by and by," said his acquaintance, composedly. "Sit here and rest yourself a while; and when you feel like moving again, there is my staff to help you along."

Without more words, he threw his companion the maple stick, and was as speedily out of sight as if he had vanished into the deepening gloom. The young man sat a few moments by the roadside, applauding himself greatly, and thinking with how clear a conscience he should meet the minister in his morning walk, nor shrink from the eye of good old Deacon Gookin. And what calm sleep would be his that very night, which was to have been spent so wickedly, but so purely and sweetly now, in the arms of Faith! Amidst these pleasant and praiseworthy meditations, Goodman Brown heard the tramp of horses along the road, and deemed it advisable to conceal himself within the verge of the forest, conscious of the guilty purpose that had brought him thither, though now so happily turned from it.

On came the hoof tramps and the voices of the riders, two grave old voices, conversing soberly as they drew near. These mingled sounds appeared to pass along the road, within a few yards of the young man's hiding-place; but, owing doubtless to the depth of the gloom at that particular spot, neither the travellers nor their steeds were visible. Though their figures brushed the small boughs by the wayside, it could not be seen that they intercepted, even for a moment, the faint gleam from the strip of bright sky athwart which they must have passed. Goodman Brown alternately crouched and stood on tiptoe, pulling aside the branches and thrusting forth his head as far as he durst without discerning so much as a shadow. It vexed him the more, because he could have sworn, were such a thing possible, that he recognized the voices of the minister and Deacon Gookin, jogging along quietly, as they were wont to do, when bound to some ordination or ecclesiastical council. While yet within hearing, one of the riders stopped to pluck a switch.

"Of the two, reverend sir," said the voice like the deacon's, "I had rather miss an ordination dinner than to-night's meeting. They tell me that some of our community are to be here from Falmouth and beyond, and others from Connecticut and Rhode Island, besides several of the Indian powwows, who, after their fashion, know almost as much deviltry as the best of us. Moreover, there is a goodly young woman to be taken into communion."

"Mighty well, Deacon Gookin!" replied the solemn old tones of the minister. "Spur up, or we shall be late. Nothing can be done you know until I get on the ground."

The hoofs clattered again; and the voices, talking so strangely in the empty air, passed on through the forest, where no church had ever been gathered or solitary Christian prayed. Whither, then, could these holy men be journeying so deep into the heathen wilderness? Young Goodman Brown caught hold of a tree for support, being ready to sink down on the ground, faint and over-burdened with the heavy sickness of his heart. He looked up to the sky, doubt-ing whether there really was a heaven above him. Yet there was the blue arch, and the stars brightening in it.

"With heaven above and Faith below, I will yet stand firm against the devil!" cried Goodman Brown.

While he still gazed upward into the deep arch of the firmament and had lifted his hands to pray, a cloud, though no wind was stirring, hurried across the zenith and hid the brightening stars. The blue sky was still visible, except directly overhead, where this black mass of cloud was sweeping swiftly north-ward. Aloft in the air, as if from the depths of the cloud, came a confused and doubtful sound of voices. Once the listener fancied that he could distinguish the accents of towns-people of his own, men, and women, both pious and ungodly, many of whom he had met at the communion table, and had seen others rioting at the tavern. The next moment, so indistinct were the sounds, he doubted whether he had heard aught but the murmur of the old forest, whispering without a wind. Then came a stronger swell of those familiar tones, heard daily in the sunshine at Salem village, but never until now from a cloud of night. There was one voice of a young woman, uttering lamentations, yet with an uncertain sorrow, and entreating for some favor, which, perhaps, it would grieve her to obtain; and all the unseen multitude, both saints and sinners, seemed to encourage her onward.

"Faith!" shouted Goodman Brown, in a voice of agony and desperation; and the echoes of the forest mocked him, crying, "Faith! Faith!" as if bewildered wretches were seeking her all through the wilderness.

The cry of grief, rage, and terror was yet piercing the night, when the unhappy husband held his breath for a response. There was a scream, drowned immediately in a louder murmur of voices, fading into far-off laughter, as the dark cloud swept away, leaving the clear and silent sky above Goodman Brown. But something fluttered lightly down through the air and caught on the branch of a tree. The young man seized it, and beheld a pink ribbon.

"My Faith is gone!" cried he, after one stupefied moment. "There is no good on earth; and sin is but a name. Come, devil; for to thee is this world given."

And, maddened with despair, so that he laughed loud and long, did Goodman Brown grasp his staff and set forth again, at such a rate that he seemed to fly along the forest path rather than to walk or run. The road grew wilder and drearier and more faintly traced, and vanished at length, leaving him in the heart of the dark wilderness, still rushing onward with the instinct that guides mortal man to evil. The whole forest was peopled with frightful sounds —the creaking of the trees, the howling of wild beasts, and the yell of Indians; while sometimes the wind tolled like a distant church bell, and sometimes gave a broad roar around the traveller, as if all Nature were laughing him to scorn. But he was himself the chief horror of the scene, and shrank not from its other horrors.

"Ha! ha! ha!" roared Goodman Brown when the wind laughed at him. "Let us hear which will laugh loudest. Think not to frighten me with your deviltry. Come witch, come wizard, come Indian powwow, come devil himself, and here comes Goodman Brown. You may as well fear him as he fear you."

In truth, all through the haunted forest there could be nothing more frightful than the figure of Goodman Brown. On he flew among the black pines, brandishing his staff with frenzied gestures, now giving vent to an inspiration of horrid blasphemy, and now shouting forth such laughter as set all the echoes of the forest laughing like demons around him. The fiend in his own shape is less hideous than when he rages in the breast of man. Thus sped the demoniac on his course, until, quivering among the trees, he saw a red light before him, as when the felled trunks and branches of a clearing have been set on fire, and throw up their lurid blaze against the sky, at the hour of midnight. He paused, in a lull of the tempest that had driven him onward, and heard the swell of what seemed a hymn, rolling solemnly from a distance with the weight of many voices. He knew the tune; it was a familiar one in the choir of the village meeting-house. The verse died heavily away, and was lengthened by a chorus, not of human voices, but of all the sounds of the benighted wilderness pealing in awful harmony together. Goodman Brown cried out, and his cry was lost to his own ear by its unison with the cry of the desert.

In the interval of silence he stole forward until the light glared full upon his eyes. At one extremity of an open space, hemmed in by the dark wall of the forest, arose a rock, bearing some rude, natural resemblance either to an altar or a pulpit, and surrounded by four blazing pines, their tops aflame, their stems untouched, like candles at an evening meeting. The mass of foliage that had overgrown the summit of the rock was all on fire, blazing high into the night and fitfully illuminating the whole field. Each pendent twig and leafy festoon was in a blaze. As the red light arose and fell, a numerous congregation alternately shone forth, then disappeared in shadow, and again grew, as it were, out of the darkness, peopling the heart of the solitary woods at once.

"A grave and dark-clad company," quoth Goodman Brown.

In truth they were such. Among them, quivering to and fro between gloom and splendor, appeared faces that would be seen next day at the council board of the province, and others which, Sabbath after Sabbath, looked devoutly heavenward, and benignantly over the crowded pews, from the holiest pulpits in the land. Some affirm that the lady of the governor was there. At least there were high dames well known to her, and wives of honored husbands, and widows, a great multitude, and ancient maidens, all of excellent repute, and fair young girls, who trembled lest their mothers should espy them. Either the sudden gleams of light flashing over the obscure field bedazzled Goodman Brown, or he recognized a score of the church members of Salem village famous for their especial sanctity. Good old Deacon Gookin had arrived, and waited at the skirts of that venerable saint, his revered pastor. But, irreverently consorting with these grave, reputable, and pious people, these elders of the church, these chaste dames and dewy virgins, there were men of dissolute lives and women of spotted fame, wretches given over to all mean and filthy vice, and suspected even of horrid crimes. It was strange to see that the good shrank not from the wicked, nor were the sinners abashed by the saints. Scattered also among their pale-faced enemies were the Indian priests, or powwows, who had often scared their native forest with more hideous incantations than any known to English witchcraft.

"But where is Faith?" thought Goodman Brown; and, as hope came into his heart, he trembled.

Another verse of the hymn arose, a slow and mournful strain, such as the pious love, but joined to words which expressed all that our nature can conceive of sin, and darkly hinted at far more. Unfathomable to mere mortals is the lore of fiends. Verse after verse was sung; and still the chorus of the desert swelled between like the deepest tone of a mighty organ; and with the final peal of that dreadful anthem there came a sound, as if the roaring wind, the rushing streams, the howling beasts, and every other voice of the unconcerted wilderness were mingling and according with the voice of guilty man in homage to the prince of all. The four blazing pines threw up a loftier flame, and obscurely discovered shapes and visages of horror on the smoke wreaths above the impious assembly. At the same moment the fire on the rock shot redly forth and formed a glowing arch above its base, where now appeared a figure. With reverence be it spoken, the figure bore no slight similitude, both in garb and manner, to some grave divine of the New England churches.

"Bring forth the converts!" cried a voice that echoed through the field and rolled into the forest.

At the word, Goodman Brown stepped forth from the shadow of the trees and approached the congregation, with whom he felt a loathful brotherhood by the sympathy of all that was wicked in his heart. He could have well-nigh sworn that the shape of his own dead father beckoned him to advance, looking downward from a smoke wreath, while a woman, with dim features of despair, threw out her hand to warn him back. Was it his mother? But he had no power to retreat one step, nor to resist, even in thought, when the minister and good old Deacon Gookin seized his arms and led him to the blazing rock. Thither came also the slender form of a veiled female, led between Goody Cloyse, that pious teacher of the catechism, and Martha Carrier, who had received the devil's promise to be queen of hell. A rampant hag was she. And there stood the proselytes beneath the canopy of fire.

"Welcome, my children," said the dark figure, "to the communion of your race. Ye have found thus young your nature and your destiny. My children, look behind you!"

They turned; and flashing forth, as it were, in a sheet of flame, the fiend worshippers were seen; the smile of welcome gleamed darkly on every visage.

"There," resumed the sable form, "are all whom ye have reverenced from youth. Ye deemed them holier than yourselves, and shrank from your own sin, contrasting it with their lives of righteousness and prayerful aspirations heavenward. Yet here are they all in my worshipping assembly. This night it shall be granted you to know their secret deeds: how hoary-bearded elders of the church have whispered wanton words to the young maids of their households; how many a woman, eager for widows' weeds, has given her husband a drink at bedtime and let him sleep his last sleep in her bosom; how beardless youths have made haste to inherit their fathers' wealth; and how fair damsels—blush not, sweet ones—have dug little graves in the garden, and bidden me, the sole guest, to an infant's funeral. By the sympathy of your human hearts for sin ye shall scent out all the places—whether in church, bedchamber, street, field, or forest—where crime has been committed, and shall exult to behold the whole earth one stain of guilt, one mighty blood spot. Far more than this. It shall be yours to penetrate, in every bosom, the deep mystery of sin, the fountain of all wicked arts, and which inexhaustibly supplies more evil impulses than human power—than my power at its utmost—can make manifest in deeds. And now, my children, look upon each other."

They did so; and, by the blaze of the hell-kindled torches, the wretched man beheld his Faith, and the wife her husband, trembling before that unhallowed altar.

"Lo, there ye stand, my children," said the figure, in a deep and solemn tone, almost sad with its despairing awfulness, as if his once angelic nature could yet mourn for our miserable race. "Depending upon one another's hearts, ye had still hoped that virtue were not all a dream. Now are ye undeceived. Evil is the nature of mankind. Evil must be your only happiness. Welcome again, my children, to the communion of your race."

"Welcome," repeated the fiend worshippers, in one cry of despair and triumph.

And there they stood, the only pair, as it seemed, who were yet hesitating on the verge of wickedness in this dark world. A basin was hollowed, naturally, in the rock. Did it contain water, reddened by the lurid light? or was it blood? or, perchance, a liquid flame? Herein did the shape of evil dip his hand and prepare to lay the mark of baptism upon their foreheads, that they might be partakers of the mystery of sin, more conscious of the secret guilt of others, both in deed and thought, than they could now be of their own. The husband cast one look at his pale wife, and Faith at him. What polluted wretches would the next glance show them to each other, shuddering alike at what they disclosed and what they saw!

"Faith! Faith!" cried the husband, "look up to heaven, and resist the wicked one."

Whether Faith obeyed he knew not. Hardly had he spoken when he found himself amid calm night and solitude, listening to a roar of the wind which died heavily away through the forest. He staggered against the rock, and felt it chill and damp; while a hanging twig, that had been all on fire, besprinkled his cheek with the coldest dew.

The next morning young Goodman Brown came slowly into the street of Salem village, staring around him like a bewildered man. The good old minister was taking a walk along the graveyard to get an appetite for breakfast and meditate his sermon, and bestowed a blessing, as he passed, on Goodman Brown. He shrank from the venerable saint as if to avoid an anathema. Old Deacon Gookin was at domestic worship, and the holy words of his prayer were heard through the open window. "What God doth the wizard pray to?" quoth Goodman Brown. Goody Cloyse, that excellent old Christian, stood in the early sunshine at her own lattice, catechizing a little girl who had brought her a pint of morning's milk. Goodman Brown snatched away the child as from the grasp of the fiend himself. Turning the corner by the meeting-house, he spied the head of Faith, with the pink ribbons, gazing anxiously forth, and bursting into such joy at sight of him that she skipped along the street and almost kissed her husband before the whole village. But Goodman Brown looked sternly and sadly into her face, and passed on without a greeting.

Had Goodman Brown fallen asleep in the forest and only dreamed a wild dream of a witch-meeting?

Be it so if you will; but, alas! it was a dream of evil omen for young Goodman Brown. A stern, a sad, a darkly meditative, a distrustful, if not a desperate man did he become from the night of that fearful dream. On the Sabbath day, when the congregation were singing a holy psalm, he could not listen because an anthem of sin rushed loudly upon his ear and drowned all the blessed strain. When the minister spoke from the pulpit with power and fervid eloquence, and, with his hand on the open Bible, of the sacred truths of our religion, and of saint-like lives and triumphant deaths, and of future bliss or misery unutterable, then did Goodman Brown turn pale, dreading lest the roof should thunder down upon the gray blasphemer and his hearers. Often, waking suddenly at midnight, he shrank from the bosom of Faith; and at morning or eventide, when the family knelt down at prayer, he scowled and muttered to himself, and gazed sternly at his wife, and turned away. And when he had lived long, and was borne to his grave a hoary corpse, followed by Faith, an aged woman, and children and grandchildren, a goodly procession, besides neighbors not a few, they carved no hopeful verse upon his tombstone, for his dying hour was gloom.

44.

CHARLES CHILD WALCUTT

Interpreting the Symbol

When I recently asked a distinguished classical scholar what his advice would be about how to teach symbolism, he replied with a single ringing word: "Don't."

The reply was, of course, facetious and appropriate to a waning August night, but it reflected an attitude as clearly as if it had been a three-hundred-word sentence. It implied, I suspect, that everybody teaches symbolism and nobody is sure about it; that some modern criticism has run symbolism into the ground; that the lunatic fringe of modern poets and prose writers had used what appear to be symbols as a means of achieving effects of profundity which are in fact only impressive façades—and often not even façades but rather false fronts of suggestive language behind which there is nothing.

It reflected, finally—this "Don't"—the belief of a precise intelligence that when people talk about symbols and their meanings they are likely, alas, to be furthest from the kind of responsible reading that good literature demands. Responsible reading. How many times have you tossed a good little

From *College English*, XIV (May 1953). Reprinted with the permission of the National Council of Teachers of English and Charles C. Walcutt.

poem into the arena (the soon-to-be-bloody arena) of a freshman or sopho-
more class and been straightway informed that every detail and word of it
"stand for" (sometimes they say "symbolize") some specific but utterly
remote notion? And when you have protested, a dying Christian, that all
those remote, specific, personal "interpretations" (as they are called) cannot
be equally right, have you not been told, by some, that that is what it means
"to me"; by others, that the test of a good poem is the variety of interpretations it excites; and by others (who may indeed be the what-it-means-to-me
people reciting a second time) that there is no way of proving what a thing
symbolizes and that therefore it must follow that one reading is as good
as another?—so long, of course, as it is a richly imaginative one?

There are several possible sources of these attitudes toward poetry: I
believe some high schools are "teaching" poetry which is too difficult for
high school students, poetry in which the complexity of thought and language is such that average or even good high school students lack the verbal
sophistication needed for its comprehension. They simply do not yet feel
language sensitively enough to be able to know, even when told, what such
poetry means; and so they substitute personal meanings for the complex
meanings that live in the language and structures of such poems. There is
also current a tendency to encourage young students to express themselves,
to think creatively about the arts; and it may be that it is difficult to cultivate
strictness and accuracy of reading at the same time. There may be teachers
who are modestly unwilling to impose their beliefs on their students—and
others who are unsure of themselves. And still others whose reading of
modern criticism has convinced them that anything goes—and who are they
to think it possible ever to be sure about what any poem means?

And the problems do not end there. The instructor who launches a full-
scale assault upon irresponsible reading is likely to achieve a curious reversal
of roles, with the students refusing to find anything but the simplest literal
statements and the instructor begging them to entertain at least the possibility
that more may be meant than can be found on this most literal level. The
unhappy instructor may find himself attacked no more severely by the
student who insists on the value and importance of his own private "interpretations" than he is attacked by that same student a few weeks later when
he has swung over to the position of a skeptic who will allow nothing that
cannot be literally spelt out of a poem. He sits back and asks, "How do you
know?"—which is just what his instructor was asking him a few weeks
previously; the instructor begs for a co-operative sympathy, for open-minded-
ness, for a willing suspension of skepticism, but he has already taught his
students to give him none of these.

Out of the oscillations between over- and underreading come modula-
tions of the dominant frequency, overtones of lagging or pronounced response which will put a class at cross-purposes with itself, the skeptics and

overeager beavers wrestling for the monkey wrench they will throw into the instructor's lesson plan. Some of these problems were illustrated for me when a student in an advanced class in poetry analysis submitted a paper on Wallace Stevens' "Anecdote of the Jar."[1]

> I placed a jar in Tennessee,
> And round it was, upon a hill.
> It made the slovenly wilderness
> Surround that hill.
>
> The wilderness rose up to it,
> And sprawled around, no longer wild.
> The jar was round upon the ground
> And tall and of a port in air.
>
> It took dominion everywhere.
> The jar was gray and bare.
> It did not give of bird or bush,
> Like nothing else in Tennessee.

The poem, he wrote, was obviously a Republican treatment of the TVA. This particular jar is Norris Dam, "on a hill" in that it joins two hills. "The jar was round . . ." refers to the shape and symmetry of the dam. Its "dominion" is oppressive, unproductive, wasteful ("gray and bare"); it stops river traffic (being a "port"); and it does not give "of bird or bush." This summary does not do justice to the student's paper, for it was full of subtlety and persuasion. When the class assailed him, the author asked them to tell him why after all the jar was placed on a hill in Tennessee, of all states? And was not the TVA the most significant unnatural establishment there?

Continued discussion brought out some conclusions about symbolism and its uses: One must begin and stay with the immediate sensuous texture of a poem, seeing what ideas or attitudes inhere in the plain language-and-situation of the poem and resisting that impulse to search for a "hidden"— which is what the tyro usually understands by a "symbolic"—meaning. "Anecdote of the Jar" must first be read as a poem about a jar placed on a wild hill in Tennessee. That is what the poem says. Examining how the poem says it, we find riches of suggestion in the words that characterize the situation. The wilderness is slovenly; it sprawls; but around the jar it takes shape and is no longer wild. Since the wilderness itself is just as wild as it was, however, the phrase "no longer wild" must refer to the new composition of the scene, with the round jar in the center. The words that qualify the jar and its effects, however, do far more than acknowledge its function

[1] Copyright 1923 and renewed 1951 by Wallace Stevens. Reprinted from THE COLLECTED POEMS OF WALLACE STEVENS by permission of Alfred A. Knopf, Inc.

of bringing order (or composition); they render an ambiguous attitude of reserved mockery, amusement, and scorn. The jar, "gray and bare" and "of a port in air," is not beautiful or impressive in itself; it has the color and texture of Norris Dam, but not its dignity; "of a port" is not magnificent or beautiful. It is plump and smug; it is insensitive to the magnitude and vigor of the wilderness over which it takes its curious dominion. Yet there is delight in the definition of these ambiguities, for they are sharply drawn.

Having got thus far by scrutinizing what the poem literally says and suggests, the class raised again the question of symbols and symbolism. It was agreed, in general, that any so-called symbolic interpretation would have to grow directly out of the tones and connotations found in the close literal reading of the poem—a conclusion arrived at negatively, after considerable discussion during which various fantastic readings were rejected. This negative conclusion is an enormous gain, for it assumes a continuum of meaning from the literal to the "symbolic." It carries with it the assumption that symbolic meanings, at their end of the continuum, will yield to the same close reading that is first applied to the literal statement. (Where the concrete particular and the abstract universal are not continuous, we have allegory—of which more later.)

Assuming the continuum, then, the class offered two propositions: (1) the jar is a symbol of Order; (2) the jar is a symbol of the quality and effects of the machine age.[2] Now which is the more general or universal idea, and which is more tenable for this poem? At first glance it would appear that the jar-as-machine-age is less general than the jar-as-Order and that the former depends on the latter. But no; testing the universal by close examination of the concrete particulars of the literal words, we discovered that the idea of Order is here included in and subordinated to the specific idea of the machine age which the jar seems most definitely to symbolize. It is not abstract Order here but the particular kind of order brought by the machine. Universal Order is majestic. Linked to the gray, bare, and portly (mason?) jar, it becomes ludicrous and also formidable. Order under its auspices is a version of divine Reason, if you like, but its glory is yoked to the gray and pompous intentions of commerce. It therefore appears here in a grotesque, evil, and frustrating guise. By this time we find that we are talking about literal meanings, tone and attitudes, and symbolic meanings all at the same time, that no one of these elements can be isolated from the others or understood without considering them. If the reading has been tested and accepted,

---

[2] This interpretation is, of course, highly debatable. Stevens' favorite theme is the order imposed by art or the aesthetic imagination. If the words characterizing the jar make it seem beautiful, it would properly be seen as a symbol of art or the imagination; if it is a symmetrical but colorless jar, it might be a symbol of Order; if it is symmetrical but ugly, it may be a symbol of the machine or of the unlovely aspects of man-made order. Much depends on one's reading of the puzzling phrase "of a port."

the continuum has been established and a fundamental method for getting at symbolism has been achieved.

Another way of getting at the objective I have defined is to explore the distinction between a particular symbol and the universal content of any concrete idea or situation. General statements can be made about any particular fact or situation, such as "The cow is a herbivorous mammal." But the cow does not symbolize the idea of herbivorous mammal. Most early student statements of what a poem symbolizes are versions of this error. A student writes, for example, of Housman's "To an Athlete Dying Young," "The athlete who is reduced to nothing in a few years symbolizes man and his illusions of perfection and greatness." This is making a good deal of

> Runners whom renown outran
> And the name died before the man,

but, even granting him the right to enlarge upon the status of these ancillary figures in the poem, we must conclude that they do not symbolize "man and his illusions of perfection and greatness." In the first place (and I dwell on this specific error because it resembles a thousand other errors of statement about so-called symbols), these runners cannot symbolize both man and his illusions. Men are one thing; illusions of perfection are of another order. What the student perhaps meant was that the relation of the runner to his fame symbolizes the relation of man to his illusions of perfection. But the runner's fame lives in the minds of others and "dies" when they forget; whereas a man's illusions of perfection are his own ideas, and they "die" when he is disappointed or disabused or just diverted. One cannot symbolize the other, for the jump from one logical pattern to another cannot be accommodated to the runner-as-symbol. There is nothing in the poem which directs the reader to see in the situation of the runners or in the word "renown" a symbol of illusions of perfection; and any brief discussion will make this fact clear.

Now (to proceed) perhaps what the student meant to mean was that, just as the loss of fame involves bitterness or disappointment, so the loss of illusions of perfection involves bitterness or disappointment. The two losses have in common that they cause, say, bitterness. This purely abstract remark —which is a simple classification, that is, the identification of a quality or aspect that is present in two items—is certainly true in so far as it shows a property common to loss of fame and loss of illusions (which is all many students require to make them cry havoc or "Symbol!"). But can the runner properly be said to symbolize "man and his illusions of perfection"? Loss of fame and loss of a new boat would cause bitterness; but this fact hardly makes the runner symbolize loss of a new boat. He might as well symbolize a nation past its glory, a garden that has withered, a wrecked airplane, or a thousand other items that partake of the same quality or somehow relate to it. Examination shows that the connection between "runners whom renown outran" and "man and his illusions of perfection" is neither logical nor necessary nor particular nor (most important) exclusive.

Whenever we come upon the problem of symbolism, we are likely to be puzzled by a double-facedness that invites misinterpretations: There is the symbol which seems to "stand" for an institution or a situation or a problem. And then there is the accompanying fact that any situation or problem suggests dozens of similar or comparable problems which ring out around it like the ripples from a pebble dropped into a pond. When Robert Frost in "Stopping by Woods on a Snowy Evening" says,

> But I have promises to keep
> And miles to go before I sleep,

he is suggesting the thousand obligations and duties which sometimes make life burdensome. They range from a call down the road, which the reader imagines, through some shopping he has promised to do for his wife, through his long-range plans for planting orchards and paying mortgages, out to the burden of life itself which man has perhaps promised his god that he will bear. These notions are suggested by the poem's "promises" and "miles to go"—but can we say they are definitely symbolized in the poem? I think not. I think the student must be shown that he is dealing with the examples or instances which any situation evokes through the imagination. A symbol must have a specific referent or a cluster of them to which it is somehow specifically attached. There may of course be ambiguities, but ambiguities are not the same as the countless examples of "promises" and "miles to go" that one could imagine. If these phrases can be said to symbolize anything, it must be the idea of duty or obligation—and nothing more specific.

If there is a symbol in Frost's poem, it is the woods—"lovely, dark and deep"—which are identified by the clause that follows them as symbolizing the impulse to escape. This is particular; it is specific; it is an idea carefully prepared for in the poem and then clearly evoked through its symbol. But, then, what about the last word in the poem? Is "sleep" a symbol of death? I should say that death is just one of many instances suggested by the tension of obligation-and-escape which gives the poem its life. Life makes us yearn for death: the thought of death makes us value life. Then can one say that the woods symbolize death, the final escape? Again, I think not, because the woods seem to me specifically to symbolize an impulse (the return to the womb, even?) but not a concept or a state like death. If we can define the specific intention of a symbol, we can then allow our imaginations to universalize the problem or situation in which it operates without losing sight of the symbol's specific reference. The important thing is to make clear the difference between a specific symbol and the general truth that any situation suggests a thousand other comparable and similar situations. Hedda Gabler's pistols are almost literally physical extensions of her personality. They are perfectly fashioned and beautiful, but precise, inflexible, hard, cold, deadly, and destructive. They are, thus, extraordinarily specific symbols of Hedda's personality and of her relation to the other characters.

Returning, now, to Housman's athlete, we find two other passages where the situation is different, where rich and precise symbols can be identified:

> And early through the laurel grows,
> It withers quicker than the rose.
>
> .   .   .   .
>
> And find unwithered on its curls
> The garland briefer than a girl's.

The laurel is a definite symbol of victory. It is placed upon the winner as a sign of victory, and it has also come, in time, to symbolize victory in a way that a blue ribbon does not symbolize victory in a dog show. The distinction is that a sign points, whereas a symbol is. Except perhaps for the ardent dog-breeder, the blue ribbon merely indicates; yet, when the blue ribbon is used to decorate beer cans and beer advertising, we can see that it is on the way to becoming a general symbol—as the laurel has already done. It has become an emotional center and force. It evokes emotions directly, because of the meanings it has acquired; and this emotional force is more than the force of what it points to. The cross and the flag are outstanding symbols which plainly evoke direct responses, in contrast to such obvious signs as "W 26 STREET" or "LOGE" which do not have general direct emotional appeal (although they may have become symbols for certain individuals).

The rose, too, is a symbol. In this poem it can only be a symbol of beauty—because that is what it has generally been and that is what the poem makes it mean within its own structure. The fame that withers sooner even than beauty becomes an object of pathos, tenderness, and pitiful regret in a way that it can do only through the poet's juxtaposition of symbols both of which are possessed of their own magic. In the last two lines of the poem the same qualities of pathos and tenderness, fragile beauty and poignant regret, are evoked by the reappearance of the symbols in a setting. Before, they were presented as general symbols. Here they appear in a tableau—the strengthless dead gathered about the victorious garlanded youth, yearning toward the life which he reveals; the youth in his prime now in the place of shades; and the image too of a young girl, the rose of whose beauty has, in this place of shades, come to a pale, immobile, perfect stillness. She is there because the rose symbol evokes her; rose, laurel, girl, athlete, and shades make a very definite scene, a scene full of concrete particulars that not merely suggest but actually contain their universal meanings. It is not "reading into" the poem to see youth, beauty, and fame there immobilized before death; these universals must be felt by the responsible reader. Considerably more subtlety and discrimination are demanded of the student who will find that the young athlete has become identified both with and in the girl. Beauty fades, but in this poem it pathetically dies; the girl's qualities of fragility and perfection become assimilated into the image of the dead athlete.

Thus real symbols have magic and life, which they bring to a complex and subtle situation. Here the meaning glows in its own living form. It does not take us off into general ideas or remote and private applications of itself. Properly grasped, it is there to be felt rather than argued about. But argument is necessary and fruitful if it can be directed to show the follies of private improvisations as contrasted with the power of a symbol that has been apprehended as a living, incarnate idea. The nature of a symbol is the nature of poetry. The special quality of each is that it is powerfully concrete and yet suggests more than can be logically accounted for, because it enjoys a dimension of felt thought which cannot be reproduced by the phrases which attempt to describe it. Because the symbol has a life of its own which eludes mere logic, the instructor may suggest, unintentionally, that its meaning is indefinite and subject to private "interpretations." Again, if he feels the full force of a symbol, he may convey his reaction more clearly than he accounts for it, so that students who have not truly felt the same symbol may (naturally!) conclude that the instructor's reaction is subjective, private, even invented—and so set about devising comparable inventions. Here, I believe, is one major source of confusion about symbols.

A second appears where the instructor, or critic, thinks and explains more powerfully than he feels, so that he may come to define "symbolic" intentions which cannot really be felt by himself or anyone else. Conrad's "Secret Sharer" is a good piece to explore in this connection. It is the story of a captain who has taken as his first command a strange ship with a strange crew in strange waters. While the captain is alone on deck at night, speculating "how far I should turn out faithful to that ideal conception of one's own personality every man sets up for himself secretly" and ironically rejoicing "in the great security of the sea as compared with the unrest of the land, in my choice of that untempted life presenting no disquieting problems, invested with an elementary moral beauty by the absolute straightforwardness of its appeal and by the singleness of its purpose," a swimmer calls softly up to him from the water. He is the mate of the *Sephora,* anchored some distance away; he has killed a truculent sailor during a storm in a fit of fury brought on by exhaustion and exasperation; he is escaping the vindictiveness of his captain, who had been overcome with terror during the same storm. Conrad's captain takes this man, Leggatt, aboard, hides him in his own cabin at great risk, and later enables him to escape, again in the night, by swimming off to an obscure island.

Conrad's captain protects this "murderer" Leggatt because he is a "Conway boy"; because he recognizes a man of similar age, background, and abilities to his own; because Leggatt has, by his own secret standards, failed in the kind of test which the captain might face but has, in fact, not had to face yet. Thus Leggatt appears to the protagonist-captain as a sort of sacrifice who has absorbed the bad luck that might have defeated him. This comes out clearly when the captain muses, "And as to the chapter of accidents which counts for so much in the book of success, I could only hope that it was closed. For what favorable accident could be expected?"—suggesting that there is a certain amount of ill fortune afloat on the winds of chance which may or may not destroy a man by hitting him when and where he is most vulnerable. The test under which Leggatt failed might very well have destroyed the captain.

Conrad's view is pagan and classically tragic. Leggatt has not only absorbed the current ill fortune. He has also acted, symbolically, as the captain's potential other self; his fate, thus, has been a ritual—a symbolic ritual—sacrifice in which the captain has seen his tragic potentialities enacted and therefore forestalled. Religious ceremonies were originally, the anthropologists tell us, incantations, charms, spells, magic—methods of propitiating, managing, controlling, or duping the gods to avert their jealousy or wrath, to forestall their greedy designs, or to gain temporary control of their powers. One kind of incantation is the dance which imitates and thereby anticipates some divine action—and in doing so forestalls its menace or assumes its power. And as the dance is a ritual incantation, just so is the symbolic action of a story. The ritual dance of evil performed by Leggatt has satisfied (or perhaps duped) the gods and given the captain a chance to gain control of his ship, his crew, and himself. The risk that the captain takes in protecting Leggatt is, symbolically, his participation in this ritual forestalling. The climax of this symbolism comes, of course, when Leggatt's hat remains floating by the ship and enables the captain to know that he has enough sternway to come about and sail free of the rocks to which, in his part of the propitiating ritual dance, he has brought his ship dangerously close. Thus ritual and reality mingle to make the reader's hair stand on end, as the most effective symbolism always does. It is in this sense that Leggatt's story symbolizes what might have happened to the captain. It is also symbolic as incantation. Like all poetic symbolism, it lives in the story; indeed, it lives and grows in the story, gathering richness and dimensions in action.

I have described this symbolism according to my notion of a continuum: The story is literally about failure (or success) in a man's first major test. It tells, literally, that Leggatt has failed and that the narrator succeeds. It also shows that the captain might have failed because any man can fail under a certain combination of forces. Thus it moves into the universal and says something about the relation of chance and freedom in life. It also recognizes the subconscious and the fact that the will-to-fail (Freud's "death instinct") microcosmically reflects the force of chance in the macrocosm; it can make the captain see Leggatt as an alter ego—not just theoretically, but a felt other self—who dramatizes the captain's struggle against his own temptation to fail by indulging his anger at his stewart, his mate, and the exasperating captain of the *Sephora*. This identification goes so far that the captain for a moment doubts the "bodily existence" of Leggatt—and frequently speaks of his "double" and his "other self." All these meanings are concretely imbedded in the literal narrative.

But how far can one go? If Leggatt has failed, as he so plainly has, can he stand as "the psychological embodiment of the reality, the destiny, the ideal selfhood which the captain must measure up to"? And can he at the same time (as this critic says) be "the embodiment of the captain's moral consciousness"? Literally, Leggatt is strong and firm because, having failed, he has no expectations. Can he "stand for" an ideal to the untested captain? Such a reversal destroys the continuum; if it is possible, anything goes, for nothing can be proved.

Another analysis says:

> Kafka's "Hunger-Artist" and Conrad's "Secret Sharer" allegorize (though not exclusively) the problem of the spiritual disunity of the isolated artist.

And, as the writer warms to his task,

> "The Secret Sharer" is a double allegory. It is an allegory of man's moral conscience, and it is an allegory of man's esthetic conscience. The form of "The Secret Sharer," to diagram it, is the form of the capital letter *L*—the very form of the captain's room. (It is hinted at, again, in the initial letter of Leggatt's name.) One part of the letter *L* diagrams the allegory of the captain's divided soul, man in moral isolation and spiritual disunity. The other part of the letter represents the allegory of the artist's split soul ("the man who suffers and the mind which creates"). The captain stands at the angle of the two isolations and the two searches for selfhood.

Now I should say that these ingenious interpretations cannot be felt in symbols. The critic has protected himself by calling these meanings allegorical. In allegory there is no continuum between the levels of meaning. One meaning is not exclusively and necessarily contained in another. Indeed, the allegorical meaning requires a key of some sort; or else, as in this instance, it rests entirely upon the word of the critic. Allegorical meanings are not generally felt in the concrete particulars of a story; they are likely to be somewhat didactically indicated by the writer; and they demand a mental shifting of gears on the part of the reader—all qualities which symbols most definitely do not possess. Now when a critic elaborates this sort of allegory in "The Secret Sharer" he implies that Conrad put it there and meant his readers to find it and therefore that he included certain definite clues to it. I find more meanings in the story that I have described in my brief analysis, but nothing so specific as the captain's involvement in two distinct searches for selfhood—or that the two parts of the letter *L* stand for "the captain's divided soul" and "the artist's split soul." These meanings can be thought, but can they be felt?

The complexity of meanings that a poet can evoke with a rich symbol is little short of miraculous; and even more remarkable than the complexity is the clearness and precision of communication through symbols. Symbols are the artist's means of creating patterns of thought and emotion which did not previously exist and of communicating what had previously been ineffable. The challenge to the reader is to penetrate these symbols, to feel and think one's way into them, and so to participate in the artist's perception and creation. Above all, one must resist the temptation to overlay and smother the artist's creation with a creation of his own. The reader, too, must keep his eye steadily on the object.

Exercises

1. Discuss the symbolism in the following poems.

TO THE VIRGINS, TO MAKE MUCH OF TIME

Robert Herrick

> Gather ye rosebuds while ye may,
>   Old Time is still a-flying;
> And this same flower that smiles today
>   Tomorrow will be dying.
>
> The glorious lamp of heaven, the Sun,
>   The higher he's a-getting,
> The sooner will his race be run,
>   And nearer he's to setting.
>
> That age is best which is the first,
>   When youth and blood are warmer;   10
> But being spent, the worse and worst
>   Times still succeed the former.

Then be not coy, but use your time;
  And while ye may, go marry;
For having lost but once your prime,
  You may forever tarry.

THE EAGLE

Alfred, Lord Tennyson

He clasps the crag with crooked hands;
Close to the sun in lonely lands,
Ringed with the azure world, he stands.

The wrinkled sea beneath him crawls;
He watches from his mountain walls,
And like a thunderbolt he falls.

THE LAMB

William Blake

  Little Lamb who made thee?
  Dost thou know who made thee?
Gave thee life, and bid thee feed
By the stream and o'er the mead;
Gave thee clothing of delight,
Softest clothing, wooly, bright;
Gave thee such a tender voice,
Making all the vales rejoice?
  Little Lamb, who made thee?
  Dost thou know who made thee?   10

  Little Lamb, I'll tell thee,
  Little Lamb, I'll tell thee:
He is callèd by thy name,
For he calls himself a Lamb.
He is meek, and he is mild;
He became a little child.
I a child, and thou a lamb,
We are callèd by his name.
  Little Lamb, God bless thee!
  Little Lamb, God bless thee!   20

THE TYGER

William Blake

Tyger! Tyger! burning bright
In the forests of the night,

What immortal hand or eye
Could frame thy fearful symmetry?

In what distant deeps or skies
Burnt the fire of thine eyes?
On what wings dare he aspire?
What the hand dare seize the fire?

And what shoulder, and what art,
Could twist the sinews of thy heart?   10
And, when thy heart began to beat,
What dread hand? and what dread feet?

What the hammer? what the chain?
In what furnace was thy brain?
What the anvil? what dread grasp
Dare its deadly terrors clasp?

When the stars threw down their spears,
And watered heaven with their tears,
Did he smile his work to see?
Did he who made the lamb make thee?   20

Tyger! Tyger! burning bright
In the forests of the night,
What immortal hand or eye,
Dare frame thy fearful symmetry?

TO DAFFODILS

Robert Herrick

Fair daffodils, we weep to see
    You haste away so soon;
As yet the early-rising sun
    Has not attained his noon.
        Stay, stay,
    Until the hasting day
        Has run
    But to the evensong;
And, having prayed together, we
    Will go with you along.   10

We have short time to stay as you;
    We have as short a spring;
As quick a growth to meet decay
    As you, or anything.
        We die
    As your hours do, and dry
        Away

Like to the summer's rain;
Or as the pearls of morning's dew
Ne'er to be found again.   20

BECAUSE I COULD NOT STOP FOR DEATH*

Emily Dickinson

Because I could not stop for Death—
He kindly stopped for me—
The Carriage held but just Ourselves—
And Immortality.

We slowly drove—He knew no haste
And I had put away
My labor and my leisure too,
For His Civility—

We passed the School, where Children strove
At Recess—in the Ring—   10
We passed the Fields of Gazing Grain—
We passed the Setting Sun—

Or rather—He passed Us—
The Dews drew quivering and chill—
For only Gossamer, my Gown—
My Tippet—only Tulle—

We paused before a House that seemed
A Swelling of the Ground—
The Roof was scarcely visible—
The Cornice—in the Ground—   20

Since then—'tis Centuries—and yet
Feels shorter than the Day
I first surmised the Horses Heads
Were toward Eternity—

STOPPING BY WOODS ON A SNOWY EVENING†

Robert Frost

Whose woods these are I think I know.
His house is in the village though;

He will not see me stopping here
To watch his woods fill up with snow.
My little horse must think it queer
To stop without a farmhouse near
Between the woods and frozen lake
The darkest evening of the year.

He gives his harness bells a shake
To ask if there is some mistake.   10
The only other sound's the sweep
Of easy wind and downy flake.

The woods are lovely, dark and deep,
But I have promises to keep,
And miles to go before I sleep,
And miles to go before I sleep.

2. Symbols occur in prose as well as poetry. Examine James Joyce's "Araby" for characters, events, objects, and places that seem to have symbolic meaning.

ARABY‡

North Richmond Street, being blind, was a quiet street except at the hour when the Christian Brothers' School set the boys free. An uninhabited house of two storeys stood at the blind end, detached from its neighbours in a square ground. The other houses of the street, conscious of decent lives within them, gazed at one another with brown imperturbable faces.

The former tenant of our house, a priest, had died in the back drawing-room. Air, musty from having been long enclosed, hung in all the rooms, and the waste room behind the kitchen was littered with old useless papers. Among these I found a few paper-covered books, the pages of which were curled and damp: *The Abbot*, by Walter Scott, *The Devout Communicant* and *The Memoirs of Vidocq*. I liked the last best because its leaves were yellow. The wild garden behind the house contained a central apple-tree and a few straggling bushes under one of which I found the late tenant's rusty bicycle-pump. He had been a very charitable priest; in his will he had left all his money to institutions and the furniture of his house to his sister.

When the short days of winter came dusk fell before we had well eaten our dinners. When we met in the street the houses had grown sombre. The space of sky above us was the colour of ever-changing violet and towards it the lamps of the street lifted their feeble lanterns. The cold air stung us and we played till our bodies glowed. Our shouts echoed in the silent street. The career of our play brought us through the dark muddy lanes behind the houses where we ran the gantlet of the rough tribes from the cottages, to the back doors of the dark dripping gardens where odours arose from the ashpits, to the dark odorous stables where a coachman smoothed and combed the horse or shook music from the buckled harness. When we returned to the street light from the kitchen windows had filled the areas. If my uncle was seen turning the corner we hid in the shadow until we had seen him safely housed. Or if Mangan's sister came out on the doorstep to call her brother in to his tea we watched her from our shadow peer up and down the street. We waited to see whether she would remain or go in and, if she remained, we left our shadow and walked up to Mangan's steps resignedly. She was waiting for us, her figure defined by the light from the half-opened door. Her brother always teased her before he obeyed and I stood by the railings looking at her. Her dress swung as she moved her body and the soft rope of her hair tossed from side to side.

Every morning I lay on the floor in the front parlour watching her door. The blind was pulled down to within an inch of the sash so that I could not be seen. When she came out on the doorstep my heart leaped. I ran to the hall, seized my books and followed her. I kept her brown figure always in my eye and, when we came near the point at which our ways diverged, I quickened my pace and passed her. This happened morning after morning. I had never spoken to her, except for a few casual words, and yet her name was like a summons to all my foolish blood.

Her image accompanied me even in places the most hostile to romance. On Saturday evenings when my aunt went marketing I had to go to carry some of the parcels. We walked through the flaring streets, jostled by drunken men and bargaining women, amid the curses of labourers, the shrill litanies of shop-boys who stood on guard by the barrels of pigs' cheeks, the nasal chanting of street-singers, who sang a *come-all-you* about O'Donovan Rossa, or a ballad about the troubles in our native land. These noises converged in a single sensation of life for me: I imagined that I bore my chalice safely through a throng of foes. Her name sprang to my lips at moments in strange prayers and praises which I myself did not understand. My eyes were often full of tears (I could not tell why) and at times a flood from my heart seemed to pour itself out into my bosom. I thought little of the future. I did not know whether I would ever speak to her or not or, if I spoke to her, how I could tell her of my confused adoration. But my body was like a harp and her words and gestures were like fingers running upon the wires.

One evening I went into the back drawing-room in which the priest had died. It was a dark rainy evening and there was no sound in the house. Through one of the broken panes I heard the rain impinge upon the earth, the fine incessant needles of water playing in the sodden beds. Some distant lamp or lighted window gleamed below me. I was thankful that I could see so little. All my senses seemed to desire to veil themselves and, feeling that I was about to slip from them, I pressed the palms of my hands together until they trembled, murmuring: *O love! O love!* many times.

At last she spoke to me. When she addressed the first words to me I was so confused that I did not know what to answer. She asked me was I going to *Araby.* I forget whether I answered yes or no. It would be a splendid bazaar, she said; she would love to go.

—And why can't you? I asked.

While she spoke she turned a silver bracelet round and round her wrist. She could not go, she said, because there would be a retreat that week in her convent. Her brother and two other boys were fighting for their caps and I was alone at the railings. She held one of the spikes, bowing her head towards me. The light from the lamp opposite our door caught the white curve of her neck, lit up her hair that rested there and, falling, lit up the hand upon the railing. It fell over one side of her dress and caught the white border of a petticoat, just visible as she stood at ease.

—It's well for you, she said.

—If I go, I said, I will bring you something.

What innumerable follies laid waste my waking and sleeping thoughts after that evening! I wished to annihilate the tedious intervening days. I chafed against the work of school. At night in my bedroom and by day in the class-room her image came between me and the page I strove to read. The syllables of the word *Araby* were called to me through the silence in which my soul luxuriated and cast an Eastern enchantment over me. I asked for leave to go to the bazaar on Saturday night. My aunt was surprised and hoped it was not some Freemason's affair. I answered few questions in class. I watched my master's face pass from amiability to sternness; he hoped I was not beginning to idle. I could not call my wandering thoughts together. I had hardly any patience with the serious work of life which, now that it stood between me and my desire, seemed to me child's play, ugly monotonous child's play.

On Saturday morning I reminded my uncle that I wished to go to the bazaar in the evening. He was fussing at the hallstand, looking for the hat-brush, and answered me curtly:

—Yes, boy, I know.

As he was in the hall I could not go into the front parlour and lie at the window. I left the house in bad humour and walked slowly towards the school. The air was pitilessly raw and already my heart misgave me.

When I came home to dinner my uncle had not yet been home. Still it was early. I sat staring at the clock for some time and, when its ticking began to irritate me, I left the room. I mounted the staircase and gained the upper part of the house. The high cold empty gloomy rooms liberated me and I went from room to room singing. From the front window I saw my companions playing below in the street. Their cries reached me weakened and indistinct and, leaning my forehead against the cool glass, I looked over at the dark house where she lived. I may have stood there for an hour, seeing nothing but the brown-clad figure cast by my imagination, touched discreetly by the lamp-light at the curved neck, at the hand upon the railings and at the border below the dress.

When I came downstairs again I found Mrs Mercer sitting at the fire. She was an old garrulous woman, a pawnbroker's widow, who collected used stamps for some pious purpose. I had to endure the gossip of the tea-table. The meal was prolonged beyond an hour and still my uncle did not come. Mrs Mercer stood up to go: she was sorry she couldn't wait any longer, but it was after eight o'clock and she did not like to be out late, as the night air was bad for her. When she had gone I began to walk up and down the room, clenching my fists. My aunt said:

—I'm afraid you may put off your bazaar for this night of Our Lord.

At nine o'clock I heard my uncle's latchkey in the halldoor. I heard him talking to himself and heard the hallstand rocking when it had received the weight of his overcoat. I could interpret these signs. When he was midway through his dinner I asked him to give me the money to go to the bazaar. He had forgotten.

—The people are in bed and after their first sleep now, he said.

I did not smile. My aunt said to him energetically:

—Can't you give him the money and let him go? You've kept him late enough as it is.

My uncle said he was very sorry he had forgotten. He said he believed in the old saying: *All work and no play makes Jack a dull boy.* He asked me where I was going and, when I had told him a second time he asked me did I know *The Arab's Farewell to his Steed.* When I left the kitchen he was about to recite the opening lines of the piece to my aunt.

I held a florin tightly in my hand as I strode down Buckingham Street towards the station. The sight of the streets thronged with buyers and glaring with gas recalled to me the purpose of my journey. I took my seat in a third-class carriage of a deserted train. After an intolerable delay the train moved out of the station slowly. It crept onward among ruinous houses and over the twinkling river. At Westland Row Station a crowd of people pressed to the carriage doors; but the porters moved them back, saying that it was a special train for the bazaar. I remained alone in the bare carriage. In a few minutes the train drew up beside an improvised wooden platform. I passed out on to the road and saw by the lighted dial of a clock that it was ten minutes to ten. In front of me was a large building which displayed the magical name.

I could not find any sixpenny entrance and, fearing that the bazaar would be closed, I passed in quickly through a turnstile, handing a shilling to a weary-looking man. I found myself in a big hall girded at half its height by a gallery. Nearly all the stalls were closed and the greater part of the hall was in darkness. I recognized a silence like that which pervades a church after a service. I walked into the centre of the bazaar timidly. A few people were gathered about the stalls which were still open. Before a curtain, over which the words *Café Chantant* were written in coloured lamps, two men were counting money on a salver. I listened to the fall of the coins.

Remembering with difficulty why I had come I went over to one of the stalls and examined porcelain vases and flowered tea-sets. At the door of the stall a young lady was talking and laughing with two young gentlemen. I remarked their English accents and listened vaguely to their conversation.

—O, I never said such a thing!

—O, but you did!

—O, but I didn't!

—Didn't she say that?

—Yes. I heard her.

—O, there's a . . . fib!

Observing me the young lady came over and asked me did I wish to buy anything. The tone of her voice was not encouraging; she seemed to have spoken to me out of a sense of duty. I looked humbly at the great jars that stood like eastern guards at either side of the dark entrance to the stall and murmured:

—No, thank you.

The young lady changed the position of one of the vases and went back to the two young men. They began to talk of the same subject. Once or twice the young lady glanced at me over her shoulder.

I lingered before her stall, though I knew my stay was useless, to make my interest in her wares seem the more real. Then I turned away slowly and walked down the middle of the bazaar. I allowed the two pennies to fall against the sixpence in my pocket. I heard a voice call from one end of the gallery that the light was out. The upper part of the hall was now completely dark.

Gazing up into the darkness I saw myself as a creature driven and derided by vanity; and my eyes burned with anguish and anger.

Language and Logic

45.

RICHARD D. ALTICK

Deductive Reasoning

[An important kind] of formal reasoning is the deductive, by which one moves from a general truth or assumption to a particular conclusion. The classic way of analyzing this process is the syllogism: a rigidly organized series of three statements, the last of which is the conclusion drawn from the preceding two, which are called the major and minor premises. From the point of view adopted in this essay—that of the critical reader—the main importance of the syllogism is that it affords us a quick way of testing and perhaps exposing the incorrectness of a statement that is assumed to follow logically from certain premises.

In our everyday reading we seldom encounter statements ready-made into syllogisms. Instead, the logical antecedents of a statement are usually only implied or half-stated. To understand the reasoning by which a conclusion has been reached, we must, therefore, work backward by reconstructing the syllogism which seems to have been in the author's mind. Beginning with the statement in question, which serves as the conclusion of the syllogism, we build a major and a minor premise which the maker of the statement seems to have assumed to be true. In order to form a syllogism, we must often change the wording of the original statement. There is no harm in doing this, *provided always that we do not change in any way the thought of the author*. The words we select for our syllogism, if different from his own, must be equivalent to them in meaning.

A *major premise* may be derived in any of three ways: (1) It may be the product of an induction, that is, a generalization based on individual instances of verifiable fact, or from the verification of a hypothesis. (This is

From *Preface to Critical Reading*, by Richard D. Altick. Copyright, 1956, © 1960, Holt, Rinehart and Winston, Inc. Reprinted by permission.

why inductive and deductive reasoning are intimately connected. The result of an induction serves very often as the major premise of a deduction.) (2) It may be an unverifiable assumption, which may or may not have a considerable body of evidence to suggest its truth, but which in any case is assumed to be true for the purposes of argument. (3) It may be the result of another deductive argument.

In most syllogisms the *minor premise* is a statement that a single individual, or a smaller class, belongs to the larger class mentioned in the major premise. Or it may state that an individual or class has a characteristic which the major premise asserts is possessed by a larger class. The *conclusion,* or *inference,* is based on the relationship of the two premises. If each of the premises is true, and if the syllogism violates none of the rules governing deductive thinking, the conclusion will be true. To be sure, the statement made in a conclusion may be true even though the syllogism is faulty; but in such a case it is true for a reason other than that indicated in the syllogism. In other words, it is in itself a true statement, but not a valid deduction from the premises given. On the other hand, if either of the premises is false, a sound syllogism—one that obeys all the rules of inference—will produce a false conclusion.

Because the "middle term" (the term found in both premises) can occur only in four different positions, syllogisms have four basic forms. We shall, however, confine ourselves to the two most commonly used:

I

(Major premise)	A is B
(Minor premise)	C is A
(Conclusion)	C is B

II

(Major premise)	A is B⎱	(One of these premises
(Minor premise)	C is B⎰	must be negative)
(Conclusion)	C is not A [Or: No C is A]

In formal logic, the major premise of each of the above syllogisms must be "universal" (*all, always, none, never*). But for our purposes we shall modify the rule to allow proportional generalization—that is, statements that such-and-such is true in most cases or few cases. Since . . . terms like *most, frequently, some, sometimes, seldom, few* . . . are too vague to be useful, a more specific statement of proportion must be given: "half the time," "75 per cent of the cases," "one out of ten instances," and so on.

Now, let us take four ordinary sentences and reshape them into syllogisms. Numbers 1 and 2 illustrate the first form given above, 3 and 4 the second form:

1. "Mr. McGuire's a Catholic, so of course he must go to Mass."

(Major premise: A is B)   All Catholics are obligated to attend Mass.
(Minor premise: C is A)   Mr. McGuire is a Catholic.
(Conclusion: C is B)   Mr. McGuire is obligated to attend Mass.

[That is, since Mr. McGuire belongs to a class all of whose members have a certain characteristic, Mr. McGuire necessarily shares that characteristic.]

2. "You're likely to find that particular brand in Graham's store, because about 75 per cent of the men's clothing stores in this city carry it in stock."

(Major premise: A is B)   About 75 per cent of the men's clothing stores in this city carry that particular brand.

(Minor premise: C is A)   Graham's store is one of the men's clothing stores in this city.

(Conclusion: C is B)   Graham's store probably carries that brand. (I.e., there's a 75 per cent chance that it does.)

[That is, while not all stores carry a given brand of merchandise, 75 per cent of them do; therefore, though it is not certain that Graham's store does, it is likely to do so.]

3. "His wife isn't well educated. She doesn't know anything about science."

(Major premise: No A is B)   No well-educated person is ignorant of science.
(Minor premise: C is B)   His wife is ignorant of science.
(Conclusion: C is not A)   His wife is not well educated.

[That is, the lady spoken of has a characteristic which is asserted not to belong to any member of a given class; possession of that characteristic therefore excludes her from that class.]

4. "He doesn't have any excessive thirst, so he can't have a fever."

(Major premise: A is B)   All fever-stricken patients are excessively thirsty.
(Minor premise: C is not B)   This patient is not excessively thirsty.
(Conclusion: C is not A)   This patient does not have a fever.

[That is, the patient does not have a characteristic that is said to be universally true of a class, hence he does not belong to that class.]

In each of these examples, the conclusion is valid (the product of a formally correct syllogism), although it may or may not be true, depending on whether or not both premises are true.

Now for a few of the most frequent errors in deductive thinking. These are *among* the reasons (there are many more) why statements which seem, at first glance, to be perfectly "logical," turn out on analysis to be derived from unsound syllogistic arguments.

1. *The terms must be accurately and consistently defined.* No matter how the major premise has been obtained—whether by induction or deduction, or simply assumed as the first link in the present chain—the wording must be as exact and clear as possible. We have seen how ambiguous and misleading are such words as *normal, typical, average.* In addition, *all* terms must be defined as precisely as possible. "The intelligence level of Negroes is higher than that of whites": what, precisely, does that mean? "Intelligence" itself has never really been satisfactorily defined, although probably one may assume that for practical purposes the arbitrary standards of I.Q. tests are meant. But what does the phrase "intelligence level of Negroes" mean? The over-all average I.Q. of southern Negroes tested between 1930 and 1950? The I.Q. of Negroes now in the colleges and universities of six midwestern states? The I.Q. of Negroes enlisting in the United States Army? And what, precisely, does "that of whites" refer to? The generalization is phrased too vaguely, too loosely, for a syllogism to be soundly developed. It needs to be an exact statement which takes into account the limitations of the data upon which it is based.

Again, just what is a "business recession"? What statistical criteria are involved—what is the difference between a recession, a panic, and a slump? What is meant by "the greatest freedom and opportunity" which "democracy" (what is *it?*) is said to afford to the individual? Every such phrase cries out for definition. If it is left undefined, for each party to the argument to interpret according to his own wishes, the argument is worthless, because the parties will not be talking the same language. . . .

Hence, one of the first things to do in testing the logical validity of a statement is to determine just what the maker of the statement means by the terms he is using, and whether his terms mean the same thing in the conclusion that they were understood to mean in the premises. Shifting definition in the course of an argument invalidates the whole sequence of thought. A recent illustration comes from the field of medicine. At a meeting of the American Psychiatric Association, the drug thorazine was announced as having remarkable powers to relieve "depression." Now in medical usage, *depression* is a technical term referring to a whole group of symptoms, both physical and mental; depression is as much a malfunctioning of certain parts of the nervous system, resulting in bodily ailments, as it is a disturbed state of mind. But in the popular vocabulary, *depression* simply means "the blues." It is not surprising, then, that when a newspaper columnist read of the report, she translated *depression* into laymen's language and announced "the invention of a new pill that chases the blues away. . . . Obviously, the world is going to heck in a hack and as far as aspirin is concerned, we have reached the point of no return. But just as mankind was about to be permanently marooned in its misery, presto! A new kind of pink pill for pale people who, emotionally, are lower than a snake's abdomen." Medical men who read that column must have shuddered at the misrepresentation of what the "new mood-lifter pill" accomplished—all because the term *depression* changed meaning in its trip from the psychiatrists' meeting to the pages of a newspaper. (The uncritical reader would have responded this way: "People who suffer from depression will be helped by this drug. I suffer from depression. Therefore this drug will help me." But the term in the major premise does not mean the same thing that it does in the minor premise.)

2. *Any qualification in a premise must be faithfully retained in the conclusion.* This is, in effect, an extension of what has just been said. Here the vital point is that if a premise allows for no exception (*all, none, every, always, never* . . .), the conclusion must retain the same idea; and similarly, if a premise contains a proportional generalization of the *some-many-few-often* . . . variety, the conclusion must contain it too. In Example 2 above, the categorical conclusion that "Graham's store *will* have that particular brand" would have been unwarranted. The major premise said that 75 per cent of the stores in town carried the brand, hence there is only a 75 per cent chance that Graham's did.

It may not be really necessary, in ordinary writing, to be so careful to qualify one's statements. In practice, the writer tacitly allows for exceptions: "The rate of fire alarms [in most cities] is highest in the slums"; "the efficiency of stenographers [in nine cases out of ten] is improved if they work in air-conditioned offices"; "the children of divorced parents [as a rule] have two strikes against them in life." The danger remains, however, that the uncritical reader, not realizing that such exceptions are implied, will follow the reasoning through to an unjustified conclusion. "Psychologists," says a magazine article, "show that boys' minds mature more slowly than girls'." "Bob and Mary are both sixteen," thinks a parent, "therefore Mary's mind is more mature than Bob's." The writer means that *as a rule* his generalization holds true. The reader instead thinks that it is always true, hence necessarily applicable to Mary and Bob in particular.

This almost universal human habit of reducing things to the simplest possible terms is the weakness on which the unscrupulous writer thrives. Clever persuaders deliberately omit such words as *always, never, only, none but, every, all* . . . because if they appear, they signal the reader to take a second, more critical look at what is being said. Without them, a statement is more likely to be accepted at its face value. If we keep always in mind the fact that a statement can be positive and sweeping only to the degree to which its implied premises are positive and sweeping, we are well equipped to expose the false dogmatism of writers and speakers.

When we first read the adventures of Sherlock Holmes, we are impressed by the uncanny accuracy of his split-second deductions. But our admiration is somewhat tempered when we realize that much of it is due to the unwarranted positiveness with which the deductions were phrased.

In "The Case of the Norwood Builder," for example, Holmes welcomed John Hector McFarlane to his Baker Street rooms with these words: "I assure you that, beyond the obvious facts that you are a bachelor, a solicitor, a Freemason, and an asthmatic, I know nothing whatever about you."

"Familiar as I was with my friend's method," writes Dr. Watson, "it was not difficult for me to follow his deductions, and to observe the untidiness of attire, the sheaf of legal papers, the watch-charm, and the breathing which had prompted them."

The implication is that Holmes reasoned in this fashion:

Men who dress untidily are bachelors.
This man is dressed untidily.
This man is a bachelor.

—and so on with the other three deductions. On that basis, we are prone to assume that there could be no question whatsoever that McFarlane was everything Holmes deduced he was. But let us phrase the syllogism more strictly:

All men who dress untidily are bachelors.
This man is dressed untidily.
This man *must* be a bachelor.

Or:

A man who dresses untidily *can only* be a bachelor.
This man is one who dresses untidily.
This man *can only* be a bachelor.

Now we have brought the vital idea of *all* or *only* (which was hidden in the syllogism as previously stated) into the open, and the weakness of the major premise is exposed. Obviously it is untrue that *all* men who dress untidily are bachelors; there must be some untidy men who have loving wives at home. Therefore the conclusion—that this man *must* be a bachelor —is invalid. Maybe he is a bachelor, but the proof does not lie in the syllogism.

Actually, of course, what Holmes did, though his manner concealed the fact, was to count on the probabilities. A somewhat sounder syllogism— though still unsatisfactory, because *most* is too vague a word and it would be hard to prove the major premise—would be:

Most men who dress untidily are bachelors.
This man is dressed untidily.
This man *probably* is a bachelor.

Thus it appears that even though the odds may have been in favor of McFarlane's being a bachelor, it was quite possible that Holmes could have been mistaken. The degree of probability in the conclusion depended, as always in such reasoning, on the degree expressed in the major premise.

To sum up this important point:

(correct)   *All* Congressmen are United States citizens.
               Mr. Benton is a Congressman.
               Mr. Benton *must* be a United States citizen.

(wrong)   Sixteen of the twenty Congressmen from this state are Republicans.
               Mr. Morgan is a Congressman from this state.
               Mr. Morgan *must* be a Republican.
               [What is the correct conclusion?]

(correct)   *Only 10 per cent* of the towns in this county have over 5,000 population.
               The town in which I live is in this county.
               My town *probably* has less than 5,000 population.
               [I.e., there's only a 10 per cent chance that it has a population of over 5,000.]

(wrong)   March *usually* is a stormy month.
               This month is March.
               This month is *bound* to be stormy.
               [How many flaws can you find in this argument?]

(correct)   *All* the rivers on the western side of this watershed flow into the Gulf of Mexico.
               Two-thirds of the rivers I'm talking about are on the western side of this watershed.
               At least two-thirds of the rivers flow into the Gulf of Mexico.
               [Why say "at least"?]

(wrong)   *All* Quakers refuse to take oath.
               Ten of the twenty witnesses in this case are Quakers.
               Most of the witnesses in this case will refuse to take oath.

3. *The conclusion of a syllogism must not be identical with a premise.* This is the fallacy known as "begging the question." Since the whole purpose of deductive reasoning is to progress from one point (the premises) to another (the conclusion), an argument in which the two points are identical gets nowhere; it doubles back on itself, and is therefore sterile. "Begging the question" usually occurs in a statement which makes the same assertion in two different ways: "The reason why Sally is so mischievous is that she has just a little of the devil in her." Which is to say, A equals A. "This ordinance will certainly reduce juvenile delinquency, because it provides for

steps which will prevent crimes on the part of teen-agers." "Because it will stir up the frictions between us and our potential enemy which will eventually ignite the powder keg, this diplomatic policy will bring us closer to war." By assuming as true the very point he ostensibly is trying to prove, the arguer changes roles: he ceases to be a counselor at the bar, presenting the evidence that supports his case, and becomes the judge, who hands down a verdict before the trial starts. (In what way are the devices of name-calling and the glittering generally related to begging the question?)

Exercises*

1. Here are several syllogisms with one statement missing. From the information given in the other two statements, reconstruct the missing one:

a. (Major premise)   More than half of the members of this class have read some American literature in high school.
    (Minor premise)   Carol is a member of this class.
    (Conclusion)   _____

b. (Major premise)   _____
    (Minor premise)   Captain Turner is a pilot.
    (Conclusion)   Captain Turner does not have defective eyesight.

c. (Major premise)   All families threatened by the flood waters were safely evacuated.
    (Minor premise)   _____
    (Conclusion)   Our uncle and his family were safely evacuated.

d. (Major premise)   _____
    (Minor premise)   The proposal to share atomic information with other governments is part of our official policy.
    (Conclusion)   The proposal to share atomic information with other governments is motivated solely by self-interest.

e. (Major premise)   There was rain on twenty-two of last July's thirty-one days.
    (Minor premise)   The day I'm speaking of was last July 15.
    (Conclusion)   _____

2. Using a syllogism wherever necessary (sometimes more than one may be needed in a single case), analyze the soundness of the reasoning in each of the following statements. Are the premises correct? Does the conclusion necessarily follow from the premises? (When you recast a statement into syllogistic form, omit rhetorical flourishes like "everyone agrees," "obviously," etc.; . . . they are often used to conceal the lack of logic.)

    a. The large increase in church membership in recent years shows that the American people are becoming more religious.

* Exercises 1 and 2 are from *Preface to Critical Reading,* by Richard D. Altick, copyright, 1956, © 1960, Holt, Rinehart and Winston, Inc. Reprinted by permission.

b. We can go on our trip as we planned. The weather man says there won't be any snow for at least forty-eight hours.

c. The revolt in that South American country was caused by the antigovernmental factions that have long been plotting to overthrow the government.

d. Let's not go to the orchestra concert tonight. It's bound to be pretty bad—most of the program is devoted to contemporary music.

e. The solution is an acid. It turned the litmus paper red.

f. If you're old enough to fight you're old enough to vote.

g. I don't deny that I copied most of the theme from a magazine article. What's the matter with that? Everybody does it.

h. Anyone who refuses to testify before an investigating committee by invoking the Fifth Amendment automatically proves that he is guilty of something.

i. The Communist party is the most democratic party because it is the most uncompromising enemy of Fascism, and everybody admits that the real test of a party's democratic principles is the intensity of its opposition to Fascism.

j. This book contains only advice that is based on scientific evidence; if you follow its rules on how to write, you can be certain that people will understand you better.

k. To beg the question is to take an argument for granted before it is proved. This is one of the most insidious of fallacies, hence one of the most prevalent.

l. Boy, look at that red hair! I'll bet she has a temper.

m. The fact that there is no direct evidence that William Shakespeare, a minor Elizabethan actor, was capable of writing the great plays attributed to him proves that he didn't write them.

n. It is degrading to a man to live on a dole or any payment made to him without his being required to render some service in return. The reason is that he thus becomes, from an economic standpoint, a parasite upon the community as a whole, a position which is inconsistent with the maintenance of an individual's self-respect.

o. There are a few typographical errors in the answers in the back of this math book, so even though my answer doesn't agree with the one in the book, it's probably correct.

p. Last year Foam detergent outsold the next three brands combined. It's the best you can buy! There's no flakes like Foam!

q. Don't hurry. The train is due now, but you know how that railroad is. We have plenty of time.

r. My daughter Desdemona has always been innocent, modest, retiring. She had no interest in men. If she actually has eloped with Othello, he must have drugged her with some sort of magic potion. And since Othello is a foreigner, of a different race from ours, that is undoubtedly what he did. Those people know all about casting evil spells.

s. I never did trust him. He always had that sneaky look on his face.

t. If you prohibit the taking of pictures while the court is in session, you are interfering with the freedom of the press, which is a fundamental right guaranteed by the Constitution.

3. Comment on the validity of deductive reasoning in each of the following syllogisms:

a. All men are mortal.
   Socrates is a man.
   Therefore, Socrates is mortal.
b. All fish swim.
   All trout swim.
   Therefore, all trout are fish.
c. All Communists favor public housing.
   The Pope favors public housing.
   Therefore, the Pope is a Communist.
d. All citizens should do their utmost to prevent crime.
   It's a crime the way Charley squanders his money on wine, women, and song.
   Therefore, all citizens should do their utmost to prevent Charley from squandering his money on wine, women, and song.
e. All A's are B's.
   All C's are B's.
   Therefore, all A's are C's.
f. No one in his right mind could ever commit murder.
   Assassins commit murder.
   Therefore, assassins are insane.
g. No X's are Y's.
   No X's are Z's.
   Therefore, no Y's are Z's.
h. No mountain is taller than Mt. Everest.
   Any mountain is taller than no mountain.
   Therefore, any mountain is taller than Mt. Everest.
i. Only men of good will can successfully bring about brotherhood.
   The congressman is not a man of good will.
   Therefore, the congressman can not successfully bring about brotherhood.
j. All A's are B's.
   No C's are A's.
   Therefore, no C's are B's.

   4. Prepare a brief report on the deductive reasoning powers of Sherlock Holmes, Hercule Poirot, Nero Wolfe, Sam Spade, or any other fictional detective with whom you are familiar.

46.

MAX BLACK

The Process of Induction

The pattern by which examination of confirmatory instances leads to the acceptance of a generalization deserves very special attention since it is the basis of all knowledge about matters of fact, whether in everyday life or in the most advanced sciences.

Let us vary our illustrations by considering the example of the generalization *poison ivy stings*. The A state of affairs is that which occurs when we have a case of poison ivy; and the B state of affairs is a certain inflammation of the skin. Each confirmatory instance takes the positive form *this particular piece of poison ivy in contact with human skin is in fact accompanied by inflammation of the skin* $(A_n \rightarrow B_n)$, or the negative form *this particular case of absence of skin inflammation was in fact accompanied by absence of poison ivy* $(B'_n \rightarrow A'_n)$. Each such confirmatory instance, positive or negative, will normally be accompanied by information tending to eliminate factors other than A and B.

If the generalization is true, there must be indefinitely many confirmatory instances—*anybody* whose skin were to come in contact with poison ivy would suffer the corresponding inflammation of the skin. Nobody, however, could hope to observe *all* of these confirmatory instances; it would be impracticable even to try to observe all the *positive* cases in which poison ivy came into contact with the skin. *In establishing the truth of the generalization we examine a sample of the relevant confirmatory instances.*

The poison ivy generalization is a rather weak one, subject to all kinds of exceptions which would have to be made explicit if we wanted to talk about the subject with scientific accuracy. But even the most firmly established scientific generalization is no exception to the rule that a generalization is established by examining a *selection* of the cases (confirmatory instances) to which it applies. The student who begins to learn chemistry very soon finds out that the liquid known as hydrochloric acid turns blue litmus solution red; and this generalization, unlike that about poison ivy, holds without exception. Nevertheless, neither the student, nor his professors, nor the scattered hosts of practicing chemists, have ever tested *all* specimens of hydrochloric acid with respect to its effect upon blue litmus solution. The generalization about the acid is based upon *sampling*.

The process by which we pass from evidence concerning *some* members of a certain class of objects to an assertion concerning *all* members of that class, is known as **induction.** To speak more precisely, we shall mean by an induction a process of reasoning in which a proposition of the form *all P are Q* is asserted on the basis of a number of propositions having the form *this P is Q* and *that P is Q* and *that other P is Q,* etc. (We prefer the formula *all P are Q* in preference to *every case of P is also a case of Q,* from this point onward, for the sake of brevity.) By the usual "process-product ambiguity," it is customary to refer to the conclusion *all P are Q* as itself *an induction* from the evidence.

We shall find it often convenient to present the pattern of induction in the following shorter form:

$$P_1 \ \& \ P_2 \ \& \ \ldots \ \& \ P_n \ are \ Q$$
$$\overline{all \ P \ are \ Q}$$

in which the evidence for the inductive conclusion has been telescoped into a single statement.

Differences between induction and deduction. Induction and deduction are both processes of reasoning, i.e. methods by which we pass from evidence to a proposition which is "based upon" that evidence. The resemblance ends here. Let us consider some of the differences between the two processes:

1. In a deductive argument, the premises constitute *all* the evidence which is relevant to the soundness of the conclusion. The validity of the conclusion is determined by inspection of the premises, and the truth or falsity of other propositions has no bearing upon the result. In an inductive argument, the truth of the conclusion is determined by inspecting the premises, but the truth of *other* propositions *is* relevant. The truth of *all P are Q* requires that every confirmatory instance which shall later come to our attention shall accord with the conclusion, and a single case of a *P* which is not a *Q* will destroy the generalization. However firmly the conclusion of an inductive argument is established, it is always subject to possible rejection in the light of further evidence.

2. In a deductive argument, the test of the validity of the conclusion is consistency with the premises. More explicitly, if we try to assert both the premises and also the *denial* of a proposition which is a valid conclusion from those premises, we shall be contradicting ourselves.

Contrast this with the case of induction. Supposing I were to maintain that the very next specimen of hydrochloric acid I tested would *not* turn the testing fluid red. I should then be running counter to the accumulated evidence of thousands of experiments many times repeated by a great many chemists. *Nevertheless, there would be no logical contradiction involved in my denial of the inductive conclusion.* If a man says "I have seen you turn the litmus solution red a thousand times by adding the acid, but I still believe that the solution will turn green the next time," he is not contradicting himself. There is a *logical possibility* that he is right in supposing a miracle will occur. For the general evidence against the happening of miracles is *inductive;* and if our skeptic refuses to trust in such evidence, the utmost we can say in reply is "wait and see." The soundness of an inductive conclusion is *a matter of fact,* not merely a question of the logical relations between the premises and the conclusion of the inductive argument.

We can understand the implications of this last point more clearly by considering what is needed in order to present an inductive argument in deductive form. Suppose we are testing the ripeness of a watermelon by the familiar procedure of cutting out a small wedge. The inductive argument takes the form:

this wedge of melon is ripe

the whole melon is ripe

(We notice here the typical process from a sample to an entire class containing the sample. The example is particularly interesting because we seem to have here a *single* confirmatory instance as sufficient evidence for the generalization.)

Somebody who is impressed by the decisive character, the "finality," of deductive argument might try to convert our reasoning about the watermelon into a deduction. In order to do this, it is of course necessary to add an assumption, as follows:

this wedge of melon is ripe
[this wedge of melon is a fair sample of the whole melon]

the whole melon is ripe

To check that this argument is valid, we need a definition of the crucial phrase "fair sample." We might suppose that to call the wedge a fair sample of the whole melon is to assert that the properties of the wedge are a safe guide to the properties of the whole melon. We are, however, not concerned with *all* the properties of the wedge (*e.g.* with the number of pips it contains) but only with its ripeness. Thus, all we need is a definition of *being a fair sample with respect to ripeness.* What this means is clear enough: To say that the wedge is a fair sample with respect to ripeness is to say that *if the wedge is ripe the whole melon will be ripe.* Thus the deductive argument proposed becomes:

this wedge is ripe
[if this wedge is ripe the whole melon is ripe]
_____
the whole melon is ripe

The argument is valid—but it is quite useless to us *if we are interested in knowing whether the melon really is ripe*. For we have been forced to make an assumption which is the very question that we are trying to settle. Naturally, if we assume that knowledge of the ripeness of the wedge is enough to ensure the ripeness of the whole melon, we can *prove* deductively that the whole melon is ripe. But the proof is useless. Our purpose is to pass from knowledge about the wedge alone to knowledge about the whole melon. And this we can do only by applying an inductive procedure, *i.e.* by concluding in a manner *which has worked in the past* that the whole melon will have the desired property.

Induction is not an inferior kind of deduction. In the light of our discussion, you should now be on guard against the temptation to regard induction as a kind of inconclusive or otherwise inferior form of deduction. The point to emphasize is that induction and deduction are processes directed toward different ends. In deduction we discover what is logically involved in given propositions: it supplies us with a valuable means of organizing and re-organizing our assumptions and our beliefs. By means of *induction* we try to discover those generalizations which are true of the world in which we actually live.

No degree of piling on the amount of *inductive* evidence for a conclusion will ever bring us nearer to turning the induction into a deduction. If everybody alive in the world spent twenty-four hours a day for a whole year turning blue litmus red by the addition of hydrochloric acid, without in that time finding a single exception—the prediction that the test would succeed the next time it was tried would still be supported by induction. The step from *ten billion cases of P have been Q* to *all cases of P are Q* is not justifiable on deductive grounds alone. That we are, in certain cases, nevertheless justified in making the transition is something we have to learn, inductively, through knowledge of the kind of world we live in.

Induction and deduction have their different and equally proper functions. A reasonable man is one who uses the method appropriate to the problem before him. It would be as unreasonable to try to prove *deductively* exactly how much rain will fall next month, as it would be to establish inductively the solution to a mathematical problem by taking a poll of mathematicians. You will have realized by now, of course, that in most inquiries, it is reasonable to use deductive and inductive methods in combination.

(The all-important difference between induction and deduction is comparable to the difference between walking and swimming. Both walking and swimming are forms of locomotion, as deduction and induction are forms of reasoning. But swimming is not an inferior *kind* of walking in water—and induction is not an inferior kind of deduction suitable for use in cases where the premises are too weak to support the conclusion.)

Exercises

1. Would you use mainly inductive or deductive reasoning to determine the following?
a. Which brand of gasoline to buy
b. Whether a certain professor is a Communist
c. A cure for leukemia
d. The desirability of the four-day work week
e. The existence of God
f. Whether a tomato is a fruit or a vegetable
g. The best college in the United States
h. Popular opinion concerning the admission of Red China to the United Nations
i. Whether the Yankees will win the Pennant next year
j. Whether a pound of butter is rancid

2. Three frequent fallacies in induction are hasty generalization (a conclusion based upon insufficient evidence), improper sampling (a conclusion based upon evidence derived from unrepresentative sources), and stereotyping (a conclusion based upon a concept of a group which fails to consider differences among individual members of that group). Identify these fallacies in the following examples of reasoning.

a. The harmful effects of comic books on young people was shown in a recent survey. Of all children convicted of crimes in Chicago during 1960, seventy-five percent admitted that they read comic books often.

b. The high school student body was very surprised to learn that the new football coach had just published a book of poems.

c. To determine the purchasing habits of the average American, the team of pollsters interviewed thousands of shoppers in an exclusive suburb of New York City on an average day in December.

d. Because her first husband was an alcoholic and her second was a miser, Mary decided that all men were weak or selfish and that she would never marry again.

e. The dean of the medical school accused the science departments in the undergraduate colleges of failing to prepare premedical students for graduate work and cited the rising rate of failure in his school in support of his accusation.

f. Mr. Clement had heard that judges were extremely austere and was very surprised and pleased when Judge Hastings was kind to him during his recent trial.

g. Students who had failed Professor Brown's course were so uniformly negative in their opinions of him that the dean concluded that Brown was a poor teacher and did not rehire him.

3. Sampling is an essential process in the inductive method. Show in detail how you would go about selecting representative samples for a study of each of the following:

a. The sexual behavior of the American male

b. Television viewing habits of the American family

c. Attitudes of college students on birth-control pills

d. The nation's favorite candidates for the next presidential election

4. Nielsen, Gallup, Harris, and Roper are all polling services which depend upon sampling for their conclusions. Do some library research and investigate the techniques of one of these firms. How do they select their samples? Phrase their questions? Analyze their results? Report your findings to the class.

47.

ROBERT H. THOULESS

Pitfalls in Analogy

In the course of explaining any rather abstract matter, it is an advantage to use an illustration in order to make one's meaning clear. In an earlier chapter, when describing the evil of allowing our brains to degenerate into automatic organs, I said that this was like using a razor for digging the ground. In another book, when trying to explain that instincts which have no useful outlet in behavior find one for themselves, I compared this with what happens to a leaky boiler. Such illustrations are a common and useful device in explanation. A mental picture is easier to understand than a form of words.

These illustrations are merely intended to give a vivid picture of an abstract matter; they are not meant to be a method by which we can find out anything new about it. When, on the other hand, we use a concrete illustration in order to deduce new conclusions, it is no longer a mere illustration, it is an argument "by analogy."

Let us suppose that after the illustration of the boiler, I had pointed out that if the steam had no outlet at all the boiler would burst, and had concluded from this that if human instincts had no outlet in behavior a serious mental upheaval would result. Then, if I had no other reason for making this statement than the alleged resemblance between human instincts and steam in a boiler, I should be relying on an argument by analogy. In point of fact, there are other reasons for saying that the damming up of outlets for instinctive behavior leads to mental disorder (actual observations of human life), so the burst boiler can quite properly be used as an illustration. If, however, we had no such observations, the analogy from a boiler would obviously be a very weak and unconvincing reason for concluding that mental disturbance would follow a complete stopping-up of instinctive outlets.

The argument by analogy is not necessarily a dishonest or crooked method of thought, although it is a dangerous one always requiring careful examination. Reduced to its bare bones, it can be expressed as the argument that because N has the properties A and B which belong to M, it must also have the property C which too belongs to M. Displayed like this, the argument does not sound a very convincing one. Things which are alike in some respects differ in others. A and B may be respects in which M and N resemble one another, while C may happen to be a property in which M differs from N. A whale resembles a fish in the general shape of its body and in the fact that it lives in water. If we knew no better, an argument from analogy would lead us erroneously to suppose that the whale also resembled a fish in breathing by gills instead of lungs. There is a well-known principle in arguing from analogy that we can only safely argue from the possession of one set of characters to another if there is a causal connection between them. Even this principle would not, however, save us from error here, because the possession of gills is causally connected with the fact of living in water. This just happens to be a character in which whales differ from fishes.

An argument by analogy is not always expanded into a clearly recognizable form. When a writer refers to "the keen edge of an argument" or to "filling the mind of the child with facts," an analogy is implied, in the one case between an argument and a knife or sword, in the other between a mind and a bucket, bag, or box. Such an analogy, implied by the choice of words but not definitely expressed, is a metaphor. A metaphor may be used merely for the purpose of illustration, but if (whether purposely or not) the user of a metaphor draws any new conclusions from the implied analogy, then he is using the argument from analogy although in a somewhat disguised form. Metaphor abounds in all our thinking about abstract matters, and leads to the dangers to straight thinking resulting from unrecognized arguments by analogy.

Against a too drastic condemnation of argument by analogy, it may be urged that analogy underlies a great part of science and that many generally accepted scientific conceptions are really analogies from familiar objects. Thus molecules, atoms, and electrons are thought of and treated as if they were tiny fragments of solid matter; the ether of space as if it were an elastic fluid with peculiar properties; the behavior of falling bodies as if it were due to an attraction by the earth. The startling success with which physics used these conceptions to build up a consistent science and to predict facts which turned out on investigation to be true left men in no doubt that such analogical reasoning was sound at bottom. Indeed, the fact that these conceptions were analogies was very largely forgotten.

Yet, in every one of the three cases I have mentioned, a point was reached at which the analogy broke down. There were properties of electrons which were not conceivably those of lumps of matter, however small; it was found that if all space were filled with an ether it must have the absurd property of both moving and being stationary with respect to the earth at the same time; and certain properties of gravitational fields could not be expressed in terms of invisible elastic threads.

So the most recent physical science turns away from all these concrete representations and expresses observable facts by means of mathematical equations. Thus it becomes entirely incomprehensible for most of us, for we must think in terms drawn from what we can see and handle—that is, by analogies. Such analogies help us very little in comprehending a four-dimensional space-time system and not at all in grasping the latest developments of the quantum theory.

We must not conclude that thinking by analogy has proved itself a thoroughly unsound method of thought. Our scientific thinking is throughout largely dependent on analogy and yet has proved an invaluable guide to the discovery of new truth. Darwin was led to his theory of the origin of species largely by consideration of analogies between the activities of the breeder and the conditions under which animals and plants survive in the wild state, and this analogy is embodied in the term "natural selection." Similarly, the very fruitful conception of "the struggle for existence" is based on an analogy between these conditions of survival and a physical struggle in which the stronger kills the weaker. Even when in physics we have succeeded in transcending the analogies by which our first steps were guided, this has only been possible because these analogies guided our thought about molecules, lines of force, gravitational attraction, etc., along right lines.

The final fate, however, even of these solidly established analogies of physical science reënforces the conclusion already suggested: analogies are a valuable guide as to the direction in which to look for truth, but are never final evidence as to what we shall discover. We must not forget too that science has also followed analogies which have misled her and that the valuable analogies are those which have been selected because of their power of predicting new truth. Combustion was at one time attributed to a material called "phlogiston," which was supposed to leave the burning object. In the same way, Lamarck was misled by a false analogy when he attributed the adaptations of organisms to a process resembling that of the changes which take place in the body when part of it is exercised by use. He supposed that the long neck of the giraffe was due to the cumulative effect of successive generations of giraffes reaching up to high leaves, just as the arm muscle of an individual who habitually lifts heavy weights will increase in girth. A similar misleading analogy in psychology was Mesmer's guess that the phenomena of hypnotism were due to a "nervous effluence" proceeding from the fingertips of the hypnotizer.

The examples we have given of successful analogies in the history of science show how very far a good analogy may prove to be a true guide. A good guide whose reliability is certain to give out somewhere can, however, only be treated in one way by sensible people—with caution. We can never feel certain of a conclusion which rests only on analogy, and we must always look for more direct proof. Also we must examine all our methods of thought carefully, because thinking by analogy is much more extensive than many of us are inclined to suppose.

Analogies also underlie much of our thinking about human beings and their institutions—that is, in psychology and the social sciences. When, for example, we speak of "distressed industries," we are thinking of these industries as if they were themselves human beings and not merely the modes of employment of human beings. Such a way of thinking may be partly appropriate, but it may also be partly misleading. When the patriot says, "What matter how I suffer, so long as my country prospers?" he is thinking of his country as a kind of super-person. This analogy may lead to the appropriate and admirable behavior of sacrificing himself for the good of his country. Some too-fervent nationalists are led by this analogy, however, into a kind of thinking which may be expressed as: "What matter how I and all my fellow-countrymen suffer so long as our country prospers?" This is obviously pushing the analogy beyond the point at which it ceases to be a reasonable guide to conduct. Common sense demands that one should remember that the prosperity of the country is only a picturesque way of expressing the prosperity of Mr. Brown, Mrs. Brown, and their family, of Mr. Jones, Mrs. Jones, and their family, and of a few million other people, and that unless the happiness of these individuals is secured, there is no reasonable sense in which their country can be said to prosper.

In psychology, too, much of our thinking has been based on physical analogies, and in the past these analogies have proved less trustworthy than the analogies we have mentioned in physics. The way of thinking of the mind as composed of separate "faculties" of memory, imagination, etc., seems to be based on analogy with the arms, legs, etc., which are parts of the body. Careful investigation has shown that many of these "parts" of the mind have no claim to existence at all. The grand theory of "association of ideas" treated ideas as if these were like separable physical things linked by physical bonds. This way of conceiving thought proved serviceable over a certain range of facts, but it breaks down on a closer study of those mental processes in which there are no separable ideas at all.

Our more modern psychological analogies should also be distrusted. "Mental energy" or "libido," for example, is thought of as if it were a stream which, if it is dammed by hindrances to love in adult life, may overflow its earlier channels of our childhood's affections. We may use such an analogy with confidence so far as actual observation of human life gives us reason to believe that it is a reliable guide; we may use it too to suggest new possibilities to be tested afterwards by actual observation; but we cannot draw new conclusions from it as to how human beings will behave and suppose that, apart from observation, these will possess any scientific validity.

So far we have been dealing with analogies that are, at any rate, the best available; they do not contain obvious imperfections although they may be of limited reliability as methods of discovering truth. In argument, however, one frequently meets with analogies which are so imperfect that their use must be attributed either to the incompetence or to the dishonesty of the user.

For example, the view that a revival of internal trade was sufficient to restore prosperity has been derided by reference to a dog living by eating its own tail. Let us consider this analogy carefully. If we assume the tail of an animal will go on growing after being bitten off (which is quite possible though not, as it happens, true of a dog), then the case of such an animal eating its own tail does present some analogy with a country living on internal trade. The body-building and energy-supplying elements in the food of the dog correspond to the consumable goods in the country. The argument is intended to prove that the country could not continue to exist without importation of such goods from outside.

On looking more deeply into the argument we see that there are vital differences between the two cases which vitiate the analogy. In the body of a dog there is necessary wastage of its food-stuffs to supply the animal with heat and movement, and no possibility of replacement of this wastage except by taking in food from outside. It is physically impossible for the dog to generate his own proteins and carbohydrates from nothing, so, however generously his tail went on growing, he would be bound to die of starvation in the end if he had nothing but that to eat. The consumable goods of a country differ in this essential respect. Wealth can be generated in a country without taking in anything from outside, and this happens whenever labor is usefully employed. Every time a man sows a grain of corn and reaps an ear, or joins together two or more pieces of material to form a serviceable instrument, he is increasing the country's goods. The point, therefore, at which the dog eating his own tail supports the conclusion of the argument is the very respect in which the analogy is imperfect. What is contended may well be true, but it certainly cannot be proved by this argument.

I have also heard the democratic election of members of Congress attacked on the ground that children are not regarded as capable of electing their own teachers. Again, however, the analogy is obviously imperfect. Adult men and women are presumed to know more about the qualities required of an efficient ruler than children know about those of a good teacher. Moreover, governing and teaching are such very different functions that a method of selection serviceable in the one case may not be in the other. In addition, the democratic selection of the governing class partly serves to secure that those who rule shall not do so in their own interest; no similar problem arises with teachers. In fact, there is so little analogy between the selection of teachers and a Congressional election that no conclusions can safely be drawn by analogy from one to the other, whatever other weighty and reasonable objections may be urged against democracy.

The worst that can be urged against such arguments as the above is that the analogies are very imperfect—that is, that they break down on examination. A still greater degree of imperfection is to be found when there is no analogy at all and an argument is used in the form of an argument from analogy when there is no reason whatever why the same concrete illustration should not have been used in the opposite way. A Victorian bishop, for example, said that virtue grew when watered by war's red rain. He might just as well have said that vice grew when watered by war's red rain, or that virtue died when watered by war's red weed-killer. Such an argument has so little logical justification that we may wonder why it is not immediately rejected.

This leads us to a point in psychology commonly neglected in theoretical discussions of analogy. Whatever may be urged against the logical convincingness of an argument by analogy, it remains true that any analogy, good, imperfect or obviously absurd, tends to produce conviction in the same immediate and unreasonable way as does repeated affirmation or a good slogan. If you make an argument in the form "*A* is *B,* just as *C* is *D*" (where *A* and *B* are abstract or controversial while *C* and *D* are concrete and familiar), then your hearers will immediately tend to believe that *A* is *B* quite independently of any real analogy between *A/B* and *C/D*. If the relationship between *C* and *D* can form a picture in the mind, this makes the process of acceptance easier, but I do not think that this is essential. The mere fact that the argument is in the form of an analogy is often enough to force immediate irrational acceptance.

There seems to be no other explanation of the extraordinary extent to which otherwise intelligent people become convinced of highly improbable things because they have heard them supported by an analogy whose unsoundness should be apparent to an imbecile. We hear them say: "Mr.

Willoughby Snooks was so helpful and convincing in his address yesterday. He said that right thinking will remove disease from our bodies just as a policeman will remove a burglar from our house. I always used to feel a difficulty about the cure of disease by thought, but I see it quite clearly now."

"But," you may protest, "getting rid of disease by merely thinking about it is not in the least like getting a policeman to put a burglar out of your house. If you must have an analogy, it seems to be more like dealing with a burglar by going to sleep again and dreaming he isn't there." Your protest is obviously right. The speaker has been led to the absurd opinion that physical disease can be cured by mental methods through his (or her) tendency to accept an argument in the form of an analogy, however loose the analogy may be.

This device of commending a statement by bringing forward an argument in the form of an analogy which has no real force is a pretty common one. At election times, thinking in words seems to be very largely replaced by picturesque metaphors and analogies. Flowing tides, harpooned walruses, opponents trimming their sails or casting away their sheet-anchors, replace the more prosaic ways of thinking of normal times. No doubt it all aids impassioned conviction, although it may be doubted whether this kind of thinking does much towards solving the real problems of the country.

Typical of this tendency is the speech of a politician who referred to a radical opponent as "sailing as near to the socialist wind as he can without upsetting his frail craft."[1] The speaker has given no reason beyond mere assertion that his opponent would be as socialistic as possible, but in a way that carries much more conviction than the bare verbal statement. The picture of the radical leader timorously edging his boat as close to the wind as he dare sticks in the mind persistently and is accepted readily: if the speaker had said bluntly what he meant instead of putting it in the form of an analogy, it is probable that his hearers would have been less inclined to believe him.

While, therefore, thinking by analogy is not to be regarded as necessarily crooked thinking, the use of an imperfect analogy may be a really crooked argument. Much more crooked is the last trick we have mentioned of using a metaphor or an argument in the form of analogy when no true analogy

[1] To object that sailing too near the wind is not liable to upset a boat, but only to make it stop, would be to lay one's self open to a just charge of "diversion by irrelevant objection." It shows, however, ignorance and incompetence to make such a slip in an analogy or in a metaphor, for, even if the objection is not made, it will occur to the minds of many hearers and interfere with the process of creating belief. Many candidates in fishing districts have aroused mirth instead of conviction by inept metaphors of fishing and sailing. Of the same order of error is the "mixed metaphor" in which different parts of the picture suggested are inconsistent with one another, such as the newspaper report of the Allied soldiers "opposed to a numerical superiority of the cream of the German army tuned to concert pitch."

exists at all. Let us call this device a "forced analogy." Although these two dishonest devices in argument may be regarded as different degrees of the same defect, it seems better to treat them as distinct errors, since they are used in a different way and demand different methods of refutation.

Imperfect analogies occur commonly in serious discussion and are best dealt with by simply pointing out where the analogy breaks down. This is, for example, what I did with the argument of the dog eating its own tail.

Forced analogies, on the other hand, are commonly found in the course of public speeches. Their looseness is too obvious to stand against the kind of criticism they would meet in free discussion. They rely for their effect on the readiness of the mind to accept immediately any vivid metaphorical or analogical presentation of a matter. When one finds oneself driven to belief by a well-worded analogy like that of virtue watered by war's red rain, one can begin by examining how close the analogy is. Realizing that it is not at all close, one can try other analogies, as that of vice watered by war's red rain. Finding that these have no less force than the original analogy, the nature of the device used is apparent and its effect in forcing conviction disappears.

Exercises

1. Comment on the validity of each of the following uses of analogy in the reasoning process.
   a. Despite the fact that three people died in a fire in his apartment house, the landlord refused to install a sprinkler system because he felt that to do so would be like locking the barn door after the horse had been stolen.
   b. I see nothing wrong with divorce. Wedlock's like wine—not to be properly judged until the second glass.
   c. Man does not attempt to negotiate with a mad dog. He properly takes a club and with one deft blow protects himself and his community from danger. It follows that the United States is foolish in humoring the mad dogs of the Kremlin in an attempt to negotiate a disarmament treaty with the Russians at Geneva.
   d. Twentieth century social history has shown that in countries like Sweden and England, where the aged and indigent were unable to procure adequate medical care, socialized medicine has been accepted despite resistance from the medical profession. Such is the situation in the United States, and we should have recognized the inevitability of some kind of government-sponsored medical program.
   e. You would never bet anyone that you'd die, that your car would be stolen, or that your house would burn down; then why buy insurance? When you do, that's exactly what you're doing—wagering that some calamity will happen to you.

f. Never lament a broken romance, because women are like street cars—if you
   miss one, there will always be another along in a few minutes.

g. We should never waste our pity on murderers awaiting their fate in the electric chair, for Nature has condemned us all to death—only with the time and
   place of execution unknown.

   2. Devise arguments by analogy based on the following comparisons:

a. The human body is a machine.

b. Ballots are really bullets and an election is a war.

c. Communism is like a cancer.

d. All the world's a stage.

e. The mind of man at birth is like a blank tablet.

f. Religion is the opiate of the people.

   3. Each of the following speeches makes a point which is based on an analogy.
Comment on the effectiveness of each analogy and discuss the extent to which
each is justified.

a. I have no respect for universities, corporations, the Congress, both Houses or
   the presidency, the office or the man who occupies it. They're supposed to
   believe in law and justice but they have done a miserable job. The church is
   like the wicked witch in Cinderella and Jesus Christ is the poison apple that
   puts the black man into a deep and profound sleep.

   (Ernie Chambers, a Black Power leader from Omaha, quoted in the
   New York Times, January 22, 1968, p. 18)

b. The United States—and most of the rest of the rapidly urbanizing world—is
   going to be a very strange country indeed if the problems of the city are not
   resolved within a reasonable period of time. The city is the heart and brain
   of an industrial society. And before we let them deteriorate and decay, perhaps we should give some thought to that famous beast, the Brontosaurus,
   who is supposed to have disappeared from the earth because it took too long
   for a message to travel from his forebrain to his hind-brain and vice versa.

   (F. J. Borch, president of General Electric, delivered November 15, 1967)

c. After Congress had established a forbidden list of hundreds of items which
   nobody in America could ship to any communist country sending supplies to
   the enemy, President Lyndon Johnson, on October 12, 1966, by Executive
   Order—in defiance of the expressed intentions and desires of Congress—
   opened up for unlimited and unlicensed shipment over 400 items of supplies
   to Russia and her satellites in Europe; and in February of this year, increased
   it by another 40. So we have about 440 of those items now being shipped.
   The argument is: "We're building bridges." My answer is that when you
   build a bridge, you ask yourself first of all: where does it lead? To what
   destination does it take you? And the bridge built toward disaster, in my
   opinion is worse than no bridge at all.

   (Senator Karl Mundt, delivered at American Legion Convention,
   August 27, 1967)

d. A little over a year ago the ship of state was heading for the rocks. The
   skipper had to change his course, suddenly, and many of his officers and most
   of his crew deserted. It was a case of all hands to the pumps, and I signed

on with my friends, not for six months or a year; I signed on for the duration, be the weather fair or foul, and I am going to stick to the ship, whether it goes to the bottom or gets into port, and I think the latter end is a good deal more likely.

> (Stanley Baldwin, stating why he did not intend to resign his post in October, 1932)

4. What analogies are implicit in the phrases *a sick society, the prostitution of ideals, the Iron Curtain, a price war,* and *a raw deal?* What other "hidden" analogies can you think of?

48.

DANIEL J. SULLIVAN

Linguistic Fallacies

No system of words, no matter how refined or elaborate, can perfectly translate the subtleties of thought or reflect the infinite variety within reality. There will always be an unexpressed margin between language and thought, and this is always a potential source of misunderstanding. Words, too, have their own way of behavior, their own patterns, relationships, and laws of association. We are sometimes inclined to assume that things themselves will behave in the same way—joined and separated, added and subtracted— as the words (or mathematical symbols) that stand for them.[1] This disparity between the universe of words and the world of concrete things creates, again, an ever-present possibility of error. Logicians must therefore pay close attention to language as one of the principal sources of fallacy.

FALLACIES OF EQUIVOCATION

Fallacies of equivocation, sometimes called *semantic fallacies,* follow upon the use of terms (words or phrases) which have more than one distinct

[1] See Aristotle: "It is impossible in a discussion to bring in the actual things discussed: we use their names as symbols instead of them; and therefore we suppose that what follows in the names, follows in the things as well, just as people who calculate suppose in regard to their counters. But the two cases (names and things) are not alike: For names are finite and so is the sum total of formulae, while things are infinite in number. Inevitably, then, the same formulae, and a single name, have a number of meanings." *Sophistical Refutations,* 164 a.

meaning.[2] These may be words written in the same way: "punch" may refer to an instrument for cutting holes, a blow with the fist, a mixed drink, a species of draft horse. Or, they may be words spelled differently but pronounced similarly: "beer" and "bier." The term "dispense" is equivocal in the druggist's sign, "We dispense with accuracy." A famous example of equivocation is Calvin Coolidge's response, "I do not choose to run," when asked if he was available for another term as President. The world is still debating whether he meant that he did not desire to run (but would do so, if pressed), or whether he meant that he had resolved (made a firm decision) not to run.

Some terms, employed in a wide variety of contexts and sometimes over centuries of time, have taken on so many meanings that it is very difficult in a long discussion to avoid slipping from one meaning to another. The word "liberal," for instance, as it was used in the nineteenth century by John Stuart Mill or Pius IX, was in one of its meanings the exact opposite of the term as used today by Walter Lippmann or Barry Goldwater. Terms of similar elasticity will readily suggest themselves: "freedom," "democracy," "conservative," "natural," "right," "duty," "progress," "pleasure," "happiness," "good," and so forth. When one important school of philosophers says that every pleasure is good, and another large group at the same time says that no pleasure is good, there is a reasonable presumption that either "pleasure" or "good" is being used equivocally.

Equivocation in argument leads to the fallacy of four terms:

Whatever is sharp is pointed.
Vinegar is sharp.
Therefore vinegar is pointed.

Since the term "sharp" stands for two different realities, the form of the apparent syllogism is really this:

Every *A* is *B*.
But *C* is *D*.
Therefore every *C* is *B*.

The sophists, who eagerly exploited the possibility of equivocation, "proved" the simultaneous existence of contraries by arguments such as the

[2] Equivocal terms should be carefully distinguished from analogical and metaphorical terms, which are equivocal only if literally interpreted.

Some logicians assimilate fallacies of equivocation to fallacies of context, on the ground that it is the context that is ambiguous rather than the terms themselves. Thus *pen,* which is equivocal in that it is applicable either to a small enclosure or to a writing instrument, is not equivocal when used as a class name for a Parker, a Waterman, etc. What all can agree on is that it is the way in which homonyms are *used* which determines whether or not they will be a source of fallacy.

following: "The same man is both seated and standing, and he is both sick and in health: for it is he who stood up who is standing and he who is recovering who is in health: but it is the seated man who stood up and the sick man who was recovering."[3] The equivocation lies in the change in the universe of discourse in which the term "man" is used—it is the man who was seated and who was sick (past tense) who stands up and is well (present tense). By a similar juggling of the verb "to be" the sophists pretended to prove that being and non-being were identical: nothing *is;* that is, what has no being is being.

The sophists' use of equivocation was often on the level of mere quibbling—a play on words which may have puzzled but did not really deceive. Some forms of humor, particularly the pun, trade on this same possibility of double meanings in language.

There is, finally, the use of ambiguous language to conceal the truth; in this sense "equivocation" has become a synonym for "lie." Adolf Hitler, in *Mein Kampf,* showed that a lie could be a source of fallacy if it were big enough. The very bigness of the lie is an invitation to belief, on the grounds that no one would affirm such an enormity if it were not true:

> . . . the magnitude of a lie always contains a certain factor of credibility, since the great masses of the people in the very bottom of their hearts tend to be corrupted rather than consciously and purposely evil, and that, therefore, in view of the primitive simplicity of their minds, they more easily fall a victim to a big lie than a little one, since they themselves lie in little things, but would be ashamed of lies that were too big. Such a falsehood will never enter their heads, and they will not be able to believe in the possibility of such monstrous effrontery and infamous misrepresentation in others.[4]

AMBIGUOUS SENTENCE CONSTRUCTION

Ambiguity in the grammatical structure of a sentence leads to the fallacy of amphiboly, or fallacies of syntax.[5] This fallacy differs from the fallacy of equivocation in that the double meaning stems not from the ambiguity of a word or phrase but from a word order that permits more than one meaning in a sentence. In English, this fallacy results most often probably from the failure to make clear the antecedents to which pronouns refer, as in this sentence:

[3] Aristotle, *Sophistical Refutations,* 165 b 39.
[4] Hitler, *Mein Kampf,* Ralph Manheim (trans.), Houghton Mifflin Company, Boston, 1943, vol. 1, chap. 10.
[5] Syntax, from the Greek word meaning "order," refers to the laws governing the arrangements of words in sentences.

Peter told Paul's friend that he would go with him.

No less than six meanings are possible here:

1. *Peter told Paul's friend that he (Peter) would go with him (Paul).*
2. *Peter told Paul's friend that he (Peter) would go with him (Paul's friend).*
3. *Peter told Paul's friend that he (Paul) would go with him (Peter).*
4. *Peter told Paul's friend that he (Paul) would go with him (Paul's friend).*
5. *Peter told Paul's friend that he (Paul's friend) would go with him (Peter).*
6. *Peter told Paul's friend that he (Paul's friend) would go with him (Paul).*

Other examples of the same kind:

He had five children, three boys and girls, the eldest of whom died in an accident.

Daumier was the son of a Marseilles glazier who wrote a little poetry on the side and who thought so much of his talent that he decided to move to Paris.

The preacher spoke briefly, much to the delight of the congregation.

The need for brevity in headlines, or in want ads, is a potent source of syntactical ambiguity:

WOMAN ENDS LIFE OF MISERY WITH PLASTIC BAG.

The failure to punctuate can also be a source of misunderstanding:

He only was mentioned in the will.
He, only, was mentioned in the will.

If he goes, then it will be disastrous.
If he goes then, it will be disastrous.

Deliberate syntactical ambiguity was the device by which the oracles of ancient Greece and Rome contrived to be on the right side, no matter what happened. Herodotus tells how Croesus, King of Lydia, was betrayed into a disastrous war by the oracle of Delphi, who ambiguously assured him that if he attacked Persia, he would destroy a mighty empire. It was Croesus' empire, of course, which was destroyed.[6]

---

[6] Cicero, in his treatise, *On Divination,* Bk. 2, 56, gives a number of instances of oracular double talk. Edition trans. by Hubert M. Poteat, University of Chicago Press, Chicago, 1950.

COMPOSITION AND DIVISION

Composition is the fallacy of taking collectively what is meant to be taken one by one. The fallacy of division is the converse: taking one by one what is meant to be taken collectively. The fallacy may concern words or things. In argument, it results in a syllogism with four terms:

The students at this school are from thirty different states.
You are a student from this school.
Therefore you are from thirty different states.

"Student" in the first premise is, of course, used collectively; in the second premise, distributively. That is, the same word stands for two different things, so that there is no true middle term.

The next example involves a transition from distributive to collective:

3 and 2 are odd and even.
3 and 2 are 5.
Therefore 5 is odd and even.

Aristotle gives it in this way:

3 and 2 are odd and even.
Therefore 3 and 2 are odd and 3 and 2 are even.

One of the common causes of this fallacy stems from the assumption that what is true of the whole must be true of the parts, and vice versa. On this basis a person may argue that, because every episode in a play or novel is plausible and lifelike, therefore the story as a whole is plausible and lifelike. Cooperative undertakings often suffer from this same illusion: a play or a motion picture must be good because every actor can be counted on for a star performance; a church jointly decorated by ten of the leading artists of the day must be a model of artistic excellence. One might argue, again, that because Americans are generous, therefore Sam Smith of Madison, Wisconsin, is generous. It is true, of course, that the whole may show the characteristics of each of the parts, or contrariwise. The fallacy consists in holding that they *must* do so just because they are related as part and whole.

Sectional and group prejudices reflect the fallacy that what holds good for the parts necessarily holds good for the whole. Thus, a high tariff against citrus fruits will increase the wealth of Florida and California, or a quota on woolen imports will augment the prosperity of Connecticut and Massachusetts. Since these states are part of the United States, it must follow that the United States as a whole must benefit from this regional legislation. The statement, "What is good for General Motors is good for the country" is another version of the same fallacy. A more sophisticated example comes from John Stuart Mill: ". . . each person's happiness is a good to that person, and the general happiness, therefore, a good to the aggregate of all persons."[7]

Still another variant of this fallacy is the one known as *sorites*,[8] which consists in piling up instances of things true of individuals, and then asserting the same things as true collectively. The spendthrift fallacy is of this nature: 10 cents for a newspaper is not an immoderate sum; nor 35 cents for a milk shake; nor 25 cents for car tickets; etc. Soon a lot of little expenditures, none in themselves excessive, have added up to an unexpected extravagance. The same illusion operates in respect to time. The night before an examination at 7 P.M., a student decides that with a long, unbroken evening of study before him he can afford to take out fifteen minutes to read the newspaper, and another thirty minutes for a favorite television program, and time for a phone call to a friend and for a coffee break. . . . Once again the accumulation of small items adds up to a large waste, and the evening is gone with very little study accomplished. Another example, frequent in everyday life: One person, after a long series of minor irritations or provocations, erupts into anger at some point which, taken by itself, is insignificant. The second person accuses the first of an exaggerated display of temper over the insignificant triviality which triggered the explosion. This is the familiar situation of the straw that breaks the camel's back, and the truth is that the outburst was caused by the trivial incident plus a great many others. The result is usually a confused and futile wrangle with neither person arguing the same point—one focusing on the single episode; the other, on the whole sequence.

The name sorites was also given in ancient times to the fallacy of continuous questioning, which insists on putting precise limits to things in themselves imprecise—by asking, for instance, on what day a lamb becomes a sheep. Hamilton gives this illustration: "It was asked,—was a man bald who had so many thousand hairs; you answer, No: the antagonist goes on diminishing and diminishing the number, till either you admit that he who was not bald with a certain number of hairs, becomes bald when that complement is diminished by a single hair; or you go on denying him to be bald, until his head be hypothetically denuded."[9]

The "gambler's fallacy" falls within the category of the fallacy of division. If a coin (assumed to be honest) comes up heads each time for twenty consecutive spins, the gambler is apt to argue that the odds, instead of being

[7] *Utilitarianism*, edited by Oscar Piest, Liberal Arts Press, New York, 1948, chap. 4.

[8] From the Greek word meaning "heap." It is the term also used for piling up syllogisms.

[9] From *Lectures on Logic*, I, 464, quoted by Keynes in *Formal Logic*, p. 253.

fifty-fifty, are considerably in favor of the coin turning up tails on the twenty-first throw. But in fact (the coin having no memory) the odds remain fifty-fifty on each individual toss. It is indeed highly probable that the twenty consecutive heads will be balanced out by a series of tails, but only over a very long sequence. The gambler's fallacy, then, consists in applying to a single case (the part) what holds good for a large group of cases (the whole). Insurance policies are sometimes urged on the same basis: John Jones's home was blown away by a tornado, and it can happen to you. Hence you are jeopardising your future if you do not take out tornado insurance. Let us note, finally, that many a house owes its furnishings to the effectiveness of this same fallacy: "$1 down will bring this combined radio, TV, and Hi-Fi into your living room." What really brings the item home, needless to say, is $1 plus $1 each week for five years—in the end, quite a large accumulation of dollars.

FIGURE OF SPEECH

Figure of speech is the fallacy of inferring a similarity of meaning from a similarity of grammatical structure—to suppose, by way of illustration, that on the analogy of words like "decompress," "decentralize," and "depopulate," the word "delimit" means to remove limits (whereas it really means the exact opposite).[10]

This fallacy is of much greater likelihood in languages that are highly inflected, such as Latin and Greek, than in English. Its incidence in English in quite low and it would probably be bypassed in most classifications were it not part of Aristotle's original classification. Nevertheless, it does crop up, and John Stuart Mill provides us with one of the more famous occurrences of it—all the more striking as coming from the pen of a noted logician. Mill argues that because "visible" means "what can be seen," so also "desirable" means "what can be desired" (though, in this context, it means "what ought to be desired"):[11]

"What ought to be required of this doctrine [that 'happiness is desirable, and the only thing desirable, as an end'] . . . to make good its claim to be believed? The only proof capable of being given that an object is visible, is that people actually see it. The only proof that a sound is audible is that people hear it: and so of the other sources of our experience. In like manner, I apprehend, the sole evidence it is possible to produce that anything is desirable, is that people do actually desire it."

[10] This fallacy is most likely to occur in the process of obverting propositions. . . .
[11] John Stuart Mill, *Utilitarianism*, chap. 4.

FALLACIES OF ACCENT

Because of the margin between thought and speech, any written or spoken sentence can have its meaning changed by varying the emphasis of its parts. The sentence, "This is a fine country" is apt to be meant quite differently by the July-the-fourth orator and the man who has just filed his income tax. A sentence such as the following takes on a new meaning with the placing of the stress on each successive word:

She will obey her superior.	(She, but not necessarily others.)
She *will* obey her superior.	(Command, as against prediction.)
She will *obey* her superior.	(She will act only under obedience.)
She will obey *her* superior.	(But not the superior of others.)
She will obey her *superior*.	(But no others.)

The sentence can be still further changed by adding exclamation and question marks.

Mistakes in argument resulting from the ambiguities which arise from variations in emphasis within a single word also are called fallacies of accent. The term, as originally used by Aristotle, applied in this way to the misinterpretation of words that differ in syllabic accent. An example in English would be the confusion of *in*valid and inv*a*lid:

Every *in*valid needs medical care.
But every fallacy is inv*a*lid.
Therefore every fallacy needs medical care.

However, the fallacy of accent, as it is now interpreted by most logicians, refers to all mistakes arising from ambiguity of emphasis within a word or phrase. And since the comparative value of words and phrases is usually determined by their context, the term is also used in a broad sense to cover all arguments which err by ignoring the requirements of context.

Fallacies of emphasis are probably more common in spoken than in written speech, for ironic, sarcastic, facetious, or mocking intonations can radically change the meaning of otherwise straightforward assertions. Many a weak argument has gained strength from a bold, confident manner of speaking. Many a truth has been clouded or subverted by those who:[12]

> Damn with faint praise, consent with civil leer;
> And without sneering teach the rest to sneer.

[12] Alexander Pope, *Epistle to Dr. Arbuthnot*, 1, 201, referring to Gibbon; in *Collected Poems of Alexander Pope*, E. P. Dutton and Co., Inc., New York, 1935.

This is not to deny that irony, humor, and similar rhetorical devices are legitimate literary and oratorical techniques. They are, however, fertile sources of misunderstanding and must therefore be handled with care. Any teacher can testify to the ease with which classroom remarks, intended ironically or facetiously, can be interpreted literally. The difficulty, too, in translating irony and whimsy from spoken to written speech is one of the reasons why letter writing is dangerous.

Probably nowhere better than in newspapers can the importance of emphasis be recognized for purposes of communication. Events tend to assume importance according to the size of the headlines they are given. Responsible newspapers usually proportion the scale of their headlines to the significance of the stories they head.

Position in the paper, too, has its effect. One time-tested way to kill a story is to bury it among the want-ads. On the other hand, any editor hard-pressed for news or with an axe to grind can start a crime wave by featuring on the front page the routine police-court news that would ordinarily be consigned to the obituary page. An influential newspaper such as the *New York Times* can elevate an issue to national importance simply by the device of emphatic repetition.

A message in large, eye-compelling letters is often qualified by unscrupulous salesmen with a line of unobtrusive small print:

SELLING OUT
(*present stock*)

Or

ALL MAKES TRANSISTOR RADIOS $15.00
(*and up*)

The small print in legal documents—contracts, mortgages, leases, and so on —has been used so often to conceal trickery that most people have now learned the advisability of a careful reading of the fine print.

The use of italics, or their omission, is another familiar device for securing a change of meaning by a change of emphasis:

{ I didn't happen to go down that street.
{ I didn't *happen* to go down that street.

{ But Brutus is an honorable man.
{ But Brutus is an *honorable* man.

The term *special pleading* has been given to one of the prevalent species of this argument. It consists in the employment of an argument in one context without permitting it in another. Thus, in religious controversy, freedom of opinion and private judgment has often been pleaded on one side but excluded from the other. Idleness among the well-to-do may be praised as gracious living, but condemned among the poor as character corroding. A man who pleads for rugged independence in one context may argue for a state subsidy in another. Bertrand Russell illustrates this tendency to be easier on ourselves than on those who disagree with us by the following conjugation:

I am firm.
You are stubborn.
He is pigheaded.

Stacking the deck is another variant of this fallacy. It consists in slanting an argument by a one-sided selection of facts. A book or a play, for instance, may be unfairly reviewed by stressing unimportant trivialities. A character may be destroyed or a cause discredited by concentrating exclusively on unfavorable factors. Cardinal Newman, speaking on the one-sided presentation of the Catholic position in England in the middle of the nineteenth century, illustrated this type of thinking with a fable. A man invited a lion to his palace, richly furnished and with a profusion of fine specimens of sculpture and painting, most of which had for their subject matter the noble lion himself.

There was, however, one remarkable feature in all of them, to which the host, silent as he was from politeness, seemed not at all insensible; that diverse as were these representations, in one point they all agreed, that the man was always victorious, and the lion was always overcome. The man had it all his own way, and the lion was but a fool, and served to make him sport. There were exquisite works in marble, of Samson rending the lion like a kid, and young David taking the lion by the beard and choking him. There was the man who ran his arm down the lion's throat, and held him fast by the tongue; and there was that other who, when carried off in his teeth, contrived to pull a penknife from his pocket, and lodge it in the monster's heart. Then there was a lion hunt, or what had been such, for the brute was rolling round in the agonies of death, and his conqueror on his bleeding horse was surveying these from a distance. There was a gladiator from the Roman amphitheatre in mortal struggle with his tawny foe, and it was plain who was getting the mastery. There was a lion in a net; a lion in a trap; four lions, yoked in harness, were drawing the car of a Roman emperor; and elsewhere stood Hercules, clad in the lion's skin, and with the club which demolished him.

Nor was this all: the lion was not only triumphed over, mocked, spurned; but he was tortured into extravagant forms, as if he were not only the slave and creature, but the very creation of man. He became an artistic decoration, and an heraldic emblazonment. The feet of alabaster tables fell away into lions' paws. Lions' faces grinned on each side the shining mantelpiece; and lions' mouths held tight the handles of the doors. There were sphinxes, too, half-lion, half-woman; there were lions rampant holding flags, lions couchant, lions passant, lions regardant; lions and unicorns; there were lions white, black and red; in short there was no misconception or excess of indignity which was thought too great for the lord of the forest and the king of brutes. After he had gone over the mansion, his entertainer asked him what he thought of the splendours it contained; and he in reply did full justice to the riches of its owner and the skill of its decorators, but he added, "Lions would have fared better, had lions been the artists!"[13]

CONFUSION OF
FORMAL AND MATERIAL USES OF LANGUAGE

A fairly common fallacy of context results from the failure to distinguish between different ways of using speech, for language may be used in either of two ways: in a consistently strict, literal sense, where each word has a precise, sharply defined, straightforward meaning; or in a freer way, where the intended meaning of the words depends upon the total situation in which they were employed. The terms "formal" and "material" have been extended to cover these disparate usages of language.[14] Language used formally limits itself to the direct, explicit, primary meanings of words. Language used materially depends upon context, mental associations, figures of speech, even on the physical environment, and the meaning is often implied, suggested, or hinted at, rather than explicitly stated. Everyday speech, where so much depends upon the circumstances of the moment—common surroundings, common moods, shared or presumed backgrounds of knowledge and experience—uses a more fluid and unconstrained speech than is found, for example, in legal documents, cookbooks, or scientific treatises, where impersonal exactitude and complete absence of ambiguity is the ideal. Either way of using language is legitimate, but to change from one usage to the other without indication, to interpret formally a sentence meant materially, or vice versa, is to invite error and fallacy. The deliberate confusion of one with the other is a favorite device of the sophist. Let us illustrate the two usages.

The following sentences are true if taken formally, false if taken materially:

The King can do no wrong.
["King" here stands for legitimate authority.]

---

[13] John Henry Newman, *Present Position of Catholics in England,* Longmans, Green & Co., Ltd., London, 1891, p. 3.

[14] See J. Maritain, *Introduction to Philosophy,* Sheed and Ward, Inc., New York, 1930, p. 253. See also John Henry Newman, *Apologia pro vita sua,* Image Books, Doubleday & Co., Inc., Garden City, N.Y., 1956, appendix 8.

The senses never err.
[The sense report in itself cannot be wrong, only the judgment based on it.]
Whatever is, is good.
["Good" as a being, which need not be morally good.]
Man is born free.
[Man is by nature a free being.]
All men are equal.
[By nature, though not by circumstance.]
Art imitates nature.
[Imitates, not in the sense of "mirrors," but in the sense that it works according to the same principles.]

These sentences may be true if taken materially, false if taken formally:

My heart is broken.	*He is a rubber stamp.*
He knows Plato well.	*She ate the whole plate.*
This picture is the President.	*Mary is a peach.*

Highly formalized speech sometimes takes on the aspect of a new language with its own specialized vocabulary, idioms, and syntax. The language of the law, for instance, as defined, qualified, and conventionalized through centuries of courtroom arguments, is an instrument well-adapted to the elimination of ambiguity and the avoidance of change, though to the layman's ear it may sound stilted, repetitious, and archaic. The language of a technical treatise in science, philosophy, or theology frequently repels the uninitiated, though it may be admirably adapted for its proper ends. Generally (though not always), the more plain and straightforward a piece of prose, the better it is adapted to clear communication.

Material speech has its proper place, too, in human discourse. The diction and style of a textbook or a law code would be inappropriate for everyday speech. Material speech offers, as well as a greater flexibility, a kind of short cut in communication; it moves at a speed better adapted to the rhythms of everyday conversation than does the slower pace of technical speech. W. W. Sawyer, in a book which aims at an exposition of mathematics in everyday language, makes this point:

Readers will find some statements in this book very puzzling if they treat every sentence as being true (so to speak) to ten places of decimals. Particularly within the limits of a small booklet, it is impossible to hedge every sentence round with the remarks and cautions that would be necessary in a textbook.[15]

There is a wider possibility of misunderstanding material than formal speech because it makes greater demands on the interpretive activity of the

[15] W. W. Sawyer, *Mathematician's Delight,* Pelican Books, London, 1943, p. 37.

hearer. But, by the same token, it is often more useful for the communication of things too difficult to be pinned down literally. Plato refused to allow his lecture on *The Good* to be published because written speech could not adequately reproduce the subtleties of spoken discourse, which alone could reach the necessary heights. St. John of the Cross remains one of the most penetrating writers on mysticism because he brought the language of poetry to the description of experiences that were beyond the power of more prosaic speech.

The writings of Plato and Aristotle offer an interesting contrast in the uses of language. Plato's dialogues were intended for a general audience, and his language, reproducing the rhythms of everyday speech, verges more on the material than the formal. Aristotle's writings, on the other hand, are the reports of lectures delivered to his students, and are in a language much more formal than material. To this extent there is some truth behind the popular characterization of Plato as poetic and Aristotle as prosaic.[16]

The fallacies which depend upon a confusion of the formal and material uses of languages are primarily fallacies of context, though they cut across the conventional categories, since almost any expression is susceptible to both formal and material interpretation. The principal ways of confusing formal and material speech are as follows:

1. Words or phrases taken out of context. This applies especially to words used materially, that is, words that directly depend for their full meaning on their context. The word "partisan," for instance, may simply mean an adherent to some party, in one context; in another, an unreasonable adherent to some cause or party; in still another, a guerrilla fighter. The term "intellectual" is a compliment in Europe; in the United States it is usually a term of depreciation. Epithets taken out of context are particularly liable to misunderstanding. Names accepted as terms of endearment when said with a smile become fighting words in another context.

2. Taking formally propositions meant materially, and conversely. Thus, "Infants are rational," a proposition that is true if taken formally (*i.e.,* infants belong to the class "rational animal"), would be false if transferred to a material context—if we said, for example, that six-months-old Peter is responsible for his actions because infants are rational.

Polite forms, such as "Pleased to meet you," "The boss is not in," "Yours to command," or "My house is your house," are meant materially. Were they taken formally, they might often be interpreted as outright lies.

Another instance in this confusion of language would be to take the various species of irony—sarcasm, understatement, and hyperbole—in a literal sense, or to take a rhetorical question as implying a real doubt in the

[16] Plato's esoteric writings, meant only for the initiates, have not survived. Aristotle, too, wrote, for general circulation, philosophic dialogues that have survived only in fragments.

speaker's mind—for example, when the preacher starts his sermon with the question, "Does God really exist?"

3. The coupling of statements meant formally in such a way that they are likely to be taken materially, or contrariwise. This is a favorite device of the sophist, for if the material implications of his speech are challenged, he can reply that he meant it formally. Prejudices of race, color, or religion are particularly susceptible to this treatment. Suppose the sandwiching of sentences of this kind:

> Crime in New York is most prevalent among the foreign-born element. The principal waves of immigration in this century have come from countries predominantly Catholic. Patterns of crime are generally a reflection of group mores. Immigrants from Catholic countries usually settle in their own community groups on arrival in this country. The incidence of crime will not decrease until the newcomers to our shores have been thoroughly Americanized.

Nowhere in the above passage has it been explicitly stated in a simple proposition that there is a direct relationship between crime and Catholicism, but this is the impression most people would take away from it.

The juggling of moral and material lends itself to certain forms of quibbling. To the question, "Are you a drinking man?" a person might answer "No," with the unexpressed context that he is not a buttermilk drinker. In a dispute in Ireland over a contested will, the witnesses for the defense kept asserting that when the will was signed there was life in the testator. The opposing counsel, Daniel O'Connell, becoming suspicious of the unvarying formula, "There was life in him," brought out the fact that the defendants had indeed signed the will themselves, but that they had enclosed a live fly in the mouth of the deceased so that they could swear there was literally life in him when the will was signed.

Our final illustration, which is also a fallacy of accent, uses emphasis to make the transition from material to formal:

> Do you have much trouble with drunkenness among the boys? . . ." "There is no drinking in the school, your Honor," said the headmaster with considerable dignity. . . . "Occasionally in the course of taking my evening stroll, I pass a few of the boys lying drunk by the roadside, but there is *no* drinking *in* the school."[17]

AESOPIAN SPEECH

A modern variation in the techniques for verbal deceit is the device called Aesopian speech, a highly developed form of double talk used by the

---

[17] Aubrey Menen, *The Prevalence of Witches,* Charles Scribner's Sons, New York, 1949, p. 249.

Communist Party to communicate with the initiated and to deceive the uninformed. The name is taken from Aesop's fables, where the moral is often implied rather than openly stated, and the technique was devised by Lenin during the Czarist regime as a way of bypassing the official censorship. By substituting specialized meanings for ordinary words, it was possible to transmit revolutionary doctrines and directives through the apparently innocuous pages of the Party publications. In one of his political tracts, for instance, Lenin bypassed the censor with an article about current problems in Japan. "The careful reader," he said, "will easily substitute Russia for Japan."[18]

Aesopian speech did not disappear with the accession to power of the Communist Party in Russia, but continues in full use today as a weapon of international intrigue. Louis Budenz, in *The Techciques of Communism,* tells how the General Secretary of the Communist International recommended "the language of Aesop" to the Italian Communists as a means "to observe the rules of conspiracy, to resort to maneuvers in order not to let yourself be seen through at once." Criticizing the Italian Communists in the same passage, he affirmed, "They have not mastered the secret of using that language of Aesop which, without diminishing its revolutionary class contact, may stir and capture the imagination of the workers."[19]

The *New York Times,* in its coverage of the trial for conspiracy of the Communist Party leaders of the United States in 1949, reported the testimony of Herbert Philbrick:

> By the use of semantic devices . . . the party could prepare the minds of its members for war without public knowledge by apparently calling for "peace," could rally them to the support of totalitarian Russia by apparently supporting "democracy," and could arouse them against the United States by apparently attacking "fascism" and "imperialism."[20]

Prominent in the Communist lexicon of esoteric speech are words such as the following:

democrat—one who favors the Communist Party.
people's democracy—the dictatorship of the proletariat.
negotiation—one-sided concession.

---

[18] Quoted by J. Edgar Hoover, *Masters of Deceit,* Holt, Rinehart and Winston, Inc., New York, 1958, p. 102. For original sources, see *State and Revolution: What Is to Be Done,* and the Preface to *Imperialism, the Highest State of Capitalism,* by V. I. Lenin; also *History of the Communist Party of the Soviet Union* by J. Stalin.

[19] D. Z. Manuilsky, *The Advance of the Revolutionary Crisis,* International Press Correspondence, Feb. 26, 1934, p. 310, quoted by Louis Budenz, in *The Techniques of Communism,* Henry Regnery Company, Chicago, 1954, p. 43.

[20] *The New York Times,* April 13, 1949.

peaceful co-existence—subversion by political and economic penetration.
imperialist—capitalist, and especially American.
colonialist—anti-Communist.
just war—one in which the Soviet Union is engaged.
unjust war—war against the Soviet Union.
patriotism—support of the Soviet Union against one's own country.

The list can be extended indefinitely, and is expanded to meet the demands of the moment, as in the invention of the phrase "agrarian reformers" to describe the Chinese Communists. Let us conclude with the warning by Harry Hodgkinson, in *The Language of Communism:* "The language of Communism . . . is not so much a means of explaining to an unbeliever what Communism means, but an armory of weapons and tools intended to produce support or dissolve opposition to Communist policies on the part of people either hostile or indifferent to them. The meaning of a Communist word is not what you think it says, but what effect it is intended to produce."[21]

Exercises*

1. Identify the equivocal words or phrases in the following:
a. He wanted to be a writer in the worst way and he succeeded.
b. Drinking satisfies thirst.
c. Headline: LIONS INVADE NEW YORK.
d. The highest form of animal life is the giraffe.
e. "I could write like Shakespeare if I had a mind to."
f. Whatever is clearly seen is visible.
   This argument is clearly seen.
   Therefore this argument is visible.
g. Some girls are blonde.
   Mary is some girl.
   Therefore Mary is blonde.
h. Aristotle is a word of four syllables.
   Aristotle is profound.
   Therefore profound is a word of four syllables.
i. What's well done is done well enough.
   The roast is well done.
   Therefore the roast is done well enough.

---

[21] Harry Hodgkinson, *The Language of Communism,* Pitman Publishing Corporation, New York, no date, Introduction, p. *v*. See also R. N. C. Hunt, *A Guide to Communist Jargon,* The Macmillan Company, New York, 1957.
   * From FUNDAMENTALS OF LOGIC by Daniel J. Sullivan. Copyright © 1963 by McGraw-Hill, Inc. Used by permission of McGraw-Hill Book Company

j. The blind man is one who cannot see.
Peter (who is sleeping) cannot see.
Therefore Peter is blind.

2. Make a list of twenty words which are easily susceptible to equivocation.

3. Construct sentences in which the following words will be equivocal: *Light, right, duck, strain, fair, fare, match, band.*

4. Bring out the ambiguity in the following sentences by rewriting in at least two different ways:

a. His father having lost his job, he was obliged to leave home.

b. How much is $3 \times 2 + 4$?

c. Testimonial: "I used your soap two years ago. Since then I have used no other."

d. Sign: "Good Clean Entertainment Every Night Except Monday."

e. He was a great admirer of Wordsworth whom he met near Windermere when he was eloping with a rich widow.

f. "The Duke yet lives that Henry shall depose."

5. Indicate whether the transition in the following fallacies is from collective to divisive or contrariwise:

a. Feathers are lighter than iron. Therefore a ton of feathers will be lighter than a ton of iron.

b. The angles of a triangle equal two right angles. *ABC* is the angle of a triangle. Therefore *ABC* equals two right angles.

c. Gold and lead are precious and useful metals; that is, gold is precious and useful and lead is precious and useful.

d. The Apostles preached everywhere.
St. James was an Apostle.
Therefore St. James preached everywhere.

e. 5 and 2 are odd and even. Therefore 7 is odd and even.

f. The Chicago Bears have succeeded in buying the best stars in the game. Therefore they will have the best team this year.

6. Tell whether the following sentences are true or false if taken formally:

a. Fiction is a drug.

b. Whatever is, is true.

c. The King never dies.

d. "Although God cannot alter the past, the historian can."

e. The divine law commands us to honor kings.

f. He's nothing but a hound dog.

g. To kill is forbidden by the Commandments.

h. The tree throws a shadow.